Harvard Historical Studies 129

Published under the auspices of the Department of History
from the income of the Paul Revere Frothingham Bequest
Robert Louis Stroock Fund Henry Warren Torrey Fund

Parish Communities and Religious Conflict in the Vale of Gloucester, 1590–1690

Daniel C. Beaver

HARVARD UNIVERSITY PRESS

Cambridge, Massachusetts

London, England

1998

Copyright © 1998 by the President and Fellows of Harvard College
All rights reserved
Printed in the United States of America

Library of Congress Cataloging-in-Publication Data

Beaver, Daniel C., 1961–
    Parish communities and religious conflict in the Vale of
Gloucester, 1590–1690 / Daniel C. Beaver.
        p.   cm.—(Harvard historical studies : 129)
    Includes bibliographical references and index.
    ISBN 0-674-75845-5 (alk. paper)
    1. Tewkesbury Region (England)—Church history—16th century.
    2. Tewkesbury Region (England)—Church history—17th century.
    3. Church controversies.   I. Title.
    II. Series : Harvard historical studies ; v. 129.
    BR765.T48B43   1998
    274.24'1206—dc21   98-16295

For my parents

Acknowledgments

Publication may be viewed as the birth of a project, as the moment of its public appearance before an audience. Yet the moment of publication also resembles a death, as a project ceases to be a process and becomes a book, an object laid in state for the scrutiny of inquisitive readers. In the seventeenth century, the moment of death demanded an account, a narrative of debts and obligations. This moment of transition in my work on the northern Vale of Gloucester seems to require its own account. I have many debts to acknowledge and many friends to thank.

I must first express my thanks to the several institutions that helped to fund the research for this study. My doctoral work received generous support from a Mellon Fellowship in the Humanities, administered by the Woodrow Wilson National Fellowship Foundation. In the last phases of writing the book, a Josephine Berry Weiss Fellowship from the Pennsylvania State University permitted a release from classes in the fall of 1994 to finish the revisions of the manuscript.

This book originated as a doctoral dissertation at the University of Chicago. I thank my dissertation adviser, Mark Kishlansky, for his criticism, advice, and friendship over the years. I thank the other members of my committee, Edward Cook and Bernard Cohn, for perspectives from early American history and historical anthropology. Keith Wrightson's work has been a source of inspiration. He generously read the entire manuscript and offered both challenging criticisms and friendly encouragement. In addition, I thank John Morrill and Conrad Russell for numerous references and for invitations to present the early results of my work in seminars at Cambridge University and the Institute of Historical Research. Sears McGee shared his knowledge of early Stuart religion, introduced me to the Bodleian Library, and offered kind hospitality for a few weeks of summer in Oxford. Finally, I thank Peter Lake for his comments on early drafts of chapters, for his intellectual generosity, and for many helpful references. Michael Adas and Traian Stoianovich directed my first explorations of early modern social history as an undergraduate at Rutgers University.

Historical research is a collaborative enterprise, and many friends have offered references and archival advice. My debts to the scholarship of others are acknowledged in the notes, but I thank Sabrina Baron, Alastair Bellany, Brian Frith, Paul Halliday, Michael Martin, David Smith, Tim Wales, and Andrew Warmington for their particular contributions to the evidence used in this book.

I had the opportunity to spend two wonderful years in the Gloucestershire archives, and many kind people opened their homes and affections to me. In Gloucester, I thank John Knowles, Rosalind and Ron Lane, Michael Martin, Terry Peters, Phyllis and Brian White, and Graham Whitehead for their friendship and support. I must also express my fond appreciation for the staffs of the Gloucestershire Record Office and the Gloucester City Library. Kate Haslem and the search room staff of the record office took the time to field countless novice questions about Gloucestershire sources. In London, I thank Maria Dowling, Joan Henderson, Julia Merritt, and Stephen O'Connor for many kindnesses and good cheer.

Many more friends than I can name here have helped me to think about the practice (and excessive practice) of history. I thank Emary Aronson, Matt Berg, Antoinette Burton, Dave Goodman, Dan Gordon, Maureen Harp, Tim Harris, Steve Johnstone, Newton Key, Caroline Litzenberger, Cathy Patterson, Steve Pincus, and Joe Ward for their friendship and criticism. I thank Edward Kishlansky for his kind prayers on my behalf at a critical moment.

I have had the benefit of much help and encouragement from my colleagues in the Department of History at the Pennsylvania State University. Paul Harvey, Sally McMurry, Jim Sweeney, and Nan Woodruff have given their time to discuss ideas, read papers, and lend critical support to a project quite distant from their own fields. Phil Jenkins, who read an early draft of the manuscript, offered helpful suggestions and references. I thank the house band, Barry Kernfeld, Dan Letwin, Mary Ann Maslak, On-cho Ng, and Bill Pencak, colleagues and friends, for mixing ideas and music. Thanks also to Patrick Sharbaugh of University Photo/Graphics, who designed the map.

I have made life difficult for friends and family in the ten years this book has been my sometimes jovial and sometimes cantankerous but always inescapable companion. I thank my parents and my sister and brother for their constant love. Janina Safran is my partner and best critic in everything. I am honored to have Michael and Jane Adas, Deborah Diamond, Greg Eghigian, Mike Kugler, and Paul White as my friends. My thanks are small return for their gifts to me.

Contents

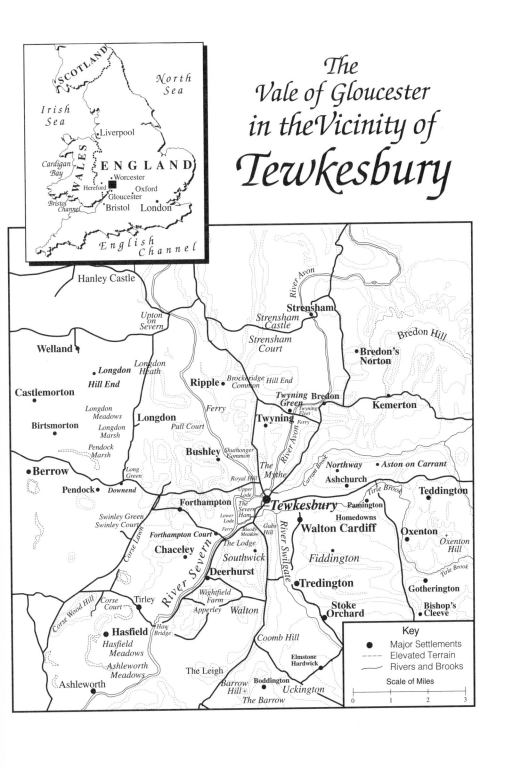

The
Vale of Gloucester
in the Vicinity of
Tewkesbury

Key

● Major Settlements
- - - - Elevated Terrain
——— Rivers and Brooks

Scale of Miles

0   1   2   3

Church History as a Cultural System

A religious symbol conveys its message even if it is no longer
consciously understood in every part. For a symbol speaks to the whole
human being and not only to the intelligence.
                          Mircea Eliade, *The Sacred and the Profane* (1957)

A society, like a mind, is woven of perpetual interaction.
                          Marc Bloch, *Feudal Society*, vol. 1 (1939)

Three incidents, separated in space and time yet related by a common
symbolism, preserve fragments of religious conflict and violence in seventeenth-century England. In May 1606 Thomas Drake, a suspended
curate, confronted his replacement, Richard Garner, over the issue of
posture in holy communion.[1] The dispute occurred in the rural parish of
Forthampton, just across the River Severn from Tewkesbury in Gloucestershire. Drake's refusal to wear the surplice had resulted in his suspension from clerical office in Forthampton, but he continued to reside in
the parish and received food and money from sympathetic families. Garner was sensitive to the issue of ceremonial posture because he knew that
several members of his congregation and their families habitually crossed
the boundaries of the parish on holy days to receive communion from
other hands. He suspected that their desertion of the parish resulted
from a desire to receive communion in a sitting or standing posture. This
form of communion violated the royal injunction to receive the sacrament in a kneeling position. Garner also believed that the practice was
contrary to the word of God and the maintenance of peace in the neighborhood. As Drake and his supporters seemed to persist in their "un-

1

charitable" practices, Garner made a list of the offenders for the archdeacon of Gloucester diocese and obtained their presentment in the diocesan court of correction.

The announcement of this presentment in the parish church of Forthampton led to the confrontation. After morning prayers, Drake strode angrily to the seat from which Garner conducted religious services. As Drake and Garner became embroiled in argument, a crowd began to gather in the front of the church. Drake invoked the authority of conscience and denied the spiritual legitimacy of the doctrinal foundation of the Church of England expressed in the 39 Articles. He reviled Garner for his malicious presentment and demanded a public debate on the scriptural authority of sitting and standing postures in communion. Garner refused to debate the sacramental issues in the open church. If Drake wanted learned discussion, he could hold his debate in the court of visitation to be held in Tewkesbury. Garner later admitted he feared such a debate in Forthampton would provoke a riot among the members of his congregation.

Controversies over religious beliefs and practices had not diminished in the early 1630s. The very different accounts of the life and times of Thomas Hickes of Tewkesbury reveal the persistence of conflict among several distinct styles of belief. Peter Studley, a clerical author, used local rumors of the divine retribution visited on Thomas Hickes and his family to demonstrate the evils of Nonconformity in his book *The Looking Glass of Schism,* published in 1633.[2] Hickes had reportedly used his authority as a churchwarden to destroy a stone cross in the churchyard of Tewkesbury. Although several unidentified neighbors had respectfully placed the loose stones from this cross beneath the church, Hickes demanded more than the physical destruction of the monument. Despite a series of monstrous births in his family that many of his contemporaries would have taken as a divine affliction, Hickes allegedly recovered the stones from the cross and used the materials to construct a trough for his pigs. The animals that used this trough immediately died from the shock of the blasphemy, and Studley described the subsequent suicide of Hickes as the final abominable act of a soul belatedly conscious of its own wickedness. Studley thus represented Hickes as a fanatic determined on the unspeakable desecration of sacred monuments.

But the multiple styles of religious belief in the neighborhood created several alternatives to Studley's representation of religious images as the divinely protected embodiments of the holy spirit. A second version of the Hickes case was scribbled in the margins of Studley's book by one of his local readers.[3] The unidentified reader denied that Hickes had ever been a churchwarden and thus removed Studley's rapacious Nonconformist from a position of authority in the parish. According to this account, Hickes had sacrilegiously stolen an image of the Virgin from the parish church, had made "a base use" of the image, and had thus earned the contempt of his neighbors. No mention was made of divine retribution, only the laconic observation that Hickes had drowned in a local well "at the latter end of a sickness." The account, which assumed a nominalist position on the issue of religious images, described Hickes' behavior in terms of "high presumption" and irreverence, rather than of blasphemy.

Yet another variant of the Hickes case expressed the interests and concerns of officers in the corporation of Tewkesbury. According to this third version, Hickes had never held office in either the parish or the corporation. After having been hired as a mason to make some repairs of the church, he had involuntarily destroyed the cross. Hickes had been prosecuted for this involuntary sacrilege, but the justices of the borough court had determined that the images engraved on the stone could no longer be recognized. This account, which represented Hickes as the victim of an epidemic, struck down after many happy years in the practice of his occupation, excluded the element of divine retribution.[4] The narrative attested to the vigilance of local officers on matters of religious orthodoxy and affirmed the local commitment to protect the monuments of the church.

An informant to the Court of High Commission in London created the fourth version of the Hickes case. The most important elements of the other narratives disappeared from this account, although religious heterodoxy, represented as the invasion of the neighborhood by a virulent *clerical* Nonconformity, once again resulted in human tragedy. In this version of the drama, Hickes appeared as an innocent victim of the Nonconformist preacher John Geary of Tewkesbury. Geary's sermons had reportedly produced such an unquietness of spirit in his congregation that Hickes was driven to suicide and consequently hurled himself into a well.[5] The significant feature of this brief narrative was its location of the deadly source of heterodoxy not in the lay community of the parish but in the official hierarchy of the Church of England.

The religious diversity implicit in these narratives assumed an explicit institutional form in the violence of the Civil War, Revolution, and Restoration. Although the Restoration has traditionally been interpreted as the end of a process, as the decisive moment in the formation of Anglicans and Dissenters, a controversy among Anglican factions in Tewkesbury in the late 1670s demonstrated the persistence of Nonconformist beliefs and practices in the parish church.[6] This controversy resulted from a fast sermon delivered in the early days of the Popish Plot, an alleged Catholic conspiracy to assassinate Charles II and restore Roman Catholicism in England. Francis Wells, the vicar of Tewkesbury, constructed his sermon as an indictment of Charles II for adultery and fornication, the causes of the crisis in church and state. On 13 November 1678 Wells delivered the sermon in the parish church despite the intervention of the senior bailiff of the corporation. This inflammatory declaration of the authority and responsibilities of conscience once again divided the corporation and the parish into hostile factions. Wells and his supporters fought locally to preserve a Nonconformist ceremonial style, but a prolonged and expensive lawsuit to control the rituals of the parish church was conducted in diocesan and metropolitan courts. In 1681 the faction opposed to Wells finally had him deprived of his benefice in the Church of England. As the case proceeded to his final deprivation, Wells defended his actions in strident protests against the Book of Common Prayer and the 39 Articles. Despite the critical differences of context and historical experience, his criticisms were remarkably similar to the arguments and sources of authority invoked in the parish of Forthampton in 1606.[7]

Although these moments were perceived by contemporaries as important local incidents or events, the events have nevertheless been selected from seventy-five years of local and national history. If a historical relationship connected the incidents, what were its characteristics? How were continuities and discontinuities interpreted by the various participants in this relationship? If continuity existed in the form of convention or tradition, how was this continuity created over time? The local actors were different in each case, and no common institutional process joined the incidents. The conflicts in Forthampton and Tewkesbury left traces in the records of the diocesan court, but the narrative events of the Hickes case have survived only in the texts of a pamphlet war. Distinctive features of time, space, and medium make the events seem discrete and difficult to compare. Despite these important discontinuities, the incidents were defined by an explicit religious symbolism. If this symbolism could be understood as a system and if the social dimensions and continuity of the system could be established, it might be possible to discuss conflicts and disputes as moments in a cultural process. The connection between the events may have consisted not in common personnel but in common symbols and in the continuous power of religious symbols to evoke social relationships and to motivate action. The incidents may thus have been related in symbolic and structural form rather than in surface characteristics.

The use of disparate local incidents to study religious conflict as a cultural process demands a consistent method to counter criticisms of selective evidence. This method should identify local incidents as expressions of structural criteria, the properties of religious symbols, for instance, and the relationship of symbols to social behavior, in order to determine continuities and discontinuities in the process of conflict over time. These events clearly affected social life in the neighborhood of Tewkesbury. In 1606 Thomas Drake received food and emotional support from sympathetic local families in Forthampton. Thomas Hickes was reportedly a victim of neighborhood retaliation. The officers of the town council in Tewkesbury claimed that neighbors killed several of Hickes' farm animals in revenge for his alleged violation of the cross. In the 1670s Francis Wells received assistance and moral support from several influential and intermarried families in the corporation and parish of Tewkesbury. The players in each drama translated conflicts over the symbolism of religious fellowship into the idiom of social relations. Yet the nature of this relationship between social solidarity and religious identity remains elusive and difficult to define.

This book explores the religion of the parish in the late sixteenth and seventeenth centuries, the complex phenomenon Patrick Collinson has described as "the religion of Protestants in its social setting."[8] Many of the questions posed in this inquiry already form a densely settled and familiar historiographic territory. The attempt to define and classify forms of Protestantism, most famously Puritanism, has produced a vast and rich historical literature over several generations.[9] Because so much of the evidence of Protestantism in the parishes comes from the records of diocesan courts, local records generally favor Collinson's more restrictive, behavioral definition of Puritanism as an attitude confined to the movement for further reformation in the Church of England.[10] If the Puritans who were convicted of nonconformity in the courts differed little in fundamental beliefs from their conformist neighbors, this shared world of belief has left no consistent record in the parish. Yet the problem of Puritanism is merely a symptom of the deeper problem of religion. As Collinson has conceded, the discussion of definitions recognizes but seldom confronts the problem of the nature of religion.[11] This latter problem identifies the particular interpretations of Protestantism and Puritanism as expressions of the way in which historians and sociologists have defined religion and have selected the evidence of it. Because this issue is seldom confronted, the persistent influence of early contributions to the discussion of "Protestantism in its social setting" is less clearly appreciated than shifts in particular debates, such as the discussion of Puritanism. These early contributions hold the key to a cultural system implicit in the academic discussion of religion and continue to provide much of the intellectual capital of church history.

Problems of method in the history of religion lead to the scene of a modern crisis in moral authority, a crisis expressed by European conceptions of "the social problem" in the early 1900s.[12] Many perceived in the vast slums and bourgeois mansions of European cities a civilization devoid of moral vision, conscience, and values, lost in a vacuous materialism. As R. H. Tawney observed in a public lecture delivered in 1922, "The question, to what end the wheels revolve, still remains; and on that question the naive and uncritical worship of economic power, which is the mood of unreason too often engendered in those whom that new Leviathan has hypnotized by its spell, throws no light."[13] This perception of crisis inspired, as part of a diverse movement for social reform, an immensely creative debate on the relationship of religion and society. The most influential contributions to the debate, for the purposes of the present inquiry, came from Max Weber, Ernst Troeltsch, and Tawney.[14] Their social histories of Christianity explicitly rejected denominational bias and polemic in order to uncover general rules governing the relationship of religion and everyday life.[15] This charismatic phase in the formation of modern church history and in the sociology of religion resulted in a "shift from denominational biographies and genealogies to sociological analyses."[16] A new language, expressing the concepts of charisma, ethos, the institutional distinction of church and sect, worldly asceticism and rationalization, transformed the social sciences.[17]

Yet in their questions, methods, and interpretations, the disciplines preserved the distinctive historical circumstances of their creation. This sociological literature sought the origins of modern society, in the form of rational individualism, the spirit of capitalism, and its problems. Diverse forces in European civilization, not least the fragmentation of the church system itself, received credit for the destruction of a common moral vision and the loss of social cohesion.[18] Scholars participated in a broad effort to reconstruct the social meaning of religion. The Holland Memorial Lectures, dedicated in the early 1920s to "the religion of the incarnation in its bearing on the social and economic life of man," exemplify the commitment to this mission.[19] The founders of this lecture series believed that the scientific investigation of religion and the public diffusion of its results might contribute to the formation of a new social policy. As a result of this connection to the scientific discourse of public policy, early ventures in the sociology of religion and the new church history tended to produce a rational conception of religion divided into systems of doctrine and ethics.[20] This framework created several famous interpretations of the Reformation as a quintessentially rational and intellectual process. Although historians have criticized the specific interpretations advanced in this literature, a rational conception of religion, defined by doctrine and ethics, continues to dominate church history and the social history of religion.

The work of this charismatic phase in the sociology of religion and church history was routinized in the 1930s and 1940s, as the rational construction of religion from doctrine and ethics became an assumption to build on rather than a proposition to demonstrate. In 1938 William Haller used "sermons, popular expositions of doctrine, spiritual biographies, and manuals of godly behavior" to discuss "how the preachers transposed the teachings of Paul and the doctrine of Calvin into a psychological pattern and a code of behavior for all men to follow."[21] Haller's work was remarkable both for the sheer volume of sermons consulted and for the inclusion of conventional lives and other printed sources to reconstruct the complex techniques used to communicate the Puritan message.[22] Haller's rationalism exploited the possibilities of the sermon as an intersection of the Calvinist doctrine of predestination and the ethical precept of the calling, but his conception of religion itself and his view of socioeconomic transition in the sixteenth and seventeenth centuries were indebted to Weber and Tawney.[23] Marshall Moon Knappen expressed a similar intellectual conception of religion in his history of

Tudor Puritanism, which was published in 1939.[24] Knappen understood the Reformation as a conflict between rational systems, intellectual compounds of realism and idealism, and he interpreted Puritanism, in the manner of Weber and Troeltsch, as a new form of ethical idealism supported, if not caused, by new forms of wealth in the sixteenth century.[25] Because of its connections to the past, Puritanism could serve as a "transitional movement linking the medieval with the modern."[26] This rational perspective enabled Knappen to view the English Reformation as a narrative, the first scene of which opened on William Tyndale's decision to leave London for Germany, a decision represented as the archetypal Puritan action.[27] Although Knappen consistently stressed the complexity of Puritanism, his narrative depended on the decisions and actions of individuals, and he perceived no contradiction in the use of the doctrinal debate between William Tyndale and Sir Thomas More as evidence of the internal development of the Puritan movement.[28] Both Haller and Knappen made significant contributions to the historical study of religion, particularly in their method and their determination to write exclusively from sources; however, the conception of religion implicit in their histories did not depart from the work of the early 1900s and tended to assume its framework.[29]

The most important contribution to theoretical capital in the study of Puritanism and the Reformation since the early 1900s did not question the rationality implicit in earlier work, the focus on "the decision to be a Puritan," but applied its precepts creatively in the field of politics.[30] Michael Walzer acknowledged the influence of Weber, but he left the priorities of the "social problem" for the imperatives of the "political problem" of revolution in the 1960s, an ideological problem that induced Walzer to explore the political activism of Puritanism rather than its social discipline.[31] He followed Haller in his concentration on the imagery of Puritan conceptions of political order and discipline communicated in sermons, particularly the metaphors of the ship of state and the conjugal family, and on the use of a certain style and mode of communication to convey the implications of Puritan doctrine for social and political life.[32] These metaphors conveyed prescribed behavioral codes, and the Puritan sermon, as the familiar bridge between doctrine and ethics, created the godly magistrate and symbolized the "political religion of intellectuals (ministers) and gentlemen."[33] Walzer used the traditional form of rationality in an innovative way, but his work focused exclusively on the conscious use of ideas, and the relationship between "thought and action" dominated his conception of Puritanism just as the relationship between economic environment and action dominated the Marxist conception.[34]

Since the 1960s the rational conception of religion has had a pervasive and productive influence on interpretations of the English Reformation and of the sociology of Puritanism. A. G. Dickens used the evidence of doctrinal connections between Lollards and Lutherans, Lutherans and Calvinists, to construct his interpretation of the Reformation as a process; moreover, an intellectual conception of the church allowed Dickens to extend this process in broad perspective in both space and time.[35] Despite different views on the pace and problems of the Reformation and despite his profound interest in ceremonial expressions of doctrinal division, Patrick Collinson expressed a similar view of the intellectual nature of religion in his early work, a view implicit in his discussion of Troeltsch's distinction between church and sect and in allusions to the "planks in the Puritan platform."[36] Collinson's later work, which considers both the rational and the nonrational elements of religion, includes assumptions of order and the problem of custom, but does not interpret their interrelationship, and his criticism of Walzer's conception of Calvinism concerns the radical content of Calvinist doctrine.[37] Collinson's notion of voluntary religion in the Stuart church returns to Troeltsch and the rational relationship of doctrine and ethics. The "ecclesiastical and social disciplines" of this voluntary religion were "concomitants of intellectual and moral constraint" imposed by Calvinism on individual action. Collinson observes "that puritan theology, especially in its application to the conscience as 'practical divinity,' emphasized increasingly the willing response of the individual within the covenant of grace."[38] This discipline eliminated the dangers of "individualism" or "anarchy" and produced the uniformity or "programmed corporateness" of Puritanism, its lack of significant local variation.

Tawney's work exerted a powerful influence on social historians and remains the most important source of intellectual capital in the social history of Puritanism. Many of the recent developments in this field can be traced to *Religion and the Rise of Capitalism*, in particular the notion of a reformation of manners, driven by the yeomen and the mercantile classes of the towns, "the citadel of the Puritan spirit," and a few gentry families, to impose Puritan standards of conduct "derived partly from the obvious interests of the commercial classes, partly from its conception of the nature of God and the destiny of man."[39] Tawney also described the two Calvinisms created by the relationship of two elements: recognition of commerce and discipline. An emphasis on the latter produced the collectivism of the Revolution in the late 1640s, but an emphasis on the former created the Puritanism of "the individualism congenial to the world of business . . . a political force, at once secularized and committed to a career of compromise . . . an ideal of personal character and conduct, to be realized by the punctual discharge both of public and private duties."[40] This idea has been brilliantly developed by Christopher Hill in his studies of the failed radical revolution inside the Puritan Revolution.[41]

The rational conception of religion in its early forms seldom involved discussion of the parish, but since the 1960s historians have involved the parish in a complex process of social change. Christopher Hill has described a dual process of secularization in the parish and spiritualization in the household.[42] Hill made economic conditions in the sixteenth and seventeenth centuries the foundation of his study. He focused on inflation and the periodic crises in traditional industries and markets that from the 1570s produced economic misery for poor families as well as a series of statutes for the punishment of "vagabonds" and the relief of the poor. The collection of poor relief and the assessment of parish rates were the most important of the "secular" tasks subsequently imposed on churchwardens, the lay officers of the church in the parish. Hill believed that the fiscal demands of the Tudors had transformed the parish from a religious community into a unit of civil government. "The most significant function of the parish," Hill argued, "came to be collection of taxes rather than provision of communal amenities."[43] Tudor emphasis on parish rates and tax collection destroyed the old social democracy of the parish and produced an oligarchy of rich families that paid most of the taxes and formed vestries to oversee the expenditure of the revenue. Puritanism was the discipline imposed by the local oligarchies in their effort to control behavior among the increased number of poor families in their parishes. This discipline sanctified self-denial and labor as it removed religious activity and sentiment from the communal arena of the parish to the more intimate environment of the household and the family. The ecclesiastical establishment of the late Tudors and early Stuarts consisted of an uneasy alliance between these Puritan parish oligarchies and the episcopal hierarchy. Hill implied that the parish oligarchies chafed against ecclesiastical authority. "As the functions of the parish became more and more secularized," he maintained, "so the responsibilities of parochial officials to the church courts became increasingly irksome."[44] The rich families of select vestries were almost ready to assume the secular domination of a class. This representation of the parish followed Tawney's rationale in its treatment of religious doctrine, ceremony, and discipline as the reflections of economic rationality.[45]

This conception of the parish, in its broad outline, has become a commonplace in the study of early modern English society. As a social phenomenon, the movement for further reformation in the Church of England, known as Puritanism, has been interpreted, in the tradition of Tawney and Hill, as the ideological expression of an economic rationality, and the introduction of the Puritan discipline in parishes has been understood as a phase in the formation of a class society. Keith Wrightson and David Levine, in an influential study of the village of Terling in Essex, pulled back from Hill's notion of the secularization of the parish but created a rich local portrait of a parish oligarchy in action.[46] This portrait is less successful as an attempt to connect the economic polarization reflected in the formation of parish oligarchies and the religious polarization reflected in Puritanism.[47] Despite evidence of the diffuse appeal of Protestantism, Wrightson and Levine conclude that "nonconformity in Terling . . . was essentially an affair of the middling sort of villager," the same group of substantial farmers identified as beneficiaries of change in the agricultural economy of the village.[48] A dramatic change in elite perceptions of traditional forms of social interaction and behavior in the village accompanied this transformation of religious discipline among the economic leaders of the parish. As churchwardens and constables, the parish elite used both secular and ecclesiastical courts to craft their Puritan sensibilities into social order. The economic polarization of the parish thus found religious expression in the reformation of belief and found social expression in the reformation of manners. The parish is represented as a rational system of social control based on the integration of economic leadership, visions of religious community, and standards of moral behavior.

This interpretation has been criticized from several different perspectives, although the discussion has not touched the conception of the parish itself and the framework of rationality that supports it. Martin Ingram has eschewed locality and focused instead on the social life of an institution in his study of the ecclesiastical courts in Wiltshire.[49] He rejects interpretations of the courts as socially obsolete and harmful to the economic interests of "the industrious sort of people" in the Puritan parish oligarchies.[50] Ingram then uses this institutional platform to question the interrelationship of religion, economy, and society and their polarization in early modern villages. His exploration of religious belief in Keevil and Wylye has uncovered religious factions among the Protestant families identified in other contexts as a Puritan movement and has established a spectrum of orthodox Protestantism as the local foundation of the church court's authority.[51] Ingram then substitutes one form of rationality for another in his analysis of the social context in which the ecclesiastical courts operated. A social and demographic system replaces the economic system as the force behind the operation of the courts. Ingram represents the church courts as the functional regulators of this system, responsible for the "maintenance and reinforcement" of a demographic regime characterized by "a relatively high mean age of first marriage for both men and women and a substantial proportion of people who never married."[52] The variation in the number of moral offenses prosecuted in the ecclesiastical courts in the late sixteenth and early seventeenth centuries, previously interpreted as a Puritan reformation of manners, is recast in Malthusian terms as a social reaction to demographic crisis, distinct from Puritan religious belief.[53]

Margaret Spufford's study of parishes in Cambridgeshire observes the failure of "rational justification" in the face of the ceremonial disturbances in parish churches after the Reformation and recognizes the power of symbols to convey meanings not clearly formed in doctrine.[54] She focuses on the early impact of the Reformation, on the socially diffuse nature of Puritanism and dissent, and on the importance of family and household in the diffusion of new beliefs.[55] Spufford's work has demonstrated the appeal of Nonconformist beliefs to both rich and poor villagers in different social structures and economies, an appeal that is in part a reflection of economic differences within families in the seventeenth century.[56] Spufford was a pioneer in the now familiar use of probate records to reconstruct the form and social distribution of lay concepts of faith and conscience, redemption and salvation, as well as the social context of their expression. Yet the result of this work is a conception of religion as an independent reality, irreducible to social relations, the economy, or local geography. "No determinism, economic, social, educational, or geographical will fully account for the existence of religious conviction; which is as it should be."[57] This conception of religion as an independent variable, which divides the book into separate parts, complicates the issue of how symbols create forms of fellowship, a question that Spufford admittedly has not made part of her project. Her discussions of religious belief and social relationship appear to represent essentially unrelated domains. Although this separation of spheres would doubtless have appealed to the spiritual sensibilities of some Nonconformists in the seventeenth century, radical separatism makes it difficult to appreciate the interaction of religious symbolism and other aspects of social life.

A short discussion cannot convey the expanse and richness of the historical study of Puritanism, but this brief introduction has attempted to identify in the key texts of this tradition a form of rationality that constituted a cultural system, a series of assumptions and conventions that classified religion and shaped interpretations of religious motives and behavior. This system classified religion as an intellectual phenomenon, composed of doctrine and ethics, most clearly expressed in the form of a sermon or a treatise. Association for religious purposes became a conscious intellectual decision. Differences could be clearly articulated and tended to result in the formation of parties or distinctive associations unless inhibited by an external force. The lack of interest in the contribution of the nonrational elements in symbol, ceremony, and performance to the creation and dissolution of communities follows from the rational conception of religion itself. If the rationality of the system is assumed, doctrine is read as a script for ceremony, and particular performances must reproduce the pattern prescribed in doctrine.

The rational sociology of religion reproduces a modern distinction between religion and society. Weber used doctrine and ethics to create an intersection between sacred and profane, ideal and material, religion and society. This intersection assumed the form of a rational ethical discipline imposed on social life. Yet the meanings of religious symbols and ceremonies are not exhausted by the rationality of doctrine and ethics, and religion has not always been experienced as a phenomenon distinct from social life or neighborhood. A second tradition in the sociology of religion, another intellectual response to the issues of "the social problem" in the early 1900s, rejected the rational individual as a point of

departure and began to investigate "collective representations" or symbols.[58] This sociology, which approached religion as a compound of rational and nonrational elements, "a complex of myths, dogmas, rites,
and ceremonies," has explored the power of religious symbols to *constitute* the cosmological framework perceived as necessary to the conduct of
everyday life and to the form of the community itself.[59]

Despite his stated indifference to this sociology of religion, Mircea
Eliade seems to offer a similar perspective on the religious *mentality* in
his determination to combine the rational and nonrational elements of
religion in a study of "the sacred in its entirety."[60] He uses evidence from
a variety of religious traditions to represent the structure of sacred space
as the primary reality in religious mentality. The experience of this sacred
space becomes a primordial experience, analogous to the foundation of
the world.[61] Eliade interprets the sacred as a series of homologies that
represent the cosmos not only in space, time, and nature, but also in the
sanctification of human life. Abstract concepts, such as orientation, direction, duration, and relationship or association, were possible only in
the context of this religious cosmos, and identity itself became inseparable from the cosmos articulated in religious symbols. Eliade recognizes a
phenomenology of religion in his distinction between the experience of
the homologies and the structure of religious systems, but he does not
develop the distinction or discuss the relationship of structure and experience. The religious mentality emerges from this work as a mode of
symbolism and apprehension, distinguished by the pattern of generation, death, and regeneration as the dominant structure of experience.[62]

This sociology of "collective representations" has attracted numerous
historians, as historical interest has focused on culture broadly defined as
"a system of shared meanings, attitudes, and values, and the symbolic
forms (performances, artifacts) in which they are expressed or embodied."[63] Keith Thomas placed the rational world of doctrine in proximity
to the diffuse worlds of magic and witchcraft as explanations of misfortune, and he connected the familiar rationality of theology to the less
familiar rationale encoded in the laws of sympathy.[64] A generation of
historians has created a sketch map of early modern European popular
culture, a cultural universe neither divorced from the rational world of
doctrine nor invariably governed by its conventions of either expression
or meaning.[65] This popular culture has been considered in relation to
the formal ceremonies of the church in order "to rediscover the 'aver-

age' Christian of past ages and to know how and to what extent he practiced his religion and lived his faith."[66] Although no consensus has been reached on the claim that the different worldviews of the past reflect the existence of "mental structures radically different from our own," historians in several early modern fields have used the techniques of this sociology to produce an interdisciplinary history of religion.[67]

The method used to reconstruct parish communities in the Vale of Gloucester draws on the ideas and techniques of social and cultural anthropology as a complement to the rational schemes created to understand intellectual aspects of religion. An anthropological approach differs from other approaches in its attention to the symbolic significance of social relations for the participants. An emphasis on the value of symbols and ritual in social life has established the creation of meaning in human society as the distinctive concern of anthropology. An important aspect of this interest in meaning has been the analysis of the roles of symbol and ritual in the creation of social continuity. Edmund Leach has defined the problems of continuity and discontinuity as fundamental problems of anthropology in his formulation of the question, "How do the discontinuities of time and space which we seem to recognize at one level tie in with the continuities which we experience at another?"[68] Leach referred to the social context of personal experience, but the same question could be asked of continuities and discontinuities in the social experience of groups. This emphasis on symbolism and the role of symbols in the continuity of social organizations makes the questions and techniques of anthropologists particularly suited to the explication of the incidents in Forthampton and Tewkesbury. Since the customs of this anthropological community are unfamiliar to many historians, it may be helpful to define a few basic concepts.

Symbol is among the most frequently used concepts in modern anthropology yet remains the most difficult to define. Despite the diversity of opinion, most anthropologists define some form of symbolism as essential to the order of human social activity. Clifford Geertz has defined a symbol as "any object, act, event, quality, or relation which serves as a vehicle for a conception: the conception is the symbol's meaning."[69] He differentiates the symbol as an "extrinsic source of information" or model of the natural world beyond the individual, as a social construct or representation of the external world based on shared associations.[70] The study of symbolism and its referential properties has become more diffuse and problematic since Geertz made this categorical statement in the 1960s, but recent anthropological studies of local societies in Britain have reaffirmed the importance of subtle forms of discursive symbolism, such as local dialect, in the constitution of group boundaries and social identity.[71] Anthony Cohen has acknowledged the universality and ambiguity of symbolism but has simultaneously sought to locate in this universe of symbols the expressions that serve as vehicles for a sense of distinctiveness or common identity.[72] This study places a similar emphasis on the symbols of personal and corporate identity in the Vale of Gloucester. The field of reference has been further narrowed to include primarily the sacred symbols of religious identity. If the focus has been placed on religious symbolism, however, it is because symbols such as the parish church, parochial boundaries, and various religious observances informed the corporate identity most frequently acknowledged in local sources.

As invocations of a shared identity, religious symbols were most commonly used in the public rituals of the parish church. The clerical performers of sacred rituals combined symbols in different styles to form complex statements about both the content of religious experience and the nature of religious fellowship. Because ritual was a conscious and a prescriptive process that required the creation of a statement in the symbolic medium, the ritual moment often furnished the most cogent evidence of differences in local responses to particular symbols and forms of identity. This study focuses primarily but not exclusively on rituals known as rites of passage, particularly the rich evidence of mortuary customs in the parish.[73] The most familiar rites of passage were performed in the crisis moments of birth, marriage, and death. These rites evoked social relationships to assist the subject or primary beneficiary of the ritual to cross a perceived boundary or threshold in the process of transition to a new status or new social position and also represented the meaning of this transition symbolically. The rites of passage were particularly sensitive points in religious culture, an intersection of diverse forms of personal relationship and symbolic notions of personal and shared identity. As moments of transition or movement, the rites represented phases in a ceremonial system. The coherence and unity of the system were expressed in the collective rite of communion as a symbolic representation of the religious identity of the person in the social context of the parish. This conception of ritual is inseparable from the form of fellowship that rituals evoked and affirmed. If symbols were the vehicles of abstract conceptions, ritual was the manipulation of symbols in fellowship, an activity calculated to achieve religious aims but inseparably linked to the social context of its performance.

Symbol and ritual were products of the social and psychological matrix represented in modern concepts of structure. The method employed in this study considers elementary structures in three distinct but interrelated forms: the symbol, the ritual, and the ceremonial system. Structure is easier to demonstrate than to define or describe. Claude Lévi-Strauss has defined the imposition of forms or schemes on content as an "unconscious activity of the mind" and has placed structure among "the unconscious foundations of social life." As the "unconscious structures" of institutions, these schemes "correspond neither to a particular model of the institution nor to the arbitrary grouping of characteristics common to several variants of the institution," but "may be reduced to certain relations of correlation and opposition."[74] Because this formulation of structure represents texts and symbols in terms of the oppositions inherent in classifications of experience, the technique has implications for narratives of the Hickes incident in Tewkesbury. If symbolism expresses an unconscious structure, the various accounts of sacrilege should disclose the essential structure of the symbol. This treatment of the text as a manifestation of structure defines structure itself in a manner susceptible to empirical demonstration. Structure must be seen to manifest itself in the creative life of a society. If the notion of unconscious structure has any validity for the analysis of social activity, the unconscious structure of the cross should be detectable in the conscious discussion of its violation.

Two additional forms of structure in ritual and in the ceremonial system may help to clarify the process of religious conflict and transformation in the Vale of Gloucester. An idea of structure as binary opposition is not sufficient for a social interpretation of ritual. Different forms of social relationship may have the same binary structure inherent in their symbolism. This structural identity cannot explain the disturbances experienced in the shift from one form of relationship to the other; therefore, the structure of a ritual should include the implicit reference of particular combinations of symbols to specific forms of fellowship. The rituals of baptism and communion performed in the parish church had the territorial and residential community of the parish as their social referent, a reference that formed an important element in their meaning. The covert assemblies of Nonconformists in Forthampton had as their social referent an exclusive fellowship of spiritually sympathetic families. These rituals may have carried many of the same binary structures in their formal symbolism, but the distinctive social formations that accompanied the rituals were included in their symbolic significance and generated violent conflict.

A similar form of structure existed in the ceremonial system. As rituals referred to local forms of fellowship, the ceremonial system as a whole embodied and represented the larger social and political worlds of the kingdom.[75] The explication of this form of structure and its shifts over time is difficult work. Because a structure of this kind combined the ideals of social and political hierarchy and the practice of ceremony, the problems of conflict and change are best approached by a consideration of prescriptive models for religious behavior, accounts of what was supposed to happen in the parish, and an exploration of the effectiveness of such models as descriptions of practice. Before the Civil War and Revolution of the 1640s and 1650s, religious factions in the Vale of Gloucester shared a model of religious fellowship in the parish. These factions represented their beliefs as authoritative blueprints for a reformed Church of England and attempted to realize their visions of order in the local church. Despite resistance to Nonconformist notions of religious ceremony and fellowship in both the parish and diocese, separation from the Church of England was not perceived as a viable alternative, although precedents for separation existed in the late sixteenth and the early seventeenth centuries. After the return of the monarchy in 1660, this notion of the inclusive parish and Separatist forms of religious identity and fellowship served as the basis of multiple communities and conflicts. These differences between the model and the reality of religious solidarity in the parish raise several questions. What were the codes of behavior conceived before and after the wars to explain the failure of prescriptive models as descriptions of religious identity and fellowship? If strategies were devised after the Restoration to accommodate religious pluralism, how were such strategies created and made authoritative? This third form of structure may help to reveal the broad social and political implications of conflicts over prescriptive models or representations of religious community, such as the ideal of the parish and its ceremonies.[76]

These concepts of symbol, ritual, and structure help to clarify the significance of the sacred in the cultural system and to address a difficult problem in the social history of early modern religion, a problem Robert Scribner has identified as the process whereby "the sacred is always experienced *within* the profane."[77] Several recent studies have identified controversies over religious symbols and moral codes or manners as elements in a unitary process of social control and religious reformation.[78] The difficulty of this interpretation, in the context of evidence from the northern parishes of the Vale of Gloucester, is the absence of Nonconformists or Puritans, who were active critics of the Book of Common Prayer and the lawful ceremonies of the Church of England, from the offices of disciplinary enforcement in the parish. The moral discipline of a parish, and the prosecution of Nonconformists for such offenses as rejection of the surplice or refusal to kneel in communion, were undertaken by a Protestant faction difficult to describe as Puritan in any sense other than its interest in a discipline that followed some of the familiar contours of godliness.[79] As churchwardens regularly prosecuted Nonconformists in the courts, it is difficult to make the case for a *Puritan* reformation of moral discipline and church ceremonies.

A solution to this problem may begin from recent efforts to recover early modern theories of the interrelationships among symbols of the sacred, rituals, and everyday life in society. The symbolism used in parish churches, in England and across Europe, expressed a conception of the sacred as the absolute reality and of the profane world as an illusion in comparison.[80] Yet the codes of behavior in everyday life, such as the codes of sexual integrity, established the proximity of the profane world to the sacred and thus to the absolute reality of religion. These prescribed codes of conduct may be appreciated even as techniques to consecrate life itself.[81] The evident difference between conflicts over manners and conflicts over the ceremonies performed in parish churches may be viewed as an expression of early modern notions of sacred and profane, and the relationship between the forms of conflict may be represented by concepts of core and periphery. These concepts are used to describe positions in a cultural system. The core included the sacred symbols of the ceremonial system and the ritual process that created the parish. The periphery contained the profane life of the behavioral codes, even the consecrated codes of family life, prescribed and sanctioned in ritual contexts. This scheme of classification represents both the differentiation of and the interdependence of symbols and behavioral codes, sacred and profane.[82] The religious symbols enshrined in the core of the system represented the ultimate source of authority or frame of reference for everyday moral conduct, and the codes of behavior incorporated in the periphery translated the order of the sacred into everyday social life. The classification of a statement or practice in the periphery does not denote marginality or insignificance in the everyday sense of the term. This classification, which positions the action or the statement in relation to the symbols of sacred power in the cultural order, makes it possible to recognize conflicts over manners that do not necessarily imply fundamental conflict over the core system of religious symbolism. As a model of the relations among the myriad representations in the cultural system, the scheme thus differentiates conflict over sacred ceremonies from conflict over manners.

A theory of the sacred is only as effective as the archive and the evidence used to explore its problems and possibilities. This book depends on a variety of evidence, but the most important sources come from the Gloucester diocesan archive.[83] The detection books created after episcopal visitations survive across the seventeenth century, and, in the absence of an effective archidiaconal jurisdiction in Gloucester diocese, these books provide the only consistent quantitative and qualitative evidence of religious conflict and parish discipline. The probate records of the court, the wills and inventories, were intimately related to experience of the sacred, particularly preparations for death. Parish records are indispensable to this kind of inquiry but unfortunately have not survived in equal proportion for the parishes included. The annual accounts of the churchwardens in Tewkesbury, which survive in a magnificent series from 1563 to 1703, attest both to the enormous expense of maintenance and to the local sense of responsibility and affection for the fabric.[84] The corporation of Tewkesbury has also left substantial records of its activities in the late sixteenth and the seventeenth centuries. A series of five minute books provides evidence of the interrelationship between the civil and ecclesiastical domains, and the account book of a local charity, linked to the corporation in its administration, preserves a chronicle of important events that emphasized the interaction of local, national, and international concerns.[85] A rich sectarian archive for Tewkesbury and its neighborhood consists of the Tewkesbury Baptist church book, a record of the members and activities of the church from the 1650s to the middle of the eighteenth century, and detailed Quaker records of weekly and monthly assemblies after the early 1670s.[86] This archive presents numerous difficulties and complexities, but the problems mean little in the abstract and are best discussed as the records are used.

The first part of this book discusses the formal characteristics of social life in the late sixteenth and the seventeenth centuries. These characteristics—the expressions of custom and place, forms of social identity and interaction, the creative power of religious symbols and ritual in notions of personal identity and the fellowship of the parish—existed continuously from the late sixteenth to the late seventeenth centuries, and indeed the temporal boundaries of this study cannot contain their histories. This descriptive interpretation is an attempt to create an ethnography of the sacred, to demonstrate the interrelationship of the sacred and everyday life. The sacred appears as an element in a variety of profane experiences, from the perception of place to the representation of friendship, physical infirmity, and mortality. Yet the discussion of ritual and social identity cannot avoid the issue of distinctive notions of fellowship and styles of ceremony in the parish and thus begins to confront the process of transformation in ceremonial system and society.

The second half of the book then focuses on the implications of religious diversity and attempts to identify a temporal process of transformation in the forms of fellowship expressed in religious symbols. This transformation was evident in the successive variants of local religious conflict and diversity. The first expressions of religious difference in the late sixteenth and early seventeenth centuries assumed the form of factional diversity in the parish. This internal diversity subsequently assumed different forms in response to crises of national magnitude. The problems of civil war and revolution created a garrison in Tewkesbury and dissolved the national church and the local parish into sectarianism. After the return of monarchy in 1660, the restored parish continued to include a spectrum of religious opinions that gradually shaded into formally invisible communities of Dissenters. Only after a further experience of revolution in 1688 were Anglicans and Dissenters incorporated as citizens in a common civic community expressed not in the ceremonies of the parish church but in the oaths of loyalty to the new monarchy and in a statutory *recognition* of religious difference, which was a decisive change in the interrelationship of religious symbols and political authority.

This study covers a century of familiar events but does not assume the form of a conventional narrative. The choice was made to cover a relatively long period of time in episodic fashion, to provide a detailed analysis of incidents from a particular locality rather than to multiply examples from more diffuse sources. This approach may help to resolve an important problem in early modern English history that is still not clearly understood in detail: the interrelationship of the crises in the Stuart regime and the uses of sacred power in the fellowship of the parish and in the intimate contexts of everyday life. If the interpretation presented here were to elevate the experience of Tewkesbury and its neighborhood as a symbol or type, such as the experience of market towns generally, the approach might present serious problems. Some specified criteria of representativeness would have to control the selection of both locality and evidence. The incidents chosen for analysis would have to stand as archetypes, as models of similar events in other localities, and would have to be placed on a spectrum of possible or likely events in the typical locality. But no such claim of representativeness is made for the events described in this study: Thomas Drake and Richard Garner, Thomas Hickes, and Francis Wells do not appear as types or as the vehicles of an abstract process. The precise form of the conflicts and transformations discussed here may well have been unique to the neighborhood of Tewkesbury. However, this limitation does not mean that the experiences of Drake and Garner, Hickes, and Wells were devoid of implications for the interpretation of other local societies. The elements involved in these experiences, such as religious symbolism and ceremony, notions of personal identity and common loyalty, and perceptions of place and status, existed in every corner of early modern England. The task of the historian is not to elevate a particular expression of the interaction of these elements as representative but to discover the range of variation and possible interaction among the formal elements of social life.

I

Social Form

1590–1690

Reverend Histories: Geography and Landscape

I do love these ancient ruins. We never tread upon them, but we set our foot on some reverend history.

John Webster, *The Duchess of Malfi* (1623)

The Vale of Gloucester has been shaped by the life of its rivers nowhere more than in the neighborhood of Tewkesbury, nine miles north of the City of Gloucester.[1] In 1712, Robert Atkyns perceived the hand of God behind the riverine forces of the northern vale and likened its physical beauty to "the garden of Eden, watered with four rivers."[2] A drawing of the Tewkesbury quay made in the early nineteenth century displays little evidence of belief in a providential design but joins the life of the rivers to the life of the town, as a team of three horses strains to pull a load of bricks from the quay, destined for new building sites in Tewkesbury.[3] The vigorous activity, commerce, and prosperity in the scene appear to flow from the River Avon in the foreground, a link to the limitless commercial potential of the River Severn on the western border of the town. This beneficent power of the rivers, the relative ease of travel on the ferries between Tewkesbury and the rural parishes of Forthampton and Twyning, was never far from the fearsome destructive power of the annual floods in the northern vale.[4] The small Carrant Brook and the River Swilgate on the eastern and southern borders of Tewkesbury, as well as the Avon and the powerful Severn, produced extensive annual floods that turned the churchyard of Tewkesbury Abbey and even the streets of the town itself into reflective pools.[5] These rivers have been brought more or less under control in the twentieth century, although the flood of 1947 left only a few forlorn streetlamps above the flood waters in Church

Street, and children in the village of Deerhurst were rowed to school in boats.[6] During the seventeenth century, floods were frequent and severe. In 1640, "the wettest summer that ever was known," the fields around Tewkesbury flooded eight times between Midsummer and Michaelmas.[7] The annual floods were less severe but posed formidable problems to travel and communication in the vale. Thomas Baskerville was told in 1678 that "in flood times [the confluence of waters] makes an island of that part of [Tewkesbury] where St. Mary's Church does stand, and in very high floods comes into the church."[8] These floods could present deadly hazards to travelers. In 1656 John Bagstaff and Margery Farmer of Bristol "upon a high flood were drowned between the town's end and the Mythe."[9]

The high ground in the parish of Tewkesbury lies north and south of the town in the rural hamlets of the Mythe and Southwick. An ancient lookout hill constructed on the red marl of the Mythe Tute commands views of the vale north and south on the River Severn and dominates the confluence of the Severn and the Avon. In 1788 the royal touch transformed this scenic mound into Royal Hill, because the stately views delighted George III and Queen Charlotte.[10] The abbey and town occupy a smaller rise between the Mythe Tute and the hills of the estate known as the Park or Lodge in Southwick, a precious forty feet above the waters. The streets of Tewkesbury retain the pattern of hundreds of years. Church Street, High Street, and Barton Street converge to form "the cross" in the center of town, a place now dedicated to the memory of soldiers killed in Britain's modern wars, but formerly the site of the market cross, demolished by the hands of revolutionaries in 1650. These roads were periodically swamped by flood waters, but in happier times the junction made the town an important hub in the commercial life of the vale. Church Street points south to Gloucester and the villages of Deerhurst, Tredington, and Norton. High Street leaves Tewkesbury in branches, north to Worcester and northeast to Bredon. The commercial prosperity of this route between Gloucester and Worcester is reflected in the timber-framed splendor of the buildings on Church Street and High Street, homes of the rich and powerful in the seventeenth century. Barton Street crosses the fields of Ashchurch to the east and turns northeast to Stow and the market town of Evesham. The floods ensured the survival of open spaces that magnified the modest elevation of the town, and the Norman abbey, constructed in the twelfth century, dominates the landscape of the northern vale from this enhanced position at the southern end of Church Street. Behind the shops and sturdy houses of the main streets, in the seventeenth century, lay the maze of alleys and lanes inhabited by the poor, deprived of sun but occasionally afforded a view of the abbey.[11] Red Lane ran like a rope between the River Avon and the riches of the High Street. Gander Lane and St. Mary's Lane snaked in the shadows behind Church Street. Behind the alleys and lanes were the fields and the water.

The Vale of Gloucester supported a rich agriculture. William Marshall described the soil of the vale in the late eighteenth century as a "rich, deep loam."[12] Tewkesbury and adjacent parishes of the northern vale were distinguished by alluvial meadows, such as the magnificent Severn Ham, a broad meadow of two hundred acres between the streets of Tewkesbury and the River Severn. In addition to its provision of hay and pasture, enriched by the Severn floods, the Ham beckoned as a racecourse. In October 1721 the Prince of Wales sponsored a race on the Ham for a gold cup valued at fifty guineas, and the horseraces in Tewkesbury routinely attracted enthusiasts from across the county.[13] The land devoted to agriculture in Tewkesbury consisted primarily of pasture and meadow.[14] The important exceptions were the Oldbury field, east of the town, and parts of Southwick around Home Hill and North Longdon Hill. Oldbury field contained substantial tracts of arable land, although the clay soil was good for brickmaking, and George Harris claimed in the 1620s that arable land in the Oldbury had declined as a result of gentlemen making "brick kills."[15] The arable fields of Southwick were the sites of experiments in commercial crops, such as woad, during the late sixteenth and early seventeenth centuries.[16]

This agricultural landscape had entered the English historical imagination as a record of the clash of Yorkists and Lancastrians at the Battle of Tewkesbury in 1471. The fields of Southwick and Gubs Hill contain Bloody Meadow, which was named for a massacre of Lancastrian soldiers in flight after their defeat, and Margaret's Camp, which was supposed to mark the Lancastrian army's position before the battle.[17] In the sixteenth and seventeenth centuries, this connection to the military trials of English royalty comprised much of Tewkesbury's limited significance in national memory. An imaginative but disingenuous newsbook writer evoked this landscape of Yorkist triumph as the site of a great *parliamentary* victory against papist forces from Wales in 1642.[18]

Tewkesbury served as a market town for the rural parishes in its vicinity.[19] Walton Cardiff lay southeast of the town, its low pasture and meadow drained by the River Swilgate, Carrant Brook, and Tirle Brook. In the seventeenth century, the burgesses of Tewkesbury did not consider Walton an independent parish, and the clerk drew accusatory hands in the town's parish registers beside the baptisms, marriages, and burials received by villagers of Walton Cardiff in the abbey church.[20] The lands of Walton Cardiff and Tredington, a lowland parish two miles southeast of Tewkesbury, had belonged to Tewkesbury Abbey before the dissolution of the monastery in 1539, and the town council believed that the revenue of its chapelries followed the abbey church itself into the property of the town. The noise of this quarrel, as well as a series of disputes in law over the authority to levy parish rates, added its discordant theme to a century of disturbance in the vale.[21] Tredington differed from its neighbors only in the extent of its arable land, complemented by tracts of meadow on the banks of the Swilgate in the west and pasture in the east. Tewkesbury Abbey had also controlled estates in the large parish of Ashchurch, two miles east of Tewkesbury on the borders of Tredington and Walton Cardiff. As a result of a lease of the Ashchurch rectory made before the dissolution of the monastery, the four main hamlets of the parish, Northway and Newton in the northwest, Aston on Carrant in the northeast, Pamington in the southeast, and Fiddington in the southwest, avoided the political difficulties of Tredington and Walton Cardiff and constituted an independent parish from the sixteenth century.[22] Ashchurch remained an agricultural parish composed of low pasture, meadow, and arable land, watered by Carrant Brook and Tirle Brook, until the introduction of light industry in the twentieth century transformed its economy. Plans made in the eighteenth and nineteenth centuries to exploit mineral waters beneath the western lands of the parish never came to fruition, as vested interests to the south confined this dream of a spa in Ashchurch to the empty, disused building on the Tewkesbury road, no rival to the salubrious waters and economic power of Cheltenham spa.[23]

Deerhurst, three miles south of Tewkesbury on the Severn, suffered the same harsh floods as the town. The mythical dragon of Deerhurst could hardly have inflicted more severe damage on the parish than the annual deluge that forced villagers to maintain raised footpaths and a system of boards or "stanks" to preserve the roads from the waters.[24]

These floods brought the usual curses and benedictions of the vale, as the alluvial lands in the southern and western parts of Deerhurst provided rich pasture and meadow to balance the arable eastern lands in the mixed husbandry of the parish.[25] Villagers from the four scattered hamlets of Deerhurst in the north, Apperley in the south, Wightfield in the center, and Deerhurst Walton in the east, attended the same church in the northern corner of the parish, a Saxon church and ancient priory, later a cell in the vast spiritual and landed empire of Tewkesbury Abbey.[26]

The roads and rivers often intermingled in the watery landscape of the northern vale. A ferry at the Upper Lode, a curve in the River Severn west of Tewkesbury, carried passengers to the rural parishes of Longdon and Bushley, northwest of the town.[27] Less than a mile south of this site at the Lower Lode, a second ferry joined Tewkesbury to the valuable tracts of woodland in the parish of Forthampton. Before the dissolution of the monastery, the monks of Tewkesbury Abbey had owned both ferries, which formed the links to abbey estates on the western banks of the Severn. Forthampton contained the most luxuriant woodlands in the northern vale. The forest dispersed human settlement on the land, and houses and farms lay some distance apart even in the hamlets of Swinley and Forthampton.[28] The clusters of dwellings in the smaller hamlets scattered across the west of the parish, known as Swinley Green, Dunsmore Green, Long Green, and Neely Green, conceded to Worcestershire in 1931, first sheltered squatters on the forested wastelands of the manor of Forthampton.[29] These woodlands supported poor laborers as well as the rich abbey and its lay successors in the sixteenth and seventeenth centuries. A third ferry joined the market in Tewkesbury to the rural hamlet of the Mythe, which was north of the town.[30] The varied features of this landscape are intimated by the tragic record of Thomas Baxter, a servant who fell to his death from an apple tree on the Wakeman estate in the Mythe in 1687.[31] After the ferry journey to Mythe Hill, a road led north from the orchards and brickfields of the Mythe to the nucleated settlement of Twyning and to the dispersed hamlets and isolated farms of Shuthonger and Green End, all situated in a landscape of meadow, pasture and arable land that supported the mixed husbandry characteristic of the northern vale.[32]

Although descriptions of local topography and landmarks, like the rational clarity of lines on a map, are useful instruments for tourists, they provide only superficial descriptions of places, an outsider's perspective. The landscapes of the sixteenth and seventeenth centuries were overlaid by complex systems of claims and rights, which were familiar to natives but invisible to outsiders. Spaces were bounded and marked in the language and symbols of custom, a pervasive but frequently unexamined mode of discourse. The language of custom created, from local actions over time, authoritative symbols bounded by the span of collective memory. Custom was a way to see and define relationships, a method of relating moral concepts and formal rules to observed practice. The symbols of custom, enshrined in the memory of parish elders, prescribed rules to protect the life of the group from the disintegrating influence of time. Customs differed from parish to parish, and this variation helps to explain subtle differences in the experiences of place characteristic of local communities in the vale.

Custom was a common mode of defining relationships. The word *custom* also referred to specific relationships or practices, but interpretations of custom based narrowly on practice can account for the frequency of disputes over customs in the sixteenth and seventeenth centuries only in terms of a breakdown in the customary system. A definition of custom based on the evidence of this creative idiom or language, which was used to form rules for relationships from the vocabulary of local practice, offers a different perspective on familiar conflicts over custom, for conflict ceases in itself to indicate a weakness or breakdown. Most of the evidence of custom in the Vale of Gloucester comes from disputes over specific practices, particularly disputes over the custom of tithe recorded in the church courts. These conflicts reveal the ways in which litigants could use the language of custom to further their own interests while sharing with opponents a basic belief in custom as a proper way to understand communal relationships.

Custom possessed wide authority and prescribed the appropriate behavior in many local contexts in the sixteenth and seventeenth centuries. In its most familiar forms, custom differentiated between claims to the yield of land and livestock. The timing and scale of tithe payments, for instance, were fixed by customs that marked significant points in the agricultural calendar. In 1593 the parishioners of Ashchurch described their customary payment of small tithes.[33] The annual cycle for farmers raising sheep in Ashchurch came to an end on Holyrood Day, when payments were made to the farmer of the tithes. The parishioners' representation of the custom allowed the tithe farmer one halfpenny for every ewe or dry sheep sold unshorn before Holyrood Day and one penny for every sheep sold after that date.[34] The timing of these payments influenced the scale of participation by local farmers in the spring fair at Evesham and also set the pattern for the late summer sale of animals to farmers in neighboring parishes.[35] The way in which the language of custom objectified practice was indicated by John Carpenter, who described the parishioners of Ashchurch as having "possessed" the custom in question ever during his remembrance.[36]

The power of custom is best illustrated by its influence on even routine movements in the landscape. James Cartwright of Tredington claimed a customary right of way through the parish churchyard and a corresponding right to use the churchyard gate. In 1613 the churchwardens allowed the existence of Cartwright's customary path but argued that the occupant of Tredington Farm, Cartwright's holding, had an equally powerful customary obligation to keep the gate in good repair.[37] Moving in this kind of landscape could be difficult for an outsider, not knowing the system of paths and private rights of way marked out by long practice. Few mistakes went uncontested, for in a relatively short time, "mistakes" might become entrenched customs.

Crossing the Severn was an everyday event in parts of northern Gloucestershire, and a complex set of customs had formed to ease the process. The passage that was called the Overlode or Upper Lode, previously parcel of Tewkesbury Abbey, was owned and farmed by the crown after the dissolution of the monasteries.[38] The parishes closest to the passage claimed an "ancient custom" whereby the occupants of particular holdings made annual payments of wheat, called "custom sheaves," to the farmer of the passage in return for crossing. The boatman, a servant of the farmer, received the occasional sheave and was entitled to a "flood penny" at Christmas. At the end of the harvest, the farmer sent the "passage cart" around the parishes of Longdon and Bushley to gather his customary payment. The practice was originally a manorial custom, and before the sixteenth century, payment had been based on the "ancient messuages where ploughs or teams have been kept."[39] This custom differentiated natives from mere travelers in the region. In the 1620s the parishioners complained that the farmer was trying to break the custom by forcing them to pay each time they passed over "as if they were strangers," although in earlier times the parishioners themselves had made an unsuccessful attempt to evade the custom, claiming payment ought not to be made in time of plague, when crossings to Tewkesbury were infrequent.[40] In a brief prepared for the case, however, it was remarked that the form of payment could only be modified if former practice was shown not to be custom.[41]

Custom was an open system, expansive and flexible in its boundaries, but because the symbols of custom implied a deference to established practices, the system was susceptible to lapses when confronted with new applications or unprecedented situations. The customary status of woad became an issue in Southwick, a southern hamlet of the parish of Tewkesbury, in 1595.[42] The cultivation of woad had taken hold in southern England during the early 1580s, but this dispute provides the earliest evidence of its cultivation in the fields around Tewkesbury.[43] The appearance of this new crop led to a controversy over the application of custom and the payment of tithes, although none of the participants in the dispute questioned the more general authority of custom. The definitive sentence of the consistory court has not survived in this case, but depositions indicate that the farmer made no headway persuading his neighbors of woad's immunity to the customary assessment of tithe.[44]

Customs were sometimes made deliberately by the collective action of a parish and could be adapted to local circumstances. Many of the symbols and rules in the customary system were older than the residents of a parish and thus appeared beyond human agency, but some customs were created in response to changing local conditions. In the summer of 1601 the copyholders of Ashchurch remembered decisions taken twenty-five years earlier that had created a new set of relationships between the hamlets of the parish.[45] Until roughly 1575 a pasture called the Homedowns, 160 acres lying between Northway and Fiddington, had been open field and common pasture for the copyholders of the five hamlets of the parish.[46] Then "the copyholders of the five hamlets, seeing the inconvenience that grew by this grazing of Homedowns as before, fell to a composition or agreement among themselves and allotted to every the hamlets a part of the Homedowns according to the condition or quality of every man's copyhold and as they esteemed and judged the same of right to belong to the several tithings or hamlets."[47] Subsequent disputes over customary relations and boundaries between the hamlets took this collective decision as their point of departure, as the moment at which the custom had been made.

The authority of custom was consecrated by the transcendent authority of religious symbols, ritual, and sanctions, as demonstrated by the ceremonial delineation of the boundaries between parishes. These boundaries were sanctified by ritual processions or perambulations that combined the idioms of custom and religion to form a powerful statement of territorial identity and spiritual unity. The bounds were walked by "the curate and the substantial men of the parish" in the early summer as part of the week of fasts and prayers before Ascension Day.[48] The curate and churchwardens led the lay community of the parish in this procession, stopping at "certain convenient places" to "admonish the people" to give thanks "for the increase and abundance of his fruits upon the face of the earth," to implore divine mercy, and to ask for a blessing on the fields.[49] The customary bounds of the parish thus symbolized a common dependence on divine power and goodwill and were the spatial expression of a distinct communal relationship with God.

The royal injunctions of 1559 called for annual perambulations during the rogation days, a penitential phase of the Easter cycle that included the fifth Sunday after Easter and the Monday, Tuesday, and Wednesday before Ascension Day, but the ceremonies seem to have taken place only intermittently during the sixteenth and seventeenth centuries.[50] This irregularity of performance is difficult to interpret as evidence of a decline in local interest or increased local conflict, indeed as evidence of social change in any form, because the pattern of intermittence remained constant. The few references to perambulations in the middle years of the sixteenth century indicate the same discontinuity of performance that characterized the seventeenth century, whereas the householders of middle rank in Tredington were active in perambulations as late as 1714.[51] No formal description of perambulation can do justice to the diversity of local practice. The ritual conveyed a message of broad Christian significance in its consecration of the physical and spiritual boundaries of the parish, but the social content of this process, the ritual actions used in the procession, and the frequency of performance varied considerably from place to place and over time. As a substantial assembly of neighbors, perambulation could have many indirect social consequences, from the resolution of conflicts to the distribution of charity. These informal aspects of perambulation were the most locally specific.[52] Perambulation, which assumed a variety of forms depending on other aspects of custom in specific parishes, is unreliable as a general measure of parochial cohesion.

In northern Gloucestershire, perambulation served as a means to transmit the knowledge of custom from one generation to the next. Age was the most important variable in the composition of the procession, although wealth and status were not insignificant.[53] The participants were usually the householders and "ancient men" of the parish, but nonhouseholders were seldom included in the procession. The ceremony expressed the unity of propertyholders, although this group included one-hearth householders as well as the wealthier residents of the parish.[54] Younger parishioners also took part, learning the bounds and customs by following and talking to the parish elders. Conversation with the older residents and observation of the perambulation were equally important for newcomers to the parish, thereby acquainting themselves with the customs of an unfamiliar environment. The parishioners who testified in disputes over custom were almost invariably male natives of the parish, but this bias was case specific and related particularly to male experience of the payment of tithes. Older women were not disqualified by gender from speaking with authority on questions of custom; in fact, Richard Sharp of Deerhurst learned the tithe customs of his village by listening to the talk of "the old men and women" of the parish. After long residence, an immigrant could also acquire the authority to speak as a native on custom, but migrants who remained in the region might find themselves called "home" to depose in the controversies of their native parish. Richard Sharp resided north of Tewkesbury at Twyning when he was called back to his native Deerhurst to help resolve a boundary dispute.[55] The close observation of processions performed in neighboring parishes was an important part of the learning process, for the balance of custom in a parish could be upset by the loss of territory to neighbors. In Deerhurst, for instance, tithes were based on the number of beasts that parishioners grazed, not on the area of tithable pasture. If fields were lost to the neighboring parish of the Leigh, Deerhurst farmers not only would pay the same tithe for less pasture but also would be forced to reduce their stock.[56]

Perambulation was an important aspect of identity and socialization in the parish. Young parishioners and newcomers learned from parish elders the practices and boundaries that set their parish apart from its neighbors and, simultaneously, observed customs different from their own in the processions of neighboring groups. Custom, as a form of distinction and relationship, was thus reproduced in the attitudes of a new generation of parishioners. The effectiveness of this educational device derived from the power of perambulation itself as a religious ceremony in which the language of custom was spoken with the authority of God.

Conflict was endemic in the world of custom, for specific customs were not invariably favorable to particular interests. Custom was a right that cut across time, no momentary interest or lapse but an authentic claim resting on a moral principle. In conflicts over custom, opposed practices were dismissed as the base accretions of time, as corruptions of custom. In 1610 the parishioners of Deerhurst allowed that the perambulations of their neighbors in the Leigh had occasionally crossed over into a disputed field but described this practice as the result of a "dirty lane" that "hindered their passage and not of any right or title they had" to enter the field.[57] Roger Darston of Ashchurch took the actions of his tenant as a corruption of customary rights and threatened to "turn him out of his house, if he did watch anymore with Fiddington men."[58] The farmer of the Overlode passage across the Severn, disputing the claims of parishioners in Bushley and Longdon, argued that "there was no ancient custom but agreed compositions between the farmers of the passage and the inhabitants dwelling near which ought not to bind the owners though the usage has been long."[59] No one disputed the authority of custom: controversy centered on the proper identification of that authority in specific circumstances. Denial of custom would have amounted to a denial of self and place.

The common language of custom used in court records often concealed diverse experiences of landscape and place. The social complexity of local communities in the vale, divided on lines of social status and wealth, age, gender, and worldview, produced different experiences of place and movement in the landscape.[60] These experiences differed between social ranks and across time; they were not the same for women and men, not the same for young women and old women, young men and old men. The almost infinite diversity of local social life resided in this intimate social landscape. A place contained as many landscapes as its social experiences, marking landscape in patterns of purely personal significance. These social or personal landscapes may ultimately help to explain the numerous conflicts in which personal and factional interests were not differentiated from the interests of a parish community, defined in terms of custom.

Status differences in the experience of landscape resulted from the different social situations in which knowledge of place was acquired. Depositions recorded in tithe disputes provide ample evidence of these situations, as officers of the church court asked people of different social rank to reveal their knowledge of ownership and the means by which the knowledge was acquired. In 1603, for instance, Thomas Alston, a gentleman of Deerhurst, deposed in a dispute between Sir Thomas Throckmorton, scion of a powerful landed family, and Robert Wells, a husbandman.[61] Alston acquired his knowledge of Throckmorton's rights in the disputed fields by "seeing and perusing" two leases. The authority of Alston's statements about relations in the landscape thus rested on knowledge gained from his reading of legal documents formally transferring ownership from Throckmorton's father and brother to Throckmorton himself. Alston's reflection on the fields in question was reflection on a relationship to Throckmorton close enough to allow access to family papers. In September 1680 Nicholas Smithsend, a gentleman, gave evidence in a dispute between Robert Wriggan, curate of Walton Cardiff, and Thomas Jeynes, a gentleman of Tewkesbury.[62] Smithsend based his discussion of rights in the fields of Walton Cardiff on his knowledge of "a grant and settlement" made by his former neighbor Fulke Read, also described as a gentleman, to the College of All Souls, Oxford. The experience of landscape and its ownership was, for Alston and Smithsend, inseparable from their experience as gentlemen sharing with other gentlemen a social world shaped by literacy and the language of law.

Those excluded from the world of gentlemen acquired their knowledge of ownership in a different but no less authoritative manner. In 1610 Hugo Hampton, a husbandman of Deerhurst, was asked for the source of his knowledge about local ownership.[63] Hampton said he knew the disputed tithes had been leased because he had "seen the parties receive, collect, and gather the tithes" from the field in question. Ten years later, the husbandman Ralph Jeynes of Northway in the parish of Ashchurch asserted Robert Hunt's right to tithe in the fields of Ashchurch, having himself paid tithe to Hunt and having seen others do the same.[64] William Worley, a yeoman, and Edward Knowles, a blacksmith, speaking in the same cause as Jeynes, both based their knowledge of Hunt's right on the visual evidence of payment and the authority of observed practice.[65] The spoken word and observed practice were the most important sources of knowledge about claims in the landscape of commoners. In 1603, Richard Harris, a yeoman of Deerhurst, had "credibly heard it reported and spoken" that Sir Thomas Throckmorton's right to tithe in the fields of Deerhurst was not expired.[66] John Jeynes recalled in 1680 "that he heard [that] Mr. [Fulke] Read gave a portion of tithes to a curate to supply the cure [of Walton Cardiff] and that the curate [had the] right to receive such tithes."[67]

These spoken and visual sources of knowledge were not spurned by gentlemen, nor was the experience of literacy a monopoly of gentlemen.[68] The pervasiveness of leasehold arrangements in the neighborhood of Tewkesbury implies the existence of a group whose experience crossed the boundary between gentle and common forms of knowledge and experience.[69] A cultural distinction can nevertheless be made between groups of gentlemen and other social groups on the basis of differences in their means of acquiring knowledge about ownership, in the authority on which this knowledge was believed to rest, and in the social context in which knowledge was acquired. Gentlemen cited practice to bolster their claims about ownership, but their knowledge often rested on familiarity with written documents bearing the authority of law. The witnessing of deeds, which were formal transfers of legal ownership, was one of the many social obligations of a gentleman, usually fulfilled in the presence of other gentlemen. Knowledge of ownership—the possession of the landscape—was thus acquired through interaction and social exchange with others of the same status group. The diverse groups that were excluded from the society of gentlemen ordinarily did not make reference to written documents when forming statements about rights in the landscape. The authority of their statements, like the authority of custom, rested ultimately on the spoken word and on a keen observation of local practice. A knowledge of ownership was usually acquired in the fields or in the casual conversation of the alehouse, situations quite different from the gentle world of deeds and the muniment rooms of gentry families.

Tithe represented a specific form of property, a claim superimposed on the other forms of absolute property vested in the individual owner of the land. The dissolution of the monastery in Tewkesbury in 1539 transferred control of the tithes to lay proprietors. In the late sixteenth and seventeenth centuries, the servants or farmers of a more powerful landholder usually collected payment from local tenants, and the unequal distribution of knowledge about claims to tithe was one of the ways in which perceptions of landscape reflected inequalities of status and economic power. These inequalities were also reflected in objective boundaries on the land. In 1617 Richard Baugh and Giles Savage, the lords of Twyning and the Mythe, decided between themselves to divide their shared common "by meets and bounds."[70] Small farmers were caught between Savage and Baugh in the dispute over tithes that resulted from this decision. Mythe common was twice as large as Twyning common, yet Baugh, as farmer of the rectory of Twyning, insisted that residents of Twyning whose cattle grazed in both fields should pay tithe to him. Baugh's power was keenly felt in the landscape, his cattle easily recognized. Farmers eventually paid tithe to both Savage and Baugh, being assured by Savage that payment would be returned if he lost his suit in the consistory court.

Perceptions of property and claims to possess the land were equally important in relations between social equals. To move across the landscape of the vale was to be confronted constantly by objective marks and boundaries of ownership by neighbors. In the everyday relations between neighbors, a commonsense construction of ownership disregarded the difference between absolute property and rented property, and bestowed a practical ownership on the person *seen* to possess, the occupier.[71] A complex system of rules and sanctions protected the boundaries of property in this densely owned environment. These rules were part of an informal code of conduct known as neighborliness, an expression of Christian notions of charity in the everyday life of the parish; and the code of neighborliness received an explicit religious sanction in the perambulation ceremony, a ritual that consecrated property boundaries even as it sanctified the boundaries of the parish.[72]

Conflicts between neighbors in the vale assumed distinctive forms, the most common being the confrontation between real and moveable property represented by straying animals. In 1618, for instance, problems associated with adjoining gardens behind the houses in Tewkesbury led to verbal abuse and defamation.[73] Some hens belonging to Margaret Shaw's father, John Harding, had escaped into the garden of his neighbor, John Higgins. In the ensuing conflict, neighbors would ordinarily have used "civil" language to emphasize the accidental nature of the event and to establish distance, the hens having wandered "by chance."[74] But the damage done was taken personally by Mary Higgins, John's wife, who was thought by Shaw to have "exceeding ill used" the hens in handling the situation. Shaw came out of her father's house to protect his property and "told Mary Higgins of her ill usage of [the hens]."[75] An argument that began as a dispute over a property boundary ended with Higgins openly questioning Shaw's sexual integrity. Yet the personal aspects of boundaries and ownership could also promote solidarity between neighbors, as neighbors and kin regularly pooled their resources in common projects. Roger Darston and his "familiar friend" Edward Drake were partners in the leasing of a pasture in Ashchurch in 1601.[76] In 1617 the husbandman Thomas Neend of Ashchurch and his kinsman Richard Jordan joined their neighbor John Deaves in a lease of some pasture across the county border at Overbury in Worcestershire.[77]

The landscapes of the poor were as rich and varied as the landscapes of gentlemen and farmers of middle rank, but the indirect nature of the evidence makes it difficult to reconstruct the patterns of spatial significance created by people with little or no property.[78] The poor seldom recorded experiences of place, and the coherence of the poor as a group or broad class was the product of administrative perception. The experience of poor householders, for example, differed fundamentally from the experience of migration and homelessness. Despite numerous important gradations within these classes, the distinction between the settled and the migrant poor was decisive in the experience of landscape and place. Poor householders belonged to the parish community and possessed a claim on its resources in time of sickness or economic distress.[79] Place was familiar, its customs known, and its fields named. The rates and rents that provided poor relief were based on the distribution of property in the parish, and the claims of poor parishioners were thus defined within the boundaries of the customary landscape.

The landscapes of the homeless reflected the marginality of vagrants in a society deeply ambivalent about all forms of mobility, social and geographic.[80] The homeless, who move namelessly through local records, occasionally receive alms, always with the firm understanding that they will move on. A "poor woman" from Ireland passing through Tewkesbury in 1656 was given four pence, and a "poor man" received the same sum later in the year.[81] Those undone by "acts of God" sometimes received licenses to beg from the bishop of Gloucester, such as "Susanna Benry, a maid, and two children, with a pass, their habitations in the Isle of Aish being drowned by the breaking in of the sea."[82] Yet boundaries were generally a warning to the homeless: anonymous threats separating nameless, unfamiliar fields. Movement in the landscape was the often surreptitious search for shelter. William Hill, the town clerk of Tewkesbury, described his chance meeting with a band of homeless beggars in 1636. On a rainy November evening, Hill took refuge with a shepherd "in a poor cottage where the rain came so fast down the chimney that it forced us from the fire, and we had much ado to be dry in any other part of the house (the barns only excepted) where were about thirty persons, men, women, and children naked in straw, and amongst them a boy (who without teaching) plays well upon the tabor and pipe." The beggars were a close band "who [admitted] no strangers to come amongst them," and the boy played them to sleep at night.[83] The migrant poor may have survived in the margins of the customary landscape, but, as Hill's account makes clear, the homeless were not without communities and customs of their own.

Boundaries in the landscape were thus complex markers of local social life: sources of anxiety or solidarity, depending on the context. But differences in social rank were not the only causes of the varied experiences of landscape and place in the Vale of Gloucester. Differences of age profoundly influenced attitudes toward the landscape, although only scattered evidence survives to indicate the different worlds of the old and the young. The fields around Tewkesbury signified freedom from the constraints of religion and the discipline of craft for the eight apprentices caught playing stoolball on the Sabbath in the autumn of 1597.[84] These fields were open spaces, sites for the ritual violence of sport and its allocation of adolescent rank and status.[85] Yet the associations of the fields were quite different for the lovers Elizabeth Cartwright and Richard Bishop, "meeting at the end of a close of pasture, near unto her mother's house in Tredington."[86] In the presence of the relatives and friends gathered in the enclosure, and "after many kind and loving speeches passed between them," Cartwright and Bishop made formal declarations of their intention to marry.[87] This assembly of family and neighbors, and the formal contract of marriage, defined the field in terms of duties and obligations and created a place marked and remembered later in court for its link to a significant event in the life cycle. The concerns of old age created similar patterns of significance from places and relationships. In the late spring of 1610 Henry Chauntrell and Thomas Tusten, both in their middle sixties, were "walking up and down the common fields in Twyning, looking of sheep."[88] Chauntrell, whose thoughts were obviously elsewhere, began talking of provisions he

hoped to make for his kindred before his death.[89] Tusten listened dutifully, and, when he was questioned three years later about Chauntrell's
final wishes, he remembered the place and the circumstances of their
walk in the fields, when his friend had spoken so abruptly of mortality. In
this context, place and event were defined by the obligations of friendship and the sacred duty to honor the final wishes of the dead.

Differences in gender and the varied social experiences of women in
the life cycle affected perceptions of landscape and attitudes to place.
Married women did not experience landscape as their own personal
possession or property. These women participated in ownership only
indirectly through the property of their husbands. Margery Carter, for
instance, described an event that occurred "next door to her husband's
house."[90] Mary Higgins was in "her husband's garden" when it was invaded by hens from the adjoining property.[91] But Higgins' violent response to the violation of the boundary indicates the depth of the claim
to property underlying the formal exclusion from ownership. This claim
was acknowledged in the overwhelming number of cases in which wives
acquired control of the family property after the death of their husbands.[92] The right of ultimate control was keenly felt and defended. In
1612, Elizabeth Greenwood found the executorship of her husband's will
contested.[93] Elizabeth Eaton claimed to have received "a deed of gift or
executorship," conveying "one Pitt's house in Tewkesbury," from Greenwood's deceased husband before his marriage. Greenwood felt betrayed
and told her friends "that if her husband had made a will or deed to
another woman before he was married to her, then all women might take
an example by her."[94] Age did not diminish a wife's customary claim to
her husband's estate. Isabell Buckle was in her eighties "at least" when
she became executrix of her husband's will. On the advice of a friend,
a joint executor was appointed to assist her in the trips to Gloucester
that the execution of a will might require.[95] The transition from wife to
widow represented a shift in a woman's experience of place, in many
instances augmenting her authority and formal control over the environment and relationships of property. The widow Elizabeth Waters of Deerhurst, making her will in the spring of 1625, specified that her grandchildren, Richard Beale and his brother, "should never have the worth of one
penny of her goods or estate, for they did scorn to take her for their
grandmother."[96] Over time, single women could also accumulate substantial property and influence.[97] The authority conveyed by property is

evident in the landscape evoked by Elizabeth Jefferies als. Yeend, a single woman of Aston on Carrant, who declared "that she would rather her goods were taken down in her close [of pasture] and set on fire than that Joanne Yeend or any of her relations should have a penny worth of it."[98] A woman's experience of place and landscape thus depended on her position in the life cycle and on her marital choices, although the significance of these elements in any particular case could be affected by the social status and wealth of her family.

The landscape of the parish was not perceived as an exclusively human domain. Social status, age, and gender had a powerful influence on experiences of place, but perceptions of landscape were also affected by an awareness of active forces beyond human society that could intervene in the environment. The vertical landscapes created by this awareness of powers above and below the horizontal plane of the earth's surface assumed a variety of forms.[99] Supernatural manifestations in the Protestant landscape were usually described as providences: divine prophecies, warnings, and benedictions expressed in the natural environment.[100] In the late 1630s, for instance, a carrier from Tewkesbury crossed the Cotswold Hills in the company of his servants. "A little before the dawn of day [he] saw most sensibly and very perspicuously in the air musketeers, harnessed men, and horsemen, moving in battle array and assaulting one another in diverse furious postures."[101] This vision was classified with other tokens, such as "fiery meteors and thunderbolts that have fallen upon sundry of our churches and done hurt," as indications that "unless God be pleased to make up these ruptures between us and Scotland, we are like to have ill days."[102]

The subtle interplay of vertical and horizontal landscapes reflected the social distribution of certain forms of learning or knowledge among gentlemen in the seventeenth century as well as more diffuse differences in religious belief.[103] An incident in southern Gloucestershire in 1685 exemplified the broad class distinctions in this metaphysical apprehension of landscape. Two laborers were digging a gravel pit beside a hill not far from Cirencester. When the pit was about four yards deep, they noticed a looseness in the ground next to the hill "and presently discovered an entrance which, appearing very strange to them and rather the work of art than nature, one of them ventured a little way in and discovered a large cavity."[104] Once inside, they found themselves in a large hall with furnishings "which they no sooner touched to feel their substance, but they crumbled into dust." The men then walked down a passage "supposed to have been for worship and devotion, by the images on the wall," into a room where "they spied a door strongly patched with iron." The door fell to pieces when pushed, "and, looking in, to their great astonishment, they saw the image of a man in full proportion with a truncheon in his hand and a light in a glass like a lamp burning before him." They were "very much affrighted" by this object, "imagining it to be the devil in that shape, or a guardian spirit set there to defend some hidden treasure." Emboldened by these hopes of treasure, one of the men ventured forward a step, "but upon his first descent the image seemed to strike at him, at which they were both so terrified" that they fled. Later that night, the laborers went to "a gentleman who [was] a famous anti-quary" and told him of their discovery. He "ordered" them to keep the matter private, promising to go with them on a return visit the next morning. After the antiquary had viewed the other rooms "with wonder and delight," the laborers took him to the place where the image stood guard. The gentleman supposed it might have been made "by some great artist" to "strike at certain times." Therefore, "without any apprehension of danger [he] went in, and as before, upon his first step the image made an offer to strike, so at the second step but with a greater force, at the third step it struck a violent blow on the glass where the light was, which broke it in pieces and quite extinguished it." Upon investigation, the gentleman decided the image was an "effigies of some Roman general, by the ensigns of martial honor which lay at his feet." On the left lay two embalmed heads, "the flesh shriveled up like parchment scorched, of a dark complexion, with long hair on the chin, one seeming red the other black." Further search of neighboring passages was cut short when "a hollow noise like a deep sigh or groan" warned of the impending col-lapse of the cave, and the party withdrew.

Despite melodramatic embellishments, the account of this incident illustrates some of the ways in which people with different social back-grounds sought to understand initially unfamiliar events and objects in the environment. The laborers interpreted their find within the frame-work of a complex cosmological landscape. The furnishings of the rooms were touched "to feel their substance," and the image was initially taken for "the devil in that shape or a guardian spirit." The decision to inform the gentleman antiquary, however, would seem to indicate local aware-ness of a different form of knowledge associated with the "reliques of antiquity." The antiquary approached the cave and the image without fear, as the inanimate products of a distant human past. The cave and its contents had an intrinsic academic interest for him, inspired by the value placed on Roman antiquity in a classical education. Yet the distance between these forms of belief should not be taken as evidence of separate elite and popular cultures. Within their own more practical frame of interest in treasure and gain, the laborers clearly appreciated and valued the knowledge that the antiquary brought to bear upon their discovery.

The settlement of Tewkesbury and the parishes in its rural hinterland conformed to the topographic constraints of the Vale of Gloucester, but language, ritual, and cultural distinctions in the communities of the vale imposed an order on the landscape itself. The common language of custom bounded parishes rich in the landscapes created by varied social experiences and interests. As a complex institution, custom possessed formidable powers to resolve the conflicts of interest. Parties in conflict, such as James Cartwright of Tredington, concerned over his customary path through the churchyard, or Richard Baugh of Twyning, defending his claim to the tithes in the commons of Twyning and the Mythe, translated personal interests into the common language of custom. Custom offered a means to demonstrate both the legitimacy of particular claims and the harmony between individual interests and the interest of the parish in order and continuity.

The invocation of custom subjected a personal claim to the close scrutiny of neighbors and forced conflict into a communal arena. The dynamism of custom in the vale reflected the distinction between the idea of landscape as a common resource and the idea of landscape as a personal possession. Perambulation and informal conversation among the parish elders inculcated in youth the knowledge of a landscape larger than personal possession, a landscape of authority and power described in terms of custom. The tendency of neighbors in conflict to describe their personal claims as parish customs suggests a subtle interrelationship of custom and interest in attitudes to place, an amalgam of the landscape custom defined as shared and the landscapes of possession or personal property. As the elements of a cultural idiom, a way to understand and describe relationships, attitudes to custom and property decisively influenced the experience of landscape and place in the Vale of Gloucester.

2

Parts, Persons, and Participants in the Commonwealth: Social Relations, Institutions, and Authority

To make all things yet clear before, as we shall go, there arises another
division of the parts of the commonwealth. For it is not enough to say
that [the commonwealth] stands by a multitude of houses and families
which make streets and villages, and the multitude of streets and
villages, towns, and the multitude of towns the realm, and that
freemen be considered only in this behalf, as subjects and citizens of
the commonwealth . . . but the division of these which be participant
in the commonwealth is one way of them that bear office, and which
bear none, the one be called magistrates, the other private men.

Sir Thomas Smith, De Republica Anglorum (1583)

A thousand of these comedies were acted in dumbshow, and only in
the private houses, at which the Devil's messenger laughed so loud
that Hell heard him and for joy rang forth loud and lusty plaudits.

Thomas Dekker, Lantern and Candlelight (1608)

The society of the northern vale is difficult to describe, in part because
historians disagree on how to convey the meaning of relationships in the
past. A storm of controversy continues to surround the word *community*
in history and the social sciences.[1] Among the important issues in this
debate have been the status of the observer and the relationship of the
observer to the object of study.[2] Many uses of the word community have
been attacked as inventions of the observer, less *descriptive* of a social
reality than *reflective* of the observer's needs and social experience. The
words used to describe the society of the vale, in this view, may furnish
little more than a narcissistic reflection of priorities in the present. Dis-

putes over definitions and the suspicion of bias and reification in the very notion of community have encouraged many historians and social scientists to abandon the concept and to discard its questions.[3]

This critique of community concentrates its fire on a form of ethnographic description known as functionalism. The functionalist use of community would describe the society of the vale as an organism, as a system of processes or functions performed by social institutions, such as kinship and neighborhood, integrated to serve the emotional needs of individuals and the needs of social order. Symbols would *express* the integration of functions in a stable social system but could not *create* communities.[4] The ethnographic evidence from the Vale of Gloucester illustrates the major problems in this approach, as the symbols of the parish could hardly express a society of dispersed hamlets and farms. The functionalist community seems rather to express a modern search for coherence and to evoke a mythic rural isolation before the arrival of industry, described in the nostalgic terms of kinship, friendship, and neighborhood in small communities.[5] A broad reaction against this use of community has explored how symbols, and conflicts over symbols in early modern societies not radically different from the society of the vale, can create and transform communities defined in cultural rather than functional terms.[6]

This obscure debate in the social sciences is relevant to ethnographic reflections on the Vale of Gloucester because the functionalist community has influenced descriptions of society in early modern England. An important synthesis of the work on rural societies in the seventeenth century describes the "arable village" in functionalist terms as "nucleated, tightly packed around church and manor house (often with a resident squire), the whole structure firmly bound by neighborhood and custom and by powerful mechanisms of social control."[7] David Underdown has broadened this vision of community to include the "small towns" in the seventeenth century, described as "what modern historians like to call 'face to face' societies, in which everybody knew everybody else."[8] Other historians doubt whether such "face to face" societies exist beyond the historical imagination. Alan Macfarlane's critique of functionalism has questioned the usefulness of the word community and has stressed the influence of nongroups or networks of individuals in local societies.[9]

These views of community represent different constructions of the road between feudalism and capitalism in early modern England.[10] Underdown sees a small road under heavy construction in the seventeenth century, its contours destined to pave over traditional village communities on the way to the drained pools and dead forests of Lower Binfield.[11] Macfarlane sees a highway already substantially completed in the sixteenth and seventeenth centuries, removes the word community from the English historical vocabulary, and points to the freedom of individuals in English social structure as the key to social change.[12] Both the use and the nonuse of community make it difficult to explain important evidence from the vale. In 1628, for instance, Elizabeth Morry of Tewkesbury presented a fine cloth to cover the new communion table in her parish church.[13] Morry's actions addressed the parish community in terms of its *symbols,* not in terms of social relationships. The language of functions and networks cannot explain this type of symbolic or imagined community among the dispersed populations of the vale.[14]

The parishes of the northern vale were complex intersections of personal relations, status relations, and imagined or symbolic communities.[15] Yet the vale displayed considerable variation, because its societies reflected subtle interrelationships of ecology and the distribution of population, of the relative power of kinship and friendship, neighborliness and status, and of the authority of symbols in its parishes and in the corporation of Tewkesbury. The evidence of surveys, probate records, hearth tax returns, churchwardens' accounts, borough council registers, and church court records survives in abundance, and used in conjunction, it discloses some important intersections of landscape, wealth, social relationship, and imaginary community in the vale. These parishes were not communities in the functionalist sense of the term. If the intimacy of the parish in communion was often difficult to separate from the fellowship of friends and neighbors, some of the most bitter parish conflicts resulted from their jealousies and rivalries.

The variation of local institutions was related to the size and distribution of population. The vale contained large parishes and varied settlement patterns in the neighborhood of Tewkesbury. Ashchurch, Deerhurst, and Twyning, in particular, present complex patterns of nucleated settlement in villages and hamlets surrounded by dispersed, isolated farms. The varieties of settlement and the distance between houses affected the formation of families and friendships, neighborly relations, attendance in parish churches, and the general pursuit of order by churchwardens and constables. The enforcement of civil and ecclesiastical order required bridges across the large open spaces of the parishes in the northern vale.

The sources for local population totals are diverse, and each source presents problems.[16] The most important and difficult source is John Smyth's survey of the Gloucestershire militia, compiled in 1608.[17] This survey includes only men fit for service in the militia, and, even in the class of men between the ages of eighteen and sixty, Smyth excluded the unfit, clerics, and the aristocracy and their servants. Yet the survey has considerable value for the study of settlement patterns because Smyth based his assessment on the manor. As the dispersal of fit men was doubtless unbiased, Smyth's survey provides an excellent guide to the distribution of population in parishes.

The ecclesiastical survey commissioned by Archbishop Whitgift in 1603 can be linked to the 1608 militia list in order to create a profile of population and settlement in the vale.[18] This 1603 survey includes estimates of communicants, recusants, and persons who refused communion, although uncertainty about the age of communion makes the proportion of the population included in the survey difficult to determine. The age of communion was between twelve and fourteen years in the late sixteenth century, but in 1604 canon law adjusted the age to sixteen years, and this canon may have become common practice in the seventeenth century.[19] Richard Thorne, a yeoman of Tewkesbury, was twenty years old in 1665 and had not yet received the sacrament.[20] If fourteen years is accepted as the age of communion in 1603, a proportion of 33 percent added to the returns will account for the younger children excluded from the survey.[21] In addition, the 1603 returns, which are based on the calculations of parish clergy, should be compared with both the record of Bishop John Hooper's visitation in 1551 and with surveys made in 1563 and 1650, in order to identify dubious estimates.[22]

The returns of the hearth tax levied between 1662 and 1689 provide a much clearer picture of local population and its distribution in the later seventeenth century, but this source too presents difficulties. The rate was assessed on every householder who owned property valued annually at twenty shillings or more. Householders whose property was valued at less than twenty shillings and persons in receipt of alms or poor relief were exempt from payment.[23] Unfortunately, many returns do not include exemptions. A full return, such as the 1672 return for Gloucester-shire, includes a list of exemptions and can be converted into estimates of population, using the standard multiplier of 4.75 to represent mean household size.[24]

This evidence yields a demographic sketch of the northern vale in the seventeenth century.[25] The parishes present a spectrum from the steady but unspectacular growth of Tewkesbury (5 percent), Forthampton (13 percent), Walton Cardiff (17 percent), Tredington (18 percent), and Twyning (30 percent), to the more impressive expansion of Ashchurch (46 percent) and Deerhurst (52 percent).[26] As the population of England doubled in the sixteenth and seventeenth centuries from approximately two-and-a-half million to five million, the experience of the vale barely approached the national trend even in the parish of Deerhurst.[27] The relationship to the trend is not changed if the comparison includes figures from the sixteenth century.[28] The vale never experienced the rapid expansion characteristic of villages in Essex, but parts of Cambridgeshire and Norfolk exhibited a similar spectrum of slow to moderate growth.[29] Across the vale, the increased population was distributed in a varied settlement pattern marked by nucleated villages and dispersal in hamlets. In the parish of Deerhurst, approximately half the population dwelt above the flood plain of the River Severn in the hamlet of Apperley, two miles south of the primary village of Deerhurst. The denizens of Ashchurch were evenly divided among the four hamlets of Aston on Carrant, Fiddington and Natton, Northway and Newton, and Pamington. This pattern of dispersal was complicated by the persistence of nucleated villages in Deerhurst, Ashchurch, and Twyning. Tredington, Forthampton, and Walton Cardiff remained the primary settlements in their parishes.

These variations in population and settlement create problems for the historian interested in local communities. As a result of dispersed settlement in the vale and the relatively slow growth of population, the worlds of village and neighborhood cannot be assumed to have been the same for all the inhabitants of a parish. Little everyday contact occurred between hamlets separated by as much as four or five miles. Those who lived in the border hamlets, such as Aston on Carrant, might be closer to their neighbors in the adjoining parishes of Kemerton and Bredon than to their coparishioners in Ashchurch. Parish communities in the northern vale were too widely dispersed to be formed and sustained by personal contact. In order to understand the power of the parish in this context, the local historian must investigate its symbolic life and ritual.

Social life in early modern England was experienced primarily in the relations of kinship, friendship, and neighborhood.[30] An imprecise or diffuse reciprocity characterized these relations in a society otherwise dominated by the prescriptive authority of hierarchy and rank. The demands, exchanges, and expectations of kinship, friendship, and neighborhood lacked strictly enforced rules. Decisions either to disregard or to recognize conventions of kinship, friendship, or neighborhood in any particular situation were commonly left to the persons involved. The roles and duties implied by each type of relationship were flexible, and the emotional value of any particular relationship could cover a considerable spectrum from indifference to deep affection. Yet the social roles of kin relation, friend, and neighbor remained distinct in rights and obligations.

Discussion of the early modern family has tended to focus on the size and organization of the residential group, and the result has been a persuasive description of the typical household as a single nuclear family, with or without servants.[31] The bonds between a household and nonresident kin have received less attention and are usually afforded only a minor role in English social life.[32] This emphasis on the nuclear family has resulted, in part, from the use of wills to reconstitute kin relations, but the primary concern at the moment of death was to provide for the material needs of dependents, particularly young children and spouses.[33] Kin beyond the nuclear family were not considered dependents and therefore tended not to receive significant bequests of property. The absence of extended family networks from testamentary records does not diminish the value of kin if help was needed to build a barn, to haul heavy materials, or to borrow money or provisions.

If the importance of the nuclear family has been overstated, the intimacy of the household made it the heart of local society in the vale. Brief glimpses of the relationships between spouses contrast sharply to the formal patriarchy expressed in law and in prescriptive literature on family roles.[34] Wills often expressed the idea of partnership, sometimes contained final statements of a husband's love for his wife, and usually gave her control of the family property and responsibility for younger chil dren. In 1613 Richard Owen of Forthampton left his wife his goods and credits "with all his heart and said that it was all too little for her."[35] A husband's duty to support his wife gave her strong claims on family resources even if the reciprocity of partnership failed to develop or survive. John and Elizabeth Fluck failed to produce children, and their marriage dissolved in mutual recrimination. The couple shared a house for twenty years but had no real marriage, as John Fluck seldom slept at home. Yet this arrangement became unacceptable to Elizabeth only when John failed to provide her "sufficient maintenance" as his wife, and she promptly sued him in the consistory court.[36] Although traditional roles prescribed a formal and public subordination of women in the patriarchal family, the values of patriarchy also protected women in their domestic roles by duties in law enforced on the husband.

Most parents felt a strong obligation to help their children get started in life, and the wills of the vale provide ample evidence of the elaborate schemes formed by parents to provide for every contingency. In Tewkesbury, John Fisher's involvement in the early adult life of his son John indicates the sacrifices that parents made to help their children. In the early 1620s Fisher honored his son's request to recall a large loan that had been made to a neighbor in order "to furnish his [son's] occasions." Once the neighbor had repaid the money, the younger John began to build a house in Tewkesbury, but the building costs quickly became too much for him to bear alone. The elder Fisher therefore paid for supplies of glass and sand that had been cut off because his son's debts had run too high. Finally, Fisher took three years off work at his son's behest, "being wholly spent in carrying and fetching of sand for him and thereby losing all my gains in fishing, which I did to help him . . . in respect of the late building of his house." Some of this aid was bestowed as a gift, but the income lost in the three years of working on the house made a serious dent in the family finances. Fisher enjoined his son to "be more careful to pay his mother the money he owes me to relieve her wants." The debt carried a powerful moral and emotional charge, as shown by the father's order to John and his brother "to show all dutiful and natural respect to their aged mother and to be helping and comfortable to her in respect of her impotency and great weakness."[37]

The practice of kinship extended the family beyond the coresidents of the household.[38] Although this observation may seem uncontroversial, efforts to measure the influence of nonresident kin on family life in the

Vale of Gloucester are beset by several intractable problems. The absence of formal genealogies for most of the local population makes it difficult to recover kinship ideology. Only the families of gentlemen constructed genealogies to represent their status and authority. This vacuum cannot be filled by ideas transferred from the prescriptive literature to the local communities of the vale. Practical kin groups are equally difficult to recover, as many of the activities likely to have attracted the assistance of kin relations did not generate archival evidence. This absence of reliable evidence has forced historians to reconstruct kin relations from the dubious evidence of wills. Yet the risk of distortion, unavoidable if wills are interpreted as kinship charters, might be reduced by a careful regard for the personal motives and social circumstances behind the creation of wills. The decision to prepare a will was first and foremost a response to mortality, a profound crisis in the family. This crisis influenced the references to family in a will as well as the choice of people to assist in its preparation. Sickness or infirmity in a household focused attention on those family members who were classified as dependents and as sufficiently close, in geographic and emotional terms, to offer help in the performance of the will. Testators therefore referred most frequently to their kin identified either as relatives and dependents or as relatives and friends. If the social constraints behind the evidence are borne in mind, wills become useful as abbreviated maps of the kin relations invoked in family crises such as death. These maps sketched a route from the potential chaos of physical death to the destination of a secure family. A circle of kin relations, who were less intimate than those in coresidence but closer than distant relations in other locales, ran the safe houses on this journey. Many other family crises, such as long and dangerous physical journeys on land or sea, required the help of an extensive network of kin, but this use of kinship is difficult to recover from testamentary evidence.

The households that were called for help in the preparation of a will often stood in different degrees of relationship to each other.[39] This network of practical kin relations provided emotional support and assistance in the hour of death. Although practical kin could stand in a variety of genealogical relationships to the deceased, kin relations as a group comprised 40 percent of the references in wills. Brothers and sisters were the most frequently mentioned. Between 1590 and 1690 bequests and other allusions to brothers and sisters furnished 13 percent to 15 percent of all the testamentary references to nonresident kin in the northern vale. Brothers were prominent in positions of trust and often served as overseers. After siblings, practical kin consisted of cousins, kinsmen, and kinswomen. As the same word was often used to describe different kinds of relatives, the use of the terms may have been determined less by abstract genealogical calculation than by a person's practical roles as relative and friend. In wills, cousins were generally the children of brothers or sisters, the same relatives signified by the term *kinsman*.[40] Kinsmen were usually the male children of brothers or sisters, or less frequently, male grandchildren or the husbands of sisters or daughters.[41] Kinswomen might be either the daughters of daughters or the daughters of brothers or sisters.[42] These practical kin relations were supplemented by less frequent references to grandchildren, parental kin relations, and relatives by marriage.[43]

The importance of kin relations beyond the household may have been greater in the Vale of Gloucester than in other parts of England.[44] These relationships lacked the intimacy of coresidence, but the bonds that joined households to kin relations in the neighborhood surfaced in moments of crisis. Birth, marriage, and death furnished the occasions of the most intense interaction among the related households of a family, illustrated in 1635 by the efforts of five households to make a will for Thomas Buckle.[45] Buckle lived in the village of Uckington, southeast of Tewkesbury, but his family consisted of dispersed households in nearby villages and included the kin relations from his parental family and from several marriages. These households interacted in a complex diplomacy that exploded in conflict after Buckle's death. In 1638 William Beale sued his relatives for the unfair exclusion of his household from the deathbed preparation of Buckle's will. Beale, who lived in Tirley, five miles from Uckington, had entered the Buckle family through marriage to Thomas Buckle's stepdaughter.[46] Beale was convinced his household should have been told of Buckle's decline and included in the administration of the estate. He pointed to the notification of relatives further removed from Uckington as evidence of a conspiracy to exclude his wife and children from his father-in-law's estate. The relatives who had been invited to assist in the will disputed this interpretation and claimed that Buckle chose not to involve the Beale household because he knew his stepdaughter lay in childbed. According to this account, Buckle feared that the news of his final sickness would alarm the household and endanger the health of the mother.[47]

This controversy disclosed the layers of early modern family life and the delicacy of relations among dispersed households.[48] Because conflict evoked different interpretations of behavior in the family, the evidence of conflict offers a rare opportunity to identify the organizational axes among the households of a kin group. The factions in the Buckle family reflected the emotional politics of complex families that frequently contained children from successive marriages. Beale may have been prone to suspect deliberate exclusion because his wife was not Thomas Buckle's biological daughter. Beale's accusations of conspiracy in the settlement of the estate consequently focused on Thomas Smith of Forthampton, the husband of Buckle's biological daughter. Smith lived farther from Uckington than Beale but had nevertheless been apprised of the will's preparation and played a prominent role in the administration of the estate. Conspiracy was difficult to prove, however, because the interaction of kin was too complex to be reduced to the axes of geographic proximity and genealogy. Practical kin relations were affected by a knowledge of affairs in the households of the kin group, and domestic conditions formed a third axis of interpretation in the conflict. The overlap between domestic crises of birth and death in the Buckle and Beale households complicated the dispute in the Buckle family. This domestic axis enabled Thomas Smith and Walter Buckle to describe the exclusion of the Beales as an expression of concern by anxious relatives, who were fearful that the knowledge of sickness and death in her family might endanger the mother in childbirth. The factions in the Buckle family reflected the prescriptive authority and manipulation of geographic proximity, genealogy, and domestic conditions in matters of kinship.

The proximity of related households affected neighborhood in the vale, as neighborliness often involved the interaction of kin, not to mention the reconciliation of angry kin factions. The politics among the dispersed households of families is further illustrated by events in the Hatton family of Forthampton. The elderly Christian Hatton shared the home of her son Henry Hatton in the 1560s. After an obscure quarrel, Christian left Henry's house, her two cows "Browny" and "Fillpale" in tow, and went to live in the house of her other son Alexander Hatton in the same parish.[49] Christian then returned to Henry's house after a short time, "disliking to continue longer" in Alexander's company. At some point during her sojourn, Christian had asked Alexander to sell one of her cows. When she subsequently bequeathed the value of this cow to

Henry, the fate of the proceeds from the sale became the focus of a bitter family dispute, pursued in the courts well into the 1580s. The near presence of kin afforded prompt mediation and distance between Henry and Christian in the first dispute. But the second incident reveals how the mediation of kin in domestic squabbles could enlarge the circle of conflict and create enduring factions in a family.

Of the relationships in the society of the vale, friendship is the most difficult to describe as a separate type. The conduct expected of neighbors and kin remained distinct, although the society of family and neighborhood often overlapped. Many families had kin outside the neighborhood and neighbors unrelated to the family. Only a handful of affluent local families, however, formed distant friendships distinct from kinship and neighborhood. Friendship was less a separate type of relationship than a quality of personal attraction that intensified a few chosen relations of family, neighborhood, or a combination of both. Friendship, family, and neighborhood were interrelated and must have seemed inseparable in everyday life. The preparation of a will separated personal networks, described as friendship, from the formal bonds of neighborhood and family; and, more than any other type of evidence, it is a will that reveals the pattern of this intricate fabric of social relations. In the social language of a will, friend often stood to neighbor as overseer to witness. A friend was usually a relative or an unrelated neighbor trusted in the family circle, and this friendship might be expressed as fictive kinship in the form of godparentage.[50] By virtue of their incorporation in the family, friends were often asked to assume active roles in moments of crisis.

The crisis provoked by a friend's death clearly defined the duties of friendship. The notion of friendship in the vale involved the execution of special duties and responsibilities rarely required in modern friendships. These duties included the division and management of family property, the arrangement of apprenticeships and marriages for children of the deceased, the evaluation of the subsequent marital choices of a spouse, and the exercise of a general authority in family conflicts.[51] In 1590 Richard Clarke of Tewkesbury made a large bequest to his daughter Alice. As Alice was still in her minority, Clarke entrusted authority over the gift to his "friend and neighbor" John Barston. Barston was asked to assume responsibility for any marital choices Alice made before she turned seventeen.[52] The obligations of friendship commonly extended to the supervision of children as well as the management of property. In 1593 Richard Labington implored his "very friends" John Bradford, Thomas Dunne, and Thomas Hawker to manage his estate and watch over his seven children during their minority.[53] Robert Olive selected his friend William Beale as one of his overseers in 1638. Beale and a second overseer chosen from Olive's kin group received discretionary power to arrange or approve marriages and apprenticeships for Olive's children.[54] Similar demands on the reciprocity of friendship were made by William Wakeman in 1681. Wakeman appointed his "trusty and well-beloved friends" Phillip Surman and Samuel Hawling to administer charities in Tewkesbury and Twyning and to manage funds allocated for the education of his children.[55]

The uncertainties of economic life marked the boundaries of friendship. In an environment of scarcity, friends were sometimes unable or unwilling to meet the demands and attendant risks imposed on overseers and executors. In 1612 Edward Guy of Deerhurst could not persuade his friends to accept responsibility for a heavily indebted estate and for the payment of substantial bequests to five sons and a daughter.[56] In 1626 the friends of William Cook of Tredington refused to execute his will. The motives for this refusal were not stated, but the terms of the will enmeshed the executors in a prolonged and potentially expensive administration of local property for a family some distance from the diocese. Since his friends refused to become involved, the administration of Cook's estate was assigned to a daughter resident in the parish.[57] The rarity of such renunciations may be taken as evidence of the moral and emotional power of appeals made to friendship in the hour of death.[58] The word *friend* had the power to incorporate neighbors in a family and to mark chosen kin for positions of special trust and responsibility.

The relations of neighborhood expressed the local character of society in the northern vale.[59] Yet the words *neighbor* and *neighborhood,* like *friend* and *friendship,* remain ambiguous as descriptions of expectations, conduct, and institutions in this varied landscape. Several modern studies, which have questioned the impact of the built environment on neighborliness, have discarded the idea of distinctive urban and rural patterns of neighborhood.[60] These distinctions are even less helpful in the early modern society of the vale, as one local description defined the neighborhood broadly enough to include Tewkesbury and the rural villages in its market area. The relations among neighbors in the vale were not demonstrably linked to characteristics of locality, and the physical environment shared by neighbors cannot explain conduct among neighbors. A more intractable problem is the interrelationship between personal and abstract forms of neighborhood. A neighbor was known less intimately than a friend and assumed a more distant place in personal networks, but neighborhood also implied a code of values. The decision to accept a person as a neighbor, for practical purposes of neighborliness or mutual aid, depended on the person's reputation or position in the neighborhood, understood in this prescriptive sense. The prescriptive and personal aspects of neighborhood were subtly interrelated in its dual nature as both a network of exchange and a moral community.

The personal aspects of neighborhood were expressed in various forms of exchange. In the most basic sense, neighbors simply lived near each other, sufficiently close for routine social contact. The regularity of contact varied from neighbors seen and evaluated daily in the streets to neighbors from villages further afield, seen on weekly market days in Tewkesbury, to the visitors seen only on special occasions, such as the festival organized by the Tewkesbury churchwardens in 1600 to raise money for church repairs.[61] But proximity and neighborliness were quite different matters.[62] The conduct of neighbors varied from limited friendship to indifference or even hostility. A neighbor often furnished credit or food to relieve a family crisis, but the limits of neighborliness became clear if substantial debts were unpaid or animals strayed from the property of their owners. Because these incidents could produce verbal abuse and insults unequal to the property damage incurred, defamation cases entered in the church court suggest that the invasion of property by neighbors or their animals may have violated notions of proper neighborly distance. The superficial friendliness and helpfulness of neighbors were clearly differentiated from friendship in the society of the vale.[63]

The fascination of neighborhood lies in the ambiguity of the term. There were objective or geographic descriptions of neighborhood, sometimes many miles in circumference, as well as the smaller neighborhoods defined by the practice of neighborliness.[64] Just as a place consisted of diverse landscapes, a neighborhood contained many social networks. The debts listed in probate records provide evidence of these networks but cannot reveal how requests for help were evaluated and how proper neighbors were identified and honored with assistance. Perhaps neighborhood spoke in the idiom of custom. In 1616, Elizabeth Best was described as a widow of "good name and fame and so repute amongst all her neighbors and *other* places and parishes adjoining."[65] Best's "good name and fame" in her parish became the basis of a claim to neighborliness. After all, custom did ascribe a special neighborliness to dwellers in the same parish, the most frequent recipients of aid in wills.

Yet the evidence of neighborliness is sparse and so cannot easily explain why some received help and recognition as neighbors and why others did not. A pronounced economic distance could reduce the sympathy between families, as neighbors were social equals in a limited sense. But even wealthy debtors were not unknown to the farmers of modest social rank in the vale. In 1602 John Wright of Twyning recorded among the smaller debts of his neighbors the sum of £2 owed him by Lady Berkeley.[66] Claims of kinship might sharpen the duties of neighborliness. Giles Fluck, a husbandman of Deerhurst, gave "the butt of a tree" to Roger Fluck, his kinsman and neighbor, "to make a must mill" yet was himself indebted to Roger for the manufacture of cider.[67] If a person was accepted as a neighbor, the exchanges between households could reflect common experiences of the life cycle as well as economic needs. An elderly neighbor might require frequent visits or need help to settle property and social affairs. Henry Wells of Deerhurst and his wife Anne, who lived near the elderly widow Elizabeth Waters, described their neighborliness in terms of regular visits to converse and pass the time.[68]

The failure of neighborliness had profound moral consequences and could be dangerous, in particular for elderly women and widows. A fine line separated the bad female neighbor from the witch, and a fit of temper could lead to accusations of *maleficium,* or harm done by supernatural means.[69] In 1667, this kind of distrust exploded in Tewkesbury between Susanna Vicaridge and her neighbor, the widow Isabell Sheene.[70] Sheene had visited the Vicaridge house and had offered cake to Susanna's children "several times" in the previous year. Although this offer was refused at first, the children were eventually allowed to eat the cake. Sheene then recommended a servant to the Vicaridges, possibly Anne Phillips, and Susanna hired her.[71] Perhaps Sheene hoped for some favor from this affluent household. When Susanna fired the servant, "not finding her for her turn," Sheene apparently expressed anger, and shortly afterwards the Vicaridge children became sick. Susanna's daughter Margaret suffered a violent seizure. After this terrible event, Susanna accused

Sheene of *maleficium*, convinced that Isabell's unneighborly anger had caused the sudden sickness in the family. As a woman of gentle status, Vicaridge rallied sixteen neighbors, including Robert Eaton, the minister of Tewkesbury, to support her account of *maleficium* and to confirm Isabell Sheene's reputation as a witch.[72] John Parsons, a gentleman, attested "to the great strength of Margaret Vicaridge while the fit was on her." Although Sheene denied the charges and abjured the "devilish art," the echoes of this accusation reverberated from the troubled neighborhood in Tewkesbury to the assizes in Gloucester.[73]

A neighborhood held considerable authority as a prescriptive moral community, despite the ambiguities in the practice of neighborliness.[74] The records of unneighborly conflict, in particular the exchange of angry or abusive words, vividly testify to the power of this community. On a summer day in 1623, for instance, Margaret Cartwright and Joanne Collett of Tredington stood in a circle of neighbors and disputed the ownership of some ducks. Collett revived the memory of an older conflict and accused Cartwright of stealing ducks. The controversy escalated, as Cartwright replied that "only a whore or a thief" would dare to make such an outrageous claim. Collett then branded Cartwright a whore and promised that others in the Cartwright family would substantiate the charge. This public accusation of whoredom against Cartwright quickly became a defamation case in the consistory court.[75]

This exchange reveals the dynamics of neighborhood as a moral community. Violence was expressed in the verbal assault on "good name and fame," or reputation. A reputation consisted of a variety of elements, combined to produce a stock of honor or credibility, and the possession of honor influenced the response to requests for economic aid or aspirations to political leadership. Many elements contributed to honor, but sexual integrity in the judgment of neighbors formed the basis of reputation.[76] The loss of a good name in sexual relations could lead to diminished credibility in neighborly exchanges, to reduced claims to material aid or fellowship, and possibly to an appearance in the church courts if allegations of sexual misconduct were not discredited. The informal codes of neighborhood and ecclesiastical law converged in efforts to restrict sexuality to the marriage bed. Churchwardens were neighbors authorized to present violators of ecclesiastical law, and the court could excommunicate and exclude moral offenders from the religious life of the community. If a victim of verbal assault had money to defend honor and good name, no public assault on reputation could be allowed to pass unanswered.

The squabble over the ducks in Tredington illustrates a common pattern in neighborhood politics. Collett and Cartwright entered the street to claim property, but instead became embroiled in a fight for reputation. After the contest for the ducks turned hostile, the women called each other "whore and thief" and used the terms of reputation to enhance their position in the watchful eyes of their neighbors. Yet the battle for reputation began as a minor property dispute. Another common form of conflict among neighbors arose from the deliberate manipulation of reputation in gossip.[77] Personal interest and the morality of neighborhood intersected in the world of gossip. The diverse uses of this kind of informal conversation in the street, the church porch, or the alehouse included the evaluation of national news, the discussion of births, deaths, and other local matters, and the vivisection of local reputations. In the sometimes vicious world of rumor and gossip, reputation became a focus of conflict rather than a means to defend other interests, such as property.

The manipulation of reputation in gossip could be particularly important in the selection of leaders, and this political use of gossip in the vale was demonstrated in 1628 by the parliamentary election in Tewkesbury. Thomas Vaughan, a local candidate, contested and lost the election to Sir Baptist Hickes and Sir Thomas Culpepper, candidates foreign to the borough. Yet the only record of this contest is the defamation suit that Vaughan brought against Elizabeth Canner of Tewkesbury in the church court.[78] Vaughan accused Canner of a public assault on his reputation. According to Vaughan, Canner and several female neighbors had convened "in the open street of Tewkesbury" to discuss the result of the election. Canner endorsed the victorious candidates. She believed that Vaughan would require eight shillings a day for expenses in London and would become a burden to his neighbors. Quinborough Johnsons, a young servant, claimed Culpepper and Hickes would cost the town as much as twelve shillings a day, but Canner then dismissed questions of finance and said it was better "such bastardly rogues and whores [as Thomas Vaughan] were hanged." Several days later, Elizabeth Canner made a second accusation of bastardy against Vaughan. The audience for this assault included officers of the borough council. As the conversation turned to the recent election, Canner denounced Vaughan as a bastard and said she "would have no bastards to be burgesses" of Tewkesbury.

Both these accusations and Vaughan's expensive lawsuit in defense of his name indicate the political value of reputation. Yet the political issues are difficult to detect and can only be inferred from a few scraps of evidence. The similar social positions of the Vaughan and Canner families may provide a key. This similarity appears in fiscal records, since persistent demands in the 1620s resulted in several assessments of the parliamentary subsidy.[79] The collection of revenue for war produced nine ranked lists of local contributors from 1620 to 1629.[80] These assessments provide a series of snapshots of Thomas Vaughan and Christopher Canner in the local status hierarchy.[81] In 1620 Vaughan and Canner, who were described as gentlemen, were assessed on £4 of moveable property. Vaughan nevertheless appeared four places higher than Canner in the assessment list. In 1622 Vaughan was only one place higher than Canner, and both men were again assessed for the same value in goods. A sharp difference in the status of the families appeared only in 1624. Vaughan was assessed for lands and removed to more exalted ranks, separate from Canner.[82] Although he was returned to the assessment for moveable property in 1626, Vaughan maintained the increase in the reported value of his goods and consistently ranked four places higher than Canner.[83] In the midst of this separation from the other families in his status group, Vaughan made his move for a parliamentary seat in 1628. Social distance and status difference suddenly became explicit among families previously similar in rank and honor. Both Vaughan and Canner had served in the office of bailiff, the highest office in borough government.[84] Elizabeth Canner's assault on Vaughan's reputation and honor may have reflected this local competition for status. Perhaps the Canners were loath to see a family of comparable position established in the circles of authority and power beyond the vale.[85]

This controversy also illustrates the dominance of sexual themes in the moral dramas of a neighborhood. An accusation of bastardy and compromised sexual integrity was the only recorded expression of the social contest between the Vaughan and Canner families. This interrelationship of status and sexuality reveals some important moral assumptions. A reputation combined notions of sexual integrity and perceptions of social position and social mobility. Movement in the status hierarchy occurred only in the face of the general fear and stigma attached to social mobility.[86] Any conscious effort to change social position required care to secure neighborly acceptance of the new position. An overly ambitious change in status could inspire fear and hostility, particularly among neighbors of similar rank. As a society of stereotypes, the neighborhood of reputations included several stereotypes of the bad neighbor, such as the bastard, the cuckold, the liar, the drunkard, the thief, the whore, the scold, and the witch.[87] An overmighty neighbor inspired the poets of rumor and gossip to use these stereotypes in defense of settled relationships.

The images of bad neighbors featured sexual license and political disorderliness in contrast to the stable authority and orderliness of the patriarchal household. If neighbors feared a family's tyranny, rumors might be circulated to diminish a reputation and to limit claims to leadership in the neighborhood. Public knowledge cannot explain the power of rumor, and it is unwise to approach rumors as descriptions of behavior.[88] On the contrary, gossip was often effective because little was known about the sexual conduct of neighbors. A rival's reputation and honor were vulnerable to attack in sexual terms because the behavior in question was private and concealed, rather than public and known. If a neighbor such as Vaughan had already run the risk of criticism as a bad neighbor, the authority of sexual innuendo increased. Because Vaughan had been born in Denbyshire, the circumstances of his birth were unknown in the vale.[89] Canner used this local uncertainty to advantage. There were few forms of criticism more destructive to male assertions of public leadership than assaults on the legitimacy of personal descent and the sexual integrity of one's parents.

Vaughan's defamation suit in the church court ventured further into the politics of credit and reputation in a neighborhood. Elizabeth Canner laid claim to the moral authority of neighborhood in her efforts to discredit Vaughan's witnesses.[90] Vaughan had little chance of victory if his supporters could be painted as disreputable characters. Canner therefore ignored the charge of defamation and attacked the reputations of Vaughan's friends. First she reviled Thomas Rayer as a cheat, and then she dismissed Quinborough Johnsons as "a poor young woman of small worth and little credit or estimation among the better sort of people and one that gets her living by knitting, spinning, and carding."[91] These assaults on witnesses point to a difficult problem in the evidence of the conflict. If Rayer and Johnsons were so obviously disreputable, why did

Vaughan select them to defend his reputation and honor? The court documents reveal a contest for the moral authority to speak on such issues as bastardy; and, in this context, the terms "better sort" and "lesser sort" seem no more descriptive than the terms "bastard," "rogue," and "whore." Both Canner and Vaughan attempted to control the moral discourse of neighborhood. Vaughan clearly placed Johnsons and Rayer among the "better sort" and requested their help to defend his reputation.

This battle for reputation between Vaughan and Canner brings together several powerful themes of social life in the vale. The diffuse reciprocity of kinship, friendship, and neighborliness were intimately linked to the prescriptive codes of neighborhood and even to the jurisdiction of the church courts. Thomas Vaughan looked to restore his reputation in the court. Elizabeth Canner attempted to use the court to protect the social position of her family. The prescriptive moral codes of household and neighborhood formed a bridge between the personal troubles of the Vaughans and the Canners and the complex hierarchy of the church courts. These courts were more difficult to manipulate than local reputations. The operations of courts and institutions of government, the authority of law in a variety of forms, imposed constraints on vale society unknown in the intimate relations of family, friendship, and neighborhood. The authority of law and the prescriptive power of custom, which comprised the common idiom of many institutions in borough and parish, narrowed the scope of political manipulation and placed limits on the uses of power in the society of the vale.

The people of northern Gloucestershire created complex social networks described in terms of kinship, friendship, and neighborhood. Yet neither Thomas Vaughan and Elizabeth Canner nor Margaret Cartwright and Joanne Collett were free to create the society of the vale in their own image. A hierarchy of authority and power imposed constraints on the social dramas of town and village. A hierarchy of status defined a formal distance between neighbors and rested on factors difficult to manipulate and control. The most important sources of status or social rank were family descent and occupation. A child of "noble" or "gentle" parents stood in a lineage ranked hierarchically in relation to other lineages.[92] The inherited reputation of a lineage could protect a family from decline in rank, but the respect of neighbors and authority of leadership, measures of honor and effective status, often required a demonstration of personal merit. A second source of status was occupation or work. A child of parents who were identified by work left the family in adolescence for apprenticeship in a craft or in agricultural labor, in the case of boys, or in the diverse tasks of domestic service, in the case of girls. The acquisition of occupational skills and, perhaps, the wealth needed to marry and start a family marked the child's entrance into adulthood.[93] A strict order of custom and law governed the distribution of status. A code of honor and precedence, the domain of the royal heralds, protected the hierarchy of lineages. The rules of companies or guilds policed the rank and file of occupation. A principle of succession further distinguished the power of status from informal social relations. Death dissolved relations of friendship and neighborliness, but the structures of rank, lineage, and guild transcended the mortality of individuals.

The differences between lineage and kinship illustrate this distinction between status and informal social relations. Many families in the vale experienced kinship as the circle of effective relations selected from paternal and maternal kin. A descent group or lineage followed a restrictive principle of patrilineal descent, a form of unilineal descent traced through the male line.[94] There is ample evidence of this principle of descent in elaborate genealogies, which were designed to trace the descent of a house from an original paternal founder as well as marital bonds to other lines or houses.[95] The lineage was understood as a body animated by the circulation of "noble and known" blood among its generations, and a prescriptive order arranged the "race" of patrilineal corporations in a ranked hierarchy of honor and precedence.[96] The honor of a lineage could be displayed in several ways, from the aristocratic pinnacle of hereditary lordships and title to the more humble possession of arms and crest common among the elite families of the northern vale. Although the genealogies recorded in visitations described only the upper reaches of the status hierarchy, families of lower rank than the aristocracy and the gentry sometimes expressed a pride of descent in the transfer of heirlooms in the male line.[97]

The distribution of honor in the status hierarchy has only recently received the attention it deserves.[98] Unlike the notions of personal honor manipulated in the politics of neighborhood, the honor and reputation of a lineage reflected its relationship to the fixed sources of authority in the English polity. The hierarchy of descent derived from the authority of the Crown. A monarch elevated a person's lineage as a reward for services, traditionally military services, and the personal honor expressed in noble or virtuous action on the battlefield was transformed into the honor of descent.[99] In the society of the vale, the ranks of noble descent did not extend beyond the commons described by Sir Thomas Smith as *nobilitas minor.*[100] The Tracys of Todington, "descended from the blood royal of the Saxon kings of England," and the Hickeses of London, represented in the vale by Sir Baptist Hickes, a prominent London merchant and financial advisor to James I, disputed pride of place in the early seventeenth century.[101] Hickes acquired an estate at Campden in 1608 and used his connections to defeat the Tracys in the battle to represent Tewkesbury after the town became a parliamentary borough in 1610.[102] The Hickes property and interest in Tewkesbury passed from Sir Baptist Hickes to his daughter Mary, her husband Sir Edward Alford, her stepson Anthony Ashley Cooper, and her grandson Sir Henry Capel.[103] Although these beneficiaries of the Hickes interest kept local estates, they did not reside in the neighborhood of Tewkesbury. Sir Robert Tracy and Sir Francis Russell of Strensham, baronet, were the only effective representatives of the order of knighthood in the northern parishes of the vale after the Restoration.[104]

Contemporary notions of honor and status did not derive rank from wealth and estate. The possession of property was essential to maintain status but could not assure its acquisition.[105] In the fight for Tewkesbury's parliamentary seat, Sir Robert Tracy decried the promotion of the Hickeses and claimed the burgesses had confused status and mere riches. Tracy observed bitterly that "not he who brings most in his truest love but brings most in his purse shall be accepted."[106] The order of rank stood on ancient custom, and the honor of a house should transcend its material fortunes. As Tracy lamented to a friend in Tewkesbury, "Their love to this family I thought until now had been long ago built on a better foundation than what my deserts could merit from them, which now I see was placed upon an ill ground, that it should be utterly thrown down by Mr. Baptist Hickes, a stranger."[107] Hickes expressed his commercial prosperity and political power in the "honorable" displays demanded of nobility. The profits and influence of a silk merchant and financial servant to the Crown became a less remunerative but symbolically potent landed estate. Tracy used the commercial interests of the Hickeses to assault their newly established position in the vale and to divert attention from the font of their success: financial and administrative service to the Crown. The Tracys claimed status by virtue of an "ancient" connection to the soil of Gloucestershire. The Hickeses rose less from the possession of riches than from the cultivation of the court and connection to the monarch. As Sir Thomas Smith assured his readers, "No more are all made knights in England that may spend a knight's lands but they only whom the prince will honor."[108]

The hierarchy of status was profoundly territorial. This territoriality reflected the authority and status inscribed in specific pieces of property. As the rector of her parish, Alice Cartwright of Tredington received an "honorable" burial in the chancel of her parish church.[109] A claim to status flowed from a manor or lordship, from the authority to govern its courts and to lead its tenants on the battlefield. A manor carried a genealogy of lordship, and its status thus combined continuity of descent and authority on the land.[110] A few families in the vale could claim this territorial status on the strength of customary manorial lordships: the Baughs of Twyning, the Casseys of Deerhurst and Wightfield, the Neasts of Swinley, and the Surmans of Tredington Court.[111] These families neither obtained rank by service nor depended on royal honors. Status inhered not in their persons or their families but in their property.

This brief sketch of the sources of "nobleness" in the status hierarchy, notions of descent, service, and territorial identity, hints at shades of difference between personal honor and the honor of descent in vale society. Thomas Vaughan cultivated the honor of his person and reputation in the continuous society of his neighbors. His demeanor in the streets and conversation in the inns were important sources of reputation for a relative newcomer to the vale. The malicious gossip of neighbors could threaten and even destroy a reputation made in this way. The honor and status of a lineage reflected the prescriptive authority of descent and custom, the charisma of the royal touch, and the landed power of lordship, which were sources of honor less vulnerable to the manipulation of neighbors and personal failures. As Sir Thomas Smith remarked, "The fame and riches of their ancestors serve to cover them so long as it can, as a thing once gilded though it be copper within, until the gilding be worn away."[112]

The male heads of the prominent families in the northern vale were usually styled "esquire" or "gentleman." The style "esquire" placed after a family name usually indicated the possession of arms as a token of honorable descent.[113] These arms or coats of arms illustrated the traditional value of violence and military leadership in the distribution of honor, since the segments of the escutcheon formed an index of reported or invented valor and its transfer across the generations. A family's arms customarily had been inscribed on the helmets and shields of their servants and had simplified identification in combat.[114] Several families carried this rank, if not its traditional military duties, in the vale: the Alyes and Bulstrodes of Tewkesbury, the Perts and Wakemans of Mythe and Mythe Hook, the Baughs of Twyning, the Dowdeswells of Bushley, and the Reads of Walton Cardiff. The nobility of the vale also included many families of gentlemen, although the "simple gentlemen" possessed neither arms nor the status of descent claimed by esquires.[115] Arms could be bought from the heralds, but scornful references to "gentlemen of the first head" expressed the marginal status of the parvenu.[116] Gentlemen acquired their rank from supposed merit or virtue rather than from nobility of descent, could afford to abstain from manual labor, and possessed the wealth and wit required to maintain the displays of rank described by Sir Thomas Smith and William Harrison as "the port, charge and countenance of a gentleman."[117] Despite the absence of arms and pedigree, the code of the gentleman was sometimes described as a genealogy of riches or virtue. Smith, for instance, included the blood of gentlemen in his hierarchy of nobleness, "for the ancestor has been notable in riches, or for his virtues, or (in fewer words) old riches or prowess remaining in one stock."[118]

The demands of manual labor marked the inferior stratum of the status hierarchy, arrayed in diverse occupations below the nobility. In the rural parishes of the vale, this stratum consisted of yeomen, husbandmen, craftsmen, and laborers. The corporation of Tewkesbury controlled local production through chartered companies of bakers, butchers, coopers and joiners, cordwainers, drapers and dyers, haberdashers or mercers, smiths, tailors, tuckers, and weavers, as well as a company of leatherworkers that included glovers, pointmakers, pouchmakers, pursers, and whittawers.[119] These companies figured prominently in numerous local activities, from everyday work to conviviality and civic pageantry.[120] Unfortunately, the distribution of work in the vale is only dimly reflected in flawed sources.[121] Militia surveys, probate records, and tax returns served different purposes, and a term used to describe status did not have the same meaning in every document. This problem of inconsistent evi-

dence adds uncertainty to the most basic sociological comparisons between the first and second half of the seventeenth century.

Land was the most important source of income and status, so that few
lives in the vale escaped the rhythms of the agricultural year. The demands of seedtime and harvest affected even the life of the town, and
occupational lists conceal the number of Tewkesbury tradesmen who
added to their incomes by small-scale farming and horticulture. In 1601,
for instance, the brewer Christopher Canner also kept a garden, and in
1609 the estate of William Wodley, a blacksmith, included a "crop of
corn as yet unthreshed."[122] Market gardens became a prominent feature
of the landscape by the 1670s.[123] The economy of the vale involved the
town and its rural neighborhood in a symbiotic relationship of agricultural production and markets. Tewkesbury held markets on Wednesdays
and Saturdays "for all kinds of grain and other dead victuals and merchandise," and a second market on Wednesdays for the sale of cattle,
wool, yarn, hemp, linen, and other material used to make cloth.[124] The
town was also the site of annual fairs held in February and August, on St.
Mathias's Day and St. Bartholomew's Day.[125]

As an economic community, Tewkesbury processed and marketed the
fruits of agriculture in the vale. The forms of work represented in the
town in 1608 reflected this economic function. Almost half of the men
listed in the militia survey either worked directly on the land, as yeomen,
husbandmen, and laborers, or prepared the produce of the land for consumption, in such trades as maltster, baker, or butcher. Just over a quarter of the men in Smyth's list produced or sold leather or leather goods,
textiles, or clothes. Another 10 percent of the men in the survey shaped
metal or wood into the myriad tools needed to farm and the furniture
required to keep a respectable house. The carriers and boatmen of the
town, servants of the channels and roads that joined the economy of the
vale to the great cities of London and Bristol, were often abroad on
extended journeys. The absence of boatmen and the small number of
carriers in the militia list almost certainly attest to the demands of this
kind of work and the small numbers actually present in Tewkesbury
when Smyth made the survey.

The forms of work in the villages offered minor variations on the
themes of an agricultural economy. Ashchurch, Deerhurst, and Twyning
supported substantial numbers of craftsmen. In the northwestern corner
of Ashchurch, close to Tewkesbury, about a quarter of the men returned

in Smyth's survey for the hamlet of Northway and Newton worked in trades. The tailor and joiner of the hamlet had the benefit of business on the main road across the parish from Tewkesbury.[126] Deerhurst and Apperley enjoyed strategic positions on the road between Gloucester and Tewkesbury, and the tailors, musician, and glover in the villages could depend on the custom of travelers as well as on local trade.[127] Three badgers, substantial grain merchants, lived in Apperley and may have carried the produce of the northern vale from the markets in Tewkesbury as far as the cloth district of Stroudwater in the south.[128] Twyning offered opportunities for its tailors and shoemaker to profit from the traffic on the road between Tewkesbury and Worcester. These commercial prospects were generally restricted to the roads. The craftsmen in Forthampton and Tredington were isolated smiths, probably not much inclined to look past the tools and metalwork required for the agricultural work of their villages. The two weavers in Walton Cardiff comprised 40 percent of the extremely small number returned for this trade in the six rural parishes near the town. In the second half of the seventeenth century, weavers may have farmed on a considerable scale to support their income. In 1608 Thomas Greene, a young man in his twenties, was listed as a weaver in Walton Cardiff. Greene, who later moved to Tewkesbury, owned cattle valued at more than £130 in the early 1640s.[129]

There is no source from the later seventeenth century to match Smyth's survey for breadth and detail, but the fragments of testamentary evidence related to occupations may indicate changes in the vale economy.[130] Although testators were a small, generally more affluent minority, shifts in the economy would be reflected in the diverse occupational styles recorded in the total population of testators. After the Restoration, the number of households in Tewkesbury involved in work on the land apparently declined from 38 percent between 1590 and 1615 to 18 percent in the last quarter of the century. The drop to 9 percent between 1640 and 1665 reflects the smaller number of wills, although scattered evidence indicates that farmers in the vale suffered from the depredations of royalist forces stationed in Tewkesbury in the 1640s.[131] A second important change resulted from an increase in the number of gentlemen. The slippery use of the term *gentleman* in records makes it difficult to grasp the scale of this change. Smyth's militia return listed fifteen gentlemen for Tewkesbury in 1608, but only five testators described themselves as gentlemen between 1590 and 1665. Of the fifteen gentlemen in Smyth's survey, eleven were in their forties or older and may well have been retired tradesmen. After 1665, the greater number of "noble" households in Tewkesbury probably stimulated the demand for agricultural provisions from the hinterland, although dealers in produce already prospered from local population increases and a lucrative trade in malt to Wales.[132] The new prominence of gentlemen in Tewkesbury may also have intensified the traditional demand for fine furniture and cloth, the province of joiners, mercers, and linen drapers.

The social changes registered in wills and probate inventories are more difficult to assess in the countryside. The small number of inventories before 1665 indicates a mean estate value of £204 for yeomen, a figure placed in perspective by the median value of £137, and a mean estate of £40 for husbandmen. In Deerhurst, Forthampton, and Twyning, the number of wills made by small farmers, or husbandmen, declined between 1615 and 1690, while the number made by wealthier farmers, or yeomen, increased. In Ashchurch, yeomen's wills increased in number from three to twelve without any reduction in husbandmen's wills. Yet estate inventories make it difficult to state the significance of this change in terms of the disappearance of the smallholder.[133] The mean value of a yeoman's estate dropped from £204 to £117 in the years between 1665 and 1690, and the median value fell from £137 to £82, as the term *yeoman* came to describe a wider range of estate values. In the same years, the mean value of a husbandman's estate increased to £57, and the median value reflected the mean at £52. The change in vale society thus consisted, in part, of an inflated use of the term yeoman among farmers who, prior to the 1660s, would have used the less exalted term *husbandman* to describe their rank.[134] As neighbors prepared estate inventories, the combined evidence of wills and inventories illustrates both the elevated claims of small farmers and neighborly acceptance of a new yeomanry. A broader access to the clothes, furniture, and other goods used to display status, conspicuous in the inventories, may have been more important in this change than shifts in the distribution of land.

The distance between rich and poor was a fundamental reality of social life in the vale. The diverse class of the "poorer sort" consisted of wanderers, local families on more or less constant parish relief, and a substantial number of households vulnerable to fluctuations in the economy. This third group of families worked in trades but suffered from sudden disruptions in the supply of basic provisions not uncommon in the vale economy. A horrific frost in the winter of 1607, for instance, caused the Severn to freeze and made it impossible to bring shipments of wood and coal to Tewkesbury. The miserable failure of supplies resulted in "a great scarcity and extremity . . . so as no man could keep his trees and hedges from cutting and spoiling by the poorer sort."[135] As this rueful note in the borough council register indicates, the most serious social conflicts resulted from assaults on property to preserve life in an economic crisis, such as a dearth of grain, firewood, or coal.[136] The significant variations in estimates of the "poorer sort" in Tewkesbury reflect the cyclical nature of poverty. In 1625 the town clerk observed the distribution of alms after the funeral of Edward Alye, a gentleman and affluent householder of the parish, and estimated the number of poor to exceed nine hundred, almost half of the population, despite the exclusion of nonresident families.[137] Just five years later, in 1630, the poor in Tewkesbury were calculated at five hundred, perhaps a quarter of the population.[138] These estimates conceal the hardships suffered by many families on the line between sufficiency and relief, pushed across the line in difficult times. Yet the local officers responsible for the reports clearly believed poverty was on the march and increased in absolute terms.

The hearth tax returns from the later seventeenth century speak in plain style, but the lists of numbers are an eloquent record of the disparity between the houses of the rich and the poor.[139] Most of the people in the vale were either too poor to pay the tax or lived in small homes of one or two hearths. Poor craftsmen, laborers, and farmers who occasionally worked for wages to increase their small incomes, composed the largest group in this class. Thomas Pritchett of Tewkesbury, a joiner, may stand for the better fortunes of this group. Pritchett's two-hearth house had a shop and a kitchen on the ground floor, with a larger chamber for sleeping and two smaller rooms upstairs.[140] A few laborers worked their way into the ranks of the husbandmen, such as Thomas Potter of Clifford Chambers, who developed a small trade in malt into an estate worth £50 at his death.[141] Thomas Etheridge of Deerhurst, a wealthy laborer, lived in a four-room, one-hearth house in 1715.[142] At the lower end of the spectrum, Robert Wintell, a poor fisherman of Apperley, lived in a crude variation of a one-room house that consisted of a "fire room" and two open chambers above for storage and sleeping.[143]

A middle group of householders included modest to wealthy craftsmen, shopkeepers, and farmers, sheltered in houses of three to five hearths. John Pumfry's house in Tewkesbury marked the line between poverty and sufficiency for tradesmen in the town. Pumfry's house had a kitchen and a butcher's shop on the ground floor, with two sparsely furnished chambers for the family and a storage room above.[144] More characteristic of this middle group was the four-hearth house kept by the Neast family in Forthampton, composed of nine chambers and two garrets over a basic ground plan of hall, parlor, kitchen, and buttery.[145]

The wealthiest families in the vale lived in comfortable houses of six or more hearths. William Deagle's six-hearth house in Tewkesbury featured nine upstairs rooms over a tallow chandler's shop, a hall, and a kitchen.[146] By the last quarter of the seventeenth century, the intimate rooms in such houses were sometimes designed around motifs and reflected a desire to create distinctive spaces in the home for the society of family and friends. Deagle's "Swan Chamber" and "White Hart Chamber" expressed this fashionable interest in the unique social uses of rooms. Townhouses at the upper end of the scale increased less in size than in comforts. John Cooke's eleven-hearth house in Tewkesbury was not much bigger than Deagle's house, but it was far better heated, as half its upstairs rooms had hearths.[147]

The references to status in probate records, the size of houses, and the value of estates are not always trustworthy guides to wealth in the vale. John Healing of Wightfield, described in his estate inventory as a husbandman, lived in a one-hearth house composed of three small rooms and a "great chamber" over a parlor and a kitchen, yet Healing's estate of £369 made him wealthier than many yeomen.[148] In addition, the executors of a will usually registered the estate inventory before the deceased's debts were paid. The fragment of estate left to Hester Farmer, widow of William Farmer of Apperley, indicates the small credit margins of vale farmers, even the farmers honored as yeomen. The median value of a yeoman's estate between 1691 and 1715 was £110. William Farmer's estate was appraised at £83 in 1711 but quickly shrank to less than £9 after the payment of debts, rents, and back wages.[149] Probate records were often created in the midst of a crisis, and neighbors were unlikely to dispute reasonable claims to status in the moment of death. Yet this reluctance to demand a match between claims to status and command of wealth also reflected the imagined social order of stationary ranks. The neighbors of the vale followed the cosmologies of Smith and Harrison in their desire to preserve a static hierarchy of ranks and to honor the ideal, if not the practice, of a fixed relationship between lineage, work, wealth, and status. The wish and the imagination clearly could not make it so. This cosmology was itself a prescriptive ideal, an abstract justification of the principles of custom. The image of an immutable social order defied the competition for status and its uncertainty for many families in the vale.

The uncertainties of status were revealed in a dispute between the Baugh and Turberville families of Twyning. The Baughs, who ranked as esquires and gentlemen, had dominated Twyning since the sixteenth century. In the militia survey of 1608, the Baugh household accounted for 18 percent of the men returned for the village, and four of the five gentlemen in the community were Baughs.[150] The Turbervilles had never been more than yeomen. In the 1620s, however, the Turbervilles began to form connections in Tewkesbury and to acquire expensive leases in Twyning. By the 1630s and 1640s the tokens of lineage had started to appear in the wills of the Turberville family. In 1631 Richard Turberville passed his sword to his brother Robert. Ten years later, Edmund Turberville bequeathed to his son the gold signet ring that had belonged to his uncle Balthrop.[151] William Turberville's lease of land in the Mythe in the late 1630s thus had a special significance.[152] Many farmers of Twyning grazed animals on the Mythe common, and Turberville made his leasehold a symbol of his family's elevated status in the neighborhood. He planted "many young trees . . . and many thousands of quicksets, and thereby making and scouring the ditches and mounds of the premises . . . did very much improve [the land's] value and revenue." Edward Baugh, "being no soldier nor officer employed by any army or parliament, but a private country gentleman," disputed this claim of status in March 1659, entering the premises with a gang of his friends "by force and strong hand, taking advantage of the bad and troublesome times." Baugh proceeded to place his own cattle on the property, and before giving up the land, he cut down Turberville's trees and hedges and broke the mounds and fences.[153] Turberville's property obviously could not secure the status of his family. Many yeomen had wealth, but relatively few placed their families among the lineages of the parish elite. Admission even to this modest nobility of the vale required a subtle combination of property, family connection, and the skill to translate such assets into the symbols of rank and effective displays of power. An acceptance in this elite still did not guarantee status, as questions of rank were seldom settled in a definitive way. Edward Baugh needed help from his friends and neighbors to defend the village hierarchy and could not simply invoke the authority of rank. The Turbervilles were among the most prosperous farmers of Twyning, but their status in the village shifted in the tumble of neighborhood politics.

The society of the vale fostered extensive personal networks of kinship, friendship, and neighborhood, but also existed as a prescriptive social order, a fixed order, a veritable object to the townsmen and villagers of the vale, usually imagined as a static hierarchy of rank and status. The distribution of position, rank, and honor flowed from blood and work, descent and occupation. This hierarchy of ranks differed from personal networks in its explicit connection of lineages and chartered groups, such as the corporation of Tewkesbury and its guilds, to the sources of authority beyond the boundaries of the vale. As officers of the Crown, the heralds certified the honor of a lineage, which was expressed in the authenticity of its pedigree. Tewkesbury existed as a corporation only because of the Crown's divinely inspired power to carve liberties from the empire of its own prerogative. The political dynamic of status made social order in the vale an extension of the power and authority embodied in the person of the monarch.

Even though these relations of kinship, friendship, neighborhood, and status were the flesh and bone of parish communities in the vale, they cannot account for the authority and cohesion of community itself. Parish communities did not arise from social relationships. Only symbols and ritual action could create communities from the dispersed settlements in vale parishes. These sacred or profane dramas—the solemn perambulations of parish bounds or the assemblies of friends in the alehouses of Tewkesbury after the weekly market—presented opportunities to join cosmology and personal relationship, to create the types of abstract association described as communities. The power of symbols to create communities justifies a momentary disregard for the "conceptions of a general order of existence" that are particularly important in religious symbolism.[154] A momentary indifference to the most *general* meanings of symbols, in favor of the sites and performance of ritual, may help to clarify how symbols marked boundaries and created communities in the vale. Both the structure of a symbol and the site or context of its use contribute to its meaning. The ritual dramas performed on the Sabbath in the parish church of Tewkesbury were repeated in every parish church across the vale. Yet the performances in the abbey created a unique parish community from the dispersed neighborhoods of the High Street and St. Mary's Lane, and the hamlets of Southwick and the Mythe. As the annual floods created islands in the vale separated by dangerous expanses of water, the rituals of each parish church generated a discrete community of insiders and outsiders, a distinctive Christian neighborhood. The symbols of status, chartered corporation, and parish created the most important communities in the vale and assimilated the culture of the vale in the communities of church and nation.

The symbols of status and lineage created household communities composed of the retinues of friends, servants, and tenants clustered around the male heads of older gentry families. A household retinue of this type accompanied Edward Baugh in his raid on the Turberville estate in the Mythe. The Baugh family arms furnished symbols of a venerable authority and status, reinforced by a large patrimony. Edward Baugh had maintained this position of leadership from the family estates and wealth, the muscle behind antiquity and social rank. After the sixteenth century, such retinues may have been less inclined to murder in the service of nobility, but Edward Baugh used the relations of obligation and clientage to intimidate his weaker rivals in a manner not uncommon among gentry families in the seventeenth century.[155] If bands of bullies slipped away from the discipline of the household, the ethos of feud could still lead to murder in the early seventeenth century. In 1607 a variant of the type of retinue attracted to Edward Baugh murdered John Vicaries in the streets of Tewkesbury.[156] This band contained the local friends of Edward Rotherham, a London merchant, and a few servants from the household of his friend Sir John Hickford of Dixton, but acted under its own leadership in the murder. The band habitually met to drink wine in the house of William Phelps, a vintner in Tewkesbury. Hugh King and his kinsmen Thomas Jelfe and John Jelfe were among the leaders of the band. The initial cause of feud lay between Edward Rotherham and William Vicaries, a brother of the murdered man, after William cut off Rotherham's hand in a fight. This bloodshed polarized the families and friends of Rotherham and Vicaries. The final act in the feud began when John Vicaries made the fateful decision to visit the Phelps house for a drink after the Saturday market in Tewkesbury. Hugh King and his companions arrived later, and, after a few drinks, King taunted Vicaries and attempted to provoke a quarrel. Vicaries, who was outnumbered, clearly hoped to avoid a fight. He tried to escape from the house secretly, but his enemies caught him in the street. King and his friends then beat back the watchmen of the town, chased Vicaries down the High Street, and killed him in the market house near the cross.

This battle against the watchmen suggests the ambiguous relationship between the symbols of traditional rank and lineage in the vale and the authority of the borough created in Tewkesbury by a royal charter of incorporation in the last quarter of the sixteenth century. Tewkesbury, which was first incorporated in 1575, received its most generous charter from James I in 1610. This Jacobean charter established a large council of two bailiffs, twenty-four burgesses, and twenty-four assistant burgesses. The corporation contained a hierarchy of ranks. Burgesses were customarily chosen from the company of assistants, and assistants were drawn from the freemen. In 1649 the corporation included three hundred freemen, perhaps 16 percent of the town's population. Burgesses served as bailiff in annual turns.[157] Status was an important prerequisite to advancement in the corporation, but, once a person was on the council as an assistant or a burgess, status flowed from seniority in the service of the town. An "ancient custom" established the order of precedence at the council table according to the date of first service in the office of bailiff. An age hierarchy governed the discussion of issues brought before the council. The youngest were to speak first "and so to ascend and go by degrees to the most ancient."[158]

The solemn rites of admission to the ranks of the corporation conveyed its status, dignity, and solidarity. After a new burgess was elected and sworn into office, he bestowed a dinner on the company of burgesses, assistants, and their wives "for the better increase of amity and society in the corporation." This banquet brought the entire company into the house of the newly elected burgess, although a friend's house could be used if privacy was preserved and the friend was not "a vintner, innholder, or victualler."[159] The humility of the host preceded admission to the company of the corporation, and the neophyte's social rank did not affect this requirement. A new burgess selected two councilors as stewards in trust to hold the sum of twenty nobles customarily spent on the dinner. Any "broken meat" left at the end of the feast was then distributed by the stewards among the poor. In the case of newly elected assistants, two were required to furnish a dinner for the burgesses and assistants. If only one new assistant entered the council, the dinner was provided for the burgesses alone.[160] Similar duties followed each advance in the ranks, as a burgess chosen to be low bailiff for the year hosted a banquet on the night of his election for members of both companies of the corporation and their wives.[161] These rites obscured personal status and used feasts and oaths to separate the candidate from the everyday society of the town. The authority of powerful office was separated from personal rank and subsumed in the social life of the council itself. This separation of the council from the town and the vale was evident in penalties imposed "for revealing the town secrets." The first offense carried a £5 fine, but the penalty for the second was dismissal from the council.[162]

The dignity of the corporation and the distinctions in its ranks were prominently displayed in public ceremonies. A conspicuous presence in the ceremonies of the Sabbath marked the small circle of the council as the most powerful source of secular authority and status in the parish. On Sundays the burgesses dressed in their formal gowns and convened at the town hall to escort the bailiffs to church, and the four burgesses elected as justices of the peace were enjoined "for the reputation of the town" to wear "twice every Sabbath day to church a gown of the partlet fashion, faced with black bughe."[163] This solemn procession in sober attire wended its way to special seats in the abbey reserved for the bailiffs, burgesses, and assistants. The seats in the abbey formed seven rows or aisles in "the body of the church" or the nave, and the front section of the middle row, looking toward the traditional site of the altar, belonged to the bailiffs. Another six seats nearby were set aside for the guild masters. Most of the burgesses sat behind the bailiffs in the middle row, and by 1638 the assistants had acquired their own section of seats. The councilors, who strictly controlled the choice of occupants for the seats nearest their own, used the council's power in the parish to stress their distinction in the church. These efforts to preserve the mystique of the council were also calculated to enhance the rank and prestige of their own households. The bailiffs' wives had special seats in the church by 1626, and local accounts mention a plan to create a separate section for the wives of burgesses in 1638.[164]

The officers of the corporation were the cynosure of the parish community on the Sabbath and on festival days. In the early seventeenth century, the civic calendar in Tewkesbury contained twelve major celebrations. The most important points in the civic year fell between the feast of All Saints in November and Whitsunday in May or June. The feast of Simon and Jude, on October 28, was election day for new officers, and the fair held on St. Bartholomew's Day in August was the only significant civic occasion between Whitsunday and election day in the middle of autumn.[165] On these "solemn days of old accustomed," the burgesses met the bailiffs at the tolsey or town hall in formal dress. Any burgess who had served as bailiff in the past was entitled to wear a special gown "faced with foins" and a tippet or short cape. Burgesses who had never been bailiff wore gowns "of the same fashion" but "faced in bughe without a tippet." Assistants were more modestly attired in "a comely, decent gown."[166] These parish festivals thus became another opportunity to display the majesty of the corporation and to reinforce the distinctions of rank on the council itself.

The councilors strained to enhance their power in the parish, the community of belief and ceremony created from dispersed hamlets and isolated farms.[167] Symbols created the cohesion of the parish, and no symbols more powerfully evoked its identity than the parish church and its ceremonies.[168] The church bells were the collective voice of the parish community. In 1613 an anonymous writer condemned the churchwardens of Tewkesbury for their decision to sell a new bell commissioned for the abbey. A poem called "The Bell Speaks" inscribed in the parish register placed a curse on the churchwardens for the crimes of corruption and sacrilege.[169] The bells sounded the start and finish of each workday and registered important events in the life of the community. In 1595 the parish officers paid the sexton "for ringing the bell morning and evening, winter and summer." As a mark of the honor and respect due to powerful visitors, the bells rang for the visitations of the bishop and the chancellor of the diocese, and the churchwardens bought beer "for the ringers" after the Lord Presidents of the Council in the Marches entered Tewkesbury in 1618.[170]

The abbey church in Tewkesbury was revered as "a great ornament to the town" and as the site of communal events.[171] The portion of the abbey used for parochial religious services had been bought from the Crown in 1542, three years after the dissolution of the Benedictine monastery.[172] In 1600 the churchwardens "undertook to build a battlement of stone" on top of the abbey tower, because the old wooden battlement had collapsed in the 1550s. This effort began as the churchwardens' personal venture, and funds were raised by means of "marts" or private contracts between the churchwardens and "such as would take of them." But it soon became apparent that this technique would not yield the money required for the new battlement. The churchwardens then acquired a license for the year "to devise some meetings to be had within the town for their help." Plays had been performed in the abbey until the 1580s, and this practice was revived to finance the new battlement.[173] In 1600 the abbey became the site of a Whitsuntide festival of plays, music, beer, and food. Substantial gifts of wheat and malt arrived from farmers in the town and its rural neighborhood, although the plays failed to raise the amount of money needed for the battlement.[174] The abbey was again the site of festivities in 1617, when a fair was organized to pay for the new "scholars' gallery" built for the pupils of the local school.[175] In addition to this platform of public entertainments, the abbey offered tremendous views across the field and water of the vale, so that sightseers who entered the tower illicitly to climb onto the roof were an occasional nuisance to churchwardens.[176]

The stolid presence of the abbey as a motive and site for local festivals illustrates the subtle interrelationship between this symbol of the parish and neighborly activities in the town. A variety of rites, duties, and activities joined the abbey to the lives of individuals and families. The rites of the life cycle occurred in the abbey, and even recent immigrants to the parish might have celebrated baptisms in the nave or mourned over burials in the churchyard. Service in the office of churchwarden involved many prominent men in the care of the church fabric. Personal bequests and gifts to the abbey were often made in the last years of life or at the moment of death. In 1618 Edward Alye "freely gave to the church a fair silver cup for the communion table." The churchwardens bought materials in 1622 to build a fence around "the trees set in the churchyard by Mr. Smith." Six years later, the widow Elizabeth Morry gave the abbey a fine tablecloth for "the new communion table."[177] These gifts acknowledged both the abbey *and* the parish, the sacred place and its neighborhood.

The mundane affairs of the local economy involved the abbey in the everyday life of town and vale. The massive fabric required constant care and attention, and this continuous demand for stone, glass, lead, tile, and other building materials, as well as occasional labor, offered precious additional income to farmers and craftsmen. The churchwardens of Tewkesbury spent an average of £43 annually on local supplies and labor in the years between 1615 and 1629. An owner of a cart or a farmer with a free day or a servant to spare could earn small sums in unskilled labor for the churchwardens, particularly during the spring and summer when work on the outside of the church involved hauling stone and sand.[178] Few opportunities to make money for the abbey were wasted. In 1609 John Saunders of Tewkesbury paid the churchwardens eighteen pence for a piece of iron "found in the vestry." John Parret later paid two shillings "for a windfall tree" in the churchyard.[179] These routine transactions extended the intimate interrelationship of abbey and town.

The symbols of the parish created a distinctive form of fellowship from elements of family and neighborhood. The order of seats in the abbey in the early seventeenth century dissolved the nuclear family into this broader religious fellowship, and it also restricted neighborhood to the territorial boundaries of the parish. Although men and women frequently shared the same pew, husbands and wives usually sat apart during religious services. Although very young children remained beside their parents, it was not unusual for adolescents to have their own places. The male children of the wealthier families often sat apart in the "scholars' gallery" or "boys' gallery" as students of the free school.[180] As young men, many would later enter the seats of their fathers, although pews were not fixed to particular pieces of property in the town. A seat was acquired by the payment of a fine. If the pews of the bailiffs and burgesses were constant symbols of corporate dignity, the acquisition of seats by other families resembled a game of musical chairs. As vacancies resulted from deaths, exchanges, or departures from the town, neighbors in search of a more prestigious accommodation quickly filled the vacuum.[181] Beyond this orderly scramble for places in the nave, the poor families of the town crowded the corners of the abbey. Many could not afford pews and therefore stood in the back of the nave or in the side aisles. Sometimes groups of six or seven pooled their pennies to buy a place, such as Thomas Harris and his wife, Benjamin Bailies, Henry Field's wife, William Field, and "old Green," who paid four shillings in 1609 for a seat "where the preacher goes through."[182] The abbey was a battlefield in the family wars of status and rank as well as a majestic stage for the neighborly fellowship of festivals.

The activities in the abbey and even its architecture joined Tewkesbury to distant towns and to the monarchy. A royal iconography in the church interior proclaimed Crown authority over the symbols of the parish. Stuart arms were prominently displayed in the abbey, and the first act of the churchwardens after the completion of a new gallery in 1617 was to pay "for oil and colors to paint the King's arms."[183] The audience in the abbey occasionally heard briefs sent from the bishop of Gloucester to parish churches in the vale. These texts ordered ministers and church-wardens to collect money for approved causes and attempted to create sympathy for the misfortunes of other towns, particularly towns damaged by fire. The modest sums collected in 1661 for the relief of Falkenham in Norfolk and in 1673 for the assistance of Knaresborough in Yorkshire indicate a steady but limited response to requests for help from distant corners of the realm.[184] Briefs read in the abbey in the 1620s attempted to promote a local awareness of the international persecution of Protestants. In 1628, a collection was made in Tewkesbury for "the inhabitants of the Isle of Ree" and "the ministers of the Palatinate, being in exile."[185]

The abbey was the primary forum for discussion of events in the world beyond the vale. In the late seventeenth century, sermons delivered in the abbey not only described and celebrated William III's victories in Ireland but also interpreted the events in metaphors of the English nation as the new Jerusalem.[186] An earlier sermon represented the imprisonment of the seven bishops in 1688 as a reenactment of Peter's trials in Rome. John Matthews, the local minister, invoked the example of the early Christians as a model for his parish and called for a similar response to persecution, in the form of prayer.[187] The interpretive schemes in local sermons, which extended to international relations, formed a stock of conventional images used to assess the behavior of other nations. "Some sins," Matthews observed in 1708, "may be specified as more peculiar to some nations. But so long as socianism [*sic*] infests Poland, atheism Italy, the inquisition Spain, excessive drinking Germany, lewdness France and most Christian nations, indifferency in religion England, and malignity to our church and hierarchy Scotland, seeing the power of Christian religion is so little visible and vice and immorality so notorious and epidemical, we cannot be at a loss to resolve the cause of these common judgments against which reformation will be the best antidote."[188]

The parish communities of the vale were governed by a system of canon law enforced in the consistory court of Gloucester diocese. This diocese had been created after the separation of the English church from Rome, and its boundaries corresponded more or less to the boundaries of Gloucestershire. The bishops received their appointments from the Crown and, in addition to their ordinary court of jurisdiction in Gloucester, held visitations and visitation courts at least once every three years to assess the moral and spiritual condition of parishes in the diocese.[189] The lay officers of a parish, the churchwardens, usually presented local offenses in the visitation court before the consistory court called the offenders to account. A verdict of guilty often led to an act of penance in the parish church, a dramatic affirmation of the morality enshrined in canon law and ceremonial orthodoxy. Yet the evidence of neighborhood has revealed how the church court might be used as a political weapon to attack the reputation of an enemy. This complex interrelationship between the parishes of the vale and the judicial institutions of the diocese may be compared with the relations among dialects in language. A faction in a vale parish might translate its political interests into the terms of authority and procedure used in the consistory court to prosecute an enemy. The visitations of the bishop and his servants reversed this process, since diocesan authority entered the parish unsolicited. Although churchwardens could attempt to control what diocesan officials were told, the visitations were the most effective means to enforce *diocesan* priorities in the vale. There were no definitive boundaries between vale parishes and diocese.[190]

To describe a local conflict in terms actionable in the church court was itself a powerful act and commonly involved the violence of the spoken word. The court judged between legitimate and illegitimate uses of this power.[191] The depositions among the records of the church court provide ample evidence of the politics behind many cases introduced in the court. The dramatic statements attributed to Thomas Moore, a cobbler in Tewkesbury, illustrate the power of words to move a dispute from the vale to the court in Gloucester Cathedral.[192] In 1606 Moore's neighbor William Little, a shoemaker, sued him for debts, and Moore's property was impounded. Moore, who felt deeply wronged in this lawsuit, contemplated revenge against the entire Little family, whom he described as "the old knave and his son, the bawdy old whore and the young whore."[193] In the heat of anger, Moore walked to Little's home and shop in December 1606. Little saw Moore approach and called to him, asking sarcastically if Moore had acquired bail for the impounded goods. Moore faced Little in the doorway of the shop. John Little, the shoemaker's son, and Ralph Nutting, a journeyman in the shop, stopped their work to observe this confrontation between their master and his vanquished enemy. Moore then announced in a loud voice that Little deserved "a cow's grass in heaven" for ignorance of the sexual disgrace in his family. Moore claimed that Little's wife Dorothy as well as his daughter were commonly known as "whores" among their neighbors and had once seduced a journeyman employed in Little's household.

Moore's words could not be ignored. The power of his speech consisted of his status as a householder in the town and his skillful use or invention of rumor to create a narrative of adultery and to poison a reputation. Moore expressed his private anger in language of public significance. The "common name and fame of a whore" and the reputation of a "cuckold" had many unpleasant consequences, from loss of credit and status among neighbors to prosecution in the church court and the shame of public penance. John Little, "being in choler moved," entered the street to "strike and beat" in defense of his mother and sister, but William Little separated from his wife for a year after the incident, and Dorothy Little clearly hoped a victory in the defamation suit would restore the family. Moore's performance, which differed from gossip in its public nature, resembled Elizabeth Canner's verbal assault on Thomas Vaughan in 1629. As Canner had invoked the term "bastard" to dishonor Vaughan, Moore used the words "whore" and "cuckold" to humiliate the Littles and to make Dorothy Little vulnerable to the disciplinary action of the church court.[194]

The interrelationship of the church court and the vale registered differences in the policies, competence, and integrity of diocesan officials as well as local distinctions of power and status. A case often came before churchwardens and apparitors as a result of genuine concern for the health of the parish community and trust in diocesan institutions as a spiritual remedy.[195] In the 1590s, for instance, Thomas Richards of Tewkesbury cajoled his neighbor William Downbell to reform his adulterous ways, several years before Richards presented information against Downbell in court.[196] The records of Gloucester diocese contain many sincere confessions and penances for involuntary violations of canon law and parish community. As a forum for confession and the distribution of penance, the court stood between the vale and the authority of God and the Crown. Yet the court had mixed success in its capacity as mediator between the divine macrocosm and the microcosm of the parish. Officers of the court were sometimes perceived to have an interest in its disciplinary cases. Many suitors used friends in the court or paid bribes to apparitors and other officials to influence a case. These ventures often depended for success on the complicity of the chancellor and the court registrar.[197] A shady history of corrupt influences on ecclesiastical justice helps to account for local distrust of the diocesan court in the late sixteenth century. As religious factions in the vale began to seek more control over ceremonies in the parish church in the 1590s and to contest the use of the surplice, the court became involved in conflicts that questioned its own authority to adjudicate issues of conscience.

Symbols created communities from the dispersed hamlets and farms of the northern vale. The existence of parish communities in this landscape of hazardous floods and scattered population is a testament to the power of culture over material obstacles. The loyalties expressed in household bands might be derived from the dynamics of personal and status relations, but the corporation and the parish were distinctive forms of *symbolic* community. As many aspects of kinship, friendship, and neighborliness depended on everyday social interaction, only *symbols* created the corporation and the parish. As status marked distance and difference, the symbols of the corporation and the parish created intimacy and common identity within their confines. The corporation formed an exclusive circle distinct from the town. Perhaps this separation made control of the parish, its ceremonies, and its symbolism the more important for officers of the corporation. These symbols of the parish formed the core of a ritual system, an orderly sequence of sacred performances that was expressed in the offices of baptism, marriage, and burial, the ceremonial commemorations of birth, sexual partnership, and death.

The societies of the northern vale in the seventeenth century seem to evoke terms of quiet continuity, perhaps because change is often explained in terms of population and economy. The dispersed population of the vale grew only slowly in the sixteenth and seventeenth centuries; the occupational structure and distribution of wealth reflected minor shifts in the local economy. Yet the dynamics of social life in the vale also indicate change might come from other sources, perhaps from sources more difficult to quantify. The social dramas of Margaret Cartwright and Joanne Collett in Tredington, and Thomas Vaughan and Elizabeth

Canner, Thomas Moore and William Little in Tewkesbury, illustrate the subtle interrelationships among kinship and neighborliness, wealth and status, the imagined communities of parish and corporation, diocese and kingdom. A conflict over the symbols and terms of imagined community might affect the *meaning* if not the structure of family, neighborhood, status, and community itself.

In this respect, the vale presents fresh possibilities for the description of community in the seventeenth century. The clear distinction between the symbols of community and the practice of social relations in dispersed hamlets reveals how the symbols could create communities *contrary* to the diffuse tendencies of social relations in the vale. This ethnographic reality limits the usefulness of many approaches to community, but the general importance of family, neighborhood, status, and parish in early modern England may provide a means to consider the ethnographic problems of the vale in descriptions of other localities. The kinds of relationships and imagined communities in the vale were present in other places, if not interrelated in the same way. A comparative method for the description of local societies might move away from functionalist types to study the distinctive patterns of interrelationship among settlement, kinship, and neighborhood; wealth and status; and the symbols of parish, diocese, and kingdom.

3

Under the Hand of God: Parish Communities and Rites of Mortality

Man in his frailty must not presume of prosperity, but prepare a kind
of stooping under the hand of God when it pleases him to strike or
punish us.

Anonymous, The Wonderful Discovery of Witchcrafts (1619)

Our apostle [Paul], resembling burying to sowing, implies a
resurrection. For as yearly experience shows us, that the same grain
does arise from the seed sown, so the wisdom of God's spirit has
pitched upon this constant operation of nature, as a proper emblem
and representation of the Resurrection.

John Matthews, Funeral Sermon (1691)

The symbols of the parish created communities in the vale from the
scattered and sometimes contradictory relations of kinship, friendship,
and neighborhood. The parish held the power of the sacred, and ritual
performances in the parish church uncovered the meanings of human
birth and death, of procreation and salvation. The bonds of kinship,
friendship, and neighborhood commonly extended beyond the parish,
but the rituals of communion, baptism, marriage, and death created a
community from its territorial relationships.

This interrelationship of symbols and social relations has left traces in
the form of sermons, registers, and other documents created to commemorate the rituals performed in parish churches.[1] Because the ceremonies were clearly important to participants, the evidence thus created
provides a point of entry to the interrelationship of religious beliefs,

symbols, and social relations. Yet the rite in the church was only a moment in a complex ritual process, and a variety of different forms of evidence are needed to understand a rite and its meanings in the total context of vale society.[2] The evidence of responses to mortality provides the best archive of any ritual process in the Vale of Gloucester. Probate records, funeral sermons, and epitaphs reveal a process in the vale parishes sufficiently common to be described as a mortuary system.[3]

The evidence of this mortuary system also reveals profound conflicts in the culture of the vale. In the late sixteenth and seventeenth centuries, disputes over the meanings of death and its ceremonies began to create barriers between neighbors and to divide households. The mortuary system in northern Gloucestershire showed traces of a broad European conflict over the nature of a scriptural Christianity.[4] This conflict involved the nature of the sacred itself as well as the sources of religious authority and community. A prolonged, painful, and sometimes violent effort to resolve the issues of this debate left an indelible mark on the mortuary system in the vale and transformed its parish communities.

Death in the vale was as much a social and cultural event as it was a biological reality. The meanings of death were symbolic interpretations of a biological condition. A good death existed *solely* in culture and could be achieved only in the society of others. These observations join the society of the vale to a vast record of human experience. The idea of an interrelationship between funerals and social order figured prominently in the earliest attempts to describe religious systems as social bonds.[5] A seminal text in the history of modern anthropology treated the transition from the familiar spaces of everyday life to the spaces of the dead as a problem of symbolism.[6]

Yet recent historical studies have focused on demographic measures of mortality, and local histories have paid scant attention to funerals or preparation for death.[7] An exception is the recent study of Whickham, a large parish in County Durham, four miles from Newcastle in northeastern England.[8] Keith Wrightson and David Levine describe different aspects of society in Whickham as parts of an interrelated system and link the structural transformation in the parish economy, a shift from agriculture to coal production, to changes in burial customs and attitudes toward death. This method provides a detailed ethnographic complement to the demographic perspective on death. A similar approach to religious conflict in the vale might join the ethnography of death to the social and cultural history of the Reformation. The probate records, funeral sermons, and epitaphs of the vale parishes are perfectly suited to this ethnographic approach.

Death evoked ambivalent responses in the Vale of Gloucester in the seventeenth century, inspiring hopes and fears of a religious and social nature. Death figured in religious symbolism as an end and a beginning. The worldly pilgrimage imposed by the Fall ended on the deathbed, and physical death marked the entrance of the Christian to eternal life in the company of Christ.[9] But death also challenged social order and threatened to destroy the continuity of social life. A decline in a person's physical health began a ritual and social process to commemorate and eliminate the afflicted person's position in the everyday life of the parish and, after death, to move the person to a new position in the social order. The elements of the ritual process have left traces in wills, funeral customs, and the epitaphs on monuments to the dead.

This mortuary system did not express a universal experience of death. The hierarchy of status meant that experience varied considerably in the vale and elsewhere. This diversity was reflected in the unequal social distribution of wills. Only a minority in Tewkesbury and its rural hinterland prepared wills before death. Yet the careful use of wills to recover aspects of the mortuary process is both defensible and unavoidable. Status did not *dictate* the decision to prepare a will, and wills survive in greater or lesser numbers for every social stratum except the transient population of the homeless poor. Gender also influenced but did not determine the decision, and many wills survive for women as well as for men.[10] The small number of testators occupied a broad spectrum of positions in the social hierarchy.

Despite the small number of testators, the process of making a will may have been a more common experience than records indicate. The surviving wills represent the documents proved in the church court, and this procedure cost money. As the burden of probate could be prohibitive for a small estate, poor families had sound financial reasons to avoid the court if the concerned parties accepted a will's legitimacy.[11] The narrow margin between poverty and wealth in the vale meant that the officers of the church court often had to prosecute for failure to prove wills.[12] The circle of neighbors likely to have some experience of wills and their meaning can therefore be cautiously extended to include most house-holders. If poor householders did not make wills of their own, they might participate in the process as overseers or witnesses in the wills of their neighbors. This process would have been familiar to most of the householders in the vale as a significant prelude in the preparation for death.

A decision to make a will most often resulted from a physical illness or a personal trauma and intimation of mortality.[13] In 1582 Edward Hatton of Forthampton fell and injured himself near his house, while working at a saw pit, a site for processing the timber of Forthampton's woodlands. Hatton feared he would not long survive the accident and immediately made a will.[14] This fear of sudden death cut deeply into the religious consciousness. Death, which was the inscrutable call of God, could come for the unsuspecting Christian at any time. A sudden death could destroy a soul unprepared for the final judgment, and the failure to prepare for death would be reflected in the disarray of the earthly properties bestowed by God. Many wills were inspired by a heightened awareness of uncertainty in a "dangerous" world.[15] Before making a will in 1664, Thomas Crumpe of Tewkesbury reflected on "the uncertain estate of this frail and transitory life."[16] Joane Hawker of Apperley in Deerhurst "had weakness of body" and promptly made her will "not knowing how soon God may be pleased to send more, even to the taking away of my life."[17] Other wills reflect a similar anxiety about the time and manner of death. In 1634 Thomas Goodman of Ashchurch stated the motive for his will as his "knowing I must die, and I know not how soon or what kind of death."[18]

In the face of human weakness and mortality, a will became a moral obligation that enabled dying Christians to separate themselves from the world while honoring their debts and providing for personal dependents. Joane Williams of Tredington defined the hour of her death as a time "to set all worldly things as God has lent me in good order."[19] William Haines of Ashchurch described himself as the mere steward of his property and believed God would demand an account of his stewardship. In this divinely appointed role of careful steward, Haines alluded to his "diverse children" and expressed his desire to "consider them as a father, according to my ability."[20] The power of the will as a moral responsibility and as a form of expiation was recognized by Edward Matthews of Tewkesbury in 1612. Matthews conceded that he "was and is a great and daily sinner yet profess and confess that I am a Christian" and therefore made his will and testament "for that it has pleased Almighty God to lend me some goods in this world, and a wife and children, and lest after my death they should contend and strive about them."[21] A will or similar form of settlement was difficult to separate from the notion of the Christian person. John Bradford of Tewkesbury made his will in response to this obligation "to perform the part of a Christian man in the disposing of my temporal goods."[22]

As a result of this Christian duty to provide for dependents, family and friends might exert pressure on a dying person to prepare a will. Thomas Leaper's experience illustrates this pressure. In 1644 Leaper was "lying sick upon his bed in his dwelling house in Tewkesbury." Being cajoled by his wife Anne to make his will and dispose of his property, Leaper replied, "I will leave all my goods to your disposing. Do you what you will with them." Leaper's family apparently considered this verbal disposition of the estate inadequate, despite the presence of witnesses. On the following day, a second group of visitors to the deathbed asked Leaper to make another, perhaps written, will to confirm his former statement. But Leaper seems to have focused his mind on his sickness and approaching death and replied impatiently, "I have done it. Trouble me no further."[23]

The symbolism of the will in the mortuary system separated a person's spiritual goods or inward estate from the material goods or outward estate. This separation enabled the dutiful to cross the boundary between the everyday material world and the transcendental spiritual world of the Christian afterlife. In 1629, John Rawlins of Tewkesbury prepared his will in the time of his sickness "to the intent that my mind should be the less occasioned to think on worldly things."[24] Thomas Porter's will expressed his determination "to bestow, set in order, and dispose my self toward Almighty God and my goods and chattels toward the world."[25] In advice to his "sickly" neighbor Alice Carpenter, Giles Flucke of Apperley stressed the importance of this separation from the world of property before death. Flucke encouraged Carpenter to make a will, saying "her goods were never the farther from her."[26] This distinction of the spiritual life from the material life of the dying person was sometimes described as a reflection, in the moment of death, of the more significant contrast between the impermanence and corruption of the earthly body and the eternal perfection of the body of Christ.[27]

The preamble of a will disposed of the spiritual goods or the soul.[28] Because several historians have questioned the significance of preambles, it is necessary to take a position on the issues in the debate before proceeding to examine the wills themselves. The most important questions for the purposes of the present discussion involve the influence of the scribe and of administrative procedure on the form and content of a will. The evidence militates against the influence of the administrative process. In the first place, a bequest of the soul was not needed to make the will and testament a lawful transfer of property, yet only a handful of wills fail to make this bequest of the soul.[29] If individual testators were too sick to devise the bequest or had no preferences about the words in the preamble, the inclusion of the formula nevertheless indicates a general belief in the necessity of a spiritual settlement. As the interpretation advanced here focuses on ritual form and not on the specific style of a bequest, it is sufficient that the makers and writers of wills considered a bequest of the soul in some form to be appropriate and desirable. In the second place, a scribe had a good deal of control over the initial preparation of a will, but the finished product had to be read back to the testator in the presence of witnesses.[30] If the preamble did not have to reproduce the precise beliefs of the testator, the form of bequest could not directly oppose those beliefs either.[31] Another important fragment of evidence is the small number of spoken wills that include a bequest of the soul.[32] These nuncupative wills generally reported the testator's deathbed speeches, and the spoken wills that survive for Tewkesbury and its neighborhood record verbal commendations of the soul to God. The bequest of the soul is difficult to dismiss as a routine addition of scribes and should be taken seriously as the reflection of a process of spiritual and material settlement in the will.

The bequest of the soul usually preceded the distribution of property. The first line of a will invoked the name of God to secure the divine presence as the unseen director, witness, and sanctifier of events. After this invocation of the divine name and presence, the soul was placed in the "hands" or "protection" of God and Jesus Christ in the roles of creator and redeemer.[33] The precise words of the bequest were most commonly a conventional formula furnished by the lay or clerical scribe.[34] These formulae, which varied according to custom and taste, were sometimes passed from generation to generation in families. Anne Butler and her son John Butler of Tewkesbury, for instance, shared a formula distin-

guished by a detailed account of the elements in the Trinity.[35] The wills of
an entire village or parish might follow an identical formula. Richard
Edwards, the curate of Deerhurst in the 1590s and early 1600s, made
many wills for the villagers of Deerhurst, Apperley, Wightfield, and Deerhurst Walton.[36] These wills placed a common emphasis on "the certain
transmutation of man or woman, most assured to death and uncertain
the hour" and used the same phrases to bequeath and "heartily com-
mend" the soul to God as "the redeemer thereof with his precious blood"
and to beseech the acceptance of the soul "into the number of the holy
company of heaven."[37] Edwards modified the formula only to indicate
distinctions in the status of the testators and in the place of the burial.
Whatever their social differences prior to death, the minister ensured
that his parishioners surrendered their souls to God in precisely the same
way.

The bequest of the soul was not invariably formulaic. Despite their
physical afflictions, many had the strength and intellect to interpret their
deaths and thus used the spiritual clause in the will to make a statement
of personal religious faith or a confession of sin and declaration of repentance. Charles Tinker of Deerhurst "confessed" to a misspent estate in
life and hoped to make amends by giving the little he had left to his
children.[38] Edward Matthews of Tewkesbury used the preamble of his
will to "manifest to the world" his daily sins and failings "for the which I
from the bottom of my heart ask forgiveness at the hand of the only
savior of the world."[39] John Hampshire, a laborer of Twyning, confessed a
"steadfast faith, wrought in me by the motion of the Holy Ghost, which
holy Trinity I do faithfully believe to be my only God, whom I worship
and fear with all my heart."[40] Thomas Symes, a gentleman and the town
clerk of Tewkesbury, made his will in good health but remembered "with
unspeakable comfort the bottomless sea of the mercies and love of Jesus
Christ" and expressed his certain faith that "in the River of Life (the
blood of my dear Savior) all the spots and stains of my sinful life shall be
washed away."[41] The spiritual settlement in the will could thus range
from a formulaic bequest of the soul to a more personal purification and
bequest in preparation for death and divine judgment.

To understand a will as a ritual phase in preparation for death, the
distribution of property must be viewed in relation to this prior separation and bequest of the soul. A renunciation of personal ownership and
property often followed the spiritual clause. This renunciation was made

in a formula that described ownership of material goods as a loan or form of stewardship, ascribed to the benign intervention and eternal goodness of God. Thomas Porter of Tewkesbury attributed his property to "the bounteous liberality of my good and gracious God."[42] Elizabeth Greenway of Deerhurst Walton dismissed her property as mere "transitory" goods "whereof during the term of life I am by God's appointment made steward."[43] Mary Turberville professed herself "an unworthy steward" of her estate, divinely appointed to oversee the property only during her life.[44] An awareness of the spiritual significance of material goods informed this notion of stewardship. The value of property in the final moments of life came not from the criteria of exchange but from the moral character of its disposal. Nathaniel Wight, minister of Tewkesbury in the 1640s, believed his goods had been "committed to my disposal" by the hand of God.[45] Richard Sellers bequeathed the bulk of his goods to his daughter's son "to be disposed by him as Almighty God shall direct his heart."[46] This understanding of the material settlement in the will as a transaction made under the watchful eyes and influence of God underlay Roger Mortimer's reference to "the worldly goods that God has given me the power to dispose."[47] As the acquisition and prosperity of property symbolized divine benediction, the dispersal of property in preparation for death assumed a religious significance. A judicious disposition of property reflected the moral strength of a soul prepared for heaven.[48] A will thus embodied a spiritually charged transfer of property unlike any transaction previously made in a person's lifetime.

The primary aim of the material settlement was the peace of the family and neighborhood. A hasty and poorly planned withdrawal could produce chaos in the form of lawsuits and could leave a legacy of bitterness among family and friends. The provisions of a will peacefully commemorated and closed the testator's position in the social order. The first and most important duty in this process was the payment of debts. Debts to neighbors were discharged before the distribution of legacies in the family, and the speed and fairness of this settlement reflected on the honor of the family as well as on the moral integrity of the deceased.[49] Yet deathbed descriptions of indebtedness were more than recitations of a fiscal balance sheet. These "confessions" of debt could become detailed recollections of friendship and neighborliness.[50] Elizabeth Flucke of Deerhurst illustrated this pattern of commemoration in 1594.[51] Her confession of debts acknowledged neighbors who had helped to provision her home at different times. She recognized her son-in-law for sowing her wheat and building her a new barn. These were important events in her life, and the loans of grain had saved Elizabeth from the endemic scarcity of the vale. Her will offered a final opportunity to remember the help she had received. The confession of debts in the presence of family, friends, and neighbors was a powerful moment of community.

The deathbed management of debt yields substantial evidence of the material settlement in wills as more than a simple transfer of property. These allusions to debt reveal the significance of credit as a marker of trust and friendship in an environment of scarce resources. Credit might be passed across generations to preserve the relationships that the debts embodied. Thomas Etheridge's debt to Lawrence Reeve of Deerhurst in 1612 illustrates this intergenerational network of credit and friendship. The debt passed from father to son until it was finally "forgiven" in 1636.[52] The deathbed transformation of debts into gifts bestowed on debtors also expressed the dual nature of debt as economic resource and token of friendship. Henry Clements of Ashchurch made £15 of a £30 debt owed him by John Clarke of Twyning into the gifts of an apprenticeship fee and marriage portion for Clarke's son and daughter.[53]

The second duty in this process of peaceful closure was provision for dependents. The definitions of dependency and moral claims on resources reflected a person's marital history and place in the life cycle. The unmarried tended to define dependency in terms of horizontal or lateral kinship. Several wills indicate the impact an unmarried sibling could have on the households of brothers and sisters. Alice Pitt, a spinster of Tewkesbury, made the families of her sister and brother the focus of her will in 1637.[54] The provisions in their aunt's will transformed the lives of her nieces and nephews. Alice divided her house and garden evenly between Obediah Face, her sister's son, and Anne Gilbert, her sister's daughter. In return for this generous bequest, Obediah and Anne were ordered to pay annual stipends to their mother, to their brothers and sister, and to the son and daughter of Alice's brother, Richard Pitt.[55] Richard Hilley of Tewkesbury, an unmarried gentleman, had a similar impact on his sisters' families in 1668. Hilley left to his sisters and their children an estate composed of a house on the High Street, a cluster of smaller tenements behind the house, an unspecified quantity of meadow in Ashchurch, and 6.5 acres of land in the Oldbury Field behind the High Street and Barton Street.[56] Hilley also instructed his brothers-in-law to make regular payments from the estate to the young children of a sister who was recently deceased. These cases attest to the power of wills as creative documents, as more than reflections of fixed relationships in families and between households. Alice Pitt's will placed her sister's children in the same house. Richard Hilley cultivated financial relations between his deceased sister's children and their uncles. Both actions suggest the power of a will to innovate in family relations. A will often established new motives for interrelationship among households, creating, in effect, a new structure for family life, in an effort to secure the peace and prosperity of dependents.[57]

Because of the frequency of death in the prime of life, provision for dependents generally focused on the nuclear family and on young children in particular.[58] This approach to dependence was occasionally made explicit. John Carpenter of Deerhurst made his material settlement "for the good of those that depend on me as wife and children."[59] Edmund Harris of Deerhurst Walton disposed of his estate "as that all my children that God has given me may have some portions as is fit they should."[60] William Haines of Pamington referred to his "diverse children" and aspired "to consider them as a father, according to my ability."[61] Yet this notion of dependence was applied to the distinctive forms of nuclear family produced by high mortality and remarriage. The deathbed settlement often forced testators to reflect on the needs and the peaceful coexistence of dependents from several marriages, children at different points in the life cycle. The fear of conflict over resources among the multiple layers of a family was a common preoccupation of the deathbed, and the material settlement attempted to mold these layers into a single family. The fiscal contortions sometimes produced by such efforts can be seen in the case of Giles Ricketts of Deerhurst. Giles reserved his house in Tewkesbury and land in Deerhurst for the care and education of his youngest children by his last wife, arranged the cash payment of marriage portions and apprenticeship fees for the children of his first and second marriages, and left a token of remembrance to an older child by his first wife.[62] Although dependence usually denoted the nuclear family, this family routinely contained more diverse relationships than is customary in its modern counterpart.

The first phase in the mortuary process separated the spiritual and material elements of the Christian person. This separation and the withdrawal of the dying person from the affairs of the world were achieved in the dual settlements of the will. The preparation of the will honored the spirit of the dying person and commemorated and closed the person's place in the social order. A spiritual settlement returned the testator's soul to the hands of God. The moral significance of the material settlement was expressed in a religious notion of property, an effort to anticipate and avoid conflict among family and neighbors, and a general concern to make a judicious settlement in the sight of God. The symbolic movement of the dying person into the liminal space between life and death, and earth and heaven, had a personal, familial, and communal significance.

Biological death began the second phase in the mortuary process. Death usually occurred in the home, and the record of witnesses to burial in woolen shrouds in the late seventeenth century seems to indicate that women, perhaps close female relatives or friends of the family, washed and covered the corpse before the funeral.[63] A public procession escorted the body to the burial place in the parish. Before the procession, however, a funeral party assembled at the deceased's house. These parties had a dual nature and social structure. As an event in the community of the parish, funeral parties brought visits from poor neighbors and occasioned the distribution of charity. John Jeynes of Ashchurch made the substantial bequest of forty shillings "to be distributed to the poor that shall resort to my house at my funeral."[64] Death was seen as a leveler, and mortuary customs such as the distribution of alms at the door of the house narrowed the distance of status. But close friends and kin, who often gathered inside the house, received a modest provision of food and drink before the movement of the body to the church. In 1634 Thomas Coles of Tewkesbury restricted this inner circle to "those men that carry my body to church and to my grave."[65] Coles left twenty shillings "which my will is shall be bestowed upon a supper and wine to make merry withal." The inner circle was sometimes even smaller. Edward George of Tewkesbury gave 4 shillings to supply drink for a gathering of his four "well beloved friends" and overseers.[66] These assemblies prior to burial were the social expression of conventional notions of a "decent" or "honest" burial. Thomas Godfrey of Tewkesbury acknowledged this relationship when he ordered "a barrel of best beer or ale and four shillings in cakes" to be furnished for his guests "to the end that my funeral be solemnized in a decent manner."[67] The expense of funeral parties varied considerably and often reflected the social status of the deceased. Richard Restell, a husbandman of Deerhurst, described his friend's promise to spend five shillings on a funeral party "in my house the day of my burial for the benefit of my wife."[68] Mary Roach, an affluent spinster of Walton Cardiff, allowed the much larger sum of £5 for her burial in 1664 and ordered the money spent on "wine, cakes, and other necessary accommodation."[69] Funeral parties thus expressed a subtle duality in the symbolism of the mortuary process.[70] This duality involved first the use of an egalitarian rhetoric to describe the removal of the deceased person from the social order and the person's transition to the order of the dead. As the funeral party illustrates, however, this rhetoric was used only in highly structured contexts. The distribution of alms, a symbol of human interdependence in the face of death, was conducted under circumstances that confirmed the symbols of structure, distinction, status, and power in the parish.[71]

The funeral party was followed by a procession from the home to the church and finally to the grave. Because the decorum of the procession reflected on the honor and decency of person and family, the arrangements were made carefully, often in the lifetime of the deceased.[72] These notions of "a decent burial" might be conveyed only in general references. Christopher Milton of Tredington wanted his friends "to see me well brought to my grave and buried as a Christian ought to be."[73] Robert Mopp, a laborer, charged his brothers to see him "brought to the earth in a decent manner."[74] Edward Willis simply asked his wife Susanna "to see me decently brought home."[75] The meaning of honor and decency in burial became more precise in Isabel Morry's request to her daughter and son-in-law to "see her buried [in Tewkesbury] according to her degree and calling."[76] The presence of neighbors and kin dignified the procession to the grave. Custom did not prescribe any strict order for the procession, but the more distant relations of neighborhood were commonly dispersed around an inner circle of close relations, in the manner of the funeral party. A personal circle of family and friends, the intimate relations formed in life, carried the body to the grave. In elaborate and costly funerals, mourning clothes identified this group, but gifts of mourning rings or pendants and gloves made similar distinctions in modest processions.[77] Alice Turberville of Twyning presented gloves to her cousins and their children and asked them "to go along at my burial with my corpse to the grave."[78] John Rowles of Ashchurch made a gift of five shillings to his brother-in-law "so that he will help to carry me to the church."[79] Mary Roach of Walton Cardiff, on the other hand, bestowed gloves and scarves on the *neighbors* "that shall attend me and carry my corpse to the grave."[80] Thomas Symes of Tewkesbury made a list of his closest friends and presented gifts of mourning rings and gloves in return "for their trouble and pains of carrying me to my grave."[81] As a further commemoration of the unique social position of the deceased, the procession to the church was never better illustrated than by the funeral of James Cartwright, a gentleman of Tredington, who was conducted to the church by his tenants.[82]

The sermons preached in the church offered the most ambitious interpretations of death in the mortuary process. Funeral sermons were often preached by ministers chosen specifically by the deceased.[83] Although sermons required fees and were usually preached only for the wealthy householders of a parish, the concerns addressed in sermons mirrored the common anxieties of religious culture in the vale. The sermons attempted to explain mortality, to furnish instruction on how to prepare for death, and to place particular deaths in a cosmological perspective. This effort to provide interpretive tools, perceived as "a precious armory against the terror of death," was the primary motive in the funeral sermons preached by John Matthews, the vicar of Tewkesbury, in the 1680s and 1690s. A close analysis of a particular sermon shows how the interpretive schemes in funeral sermons might intersect the concerns of bereaved families, friends, and neighbors. Matthews preached in 1691 on the biblical text "sown in dishonor, raised in glory."[84] Having explored the notion of death as a form of dishonor, Matthews assured his congregation that the transformation of the flesh into an incorruptible body at the Resurrection removed this dishonor. The minister began his message of comfort with a long discourse on the body's disintegration in death and its horrible smell, such an effect of corruption that "all the spices of Arabia cannot secure the breathless body from some degree of dishonor." Matthews invoked the power of the grave as a social leveler that exposed all humanity to the same dishonorable physical humiliation. According to Matthews, this "natural dishonor" was the reason that human bodies were customarily buried, and the consignment of bodies to "the wardrobe of the grave" was described as both the repayment of an original debt to the earth and as insurance "that the dishonor of our nature should not be manifest to the sun." These images were metaphoric plays on the common concern to pay debts and preserve honor in the mortuary process. Matthews completed the performance of his clerical role by removing the dishonor of death, using biblical forms relevant to the experience of his congregation.[85] The pattern of human life and the burial of the dead were compared with the cycle of the agricultural year and the sowing of crops. Matthews preached the destruction of dishonor by the elevation of a pure body at the Resurrection and asserted "the credibility of it by the winterly dying of trees and corn and their summers reflourishing and fructifying again." Dead children, denied the full years of the life cycle, would be "raised up in a perfect state, for such Adam was created in, and so infants and minors will be advanced to the state of perfection to which full age would have brought them." This perfect body would "shine as the stars, nay as the sun in the firmament." Matthews encouraged his audience "confidently [to] presume that the heirs of salvation shall be adorned with glorious robes of light and immortality." The death of Joseph Laight, a maltster of Tewkesbury, was then celebrated as a model of pious concern for "the ancient and venerable place of religious worship and the good old paths and ancient ways."

The burial was bounded by the sacred sound of bells. The Church of England allowed the use of bells at four distinct points to mark different moments in the mortuary process: one toll as the person passed from life, one short peal after death, one toll before the burial, and one final peal following the burial.[86] The first toll of the passing bell admonished the living to reflect on their own mortality and to recommend the weak condition of the sufferer to God.[87] After the short peal of bells that signified death, any further petitions were scorned as "superstitious" prayers for the dead and officially banned from the Protestant ceremony in the Book of Common Prayer. The movement of the body into the grave occasioned a single toll of the passing bell.[88] But the primary concern in funerals seems to have focused on the final peal.[89] The evidence on this point is weak, but the final peal of bells may have marked the deceased's status. Bequests of sums as large as six shillings were left to ringers, and additional payments sometimes made the bells ring in more than one parish.[90] A clear hierarchy existed among the bells in the abbey, and the payment of significant sums to the ringers may have ensured that the great bell commemorated the final passage from the life of the parish.[91]

Place of burial was a less ambiguous mark of status. In the village of the dead, which was represented by the elaborate tombs and memorials built in the church and churchyard, burial inside the church constituted an important political distinction in status and authority from burial in the churchyard. Burial in the church conveyed several benefits, from proximity to the most sacred places in the parish to protection of the memorial and epitaph from destruction by the elements. The families buried in the church achieved an individuation lost in the churchyard, as the erosion of memorials reduced the population to a more or less undifferentiated mass. The rationale for burial inside or outside the church derived in part from the deceased's position in the status hierarchy and in part from local orders of precedence difficult to reconstruct.[92] Gentlemen almost invariably received burials inside the church. The lone gentleman who was buried in the Tewkesbury churchyard in 1666 proves the rule, as Thomas Chester had renounced the privileges of status and had requested burial outside the church "in a comely Christian manner, without any worldly pomp or vanity."[93] Other ranks are less dependable as indicators of a burial site. As a rule, yeomen farmers were more likely to be buried inside the church than husbandmen, but the evidence for Tredington and Twyning suggests that parishes used different criteria to mark a "yeoman" from a "husbandman" and observed different customs in the social distribution of burials in church and churchyard.

Several individual cases illustrate the subtleties of the prescriptive order that decided place of burial. Some church burials honored the possession of specific forms of property. Alice Cartwright was buried in the chancel of Tredington church as the proprietor of the parish rectory.[94] Yet status often seems to have been accorded to particular families for reasons now obscure. The Bingley family of Deerhurst received church burials despite a lack of continuity in formal status and occupation.[95] These cases may indicate the authority of custom in church burials. If a relative, especially a father, had been afforded this honor, the family and kin might attempt to claim similar recognition. In the early 1680s John Millington of Tewkesbury claimed a church burial in his father's grave.[96] William Joblyne had made a similar appeal for burial in the church "amongst his kindred" in the 1640s.[97] These claims were not guaranteed of success, and the prescriptive order could differentiate between claims to status in a family. Prudence Bicke of Tredington belonged to the small gentry family of Izode in Toddington, a village several miles east of Tewkesbury, and was therefore honored with a burial in the church of Tredington, but her husband Charles Bicke, a yeoman farmer, was buried in the churchyard.[98]

Despite the decisive influence of status, place of burial might reflect the power of emotional bonds formed in life. Several testators expressed a desire for burial close to loved ones.[99] Jane Carte, a widow of Tewkesbury, asked for burial in her husband's grave.[100] Thomas Symes hoped for a place in the church "between the pillar and my dear wife's grave."[101] Robert Shatterthayte of Tewkesbury desired burial in the churchyard "near unto my last wife."[102] The dying could receive comfort from the knowledge that death brought them closer to absent friends. Although these affectionate bonds could not span the distance between church and churchyard, within the ranks of both places, emotional attachment affected the choice of burial site. Status remained the most important determinant of burial in the vale, but it would misrepresent the evidence to describe this aspect of the mortuary process as a cold calculation, uninfluenced by affective bonds.

The final phase in the mortuary process was the creation of a monument and an epitaph for the deceased. A marker could be placed anytime after the burial, and a relative or friend usually prepared the inscription.[103] These "speaking stones" translated personal life into the moral terms of parish community, and epitaphs thus created metaphors of the moral code.[104] An epitaph used a life history to fashion an emblem of familial virtue, friendship, neighborliness, charity, or piety. The family and its gender distinctions were a dominant theme in this form of representation. Frances Boylston became "the mirror of her sex for virtue and true piety, a pattern fair and clear index for meekness and sobriety." These feminine "virtues" were incorporated in a universal model of piety in the closing exhortation, "God grant us all, while glass does run, to live in Christ as she has done."[105] John Millington's epitaph was a metaphoric play on his love for Patience, his predeceased wife, and his Christian restraint of the desire to follow her in death: "His Patience died and went before, his patience lived by which he bore affliction great with Christian cheer, read Patience here as well as there."[106] These epitaphs used elements of personal histories to create stereotypic images of a wife and a husband, images that asserted the formative power of Christian values in domestic order. The social education inculcated by the inscriptions on graves was not confined to family life. Thomas Merrett of Tewkesbury, a barber surgeon, became a model of piety and professional integrity "who like a faithful steward repaired the church, the poor and needy cured." This epitaph formed an acrostic and derived the values that Merrett's life represented from the letters of his name.[107] Other memorials described the dead as embodiments of the principles of neighborliness, charity, and piety. Anne Slaughter was commemorated in her public role as "sincere professor and honorer of pure religion and a patroness of the religious."[108] John Roberts of Fiddington became a metaphor of the neighborly care "to maintain tillage, the maintenance of mankind." The qualities of a good neighbor were inscribed on Roberts' memorial as the fear of God, a faithfulness to country and friends, charity to the poor, and loyalty to the commonwealth.[109] The monuments of the dead offered both a reminder of human mortality and an interpretation of social conventions. As the epitaphs indicate, the dead did not leave the social and political life of the parish but assumed a metaphoric, essentially didactic form in the sacred space of church and churchyard.

The inscriptions on memorials also furnish evidence of the egalitarian rhetoric used to ease this transition. The emphasis on structure and hierarchy in the mortuary process makes it possible to interpret this rhetoric as a metaphor of movement from one form of social order to another. The *symbolic* problem of death in the vale was the problem of movement from a hierarchy of flesh to a community of spirit, and a rhetoric of common humanity expressed the closure of one position in the process of movement to the other. This rhetoric of transition can be detected in memorials for individuals of virtually every social rank. The epitaph prepared for a gentry family in Miserdean church in the 1640s stressed the impermanence of social distinctions and the corrosive power of death: "See here that wealth, blood, honor, power, must return their owner to their mother dust."[110] A similar commentary on death as a social leveler occurred in an epitaph for a gentleman in Flaxley church: "Thus prince, nor peer, nor any mortal wight can shun death's dart. Death still will have his right."[111] An anonymous inscription from the 1680s in Rodborough churchyard celebrated death's obliteration of distinctions among the rich and poor: "This world's a city full of crooked streets, death is the marketplace where all men meets. If life were merchandise that men could buy, the rich would live, the poor would have to die."[112] The metaphors of a common humanity in the grave expressed a social mobility specific to funeral rites. These metaphors acquired meaning only in the context of rituals that reaffirmed notions of hierarchy, honor, and lineage.

This account of the mortuary system in the Vale of Gloucester has focused on ritual phases of separation, transition, and incorporation.[113] As an ethnography of the ritual process in the vale, the description suffers from its dependence on the historical record, composed primarily of wills, sermons, and epitaphs. Yet this imperfect archive illustrates the personal, familial, and communal meanings of the symbols used in mortuary rituals, the interrelationship of social life and religious symbols. A funeral in Tewkesbury, for example, evoked sacred duties and speeches from the family, friends, and neighbors of the deceased; and the *meaning* of this ceremony was inseparable from the fellowship of family, friends, and neighbors in a moment of grief. The form and process of the ritual reveal how symbols created parish communities. At the same time, an emphasis on the form of ritual creates the illusion of consensus but ignores the evidence of bitter religious conflict in the seventeenth century.

The northern parishes in the Vale of Gloucester experienced economic and religious crises in the seventeenth century, which affected the mortuary system in different ways. The parochial responses to crisis in the economy, unrelated to the mortuary system, and crisis in the parish itself, directly related to its symbols and ceremonies, offer a chance to assess the authority and resilience of religious symbolism in the vale. A wave of famine and plague in the 1590s created this economic crisis and sharply increased the number of poor families in the vale. The traditional ritual response to this kind of pressure on resources was an appeal to the principles of neighborhood and charity. The alms reserved in wills and distributed in funeral rites in the late sixteenth and early seventeenth centuries helped to support poor householders in the parish and to alleviate the worst effects of the crisis. The religious crisis resulted from disputes over burial rites and many other ceremonies, aspects of a broad process of Protestant reform and resistance in the national church and in the vale parishes. These disputes created bitterness, alienation, and new forms of selective, nonresidential religious community from sympathetic families scattered across the vale. Among the casualties of this transformation were the traditional notions of charity and personal responsibility for the poor householders of the parish.

The parish community dominated the mortuary system in the early seventeenth century.[114] The first lines of a will classified the testator in a parish and its status hierarchy and often made bequests to enhance the architectural and social fabric of the parish in one form or another. These gifts generally endorsed specific "improvements" to the church or alms to poor households.[115] John Jeynes of Fiddington and John Thurle of Pamington left money for the care of the bells in their parish church.[116] The condition of the "churchways" or customary paths across the parish to the church was another perennial source of concern.[117] Robert Maile of Forthampton left a shilling to maintain a churchway in a densely wooded corner of his parish. Bequests sometimes addressed nuisances and dangerous places in a parish. John Rowles of Tewkesbury contributed ten shillings "towards the making of a bridge joining to Francis Haines his meadow for passage there in the flood time."[118] This use of precious resources to build up the parish indicates a sense of personal responsibility for the public landscape. Thomas Hawker's burial in Deerhurst illustrates the close association of personal identity and the parish community. Hawker presented £10 to the poor and, in return, asked the parish to "engrave upon the stone under which I am buried, at their own costs and charges, my name and the sum of money given by me to the parish."[119] This sense of personal responsibility for the parish was just as clear in less exalted bequests to the poor.[120] Richard Man of Forthampton, a yeoman, left six pence for every poor householder in his parish but emphatically excluded any nonresidents or wanderers. Man allowed the benefits of his gift only to "such as are relieved by the devotion of the parishioners."[121]

Although the relations of kinship and neighborhood intersected the society of the parish, the relations of godparentage directly expressed the notion of parish community. Godparents were responsible for the religious instruction and general social welfare of their godchildren and often provided the child's name.[122] The diversity of the nominees reveals the flexibility of this fictive kinship bond. Godparents might be close relatives, friends, or neighbors of the parents.[123] Persons of wealth and rank acted as godparents to the children of poor families, and the accumulation of many godchildren enhanced the godparent's status.[124] As a parental bond created in the baptismal rites of the parish church, godparentage conveyed symbols of kinship into the culture of the parish and imposed the symbolism of the parish community on relations of kinship, friendship, and neighborhood. Although this form of spiritual or religious kinship was not universally acknowledged in preparation for death, 16 percent of the wills made in the vale before 1640 provided for godchildren.[125] The metaphor of the parish as a spiritual family may help to account for the importance of bequests to the parish in the settlement of an estate. If the will was an attempt to provide for dependents, the frequency of charitable bequests to the parish poor was a communal analog to the provision of parents for their children.

The parishes of the northern vale confronted economic and demographic crises that sharply increased the number of poor families. Tewkesbury faced the disasters of dearth or plague in 1591, 1592, 1593, 1597, 1598, 1604, and 1607. The grim result of these disasters should have eased pressure on resources but appears to have been offset by increased rates of immigration. In 1623 the borough council complained that "diverse persons in this town have of late time for their own private lucre and gain not only here erected in places remote and obscure diverse small cottages but have also converted stables, barns, beast houses, and pigscotes to houses of habitation." Many families were packed into small rooms in subdivided houses, and "the better sort of inhabitants are scarce able to relieve them . . . whereby the state of this town is like in short time to be utterly overthrown . . . the better sort being much thereby discouraged to make their abode here." The council not only attempted to control the construction of new houses but also blamed the uncontrolled immigration of strangers and "persons of dissolute and disorderly life" for an increase in the scale of poverty that threatened the parish's ability to relieve the indigenous poor.[126]

The cyclical nature of poverty in the vale economy may have sharpened perceptions of the status distinctions in mortuary ritual. Death cost money in the seventeenth century, and economic hardship may have meant that families on the margins could not afford the funerals their occupational rank and income would have promised in better times. There is no systematic evidence of funeral costs in the vale. The churchwardens' accounts indicate that the usual price of a *grave* was 6s 8d for an adult, and 3s 4d for a child. A gravestone could cost anywhere from one shilling for a child's marker to £5 for an elaborate monument in the church.[127] In 1614 Walter Turner, an apprentice or servant, left twenty shillings for his funeral in Tewkesbury.[128] Some families refused to compromise on funeral costs. John Mayde, a mercer of Tewkesbury, reserved £5 for his funeral and ordered the money to be subtracted from his children's legacies if the residue of his estate did not cover the costs.[129] In 1648 Anne Driver of Tewkesbury, a spinster, allowed only forty shillings for her funeral, despite her burial in the church.[130] This impressionistic evidence of prices suggests that an economic crisis could make it difficult for families of middle and lower estate to meet death's financial demands.

The recurrent famine and pestilence of the 1590s may have increased the distance between the social ranks displayed in funeral rites, but evidence also indicates that the mortuary system in the vale parishes redistributed wealth in the form of charity.[131] Donations as large as £100 endowed permanent charities in Tewkesbury and adjacent parishes.[132] Smaller bequests often ordered the distribution of food or clothes directly to poor families. Alice Clarke of Tewkesbury wanted her gift "bestowed in corn and baked in bread."[133] In 1614 Richard Sutton of Deerhurst presented a general gift of money to the parish poor and left his everyday clothes to a smaller group of poor neighbors.[134] The number and variety of these gifts to the parish before 1640 indicate that the moments of crisis in the vale economy were also the moments of most intense concern and fear for the social welfare of the parish. The administration of larger gifts reflected changes in the scale of poverty. The officers of Giles Geast's charity in Tewkesbury, founded in the 1550s, stopped giving alms from house to house in the 1630s because "strangers sped as well as town poor."[135] A new system preserved the customary procession through the streets of the borough, but names were checked in a book as the relief money and coal were distributed. The need for this reform became apparent in 1649, when a brief return to the earlier system resulted in violence and an unfair distribution of relief among the poor households in St. Mary's Lane and around the Mill Bank.[136] The formality of the new system protected traditional forms of charity, and the evidence of parish gifts suggests that the crises of the 1590s and early 1600s modified but did not transform the mortuary system in the vale parishes.

A decisive change in this system and in the nature of parish communities resulted from the religious controversies of the late sixteenth and seventeenth centuries. These controversies had their source in the problems of dissent from the settlement in the Church of England. The establishment of a Protestant national church in the sixteenth century produced a small number of radicals familiar to historians as Puritans or Nonconformists.[137] An objection to the ceremonies and government of the national church, seldom expressed in separation from the parish before 1660, distinguished the Puritan movement in the Church of England. After the 1590s, lay and clerical Puritans in the vale attempted to promote a more radically Protestant "purification" of ceremonies in parish churches. The advocates of this further reformation invoked the authority of scripture and the inner bond of conscience over the authority of law and the territorial bond of the parish. As an assault on the mortuary rites of the parish, the campaign for further reformation focused on the ceremonial role of the minister, the Book of Common Prayer, and the funeral sermon.[138]

The best local source for this conflict is the sermon John Matthews preached in 1691 at Joseph Laight's funeral in Tewkesbury.[139] Yet the study of earlier conflicts from evidence in this sermon may seem questionable and requires some introduction. By the 1690s a variety of views more or less uncomfortably included in the national church before the Civil War had become the basis of communities separate from the parish, known collectively as "Dissent." Matthews' sermon is a valuable source for earlier disputes because the separation of dissent from the national church did not end the controversies over mortuary rites. The sermon pursued several traditional themes in the debate. According to Matthews, Laight lived in the neighborhood of Barton Street "when a pestilential air of separation had almost infected the whole street." Laight had friends among the Dissenters, and several apparently attended his Anglican funeral. Matthews relished this captive audience as a chance to proclaim Anglican superiority in views of death and resurrection.

The sermon identified the main sources of dispute as the nature of the afterlife and the ritual performed at the grave. The doctrine of the Resurrection provoked heated controversy. Matthews and the Church of England officially endorsed the idea of a literal resurrection, a revivification and perfection of the material particles of the body. The dead would receive restored bodies on the Day of Judgment, and a significant portion of Matthews' sermon consisted of speculation about the nature of this resurrected body. Many Nonconformists shared this view, but Matthews attempted to link separation from the parish to a more radical view of the Resurrection. A small minority of sectarians had long believed in a metaphoric resurrection, based on a view of St. Paul's directions to the Corinthians that was quite different from Matthews' explication of the text.[140] "When the great Oracle of heavenly wisdom, the Judge of Quick and Dead, and St. Paul who was caught up into the third heavens, so expressly declare a real, numerical resurrection of our corruptible bodies,"

Matthews solemnly intoned to his audience, "shall any of us be so deluded as to teach that it is only a spiritual resurrection, a rising from sin into newness of life?" Although a small number of Quakers might have answered in the affirmative, most Nonconformists in the funeral party would have scoffed at this conflation of their opposition to the Anglican office of burial and the radical mystical view of the Resurrection.

Many Puritans loathed the office of burial in the national church and denied any scriptural warrant for the view of burial as a religious ceremony.[141] The neighbors of the deceased ought to carry the corpse reverently to the grave, but neither the minister's presence nor the office of burial were necessary or appropriate. In 1691 John Matthews invoked the authority and comfort of this formal office in the Book of Common Prayer. He chose the text for his sermon from the chapter in Corinthians used in the funeral lesson of the office. The sermon's preface bemoaned the exclusion of St. Paul from many gravesides and decried the commission of bodies to the earth in little more than "pagan" silence. Matthews grieved "that some should behave as if they counted it a matter of abomination to speak over the graves of the dead the words of eternal life and to comfort the surviving with the infallible promises of a glorious resurrection and eternal, incorruptible life." This sermon shows traces of a bitter fight to determine the meaning of death, to establish the symbols and ceremonies fit to honor the human flesh bereft of its soul.

The wills from the vale sometimes expressed dislike of both the office of burial and of many other aspects of the customary funeral, in terms of a renunciation of vanity and worldliness.[142] The Nonconformist style of burial in the 1630s and 1640s was a plain style marked by minimal ecclesiastical intervention. Thomas Merryman, a yeoman farmer of Twyning, instructed his executors in 1638 to avoid the customary form of burial and to see his body interred "without worldly vain pomp."[143] William Homer of Twyning ordered his body buried "without worldly pomp."[144] Nathaniel Wight, the minister of Tewkesbury in the early 1640s, consigned his body in a similar but more ambiguous fashion to "the ordinary manner of Christian burial."[145] After 1660 uncertainties and conflict over the office of burial in the Church of England survived. Thomas Chester rejected the customary burial rites of a gentleman in 1666 and asked for a quiet burial in the churchyard "in a comely Christian manner without any worldly pomp or vanity."[146] In 1664 John Pinnock's request for a "decent" burial, "according to the order of the Church of England," implied the several meanings of a "decent" death in the vale.[147]

This kind of religious conflict divided parishes and ultimately transformed the nature of the communities created in mortuary ceremonies. As religious hatreds escalated in the violence of civil war, the symbols and rituals of death came to signify small communities composed of sympathetic families, often scattered across the vale; moreover, for many people, the territorial parishes became the enemies of community. The testamentary evidence indicates that the kinds of personal relations invoked in wills remained constant from 1590 to 1690, but allusions to the parish virtually disappeared after 1660.[148] The diverse gifts to build or repair the infrastructure of the parish or to relieve the parish poor in the vale were casualties of the Civil War. The invidious distinctions in gifts of the 1630s and 1640s and the withdrawal of charity from parochial control add an acerbic flavor to this decline in deathbed allusions to the parish. In 1635 Edward Jorden of Ashchurch left £10 not to the poor of his parish but to John Geary, the suspended Nonconformist minister of Tewkesbury. Geary was ordered to distribute the money only "to honest godly ministers and to honest poor."[149] In 1642 John Jordan of Forthampton presented £10 not to the many poor families of his parish but to the same Nonconformist minister, John Geary of Tewkesbury, to be reserved for "honest godly poor Christians."[150] These gifts provide early hints of a distinction between territory and community in the vale parishes by the middle of the seventeenth century. A few fragments of evidence survive to suggest this important change in the creative power of parish symbols to evoke communities from fixed territories and scattered social relations. Few institutions captured the metaphoric riches of parish community in more eloquent terms than godparentage, a spiritual kinship formed in baptism and honored in death. Yet only 4 percent of wills made after 1640 provided for godchildren.[151] Perhaps the most succinct expression of the change in the mortuary system was the separation of Anglican and sectarian graveyards in Tewkesbury after the Civil War.[152]

The symbols and ceremonies of the parish created communities in the vale. These parish communities drew on notions of charity and neighborhood to relieve families exposed to hardship in the famine and pestilence of the 1590s and early 1600s. Although the effectiveness of the relief efforts is open to debate, clearly the response to the crisis was to build a wall around the parish but not between the rich and poor inside it. The heated religious debates of the sixteenth and seventeenth centuries gathered momentum more slowly in the vale, but these debates questioned the nature of community itself and were not easily resolved. The opposed views of religious symbols in the parish began to create boundaries between neighbors. An increase in poverty could be explained and managed in parish communities. A violent disagreement over religious symbols could neither be contained nor resolved in the parish, and, ultimately, the notion of personal responsibility for the parish poor was among its casualties.

The social life of the Vale of Gloucester refuses to fit neatly into the analytic terms of form and process. The ceremonies of the parish created communities no less real for their symbolic or imagined nature. But the meanings of symbols, ceremonies, and communities changed profoundly in the seventeenth century. A discussion of form must become a consideration of process. The mortuary system in the vale involved a decision to prepare a will, a funeral procession, and a burial, as well as a decision to construct a memorial, and the presence or absence of any particular element varied the experience of death. These phases of the ritual process commemorated and closed a person's place in the social order and offered a narrative of transition to the afterlife. Death was the moment for settlements, to prepare the soul, to support dependents, to acknowledge debts.[153]

The meaning of death, the symbols used to convey its meaning, and the community evoked in this ceremony did not remain constant over time. The economic crisis of the late sixteenth and early seventeenth centuries in the vale sharpened differences of status that were expressed in mortuary ritual. Yet such crises were not uncommon in the vale economy, and codes of charity and neighborhood in the mortuary system helped to relieve some of the hardship. These attitudes did not survive the bloody conflict over the legitimacy of the parish itself. The institutional charities, such as the Giles Geast charity in Tewkesbury, continued to operate according to custom, but the notion of personal responsibility for the parish, expressed in modest householders' gifts to poor families, virtually disappeared. A bitter debate over the meaning of death and many other issues began to create new communities from scattered families of similar views, so that for many, the parish ceased to exist as a territorial community. The second half of this book considers this process in detail.

II

Social Process

1590–1690

4

Circumcisions of the Heart:
Church Courts, Social Relations,
and Religious Conflict, 1591–1620

For he is not a Jew, which is one outwardly; neither is that
circumcision, which is outward in the flesh. But he is a Jew, which is
one inwardly; and circumcision is that of the heart, in the spirit, and
not in the letter; whose praise is not of men, but of God.

Romans, 2: 28–29

Christ's gospel is not a ceremonial law, as much of Moses' law was, but
it is a religion to serve God, not in bondage of the figure or shadow,
but in the freedom of spirit . . .

Book of Common Prayer (1559)

These selections from definitive doctrinal sources of the Reformation
movement can only begin to convey the powers of cohesion and division
in the Christian religion of the sixteenth and seventeenth centuries.[1] The
general relationship of identity, ceremony, and spirit or belief remained a
commonplace. Yet the more specific relationships of the flesh or the
letter and the heart or the spirit, the outward face of religion and the
inward religion of conscience, the religion of human custom and the
religion of God, became subjects of unprecedented debate and sometimes violent conflict in parish churches and village streets of early modern England and across Europe.[2] A broad spectrum of positions formed,
in Catholic and Protestant communities, in lay and clerical classes, on
the authentic Christian relationship of scripture, ceremony, and conscience. Yet many "street wars" never ended in a conclusive peace, particularly the wars, fought just as fiercely in diaries, pamphlets, and legis-

lation as in the open streets, over the relative authority of scripture and human custom in religion and the power of doctrinal conformity to promote authentic religious identity.[3] The discussion "of ceremonies, why some be abolished and some retained," included in the Book of Common Prayer in 1559, described how certain ceremonies, perhaps "of godly intent" in their first institution, had "turned to vanity and superstition . . . grew daily to more and more abuses," had "much blinded the people and obscured the glory of God," and were therefore "worthy to be cut away and clean rejected."[4] The Puritan "admonition to the parliament" in 1572, however, contrasted the administration of the sacrament in the primitive church, "plainly" and "simply as . . . received . . . from the Lord," to the "singing, piping, surplice, and cope wearing" in the Church of England, a sacrament administered "sinfully, mixed with man's inventions and devices."[5] Yet an identical contrast of ceremony and spirit could be perceived in the Puritan discipline itself. Despite his meticulous performance of the ceremonies and exercises deemed proper to a reformed Sabbath, Samuel Ward regularly lamented his inability to "receive Christ by faith, in the sacrament" and to "delight in hearing God's word or in keeping his Sabbath." Ward attributed this failure to a "hardness of heart," a dullness or idleness of the spirit.[6] Several distinctive religious attitudes and styles, more or less Protestant, more or less clearly articulated in the religious culture of local parishes, claimed in the late sixteenth and early seventeenth centuries to express the authoritative calculus of human custom, scripture, and conscience in religious ceremonies. The Reformation process became a "street war" in subsequent fights over the best means to create, preserve, and promote the authentic Christian spirit or "circumcision of the heart."

These conflicts could have an enormous impact on everyday life in parish and village. The connection between religious identity and obedience to secular authorities had been a deadly issue from the earliest years of the Reformation.[7] Historians of church doctrine have represented this problem of allegiance as a result of the late medieval disintegration of the scholastic synthesis and the consequent stress on a distinction between gospel and positive law.[8] Although the grounds of legitimate resistance seldom acquired such clarity in the local context of the parish, the religious revolution of the sixteenth century in England could lead to serious problems of allegiance, as the monarchy and its laws became supreme head and authority of a divided church. If a royal order contradicted the precedents of scripture, would Christians owe their primary obedience to God or to the monarch? Archbishop Grindal invoked the authority of scripture in defiance of a royal command in 1576. Grindal pleaded in his own defense that scripture and conscience had revealed the "public harm of God's church" implicit in Elizabeth I's order to suppress Puritan prohesyings and to reduce the number of preachers in the church.[9] Peter Wentworth's comment in 1576 on an earlier order to prohibit parliamentary discussion of any religious matters not introduced by the bishops furnished a more general statement of the need to reconcile the demands of scripture and royal authority. "And let it be held for a principle," Wentworth declared, "that counsel that comes not together in God's name cannot prosper."[10]

If the problem of allegiance presented itself in this extreme form only to the most committed of the godly, its presence in this context adds some familiar shades to recent interpretations of the politics of religion and, in particular, places limits on the reciprocal relationship of Puritanism and the established order in church and society.[11] Clearly in many local communities the issues did not arise in this confrontational form. Several important examples of the local reformation reveal the cooperation of godly ministers and magistrates in the creation of reformed communities in parish and village or borough. A variety of elements—in particular, the presence of a reformed ministry, catechism, and sermons, the effective dissemination of John Foxe's accounts of Protestant martyrdom, and the conversion of influential lay families—produced in a substantial minority of residents in such communities a sense of direct participation in the sacred history of scripture. This version of Reformation history sanctified the role of the Crown in the religious revolution and consequently resolved the problem of allegiance. Only divine intervention had saved the Protestant monarchy personified by Elizabeth from destruction under Mary. Obedience to the monarchy and its laws became, in this historical vision of the English nation, obedience to the providential design itself.[12] Yet many parishes, both urban and rural, never formed this alliance of godly ministry and magistracy, and instead experienced episodic conflict in the pursuit of further reformation. Several parishes in the northern vale, particularly Tewkesbury and Forthampton, furnish important evidence of this pattern.

Religious identity, ceremony, and belief possessed the same creative power in local context as in the broader context of the kingdom and its hierarchies. The ritual idiom of Christian symbols created the religious and moral community of the parish from the dispersed settlements scattered across the local landscape. The performances of ministers, nominally prescribed by the Book of Common Prayer, were the primary local manifestations of the sacred in the late sixteenth century. These ceremonies used vernacular scripture, read in fixed cycles, to educate the parish community into an authentic, because scriptural, appreciation of the Christian view of history and the salvation of humanity in Christ's sacrifice.[13] The cohesion of families in parish and borough, assembled in ordered ranks on Sundays, was thus incorporated in a sacred cosmology revealed by scripture. These Prayer Book ceremonies revealed both divine and human inspiration and expressed the compound authority of scripture, custom, and law.[14] The Act of Uniformity, included in the Book of Common Prayer in 1559, made the prescribed ceremonies into strong statements of support for the monarchy, with the result that criticism of Prayer Book ceremonies might be construed as criticism of the royal supremacy in the church.[15] Despite recognized difficulties of historical reconstruction, the appeal of this Prayer Book religion has been a compelling refrain in recent discussions of English Protestantism.[16] The prosecution of experienced curates in the Gloucester diocesan court for failure to perform ceremonies in the style of the Prayer Book, and particularly for failure to conform to the official code in the use of vestments, illustrates the local demand, or at least the churchwardens' demand, for conformist ceremonies in the late 1590s.

These sacred ceremonies asserted a prescriptive authority over the conduct of everyday life. The sacred rituals and texts of the parish community were the most obvious and important sources of the moral codes, formal rules of conduct, and stock interpretations of behavior that imparted structure and meaning, indeed conveyed a kind of sanctity, to everyday social interaction in household and neighborhood. The "order for the burial of the dead" in the Book of Common Prayer inculcated an awareness of mortality and a discipline derived from reflection on the eternal principles of salvation. "In the midst of life we be in death. Of whom may we seek for succor but of you, O Lord, which for our sins justly are displeased."[17] These worlds of sacred and profane action may be represented as the core and periphery of the parish, seen as a cultural form. The sacred symbols, texts, and performances in the parish church constituted the parish community. The prescriptive codes of moral con-

duct, presented and justified in the sacred circle of religious performance, communicated a religious significance to the profane world of
everyday routines, relationships, and institutions in the parish. This distinction between ritual forms and prescriptive codes, between core and
periphery, became particularly important in the religious conflicts that
transformed local societies in the seventeenth century.

Since contemporaries did not make this distinction in the cultural
form of the parish, its use demands justification. Puritanism as a religious mentality and the reformation of manners as a social discipline have
been conflated, and this conflation has produced a view of religious
conflicts in the Reformation as the ideological expressions of a class
movement to control the behavior of social inferiors.[18] Yet contemporaries made a clear distinction between the issues of ceremonial conformity
and the introduction of "godly discipline" in everyday life. Churchwardens presented Nonconformist ministers and lay supporters of Nonconformity for violations of the ceremonial order despite common interests
in the promotion of "godliness" in parish society. On the other hand, the
prosecution of certain kinds of misdemeanors, particularly sexual misdemeanors, in the church courts often reflected the local differentiation of
rich and poor households. The distinction between ritual forms and
prescriptive codes, core and periphery in the culture of the parish, allows
historians to recognize this pattern in the evidence and to interpret the
subtle ways in which religious symbols, rituals, and discipline *created*
distinctions in early modern English society or, alternatively, *reflected*
established social distinctions, in different contexts.[19]

This approach is particularly valuable in the interpretation of the divided communities in the Vale of Gloucester. The traditional interpretation of Tewkesbury as a Puritan town seems to rest primarily on the
mistaken impression of borough ordinances created in 1608 as evidence
of a strict local Sabbatarianism.[20] A form of Sabbatarianism certainly
existed in Tewkesbury, supported by the borough council and enforced
by the cooperation of the constables, churchwardens, and sidesmen, the
assistants of the churchwardens. Yet the nature of this Sabbatarianism
and its Puritan character are less clear. The ordinances in question declared only that "the constables shall every Sabbath day call upon the
sidesmen and with them to make diligent search throughout the town, as
well as in common inns, taverns, and alehouses, as all other places for all
drunkards, idle persons, and others absenting themselves from church in

time of divine service, as it is required of them by statute and their oath, and to present the offenders' names before the bailiffs or one of the justices in writing."[21] These "common inns, taverns, and alehouses" had to close their doors during divine service but could keep one window open to serve customers "until the little bell shall be ringed to divine service."[22] As the local evidence of the consistory court also demonstrates, the Sabbatarianism enforced in Tewkesbury in the 1590s and early 1600s placed strict boundaries around the sacred time of divine service but differed from the general Sabbath, the prohibition of games and other diversions "in any part of the day," created by local ordinance in the Puritan towns of Lancashire, Suffolk, and Essex.[23] Churchwardens responsible for the enforcement of this limited Sabbatarianism were also active in the prosecution of ceremonial Nonconformity.

Ultimately, ceremonial conformity and even a limited Sabbatarianism required the authority of the ecclesiastical courts. Despite earlier notoriety for corruption and incompetence under the administration of chancellor Thomas Powell, the diocesan courts in Gloucestershire became the most important local agent of Reformation in the later sixteenth century.[24] Yet the restoration of the court's authority testified less to the administrative genius of diocesan officials than to the resilience of the cultural importance of the courts in the creation and enforcement of moral community in local parishes. This moral community represented the indispensable profane counterpart of a right spiritual relation to God in the parish. As a vital instrument of moral discipline, the church court helped to preserve this harmonious relationship of macrocosm and microcosm, the great world of the heavens and the little world of the parish. Discipline became particularly important in the moments of crisis presented by plague, famine, fire, or flood. An anonymous pamphlet published in 1606 represented the disastrous floods in Gloucestershire and Somersetshire as a monstrous birth, a "misshapen creature," visited on humanity as a punishment for sins.[25] Conventional signs identified the event as an act of divine providence. At Barnstaple, in Devon, "an apparition of fire, strangely burning" appeared in the aftermath of the floods, "and a black dog was seen to pass through one of the arches of the bridge."[26] The author did not doubt the cause of the disaster. "Sin overflows our own souls. The seas of strange impieties have rushed in upon us. We are covered with the waves of abomination and uncleanness, we are drowned in the black puddles of hellish iniquity. We swim up to the throats, nay even above the chins in covetousness, in extortion, in sensuality, in every one against the other, in contempt of our magistrates, in neglect of our laws, and in violation of those divine statutes, the breach of which is a condemnation to death, and that death, an everlasting living in hell's fire."[27] This interpretation of misfortune reflects the familiar notion of the providential design, the divine plan of salvation facilitated by occasional disasters, intended as "gentle warnings" to restore human societies to the path of righteousness.[28] As a consequence of the corporate conceptions of society and sin in Christian cosmology, individual crimes, unpunished by the officers of church and state, accumulated to form the collective abominations, punished by divine providence in the visitations of plague, flood, and famine.[29] Church courts enforced a moral discipline essential to the corporate integrity of the parish, and the increased local reliance on the diocesan court in Gloucestershire in the 1590s illustrates both the resilience of this cosmological frame and the severe impact of plague and famine on local perceptions of community.

The church courts imposed rituals of penance perceived as a necessary means to reverse the moral disintegration of the parish, but the prosecution of religious Nonconformity made visible the religious differences in the parish, resulted in deep divisions, and sometimes generated open conflict. Yet no easy distinctions existed between Anglicans and Puritans, between a church Puritan faction and a godly faction, divided in the early 1600s over the problems of further Reformation and in the early 1640s over the problems of popery and arbitrary government. The most obvious difficulties arise from the limited capacity of local evidence to support the assumptions implicit in the language of religious factionalism. Disputes between ministers and their parishioners could have complex sources. Anthony Fletcher has drawn attention to the subtle interrelationship of personal animosity and religious difference in the problems of Henry Kent, vicar of Selsey in Sussex.[30] Nor can the identifiable Nonconformists who were prosecuted in local courts invariably be linked to the continuous activities of a faction. Many Nonconformists prosecuted in the early 1600s recanted in the church courts and promised conformity. The persistence of Nonconformist attitudes and discipline in the form of fellowship can be extremely difficult to demonstrate before the formal sectarianism of the 1640s and 1650s. If Nicholas Tyacke can express uncertainties in the reconstruction of a Puritan faction even in the literate society of the Hampton Court Conference, the less articulate, inconsistently documented expressions of Nonconformist Puritanism and conformity in local parishes demand the more caution and skepticism.[31]

The religious conflicts of the 1590s illustrate the value of a distinction, in the cultural form of the parish, between the core ritual performances of the sacred world and the prescriptive moral codes of the profane world. Churchwardens began to use the consistory court systematically in the 1590s to reform religious attitudes and moral discipline in their communities. This campaign to reform Christian discipline in the parish asserted strict boundaries between sacred and profane but left intact the framework of customary behavior. The increased activity of churchwardens marked a time of local crisis, when Tewkesbury and its neighboring parishes were struck repeatedly by plague.[32] Presentments increased in the church courts as a process of purification whereby the parish community restored its right relationship to God. The ratio of presentments to population remained low, but the more conspicuous offenders were publicly punished and the boundaries of the moral community were seen to be reasserted.

This use of ecclesiastical courts in the 1590s to enforce a vision of moral and religious order was an attempt to reform customary religious practice and social discipline in a time of crisis, when violations of the behavioral conventions enshrined in ecclesiastical law seemed especially pernicious. In this context, the prosecution of specific actions as sinful reflected a heightened local perception of disorder. Much of the anxiety about sinfulness in local societies focused on sexual behavior and the integrity of the patriarchal household. The campaign by churchwardens to remove perceived sources of sexual pollution, more than any other form of conflict in the courts, followed the socioeconomic distinction between wealth and poverty. Many cases presented as sexual offenses involved the poorer members of local society, and in such presentments the sexual code affirmed in the ecclesiastical courts was frequently a moral code imposed by wealthier families of local office holders upon their poor neighbors.[33]

Conflicts over the symbols and religious assumptions that constituted the sacred core of parish life were also prominent among the causes of presentment in the 1590s, but their power to cut across social boundaries distinguished disputes over ritual behavior from other forms of conflict in the church courts. Shared religious beliefs were not uncommon among neighbors of different status and wealth. Disputes among neighbors over the meaning of ritual signified a growing uncertainty about the source of authority in religious life, for the rites of the Church of England were established by law as symbols of the uniformity and spiritual obedience demanded in a divinely ordained political order. Religious symbols themselves thus created social difference in the context of formal ceremony, as neighbors became aware of divisions in the sacred world of religious belief and authority within the parish community. Historians have frequently viewed the moral reformation of the 1590s and conflicts over religious ceremonies in the same period as dual aspects of a "godly discipline" imposed by local oligarchies on parish communities. This interpretation is now difficult to accept, as much of the local evidence indicates that the ritual nonconformities of the "godly" were frequently presented in the church courts and thus seem to have counted among the manners to be reformed.[34]

The parish was never an isolated or self-contained community. Churchwardens on their own did not possess the authority to direct reforms of customary practice in the parish. The peaks in presentments reflected local perceptions of moral and spiritual crisis, but the continuity of interest in specific issues, particularly the separation of the sacred order from the everyday routines of profane life, implemented directives sent to churchwardens from the higher authorities in the English church. The articles of enquiry purchased by churchwardens prior to episcopal and metropolitical visitations reveal an ambitious campaign to reform religious practice from above.[35] These directives were not invariably followed, and churchwardens remained free to enforce the articles most relevant to local concerns, but the campaign to reform traditional religious practice was clearly the result of interaction between local inclinations and a broader reform movement in the church.[36]

The instrument of reform was the consistory court of Gloucester diocese, an institution viewed by historians as a symbol of ecclesiastical corruption and the decline of church authority under Elizabeth. F. D. Price, in a series of articles published since the 1930s, has focused almost exclusively on allegations of corruption in the consistory court and on popular "contempt for the spiritual censures."[37] This account of venality and decline is less persuasive for the 1590s than for the 1570s. Price has attempted to extend his interpretation of the court into the 1590s in an essay on the dispute between Bishop John Bullingham and Chancellor William Blackleech. But the conduct of the court under Blackleech never approached the notorious excesses of Thomas Powell's administration in the 1570s. The local evidence of detections, the presentments resulting from episcopal visitations, indicates a recovery of the court's power of enforcement, only briefly interrupted by the confusion of the early 1590s, when Bullingham and Blackleech held separate courts. Despite the administrative uncertainty produced by this conflict, most of the defendants cited by the court from Tewkesbury and its neighborhood made their required appearances. Of twenty-three defendants cited in a span of fifteen months between 1591 and 1592, seventeen dutifully appeared in court. These appearances came in the midst of the schism in diocesan administration described by Price as so "damaging to the reputation of the ecclesiastical authority."[38] Blackleech appears to have strengthened ecclesiastical jurisdiction by a more vigorous use of inquiries to distinguish accurate detections from malicious gossip. Although more often noted for his ingenuity in securing fees, Blackleech occasionally remitted court fees when excommunication had resulted from minor oversights, such as delay in submitting a certificate of penance to the court.[39] In 1592 when relations between Bullingham and Blackleech became more stable, the jurisdiction of the church court was stronger than it had been at any time since Hooper's episcopate in the 1550s.

The diocesan archive does not provide a complete record of episcopal administration in the sixteenth and seventeenth centuries, but the abundant survival of visitation records—and particularly the runs of detections and subsequent actions in the consistory court—furnishes a coherent archive for study of the complex interrelationship between the court and the parishes in the northern vale. A particular disappointment in many other diocesan archives would be the lack of archidiaconal court records and the subsequent need to rely on the consistory court for the statistics of church discipline. Yet the absence of an archidiaconal archive is less important in the diocese of Gloucester, as here the archdeacon had lost his independent jurisdiction by the early seventeenth century and may never have held the broad jurisdiction characteristic of other dioceses.[40] In 1632 Francis Baber, chancellor of the diocese, described a summons delivered from the archdeacon's court to the churchwardens of Mickleton as an "innovation" and the presentment of local bills of detection before the archdeacon as a violation of the consistory court's jurisdiction.[41] The evidence indicates that some presentments may have been made before both the chancellor and the archdeacon, but chancellors of the diocese considered preference of the archdeacon's court a violation of the bishop's jurisdiction. Thomas Drake, the curate of Forthampton, appeared before both the chancellor and the archdeacon in 1605 to answer charges of ceremonial Nonconformity, but the consistory court declared his suspension.[42] Detections that were produced by the churchwardens primarily but not exclusively in the course of episcopal visitations of a parish, conducted triennially, and later prosecuted in the consistory court, almost certainly represent the great majority of misdemeanors handled by the ecclesiastical jurisdiction in Gloucester diocese.[43]

Yet the constraints and idiosyncrasies of institutions in the seventeenth century must qualify any account of increased presentments in the 1590s as a movement or campaign. Churchwardens seldom held office for more than one year, and the church court's effectiveness varied with the local commitment to enforce its authority. Concern for public morality and social discipline in the community did not necessarily extend beyond the term of office. In 1591 William Clevely and William Gilbert, churchwardens of Tewkesbury in 1590 and 1594, respectively, appeared in the church court for "playing at tables on a Sunday at the time of evening prayer."[44] Because the system of detection relied heavily on the "public voice" or "common fame" of a person's behavior and values, presentments inevitably reflected local perceptions of disorder.[45] This dependence on the "public voice" in the detection and punishment of moral offenses helps to explain why spreading false rumors was itself a presentable offense.[46] The "public voice" was the residue of gossip among neighbors and formed the stock of knowledge neighbors possessed of each other's actions. This stock was not composed of neutral observations but contained critical assessments of observed and reported behavior. It was understood that moral rectitude and social discipline in human societies reflected a right relationship to God, a harmonious relationship of macrocosm and microcosm. Local perceptions of moral and material health in this cosmic framework affected the neighborly judgments expressed in gossip and the moral evaluation of particular actions. Disasters in the macrocosm influenced local perceptions of public morality in the microcosm. Presentments in the church courts were correspondingly numerous between 1594 and 1597, the most violent years of plague, high prices, and economic scarcity.[47] Churchwardens frequently fell back on the formulaic presentment of "*omnia bene*" after the sense of emergency had passed, and this cyclical pattern of prosecution expressed the powerful influence of local conditions on the assessment of public morality and public health.[48] In this culture of enforcement, attempts to reform social discipline and religious practice were necessarily discontinuous and haphazard.

The numbers of presentments varied considerably over time, but the forms of offense were more or less constant. Priorities evident in the first prosecutions of 1591 remained the dominant concerns of churchwardens in the decades before the Civil War. Sexual offenses of various kinds formed the largest class of prosecutions. Perceptions of disorder in the vale frequently focused on behavior that seemed to undermine the sacred foundations of ordered family life. As the sexual and social honor of the family figured prominently in religious performances, the violation of sexual mores seemed to subvert the moral structure of everyday life and even to contaminate the sacred community. The demands made on parish resources by illegitimate children and broken families symbolized, for their neighbors, the corrosive social effects of chaos in the form of sexual immorality. This emphasis on family discipline in local perceptions of the sacred and profane orders was reflected in the consistent prosecution of fornication, prenuptial fornication, bastardy and illicit pregnancy, fornication with domestic servants, adultery, and other perceived violations of premarital propriety and prescriptive roles in the family or household.[49]

Churchwardens enforced a particular social discipline in their campaign to protect the moral integrity of the patriarchal household and the welfare of the parish community. A distinctive feature of the patriarchal system was the principle of male responsibility for sexual relations and procreation. Of twenty-five prosecutions for sexual offenses in the church court between April 1591 and September 1592, sixteen were prosecutions of men. These figures conceal a deeper patriarchal bias. Of seventeen individuals, rather than couples, who were forced to accept responsibility for alleged sexual offenses, twelve were men.[50] The primary goals of churchwardens in cases of bastardy and illicit pregnancy were to establish paternity and to compel paternal support of the child. Yet unwed mothers were frequently prosecuted alone if they refused to reveal the father's name or if the father was beyond the reach of the court. Alice Barwick, a poor woman of Twyning, appeared before the court in June 1592 for having a child by William Johnson, a servant to

Mr. Twyselton of Burton in distant Lincolnshire.[51] This determination to establish the identity of the father resulted from the often justified fear that fatherless families would prove economically unviable, become dependent on parish poor relief, and thus increase demand on the resources of the parish.[52] A similar emphasis on male control and authority in sexual relations was apparent in cases of *suspected* impropriety, as local officers usually attempted to secure the male defendant to answer the accusation in court. In three of the four cases in which a couple was under suspicion, the man appeared to answer the charge. The fourth case seems to prove the rule, as the man was in prison and unable to appear in court.[53] Both suspected and proven offenses forced the accused to participate in discussions of sexual mores, sometimes to confess their sins and perform penance. The process of presentation and discipline in the court thus transformed behavior that was perceived as outside the Christian boundaries of patriarchy into an affirmation of customary familial roles and gender relations.

The sanctity of church festivals, the Sabbath, and the time of worship were issues of only modest concern to local churchwardens in the early 1590s but became increasingly important later in the decade. The desire to separate the time of worship from everyday routines and diversions, to enforce more rigid boundaries between the sacred and profane worlds of the parish, lay at the heart of the effort to reform customary religious practice. Before the wave of presentments in the 1590s, local conceptions of the sacred and involvement in the ritual life of the church had focused primarily on the crises of the life cycle.[54] The official insistence from the late 1540s on regular church attendance and annual communion elevated the position and significance of the Sabbath in relation to other sacred events and performances.[55] This church discipline made the regular observation of the Sabbath and the communion in prescribed form into the primary symbols of the inner faith in Christ's sacrifice binding the external, spatial community of the parish, and of the conformity of this parish religion to the official Protestantism represented by the Book of Common Prayer. Only four presentments for the profanation of sacred time occurred in 1591 and 1592. William Clevely and William Gilbert of Tewkesbury were presented for playing at tables during evening prayer on a Sunday. They were warned and dismissed.[56] Robert Dale and Thomas White of Tewkesbury were presented for working at their trades on the feast of Simon and Jude. Dale, a poor man, was dismissed after he had explained the circumstances of his case. White also appeared and confessed, but judgment in his case was referred to the bailiff of Tewkesbury and has not survived.[57] This lenity stands in stark contrast to the more numerous presentments and stiffer sentences of the crisis years between 1594 and 1597.

The attempt to reform church discipline and conceptions of the sacred included the enforcement of rigorous standards of conduct for local servants of the church. The prosecution of local churchwardens and ministers for failure to execute their duties in the manner prescribed by law and the Book of Common Prayer became increasingly common in the 1590s. John Audrey, curate of Tewkesbury, was presented in April 1591 for marrying three couples in the forbidden time of Shrove Monday and Tuesday without a license from the bishop. After its separation from Rome, the Church of England had retained the traditional prohibitions of marriage from Septuagesima to Low Sunday, Rogation to Trinity, and Advent to Hilary.[58] These seasons constituted a sacred interlude, separated from the profane time of everyday life to commemorate the miraculous history of the risen Christ. In this context, human sexuality was perceived as a dangerous source of pollution. Only the bishop had authority to remove the prohibition by his license. Although the low number of conceptions in the prohibited seasons, particularly in the period between Lent and Easter, suggests general support for the church position on this matter, its opponents perceived the licensing power of the bishop as a remnant of popish magic.[59] Audrey claimed to be unaware of the law and pleaded that publication of the banns before Shrovetide made the subsequent marriages lawful. His case may have amounted to more than simple ignorance. Audrey was an active preacher, and failure on the part of this kind of minister to respect the official holidays and fasts of the Church invariably raised questions about his orthodoxy. The episcopal reformation of local religious customs included prosecution in both kinds: ceremonial innovations as well as forbidden devotion to the prohibited ceremonies and discipline of the past. Audrey's case was referred to the personal arbitration of Bishop Bullingham.[60]

The bishop and his court also licensed and supervised local schoolteachers and physicians. The success of the official reformation depended on the education of the local population into its merits, and bishops accordingly sought to regulate the instruction provided in the schools of their dioceses.[61] Yet the unlicensed practice of either profession might also reflect unfavorably on the personal authority of the bishop. Churchwardens were consequently under increased pressure to prosecute unlicensed schoolteachers and physicians in the 1590s and early 1600s. William Symes of Tewkesbury was presented in 1592 for practicing "physic and surgery" without a license, although he described himself in court as little more than a consultant.[62] As part of a general campaign against religious Nonconformity, the court sought in 1606 to suppress an unlicensed school run by the suspended minister Thomas Drake in Forthampton.[63] The bishop's concern about professional licenses usually focused on the schoolteachers, but the prosecution of Symes indicates the court's desire to bring a wider range of unlicensed activity under control.

The consistory court used a variety of sanctions to enforce its authority. Penance was the most common punishment. The chancellor or his surrogate ordinarily declared the penance after a person's confession in court. The ritual of penance varied slightly from one case to another but followed a discernible pattern. Penitents were compelled to stand in their parish church on the Sabbath, usually during a particular segment of divine service, as John Surman of Forthampton was directed in 1591 "to stand in his parish church during the reading of the epistle and the gospel."[64] Multiple appearances were often required, and penitents sometimes stood in more than one local church, confessing their sins to a neighborhood of parishes on successive Sundays. Penitents from isolated rural parishes might be forced to stand in a public place in the nearest market town. John Parker, a resident of rural Forthampton, did penance in the parish church of Forthampton and in Tewkesbury Abbey. Penance might also be performed in the cathedral church of Gloucester itself. Steven Cooke of Tewkesbury was ordered to appear in both Tewkesbury Abbey and Gloucester Cathedral.[65] Special clothes and props were employed to represent penitent status, and suitably humble forms of demeanor were also prescribed. The penitent wore a white sheet (*lintemine induto*), held a white rod (*alba virgula*), and stood or knelt before the assembled parish to confess sin and implore divine mercy and forgiveness. Less severe forms of penance allowed the penitent to appear in everyday clothes (*in usitatis vestibus*).[66] Because penance was a deeply humiliating social experience, many petitioned to have their sentences commuted to money payments. Fines of this kind usually went to relieve the poor, as in the case of fines allocated to impoverished prisoners in Gloucester castle.[67] The rituals of penance, broadly considered, thus sought to transform the corrupting force of sin into the sanctifying force of love, in the form of either absolution or charity.[68]

These performances were important religious events, since the spiritual health of the parish community depended on its identification and correction of sin. The statements of the "public voice" identified suspects, and the process of detection and prosecution was a collective process that made gossip and other forms of neighborly interaction into important police agencies. The communal significance of penance lay in its relationship to this collective process. Tewkesbury had only two churchwardens, and the moral supervision of even a small town was unthinkable without the stock of local information contained in neighborly gossip and rumor. Most penitents had been previously identified in the everyday talk of their neighbors as offenders against the public morality of the parish. The confession of sin and request for pardon in the parish church returned the penitent to the source of accusation, and the ritual of penance was the means by which the soul and reputation of a suspected neighbor were seen to be healed. In this context of collective presentment and ritual forgiveness, statistical assessments of the court's effectiveness become less persuasive. The social discipline or sense of order in parish communities was not mechanically imposed by the church court in Gloucester. The prosecution and visible punishment of the "moral offenders" previously identified by the collective conscience or "public voice" of the parish played an important creative role in social order. Many of the key participants in this creative process—the churchwardens responsible for introduction of the reformed discipline in Tewkesbury in the 1590s and early 1600s, such as Richard Bradford, John Cooke, Thomas Deacons, and William Hitches—later served in the highest offices of magistracy in the corporation.[69] The detection, prosecution, and punishment of behavior identified as sin served as a common preparation for office in borough government. This punishment, in the form of penance, was structured by the public morality of the parish but simultaneously made this public order visible in the form of powerful religious dramas, which were organized around the detection and destruction of sin.

The most powerful sanction at the disposal of the church court was excommunication.[70] Two degrees of excommunication, the lesser and the greater, existed in legal theory, but the greater was the form most commonly used in the late sixteenth and early seventeenth centuries. This sanction signified the ultimate exclusion of the "sinner" from church and society. Christians who knowingly associated with the excommunicate, even for the purpose of routine exchange in the marketplace, might be excommunicated themselves. Severe legal disabilities compounded this isolation from the neighborhood and parish. The excommunicate could not act as plaintiffs or witnesses in lawsuits, were forbidden to serve as executors, administrators, or guardians, and were thus denied access to virtually every form of secular power in Christian society.[71] This punishment was not, however, intended as an end in itself. The threat of excommunication was used to secure a prompt appearance in court or obedience to a sentence. An excommunicate who failed to apply for absolution, remaining obstinate for at least forty days after denunciation in his or her local church, could be signified (*significavit*) to chancery, and a writ *de excommunicato capiendo* could then be issued, instructing the sheriff to imprison the offender.[72] Yet the churchwardens, neighbors, and officers of the court ultimately wanted confessions of sin and petitions for absolution, not confiscations of property. Penitents could easily obtain absolution and readmission to the moral community. An oath of obedience and the performance of penance were the usual conditions of forgiveness.

The series of prosecutions that formed the broadest sustained effort to reform customary religious practice and social discipline, before the campaign of the 1630s, was concentrated in the short span between 1594 and 1600. Just over half the prosecutions surviving for Tewkesbury and the adjacent parishes from the years 1591 to 1617 occurred in this seven-year period.[73] Significant increases in presentments of every kind reflected general concern for the preservation of public order in parishes confronted by the multiple crises of plague and scarcity.[74] The prosecution of sexual offenses, so closely related to local economic cycles and the perceptions of public morality sharpened by crisis, declined after 1600, but the wave of presentments in the 1590s marked only the beginning of organized support in the vale for the movement in the national church to reform conceptions of religiosity and the sacred. By the first years of the seventeenth century, the number of prosecuted sexual offenders had fallen below the level of the early 1590s. Presentments for violations of the Sabbath and religious discipline fluctuated considerably but never returned to their earlier levels.[75]

The annual presentments of sexual offenses nearly doubled in the 1590s from an average of twelve in 1591 and 1592 to an average of twenty-two between 1594 and 1597.[76] This increase in prosecutions for sexual offenses resulted, in part, from the impact of economic recession on marriage formation. "The sudden rise in prices before the harvest" in 1595 had led to a royal proclamation limiting the price of grain, yet the situation had remained grave. In 1597 "all grain was dearer than ever known in our memory," and "it proved before harvest that if great quantities of rye had not been by the merchants provided from the east countries, the realm had been in great scarcity and danger."[77] The decision to marry, like all decisions that involved considerations of property, was heavily influenced by the economic context. Most couples married late, after first acquiring the resources to establish a household.[78] Poor couples often had difficulty acquiring permission to marry because churchwardens and overseers of the poor feared increased pressure on the system of poor relief. Scarcity could therefore seriously disrupt preparations for marriage among families on the social margins.

Many persons prosecuted for sexual offenses left no trace in other local sources and so may be assumed to have been poor. Poverty was undoubtedly a factor in the prosecution of William Burges als. Hooper and Joanna Skull of Tewkesbury in 1594 for "living incontinently together" and claiming to be married. These names do not appear in the sixteenth-century parish register, although the name Skall does appear in a list of the recipients of funds from the Giles Geast charity in 1636.[79] In more affluent families, economic circumstances did not have such a decisive influence but could increase dependence on parental property and favor, thus affecting the bargaining positions of parents and children on such issues as the choice of a spouse. In 1594 Giles Flucke and Katherine Kirkham of Deerhurst may have used sex to force Giles' father, William Flucke, a yeoman farmer of Deerhurst, to accept their courtship. The fact of pregnancy, it was hoped, might persuade the father to support a marriage rather than see the family incur public disgrace in the church court. This plan backfired, as the elder Flucke allowed his house to be used for the birth but apparently refused to be blackmailed into the marriage. Kirkham consequently performed penance for bearing a bastard child, and William Flucke was himself prosecuted for the suspicious circumstances of the birth in his house.[80]

If economic scarcity often led to forms of behavior presentable in the courts, the same local evidence from the 1590s suggests that churchwardens and neighbors in the vale perceived a broader range of behavior as illegitimate or suspect. The perception of sexual relations in the time between the conclusion of a marriage contract and the marriage ceremony provides an index of this shift in attitudes. Sex before the ceremony was officially prohibited, but only one incident was prosecuted in 1591 and 1592. This figure increased dramatically to eighteen presentments for fourteen cases in the years 1594, 1595, 1596, 1597, 1599, and 1600.[81] Thomas Jefferies of Twyning was prosecuted in 1596 for sexual relations with his wife before marriage. Jefferies protested that a contract of marriage had preceded the consummation of courtship, but the court ordered husband and wife to perform penance. Despite their subsequent marriage and the ample local precedent for their conduct, the Jefferies appeared before their neighbors as sex offenders and penitents.[82] Behavior previously perceived as innocuous had become culpable in the mentality of economic crisis and plague. Michael Taylor of Tewkesbury was presented in February 1595 on suspicion of "fornication" with one of his domestic servants. Taylor argued in court that similar rumors had circulated ten years earlier, when the woman had first entered his service, without any prosecution. He swore to his innocence of the charge, and the court dismissed him.[83] Many of the cases brought to court between 1594 and 1600 were dismissed in similar fashion. In November 1596 Thomas Hayward of Forthampton was presented on a charge of "fornication" with his servant, Anne Jacksons. He responded indignantly that no such rumor had come to his notice, swore to his innocence, and was dismissed.[84] Richard Willis of Tredington was suspected of sexual "incontinence" in February 1594 on the grounds that "one Margaret Tiler continued in his house for the space of seven or eight days." Willis appeared and explained that Tiler, who lived in Worcestershire, was a former servant of the family and had agreed to spend several days with his wife in his absence. The case was quickly dismissed.[85] This rapid discharge of cases in the 1590s indicates an awareness, among officials of the court, that local rumor could be unreliable as a basis for prosecution in times of crisis. The "public voice" did not register behavior in any simple way but represented shifting local perceptions of the moral health of the parish community.

The prosecution of clerics for violations of episcopal authority and church discipline and for the profanation of sacred things also increased dramatically in the 1590s but did not decline once the local crisis had passed. A campaign of reform and renovation began with the present-ment of churchwardens and other lay servants of the church on varied charges of negligence following the episcopal visitation of 1594. The churchwardens of Twyning were prosecuted in February of the same year for furnishing only one psalter, failing to replace their torn Bible, and allowing the church and churchyard to fall into decay. At the same time, the parson of the parish was reprimanded for the "great reparations" required by the chancel as a result of his inattention. The churchwardens from four other parishes and the parson of Ashchurch were also pre-sented in February 1594 for similar offenses.[86] This episcopal pressure on churchwardens was partly responsible for the closer local scrutiny of curates and schoolteachers whose lax attitudes on certain disciplinary issues, particularly episcopal oversight and licenses, began to be per-ceived more consistently as abuses and debasements of their office. Be-tween 1594 and 1605 curates such as Richard Curtis of Tewkesbury, and William Rickardes and John Graver of Ashchurch, were prosecuted for failure to renew their licenses or for their connection to the lucrative local market in clandestine marriages.[87] Schoolteachers practicing their profession without a license or failing to bring their scholars to hear divine service were also summoned before the court. This issue of li-censes and discipline concerned both the integrity of episcopal authority and the material income of the diocese, but the primary aim of prosecu-tions was to confirm the authority of the bishop in the conduct of cere-monies and in the practice of the professions. Thomas Rogers of Tewkes-bury, a poor man prosecuted as an unlicensed schoolteacher in 1594, was remitted most of the cost of his license at the petition of the inhabi-tants of Tewkesbury.[88] The unseemly conflicts that sometimes resulted from this enforcement of episcopal licenses could become counterpro-ductive. In 1595 an overzealous churchwarden of Forthampton was him-self prosecuted after he ripped the surplice from the back of a curate whom he knew to be unlicensed.[89]

The distance between law and practice in both the spiritual and tem-poral life of the church had formed an important element in the higher circles of English ecclesiastical culture since the humanist criticisms of the church before the Reformation. As early as 1511 John Colet had expressed belief in a reformed clergy as the necessary prelude to a re-formed laity.[90] Yet reform was seldom simply decreed from above. Criticisms of clerical discipline and occasional prosecutions of clerics by churchwardens and civil officers of the parish formed an important element in local variants of anticlericalism.[91] These local standards of propriety in the service of the church were profoundly influenced by the curates who began to enter the parishes of the northern vale in the early 1590s.[92] The local establishment of the pastor's role as a behavioral paradigm, representing in his own life the values exalted in Christian worship, was the result of standards set by John Audrey, Richard Curtis, and Humphrey Fox of Tewkesbury; John Wright and John Ashby of Ashchurch; and William Blackwell, the curate of Beckford and later of Tewkesbury.[93] The increase in presentments for clerical incompetence and profanation of the Sabbath occurred in the wake of their arrival, the pressure from diocesan authorities being refined by a heightened local awareness of the importance of preaching and the power of the sacred.

The new local standards of clerical behavior were reflected in the case of Richard Winsmore, curate of Forthampton. Winsmore was prosecuted by one of his own parishioners in February 1602 for numerous acts of misconduct in office.[94] The court papers generated by this prosecution stand close to the intersection of religion and everyday life. In 1601 Winsmore stood in the street in Forthampton, talking with a group of his parishioners, while nearby a sow-gelder spayed one of Winsmore's pigs. As the gelder worked, he was regaled with jests about the animal's plight, to which Winsmore replied, "God save my bitch, the man fears god and loves his church." Winsmore thus invoked the name of God to protect his animal and connected the Christian integrity of the gelder to this concern for the mundane material interests of the curate. George Crumpe of Tewkesbury then asked a friend, "Is this your minister? I think he be one of Jeroboam's priests, to use or abuse the name of god thus in vain." Crumpe tried to separate the sacred world of religion from the profane world of the streets. He invoked from scripture the religious crimes of Jeroboam, who had profaned sacred places and raised "the lowest of the people" to the status of the priesthood.[95] His comment might also have been interpreted as a dangerous indictment of the regime that permitted curates such as Winsmore to officiate in the sacred places of the parish. Winsmore became enraged, seized Crumpe's staff, and hurled it over a hedge, calling him "rascal and knave." When Crumpe went to retrieve his staff, Winsmore swore "by god's wounds" to throw "the rascal" in a nearby pool, "and he caught Crumpe with all his force and might, endeavoring to throw him into the pool and do him hurt."[96]

Winsmore was also a legendary drinker, fond of a ritual he had apparently invented with his friends, called "three bare words." The ritual was simple, consisting of the words "wine, good, out" spoken in unison by the drinkers and followed by the downing of a bowl of wine. In March 1599 Winsmore engaged in a particularly uproarious version of this ritual at the Ram, an inn in Tewkesbury. After "divers bowls of wine," he began to have trouble speaking the three words, ending up "senseless and unable to stand alone or speak perfectly." A "friend" then gave Winsmore a lit pipe of tobacco, "to try what he would do with it." Raucous laughter ensued, as Winsmore placed "the fired end" of the pipe in his mouth, and "all the company manifestly understood that he was drunk." A churchwarden of Forthampton, who had observed this performance sourly from a distance, helped Winsmore to a bed in the house and ordered the chamberlain to see that Winsmore consumed no more wine when he regained consciousness.[97] At the episcopal visitation in the spring of 1602, Winsmore was pointedly assigned to recite a passage from scripture against drunkenness. He was eventually suspended from his cure pending the determination of the case against him.[98] No record of the court's judgment survives, but Winsmore was no longer curate of Forthampton at the next visitation in 1605.[99]

The campaign to reform standards of clerical conduct was part of a broader movement to reform local religious attitudes and behavior. This reform movement reflected a shift in conceptions of religious ceremony, in the significance of the Sabbath, and in the perceived position of ceremony in the hierarchy of sacred and profane activities, as well as in perceptions of proper clerical behavior and leadership. Churchwardens and their neighbors in the parish insisted on the new code of ministerial conduct because the educational duties of the ministry and the sacred ceremonies performed by local ministers on the Sabbath had acquired a new significance. The elevation of the clerical office had its ceremonial counterpart in an emphasis on regular church attendance and the annual reception of communion. Presentments for absence from church and for failure to receive Easter communion had been nonexistent in the early 1590s.[100] Between 1594 and 1600 the campaign to reform customary religion produced eighteen presentments for absence from church and twenty-four presentments for failure to receive communion.[101]

This reformed church discipline criticized both traditional conceptions of ceremonies and patterns of personal devotion. Yet responses to the accusations of impiety made in the church court reveal the perceived strangeness of the new practices and standards. John Fisher of Tewkesbury, presented in 1597 for negligence in coming to church, objected that many of his neighbors had also been absent and were irregular in their attendance. Fisher promised to attend more diligently in the future and was ordered to certify the reformation of his habits under the hands of the minister and churchwardens of the parish.[102] John Jordan of Tewkesbury was prosecuted at the same time for his indignant dismissal of an order from the churchwardens to appear in church. Jordan also agreed to attend church more regularly in the future and was then dismissed.[103] The conception of communion as an annual statement of personal faith, a sign of the communicant's exclusive dependence on Christ's sacrifice as the only means to salvation, was equally unfamiliar in the 1590s. Many local residents perceived communion as a collective event. The undivided body of the community was reflected in the ritual consumption of the body of Christ. As it commemorated Christ's sacrifice, the ceremony organized around the communion table, in the center of the church, signified the "charity" between neighbors in the parish. Anxiety or conflict among neighbors was considered sufficient cause to abstain from communion. In 1599 Thomas Perkins of Deerhurst justified his failure to receive communion on the grounds of unspecified disagreements with neighbors.[104] John Turrett of Forthampton, prosecuted in 1602 for abstinence from Easter communion, protested that "he was not in charity with a gentleman dwelling there and further said he had rather stand to the extremity of law than to receive, being out of charity."[105] Presentments for nonattendance at church and nonreception of communion remained high in the early seventeenth century, as ministers and churchwardens sought to establish regular church attendance and annual communion as core customs of a reformed parish community.[106]

The reformed parish was identified by its distinctive prohibitions as well as by its enforcement of church attendance and communion. Among the most important religious objectives of the new discipline was the strict separation of sacred time, reserved for public worship, from the everyday routines of parish life. This separation was justified in the eyes of its local supporters by the broader movement to create a gospel Christianity, purged of human corruptions and visually represented in the sober discipline of the local minister and his parish. George Crumpe's acid criticism of Richard Winsmore, in its contempt for the profane customs of Jeroboam's priests, expressed the notion of separation and its scriptural sources. As presentments for nonattendance and nonreception of communion increased in the late 1590s, the prosecution of behavior perceived as irreverent, as a profanation of the Sabbath, became more frequent. Only four presentments were made in 1591 and 1592 for violation of the Sabbath, but presentments for various forms of irreverent behavior increased to forty in 1594, 1595, 1596, and 1597. This yearly average of ten prosecutions rose to thirteen in 1599 and 1600.[107] Nor were the limits of prosecution narrowly defined by the boundaries of public worship. Crumpe reacted to Winsmore's invocation of God's name in a casual conversation. Drunkenness, swearing, and scolding extended the notion of "irreverence" beyond the sacred time of worship to include behavior perceived as harmful to the moral environment in which respect for the sacred and the principles of Christian neighborhood were cultivated.[108]

Most prosecuted offenses, however, were committed during divine service. In its most common form, a profanation of the Sabbath resulted from the performance of mundane work on Sundays. Thomas Palmer of Twyning "profaned the sabbath day" in 1597 by shaking pears and having his corn ground at a nearby mill. The court had often warned and dismissed previous offenders, but Palmer was ordered to perform penance and to pay ten shillings in fines, since penalties for violation of the Sabbath had become more severe by the mid-1590s.[109] The pursuit of sensual gratification and amusement during the time of divine service was another common form of profanation. In 1597 a group of Tewkesbury apprentices was prosecuted for playing stoolball in service time. Edward Roots of Twyning was presented in 1599 for his performances upon the tabor and pipe "on the sabbath days in time of prayer." A group of nine Tewkesbury residents was prosecuted in 1599 for spending their Sundays drinking in an alehouse and playing cards.[110] These offenses introduced the profane routines and pastimes of everyday life into the sacred world of the Sabbath. The reformers in diocese and parish did not seek to abolish such forms of conviviality but to place profane diversions in a separate and subordinate relationship to the sacred ceremonies of public worship.

The separation of the Sabbath from the profane world of everyday

labor and diversion left the customary practices of no social class unaffected. Rowland Baugh, scion of the armigerous Baugh family of Twyning, was prosecuted in 1599 for allowing his servant to work on the
Sabbath, just as Margery Addis and Anna Clenson, poor women of
Tewkesbury, had been presented in 1597 "for selling peas and beans at
sermon time in the churchyard."[111] In January 1599 Richard Cotton and
"his neighbors of the better sort" were prosecuted for carousing over
dinner and playing cards for a pint of wine during the time of public
worship.[112] The reformed discipline of the parish was a communal phenomenon, an attempt to preserve and protect the sacred in the customary framework of the parish, not a scheme to control the behavior of any
particular social class.

The reformed religion enforced by the presentments of the 1590s and
early 1600s assumed in its ritual form a particular kind of religious
community. The prominent role of churchwardens in the local enforcement of discipline entailed frequent reference to the church court and
affirmed the territorial authority of the diocese and parish, forms of
community in which shared space denoted a shared faith. This conception of religious community and the structure of worship in which it was
represented were not uncontested. The religious culture of the late sixteenth and early seventeenth centuries was marked by conflicts of varying intensity between the vision of the sacred and the form of discipline
that was enforced in the courts and alternative interpretations of Christian symbols, religious authority and forms of church government, and
styles of discipline. These alternatives led a rather shadowy life in parish
communities. The Catholics were the only group with a formal institutional identity outside the Church of England, but local Protestantism
comprised a spectrum of attitudes including support for the church discipline of the early Elizabethan Reformation; the conformist Puritanism
or "mere Puritanism" of the reformed discipline enforced in the courts;
and the advocacy of a more stringent reformation of the Church of England, fervently sought as the only means to remove Roman Catholic
corruptions and to restore a gospel Christianity. This amorphous local
support for further reformation occasionally coalesced to form conventicles, as the clandestine meetings of the godly were known, and on its
fringes became a Saturday Sabbatarianism not far from sectarianism. The
local Catholics were closely watched and occasionally presented in the

courts but were not persecuted systematically. The fundamental challenge to the reformed discipline of the established church came from the alternative visions of religious community implicit in the ritual practice of Nonconformists.

The Nonconformists were differentiated from their neighbors, and frequently from each other, by distinctive preferences in matters of ritual and by the form of religious community that their preferences assumed.[113] Broadly considered, Nonconformist attitudes to ritual stressed the authority of scripture and conscience over the demands of law, the circumcision of the heart over the circumcision of the flesh. Belief in the inherent efficacy or value of ritual itself, as distinct from the moral and spiritual condition of the participants, was rejected as a form of idolatry. The sign of the cross consequently disappeared from the ritual of baptism, and communion was received while sitting or standing, rather than while kneeling as the law required.[114] Nonconformists generally preferred the use of common bread in communion. The expression of this preference became overtly political in a local woman's assertion that "the bread allowed in the Queen's injunctions for to serve the communion was made with dog's grease."[115] Many Nonconformists also objected strenuously to the use of the surplice, the vestment of white linen that the law required clergymen to wear during public worship. The "hotter sort of Protestants" decried the surplice as a remnant of the superstition and idolatry of Roman Catholic ceremonial discipline or "priestcraft."[116] A Nonconformist curate of Tewkesbury probably spoke for his local supporters when he expressed contempt for the surplice in 1602, protesting in the church court that when it was worn, "none came to receive [communion] but drunkards."[117] According to this view, the use of the surplice in the ceremony destroyed the sacred symbolism of the wine and reduced its efficacy to the profane power of inebriation. The controversy over vestments provides the clearest illustration of the way radical Protestant culture identified itself in ritual as the inverse image of Catholicism.

An important combination of Nonconformist attitudes identified this rejection of ceremonial elements as an unavoidable consequence of insistence on scriptural authority for religious ceremonies and intense concern for the moral and spiritual condition of the soul confronted by the demands of law. This style of Nonconformity or godliness made preaching and the singing of psalms the core of Christian ritual. The "mere

Puritanism" of the reformed discipline supported preaching as a vital didactic element in public worship, but this particular Nonconformist style was distinguished by a refusal to acknowledge any value in the other elements of the liturgy. The male converts to this style of evangelical Christianity signified their disapproval of reading or reciting from prepared texts in public worship by the wearing of a hat during divine service and by its removal only for the sermon or the singing of psalms.[118]

An extreme insistence on the literal translation of scripture into religious life revived the ancient debate over the nature and authority of Christian Sunday observances, a debate expressed locally in the Saturday Sabbatarianism of George Shaw, Edward Hill, and Roger Plevy. This form of scripturalism rejected as human innovations both the Christian Sabbath and the conception of the fourth commandment as a *moral* law only, insisting instead on the ceremonial *and* moral authority of the commandment and the inviolability of the seventh day as the proper "proportion of time" for a Sabbath. Shaw, Hill, and Plevy held offices in borough government, Shaw as a burgess and Plevy and Hill as assistant burgesses, and this prominence in the civil hierarchy magnified the pollution and danger of their Nonconformity. The combination of high political office and the assault on an ancient foundation of the Christian church seemed to other local officers a subversion of order in both church and state. On June 2, 1620, the Tewkesbury borough council ordered Shaw, Hill, and Plevy to recant their views or face removal from their places on the council. The council gave the accused one month to "acknowledge the fourth commandment to be a perpetual moral law of God, and the Christian Sabbath or Lord's Day to be God's holy ordinance, and that it is not in man's power to alter the number of one day in seven for a Sabbath to any other proportion of time."[119] This ultimatum "was diverse times publicly read [in the council chamber], and it was required that if any man assented not to it, he should speak, but all were silent, and a general approbation of it." George Shaw had attended the meeting but remained silent, and the council directed the town clerk to make a copy of the order for "George Shaw and the other sectaries." On Sunday, July 2, in the evening, the bailiff of the borough council, Edward Tovy, summoned a dozen councilors to his home in anticipation of Shaw's response to the council's demands. As the only burgess among the accused, Shaw seems to have been perceived as the leader of the "sectaries." His resistance was understated but firm and, in the eyes of the assembled councilors, intolerable. Shaw "said he was busy" and refused to appear, despite repeated summonses, until the next day and then "absolutely refused to answer the questions concerning the sabbath." Between July and November 1620, the borough council brought the "dangerous opinions" of its Nonconformists to the attention of the Council in the Marches of Wales. The Council sent a pursuivant to take custody of the offenders, further evidence of the seriousness of the crime, and ultimately "bound them over before the high commission." Thomas Chamberlain, Lord President of the Council, Sir Henry Townsend, and Mr. Overbury added their own signatures to the borough council's formal complaint and praised the council's vigorous action against Nonconformists in its midst. The combined pressure of the borough council, the Council in the Marches, and the Court of High Commission crushed local resistance. On November 7, 1620, Hill and Plevy "being again demanded their opinion concerning the sabbath, did then acknowledge the Christian Sabbath or Lord's Day, now observed, to be a divine ordinance, begun and set up by such as were inspired by the Holy Ghost, and that they believed it is not in the power of any church to alter it to any other proportion of time." Shaw recanted later the same day in the open council chamber, and the council then restored the suspended councilors to their places. This brief but intense controversy over the nature of the Sabbath reveals the variety of Nonconformist styles or expressions of godliness. Yet the fluid boundaries between the distinct styles of Nonconformity expressed a common disbelief, varying in its intensity, in the scriptural authority of the Book of Common Prayer and the 39 Articles.[120]

Despite its amorphous qualities, the Nonconformist attitude and ritual discipline, founded on the authorities of scripture and conscience, represented in its various forms a reconception of religious community, which was perceived by its initiates as a restoration of the authentic religious fellowship of gospel Christianity. The external, spatially defined community of the parish was superseded by an internal, metaphysically conceived community of shared belief. Nonconformists, who perceived parish boundaries as an affront to the demands of conscience and to the spiritual affinity of coreligionists, were regularly presented in the courts for attending church in neighboring parishes where the form of service was more congenial or the preaching inspired.[121] This spiritual fellowship of inner conviction was marked by its exclusivity and conducted its affairs, from the study of the Bible to the discussion of strategy for further religious reform, in conventicles. Churchwardens prosecuted Mrs. Leight of Tewkesbury in October 1605 "for suffering conventicles at her house for Mr. Fox and others" and "ordered [her] to enter bond that there shall be none hereafter in her house." Similar clandestine assemblies formed across the Severn in Forthampton.[122] Neighbors interpreted the exclusivity of Nonconformist discipline as a spiritual slap in the face and an affront to their own conceptions of the sacred. William Restell, a yeoman of Forthampton, articulated this perplexity when he complained that his neighbor Thomas Drake refused to "give any reverence at all to divine prayers more than if he were sitting in an ordinary man's house."[123]

Paradoxically, the style of Nonconformity practiced in conventicles in Tewkesbury and its neighborhood disdained separation from the national church and, rather than presenting a distinct alternative to the church, promoted an image of a purified church, restored to its gospel heritage.[124] The more skillful initiates into this discipline were local curates last encountered as the influential agents of the reformed church discipline of the late 1590s. Ironically, the vigorous clerical effort to educate the laity into the sacred duties of ecclesiastical office regularly resulted in the prosecution of the same zealous curates by their own parishioners. In 1596 the church court forced John Ashby, curate of Ashchurch, to apologize to his parishioners for the conflicts occasioned by irregularities that he had introduced into public ceremonies. Ashby was enjoined to perform the lawful ceremonies in his surplice on the next Sunday and to follow the service with "a sermon of charity and love to be held between neighbors." Ashby then had to appear before the bishop to subscribe and declare his support of the Book of Common Prayer and the 39 Articles, promising to "perform the same in all respects, both in saying the service, ministering the sacraments, and using the ceremony allowed in the Church of England."[125] Humphrey Fox and his friend Thomas Drake were prosecuted in the court and eventually suspended from their respective cures of Tewkesbury and Forthampton for Nonconformity. Fox was suspended from Tewkesbury in 1602. The churchwardens responsible for his prosecution, John Cooke and Thomas Deacons, later served in the highest offices of the corporation of Tewkesbury.[126] Drake received suspension from Forthampton in September 1605 for hesitating when asked whether he would wear the surplice. Fox remained suspended, but Drake had been reinstated by the summer of 1607.[127] Henry Hatton, a resident of Forthampton, informed the visitation court in September 1607 that Drake allowed Fox to be present in the parish church of Forthampton during the catechism.[128] The intensity of this local response to Nonconformist practice illustrates the way in which a Nonconformist curate could make many parishioners feel like outsiders in their own church.

A distinguished tradition of historical writing has sought a socioeconomic explanation for this diversity of religious opinion and experience in the sixteenth and seventeenth centuries.[129] The problems inherent in this approach to religion surface clearly in the different social distributions of Nonconformity uncovered in Tewkesbury and Forthampton, although the interpretive problems are again compounded by uncertainties of evidence. Church court books of the late 1590s and early 1600s and an isolated entry in the Tewkesbury borough council register for 1620 indicate that local officers in Tewkesbury and Forthampton prosecuted twenty-nine Nonconformists, fourteen from Tewkesbury and fifteen from Forthampton, as either recipients of communion in the Nonconformist style or advocates of a literal interpretation of the fourth commandment and a Saturday Sabbath. The names of offenders can be linked to the ages, occupations, and places of residence given in the militia survey prepared by John Smyth in 1608.[130]

This method requires further discussion of both the definition of Nonconformity and the meaning of the church court evidence. What distinguished Nonconformity from legitimate religious attitudes and styles in the late sixteenth and early seventeenth centuries? How did Nonconformity differ from the "mere Puritanism" of the discipline enforced in the church courts? The distinction between Puritanism and Nonconformity might be criticized as yet another anachronistic division of the religious spectrum, founded on modern conceptions of the distinction between the Church of England and Dissent. On the other hand, the notion of a religious spectrum does not lessen the importance of distinctions and even conflict among Protestants. One distinction frequently made by contemporaries involved the acceptance or rejection of authorities other than scripture in matters of religion. A variety of opinions existed on either side of this distinction, but the distinction itself remained significant. The behavior described as Nonconformity, a particular style of communion and a literal interpretation of the fourth commandment, resulted from just such an insistence on scriptural authority and a rejection of the independent authority of the church.

To describe this behavior as Nonconformity does not mean that it has a general significance and power to identify Nonconformists in quite different local contexts. If Nonconformist Puritanism is viewed as a style rather than as a closed system of prescribed attitudes and behaviors or a checklist of attributes, the boundaries of religious difference and the problems of interpretation become very subtle.[131] Advocates of a return to the scriptural foundations of church and society perforce attempted to practice their discipline in a variety of local circumstances. These local circumstances often determined the attributes stressed in the Nonconformist style.[132] In Forthampton, Tewkesbury, and the northern vale generally, posture in communion became an extremely important sign of Nonconformist attitudes. Humphrey Fox, the curate of Tewkesbury, was prosecuted in 1602 "for administering communion without wearing the surplice and for administering the sacrament of the Lord's Supper to diverse parishioners sitting down, to the disturbance of the rest that were present of the congregation."[133] Yet in other English parishes, particularly in the crowded parish churches of London, sitting or standing in communion had become the unquestioned local practice of the established church.[134] Although insistence on scriptural authority in religious affairs formed a general framework for action, Nonconformity assumed a distinctive shape and emphasized different attributes in response to the local discipline of the established church in particular parishes. This local dimension of Nonconformity—its power as a political, ceremonial, and disciplinary style to recreate the European movement for a gospel Christianity in diverse local circumstances—remains among the least explored and most significant elements in the process of reformation.

This distinction between Puritanism and Nonconformity thus recognizes a contemporary perception of difference. The churchwardens and officers of the church court understood their enforcement of the reformed discipline in the 1590s and early 1600s as the local expression of a general process of further reform in the Church of England. Both officers and campaign acquired motive and direction from assumptions and attitudes conventionally identified as Puritan; but the subsequent prosecution of ceremonial Nonconformity identified in this Nonconformist style of communion a dangerous departure from lawful forms of ceremonial conduct, a departure clearly perceived as significantly different from the pursuit of further reform in the framework of episcopal government and discipline.

A second order of question concerns interpretation of the court process itself. What was the broader significance of prosecution in the church courts? If the process ended in confession and recantation and if the offense never recurred, is it permissible in the absence of further evidence to magnify the significance of the presentment by describing the accused as a Nonconformist? In the 1630s Humphrey Fox had his sons educated in Scotland and continued to conduct ceremonies in the Nonconformist style despite his suspension from clerical office, but many lay offenders have left no such evidence of persistence. These offenders frequently appeared only once in the court documents, then recanted or were excommunicated, and subsequently disappeared from the record. Does this behavior constitute evidence of Nonconformity? Current historical practice suggests a skeptical but ultimately affirmative response. If the evidence of prosecution in the church courts cannot be used as a measure of Nonconformity, the problems of historical detection become insurmountable. This practical necessity must be acknowledged. Yet the statistical measures of Nonconformity become less important if the questions focus on the attraction of diverse religious styles and attitudes and on the influence of religious difference and Nonconformity on social cohesion, and if the measurement of Nonconformity and other religious mentalities is then confined to specific moments or crises. Scarce evidence of local persistence in any religious discipline then becomes less serious, because the persistence of attitudes and styles, irrespective of statistical representation in the population at any particular moment, is a primary concern. These problems of definition and sources, although not unique to this archive, qualify any generalizations from the evidence of religious conflict in the vale.

This evidence suggests that urban Nonconformity in Tewkesbury was diverse in its social distribution and generally lacked formal cohesion.[135] Roger Plevy, a tanner and resident in the affluent neighborhood of the High Street, presented to the High Commission in 1620 for Saturday Sabbatarianism, was the only Nonconformist among the prestigious craft groups. George Shaw was a wealthy trowman also presented in 1620 for his views on the Sabbath. The other residents of the borough prosecuted for Nonconformity included Thomas Perkins, a yeoman farmer; Charles Wood and Thomas White, tailors; John James, a glover, and his wife

Elizabeth James; Thomas Woodward, a smith, and his servant William Woodward alias Blanket; George Walker, a cutler; John Severne, a weaver; and George Alcocke, a schoolmaster. In Tewkesbury, the occupational status of eleven of the fourteen identified Nonconformists cut across the gradations of poor and middling craft groups. The geographical distribution of Nonconformists in the borough violated, in similar fashion, the sometimes subtle socioeconomic distinctions between neighborhoods. Of the nine members of the group whose residences can be established, three had dwellings in the poor neighborhood of Barton Street, three in the affluent neighborhood of High Street, and three in the less clearly differentiated neighborhood of Church Street. Nonconformists were seldom chosen to serve in local offices but were not devoid of political influence.[136] George Shaw, Edward Hill, and Roger Plevy, prosecuted in 1620 for Saturday Sabbatarianism, had sufficient status and reputation to be members of the borough council in Tewkesbury.[137] These councilors may have been able to protect friends from the expense of frequent presentation in the courts, but their own prosecution before the Council in the Marches of Wales and the Court of High Commission indicates that the councilors were under a great deal of pressure to conceal their beliefs.

Perhaps because of its powerful political significance and the repressive action of local officers of the church, Nonconformity in Tewkesbury was generally diffuse and lacked cohesion. There is virtually no evidence of a sustained Protestant communal life or a sectarian identity beyond the boundaries of the Church of England. In 1606 Mrs. Leight of Tewkesbury held conventicles in her house for Humphrey Fox and his friends, and Fox formed a connection between the conventicles in Tewkesbury and similar assemblies in Forthampton.[138] After his suspension from Tewkesbury, Fox remained close to Edward Alcoke of Forthampton, a friend and supporter of the curate Thomas Drake, and even helped Drake to administer a catechism in the parish church of Forthampton in September 1607.[139] On appearance in the consistory court, however, eight residents of Tewkesbury, presented alongside Fox for receiving communion in a sitting posture, declared their willingness to kneel. Charles Wood implied he had wanted to receive communion in the prescribed form (*non sedentibus sed flexis genibus*) but "had no room to kneel conveniently." Only Roger Plevy defended the sitting posture as "the best and fittest way" to receive the sacrament.[140] Shaw, Plevy, and Hill, the Saturday Sabbatarians, were presented as a group in 1620 and were described by their opponents as sectaries, but no independent evidence survives to demonstrate their solidarity.[141] The Nonconformist style could produce more or less distance from the ceremonies and discipline of the established church and could even produce in Saturday Sabbatarianism a mentality very close to Separatism; however, as the public recantation of the Saturday Sabbatarians suggests, Nonconformity did not create autonomous communities distinct from the parish. Nonconformists in Tewkesbury were socially heterogeneous and occupied a vulnerable position on the margins of political life.

The social distribution of Nonconformity in Forthampton, a rural parish across the Severn from Tewkesbury, was limited only by the agricultural economy of the parish. In 1606 a violent dispute in the parish church had been occasioned by the prosecution of fifteen Nonconformists from the village. Although no one who was prosecuted in this conflict held a rank higher than husbandman in the militia survey of 1608, important differences between prosperous and subsistence farmers can be detected in the Nonconformist ranks. Robert Mayle appeared as a husbandman in the survey, but he called himself a yeoman and had sufficient influence in the parish to serve as churchwarden in 1603.[142] Mayle had a lease of the house in which the Nonconformist curate Thomas Drake taught an unlicensed school in 1606.[143] The Alcockes and Heywards stood among Forthampton's more prominent farming families and had ostentatiously furnished Drake with money and provisions during his suspension from the cure of the parish.[144] But the appeal of the Nonconformist style spread beyond the circle of substantial local farmers in the parish elite. Status can be determined in five further cases, involving the Hatton, Turrett, and Lane families, and here the Nonconformists were farmers on a small scale, not necessarily poor but undistinguished by service in parish office or by anything other than the conviction that kneeling in communion was contrary to the word of God.[145]

Unlike the pattern of Nonconformity in Tewkesbury, the Nonconformist style produced in rural Forthampton a cohesive circle of godly families.[146] The reasons for this cohesion are not clear. Punitive measures were certainly enforced more rigorously in Tewkesbury. Officers of the church and the borough used both the secular court of the borough council and the consistory court to prosecute religious Nonconformity. Under this disciplinary pressure, Nonconformists who were presented in

1602 and 1620 recanted. The supporters of Thomas Drake in Forthampton, on the other hand, never appeared in the consistory court, either for improper comportment in communion or for support of a suspended minister. Richard Garner, the curate of Forthampton, probably initiated the office case against his rival Drake in the consistory court, and this office case generated the surviving evidence of broader conflict.[147] The villagers who were accused of ceremonial improprieties Garner merely cited to appear before the archdeacon in Tewkesbury.[148] Another important factor in local cohesion may have been the marriage of the clerical leadership into the community. Drake, the Nonconformist curate, had married Alice Alcocke of Forthampton, and the Alcocke family became an important source of support during his suspension.

Whatever the explanation, the pattern of cohesion in Forthampton is unmistakable. A small contingent of neighbors who were described by the churchwardens as a conventicle mobilized to assist Drake after his suspension. Drake received "four or five shillings" from his relatives Edward Alcocke and Margery Alcocke. John Hatton furnished a pig and some wheat. Thomas Heyward or Joan Heyward, his wife, provided corn, and Henry Hatton, the younger, Edward Lane, William Turrett, and Richard Turrett made unspecified contributions.[149] These neighbors also shared religious activities beyond the parish. On three successive Sundays before their prosecution, Drake, the younger Hatton, Edward Alcocke, Lane, and the Turretts traveled to Beckford, five miles from Forthampton, "to hear Mr. Blackwell preach."[150] Garner's citation claimed that the same "virulent" neighbors had received communion "some sitting and some standing" from Mr. Jawnsey of Oxnall.[151] Nonconformists from Forthampton clearly attended divine service in other parishes as a distinctive godly regiment. Drake, Mr. Edwards, another suspended clergyman, the younger Hatton, Edward Alcocke, and Lane, leaders of the conventicle in Forthampton, displayed their fellowship openly in the streets of both Forthampton and Tewkesbury.[152] These Nonconformists did not separate from the parish, despite their public rejection of the 39 Articles, but came closer than any other local expression of the Nonconformist style to the creation of a sustained, visible alternative to the reformed discipline of the established church.

The movement for further reformation, in both its conformist and Nonconformist Puritan forms, has generally dominated the historical discussion of religious conflict in the late sixteenth and early seventeenth centuries. This emphasis is appropriate, given the enormous documentation produced by the similar concerns of contemporaries, but exclusive concentration on the various forms of Puritanism has tended to oversimplify the spectrum of Protestant opinion on the issue of further reformation. Recently historians have become more interested in Protestant opponents of further reformation in the second half of the sixteenth century. A small quantity of local evidence, primarily from the consistory court, suggests the outline of a distinct religious style expressed in the remnants of the traditional liturgy. This style produced no articulate statement of position, but its practice implied an emotional attachment to the formal ceremonies and customs of the church and an aversion to the reformed discipline enforced in the consistory court. The ceremonial style emphasized the customs and occasions of the church left intact by the first phase of the Elizabethan Reformation.[153] Several historians have described this attitude as Catholic, but little evidence survives to demonstrate any local interest in the restoration of the mass, much less the formal structure of traditional Roman Catholicism. As a Protestant discipline, this religious style appeared to endorse a church independent of Rome and never advocated the restoration of Roman Catholicism, but instead it desired a church founded on the liturgical style expressed in the Book of Common Prayer and in its ornaments rubric as well as venerable local custom.[154]

This ceremonial style bore little resemblance, in the second half of the sixteenth century, to traditional Catholic cults. Yet some elements survived and may have been the more deeply revered for the abbreviation of traditional ceremonies. In 1585 the liturgical equipment in Tewkesbury still included "the best cope of tinsel with red roses," three "awles" or albs, an "amyae" or amice, the linen cloth worn around the neck of the priest in the celebration of the eucharist, and a bell, possibly a small altar bell, traditionally rung during the eucharist at the elevation and communion.[155] Despite changes in the liturgical framework of parish religion, some parishioners remained loyal to the temporal framework of devotional routines expressed in the ringing of bells. The sound of the bells in Tewkesbury Abbey had traditionally marked the passage of time in the sequence of divine service, had signaled the arrival of church holidays, and, in emergencies, had placed a protective shield of sound between the community and evil spirits of the air.[156] Comparative silence ruled the Protestant parish. Bells announced civic occasions and important events in the hierarchy of the church, such as episcopal visitations, but the Protestant liturgies of the Church of England limited the ceremonial uses of bells. Walter Rogers or Richard Curtis, curates of Tewkesbury in the late 1590s, extended the ban to traditional religious holidays, and the implied restriction of devotions to one day in seven affirmed the Sabbatarianism enforced in the courts.[157] In 1595 Francis Bradbury of Tewkesbury protested against the silence and disobeyed the order forbidding the bells to be rung on holidays at the beginning of prayers. Bradbury and his friend Glover rang the bells in despite of the curate "and afterwards went into the pulpit and reviled him and brawled against him in very disorderly manner."[158] This incident reveals a keen awareness of the pulpit as a partisan platform, despite local differences on the importance of the sermon in the ceremonial discipline of the church. Protestants uninterested in further reformation generally disliked the Puritan emphasis on sermons and relative disdain for the Book of Common Prayer. John Audrey, curate of Tewkesbury in the early 1590s, attempted to make sermons an important element in his ministry, but his parishioner Henry Turner responded violently to Audrey's sermons, proclaiming publicly in the winter of 1592 that henceforth "when Mr. Audrey went to preach, he would go to shit."[159]

Sacred authority conveyed specific rights to worldly resources, and traditional ceremonies incorporated an elaborate system of fees in a distinctive interrelationship of sacred and profane elements. The transfer of many traditional church fees into lay hands after the separation from Rome created a fiscal motive for loyalty to traditional symbols and ceremonies. In 1626 William Hitches, farmer of the rectory of Tewkesbury, used the church court to protect a payment of six pence in lieu of a "chrisom cloth" for every child christened in the parish. The chrisom had played an important symbolic role in the complex of traditional ceremonies surrounding birth and death. This white linen cloth or robe, embellished with a cross of red silk, symbolized innocence and was wrapped around a child after baptism. If the child died within the month, the chrisom then became a shroud, its message of innocence a form of protection in the grave.[160] In the customary ritual of purification known as churching, the midwife carried the chrisom before the mother as she processed to the church.[161] The family then paid the value of the cloth to the parson or proprietor of the rectory. Originally the exchange had involved the cloth itself as a gift, but by the early seventeenth century the value of a chrisom had been set at six pence. Poor parishioners unable to make this payment in cash might use a cloth of lower value to pay the fee in kind.[162] In the 1620s Nicholas Smithsend refused to make any payment, claiming that the chrisom was a "relique of popery and superstition."[163] Hitches asked Margery Balthrop, Joanna Flucke, Joanna Wyatt, and Margaret Phillips, four women of Tewkesbury aged between seventy-five and eighty, to substantiate his customary right to the fee.[164] The women denied any knowledge of customs "in the time of popery" but spoke at length of the many colors in which chrisoms had formerly been made and testified to the vitality of the custom before its omission from the ritual of baptism in the 1590s. Only the use of the cloth ceased in the 1590s, not the payment of the parson's fee.[165] Yet this style of Protestantism seldom received the support of the church court on ceremonial *or* financial matters. Despite the local corroboration of his claim, Hitches lost the case. The court not only excused Smithsend from payment of the fee but also, rarest of rarities, abolished a source of ecclesiastical revenue.

The resistance to further reformation remains an elusive element in local Protestantism, an attitude rather than a movement. As a reaction to the reformed discipline introduced in the 1590s and early 1600s, the attitude contrasted the familiar sounds and colors of church holidays and traditional ceremonies to the harsh and empty discipline of further reformation. These Protestants perceived the emphasis on the Sabbath not as a glorious return to the sacred foundation of scripture but as a reduction of godliness, an exclusion of God and religion from the parish on the historic festivals of the church. The transfer of ecclesiastical fees into lay hands after the separation from Rome also created vested interests in the lay community that were opposed to any modification of traditional ceremonies likely to disturb the financial infrastructure of church discipline. Yet this resistance to further reformation differed significantly from the attitudes and assumptions of Nonconformity. Conflicts over bells and chrisom cloths did not extend to conceptions of religious community. Despite their emotional intensity, these ceremonial disputes focused on the proper ritual expression of traditional conceptions of religious fellowship. The local resistance to further reformation thus produced a distinctive style of worship, a particular vision of how the church should look and feel, but the conception of religious community implicit in its ceremonial style remained the territorial community of the parish and diocese.

The styles and attitudes of Catholicism differed from local expressions of Protestantism in several obvious ways.[166] Catholicism existed as a separate church and community. The hierarchy and discipline of the church incorporated local Catholics in an institutional structure of international complexity, a vast religious community frequently represented by both Catholics and Protestants as the inverse image of the Protestant parish, diocese, and nation. If the diverse styles of Protestantism expressed particular conceptions of the Church of England, the Catholic style and discipline denied the English church any status as a sovereign church distinct from Rome. Yet Catholics were both friends and strangers in the parish, striving to preserve the integrity of their faith and their status as neighbors. Survival as a Separatist minority in the parish depended on the ability of local Catholics to acknowledge the symbols of parochial authority and community while avoiding participation in a communion perceived as heretical. The relationship of Catholics and Protestant Nonconformists to the ceremonies conducted in the parish church thus assumed an ironic similarity. Catholics often attended public services on Sundays in deference to the authoritative symbols of the parish. But formal Catholic ceremonies and discipline survived in the private dwellings of the faithful. This clandestine community had a hierarchic organization, and its ritual life centered on the households of prominent Catholic families, such as the Hickfords of Twyning, the Casseys of Deerhurst, and the Renfords of Tewkesbury.[167] Catholics of poor and middling social status depended on the more powerful families to reproduce the faith and often sent their children to serve in the households of affluent coreligionists.[168] Perhaps because of the prominent local families concerned, officers of the church courts generally left Catholics unmolested. John Eagles, a husbandman of Deerhurst, had for many years organized his life according to "the faith we call catholic" and hoped to "finish his days" in the same faith. Eagles prepared the will containing his statement of faith in 1623, and it passed probate in the consistory court without modification in 1624.[169] The uneasiness of informal toleration became apparent, however, when the strict conditions of coexistence were perceived to be violated. Elizabeth Waters of Deerhurst was prosecuted in 1605 for absenting herself from the parish church for three years and for "instructing her servant in her popish religion."[170] The local tolerance of difference, shallow at the best of times, tended to evaporate completely once a Catholic had been presented in the church court. The penance demanded by the court regularly included certification of communion in the parish church, and prosecution in the court could thus become the first phase in a process of harassment ending in excommunication.

These diverse religious attitudes and disciplinary styles produced a complex response to the local activities of the church court and make it impossible to link a reformation of manners to any particular local faction. Protestant notions of godliness lacked the cohesive force necessary to form a faction. The relative ease of movement across boundaries, from conformity to Nonconformity to recantation in the parish church and a return to conformity, suggests that local religious behavior might be more appropriately described in the fluid terms of attitude and style than in the concrete terms of movement, group, faction, or sect. Protestant attitudes and disciplinary styles attracted interest in a broad range of status groups in town and village, and this broad appeal casts further doubts on the connection between godliness, reformation of manners, and a particular social class. As religious mentalities, each form of Protestantism and Catholicism shared a moral opposition to profanation, drunkenness, fornication, and adultery. Yet this consensus on moral discipline, on the principles of Christian conduct in the profane world, did not lessen the danger of difference in conflicts over the authority of scripture, ceremonies, the nature of the Sabbath, and the legitimacy of the Church of England itself. The inclusiveness of the English church minimized the significance of Protestant differences in the 1590s and early 1600s, as a conformist Puritan element in the church hierarchy and in the localities cooperated in the introduction of a reformed church discipline. Only a small number of extreme Sabbatarians and imprudent Catholics failed to find some form of accommodation in this discipline.

Historians have made a distinction between the different types of reformation produced by the diverse religious attitudes and styles of the sixteenth and seventeenth centuries: the reformation of religion and the reformation of manners. These reformations have been interpreted as the dual projects of a parish elite or faction that described itself as "the godly" and that used the power of sacred and secular offices to impose a strict discipline on poor families in the parish community. Religion served as a system of social control, a means to restrict the behavior of the poor in the interests of the rich and to promote the behavior conducive to work, the creation of wealth, and the protection of property.[171]

This perspective remains important as an attempt to establish *a* social context of the Reformation in particular villages but has been unwisely generalized as *the* social context of Reformation in England and across Europe.[172] Although the social and economic divisions of villages and parishes in the vale help to make sense of sexual offenses and prosecutions in crisis moments of famine and plague, the importance of such offenses as evidence of a cultural transformation is doubtful.

Nor can this approach explain the evidence of deeper religious conflicts in the vale in the 1590s and early 1600s. The Nonconformist style of Puritanism signified more than a reformation of manners and was itself prosecuted vigorously in the church courts. Although some parish leaders doubtless supported the campaign for a reformed Puritan church discipline as a response to the multiple crises of the 1590s, the primary appeal of the reformed discipline lay in its power as an orientation to the sacred. This orientation had a significant impact on moral codes and expectations of moral behavior, but to describe social control as the goal of the campaign is to misunderstand its motives. The reformed discipline, a limited Sabbatarianism, enforced strict boundaries between the sacred and the profane but did not attack custom itself. Officers of the church perceived their own activities as an attempt to restore the sacred time of divine service and the customary diversions of the parish to their proper places in the classificatory scheme of communal life. This reform interest existed in the traditional framework of authority constituted by the law and the institutional form of a territorial church.

The Reformation came to the Vale of Gloucester in the late sixteenth and early seventeenth centuries but not in the conventional form of godliness, the alliance of ministry and magistracy, and the strict Sabbatarian discipline made familiar by intensive historical study of the Reformation experience in eastern and southeastern England. These views of reform lacked broad support and existed as distinctive local styles in religion. On the other hand, the use of the church courts to reform parish morality and to forestall further divine judgments of plague and famine intensified religious differences in vale communities. The new church discipline enhanced the authority of the parish, although several alternative attitudes and styles, Protestant as well as Catholic, contested the assumptions of the territorial parish community. The enforcement of a reformed discipline in the courts exacerbated this conflict among notions of religious community in the vale and sharpened the perception of difference among religious attitudes and styles. These attitudes shared a belief in the priority of the sacred and the necessity of personal discipline but differed importantly on core ceremonies and on the forms of "imagined community" signified by their ceremonial discipline. The authority of religious symbols, the power of a symbol to signify the humanity of the inner person, ensured a clear distinction between neighbors of different views. The powers of differentiation that contemporaries perceived in religious symbols must be appreciated before the subtle religious differences in the vale can begin to form a pattern in the evidence.

5

A Circle of Order: The Politics
of Religious Symbolism, 1631–1640

And lastly, his Majesty does hereby give assurance to all to whom it may concern, that such as shall take the boldness willfully to neglect this his Majesty's gracious admonition, and for the satisfying of their unquiet and restless spirits, and to express their rash and undutiful insolencies, shall willfully break the circle of order, which without apparent danger to Church and state may not be broken, that his Majesty shall and will proceed against all such offenders and willful contemners of his gracious and religious government with that severity as upon due consideration had of the quality of their offenses and contempts they shall deserve, that so by the exemplary punishment of some few, who by lenity and mercy cannot be won, all others may be warned to take heed how they fall into the just indignation of their Sovereign . . .

    Charles I, "Proclamation for the Peace and Quiet of the Church" (1626)

The 1630s have recently become a hotly contested forward position in the debate over the causes of the English Civil War. As the division of Crown and parliament has ceased to appear the inevitable result of decades of opposition, attention has focused on the more immediate relationship between religious conflicts in the 1620s and 1630s, the Bishops' Wars, and the formation of parties in the aftermath of defeat in 1640.[1] Nicholas Tyacke has described this partisan religious conflict as an Arminian counterrevolution against the Calvinist consensus in the Church of England. According to Tyacke, the conflict intensified and became more open and embittered after James' death in 1625 and the Arminian victory at the York House Conference in 1626, a select conference of lords and bishops that convened at the Duke of Buckingham's residence in London to debate the merits of Richard Montagu's publications, which were reviled by opponents as an Arminian defense of the Church of England.[2] Charles' declaration of "the circle of order" in 1626 and his protection of Montagu reflected this partisan conflict insofar as both actions affirmed the recommendations of the Arminian bishops included in the York House Conference.[3] Tyacke has stressed this link between the monarchy and Arminianism in the 1620s as an important source of a broad Calvinist resistance to royal policy in the 1630s and early 1640s.

Criticism of this interpretation has focused on the contours of the Calvinist consensus in the Church of England, on the severity of the conflict between Calvinism and Arminianism, and on the nature and coherence of Laudianism, a general reference to William Laud's policy as Archbishop of Canterbury. Kevin Sharpe has rejected Arminianism as a political force in the Personal Rule. Sharpe defines Laudianism as the ecclesiastical expression of a general Caroline vision of orderliness and interprets religious differences in the 1630s, particularly before the Bishops' Wars, as "tensions and grievances" rather than deep divisions.[4] Peter White views the doctrine of predestination, which is essential to the opposition of Calvinism and Arminianism, as the product of subtle interaction among positions on a Protestant "spectrum" and links Tyacke's conception of violent confrontation between partisan extremes to the contemporary polemics of William Prynn and Peter Heylyn.[5] As if the discussion of Calvinism, Arminianism, and Laudianism has not rendered the politics of religion in the 1630s sufficiently obscure, Julian Davies has recently added Carolinism to this complex historiographic dialect. Carolinism defines the ceremonial innovations of the 1630s as the political religion of Charles I, designed to promote his vision of "sacramental kingship" by the development of the royal supremacy in the church. Carolinism subordinated the doctrinal squabbles of Calvinists, Arminians, *and* Laudians to "social uniformity and civility" in religion, but this Caroline cult of royal authority and interventionism in church affairs ultimately destroyed both monarchy and church in the 1640s.[6]

This book can contribute little to recent scholarship on the nature and extent of conflict in the circle of government and on the intellectual sources of policy in the 1630s. Yet the evidence of local responses to ecclesiastical policy in the 1630s may promote a useful discussion of research priorities. The current debate focuses on doctrinal issues as the most important elements in the creation of policy and the reaction to policy and has consequently expressed a distinctive historical method. After the doctrinal sources of conflict—in this instance Calvinism and Arminianism—have been identified in the universities, in the institutions of church and state, the evidence of parish religion then becomes important as a means to demonstrate the existence of the distinctions in local communities. This approach tends to assume rather than demonstrate "the sense of a constant struggle between warring factions."[7] The local evidence on doctrinal issues is sparse, and complex behavior cannot be reduced to the expression of doctrine to compensate for the deficiency. Tyacke has questioned the ability of the "average parishioner" to recognize an Arminian sermon, but the implications of this question remain difficult to accept for historians who are determined to demonstrate the pervasive effects of doctrinal difference.[8] The evidence of local reactions to ceremonial innovations in parish churches, particularly after Laud's metropolitical visitation of Gloucester diocese in 1635, provides an opportunity to explore more than the extent of religious difference. The symbols used in religious ceremonies *created* parish communities, and disturbances in this cultural process reveal the intricacies and the *politics* of the process itself. Charles created a circle of order around his person in 1626, but religious symbols had constituted a circle of order, intimately related to royal authority, in parish communities since the sixteenth century. Although the politics of religious doctrine remains important in this statement of the problem, the contested *symbols* in ceremonial disputes open new perspectives on the interrelationship of local and national issues in the 1630s.[9]

The divisions in the church hierarchy in the 1620s have left little impression in a local archive impoverished by the absence of detection books for the northern parishes.[10] Only general comments on the early Caroline regime have survived, and the comments seem to stress political continuity. The visitations of "pestilence" in London, Westminster, Oxford, and Tewkesbury itself dominated the first year of Charles' reign. A local observer, an officer of the Giles Geast charity, perceived these disasters as a matter of course in earthly polities and remarked on the similar cosmological causes behind the disturbances in 1625 and the "infections" after Elizabeth's death in 1603, "so that princes die not alone but, being the heart of the commonwealth, other members suffer with them."[11] This broad acceptance of the framework of royal authority, as

well as the disinclination to invoke providence in criticism of specific
royal policies in the 1620s, characterized a local comment, which was
also inscribed in the account book of the Giles Geast charity, on the Duke
of Buckingham's assassination. Richard Bradford, a gentleman of Tewkesbury and bailiff of the corporation in 1616 and 1629, claimed to have
seen a prophecy of Buckingham's assassination in Trinity term, 1628.[12]
This prophecy had reduced the name "Georgius dux Buckinghamiae" to
the nine numerical letters "M, D, C, X, V, V, V, I, I, I" and had added the
numbers to produce the sum 1628.[13] The assassination had then occurred in August 1628. Yet Bradford saw no providential comment on
the policies of church and state in Buckingham's death. Despite its dark
overtones, the prophecy represented Buckingham's assassination as the
fulfillment of a personal destiny, and therefore Bradford did not read in
the event any implications for the destinies of parish, church, or nation.

Parishes in northern Gloucestershire contained advocates of several
different religious styles in the early seventeenth century but did not
experience permanent factions or separation from the church. Although
religious differences existed and occasionally produced violent conflict,
as in the early 1600s in Forthampton, the intervention of the church
court and the processes of presentation, repentance, and pardon transformed even extreme differences, such as Saturday Sabbatarianism, into
external conformity and inclusion. The cooperation of churchwardens
expressed a confidence in the court's power to enforce proper standards
of ceremonial conformity and moral conduct. After the early reform
efforts of the 1590s, the standards enforced in the courts, based on the
Prayer Book and the 39 Articles, acquired the customary authority of
continuous administration. These standards did not depend entirely on
the personal disposition of the bishop. Miles Smith had a reputation
for lenity in the reconciliation of religious differences, but under his
administration the consistory court refused to license Humphrey Fox,
the Nonconformist curate of Tewkesbury and Forthampton, in 1616 and
suspended him in 1619.[14] Godfrey Goodman favored the revival of ceremonialism in the Church of England, but his consistory court left John
Geary, the Puritan minister of Tewkesbury, undisturbed in his benefice in
the 1620s, before Geary's rejection of "the canons and constitutions" of
the Church of England led to his suspension in 1634.[15]

The limited Sabbatarianism and ceremonial conformity enforced in
the court became a circle of order used by local officers to measure the

obedience of their neighbors to sacred and secular law. This order depended on the abstract symbol of the Sabbath, represented by the time of divine service, but the Sabbath in this form embodied the authority of both church and state in obedience to the Prayer Book and the Articles of Religion. Archbishop Laud's metropolitical visitation in 1635, intended to enforce a *Caroline* circle of order, created difficult problems of conscience for conformist ministers, churchwardens, and their neighbors. Laud's commissioners introduced several stylistic innovations in parochial religion and generally emphasized the objective qualities of the sacred, its immanence in the fabric of the parish church, and its unique concentration in the fixed communion table. The visitors' instructions had clear implications for the use of space in ceremonies and for the visual representations in parish churches. Laud's commissioners ordered the churchwardens to move communion tables farther back from the nave to a fixed north and south position in the upper end of the chancel and to construct a boundary of rails around the tables.[16] Orders that were related to the use and appearance of parish churches reflected a similar objectification of the sacred, particularly Laud's interdiction of animals in the churchyard, contrary to the customary use of this space for economic purposes. The visitation thus attempted to enforce a circle of order that differed in subtle but important ways from the limited Sabbatarianism enforced in parish communities since the early 1600s. The spatial metaphor of the circle sheds additional light on this partisan politics of religion, as it conveys the power of church discipline to designate insiders and outsiders in local, national, and cosmic communities.

Although the doctrinal distinctions vital to recent discussions of the politics of religion in the 1630s are absent from the evidence of parish religion in the vale, the ceremonialism implicit in Laud's visitation orders had a discernible effect on local perceptions of religious styles and attitudes present in parish communities since the early 1600s. The visitation seemed to divide Protestant conformists into the supporters of a hotter sort of Protestantism, a measured resistance to this episcopal intrusion into the local circle of order, and the advocates of the visitation order as the standard of proper submission to royal authority. After the visitation, some churchwardens perceived ceremonial Nonconformity as the forward defense of the local circle of order and hesitated to prosecute behavior not openly disdainful or contemptuous of royal authority. The consistory court seemed to be implicated in the disturbance of local churches, and presentments for ceremonial Nonconformity declined. Laud's metro-political visitation did not destroy the important interrelationship of church court and parish community, but the orders of the visitation court effected subtle shifts in the local politics of religious styles and intro-duced an element of distrust into the relationship that surfaced more clearly in the debates on episcopacy in the early 1640s.

The churchwardens' efforts in the vale to reform attitudes to the sacred had reached a peak of intensity in 1605 and had then declined gradu-ally before 1620, as the number of presentments for violation of the boundary between sacred and profane dropped from fifty-one in 1605 to fifteen in 1617.[17] Despite this decline, the priorities expressed in the presentments continued to influence local attitudes to the sacred, and the number of prosecutions never returned to the relatively low levels of the early 1590s. Churchwardens invoked the authority of the court in response to local assessments of the moral health of the community. The rituals of penance and pardon in the parish church helped to heal divi-sions among neighbors, to absolve sins, and thus to forestall the greater calamities of divine retribution. As a result of this intimate interrelation-ship between the consistory court and parish communities, the distur-bances understood as divine judgments usually increased appeals to the authority of the court. Unfortunately, the causes of renewed local efforts to reform lay perceptions of the sacred in the 1630s cannot be deter-mined precisely for parishes in the northern vale. Detection books have not survived for Winchcombe deanery in the 1620s.[18] The increased activity of the early 1630s may represent the continuation of a process already under way in the 1620s. Visitations of the plague in 1624 and the Duke of Buckingham's assassination in 1628 created a modicum of local anxiety. If the causes must remain uncertain, it is beyond doubt that presentments for violation of the sacred and for various forms of misconduct by local servants of the church had increased significantly by 1631.[19]

The priorities of reform in the early 1630s shared several features of the campaign to reform local perceptions of ecclesiastical roles and relig-ious discipline in the 1590s. Presentments for sexual offenses remained relatively insignificant, despite small increases in 1635 and 1637. The prosecution of sexual offenses in the 1630s never approached the consis-tently high levels of the 1590s.[20] An annual average of more than twenty sexual offenses had been processed by the consistory court between 1594 and 1600, but the increase to sixteen presentments in 1635 and eighteen presentments in 1637 represents the peaks of court activity in the 1630s. If presentments for 1635 and 1637 are excluded, the average number of sexual offenses prosecuted between 1631 and 1640 falls to six.[21] Yet the highest priorities retained their importance. Churchwardens in the 1630s were as concerned about regular church attendance and annual communion as their predecessors in the 1590s. Of the thirty-two presentments for miscellaneous violations of the sacred in 1631 and 1632, nineteen involved failure to receive communion or irregular church attendance.[22] A similar continuity is evident in presentments for profane work in sacred time, for drinking and providing a place for drinking during divine service, and for participating in profane amusements during the time of public prayer. In 1631 John Downbell and James Greene of Tewkesbury, among others, were presented for their violations of the Sabbath, Downbell for "carrying wares" and Greene for "keeping tippling" in his house "in the time of divine service or sermon."[23] These kinds of presentments were not confined to Tewkesbury, since the churchwardens of Deerhurst prosecuted Phillip Hampton and three of his friends in 1631 for playing kettles or skittles, a form of ninepin bowling, during public worship. Hampton confessed to bowling on the Sabbath but denied any violation of "prayer time" and so received a light penance.[24] Thomas Hickes and Thomas Brewer of Deerhurst were also presented in 1631 for playing the fiddle on the Sabbath "in time of divine service" and "drawing a company about [them]."[25] Churchwardens continued to use prosecutions for profanation of the Sabbath, defined as the time of public worship in the parish, to protect the sacred boundaries of divine service. This limited Sabbatarianism had characterized the local reform movement in the 1590s and persisted into the early 1630s.

The church discipline articulated in the Book of Common Prayer, which was introduced slowly and unevenly by the combined and sometimes contradictory actions of the consistory court, the ministry, and local churchwardens, had surfaced in identifiable form in the parish communities of the northern vale. Yet visitations still inquired into local possession of the proper liturgical equipment and corrected the more spectacular failures. The court ordered the churchwardens of Tredington in 1636 and 1637 to purchase a Book of Homilies.[26] The churchwardens of Forthampton had received similar instructions in 1631 but insisted that the book had already been acquired.[27] Directives from the court, frequently made in response to the local demands of churchwardens, held curates to standards of ceremonial order prescribed in the Book of Common Prayer. Robert Smith, curate of Deerhurst, was admonished in 1631 "for not reading prayers on weekdays and not going on procession."[28] Ralph Dutton, curate of Forthampton, was also reprimanded in 1631 for his failure to conduct perambulations of parish boundaries.[29] This combination of Prayer Book services and a rather limited form of Sabbatarianism in the local church discipline may explain the absence of controversy in Tewkesbury, Ashchurch, and Tredington over certification "that the king's majesty's declaration for sports were read in the church" in 1634.[30] The Book of Sports declared the priority of "duty to God" and church attendance as the sacred counterparts of recreation on the Sabbath, in the form of sports or customary pastimes, such as football, stoolball, and dancing, and local constructions of the declaration may have stressed this formal resemblance to common practice on the Sabbath.[31] Churchwardens did not perceive the Book of Sports as a "cultural counterattack" on the local Sabbath, and its promulgation did not produce in northern Gloucestershire the bitter conflicts characteristic of strict Sabbatarian regimes in other parts of the country.[32]

This church discipline, like the reformed discipline of the 1590s, was a collective discipline enforced irrespective of distinctions in social status. John Cowles, a gentleman of Tewkesbury and farmer of the rectory of Tredington, was presented in 1633 for allowing the chancel of Tredington church to fall into disrepair.[33] John Downbell, a wealthy baker, was prosecuted in 1631 for "carrying wares" on the Sabbath. He had inherited substantial property from his father, described as a yeoman in 1609, including a meadow in Oldbury field and a house in Barton Street, as well as the family "dwelling house" in Church Street.[34] Downbell was not the only middling tradesman presented in the early 1630s. Of the twenty men prosecuted by the churchwardens of Tewkesbury between 1631 and 1633 for sexual misconduct or profanation of the sacred, eleven were freemen of the corporation whose status as freeman suggests social rank among the upper 70 percent of the working population.[35]

The social diversity of those prosecuted in the court illustrates the complexities of status in the vale. The composition of a group presented in 1631 for playing "kettles" or skittles in Deerhurst on the Sabbath reveals a society in which differences of wealth and status did not preclude common leisure activities. One of the players, Phillip Hampton, belonged to a yeoman family. The Hamptons had served as church-wardens of Deerhurst and maintained important bonds of friendship to the Smithsends, a family of gentle rank in Tewkesbury and Walton Cardiff. Phillip's father, the yeoman John Hampton of Apperley, described the Smithsends as "my well-beloved in Christ" and appointed Nicholas Smithsend, the elder, and Nicholas Smithsend, the younger, as the overseers of his will.[36] Another player, Francis Stocke, came from a family of laborers joined to the Hamptons by bonds of friendship and obligation. The Stocke family was close enough to Phillip's cousin, Lawrence Hampton, to borrow twenty shillings.[37] William Heale, son of a husbandman of Wightfield, also played in the game.[38] The differences of wealth and status in this group suggest that the reforms of the 1630s, like similar efforts in the 1590s, were reforms of a communal culture, not the discipline of wealthy householders imposed on poor neighbors.

The Protestant reforms of the 1590s and 1630s were separated by only the most subtle shades of difference. Several cases brought before the consistory court in the 1630s addressed issues of behavioral decorum in the church that were encountered less often among churchwardens' priorities in the 1590s. It seems that regular church attendance and annual communion were not invariably considered sufficient manifestations of religious probity in the early 1630s. Churchwardens, perhaps under the influence of the reformed church discipline itself, began to insist on personal comportment suited to the solemnity and moment of the ceremonies in the parish church. In the 1630s failure to observe proper demeanor in worship, even the inadvertent failure of sickness, might be punished as severely as failure to attend church altogether. The church-wardens of Deerhurst prosecuted the unfortunate James Carpenter in 1636 for "vomiting in the church."[39] William Hickes and John Kent of Ashchurch were presented and ordered to perform penance for "laughing and grinning in the church in time of divine service and sermon" in 1634.[40] These churchwardens were not Puritans determined to impose godly standards on the unregenerate of the parish. Yet certain kinds of behavior, common enough in the parish churches of the late sixteenth and early seventeenth centuries, may have been perceived in the 1630s as mild forms of sacrilege.[41] This interrelationship of belief and demeanor expressed precisely the inner Christian community implicit in the reformed discipline of the early 1600s. The presentment of behavior perceived by the churchwardens and sidesmen as improper or unsuitable in church became increasingly common in the 1630s, as thirteen of the fifteen cases of disorderly behavior in church presented between 1631 and 1640 were presented after 1635.[42]

The relationship between local officers and the consistory court also changed in the 1630s, as diocesan officials increased the pressure on churchwardens in the government of the diocese. Churchwardens had long been expected to communicate any local incidents related to the spiritual or material welfare of the church, a duty ordinarily discharged in the bills of presentment made at Michaelmas and Easter. An active archdeaconry conducted semiannual visitations and required two bills per year, but churchwardens in the vale, perhaps because of the weakness of the archidiaconal jurisdiction in the diocese, seldom prepared more than one bill per year before the 1630s.[43] Between 1591 and 1619, diocesan officials prosecuted churchwardens only four times for inadequacies in bills and accounts.[44] But the court demanded more frequent presentments in the 1630s. Between 1631 and 1640, churchwardens were prosecuted twenty-nine times for failure to present more than one bill or for deficiencies in their preparation of bills and accounts. This administrative pressure appears to have increased after Archbishop Laud's metropolitical visitation in 1635, since nineteen of the twenty-nine presentments for inadequate bills and accounts occurred between 1636 and 1640.[45] The court attempted to make churchwardens more effective instruments of church policy in the 1630s, and this administrative reform became increasingly important after 1635, as Laud's policy depended on the cooperation of local officers.

The process of reform in the early 1630s continued to use the authority and discipline of the consistory court to protect the sacred boundaries of divine service, as defined in the Book of Common Prayer, and to inculcate a general moral code. This didactic process assumed the territorial community of the parish and the persistent authority of custom. The actions of churchwardens and their neighbors were part of an intermittent debate over moral boundaries and over the relationship between sacred and profane in the parish community. This debate was couched in the common cultural terms of the parish and accepted its core symbols and ceremonies as established in the Protestant, episcopal settlement of the church. Conflicts focused on the codes of conduct sanctified in parish ceremonies and on the calculus of Christian ethics in particular situations, such as the decision of poor craftsmen to work on Sundays or holidays, but these conflicts did not extend beyond the rational problems of ethics to question the constitutive symbols of the parish.

The continuity and persistence in the disciplinary activities of the consistory court and its local officers secured the ceremonies and pastoral conventions of the Book of Common Prayer in the Vale of Gloucester in the early seventeenth century. Yet the intricate cultural interrelationship of court and parish, a vital factor in the local process of reformation, acquired in the 1630s some of the adversarial qualities characteristic of the general hierarchy of the church. Nicholas Tyacke has described the late 1620s and early 1630s as a decisive moment in the conflict between Calvinists and Arminians in the church hierarchy, as the doctrinal differences of the 1620s became the policy differences and ceremonial differences of the 1630s.[46] Peter Lake connects the doctrinal differences of Puritan and Arminian factions to distinctive notions of idolatry, conspiracy, and politics, which were derived from the assumptions of antipopery and used to explain the vexatious political conflicts and failures of the 1620s.[47] The Puritans attributed failures in foreign and domestic policy to a popish and anti-Christian conspiracy designed to subvert true religion, the religion of faith and conscience, in the Church of England. Arminians or Laudians perceived the wrecked parliaments of the 1620s as strong presumptive evidence of a Nonconformist conspiracy to subvert monarchy and to destroy ceremonial order in the church.

If factions that were based on clear doctrinal distinctions remained uncharacteristic of most parishes before the early 1640s, the literature created by this doctrinal division in the church helped to foster local belief in the existence of overt and covert religious enemies, beliefs embodied in the figures of the Sabbath-breaker and the image-breaker. Although these caricatures could never have caused a civil war, in moments of crisis the existence of stereotypic enemies could conceal "the common ideological ground" contained in the different beliefs and ceremonial styles uneasily incorporated in the Church of England, a process of polarization that Anthony Fletcher and Peter Lake have identified as a definitive aspect of antipopery and anti-Puritanism.[48] The creation of enemies assumed its most obvious forms in certain kinds of literature, such as cautionary tales, which were intended for a general audience. The monsters created by Peter Studley in *The Looking Glass of*

Schism, which was first published in 1633, and by Henry Burton in *A Divine Tragedy Lately Acted,* which was published in 1636, crawled from this dark imagination of religious conflict and conspiracy.[49] Close analysis of the texts reveals the political context of religious difference in the 1630s, and this politics of difference, in turn, helps to explain the local evidence of change in the relationship between diocesan courts and parish communities.

As stories of religious symbols and desecration, iconoclasm, and profanation, both Puritan and anti-Puritan cautionary tales also reveal important evidence of the cultural process whereby parishes were created and sustained. Burton and Studley inevitably identified the creative powers of religious symbolism in their stories of iconoclasm and profanation. These stories illuminate the structure of the parish as a cultural form. Burton's accounts of the Sabbath and its desecration prowl the border between the core symbols of the parish and the codes of conduct in the profane world, a distinction inculcated in parish ceremonies and inseparable from its everyday life. Studley's lamentation for a profaned cross reveals the influence of religious symbols on perceptions of everyday relationships, the power of symbols to classify, to create identities, and to impose meaning on the contingencies of life. This creative power is not easily demonstrated from the behavior ordinarily preserved in church court documents. Printed sources furnish a different order of evidence, shaped by the strategies that authors use to persuade readers. Because these strategies often exploit the attributes of particular symbols and images, the printed word may thus reveal a mental world of religion present but obscured in the records of behavior.

Henry Burton, the Puritan minister of St. Matthew's in Friday Street, devoted much of his literary career to the study of Antichrist's machinations. Years of scholarly commitment and personal observation, always guided by the prejudices of antipopery, deepened Burton's passionate belief in a connection between Arminian officers in the church hierarchy and a popish conspiracy to subordinate the Church of England to Rome.[50] Burton retained his benefice in the late 1620s despite prosecution for ceremonial Nonconformity and used this platform in 1628 to proclaim his vision of the popish plot against church and state.[51] His opposition to the Book of Sports in 1633 resulted in Burton's book of cautionary tales, *A Divine Tragedy Lately Acted,* a collection of spectacularly violent stories intended to convey both the resilience of God's glory in the face of human presumption and the many forms of divine retribution in store for profaners of the Sabbath.[52] Burton's stories, like the prejudices of antipopery itself, relied on simple but essential oppositions to form boundaries between different religious beliefs.[53] These boundaries reveal the classificatory power and irrational content of religious symbols more clearly than any other evidence.

The stories contained in Burton's collection clearly express the cosmic distinction of sacred and profane, embodied in the symbols of Sabbath and sport. As a symbol, the Sabbath expressed a familiar aversion to the confinement of divine power in objects and instead represented a pattern of scripturally prescribed human attitudes and activities in response to a divine commandment. Burton's strict notion of a Sabbath extended its separation of sacred and profane, purity and pollution, beyond the boundaries of divine service, prescribed by the Prayer Book and the Book of Sports, to cover the activities of the entire day. A radical break differentiated the Sabbath, which was signified in many of the stories by devotion to scripture, sermons, and sober processions to the parish church, from Burton's profane symbol of sport, which was signified by maypoles, dances, football, and alehouses.[54] A dense accumulation of further oppositions articulated the sacred boundaries of the Sabbath and protected it from profanation. Yet the secondary oppositions life/death, reason/sense, society/individual, and human/animal formed a recurrent pattern in stories used to communicate Burton's extreme Sabbatarian perspective.

The boundary between sacred and profane frequently separated life and death in Burton's stories. Because the profane activities of sport expressed sinful sensuality, participation in sport on the Sabbath destroyed the only honorable purpose of human life, conceived as the glorification of God. The Sabbath-breaker usually came to an abrupt and painful end. At Baunton, in Dorsetshire, some villagers played bowls on the Sabbath in 1634, until one of the villagers suddenly hurled his bowl at a fellow bowler and "hit him on the ear, so as the blood issued forth at the other ear, whereof he shortly died."[55] Bally Hawks of Oxford, a butcher, made plans to mend his ditch on a Sunday in the summer of 1635. His wife admonished him to remember the Sabbath, "but he said he would go and make an end of his work, which he did, for suddenly he was struck dead in his ditch, and so made an end of his work, and his life together."[56] Death sometimes assumed the form of conventional divine judgments, especially plague, visited on an entire parish. A wedding celebration held on the Sabbath in the parish of Cripplegate, London, in 1634 included a feast and an afternoon dance in a churchhouse attached to the parish church, but this pollution of the Sabbath and the church brought swift retribution to the community only a week later, as plague struck the house of the newlyweds, destroyed the family, and spread into the parish.[57] Many similar stories represented inclusion in the sacred and in the activities of a strict Sabbath, as essential to the preservation of human life. Beyond the protective environment of Sabbatarian discipline, isolated in its disobedience, human life withered in the face of divine retribution.

The opposition reason/sense reproduces in shorthand the paths to life and death in Burton's stories. Only the application of reason to worldly events could forestall the disasters of promiscuity and death. Burton enjoined readers to be wise and observant, to understand and apply the lessons encoded in the divine punishments of profanation, in order to "understand the loving kindness of the Lord" and to avoid destruction.[58] A handful of Sabbath-breakers escaped the punishment of death by this rational appreciation of their predicament. On April 18, 1635, a Londoner decided to travel on the Sabbath, despite the solemn admonitions of his employer, and so proceeded on his way until his horse "suddenly fell and broke both his forelegs" on a clear and easy descent. The Sabbath-breaker understood "this not more sudden than strange disaster" as a divine judgment and proclaimed "this example should be a warning unto him for ever traveling on the Sabbath day again."[59] But most Sabbath-breakers existed in a world of sensual motives, devoid of rational direction. After a Sabbath spent in drunken sensuality at a wake, a villager from the parish of Otley at Baildon, in Yorkshire, struck and killed his companion with a hatchet, "and being hotly pursued, leaped into a river and drowned himself." Burton lamented such "fearful fruits of carnal liberty."[60] These prisoners of sense were marked for death and could only provide "examples" for others, who were perhaps more reasonable, to read their own danger in the punishment of sins, a process made easier by God himself "for that the punishment inflicted was stamped with the resemblance of the sin convicted."[61]

The capacity to find the sacred, to construct the discipline of the Sabbath by the application of reason to scripture, differentiated a unique human nature from the common animal attributes of sense. Burton frequently used animal figures, primarily conventional figures from scripture, to differentiate the reasonable human world of the Sabbath from the profane, dangerous world of wolves and lions beyond the sacred boundaries of human community.[62] A young man of Northampton had seen "the example of good people," had reformed his life, and had "learned to frame his conversation according to God's word, and that in the well-keeping of the Sabbath . . . and spending the whole day in the public and private duties of it." Sadly but not surprisingly, publication of the Book of Sports induced this young man to "run riot" and return to "wallowing" in the sin of thievery "for the which he suffered death."[63] The stereotypic Sabbath-breakers failed to develop the rational skills of piety necessary to humanity and "like untamed colts have thus learned to take the bit between their teeth, and so run at a gallop into all excess of riot."[64] This mildly sympathetic figure recognized the youthful impulsiveness of many Sabbath-breakers, like that of "untamed colts," and also implied the unavoidable persistence of animal qualities in adult human nature. The tone of Burton's "examples" more often resembled his dismissal of Sabbath-breakers as "rats and swine" addicted to "filthy fleshliness" and the dishonor of God.[65] Burton even confessed a disservice to animals in this regard, as many beasts seemed to honor God better than Sabbath-breakers.[66]

On the Sabbath, Christians exchanged obedience, duty, and honor for divine protection and love. Burton represented this exchange as the source of coherence in human relations, as the model for orderliness in the human community. Because human society existed to glorify God and because the Sabbath had been divinely instituted as the perfect form of glorification, orderliness in human society could never contradict the demands of the Sabbath. The Sabbath-breaker invariably violated the moral codes of human relationship, renounced worldly obedience and duty, and rejected everyday notions of honor in pursuit of selfish interests and sensual gratification. In 1634 Richard Jones planned to travel from his parish in the neighborhood of Dorchester to Stoke in order to play fives on the Sabbath. His mother "severely admonished" him to abandon this frivolous scheme, but Jones refused to listen and ultimately died in a brawl on the journey home, "a terrible example of disobedience to God's holy commandments."[67] A servant from London rebelled and decided in 1635 to travel on the Sabbath, despite the good example of his godly companions and the explicit orders of his mistress "to observe the Sabbath and not to travel on it."[68]

This confusion of relationships reflected the pollution of their sacred source. Officers of the diocese and parish had failed to protect the Sabbath and the social order, since bishops and apparitors, churchwardens and ministers, appeared regularly among Burton's agents of selfish indulgence.[69] The decline of Sabbath discipline undermined respect for the fifth commandment, and "inferior persons [exalted] in high contempt against their superiors, as the common vulgar against the magistrate and minister, servants against their masters, children against their parents, and wanton wives against their husbands."[70] The opposition society/individual added the inseparable relationship of Sabbath and human society to the layers of distinction in Burton's stories. Pollution of the Sabbath dissolved human social relations into selfish actions, motivated by animal sense. An epilogue described the process whereby the sanctified exchanges of the Sabbath created and perfected the coherence of the Christian society. Burton enjoined all "parish priests" in his province to "admonish the people" to avoid "prohibited works" on the Sabbath, to attend "cordially and religiously . . . all sacred mysteries of the church and . . . the preaching of God's word," and to perform "works of piety in relieving the poor, comforting the afflicted, and in doing other pious things, wherein Christian profession and charity do most of all shine forth."[71]

These stories of profanation and retribution appealed directly to local belief in providence, in the intimate relationship of spiritual purity, moral probity, and material prosperity. The blasphemies and impieties of Sabbath-breakers could cause enormous collective harm in the parish, even if the activities involved did not violate the boundaries of divine service. Despite their different notion of the Sabbath, readers unsympathetic to a strict Sabbatarianism could recognize Sabbath-breakers as the enemies of God and humanity, as dangerous sources of sin and dishonor in local communities. Burton violated the Caroline circle of order and identified the introduction of the Book of Sports as the source of this dishonor. He manipulated common local anxieties over divine judgments, such as the plague, in order to convert a more general audience to the strict Sabbatarian position on the Book of Sports, a relatively uncontroversial measure in many parish communities. The boundaries of the Sabbath *and* its Prayer Book ceremonies, Burton insinuated, had enemies in the local ministry, certainly in the episcopal hierarchy, and thus inside the circle of order itself.[72] "What could the Pope have done more," Burton lamented, "than some of our prelates have done in this kind, for the darkening of Christ's kingdom, and for the setting up of Antichrist's throne again in this land?"[73] These enemies of the Sabbath represented the essence of evil in both government and local neighborhood and could never be appeased. Burton used the forms of petition and prayer to request the withdrawal of the Book of Sports, but the continuous pollution of the Sabbath created a dangerous environment exposed to divine retribution.

The Sabbath-breaker was not the only literary monster abroad in the 1630s. An anti-Puritan counterpart of this Puritan conception of the enemy, the image-breaker, appeared in the publications of Laudians and Arminians as the embodiment of a Puritan conspiracy against the monarchy and the ceremonial order in the church. Peter Studley, vicar of St. Chad's in Shrewsbury, explored the violent delusions of Puritan enemies of church and state in his collection of anti-Puritan cautionary tales, *The Looking Glass of Schism,* published in 1634.[74] Studley used accounts of the anti-Christian obsessions of Puritans to defend the circle of order, which was represented as "the glory of [God's] most sacred name, the honor of our king in the vindication of his laws, and the desire of our church's tranquillity and peace, now torn into pieces by willful schism, proud faction, and peremptory disobedience to prudent and peaceable government."[75] Puritans introduced "the desperate effects of Satan's illusions" into parish communities in the form of "a spiritual pride" and assurance of election, "the imaginary sense of their adoption," and this fantasy transported its prisoners "beyond the bounds of Christian humility" to "expound the sacred scriptures agreeable to their own deluded fancies."[76] These enemies made equally delusive claims to revere the prince, but in Studley's view, Puritan disobedience placed a curse on the circle of order. "He that obeys not the law, which is by command of princely power and justice imposed on him, curses that law which he refuses to obey, for between obedience and cursing there is no medium or mean in the sense of God's spirit."[77] As a result of the intimate interrelation of the royal person and royal law, Puritan disobedience cursed the "sacred person" of the king.[78]

Studley's assault on Puritanism included a detailed account of the "extraordinary case" of Thomas Hickes, a mason of Tewkesbury. Studley introduced Hickes as "a strict, austere, and rigid Puritan" pursuing a "mechanical" vocation. Upon becoming a churchwarden of Tewkesbury in the late 1610s, Hickes was moved by "proud contempt of all ancient monuments" to pull down "a cross of stone" that had been standing in the churchyard "time out of mind." The stones of the cross were placed under the church wall and left undisturbed, "for it seems the people of the neighborhood made conscience of sacrilege." Divine retribution came swiftly to Hickes and was described by Studley with epic complacency. The next two children born to Hickes and his wife "proved deaf, lame, and deformed by monstrosity of body." Hickes nevertheless persisted in "his former opinions of schismatical disobedience," never suspecting "the hand of divine correction" to be laid upon his family "for his own disobedience to his prince or for his violation and defacing of the ancient monuments of other men's devotion." Hickes attributed his misfortunes to "secondary causes and errors in natural operations frequent in the world." He "never looked up to the hand of heaven." Some years after his first election, Hickes served a second term as churchwarden. During this second term, Hickes took the stones of the demolished cross "and, by cementing them together and hewing a hollow gutter in them, converted them into a swine trough for his own use." The unfortunate pigs that fed from this trough were instantly driven into "a raging madness" and died. Hickes was cut to the quick by misfortunes in his stock that had been lightly passed over in his children. He reflected on his past conduct and discovered, by the "terrible testimonies" of divine wrath, "the wickedness of his own heart, in abusing things once dedicated to conserve the memorial of the Lord his passion for our redemption." Hickes was subsequently so overcome by "the gripes, pangs, and tormentng terrors of a wounded soul" that he threw himself into a neighbor's well "and was taken up bruised and drowned."[79]

This narrative lends itself to the same method of interpretation applied to Burton's horror stories. Studley's narrative acquired its meaning from the five pairs of oppositions in its structure. The primary opposition in the text was the familiar distinction of sacred and profane. Hickes violated the boundary between the purity of the sacred order and the pollution of the profane world. The motive force behind the narrative was the process of divine retribution that followed this act of profanation. This separation of sacred and profane, purity and pollution, became the basis of further boundaries and distinctions in the narrative. The four sets of oppositions subsequently marked in the text assumed a position and a value in relation to each other and in relation to the definitive opposition of sacred and profane. These secondary distinctions, which closely resemble some of the elements detected in Burton's stories, are expressed by the oppositions nature/unnaturalness, providence/chance, human/animal, and society/individual.

The evidence of consistory court and pamphlet literature reveal, as a common assumption, the belief that moral and religious consequences of human action could be detected in nature.[80] The opposition nature/unnaturalness expresses this complex interrelationship of divine power, human society, and the natural world. The order of nature reflected, in the physical environment, the proper metaphysical boundaries of sacred and profane in human society. Yet natural causes could serve as channels of divine communication, and the physical environment might usefully be imagined as a text in which divine judgments of human behavior were inscribed. Violations of sacred order provoked reactions in nature proportional to the magnitude of the disturbance. In the context of the narrative, the consequences of his profanation of the cross were visited on Hickes in the monstrosity of his children, since distortion of the natural process of birth reflected divine disfavor, and in the unnatural death of his swine, since the magnitude of their master's sacrilege turned their food to poison.

The tension between providential and mechanical elements in the "natural operations" of the world introduced a politics of theodicy into the discourse on nature. In the structure of the narrative, the opposition providence/chance expressed this tension between conceptions of a world animated by divine purpose and conceptions of a self-contained world governed by mechanical laws. Burton assumed the operation of providence in his stories and seemed to assume his own capacity to interpret the providential design; moreover, his Sabbath-breakers, usually incapable of rational reflection on their actions, seldom presented alternatives to the providential conception of the world. The importance of this opposition in Studley's narrative seems to indicate a self-conscious need to capture the authority of divine providence, to reclaim the authority usurped by deluded Puritans such as Burton, enemies identified as image-breakers and schismatics. This process of reclamation had a quite subtle context in the story. Hickes, in his pursuit of a "mechanical" vocation, embodied the notion of the engine or machine as a self-contained unit. The vocation ultimately reflected a philosophy of life, as Hickes attributed his misfortunes to chance, to the accidental interplay of "secondary causes" in the world. This mechanical understanding of worldly events blinded him to the providential symbolism of the cross, an "ancient monument" maintained in the churchyard time out of mind. Studley represented the cross as an aid to human memory of the passion and of the providential design. As a memorial, the cross worked through human memory to transform the chances and events of the world into a reminder of the divine plan for human redemption. The opposition providence/chance acquired further significance from the distinctions sacred/profane and nature/unnaturalness, as the mechanical philosophy ascribed to Hickes produced a kind of atheism, a "monstrous" contempt for the symbols of divine order in the world.

Both Burton and Studley found a potent source of the evil and horror of enemy behavior in the power of religious symbols to differentiate humans from animals. The human possessed a unique relationship to the source of supernatural power and a heavy responsibility to protect this relationship in its proper sacred form. Hickes' decision to use stones from the cross to build a trough for pigs violated this unique human relationship and incorporated in the narrative a boundary expressed by the opposition human/animal. The cross was a symbol of human redemption and the promise of eternal life, a marker of the special relationship between human society and divine power. A wall of grace separated "human" and "animal" as cultural categories. The picture of Hickes as a breaker and defiler of images and his use of a cross to make a feeding trough for animals linked Puritanism to stultification of the divine plan for human salvation and to violation of the hierarchy of creation. This violation became an act of cruelty insofar as it exposed lower animals to a fatal power beyond their comprehension.

Studley's narrative used abstract distinctions and boundaries to form a representation of the social order. The opposition society/individual in the narrative linked the protection of religious symbols to the survival of human society, celebrated duty and obedience in the parish, and distrusted Puritanism as a minority interest. Hickes perverted the office of churchwarden in the commission of his sacrilege. Destruction of the cross violated the churchwarden's primary responsibility to protect the church and its symbols. This transgression of office represented an act of disobedience to the "prince and governors" and a violation of local trust, as Hickes usurped the power of parochial office to express his personal contempt for "ancient monuments" revered as objects of religious devotion by his neighbors. Hickes betrayed a sacred trust, a heinous sin reflected in the response of neighbors who "made conscience" of sacrilege. This pursuit of personal gratification in the name of duty became a model of the Puritan delusion. Hickes "pleased himself in his irregular courses" despite signs of divine disfavor. His decision to convert an object of communal devotion into an agricultural implement for his personal use completed the representation of antisocial Puritanism.

This interplay of oppositions created an image of Puritanism as a nihilistic and destructive perversion of Christian beliefs. As the enemies of true religion, Puritans pulled down the "ancient monuments" of their neighbors' faith and left only a barren, anti-Christian landscape. The boundaries in the Hickes narrative marked distinctions between the religion of the Church of England, which was based on traditional notions of God and providence expressed in the objective memorials of sacrifice, and the antireligion of Puritanism, which was based on conceited delusions of election and was committed to destroy the memorials of sacrifice. Yet Burton's collection of stories demonstrates how many of the structures implicit in the Hickes narrative could be used to support Puritan and Nonconformist counterattacks on opponents in the Church of England. In the 1590s, the opposition human/animal had informed the Nonconformist assertion that "the bread allowed in the Queen's injunctions for to serve communion was made with dog's grease."[81] Burton and Studley manipulated the oppositions implicit in religious symbols in order to create a conception of the enemy, to communicate the message of conspiracy on a national, international, and cosmic scale. Charles had prohibited this partisan conflict in religion as uniquely dangerous to church and state, and a close analysis of religious symbols and texts reveals a cause for concern. These symbols embodied classificatory schemes, used to create and interpret the order of the world beyond the immediate context of ceremony. Conflicts over religion possessed an expansive power, a power to evolve into deeper controversies over the meaning of everyday experience.

Burton and Studley represented powerful lay and clerical interests, but the politics of religion in the 1630s cannot be reduced to the conflict of Puritans and anti-Puritans. The authority of religious symbols ensured that controversial events, such as the events described in the Hickes narrative, resulted in multiple interpretations, as diverse interests attempted to capture the power and influence of religious symbols. This "extraordinary case" of Thomas Hickes survives in four distinct versions. Studley recorded one version. Another was scribbled in the margins of a copy of Studley's book possessed by the local historian James Bennett in the nineteenth century.[82] Bennett believed that the notes had been written by someone close to Hickes, but the statements could just as easily reflect local rumor. This anonymous account claimed that Studley based his version of events on misinformation. Hickes had never been a churchwarden.[83] He had been hired as a mason to work on the roof of the church and had "sacrilegiously" stolen a carved stone, "said to be an image of the blessed Virgin." The writer of the notes attributed no particular power or significance to the image and described Hickes' thievery as an act of "high presumption" only insofar as the stone "was not his, nor in his power to move." Yet Hickes' conversion of the image into a swine trough elicited the acerbic comment that the "base" use of the stone had added "vile contempt" to "greedy sacrilege." The informant observed in conclusion that neighbors had found Hickes dead in a well near his house in the final days of a sickness.

This anonymous account of local events challenged many aspects of Studley's narrative. The anti-Puritan stereotype had depended on the connection of Puritanism to the abuse of local office. According to this second version of the story, Hickes had never been a churchwarden. His profane use of the image was represented as an act of personal depravity but not as the betrayal of a collective trust. The sacrilege itself involved a different religious symbol, an image of the Virgin rather than a cross. This Catholic symbol possessed little power of retribution in the Protestant community, and the informant's indignation focused instead on the "high presumption" of its unauthorized removal from the church. Although the opposition sacred/profane still informed this interpretation of events, the sacred status of the image reflected its connection to the fabric of the church, not to properties inherent in the image as a representation of the Virgin. Hickes committed sacrilege in his violation of the reverence that was due to the fabric and property of the church. The events subsequent to the act of profanation were never represented as a process of divine retribution. Hickes was said to have died at the end of a sickness, and his mysterious fall into the well was not described as suicide.

These notes offered an alternative to Studley's interpretation of Puritanism in local society. The informant did not dispute the legitimacy of abstract distinctions, only their application to Hickes. In this process of negotiation, dispute of "the facts" became a means to contest the interpretation of events. A few elements of Studley's narrative remained, such as the opposition human/animal in the disgust for Hickes' use of the image as a trough. But this second version of the story attempted to protect the moral boundaries of the parish from the effects of Hickes' actions. A protective distance separated Hickes from the local officers sworn to defend the fabric of the parish church. Hickes had acted neither as churchwarden nor as servant of the corporation, and the sacrilege was thus a depraved individual's isolated action. Most importantly, the political perspective of this second interpretation differed from Studley's account, as the corporation and its officers were acquitted of any complicity in the destruction of the visible symbols of the parish.

The bailiffs, justices of the peace, and churchwardens of Tewkesbury articulated the issues and motives of this debate more clearly in a third version of events, prepared in 1634.[84] This version of the story was included in a certificate sent by the officers of the corporation to Richard More, a justice in Shropshire. More perceived Studley's account of Enoch ap Evan's axe murders in Shrewsbury as an affront to the honor of religion and magistracy in his neighborhood, and he collected local evidence to refute Studley's interpretation of Puritanism.[85] The certificate described Hickes as a man of good reputation among his neighbors, being "very honest" and "painful in his profession" but "never of ability to be near the place of a churchwarden or in the corporation" or in any other office. In 1618 Hickes had helped to repair the roof of the parish church but had not harmed the cross. A second workman had removed the head of the cross "in order to place a sundial of value" presented to the parish by "a skillful mathematician" to direct the ringing of the bells. As the south side of the church was enclosed, no other place was so convenient for the sundial. The churchwardens added the stone from the cross to other "refuse stones" in the church. When Hickes later requested materials to make a trough for a grindstone, one of the churchwardens gave him this hollow stone from the cross. Hickes never built this trough, and his wife converted the stone into a feeder for young pigs. After a neighbor complained of the sacrilege to one of the bailiffs, the justices of the corporation imprisoned Hickes and bound him to his good behavior. But the case was dismissed at the next sessions. The justices ruled that the stone had been too badly defaced to determine the "images or pictures" formerly engraved on it. The court also heard that unidentified neighbors had killed Hickes' pigs in revenge for the sacrilege. Then twelve uneventful years passed. In 1631 Tewkesbury suffered an epidemic of purple fever or purpura, a disease of the blood, and Hickes contracted the disease. During his illness, he consulted an eminent doctor who "prognosticated some distraction." On the next day neighbors found Hickes drowned in a well. No evidence could be discovered to determine how Hickes had entered the well. The jury for the coroner's inquest, being "pressed by authority" for a specific verdict, found that "by the violence of disease, being out of his senses, he cast himself into the well." Several of the jurors had to be threatened before they would declare whether Hickes had entered the well by choice or chance, voluntarily or accidentally.

This third version of the story contained no trace of the elements in Studley's narrative. The officers of the corporation represented the actions taken in the business of the cross as an index of efficiency and good government and thus stressed the integrity of local administration. The head of the cross, in this account, was replaced by a sundial only to facilitate the ringing of the bells for divine service, the heart of the Sabbath. In similar fashion, the certificate described the churchwardens' decision to sell unwanted stone as a public service. The justices of the borough ruled that the cross was a broken symbol and that the images engraved on the stone were unrecognizable, and acquitted Hickes from the charges of sacrilege. A complete exclusion from the circle of local office placed further distance between Hickes and the corporation. The account carefully created an image of corporate government as the guardian of established religion. This solicitude was expressed in the extensive repairs Hickes and his coworkers made under the direction of the churchwardens. The rapid response to the complaint against Hickes reinforced this impression of corporate loyalty to the church and discredited Studley's representation of local officers as openly hostile to orthodox religion. The certificate also eliminated the process of divine retribution from the story, as Hickes succumbed to illness only after many years "cheerfully in business."

These three versions of the Hickes story and Burton's collection of cautionary tales shared a rhetorical strategy designed to capture the power of religious symbols for political purposes. Studley used the oppositions inherent in symbols to brand Puritans as the enemy. He represented Puritanism as a form of sacrilege, destructive of natural, social, and political order. Studley hoped to attract the attention of a government concerned to preserve this circle of order and to pressure local officers, represented as sympathetic to Nonconformists and indifferent or hostile to orthodox religion, into a more systematic prosecution of Puritanism as Nonconformity.[86] This pressure should not be underestimated, as the earliest version of the Hickes story, a mere sketch compared with subsequent narratives, had prompted the Court of High Commission to intervene in local affairs. An anonymous informant claimed that the inflammatory sermons of the local preacher, John Geary, had created a restlessness in his congregation and had culminated in Hickes' suicide.[87] The case came before the High Commission in 1631, prior to the publication of the other accounts. William Laud, then Bishop of London, used this opportunity to inquire more closely into Geary's conformity and eventually presented the case, as the advocate "was not satisfied about the lawfulness of some of the ceremonies."[88] Studley's description of Hickes, perceived by local officers in Tewkesbury as "an high offense done against the purity of the place," thus raised the specter of local intervention by the High Commission. No corporation interested in the security of its charter and privileges could allow its officers to be connected so explicitly to religious Nonconformity.

If Burton used religious symbols to promote a strict Sabbath, and Studley employed similar methods to advocate the prosecution of Nonconformists, the corporation's certificate evoked the image of an inclusive church and identified Nonconformists as errant neighbors to be corrected and restored to the parish community. This representation expressed the firm but deliberate policy of the local justices in their response to the allegations against Hickes. The corporation became the local ally of the church and used the law to discover and reform any departures from orthodox religion. Unlike outsiders, local officers understood the peculiar circumstances of each case, and problems could best be resolved by local application of law. This mentality rejected both Puritan and anti-Puritan representations of the enemy. Churchwardens in the early 1630s prosecuted clerical Nonconformists in order to isolate hardened radicals and continued to require only repentance to restore misdirected neighbors to the orthodox community of the Prayer Book and the parish.

Despite differences in the specific representations of Sabbath and cross, the Puritan and conformist accounts of sacrilege illustrate the powers of religious symbolism. These symbols created the parish com-

munity and, in the process, expressed its relationship to royal government, to the church hierarchy, and to God. As a result of this creative
power, conflicts over symbols and ceremonies in the parish differed fundamentally from other forms of conflict. Partisans of Puritan and anti-
Puritan notions of the religious enemy claimed the cause of a general
humanity and reviled their opponents as the servants of demons. These
stereotypes of the enemy demanded a political response to the presence
of evil. Burton advocated the withdrawal of the Book of Sports to protect
the Sabbath from pollution. Studley used the questionable conformity of
local officers to justify the more decisive intervention of institutions such
as the High Commission to promote religious uniformity. The corporation of Tewkesbury linked the interests of orthodox religion to the local
enforcement of law and represented local officers as the most effective
defenders of the circle of order against both strict Sabbatarians and mis-
informed clerical pamphleteers.

The local response to Nonconformity in the early 1630s took the form of
an assault on its clerical leaders in the Church of England. This response
may have been forced on churchwardens by the increased scale of Nonconformity but also expressed a common view of extreme Puritanism
as the disruptive behavior of a few clerical malcontents. An uncharacteristic flurry of activity against lay Nonconformists in response to Laud's
visitation in 1635 reveals the increased numbers attracted to the Nonconformist style since the early 1600s. Churchwardens in Ashchurch
prosecuted forty of their neighbors in 1635 for absence from the parish
on the Sabbath. These delinquents preferred the services conducted by
the Nonconformist preachers John Geary in Tewkesbury and William
Blackwell in Beckford.[89] Churchwardens in Tewkesbury presented thirty
Nonconformists in 1635. A refusal to kneel in communion and to stand
at the prescribed moments in divine service continued to mark the Nonconformist style.[90] Much of its attraction emanated from charismatic
clerical leaders such as Humphrey Fox and Benjamin Baxter of Forthampton, John Geary of Tewkesbury, and Robert Huntington of Deerhurst. These ministers, frequently on the outskirts of conformity if not
suspended from their benefices, understood the importance of mutual
aid and communication in the survival of their discipline. William Blackwell and John Geary were close to Humphrey Fox, the former curate of
Tewkesbury and Forthampton, who was suspended for Nonconformity

in 1630.[91] Local officers focused their attention on this clerical leadership as the source of lay Nonconformity. Only six presentments made between 1631 and 1634 involved Nonconformists beyond the circle of clerical leaders.[92]

Humphrey Fox's career exemplified this assault on prominent clerical Nonconformists. Fox became the curate of Forthampton in 1616, after suspension from the cure of Tewkesbury in 1602.[93] Robert Mayle, the most powerful supporter of Thomas Drake in the violent dispute over ceremonies in 1606, had acquired the manor of Forthampton in 1612 and probably nominated Fox for the cure. The lord of the manor paid the curate's stipend and held a customary right to make the nomination.[94] Bishop Miles Smith and his chancellor, John Seman, apparently suspected Fox's attitude toward Prayer Book ceremonies and refused to license his curacy in Forthampton. Smith seems to have forgotten his "sweet and soft words of meekness" and reconciliation. Fox heard only "the voice of thunder," suspension, and excommunication between 1619 and 1622.[95] After five years of relative peace under Bishop Goodman, who was not noted for his conciliatory attitude to Nonconformist preachers, Fox received his final suspension in 1630.[96] Fox retained a measure of support in the neighborhood, despite the interdictions of the court, and local officers in the 1630s could not prevent him from conducting services in contempt of his suspension. In 1634 Fox violated his suspension and several parish boundaries to preside over a baptism held in Deerhurst for Thomas Smith's child of the Leigh.[97] Smith doubtless solicited Fox's presence because of his known willingness to omit the sign of the cross in baptism. This kind of vigorous prosecution, despite mixed success in Humphrey Fox's case, did make it more difficult for clerical Nonconformists to clothe themselves in the authority of the established church. These tactics enabled churchwardens to force Nonconformist preachers and their followers to face the choice between separation and conformity.

Despite Laud's complaints of Bishop Goodman's heterodoxy and incompetence, it appears that the local officers of the church made a serious attempt to enforce ceremonial conformity, as several Nonconformist ministers, in addition to Fox, were prosecuted by their churchwardens in the early 1630s.[98] John Geary of Tewkesbury was suspended in 1634 for refusal to conform to the "canons and constitutions" of the Church of England.[99] Robert Huntington, the curate of Deerhurst, was prosecuted in the same year for failure to wear the surplice. More seriously, Huntington allowed Humphrey Fox to conduct baptisms in the Nonconformist style and "to officiate part of his ministerial function in Deerhurst" in defiance of his suspension.[100] The churchwardens of Tredington presented their vicar William Jones before the High Commission in 1635 for "undutiful speeches against the queen" in his sermon.[101] These efforts demanded cooperation and even a certain initiative on the part of churchwardens to impose ceremonial conformity and the decorum of the circle of order on local clerics.

Yet the efforts failed in their main objectives for reasons related to the increased power and organization of Nonconformity in the vale. The benefices in northern Gloucestershire were poor and often inadequate to sustain a family. Before the augmentations of the later seventeenth century, the living of Ashchurch was valued at £10, Deerhurst at £6, Forthampton at £10, Tewkesbury at £10, and Tredington at £8.[102] The curates of such impoverished benefices often acquired local property to avoid dependence on meager stipends. Humphrey Fox leased over ninety acres of Lady Mary Cooper's land around Tewkesbury at a nominal rent in 1632, and a local report described him in 1640 as "a deprived but wealthy man."[103] Property on this scale placed ministers beyond the financial control of the bishop and afforded suspended ministers the economic security to take up permanent residence in their former benefices. Unlike Thomas Drake of Forthampton in the early 1600s, deprived of his official income and forced to depend on "relief and maintenance" from sympathetic parishioners, Fox could rely on the support of neighbors and maintain himself in modest comfort. He could afford to resist diocesan pressure to conform.[104] The clerical leaders of Nonconformity could thus make the issue of ceremonial conformity a test of commitment to the movement for further reformation.

The solidarity of Nonconformist leaders ensured both economic and ceremonial survival. Since the pursuit of Nonconformist clerics did not consistently cross parish boundaries, the ministers were seldom completely silenced. Because the ceremonial style and fellowship of Nonconformity were essentially nonparochial, the persistence of a small number of Nonconformists in local cures meant open pulpits for the suspended brethren. Robert Huntington allowed Humphrey Fox, under sentence of suspension and excommunication, to conduct Nonconformist baptisms in Deerhurst.[105] John Geary continued to preach after his suspension in 1634 because Nathaniel Wight, the curate of Tewkesbury, and Walter

Fones, the curate of Tredington, permitted him the use of their pulpits. Fones was an incompetent curate, who was prosecuted in February 1638 for his failure to catechize and to read prayers on Wednesdays, Fridays, and Saturdays.[106] Geary preached monthly sermons in Tredington and reportedly paid Fones £4 annually for the use of the pulpit.[107] The mixed success of local efforts to eliminate Nonconformity reflected the indifference of Fones and other poor curates as well as the solidarity in leadership. Archbishop Laud's metropolitical visitation of the diocese in 1635 became the occasion of a more systematic assault on Nonconformity in the wake of this failure to silence its clerical exemplars.

As the system of presentation and penance overseen in the diocesan courts was important in the culture of parish communities, both episcopal and metropolitical visitations conventionally served in this system as a means to apply higher authority to local problems. The metropolitical visitation of 1635 started in the pattern of its many predecessors. Laud's visitation confronted two of the most intractable local difficulties in the 1630s: a hard core of clerical Nonconformity and the physical decay of parish churches. As the visitation moved forward in the early summer of 1635, most signs pointed to a convergence of local interest and church policy.

Many parish churches in the vale needed extensive repairs in the 1630s. Ambitious improvements or repairs placed a heavy burden on local resources, and most churchwardens were reluctant to undertake such projects. But modest repairs, the everyday care and maintenance of the church fabric, depended on local initiative. Churchwardens frequently prosecuted neighbors who hindered this work of preservation. Richard Beale of Deerhurst was presented in 1631 for damaging the churchyard wall.[108] In 1634 the churchwardens of Tewkesbury presented five people who refused to pay a rate for the repair of the church and bells.[109] In 1633 and 1634 John Cowles of Tewkesbury, the absentee impropriator of Tredington parsonage, was prosecuted by the churchwardens of Tredington for his failure to keep the chancel in good repair.[110] The condition of the fabric was an important aspect of the church's local reputation and a primary concern of visitations. Visitations tended to reinforce the position of local officers and placed the stamp of diocesan authority on orders for the care of the church fabric.

The disrepair of local churches received added poignancy from fears of moral disintegration, linked to the increased visibility of Nonconformity.

In Ashchurch, substantial farm families had been drawn to John Geary of Tewkesbury and William Blackwell of Beckford, and Nonconformity became difficult to dismiss as the antisocial behavior of a few clerical malcontents. The churchwardens of Ashchurch presented forty of their neighbors in 1635 for abandoning public worship in their parish to hear the sermons of Geary and Blackwell.[111] These "gadders to sermons" came primarily from families of modest rank but also included yeoman families, such as the Slicers of Aston on Carrant. The ceremonial appeal of Nonconformity enhanced other forms of attraction, and the Slicers, Salisburys, Jordens, and Ockells, families included among the delinquents in 1635, had formed bonds of kinship since the early 1600s.[112] Although solidly represented in the middle ranks of parish society, lay Nonconformists lacked the confrontational confidence of their clerical leaders and found it difficult to stand apart from their neighbors. Of forty delinquents from Ashchurch presented in the court, thirty-six recanted and the other four agreed to certify proper attendance in the future.[113]

The churchwardens of Tewkesbury prosecuted thirty Nonconformists in 1635. These cases, which present a microcosm of the urban economy, include a carpenter, a joiner, a cooper, two tailors, two weavers, two hosiers, two cutlers, a painter, a mason, a tanner, a saddler, a glover, a shoemaker, two husbandmen, and two maltmakers.[114] Six Nonconformists and their families were sufficiently poor to require aid from the Giles Geast charity in 1635. The charity list included Valentine Little's wife in Salter Lane, Thomas Holtam's wife in Barton Street, Henry Lane, Francis Godwin's wife, George Windows, and Richard Brush's wife in the High Street.[115] The scale of Nonconformity is more difficult to assess in Tewkesbury than in Ashchurch, because the churchwardens presented individual men rather than families. Unlike the pattern in Ashchurch, the presentments in Tewkesbury create the impression of isolation and now included no gentlemen, no leaders of the corporation. This impression is reinforced by the rapid recantation of all the accused.[116] Despite the fears of lay Nonconformists and the speed of recantation in the courts, an anonymous resentment of the church hierarchy remained. A playful caricature of diocesan authority followed the public citation of Humphrey Fox in Tewkesbury for heterodoxy in the conduct of baptism. Robert Carter, the apparitor, complained that someone in the church "pinned a rag upon his back" to show contempt for the citation, perhaps in mockery of the surplice.[117] As the scale of presentments indicates, local officers embraced Laud's visitation in the summer of 1635 as an opportunity to halt the process of spiritual disintegration in parish communities.

These perceptions of the visitation as a means to resolve intractable local problems did not survive the summer because the metropolitical visitation of 1635 was not a conventional visitation. Laud had full royal support in 1635 and used the visitation to make his ceremonial vision of the church into local religious practice.[118] The commissioners who were employed to conduct the visitation carried into the parish communities of the vale, in the form of ecclesiastical policy, the notions of the enemy that had been created by the conflict of Puritan and Arminian factions in the church. Laud's ceremonialism was a stylistic departure from the reformed church discipline, the limited Sabbatarianism, introduced in parish communities in the 1590s and enforced in the early 1600s. The Book of Sports had only confined sermons to the conventional order of divine service. Laudian ceremonialism reduced the importance of the sermon in the context of divine service itself. Laud stressed the authority of sacred *objects*, a view expressed visually in fixed communion tables, surrounded by rails and separated from the community in the manner of traditional altars, and also expressed in efforts to protect the sanctity of church property.[119] This view of symbols and ceremonies departed from the reformed emphasis on the abstract nature of the Sabbath, on the inner Sabbath and the circumcision of the heart as a necessary prelude to the sacred knowledge communicated in the Prayer Book. Laud appeared to renounce the reformed notion of the sacred as represented but never contained in objective forms and symbols. The circle of order in church and state had not been redrawn so decisively in local life since the early days of the Reformation.

The visitation had an immediate impact. In Tewkesbury, special commissioners appointed to conduct the visitation on Laud's behalf gave detailed instructions for the movement of the communion table. These orders moved the table, fashioned from a large marble stone, east to "the uppermost part of the chancel ending north and south" and placed rails around it, supposedly "to keep out dogs" and other "noisome" creatures. A rhetoric of pollution and violation, which was used extensively in the visitation, carried into the discipline of local churches the rhetoric Studley had used to such dramatic effect in the Hickes narrative.[120] A second detailed list of instructions concerned the physical condition of the church and churchyard. The offenses and orders included minor concerns like whiting and paving as well as major structural repairs for the roof and the tower, where "ruinous" leads, the sheets of lead used in roofing, had started to damage the timber. This culpable neglect of the church fabric was compounded by ceremonial deficiencies, such as the failure to display the proper symbols of authority in the church interior. Churchwardens had neglected the royal arms, the Lord's Prayer, the Creed, and the Ten Commandments. The commissioners also chastised the churchwardens of Ashchurch and Deerhurst for the "indecent" condition of their churchyards and articulated a general impression of negligence and pollution in their complaint that local officers and parishioners allowed pigs to lie in the churchyard for want of a gate.[121]

These orders transformed the ceremony and economy of the parish church. The movement and separation of the communion table created a *framework* of ceremony and communion visually quite similar to the traditional Catholic framework, despite the persistence of Prayer Book ceremonies in this new framework. Laud's apparent confinement of the sacred in fixed objects, such as the railed communion table, contravened local efforts since the 1590s to build the parish community on the unseen spiritual foundations of the sacred implicit in the Prayer Book Sabbath, an unwritten article of inner faith. Laud's visitation appeared to reassert the primary authority of external objects in religious devotion. His closure of the local churchyards seemed to imply a sacred quality inherent in church property. The churchwardens of Tewkesbury customarily rented the churchyard as pasture and sold the manure at the end of the year. Before the prohibitions of the 1630s, this agricultural income yielded important revenue to the church, and subsequent local resistance to official demands for the beautification of parish churches must be understood in the context of diminished customary revenue. Laud's interdiction disrupted the local economy of the church, as the closure of churchyards forced churchwardens into a greater dependence on unpopular parish rates to repair and improve the church fabric.[122] The reaction to this visitation in the vale gradually divided parish communities from the church hierarchy on questions of ceremony. By the autumn of 1635, the general persecution of lay and clerical Nonconformists, so prominent in the early days of the visitation, had ceased.

The evidence of local reaction to Laud's metropolitical visitation is difficult to interpret. Julian Davies is mistaken in his account of the "rigorous" implementation of visitation instructions in the vale. Davies rather curiously refers to the churchwardens' accounts for 1627 in order to demonstrate compliance and the execution of the altar policy in Tewkesbury after 1635, but even the correct accounts for 1635 and 1636 allude only to the repair of rails in the churchyard.[123] After the visitation, Goodman summoned the churchwardens of every parish in Winchcombe deanery to appear before the court. The enigmatic phrase "to show cause," written under the churchwardens' names in the court book, seems to indicate the unsatisfactory implementation of the visitation orders in Tewkesbury. Goodman sent a servant to inspect Tewkesbury Abbey in 1636, and in the same year an emergency rate in the parish helped to finance some of the repairs that Laud's commissioners had ordered. This collection followed close on a rate of £125, assessed in 1632 to recast the bells and repair the church fabric. All told, the churchwardens spent £80 on the upkeep of the abbey in 1636, about four times their usual expenditure.[124] But the only initiative to promote uniformity in the internal architecture of the church, an important issue in the visitation, was the acquisition in 1638 of a table of the forbidden degrees of marriage.[125] Tredington and Deerhurst had not even certified the location of their communion tables as late as 1638.[126] The churchwardens also disregarded Laud's closure of the churchyards. Although the churchyard in Tewkesbury was not rented in 1635, churchwardens rented the land as pasture for the remainder of the 1630s.[127]

The important consequences of Laud's visitation appeared less in the actual modification of local religious practice than in the creation of distrust between parish communities and the church hierarchy.[128] The ceremonial view of the sacred reflected in the visitation orders narrowed the distance between Prayer Book Sabbatarianism and Nonconformity in the vale. These disciplinary styles had been close in the 1590s and became closer after 1635, as Nonconformity became the vehicle for active support of a broader reformed view of ceremonies. This shift in the politics of religion helps to explain the disintegration of local efforts to purge Nonconformity from the parish. Churchwardens in the northern vale parishes presented only three lay Nonconformists in the years after Laud's visitation, although dearth in 1637 and 1638 caused presentments of other kinds to increase.[129] The subtle affinity between Nonconformity and Prayer Book Protestantism after 1635 culminated in the election of an avowed Nonconformist to the churchwarden's office in 1639. Nicholas Mearson served as churchwarden of Tewkesbury in 1639, despite his conviction "for sitting at the time of divine service" in 1635. The parish assembly made an even more emphatic statement the next year in its election of Mearson and William Haines, prosecuted in 1635 for his refusal to kneel for the sacrament.[130]

Peter Lake has described the emergence of a similar Protestant solidarity in the neighborhood of Shrewsbury.[131] Yet mutual suspicion rendered the solidarity of conformists and Nonconformists uncertain in the Vale of Gloucester. Churchwardens continued to prosecute public statements of sedition or Separatism. In 1637 George Richards of Tewkesbury denied that the Church of England was a true church, and his neighbor Richard Walker said "that the word of God was not preached as it ought to be, that the Lord's Prayer was not a prayer, and that he was sorry [the people of] England were so simple" as to mistake it for a prayer.[132] Richards never appeared in court after his citation in Tewkesbury Abbey and quietly disappeared from the court records. Walker was already excommunicated for previous offenses and, indeed, had been prosecuted for failure to seek absolution. The court noted his excommunicate status but declined to pursue civil penalties. Despite the ineffectiveness of the prosecutions, the churchwardens continued to use the consistory court to confront extreme statements of alienation from the Church of England.

The visitation failed to inculcate an attitude of reverence for the Laudian ceremonial order, but neither could it destroy decades of cooperation between parish communities in the vale and the consistory court. In 1637 the churchwardens of Tewkesbury prosecuted their minister, the conformist Nathaniel Wight, because he allowed John Geary, a suspended Nonconformist, to preach in the abbey. Bishop Goodman had lifted this suspension earlier in the year in exchange for Geary's promise to leave the diocese forever, but Geary soon returned to preach in Tewkesbury, and Goodman therefore renewed the suspension.[133] Geary and the other Nonconformist clerics in the vale not only resisted the Laudian order but also raised the specter of disloyalty to the Crown. The Book of Sports, introduced peacefully in 1634, became a problem after the metropolitical visitation, when Benjamin Baxter, the curate of Forthampton, began to preach sermons on Sunday afternoons in 1637 "contrary to the King's instructions."[134] Suspicions of Nonconformist loyalties appear to have intensified after 1637 and may have reflected conformist fears of local support for the Scots. Humphrey Fox was known to educate his sons in Scotland, and local officers, supported by Bishop Goodman and William Hill, town clerk of Tewkesbury, responded immediately when the privy council ordered a search of Fox's study in 1639.[135] These sensational but isolated examples of distrust hardly compare with the vigorous pursuit of Nonconformist leaders in the early 1630s or the prosecution of the rank and file in 1635. Despite the recantations in court, it cannot be assumed that lay supporters of Nonconformist clerics quietly conformed to Laudian standards of ceremonial propriety in the 1630s. As Bishop Goodman himself admitted, John Geary defied suspension in the late 1630s and continued to preach in Tewkesbury and Tredington. Benjamin Baxter of Forthampton "spared not to excuse, if not to justify, the Scots in their holy proceedings."[136] William Jones of Tredington remained "the very face" of "schism and malice."[137] Yet the prosecution of ceremonial Nonconformity in the consistory court declined dramatically in the late 1630s. Churchwardens continued to present the ministers and the more vocal lay Nonconformists for behavior or speech perceived as disloyal to the Crown, but Nonconformity in *ceremonies* had lost its strict semantic connection to sedition.

Laud's intrusion in parish churches diminished local trust in the ecclesiastical court as the means to enforce a reformed church discipline in the vale. The visitation also contributed to a more general atmosphere of distrust and anxiety, perhaps a distant reflection of conflicts in the civil government and church hierarchy. Local fears of political disorder surfaced in the proliferation of omens after 1634. These omens conveyed the unfocused anxieties of local leaders in the metaphoric terms of extreme heat and cold or of violent thunder and were dutifully inscribed in the records of the corporation of Tewkesbury by four different hands. In January 1635 Tewkesbury suffered "the greatest snow seen in the memory of man," a storm "so extreme cold, violent, and tempestuous that diverse going home from this market and elsewhere were smothered and starved to death." Despite the "extreme" heat of the following summer, snow and ice produced by this storm remained in Brockington Quarry until August, and crowds of local people gathered to witness the marvel.[138] On Sunday night, August 16, 1634, the summer before Laud's metropolitical visitation, Tewkesbury had been threatened by "a great and terrible thundering and lightning," in which "sparkles of fire flew amongst the lightning," and some houses were shaken by the thunder, "the like has not been seen or heard of."[139] These storms and afflictions, like the cosmic disturbances caused by the deaths of Elizabeth and James, were not linked to any particular event but seemed to portend some great change.

The specificity of omens increased in the late 1630s, after Charles had attempted to introduce the Book of Common Prayer in Scotland. William Hill, town clerk of Tewkesbury, entered a version of the "Scottish Prophecy" in the corporation records. This prophecy, attributed in the *Polychronicon* to a "holy anchorite" in the reign of Ethelred, King of Wessex, listed the common sins of the English as "drunkenness, treason, and recklessness of God's house" and foretold the punitive conquest of the country "first by Danes, then by Normans, and the third time by Scots." According to the prophecy, the final conquest by Scots would initiate a period of fearful instability so "diverse and variable" that "the unstableness of thoughts shall be betokened by many manner diversity of clothing." Hill also recorded Peter Heylyn's rather optimistic assertion that the prophecy had been fulfilled by the arrival of King James in 1603.[140] Similar fears of cosmic instability and political disorder were reflected in a Tewkesbury carrier's vision of soldiers fighting in the early morning sky over the Cotswolds. The vision was interpreted as an omen of evil days to come unless God composed the "ruptures" between England and Scotland.[141] These kinds of omens and prophecies exercised a continual fascination in the seventeenth century, but the unusual decision of local officers to record omens in the 1630s created a local register of deep divisions in the church hierarchy, the literary creation of monstrous enemies, and the proliferation of dark conspiracies to break the circle of order.[142] The echoes of distrust are heard in the proliferation of omens after 1634.

The anxieties of the late 1630s fueled local anticipation of a parliament in 1640. As early as December 1639 a letter from William Hill to the Earl of Middlesex carried bad news for children of the aristocracy in search of borough seats. Hill expressed doubts about the candidacy of Middlesex's children and believed that the corporation would look to its high steward, Lord Thomas Coventry, for leadership and direction in their choices. "I find in this town and everywhere," Hill warned, "an extraordinary care in elections of this time, when religion is so much concerned and the good of the commonwealth never more."[143] In October 1640 the corporation expressed similar sentiments when Middlesex proposed his eldest son, James Cranfield, as a member of parliament for the town. "Touching which business," the bailiffs informed Middlesex, "we caused an assembly of our common council to treat and consult. And however we all acknowledge ourselves much bound to your lordship as to desire so far to honor our corporation, yet this parliament being of infinite consequence both to church and commonwealth, we find in them and in other places an extraordinary care to choose gentlemen of age and experience."[144] The bailiffs and corporation attempted to manage the elections in 1640 and to exclude the general local concern over religious issues from the political process. This effort succeeded in the corporation's election of Anthony Ashley Cooper and Sir Edward Alford to parliament in April 1640.[145] But the council failed to manage the next election in October, and the town experienced a "great difference" over its candidates and its franchise.[146] A crowd assembled on election day, and the bailiffs allowed some freeholders to vote, although the charter did not clearly extend the franchise beyond freemen of the corporation to include freeholders of the town.[147] The result was a triple return and four members of parliament. Roger Plevy, the senior bailiff, returned Sir Robert Cooke and Edward Stephens for the inhabitants of the town. Thomas Hale, the junior bailiff, returned Sir Edward Alford and John Craven for the bailiffs.[148] Two indentures returned Cooke and Stephens, and a third indenture elected Alford and Craven.[149] Alford, Cooke, and Craven attended the parliament for several months before the Commons quashed the election and issued a new writ on August 6, 1641.[150] A second election in October 1641 produced a double return, when the bailiffs chose Sir Robert Cooke and Sir Edward Alford, and the inhabitants elected Sir Robert Cooke and Edward Stephens.[151] This return at least narrowed the contest to Alford and Stephens. In 1643 Alford was finally seated for Arundel, and Stephens received Tewkesbury's seat.[152] These double and triple returns implicitly petitioned the parliament to adjudicate conflicts that the town could not resolve.[153] The common council placed its faith in experience and favored traditional candidates, the heirs of the Hickes interest and families of landed estate in the neighborhood. The inhabitants of the town chose members close to the Nonconformist faction of Humphrey Fox, John Geary, Benjamin Baxter, and William Jones.[154] The bailiffs returned both choices and left the issue of the franchise in parliament's hands.

The parliament became a means to redress Laud's violation of the Prayer Book Protestantism enforced in the vale since the 1590s. In May

1641 the local reaction to this violation culminated in support for the Protestation, a "national covenant" to defend "the true reformed Protestant religion, expressed in the doctrine of the Church of England, against all popery and popish innovations."[155] John Geary, styled a "preacher of God's word in Tewkesbury," delivered a powerful sermon in praise of this national fellowship for "true religion."[156] "If ministers now be silenced against law for preaching down innovation, or people vexed for refusing subjection to them," Geary declaimed, "they may go to any peer or parliament man and, by his national covenant (he himself having first taken it), require and enjoy his assistance to be righted and to have his oppressing persecutor punished, whatever he be, layman or prelate."[157] Yet the published sermon rejected separation from the church and stressed the Protestation's service to the cause of God *and* the person, honor, and estate of the king.[158] After Geary's performance, four hundred inhabitants of Tewkesbury reportedly entered into the Protestation.[159] On the other hand, some local officers continued to fear ceremonial nonconformity as disobedience to the Crown. A codification of the borough "ordinances and constitutions" in 1639 not only had barred anyone known to hold "popish opinions" from the office of burgess but also had attempted to exclude the advocates of "any opinion contrary to the articles of Christian religion now set forth by public authority."[160] An atmosphere of conflict and uncertainty hardened positions and militated against compromise. Divisions among conformists over Laud's ceremonialism and vision of church government disturbed the cultural process whereby the consistory court, the local minister, and the churchwardens had helped to create and enforce moral and religious identities in the parish.

The petitions presented to the parliament in the early 1640s contain further evidence of this division. Two petitions circulated in Tewkesbury in 1642. The first petition defended episcopacy.[161] On February 19 Edward Stephens of Sodbury, junior member for Tewkesbury, presented to the House of Commons the petition of George Whitledge, a resident of the town, "in which he showed that Conway Whithorne [of Tewkesbury] and others had pressed him to set his hand to a petition for the continuance of bishops and had spoken scandalously concerning the House of Commons, and that upon his complaint to the bailiffs of Tewkesbury, [Kenelm Mearson and John Sclicer], instead of doing him right they had bound him to his good behavior."[162] As a supporter of Humphrey Fox, Whitledge had refused to attend church or receive communion in 1635 but had recanted after prosecution in the consistory court.[163] Stephens had carried the election in November 1640 as the candidate of a broad franchise in the corporation, a franchise of inhabitants rather than freemen, and hostile local rumor made him a companion and confederate of Fox, Geary, Baxter, and Jones.[164] On May 27 Sir Robert Cooke of Highnam, near Gloucester, senior member for Tewkesbury, suspected of complicity in this Puritan conspiracy, introduced in the Commons a petition that purported to be from the borough itself, "containing thanks for our indefatigable pains and for the good procured by us both to the church and kingdom, with diverse particular expressions much after the form of other petitions delivered in to us by several counties."[165] Laud's visitation raised unprecedented questions of religious authority and helped to create these distinctive positions, perhaps best described as ceremonial conformity and Sabbatarian conformity. The culture of the parish required a solution to these related problems of authority and ceremony, and the intense religious debates in the parliaments of 1640 expressed the urgency of this cultural problem.

The church discipline introduced in parish communities in the early 1600s, a discipline that was based on the Prayer Book and a limited form of Sabbatarianism, became a hotter sort of Protestantism as a result of the politics of religion in the 1630s. Puritan and Arminian controversialists used sermons, books, and pamphlets to connect powerful symbols of parochial religion, particularly the Sabbath and the fabric of the parish church itself, to partisan visions of the Church of England and its enemies. Henry Burton and Peter Studley, among the more strident controversialists, promoted Puritan and anti-Puritan stereotypes of the enemy, the Sabbath-breaker and the image-breaker, in order to advance political solutions to the problems of divine retribution, conspiracy, and the pollution of the national church. Local reactions to religious difference in the parish and in the church hierarchy shifted in the 1630s, as the rhetoric of this partisan politics exerted a subtle influence on the spectrum of conformist positions. Churchwardens and most of their neighbors in the Vale of Gloucester perceived Nonconformity in the early 1630s as the result of irresponsible behavior by a small number of clerical radicals. To preserve the parish, local officers attempted to secure the recantations of lay Nonconformists and the prosecution of their clerical leaders in the consistory court.

Bishop Godfrey Goodman and the consistory court emerge from the evidence of detections in the early 1630s as being more active in the pursuit of conformity than historians have supposed. The same general attitude to religious difference continued to motivate the prosecution of Nonconformity in the early days of Laud's metropolitical visitation in 1635, which was the last concerted effort to enforce religious uniformity in the vale. Yet this visitation introduced Laudian notions of ceremonialism and sanctity in parish churches and generated controversies over church repairs and altar policy similar to the conflicts that Andrew Foster has uncovered in the diocese of York and elsewhere in the northern province.[166] The significance of Nonconformity shifted in the aftermath of Laud's visitation and in the local resistance to his instructions. An element of distrust entered the relationship of consistory court and parish, as the prosecution of ceremonial Nonconformity declined in the late 1630s and a Puritan front formed, a hesitant alliance composed of Nonconformists and conformists fearful of Laudian ceremonialism. As the hotter sort of Protestantism acquired a new political significance, the common council of Tewkesbury violated the spirit of their own ordinances in electing Roger Plevy, a burgess convicted of Saturday Sabbatarianism in the 1620s, to the office of senior bailiff in October 1639, and the parish assembly of Tewkesbury chose avowed Nonconformists as churchwardens in 1639 and 1640.[167] The restoration of trust in diocesan institutions became a major issue in the religious debates of the early 1640s.

6

To Unchurch a Church: Civil War and Revolution, 1642–1660

It is no small change to unchurch a church, to unminister a ministry,
and to unworship a worship.

Robert Abbot, *A Trial of Our Church-Forsakers* (1639)

And "Do you hear the news" was commonly the first word I heard. So
miserable were those bloody days in which he was the most honorable
that could kill most of his enemies.

Richard Baxter, *Reliquiae Baxterianae* (1696)

Before you live you must die, and before you be bound up into one
universal body all your particular bodies and societies must be torn to
pieces; for the true light is coming now once more, not only to shake
the earth (that is, Moses's worship) but heaven also.

Gerrard Winstanley, *Fire in the Bush* (1650)

The violence of civil war destroyed parish communities in the Vale of
Gloucester and evoked new forms of community from diverse religious
styles evident since the early seventeenth century. The armies of both
sides came to the vale early and often, as Tewkesbury commanded the
only ford of the River Avon between Gloucester and Worcester, offered
convenient access to the bridge over the River Severn at Upton, and
controlled the agricultural market of the northern vale as far as Evesham,
a vital source of provisions for Gloucester.[1] An army in possession of this
site could block movements into northern England and Wales and dominate the wealth of the vale north of Gloucester. As a result of its strategic
importance, the town changed hands several times in the early cam-
paigns of Prince Rupert and Sir William Waller and in the garrison

warfare fought in 1643 and 1644 by Parliamentarian forces in Gloucester and royalist armies in Worcester. Before the war, the corporation of Tewkesbury had constituted a separate county in all but name. Once the war started, a military calculus reduced the town to its strategic position between the powerful garrisons of Gloucester and Worcester, as street skirmishes and raids became a local routine.

The constant presence of soldiers and a military governor in Tewkesbury reduced the corporation's authority in the governance of the town. Practical necessity and the inner rationale of the charter, a document that never envisioned Crown and parliament as distinct or opposed sources of authority, induced officers of the corporation to accommodate the demands of royalist and parliamentary armies. To satisfy the economic needs of occupying armies, corporate and military officials constructed a new framework of authority and government in the vale. The new arrangement afforded civilian and military officials a greater power to intervene in the everyday life of the neighborhood. The construction of this system, the organization of forced labor, and the extraction of revenue made some of the hardships of war into administrative routine. By the late 1640s the denizens of the vale were accustomed to heavy taxes, quartering, and demands for manual labor by the armed forces.

The military administration of the vale in the 1640s, contrary to its avowed objectives of control and orderliness, proved a fertile soil for forms of religious fellowship implicit in the diverse culture of local parishes. Symbols of parochial discipline, as well as the cultural process of its enforcement, were among the first casualties of the conflict between Crown and parliament. The church court lost its power in northern Gloucestershire in the summer of 1641, as the same statute that eliminated the Court of High Commission abolished the coercive powers of ecclesiastical courts.[2] In the absence of the visitations and of the solemn administration of oaths, presentments, and acts of public penance that had formed the ritual idiom of territorial community, much of the institutional hierarchy and authority of the national church dissolved.[3] The religious discipline and ethos of the parish—the core and periphery of its cultural form—had been a product of the interaction between court and locality. The demise of the consistory court suspended the cultural process whereby the parish community had been created and sustained.

The parish subsequently dissolved into several religious fellowships, each expressed in a distinctive discipline. These new forms of fellowship and the process of their creation raise difficult questions of authority and order. Historians have often treated the crisis of the 1640s as a "breakdown" in the structure of authority.[4] This approach makes the proliferation of religious groups an aspect of disorder. Yet the process of religious division in the 1640s, as revealed by the evidence from the Vale of Gloucester, cannot be explained by models of order and disorder. Many different forms of authority, both personal and institutional, composed the distinctive texture of social relations in the seventeenth century.[5] Despite elaborate metaphysical images of uniformity and hierarchy, the diverse forms of order and community in the nation never became a monolithic social, religious, and political order. As local evidence has demonstrated, the English polity in the seventeenth century contained a variety of competitive and sometimes contradictory forms of relationship.

The religious pluralism of the 1640s and 1650s expresses a more subtle and ambiguous process if symbols of authority are approached as a language, constrained by complex conventions but rich in capacity to accommodate its statements or patterns of significance to new circumstances. This approach focuses on the cultural process whereby new and potentially revolutionary patterns of community incorporated the attractive and persuasive authority of traditional symbols. The revolution in religion becomes less a breakdown of order than a diffuse expression of new forms of community, implicit in the diverse religious styles of the Jacobean and Caroline parish and in the familiar symbols of orderliness. As Gerrard Winstanley intimated in his mixed but evocative metaphor, the "true light" revealed in the dangerous circumstances of the 1640s could "shake the earth" or convey new significance to familiar symbols. This reconstruction and use of traditional symbols formed a cohesive element even in groups defined by a radical separation from parish custom. The coherence of the Baptist and Quaker movements in the vale, for instance, depended on the sectarian reconstruction of the traditional symbols and ethos of the family.

The revolution of the 1650s rationalized many features of the garrison community created in the war. The execution of the king dislocated the hierarchies of monarchy and episcopacy. As the parish communities of the early seventeenth century revealed many traces of the royal touch, the imagined religious communities of the 1650s reflected important features of the revolution's leadership. Cromwell built his regime on a radical separation of the symbols of civil and religious authority. The martial priorities of the 1640s furnished the symbols of civil order that were essential to Cromwell's style of leadership. This style combined the elements of moral vision, physical stature, and martial prowess to form a personal image of leadership. Cromwell led because he possessed the necessary qualities in his person, not because he embodied an institution or a divine right. Andrew Marvell, in particular, emphasized Cromwell's unkingly origins and "the force of angry heaven's flame" as the sources of his power for decisive political action.[6] Marvell's commemoration of the Protector's first anniversary in power described the Instrument of Government as the divine gift and Cromwell as a competent seaman, able to steer the ship of state away from the "sands and rocks" of radicalism.[7] Marvell also contributed to the image of the fallen warrior in his elegy for Cromwell.[8] Depictions of Cromwell as an instrument of divine providence, rather than as a direct representative of God, signified the distinctive sources of religious authority behind this personal style of leadership and differentiated it from kingship. The rhetoric of providence underscored Cromwell's merely instrumental relationship to God, a lowly and subordinate position of simple strength and plain heart, expressed by his refusal to reign as a monarch or to represent ecclesiastical authority in his own person.[9] Cromwell posed as the divinely appointed means to liberate the many Christian voices in the English church but disclaimed the authority to designate any particular voice as the sacred speech and language of salvation.

The ecclesiastical result of this posture has recently become the subject of renewed debate, as uncertainties over the nature of Cromwell's personal religion have been carried into discussions of the nature and cohesion of the church in the 1650s.[10] This open church adopted no articles of religion or common liturgy and appeared to insist on little save a broad toleration for Protestants. Claire Cross has argued for coherence in this Cromwellian church, on the basis of the continuous effort of the parliament to improve the financial conditions of the ministry and the critical activities of the tryers and ejectors in the 1650s, but she concedes the voluntary nature of the Presbyterian discipline and its dependence "on the initiative of the local clergy and laity."[11] J. C. Davis and Anthony Fletcher have attempted to shift the focus of discussion from ecclesiastical institutions to religious mentality.[12] Davis has emphasized the antiformalism in Cromwell's personal religious perspective as the source of his consistent refusal to embody his providentialism in a positive church settlement. This antiformalism represented the forms of faith as human inventions, harmful to the spiritual substance of religion and the purposes of divine providence.[13] Fletcher has focused on Cromwell's conception of godliness and his attempt to create a reformed ministry in a "nondidactic and nondirective" church structure.[14] The authority for religious practices in the 1650s resided in scripture and conscience, and the boundaries of the church constituted no obstacle to the peaceable search for Protestant truth, the liberty of conscience.[15]

This vision of diverse religious communities united by a common loyalty to the instrument of providence followed Cromwell to the grave in 1658. The "humble petition and advice," a response to the perceived excesses of radical sectarianism, had reintroduced elements of hierarchy and perhaps rehabilitated the royal office itself, even before Cromwell's death.[16] The symbols of royalty, such as the imperial crown, the cap of regality, and the orb, figured prominently in the public display of Cromwell's funeral effigy in 1658. This spectacle confirmed the royal office implicit in Cromwell's regime after the reinvestiture of 1657 and attempted to solidify the "precarious alliance of personality and chance" that underlay the Protectorate.[17] As his regime had reconciled contradictory interests by little more than the force of personal authority, Cromwell's death initiated a period of intense factional conflict that culminated in the Restoration.[18] Yet the accession of Charles II represented neither the end of a process nor the restoration of undivided loyalties in the Vale of Gloucester. The territorial communities created in parish churches had died in the Civil War. In the restored parishes of the 1660s and 1670s, religious belief and ceremony focused on the cohesion of the family, although particular configurations of families often used the symbolism of the parish to express their beliefs. Although the Restoration settlement constructed protective boundaries around an episcopal church and redistributed power among religious factions, it could not restore the parish of the early seventeenth century and did not decisively alter the spectrum of factions created in the 1640s and 1650s.

The choice between king and parliament in 1642 devastated the interrelated communities of corporation and parish in northern Gloucestershire. Tewkesbury may have "submitted passively" to both sides in 1642 and early 1643—certainly John Corbet believed that the town had lost its

"zeal of religion" and "former inclination to liberty" as a result of "frequent changes under many lords"—but this submission followed painful
public discussions of political duties and military prospects.[19] Defense of
the borough against the requests of either side appeared to violate the
principles of a chartered corporation. The civic culture and constitutional order of the corporation occupied a distinctive place in the hierarchy surmounted by king *and* parliament. The difficult local choices in
the crisis of 1642—the creation of royalists and Parliamentarians—undermined the symbols of corporate and parochial authority. The order
subsequently imposed by royalist and parliamentary garrisons was intended to ensure control of a strategic position and to maximize the
resources extracted from the vale for the prosecution of the war. Military
governors were more concerned to rebuild fortifications than to reconstruct lost communities. As traditional symbols comprised the most important field contested by the armies, the symbols of authority in corporation and parish lost their power to resolve or contain conflicts among
different religious disciplines. Diverse factions began to separate from
these traditional communities.

The first report of combat in the neighborhood of Tewkesbury is a
remarkable piece of invented history.[20] A newsbook published late in
1642 described a pitched battle between four thousand Parliamentarian
soldiers under Henry Grey, Earl of Stamford, and a mixed army of seven
thousand English cavaliers and Welsh papists under William Seymor,
Marquis of Hertford, and Edward Somerset, Lord Herbert of Raglan, that
was fought on the site of the Battle of Tewkesbury. Not only has this
battle left no trace in any other record, but in addition, the newsbook has
the marks of an ingenious if misdirected fiction, an attempt to use the
iconography of Yorkist victory over the Lancastrians in Tewkesbury to
assert the nobility of the parliamentary cause. A Shakespearean solemnity attended the players in this drama. The stern Protestant soldiers in
Lord Stamford's command "stepped upon the theater of death and danger, and, like good actors, performed their parts resolutely." On the other
side, stereotypes of the Welsh furnished stock images of the Catholic
enemy. The "wild Welshmen" and "demidevils" under Lord Herbert, "a
notorious papist," were described as "a horde," were "very bad firemen"
as musketeers, and naturally "took themselves to a shameful flight" at
a critical moment in the battle, a mirror image of the Lancastrian flight
across Bloody Meadow. The Parliamentarians cut down the terrified

Welsh foot soldiers "who, poor misled creatures, came as so many asses to the slaughter, many of them flung away their arms, and cried out for mercy, which the Earl of Stamford very nobly granted [and], after a modest reproof for their boldness in taking up arms against the parliament, making them sensible and sorry for their error, [he] sent in peace to their houses." This fiction reveals important cultural aspects of the war in the vale, as local records often describe Welsh soldiers as little more than animals, certainly "poor, ignorant" cowards. But the account's unique feature is the "plain near Tewkesbury, where the great battle was long ago fought between Edward IV and the followers of Henry VI," used to frame early stereotypes of the papist enemy and heroic models of parliamentary leadership in the field.[21]

Despite the intense factional conflict in the vale over the early religious debates of the parliament, the initial response to the prospect of armed conflict between king and parliament followed no predictable pattern. The borough council register in Tewkesbury provides some evidence of the uncertainty and alarm occasioned by local perceptions of parliamentary aggression. The observations that were recorded by William Hill, the town clerk, referred to "great men questioned" by "the unhappy parliament" in November 1640. The list of "unhappy" consequences included the charges of high treason against the Earl of Strafford, Sir Francis Windebank, Archbishop Laud, and Sir Henry Finch. A later hand altered the word "unhappy" in the council register to create "the happy parliament."[22] The corporation divided between September 1642 and February 1643, but the interplay of factions is difficult to reconstruct. Unfortunately, the most informative accounts of political relations in Tewkesbury in 1642 are contained in the depositions made in 1646 as part of an investigation of Richard Dowdeswell, a local gentleman accused of royalism. Because both William Hill and Thomas Skey were anxious to assert Tewkesbury's early enthusiasm for the parliament, their depositions misrepresent the defensive mentality of September and October 1642.[23] The early alignment of the borough does not appear to have been based on a perception of king and parliament as ideological poles. In September 1642 the royal cavalry "flashed through the land, as the lightning that strikes from one quarter of the heaven to the other," but in the same month Prince Rupert retreated across the Severn, allowing the Earl of Essex and his army to enter the nearby town of Worcester.[24] Essex used "great severity" to the royalist citizens and sent their leaders to London as prisoners.[25] After this occupation of Worcester, Essex sent a commission to Tewkesbury to raise money, horse, and plate for the use of parliament.[26] He was careful to respect local influence in his approach to the borough and allowed the coercive power of his army to furnish a silent persuasion from Worcester.

Richard Dowdeswell, who was a well-connected local landholder and former estate agent of Sir William Russell, a prominent royalist in Worcestershire, prepared and delivered the commission from the Earl of Essex. Dowdeswell named William Hill, the town clerk, and several other members of the corporation in the commission.[27] The commissioners addressed the corporation in the council chamber, and the voices of insiders made the argument for support of the parliament. Dowdeswell described contributions to parliament as loans and assistance to Essex as a precaution undertaken on "the public faith" for the safety of the borough. Yet the appeals had a menacing tone. Dowdeswell declared that "if the money [the burgesses] lent then upon the public faith were lost, he would not give them two pence for the rest of their estates."[28] After the royalist desertion of Worcester and the example of its punishment, cooperation with Essex appeared to be the best means to ensure the security of the corporation. Protection and defense were the primary local concerns in this early phase of the conflict, a defensive mentality further expressed in a detailed survey of the weapons possessed by the corporation and citizenry.[29]

The basis of participation in the war and the meaning of allegiance had shifted dramatically by February 1643. The peace overtures made by parliament before the fall of Cirencester contained a systematic presentation of the parliamentary position on the causes of the conflict and on the measures required to restore peace. The "humble desires and propositions" not only used the familiar device of "evil councilors" to explain the distance between Charles and his parliament but also stressed the royal contribution to the perilous situation of religion, law, liberties, and the privileges of parliament

> by the raising, drawing together, and arming of great numbers of papists, under the command of the Earl of Newcastle; likewise by making the lord Herbert of Ragland and other known papists commanders of great forces, whereby many grievous oppressions, rapines, and cruelties have been, and are daily, exercised upon the persons and estates of your

people, much innocent blood has been spilt, and the papists have attained means of attempting, with hopes of effecting, their mischievous designs of rooting out the reformed religion and destroying the professors thereof.[30]

These propositions made parliament the vehicle of a radical program of religious reformation that included the disarming and formal political exclusion of Catholics, the abolition of episcopacy, and other measures "for the rooting out of popery out of this kingdom."[31] Charles curtly expressed his support for the suppression of popery and his particular interest in new legislation to protect the Book of Common Prayer from "the scorn and violence of Brownists, Anabaptists, and other sectaries."[32] The shadows of familiar enemies, the Sabbath-breaker and the image-breaker, loomed in the background of this discussion. Clarendon observed a difference in both Parliamentarian and royalist attitudes after the presentation of the propositions, as the parliament in particular began to make heavier financial demands to prosecute the war.[33] The representation of Parliamentarian and royalist differences in terms of anti-popery and antisectarianism made the local choice between king and parliament more difficult to defend on the grounds of convenience or security.

Before the conclusion of peace negotiations, the storming of Cirencester by royalist forces under Rupert had compromised the Parliamentarian position in Gloucestershire.[34] Both the manner and the scale of the defeat assumed gigantic proportions in local imagination and contributed to the fearsome reputation of royalist armies. William Hill's account of the assault mourned the "many hundreds sent prisoners to Oxford in cruel and barbarous manner."[35] Another local account contained a wild estimate of 1,500 soldiers captured.[36] This defeat rendered the small garrison in Tewkesbury extremely vulnerable. The bailiffs of the borough began to doubt the commitment of the Parliamentarian army in Gloucester to defend such remote northern outposts as Tewkesbury, and Colonel Edward Freeman, the military governor of the Tewkesbury garrison, requested 60 or 120 musketeers as reinforcements.[37] After a council of war in Gloucester, Colonel Edward Massey confirmed local fears of abandonment. "Hitherto [Gloucester] had been lodged in the midst of many out garrisons, as the heart in the body, but now it had enough to do in its own safety, and the remote parts must be pared off, that a liberal nourishment might preserve and foster that place which was the seat and fountain of life to these parts of the kingdom."[38] Such was the view from Gloucester. Massey declared the loss of soldiers at Cirencester left him no choice but to withdraw forces from Tewkesbury.[39]

The departure of the first garrison of Parliamentarian soldiers was a decisive moment in the local experience of the war. The officers of the garrison joined a session of the common council to discuss the options open to the burgesses in light of the royalist advance. A military defense of the town appeared unlikely to succeed, as Tewkesbury occupied "a wide and open place, not easy to be held," and villages in the vicinity had volunteered neither soldiers nor arms in response to the borough council's pleas.[40] Despite later efforts to describe Tewkesbury's surrender to the royalists as a unanimous decision, accounts of the process cannot conceal the differences of opinion in the corporation and the new significance of allegiance. Nathaniel Wight, minister of Tewkesbury, and a lieutenant in the garrison named Beachor opposed the council's decision and rode to Gloucester in a final attempt to persuade Massey to defend the town. The council suspended its resolution, as the burgesses waited overnight for Wight's return from Gloucester.[41] This mission failed, and the corporation divided in the wake of the Parliamentarian retreat. Five boats of local families and their property followed the soldiers down the Severn to Gloucester.[42] These families may have viewed their action as little more than a tactical withdrawal. In March 1643 an expedition under Captain John Fienes attempted to restore "the well affected of [Tewkesbury] that abode in Gloucester," but a swift counterattack by Lord Grandison's brigade of horse, stationed in Cheltenham, forced the refugees back to Gloucester.[43] Many would not see their homes again until the late 1640s.

These families rejected surrender to the royalists as "dishonorable" and carried a measure of the corporation's authority and integrity into exile.[44] The burgesses who left the town in 1643 are difficult to identify, but the names of Christopher Atkinson, John Bach, John Lies, and Richard Yerrow, radical supporters of the Commonwealth in the late 1640s, return to the corporation records only in 1647.[45] This separation of council families brought the processions, robes, communal feasts, and other symbols and rituals of chartered authority into the field of dispute. The garrison was no longer a compromise made in defense of a shared interest. The corporation's submission in February 1643 articulated royalist and Parliamentarian positions on the nature of the Civil War and the allegiance of the borough. The council met on February 6 to determine whether the town should surrender to Sir William Russell or Lord Chandos. Russell seemed the best choice, being "a near neighbor and a sworn burgess formerly" of Tewkesbury, and the council hoped "to receive more kindness from him."[46] Thomas Jeynes and John Orrell, later charged as royalist delinquents, rode to Worcester to present the corporation's plan to Russell and to negotiate articles of surrender.[47] The council solicited the presence of Richard Dowdeswell, former estate agent and attorney to the Russell family, to make "some small present" from the town to Russell, to ensure the strict enforcement of the articles of surrender, and to seek clemency if Russell's soldiers "should offer any violence or unfairness to any of the town."[48] On February 7 Sir William Russell and his army entered Tewkesbury to levy the negotiated sum of £500, the same sum that Tewkesbury had previously contributed to the parliamentary cause.[49]

After the surrender to the royalists, the routine affairs of borough government remained the council's responsibility, but the separation of prominent families damaged its status and its power to resist the garrison's demands. The sudden departure of many experienced burgesses increased the council's dependence on the company of assistants. William Hill, the town clerk, remained in Tewkesbury after its surrender but later described his withdrawal from local government. By his own account, Hill pretended to have an attack of gout, remained secluded in his house for "diverse weeks," and "never went forth into the street" because "he would do [the royalists] no service."[50] The patchy council records of the 1640s make it impossible to assess the scale of the assistants' new activities, but the company helped to prepare a levy for the royalist garrison in January 1644. Before the schism in the corporation, the assistants had virtually no power or practical duties in local government.[51]

The symbolism and structure of military occupation imposed a new system of priorities and relationships on the corporation, the town, and the vale. Both the royalists and the Parliamentarians appointed military governors to control strategic towns. The successive governors of Tewkesbury in 1643, 1644, and 1645 received their orders from Gloucester or Worcester, depending on the garrison's allegiance.[52] The corporation was reduced to a civilian bureaucracy, which was allowed to oversee the routine administration of the town and to collect revenue for the garrison but was subordinate to the governor. The borough council's authority was not needed to collect the arrears of military rates. Officers of the corporation merely certified the defaulters' names to the governor, and soldiers then collected the arrears.[53] The council also lost control over public spaces and no longer convened in the Tolsey, the market house and town hall near the cross, a symbol of civic identity and public authority. The new order confined the council sessions to private houses.[54] A series of public embarrassments accentuated the corporation's humiliation and loss of status, in particular its powerlessness to resist Sir William Russell's decision in 1643 to disarm the town and send its weapons to the armory in Worcester.[55]

The division of the council and the departure of important families in 1643 also affected the order of the parish, although the abolition of the church court in 1641 had compromised the parish communities in the vale even before the war started. The corporation's traditional duties included the supervision of churchwardens and the annual inspection of their accounts.[56] Churchwardens in Tewkesbury found it increasingly difficult in the 1640s to enforce their authority and to levy local rates. By 1645 the churchwardens simply hired soldiers to collect the arrears.[57] The abolition of the diocese and the reduction of the corporation's authority in its parish had a profound impact on the exercise of religious discipline in the vale. Most denizens of village and town continued to experience religious community through the symbols of the territorial parish. The churchyard and church fabric remained powerful symbols of local identity, and the ceremonial discipline of the parish retained its appeal for a majority of Protestants despite the shift from the Common Prayer to the Directory of Worship in 1646. Although the evidence of local responses to the Directory is sparse, the churchwardens of Twyning, north of Tewkesbury, surrendered their Prayer Book to the county committee and purchased a Directory in 1646, and then acquired a copy of the parliamentary ordinance for observation of the Sabbath in 1647.[58] This shift to a strict Sabbatarianism and a spare Presbyterian ceremonial style apparently did not affect the number of communicants in Twyning between 1640 and 1646. The churchwardens spent £1 8s on bread and wine to celebrate communion in 1640 and £1 9s 8d in 1646. Since a communion ceremony for one person cost seven pence, the number of communicants may be estimated at forty-eight in 1640 and fifty-one in 1646, figures that represent 17 percent and 18 percent, respectively, of the parish population in 1650.[59] This admittedly dubious evidence may indicate a familiar pattern of resistance to annual communion, although the problem does not appear worse in 1646 than before the war. Parish churches in the vale were not empty in the 1640s, and a substantial minority continued to receive communion, but the authority to *enforce* a particular discipline and form of community in the rituals of penance, weekly church attendance, and annual communion had been lost.

Despite the suspension of diocesan authority in the parish, church-wardens assisted in the local management of the war, particularly in the rural parishes of the vale. The churchwardens of Twyning helped to collect assessments imposed on the parish by the governors of the Tewkesbury garrison. Unfortunately, the wartime accounts of Twyning's parish officers have not survived, but the churchwardens' activities after 1646 reveal a new pattern of local administration. The constables and tithing-men collected most of the revenue for the garrison.[60] In 1646, however, the churchwardens collected the subscriptions for maimed soldiers and for captives in the King's Bench prison and the Marshalsea.[61] Although local evidence on this point is thin, churchwardens' duties in wartime apparently extended beyond care of the church fabric, as the garrison brought the office holders of adjacent parishes into its service. The several governors of the town subordinated the administrative powers of the council officers in Tewkesbury, and the churchwardens and constables in the rural parishes of the vale, such as Twyning, to the garrison's authority and purpose. The culture of parish communities had drawn power from churchwardens' authority to enforce an orthodox discipline in the courts and to punish violations of the sacred. As this culture lost its judicial rites of repentance in the diocesan courts and as parish officers were drawn into the garrison's administrative service, alternative forms of religious fellowship began to contest the authority of parish communities in the vale.

The demands of the garrison transformed the corporation and parish to create a distinctive order, its primary rationale being the extraction of resources for the war.[62] Ann Hughes has discussed the contribution of the evidence—its nature and the process of its creation—to historical perceptions of this military regime.[63] Because the local evidence of the regime reflects its financial demands, the community that it created tends to resemble a machine driven by the material demands of war. There is little local evidence of personal relations among soldiers and civilians, the human face of garrison life. A few examples of friendliness and mutual aid only hint at the garrison's partial assimilation in familiar patterns of neighborliness. Yet the distinctive order of the garrison society is clearly expressed in its practical schemes for taxation, the quarterage of soldiers, and the organization of forced labor to maintain the fortifications.

The royalist levies were heavier but less frequent than the weekly assessment demanded by the Parliamentarians. Sir William Russell required a £500 contribution to the royalist war effort as a condition of Tewkesbury's surrender in 1643, a gift intended to match the sum collected locally for the parliament.[64] Russell used an unpopular system of seizure and composition to raise money in the first months of the royalist occupation. His soldiers invaded the neighborhood of the town, seized cattle, and returned to Tewkesbury, where the owners petitioned and paid Russell to return their property.[65] A system of rates eventually replaced this crude form of organized plunder but could not eliminate the arbitrariness and irregularity of demands. In January 1644 a new royalist garrison under Sir William Vavasour faced short provisions, so that the denizens of Tewkesbury were forced to raise over £160 in relief.[66] The royalists needed winter provisions for a steady force of perhaps 1,500 horse and foot.[67] Two assessments were imposed in January. The first raised £22 6s 1d to buy coals and candles for the soldiers. The second, described as a loan but never repaid, delivered £140 to Sir William Morton, the sheriff, and Colonel Pagel, who were the garrison's receivers.[68] The close interrelationship of the corporation and the garrison softened the impact of demands on particular households, as the rates were assessed by street and took account of local differences in wealth and status. The residents of High Street, the wealthiest neighborhood in town, contributed £12 14s 9d for coals and candles. Church Street and Barton Street were assessed at £5 10s 4d and £4 2s, respectively. Officers of the corporation were useful to the garrison for the local knowledge brought to bear on the preparation of assessments.[69]

The Parliamentarians brought a precision and order to the collection of revenue that the royalists had never achieved. Massey created a new garrison in early June 1644, and a weekly assessment of £5 was imposed on the borough in August as part of a scheme to collect £117 per week from the northern vale to support the Tewkesbury garrison.[70] The assessors calculated the weekly cost of a company of soldiers at £21 16s. The governor's company was more expensive, since it contained 110 soldiers rather than the usual 80, and included the governor's salary of £5 5s among its expenses. The small parliamentary garrison consisted of four companies, and its basic cost was £97 15s per week.[71] Originally this weekly assessment was to last only five months, but the rate was collected well into the summer of 1645. The parliamentary garrison eventually took over £5,200 from the northern vale between August 1644, and July 1645. Tewkesbury paid £212 9s 8d, roughly 4 percent of the total collected.[72] This rate was assessed by street, like the royalist levies, and made allowances for poverty and incapacity, as the High Street paid £12, Church Street £6, and Barton Street £3. The borough's contribution to the garrison increased by £10 in January, February, and March 1645, to furnish "coals and candles for the guards" and to repair the bridges and bulwarks.[73]

The governors of the garrison, whether the royalists Sir Matthew Carew and Sir William Vavasour or the Parliamentarians Edward Freeman and Sir Robert Cooke, had to provide secure quarters for their soldiers, and this concern was a constant source of conflict between the military regime and its civilian subjects.[74] Soldiers in a garrison often received food and shelter in civilian homes, either in the garrison town itself or in nearby villages, in the system known as quarterage. The rules and impact of quarterage in the vale are difficult to ascertain before parliament imposed limitations on the practice in 1649.[75] Both sides practiced a system of unlimited quarter. In 1643 John Weaver of Boddington, five miles south of Tewkesbury, recorded a loss of £2 for his three weeks' quarterage of two royalist soldiers and their horses during the siege of Gloucester, and the time of quarter thus included most of the siege.[76] The repayment of quarter was rare and usually fell short of expenses. The value of provisions consumed by the company of 110 horse quartered for one month in Tewkesbury in 1648 must have exceeded the monthly assessment of £40.[77] The distribution of these soldiers led to disputes in the parish, as rural hamlets complained the town did not carry its share of the burden. A portion of the Mythe lay in the parish of Twyning and should have been deducted from the hamlet's responsibility for soldiers. The wealthy hamlet of the Park or Lodge, south of Tewkesbury, contained only three houses but was assessed at £6 and thus quartered sixteen soldiers. Because this distribution of soldiers followed the division of the monthly assessment, the town received only fifty soldiers, while the small number of wealthy households in Southwick, the Park, the Mythe, and Walton Cardiff quartered sixty soldiers.[78]

The practice of quarterage imposed the garrison's needs on the daily lives of civilians, but no consistent record of this intimate relationship has survived. If civilian hosts asserted their status, mutual suspicion could lead to conflict. During his quarterage at Pull Court, Richard Dowdeswell's seat, a corporal for the parliament quarreled with his host, using "very offensive words" and showing deliberate malice.[79] On the other hand, soldiers quartered in a place for an extended time could become accepted and valued members of a household. Another parliamentary soldier from Tewkesbury, who was quartered in Dowdeswell's house, helped his host's friends and servants to navigate a boat up the Severn to the lockstake at Dowdeswell's estate. Once the boat was secured, the soldier was invited to sit by the fire and to share food and drink.[80] Such scenes occur too rarely to support a general impression but hint at the potential for either friendship or animosity in the system of quarterage.

Since the garrison had to fight the local landscape to achieve tactical security, the soldiers employed Tewkesbury residents as manual laborers on the town's bridges and fortifications. The defenses in 1643 and 1644 included embankments, trenches, and two drawbridges at the town's northern and southern entrances.[81] The first evidence of forced labor appears early in 1644, when the royalists rebuilt the works "slighted" by Sir Robert Cooke and his Parliamentarian soldiers on their departure the previous summer.[82] The garrison soldiers ordered residents of the three main streets to work a specified number of days each week. Barton Street worked on Mondays, High Street on Tuesdays, Wednesdays, and Thursdays, and Church Street on Fridays and Saturdays. As in the traditional parish, however, this work was forbidden on the Sabbath. Sir William Vavasour, the governor, appointed an overseer of the works, and each morning a constable gave the overseer a list of workers to be summoned the next day.[83] The wealthy commuted their workdays to money payments, and the schedule of payments thus reflects the town's social structure. This schedule lists the names and streets of citizens eligible for work who wished to compound for their labor, the names marked by numbers from one to four. The mark "1" indicated a minimum payment of six pence. Of the householders able to escape forced labor, 130 lived in High Street, 98 in Church Street, and 47 in Barton Street. The soldiers collected £5 8s from this kind of commutation.[84] The Parliamentarians adopted the same basic scheme in the early summer of 1644, although the use of local leaders for the residential work groups made supervision of the labor force more effective.[85] In 1648 Anthony Norris of Worcester attested to the importance of forced labor in the discipline of a garrison society. He described how the royalist governor of Worcester had compelled Norris and the other inhabitants of the town to train and march alongside the soldiers of the garrison on pain of exile or consignment to the works.[86]

The arrival of soldiers and the formation of garrisons brought little more than fear and expense to the Vale of Gloucester. As the corporation and parish divided in Tewkesbury, the authority of the garrison became the primary source of order in the vale. The garrison's rationale restored a measure of routine to daily life but could not resolve many of the uncertainties of war. After the Parliamentarians' withdrawal from Tewkesbury and the town's surrender to the royalists in 1643, local loyalties become difficult to divine from the evidence of behavior. The civilians in Tewkesbury and its vicinity met both royalist and Parliamentarian demands for money, quarterage, or labor in return for a tenuous security. Many fears underlay the surface of routine, but the most terrifying nightmares of civil war in the vale, the fears of sudden and violent death, were realized in the raids and combat in the streets, the soldiers in search of plunder, and the proliferation of violent bands of criminals.

The local experience of combat in 1643 and 1644 included major and minor battles in the streets of Tewkesbury and in the narrow lanes of the Mythe, Twyning, Boddington, and Corse Lawn. In early April 1643 soldiers from Gloucester under Colonel Massey launched a surprise attack against the garrison in Tewkesbury, cut the bridge of boats that Prince Maurice had used to ferry his soldiers across the Severn, and killed royalist soldiers in the streets.[87] On April 12 Sir William Waller joined Massey in the town and led an army north from Tewkesbury on the next day to confront the royalists under Prince Maurice in the fields and lanes near the village of Ripple, northwest of Twyning.[88] The silent, empty landscapes in which the soldiers moved furnish the only evidence of local anxiety. On the morning before the fight at Ripple, Richard Dowdeswell and a royalist soldier, riding in the vicinity of Upton, met only Henry Spilsbury, a local minister on his rounds. Prudence demanded this withdrawal, as anyone seen in the vicinity of an army might be arrested as a spy. Dowdeswell himself, a gentleman of influence, had been stopped by a royalist soldier and, despite his protestations, taken to Prince Maurice for interrogation.[89]

Many dangers lurked in tactically important villages such as Upton, the site of a Severn bridge that Waller intended to seize or destroy on his march into the rural villages north of the town.[90] As the royalist cavalry secured the bridge first, Prince Maurice crossed the Severn, and a confused fight in the narrow lanes, hedges, and ditches of Ripple and the Mythe scattered casualties of both armies across the fields north of the town. Waller made an orderly retreat to Tewkesbury and installed a garrison under Sir Robert Cooke.[91] Yet neither side could maintain sufficient forces in the northern vale to secure its peace. Cooke made Tewkesbury's defenses useless to the royalists and quickly left the town.[92] There was further combat in the neighborhood after the Earl of Essex moved his army north from Gloucester in September 1643 and took heavy casualties in a royalist night raid on cavalry stationed in Oxenton, three miles east of Tewkesbury.[93] Sir William Vavasour and a royalist garrison in Tewkesbury contested parliament's control of the Vale of Gloucester in late autumn and winter, 1643 and 1644, and Vavasour leveled cannon at Boddington House, a small post three miles south of Tewkesbury created to secure Gloucester's provisions from the vale.[94] This war of attrition continued even after the royalists lost Tewkesbury in June 1644. Nicholas Mynn, the royalist commander, planned to assemble an army in Corse Lawn, four miles southwest of Tewkesbury across the Severn, to effect "the utter devastation of the parts about with fire and plunder, and to burn up the corn on the ground, it being then near harvest." Massey assembled a small force of 220 musketeers from Gloucester, 100 musketeers from Tewkesbury, and a number of "country inhabitants, armed with muskets and good resolutions," to disrupt the rendezvous of Mynn's army. These "country soldiers" viewed the Parliamentarian garrison in Gloucester as a defensive association. Richard Clarvo of Corse, a blacksmith, "was a soldier for the parliament as a countryman, the whole country associating with Colonel Massey for preserving the country."[95] John Canner of Eastington, a husbandman, served under parliament for six months in 1643, then quit for lack of pay "and afterward was a soldier in the country, as were many country people."[96] The battle among the "frequent enclosures" of Eldersfield and Corse Lawn left the bodies of Mynn himself and perhaps 170 slain royalists in the fields.[97]

Tewkesbury could not avoid the terror of street combat, although fighting in the town was mercifully light, given the frequent presence of soldiers in 1643 and 1644. In October 1643 Sir William Vavasour formed a garrison of poorly paid and discontented Welsh soldiers in the town, "styled himself the governor of Tewkesbury, [and] invited the country with promises of moderation and candor in all his proceedings."[98] Massey led an army north from Gloucester against this winter garrison, met little resistance from Vavasour's dispirited troops, and may have killed as many as 300 soldiers in the streets of Tewkesbury.[99] Demoralized Welsh soldiers fled across the bridge at Upton and, in John Corbet's words, "did scarce look back till safe in their own country, and it was to be suspected that many late knocks had beaten out their spirits, but chiefly that they were afraid of this country air, in which they could never thrive."[100] Vavasour returned in January 1644 to build a stronger garrison, and the severe floods hampered Massey's operations in the northern vale for much of the winter.[101] There was no further fighting in Tewkesbury until Massey surprised the garrison in June, and his army of 450 horse and foot "charged through the streets" to take the town by storm. The fragile discipline of garrison soldiers dissolved in the rush of this assault. Before victory was secured and the town cleared of royalist forces, the Parliamentarian soldiers entered houses in search of plunder. Corbet furnishes some slight evidence of the effects of garrison life on local allegiance. After darkness had fallen, Massey and the Parliamentarians might have secured the town more quickly, as the royalist soldiers had left their positions and fled north to Worcester, but "the townsmen, through fear, dared not give the least intelligence of what had happened."[102]

Soldiers in search of plunder occupied the darkest corners of this landscape of fear.[103] Sir William Russell, the first royalist governor of Tewkesbury, released his soldiers in the countryside to impound livestock as part of a scheme to raise money for the royal cause. The victims were forced to pay £1 per beast for the return of their property.[104] Soldiers of both armies plundered John Weaver of Boddington. In 1643 Captain Scriven, the Parliamentarian governor of Boddington, seized 19 bushels of Weaver's corn, valued at £3 10s, and Weaver then lost £10 in cash, corn, and goods to the royalists in their assault on the village.[105] Plunder often meant violence against groups or villages perceived as enemies of the cause. In September 1642 Parliamentarian soldiers from Gloucester and Tewkesbury, under Captain Scriven's leadership, assaulted and looted the house of Rowland Bartlett, a prominent Catholic in Castle-morton. Bartlett may have lost more than £650 in this attack, and his house was plundered several times in the course of the war.[106] These incidents and rumors of more brutal assaults gave credence to the threats of plunder and violence sometimes used to extort revenue or secure the cooperation of a village. Prince Rupert, reviled in the Parliamentarian press as "the Duke of Plunderland," reportedly threatened "fire and sword" to any farmers found to support the garrison at Gloucester.[107] In 1645 Sir Henry Bard, the royalist governor of Worcester, warned the "delinquent" villagers of Twyning either to pay their arrears or to expect "an unsanctified party of horse amongst you, from whom if you hide yourselves (as I believe each of you has his hiding hole), they shall fire your houses without mercy, hang up your bodies wherever they find them, and scare your ghosts into dribbling garrisons to make new committee men."[108] The familiar ethnic prejudices intensified the local response to soldiers. In 1643 and 1644 hundreds of Welsh and Irish soldiers served in Tewkesbury, soldiers who were feared and loathed as papists and cowards.[109] In 1649 parliament exploited the anxiety that the soldiers had created and authorized magistrates to "send soldiers" if anyone refused to pay their share of an assessment.[110]

These incidents reveal the shock and terror that soldiers carried into the vale, but the garrison's cumulative impact disrupted the local economy for much of the next decade. William Underhill of Forthampton, a farmer and factor for the Earl of Middlesex, described the garrison's devastation of the countryside around Tewkesbury in May 1643 after Massey's assault had placed Sir Robert Cooke in control of the town.

> I make bold to show your honor what misery we are in by reason of this powtrey town of Tewkesbury. It has been won and lost some five or six times, which will be to the utter ruin of the town and countries thereabout. For my own part, have taken away 12 oxen at one time, besides provision as hay, corn, and what not besides. We pay great payments daily. Mr. Dowdeswell is plundered of all his cattle, horses, and sheep, besides they have taken away Tewkesbury Ham and eat it with their horses, and would fain take him. Your tenants at Forthampton have been plundered of horses, cattle, and goods to a great value, and as for your grounds, there is no man will rent them upon any terms, for they think they will be eaten up from them, and as for your rents, men will not pay any. We are all [full of fears] as long as Tewkesbury is a garrison town, where all the armies lies daily upon us, so we shall be utterly

ruinated of all we have unless God out of his great mercy and goodness send us a speedy peace.[111]

Underhill wrote a second letter in September 1643, after the siege of Gloucester had ended and the Earl of Essex had moved an army north to Tewkesbury. The villagers of Forthampton "paid great payments of moneys to the one side and the other" and could not afford their rents. Essex's army in Tewkesbury imprisoned Underhill, forced him to compound for the twentieth part of his estate, and then seized another twenty "beasts and horses" before its departure.[112] William Underhill had made his service to the Earl of Middlesex a point of honor in 1634. "If this wars do hold, as likely it is," he lamented in 1643, "your lordship must take your farm, for I shall not be able to pay your rent nor to dispose of your grounds."[113]

Soldiers were not the only sources of violence. The assault on traditional sources of order in the vale, the assimilation of corporation and parish in the new order of the garrison, increased the power of small groups or bands. These groups, in a variety of forms, had always existed in town and countryside. Parish communities contained numerous coalitions expressed in terms of kinship, friendship, and neighborhood. Yet the violence and division in the corporation, parish, and nation enhanced the practical power of small scale coalitions. The important consequences of this shift included bands of criminals, often composed of wealthy householders and tradesmen. One night in January 1644, Richard Dowdeswell lost six sheep from his estate at Pull Court and sent his servants into the countryside with warrants to search for the lost animals. These servants heard reports of "a pack of knaves" in the vicinity of Upton, suspected in the neighborhood for thefts of sheep and other animals. Dowdeswell's servants questioned several Upton villagers about the lost sheep and were directed to the houses of the Branderds, a family of butchers, and of George Chandler, a glover. A search uncovered a stock of mutton and wool, and Dowdeswell's servants were convinced that it came from their master's sheep. The issue was settled when a member of the gang produced a gun and ended the search. Dowdeswell's impotence reflected local fear and respect for the power of this band of thieves. He resolved to question the gang members for felony "so soon as the times were fit for it" but in the meantime to forbear any further meddling in the business.[114]

The circumstances of war frequently undermined the conventions of order in the vale. A variety of personal relations, the conventions of the garrison, and the fragments of corporation and parish preserved in the military regime constituted the new order of the 1640s. This experience of violence, division, and fear may help to explain local reactions to the execution of the king and to the Revolution in the late 1640s and 1650s. The news of the execution and subsequent developments in the Revolution came to Tewkesbury from London. A chronicle kept in the Giles Geast charity accounts recorded the execution in just a few words. "This year, the 30th day of January, *anno domini* 1649, King Charles was beheaded upon a scaffold erected over against the banqueting house at Whitehall."[115] The laconic style of this brief note leaves an impression of disbelief and provincial distance from political and judicial processes in London. Yet the form and consequences of the Revolution in the Vale of Gloucester reflected the local experience of war and religious division in the 1640s. The execution divided the corporation once more, but many others seem to have accepted it as a means to end the privations of war. The occasion evoked no protests or demonstrations of support for the Stuarts. Charles served as a sacrifice, and the judicial elimination of a party to the conflict removed a stubborn obstacle to peace.

The Revolution in the Vale of Gloucester involved the interrelated efforts of the remodeled parliament and the new model army to express the providential identity of the English nation in local institutions and to restore the symbols of the corporation and parish in a purified form, appropriate to this providentialism. The first experience of revolution had been the exclusion of Tewkesbury's parliamentary representatives, Edward Stephens and his younger brother John Stephens, from the House of Commons on December 6, 1648, in Pride's Purge.[116] John Stephens, like his brother a Presbyterian, a supporter of the compromise settlement to end the war, and a member of the middle group in parliament, was restored to the Commons in 1651, perhaps for his moderate views and expertise in the law, but Tewkesbury lost its parliamentary representation in the early years of the Revolution.[117] The Revolution in civil government amounted to little more than an extension of the garrison system and the formation of a military dictatorship. But the attempt to restore and purify the symbols of the corporation and parish communities had a profound impact on the vale, as the process of reconstruction brought different interpretations of the war into local political arenas and led to recurrent conflicts over the meaning of the Revolution.

The Revolution in civil government created an institutional order and a political culture deeply influenced by the martial experience and mentality of the 1640s. The parliament imposed a new system of oaths to bind corporate officers to the Commonwealth, but the continuous presence of soldiers made Tewkesbury into a frontier garrison and the Revolution into a military event, a form of conquest.[118] In 1646 parliament had reduced the size of its garrison in Tewkesbury but continued to station 110 soldiers in the town in 1648.[119] Cromwell's maneuvers around Worcester in 1651 restored a powerful garrison in Tewkesbury.[120] The Gloucester council book records "dozens of bread sent by the several bakers of this city to Tewkesbury for the Lord General Cromwell's army."[121] This military presence occasionally provoked a hostile response. In 1651 the Tewkesbury churchwardens complained that the rental value of the churchyard had dropped from fifteen shillings in 1650 to five shillings in 1651 "by reason the soldiers brought their carriages into it."[122] But local officers generally avoided formal complaint and were accustomed to soldiers in the neighborhood.

The garrison provided a new framework for local government in the 1650s, and a network of garrisons became the administrative matrix for provincial towns and villages. The Tewkesbury garrison included parts of Cheltenham, Deerhurst, Tibblestone, and Westminster hundreds, as well as the upper and lower divisions of Tewkesbury hundred, in disregard of traditional administrative boundaries.[123] The garrison furnished the institutional framework of revolution, and its advocates derived its authority from the sacred instruments of divine providence, the Lord General and his army, hallowed by a succession of victories in the field. The interrelationship of local government and the military structure of command became more obvious after Cromwell's elevation as Lord Protector in 1653 and after the administrative division of the country, two years later, into the provincial commands of the major generals, who were the military governors in control of the army and militia.[124]

The Revolution made the garrison a governmental fixture, although more equitable methods of military taxation refined the system practiced in the war. The reformed system created rules to resolve such intractable problems as the duties of landlords and tenants. After the first Civil War, tenants were allowed to deduct the assessment from their rents.[125] Parliament also devised a new scheme to provide food and shelter for soldiers in civilian homes. This procedure restricted the kind and quantity of goods that soldiers could demand in private houses and limited the period of time that soldiers could be billeted in a neighborhood. If the inns, alehouses, and victual houses could provide for the soldiers, private houses were to be discharged from quarterage after two nights. The order limited all forms of quarterage to seven days. These rules applied to soldiers on the march, rather than soldiers in garrisons, but rational methods to accommodate shifts in the number of soldiers quartered in a neighborhood addressed an important civilian hardship.[126] The new rules to repay civilian loans made to Parliamentarian soldiers helped to curtail financial coercion and enhanced local confidence in the new order. John Man and Christopher Atkinson, the bailiffs of Tewkesbury in 1648, noted an improvement in fiscal responsibility. The corporation loaned £100 to quartered soldiers in 1648 "which was duly repaid within a month or six weeks."[127] The new rules of quarter on the march became law on May 12, 1649, and the corporation's officers made a detailed record of the law's provisions in the council register.[128]

The abolition of monarchy and the formation of a military government succeeded in the 1650s only because the representation of Cromwell as the Lord Protector encompassed a broad spectrum of religious symbols, sentiments, and interpretations of the Revolution. This spectrum varied in local communities and is impossible to separate from prior experience of the Reformation. The symbolism and meaning of revolution must therefore be explored in the myriad local religious settlements of the 1650s. Cromwell and other leaders of Commonwealth and Protectorate made a commitment to raise the standard of the ministry and to improve the income of impoverished local benefices, but, apart from reforms to promote a general Puritan vision of the godly nation, neither parliament nor Cromwell imposed an effective national religious settlement beyond the abolition of episcopacy in 1646. The Committee for Plundered Ministers and the Committee for Reformation of the Universities attempted to improve poor benefices in the late 1640s and 1650s, and committee decisions bolstered the low ministerial incomes in the Vale of Gloucester. In 1650 the vicarage of Twyning furnished a salary of only £24 and received an augmentation of £50 from the Committee for Reformation of the Universities.[129] Then a series of decisions in 1646, 1649, 1650, and 1651 raised the value of the Tewkesbury benefice from £10 to £60, and the Committee for Plundered Ministers made a further allowance of £50 for an assistant to the minister.[130] The additional funds came from sequestered tithes, formerly the property of the Dean and Chapter of Worcester Cathedral and local recusant families. In 1646 the Committee for Plundered Ministers used the tithes from the rectory of Wightfield, which had been seized from Henry and Thomas Cassey, prominent Catholic recusants in Deerhurst, to endow the new assistant's salary in Tewkesbury.[131] The sequestered properties may have failed to yield the desired revenue, since local officers certified the minister's income to the Committee for Reformation of the Universities as only £10 in 1651 and received a further grant of £50.[132] These decisions acted on the infrastructure of parishes and on the size of ministerial incomes but had little effect on the subtle local politics of religion in the 1650s. The Revolution in parish communities did not result from the decisions of committees and parliaments, as important as such decisions could be, but from diverse local histories.

Parish communities in the Vale of Gloucester were transformed in the 1640s and 1650s. The bitter factions in the church, the separation of sects, and the presence of several communities in the territorial parish made this process of transformation fundamentally different from earlier forms of religious conflict. Despite much fine scholarship on sectarianism and the revolution in religious mentality, historians have barely begun to explore this break in the traditional culture of religion.[133] The key problem in the history of Separatism is the symbolic representation of religious difference and its impact on social order, the power of the symbols of separateness to create new communities. These communities did not conjure cohesive power from the air, despite the claims of their enemies, and movements to break from the conventional order used forms of organization and symbolic power implicit in the traditional religious culture. The sectarian communities created a new cultural space in defiance of parish boundaries, but Presbyterian and Independent factions carried on the fight to control the corporation and the symbols of parish community. This conflict reached a peak of public intensity in the autumn of 1649.

The victors prosecuted relatively few former enemies in the neighborhood of Tewkesbury before 1649. The list of delinquents prepared by the county committee in 1648 included only the wealthiest and most prominent supporters of the royalist cause and a few unfortunate participants in royalist victories.[134] Thomas Jeynes and John Orrell had surrendered

Tewkesbury to the royalists in 1643.[135] Richard Dowdeswell had an active if murky role in Sir William Russell's garrison after the surrender.[136] John Man had served in the corporation's highest offices, and Thomas Millicheap and John Hilly came from prominent families on the common council.[137] In 1643 Theophilus Alye had held office in Tewkesbury, but the Alyes then followed the royalist garrison to Worcester, and William and Edward Alye of Worcester compounded for their estates as delinquents after the war.[138] Conway Whithorne had been a vocal supporter of the county petition for episcopacy in 1642.[139]

The number of prosecutions in the villages near Tewkesbury was even smaller. Anthony Rowles and John Roberts came from families of gentle status, owners of estates in Ashchurch and Tewkesbury.[140] Richard Gwynnett had his property sequestered as a delinquent from Tewkesbury, but the family estate lay in Wormington, ten miles northeast of the town, and Gwynnett, like many country people, may have moved into Tewkesbury during the war.[141] Several delinquents owned property in the vale but lived elsewhere. Timothy Cowles of Hatfield in Herefordshire lost tithes in Tewkesbury valued at £400.[142] Sir Edward Alford commanded a large estate in Tewkesbury and, as heir to the mantle of Baptist Hickes, Viscount Campden, had been returned as a member of parliament for the town in 1640 and 1641.[143] Alford retained his influence in the neighborhood, and the county committee accused him of complicity in a scheme to elect Sir William Russell for Tewkesbury in the "pretended" royalist parliament at Oxford in 1643.[144]

This assault on conspicuous royalists included the "papist" enemy, as the county committee seized property from the small number of local Catholics in the vale. The committee used Sir John Hayles' tithes in the parish of Ashchurch, valued at £200, to augment ministerial incomes in poor benefices.[145] Henry Cassey of Wightfield and Thomas Cassey of Deerhurst lost lands and revenue appraised at £566 per year, and Henry Cassey forfeited at least £140 annual income from the tithes of Deerhurst, reserved in 1646 to pay an assistant minister in Tewkesbury.[146] Edward Wakeman of Beckford lost £401 18s in land and £90 in tithes from the Mythe "to be paid to ministers."[147] The committee impounded smaller estates of £30 from Richard Reed of Twyning and John Vicaridge of Natton in Ashchurch.[148]

The brutal treatment of a few prominent royalists and "papists" apparently healed wounds in the corporation and eased memories of the "dishonorable" surrender to the royalists in 1643.[149] By the autumn of 1647 most families had returned from the voluntary exile in Gloucester and quietly resumed places in borough government. The divisions of 1649 were not apparent in September 1647, when a group of twenty-three burgesses that included veterans of the royalist occupation, such as William Hill, John Man, Thomas Hale, and William Whitledge, as well as such prominent exiles as Christopher Atkinson and John Bach, signed a pact of mutual assistance against the small hamlet of Walton Cardiff, east of Tewkesbury, and its campaign for independence from the town's burdensome rates.[150] These burgesses also agreed to share the expenses of litigation against "any person who shall refuse to be sworn either an assistant or a principal burgess and against any other who shall detain any money due to the corporation."[151] The council recognized its new dependence on authority beyond the corporation and admitted uncertainty about the intentions of this external authority, in provisions for any law schemes to receive prior approval from William Shepherd of the county committee in Gloucester and Richard Dowdeswell.[152] The truce in corporate affairs ended abruptly in January 1649, as the execution of the king divided the common council and the realm into rival factions. These factions used all available techniques and institutions in Gloucestershire and London to promote distinctive visions of settlement in the corporation and parish. A fragmentary record of the controversy, consisting of the petitions of local factions, the scribbled notes for a new charter in the council register, and a few wills, reveals an impassioned debate over the nature of authority and community.

A faction of Independents wanted to reduce and purge the common council and to form a religious fellowship that its opponents described as Independent. Although the faction's connection to Independency in the strict sense is difficult to demonstrate in detail, the term has the advantage of local currency, since opponents described the faction's candidate for local office as an Independent.[153] The Independents' religion can be inferred only from preachers whom they endorsed, but clearly it inclined to Nonconformity. Of the twenty-two persons named in the petition of the Independents to parliament, thirteen had expressed or would express Nonconformity in public action. William Crafte, John James, John Lies, and Richard Yerrow were prosecuted in the 1630s for their refusal to receive communion and for remaining seated during divine service.[154] Samuel Mosse and Francis Jefferies became Quakers in the 1650s, and the family names of Thomas Waters and Samuel Tovy were linked to Quakerism in Tewkesbury.[155] John White was prominent among the Baptists in 1663, and Henry Smith's views on the Sabbath, reminiscent of local Saturday Sabbatarianism in the 1620s, briefly divided the Baptist community in 1661.[156] Crafte, Lies, Yerrow, John Bach, Jonathan Crafte, and Thomas Jeynes signed a remonstrance from the Gloucestershire Independents to Cromwell in 1656.[157] Only Bach, Christopher Atkinson, William Crafte, and William Neast were burgesses, and the assault on the common council in the petition of 1649 may have been part of a scheme to gain more influence over the selection of a local minister.[158] The Independents accused their opponents of conspiracy to establish a minister of "violent spirit" against the recent actions of the House of Commons, a reference to Richard Cooper, minister of Tewkesbury in 1648 and a signatory of the Presbyterian *Gloucestershire Ministers' Testimony*.[159] The Independents' appeal to religious allies outside the council expressed a politics of religion, and in this sense a politics of election, but implied no position on earlier disputes over the franchise or on the political interrelationship of town and corporation. The faction's leaders, who had no desire to broaden participation in the corporation, imagined the reformed council as a smaller assembly drawn from families of religious integrity and proven loyalty to the Commonwealth. A similar interest in control of the political process snuffed the broader understanding of the parliamentary franchise expressed in the elections of 1640. The Independents in control of the council returned Valentine Desborough as member of parliament for Tewkesbury in 1656 on the strength of only one hundred signatures.[160]

The social structure of this Independent faction presents a microcosm of the hierarchy in the vale. The leaders claimed gentle status. William Neast of Twyning, a gentleman appointed to the common council in 1649, built his political interest on the Independents in Tewkesbury. Neast had served as a captain under parliament, as a justice of the peace, and later as a member of parliament for Gloucestershire in 1653 and 1656.[161] Neast's relatives and friends formed the core of leaders in Tewkesbury. Christopher Atkinson, his son-in-law, led the campaign for a petition to parliament in 1649, and Neast's "loving friend" Thomas Jeynes also stood behind the petition.[162] Yet bonds of friendship unrelated to Neast's influence were a significant factor. Atkinson remained close to Robert Fletcher after the Restoration and witnessed Fletcher's will in 1684.[163] Thomas Bulstrode, a barrister and a colonel in the service of parliament, may have joined the Independents in anger over the management of soldiers. Bulstrode was a newcomer in Tewkesbury but had married into the Hatch family and served as recorder in the borough courts.[164] William Hill believed Bulstrode's disaffection stemmed not from support for Independency but from the council's refusal to exempt him from payments and quarterage of soldiers.[165] This politics of quarterage exercised an important if indeterminate influence on factional politics. As bailiff in 1650, John Bach became embroiled in a dispute over the bailiffs' assignment of soldiers.[166] The Independent faction expressed differences of wealth, status, and occupation. John Bach, a gentleman and burgess, left an estate of £459, but Robert Fletcher's property was valued at only £31.[167] Richard Yerrow followed the lucrative trade of maltmaker, but William Crafte, a tailor, John James, a glover, and John Lies, a cutler, practiced trades of lower rank in the corporate hierarchy.[168]

The Independent faction confronted its opponents on the council in September 1649.[169] Although the Independents described their enemies as royalists, this second faction contained many burgesses active for the parliament before Massey's withdrawal from Tewkesbury in 1643 and may have had Presbyterian sympathies. The first election of bailiffs after the king's execution provided the immediate cause of dispute.[170] Christopher Atkinson, junior bailiff in 1648, accused John Man, senior bailiff in 1648, Thomas Hale, the younger, William Hill, Phillip Hilly, Edward Jennings, John Slicer, Edward Wilson, and William Wilson of a conspiracy to promote royalists in the corporation and to exclude candidates of "unquestionable fidelity" to the Commonwealth.[171] Atkinson prepared a petition to the House of Commons and used allegations of royalist conspiracy as a springboard for an ambitious plan of reform. He described the election as part of a darker design. This nest of royalists had repeatedly denied office to a proven friend of parliament because of his Independency and also had conspired, in Atkinson's absence, to settle an antirepublican minister in the parish. As far as Atkinson and his friends were concerned, only the reenactment of Pride's Purge in Tewkesbury could defeat this design. The petition called on the Commons to reduce the number of burgesses, to displace the disaffected, and to promote the faithful servants of the Commonwealth in their place. Atkinson criticized the inefficiency and cost of the county committee as "great discouragements in your service" and requested the arbitration of the dispute by

Sir William Constable, the governor of Gloucester, and Colonel Thomas Harrison, the major general of the region and a regicide.[172]

This complaint evoked a counterpetition from the accused of the common council, a petition based on the corporate charter as a symbol of order and authority.[173] The burgesses recited a litany of charters, "above three hundred years' continuance," as evidence of the "ancient corporation," invoked their record of aid to parliament, and attacked their enemies' scheme to promote candidates for corporate office out of turn, contrary to the charter. To prove the corporation's commitment to the national movement for godly reformation, the petition described, rather disingenuously, how the inhabitants had "for above 50 years last past at their own charge, by way of benevolence, maintained pious and learned ministers who constantly did and still do preach twice every Lord's day."[174] The opponents of John Slicer and Richard Berrow, the newly elected bailiffs, became a small group of "turbulent spirits" that was composed of selfish malcontents and even included one of the alternative candidates and his son-in-law. This allusion to the Independents makes William Neast a likely candidate, as Neast became a burgess in 1649 and could not have served as a bailiff under the rules of the corporation. Atkinson, his son-in-law, made the original complaint to parliament.[175] The ambitions of this disorderly faction were outlandish and unreasonable, according to the second petition, so that help finally had to be sought beyond the common council. As the petitioners calmly assured the Commons, the *responsible* burgesses endorsed the election as a legitimate expression of the ancient corporation. Of the twenty-four burgesses on the council, eighteen subscribed their consent to the election of the controversial bailiffs, Slicer and Berrow, both veterans of the royalist occupation of the town.[176]

Later developments reveal the maze of intentions beneath the surface of these petitions. The Commons sent the controversy to its committee at Haberdashers' Hall in October 1649; subsequently, the committee appointed local commissioners acceptable to both factions and set dates to examine witnesses.[177] The committee honored Atkinson's request for Constable to mediate the dispute, but never mentioned Harrison, and instead added Robert Holme of Netherton and Giles Hancock of Cirencester, justices of the peace in Gloucestershire. John Slicer, William Hill, William Wilson, and others in Tewkesbury complained of the commissioners' distance from the town, which would be prejudicial to their witnesses, and the committee expanded the commission to include William Leigh, William Shepherd, and Silvanus Wood, also justices of the peace in the county, at the petitioners' request.[178] After this accommodation of local concerns, the commissioners never examined any witnesses but quickly composed the differences of the factions in December 1649, and the controversy ended in a unanimous resolution to seek renewal of the charter.[179] The assembled factions chose Bulstrode from the Independents and Richard Dowdeswell to represent Tewkesbury "touching the renewing the charter of the town in order to the present government established by act of parliament." Since Tewkesbury had lost its members of parliament in 1648, four current members were chosen to act as "referees" in the "regulation" of the corporation. The Independents chose Sir Henry Mildmay and Isaac Pennington. The Presbyterians or royalists, to use their enemies' terms, nominated John Venn and Luke Hodges of Bristol. This rapid composition of the dispute in December 1649 makes the dance of petitions appear as a carefully arranged prelude to a negotiated settlement.

The Independent faction used accusations of disloyalty and royalism in the corporation to increase its influence in the parish, particularly over the choice of a minister and the form of local ceremonies. Atkinson's petition alleged an opposition to Independency in the corporation, yet the council subsequently invited the Independent ministers Thomas Burroughs and John Wells to hold the benefice in Tewkesbury.[180] The local circumstances of the factions support this hypothesis, as the Independents could ease the renewal of the charter in exchange for a voice in the selection of a minister, but Neast and his small number of friends on the council could not expect to change the structure of the charter. After the negotiations, the reformed charter that was sketched in the council register reduced the company of assistants, cited as a source of support in Atkinson's petition, from twenty-four to twelve and left unchanged the company of twenty-four burgesses, a majority of whom supported the second petition. Neast's faction did not insist on more decisive reforms in the council.[181] Yet the charter may not have been the only important issue in this conflict. The accusations of royalist conspiracy used the new political situation of 1649 to enhance the influence of a small faction on the margins of the corporation and the parish.

The factional conflict after the execution of the king revealed fundamental divisions in the corporation: the compound expressions of religious difference, experiences of war, and perceptions of the Revolution. These divisions reflected different notions of the corporation and of the parish and thus undermined the local forms of mediation customarily used to resolve conflicts. Despite the failure of *local* mediation, however, the parliament, the governor in Gloucester, and the justices of the peace in the county managed to compose the differences in dispute. This form of accommodation depended on the recognition of parliamentary authority, which was expressed in the local petitions, but parliamentary authority itself dissolved early in the Protectorate. After Penruddock's rebellion in 1655 and a second round of accusations and complaints of royalism in the corporation in January 1656, General John Desborough conducted a purge of the common council and removed Thomas Hale, Nathaniel Hill, son of William Hill, Phillip Hilley, Edward Jennings, John Man, John Slicer, Edward Wilson, and William Wilson, who were the suspected royalists of 1649, the veterans of corporate government in the garrisons of 1643 and 1644, and the electors of John Slicer and Richard Berrow in the corporate election in 1649.[182] In 1656 the remodeled council and its friends in the corporation showed their gratitude to the general and elected his eldest son, Valentine Desborough, to represent Tewkesbury in parliament.[183]

The Presbyterian faction, identified as the royalist interest in the 1650s, used similar links to sources of authority beyond the corporation to retain a measure of control over parochial affairs. This faction supported George Hopkins as a lecturer in the parish and perhaps as an alternative to John Wells, the Independent minister. Hopkins, the vicar of All Saints in Evesham, had been a chaplain in the Parliamentarian army and had participated in the Worcestershire Association, described by Richard Baxter as "mere catholics, men of no faction nor siding with any party, but owning that which was good in all as far as they could discern it, and upon a concord in so much, laying out themselves for the great ends of their ministry, the people's edification."[184] In 1656 Sir Anthony Ashley Cooper recommended a division of Tewkesbury's augmentation, contrary to the wishes of John Wells, and secured a salary of £30 for Hopkins as an assistant to the minister.[185] Cooper had been elected to parliament for Tewkesbury in 1654, the last election in which the Presbyterian or "mere catholic" faction had influence on the common council.[186] John Wells repeatedly petitioned the Council of State in 1657 and 1658 to free his ministry from this "malignant lecturer" introduced by his enemies. As the petitions failed to achieve the desired results, Wells hired Thomas Holtham in August 1658 to confront Hopkins at the church door before the Tuesday lecture. This show of force alienated even Wells' supporters, and Thomas Jeynes, the bailiff, imprisoned Holtham and indicted him in the borough court "on the act for disturbing ministers on the Lord's day."[187] Both factions clearly had powerful contacts beyond the boundaries of the corporation. The routine use of such contacts in factional conflicts survived the restoration of monarchy in 1660 to become the most important political consequence of the Revolution.

An example of this new pattern of politics followed the discovery of a packet of scandalous books in December 1655, just before Desborough's purge of the council.[188] An unidentified source in London sent the books via the town carrier to John Wells in Tewkesbury. When Wells unwrapped "the handsome single brown paper," he discovered, to his horror, three polemical tracts against the Protectorate and a note of advice "to communicate this to best advantage."[189] The parcel contained such political shockers as a "hellish" account of Cromwell's sinister plans for "the Anabaptists in the army and all such as are against his reforming things in the church." The title of "the greatest book" spoke for the entire "treasonous" collection: "The Protector (so called) unveiled, by whom the mystery of iniquity is now working; or a word to the good people of the three nations of England, Scotland, and Ireland, informing them of the abominable apostasy, backsliding, and underhand dealing of the man (above mentioned) who (having usurped power over the nation) has most woefully betrayed, forsaken, and cast out the good old cause of God and the interest of Christ, and has cheated and robbed his people of their rights and privileges."[190] Wells reported the books to his friends John Lies, Richard Neast, John Bache, Thomas Jeynes, and Thomas Smith.[191] The response to this crisis reflected the shakiness of the corporation and its new dependence on external sources of authority. Both factions immediately sent letters to Cromwell to express outrage over the plot, determination to prosecute the villains, and a fond hope "to live and die" under the "happy government" of the Protectorate.[192] John Wells and his friends on the council composed their letter "in a deep sense of such heady, hellish, and treasonable plottings to pour contempt upon your person, to overthrow the government, and to bring the churches and saints of the Lord Jesus under the vile scandal of malignancy and disaffection, a thing most abominable to our thoughts and spirits."[193] The letter ended in praise of the new military government. Thomas Hale, William Hill, Edward Jennings, Edward Phelps, Edward Wilson, and William Wilson, five of the eight burgesses purged from the council in January, sent their own letter several days later. After news of the event had broken, the burgesses sent an officer to interrogate Wells, "and we have used other means to have a light of the said books, that so we may proceed therein, according to the duty of our places, which we hold under your highness."[194] In conclusion, the burgesses invited Cromwell to a "further examination" of the case and promised their "lives and fortunes" to the "happy government" of the Protectorate.[195] The experience of war and the new institutions that it created had eroded the political mentality of the 1630s that had been so determined to handle such issues as the desecrated cross in the borough court and to exclude other jurisdictions from the corporation.

The local leaders of the Revolution made fundamental innovations in the ritual and symbolic landscape of the parish. The eradication of the stone cross in the center of Tewkesbury liberated the revolutionary landscape from the symbols of popish idolatry. The ancient and elaborate structure of the cross stood at the intersection of Church Street, Barton Street, and High Street to mark the center of the parish and, next to the market house, had served as the customary focus of the local market. William Hill of the Presbyterian faction and John Bach of the Independents, bailiffs of the borough in 1650, destroyed the cross as a popish objectification and profanation of divine power.[196] This revolutionary assault on crosses had been anticipated on a small scale in 1641, when the churchwardens, Christopher Atkinson and Edward Jennings, had paid laborers "to dig up and carry the stone of the cross," perhaps rubble from the controversial cross of the Hickes affair in the 1630s.[197] These symbols of superstition and idolatry were purged from the godly landscape; however, the loss of their spiritual efficacy enhanced their practical utility, in that the bailiffs used the stones from the cross demolished in 1650 to strengthen and repair the Long Bridge over the Avon to the Mythe "for flood times."[198]

The interior architecture of parish churches became sites of godly revolution in the 1650s. The revolutionary innovations in the abbey not only imparted a greater value to the chancel in relation to the other parts of the church but also transformed the church itself into "the public meeting place" and thus differentiated the godly architecture of the 1650s from the Laudian blasphemies of the 1630s.[199] As bailiffs in 1650, Hill and Bach repaired the chancel and constructed a pulpit on the site for the lecture sermon, "very useful especially for the sacrament and when the minister has a low voice."[200] The pulpit had formerly occupied the boundary between the choir and nave. This new arrangement brought the sermon and communion ceremony into closer proximity. The discourse of the word in the sermon moved from the body of the church, the nave, into the heart of the church, the chancel. As the chancel had become the site of both the lecture and the communion ceremony, the changes may indicate a general shift of divine service in the direction of the narrow space of the choir and perhaps a smaller, more exclusive lay attendance in the church. An assault on the fonts in parish churches represented the ceremonial counterpart of the godly attacks on crosses in the landscape. In 1653, two years after Francis Harris, an Independent, became the curate of Deerhurst, William Haines and John Hampton, churchwardens of Deerhurst, "pulled down" the font in their parish church. As churchwardens of Tewkesbury, Richard Cooke and Thomas Smith removed the stone font from their church in 1657, and Cooke placed the stones in his "backside" or garden. Haines and Smith expressed their views more clearly as messengers from Tewkesbury to the Baptist assembly in Morton Henmarsh in 1655.[201] The desire to remove the fonts reflected the same suspicion of idolatry and blasphemy expressed in the destruction of crosses.

Another set of changes in the abbey interior expressed the moral vision of the godly nation. These changes directed the godly to translate the prescribed values of sermons into social practice and to dissolve the artificial boundaries between sacred and profane. Hill and Bach, the bailiffs in 1650, ordered "that weekly in every week forever one shilling, being the fee of a single *capias,* whereof half is due to Mr. Bailiffs and the other half to the town clerk, shall be bestowed in 14 penny loaves which every Lord's Day, for the encouragement of others, shall stand in some convenient place in the church and, after the end of morning sermon, shall be, by the churchwardens or one of them, distributed to 14 poor people, whereof six to be nominated by Mr. Bailiffs for the time being and six by the town clerk and two by the churchwardens."[202] If the display of this bread provided examples to affluent families of the forms of neighborliness and charity required in the godly nation, the recipients of the bread provided examples to poor families of the kinds of poverty that local officers and godly neighbors recognized and honored by their charity.[203] The selection of recipients depended first on attendance in the abbey and attention to the sermon: a beneficiary of the charity would demonstrate godliness. Yet this expression of godliness would doubtless extend beyond attendance in church to include work in a trade and a disciplined family. The interior of the abbey thus became a microcosm of the godly revolution, a prescription for the spirituality and social form of the godly nation, a representation of the godly rich and the idle rich, the godly poor and the idle poor, insiders and outsiders in the new parish. In 1651 Lord Thomas Coventry's "charitable gift" of £200 to the corporation, intended to furnish a stock of goods to put the poor to work, conformed to this notion of the godly, industrious poor as a shared responsibility of charitable citizens in the godly nation.[204]

The scent and sound of the abbey changed in the late 1640s and 1650s to match the new internal and ceremonial architecture. In the early 1640s, the churchwardens continued to invest in baize cushions and the rosemary, emblematic of honor and remembrance, that was used "to perfume the church" in preparation for Christmas, although the practice was suspended in 1644, during the Parliamentarian occupation.[205] This custom disappeared from local accounts after 1645 and returned only in 1661, when the churchwardens once again "dressed the church for Christmas."[206] After the reduction of the traditional church calendar and the demise of the diocesan calendar of visitations, the bells in the parish came to express the providential calendar of the godly nation. Giles Blissard and Joseph Hambidge, the churchwardens of Tewkesbury in 1647, raised a parish levy of £15 18s 8d to meet the extraordinary expense of £33 11s 8d required to recast the great bell in the abbey.[207] This great bell became the voice of the revolutionary cause, sounded on "the routing of the Scots" at the Battle of Preston in 1648 and at the Battle of Dunbar in 1650, on the proclamation of Cromwell as Protector in 1653, on November 5 annually to commemorate the Gunpowder Plot, and on seven other days of thanksgiving declared under the Commonwealth and Protectorate.[208]

Changes in the local performance of religious ceremonies are more difficult to assess, but the Revolution clearly transformed the ceremonies of marriage and communion. In 1653 a new statute denied the church's authority to consecrate marriages and instead created a civil ceremony.

Parish registers announced a couple's intentions in a marketplace or in a church, issued a certificate of approval after three announcements, and a justice of the peace then performed the ceremony.[209] The local markets in Tewkesbury replaced the parish church as the crucial arena for the public scrutiny of matches. Michael Walzer has interpreted this change in marriage customs as part of a transition from a sacred to a secular form of political sovereignty, but the changes more closely resemble a transfer of the power of sanctification from the minister to the instrument of divine providence.[210] The boundary between spiritual authority and civil authority in the Protectorate remained rather murky, and support for the exclusion of the church from marriage rites did not necessarily signify a secular interpretation of marriage. Officers of the Protectorate regularly claimed providential authority for their actions. The clerical power to perform weddings and to keep the register of births, marriages, and deaths in a community lacked the scriptural authority required of institutions in the godly nation and so became symbols of the popish church's former monopolies and its fleshly ceremonies. The revolutionary church repudiated this monopoly. Cromwellian marriage customs reflected the vision of a godly nation constituted by scriptural authority and united in loyalty to the Protector as the servant of providence.

The most powerful expression of the Revolution occurred in the core ritual of communion. Since the late sixteenth century, communion had become an annual duty in the parish. An inclusive conception of the ceremony expressed a common hope of salvation for coresidents in the parish. In the 1650s the ceremony celebrated an exclusive spiritual community created by the experience of election. An internal bond, a shared consciousness of divine grace, united the saints predestined for salvation, and this bond transcended the profane accidents of coresidence expressed in the territorial parish. An authentic parish contained only godly families. "The people of God are alone his house," John Wells, the Independent minister of Tewkesbury, declared in 1653, "God dwells in the hearts of his saints."[211] The unregenerate of the traditional parish posed disciplinary problems for the saints, but the godly community's spiritual survival depended on the strict exclusion of corrupt souls from the core ceremonies of the new parish. Unfortunately, little evidence survives to record the everyday discipline of this new parish. Yet John Wells expressed his formal beliefs in a public debate that was held in the parish church of Winchcomb in 1653, on the question "whether it be lawful to minister and receive the holy sacrament in congregations called mixed or in our parish churches."[212] Clement Barksdale of Sudeley and his friend William Towers of Todington, who were described in the published account of the debate as "orthodox divines" and resident, in the early 1650s, near the royalist interests of the Brydges and Tracy families, defended the traditional church order and the administration of the sacrament according to the Book of Common Prayer.[213] John Wells, vicar of Tewkesbury, Carnsew Helme, vicar of Winchcomb, and William Tray, rector of Oddington, who were described as Independents, and Mr. Chaffey, rector of Naunton, and Colonel Richard Aylworth, a justice of the peace for the county, rejected the institutions of dioceses and the traditional practices of parish churches as popery and reserved the sacrament for regenerate souls in the church of the elect.[214] Wells contributed frequently to the debate and occasionally became heated, particularly on the subject of popery. He rejected the description of parish churches as houses of God because "the house built in the reign of popery and for the honor and adoration of saints was not built for the honor and service of God."[215] Wells also spoke in defense of gathered churches and responded violently to a reminder of the traditional church calendar. "At the mention of the word Christmas," Barksdale observed, "[Wells] was startled and cried popery."[216] To Barksdale's defense of the traditional episcopal church, Wells expressed contempt and hatred. "We have enough of you already," Wells interrupted sharply, "I would not go over the door sill to dispute with one upon whose spirit I see so much of the pope."[217] Barksdale advised Wells to reflect on the book of John Geary, his predecessor at Tewkesbury, entitled *Vindiciae Ecclesiae Anglicanae* and vehemently opposed to separation from the church.[218] After the debate, Wells remained close to his fellow Independents, and William Tray preached a sermon at Tewkesbury in 1653.[219]

These scattered fragments of revolution in landscape and ritual furnish the only evidence of the crucial transformation of religious communities in the Vale of Gloucester. Although methods cannot replace evidence, an interpretation of the Revolution in the vale as a cultural event may help to make sense of a fragmentary record. Several studies of symbolism have explored how the modification of particular elements or symbols in a system affects the other elements.[220] Any shifts, for example, in the form and meaning of religious symbols may affect an entire system of symbols and meanings and thus produce changes in symbols of place, authority, or status. If the innovations of the 1650s are considered in relation to local religious culture before the war, the implications of the changes form in layers and provide some small insight into the Revolution's impact on communities in the northern vale.

Symbols created the sense of shared place and cohesion in the parish communities of the early seventeenth century. Symbols such as the cross, which was an object in the landscape, evoked diverse attitudes and practices described in the first half of this book as the customary system. This system not only expressed shared beliefs and a common identity in the parish but also articulated personal histories in the many landscapes superimposed on the landscape of custom. The cross formed a focal point of collective and personal associations and joined the transcendental significance of redemption to the world of custom. The position of the cross in the system of ceremonies and seasonal practices that created the symbolic boundaries of the parish was a motive for its destruction. Traditional symbols of the parish, which represented such controversial customs as the collection of tithes, became obvious targets of the revolutionary campaign to separate the church from popery. The revolution in religious symbolism became an assault on the most important sources of community in urban and rural society. Unlike familiar forms of conflict, this radical assault in the 1650s attempted to destroy the symbols and authority of custom itself.

The destruction of ceremonies carried this assault into the core symbolism of the parish. The traditional forms of wedding and communion situated a bride and groom or a communicant in the moral and spiritual world of the parish. The intimate circle formed on ritual occasions, as well as the more diffuse presence of neighbors as spectators and critics, translated abstract notions of parish community into the familiar terms of family, friendship, and neighborliness. In the 1650s Wells and Borroughs insisted on scriptural authority as the exclusive source of discipline in the godly community and also eliminated customary ceremonies. The symbols of the parish became irrelevant in the godly wedding, as civil officers announced engagements in the Tewkesbury market. This separation of the marriage ceremony from the abbey transformed a public ritual, performed in the presence of neighbors, into a private ceremony undertaken by civil magistrates. To John Bach, Thomas Jeynes, William Neast, and John Wells, leaders of the Revolution in Tewkesbury, these changes signified the destruction of popish ceremonies and the corrupt fellowship of the traditional parish, a necessary prelude to the creation of a godly community and the circumcision of the heart.

The Independents created an alternative to the parish in their reformation of communion. Since the late sixteenth century, this core ceremony had become an important annual statement of belonging in the parish. Disputes perceived as violations of charity could lead to withdrawal from the ceremony, and the decision to participate affirmed its representation of Christian neighborhood. Wells and his faction described the community expressed in the ceremony as a "gathered church" and excluded many neighbors from communion. This system classified neighbors as "regenerate" or "unregenerate" souls. The saints discovered spiritual affinity and community not in the corrupt form of neighborhood but in the eternal form of grace. A new style of communion rejected the territorial parish and instead created a godly community from the internal qualities of the soul.

This revolution in religious symbolism ultimately produced the Separatist movements. The destruction of the cross in 1650 promised a strict exclusion of popish customs from the Church of England, but the persistence of tithes must have alarmed the forward members of the Independent faction, such as Samuel Mosse and Francis Jefferies, converts to Quakerism, and John White and Henry Smith, advocates of particular Baptism.[221] Popish corruption flourished, as the council in Tewkesbury continued to collect the tithes attached to the benefice, and parliament granted further tithes from the confiscated estates of Worcester Cathedral and other local rectories to augment the benefice.[222] The absence of alternative means to support a godly ministry, as well as major property issues, blocked the process of national reformation and seemed to imprison the godliness of the Revolution in worldly compromise. The Independent faction consequently splintered into several groups, determined to achieve a further reformation in voluntary separation from the parish. The radicalism and, for many contemporaries, the horror of the Revolution lay in this sectarian break in the cultural order.

The fortuitous survival of the Tewkesbury Baptist church book, a record of the articles of faith, church membership, and disciplinary system of the local Baptist community in the 1650s, makes it possible to examine the early experience of separation in this Baptist community in far greater detail than is possible for any other sectarian group in the vale.[223] The particular Baptists in Tewkesbury left the parish and the national church in the 1650s to escape "the hardening of the people in their idolizing of the Temple."[224] This effort to create a break, an open space, in the conventional order of religion produced subcultures, sectarian groups identified by representations of distinction from this conventional order in symbol, behavior, and ritual.[225] Yet the creation of identity in the rejection of the national church's "idolatry" formed a subcultural dependence on the symbols of the parish and held the sect in a dialogic relationship to the dominant order. Sectarian groups never demonstrated their dependence on traditional religious culture more powerfully than in their rejection of it.

The symbols and metaphors used to create the Baptist community also convey its dialogic relationship to the church.[226] Baptist communities described their cohesion as a form of Christ's mystical body, a metaphor radically opposed to yet related to the traditional corporate metaphors used to describe the church and state. As the structure of authority under the monarchy and episcopacy had been represented in elaborate corporate metaphors, the local Baptist association described its fellowship in 1655 as "members of the same body of Christ." This metaphor, which assumed different forms, could convey either the equality of members in Baptist fellowship or the subordination of this fellowship to the authority of Christ and the kingdom of God. An invocation of the body of Christ expressed the mystical unity of local associations in the national movement. This metaphor assumed a slightly different form, in discussions of authority and subordination, to signify Christ in his executive capacity as "the head of the body of the church." These metaphors helped to create an independent corporate structure for Baptist communities and furnished powerful admonitory symbols of union and obligation to prevent withdrawal from the group. As a local ordinance judiciously intoned, "There ought to be no schism in the body of Christ."[227]

A complex system of positive and negative ritual and demeanor articulated this conception of community. The interdictions in negative ritual signified a rejection of conventional religious practices and the separation of Baptist communities from the "heathen and publicans" of the world. Baptists stressed a refusal to hear the "Babylonish" preachers of the parish and a withdrawal from parish assemblies as marks of their spiritual difference from neighbors. Yet negative ritual also expressed an ironic dependence on the national church. Because the symbols and behaviors celebrated as Baptist were often reactions to the "corrupt" and "polluted" customs of parish churches, Baptist identity is impossible to separate from the cultural order of the parish that it rejected. This reciprocity between symbols of the parish and forms of negative ritual helped the Baptists to separate from the dominant culture. The importance of tithes in the formation of sectarian boundaries illustrates this creative reciprocity. Baptists rejected tithes as a system of "enforced maintenance" for mercenary preachers. By the late 1650s a repudiation of tithes became a vital mark of separation from the fellowship of the parish.[228]

An injunction to make their difference from the world manifest affected Baptist responses to many everyday situations. Baptists refused to say grace and thus stressed their rejection of "visible unbelievers" and the unhallowed prayers of unregenerate souls. The Baptist code prohibited any part in this ritual, because "the sacrifices of the wicked are abomination to the Lord, therefore his prayers also, and that we are not to be unequally yoked with unbelievers nor to be partakers of other men's sins." The local association enjoined Baptists to bear witness against such practices in a "discreet, sober way," but the structures of everyday life in the vale presented many challenges to the boundaries of Baptist fellowship. In 1657 the association of Baptist churches considered the plight of a lone Baptist or "visible godly person" who was asked to pray among unbelievers, "either as craving a blessing on God's creatures or praying for a sick person." The association found such prayers acceptable only if the unbelievers were clearly excluded from the act of prayer.[229]

This system of prohibitions makes sense only in relation to a core of positive ritual. The gestures of renunciation proclaimed difference, but Baptists expressed their fundamental beliefs and their motives for separation from the parish in positive rites. The ritual of adult baptism contained the definitive symbols of Baptist community, initiated its members, and constituted its distinctive ceremonial style. Baptists conceived of this style as a return to the traditions of baptism described in scriptural sources. The ceremony became a metaphor of the conversion process induced by a consciousness of grace, and evaluation as a candidate required a profession of faith and evidence of election. The "gospel ministers" or "gifted brethren" of the church then performed the ritual of baptism "not by sprinkling" but by "dipping of the person in water" to symbolize the death, burial, and resurrection of Christ. A simplified communion expressed the bond created in this common experience of baptism. The saints walked in "distinct churches or assemblies of Zion," and their communion represented the "breaking of bread" among spiritual companions.[230]

The allusion to Baptist communities as manifestations of Christ's body drew on mystical notions of an invisible church, and the forms of ecstatic religion in both rite and belief differentiated the Baptists from their neighbors.[231] Scriptural ecstasies, known as "gospel prophesyings" in Baptist parlance, articulated a belief in the direct religious experience of "gifted brethren." This rite is described as a scriptural ecstasy because its conventions, the discipline imposed on gifted brethren in gospel prophesying, derived from Paul's injunction to speak to the edification of the church and clearly distinguished the rite from personal, charismatic forms of mystical experience, such as speaking in tongues.[232] Saints represented this intimate knowledge of the spirit in their mundane actions. The Baptist discipline required the elect not only to bear witness against the shameful practices of the profane world but also "to shine forth in conversation as lights in the world."[233] A belief in the imminent arrival of Christ's rule on earth intensified this evangelical spiritualism. Baptist anticipation of the millennium was understated compared with other forms of millenarian belief, but the importance of the millennium as an injunction to prepare for the kingdom of God was clearly pronounced in fears of a "sluggish and drowsy frame of spirit" likely to overtake "the wise as well as the foolish virgins" in the final days.[234]

The separate identity expressed in ritual and metaphor was enshrined in a discipline, a system of rules to protect the boundaries of Baptist fellowship. The Bible served as a handbook and practical guide to the creation of a godly community, and every Baptist ordinance rested on multiple citations of scripture. The first article of faith described the narrow constitution of the elect and the spiritual affinity of "due believers," a shared consciousness of grace. This attraction culminated in the voluntary association expressed in adult baptism. Yet spiritual affinities and voluntary association did not altogether exclude traditional attitudes, and spatial stability, as distinct from territorial solidarity, remained an unspoken principle of association. As the association of Baptist churches declared in 1656, "baptized believers in a troop or regiment" could not constitute a gathered church because of the vulnerability of transient groups to dissolution and their inability to follow "the rule of the word" in the recruitment of members.[235]

The principle of voluntary association in the creation of the community did not preclude an emphasis on self-denial in its discipline. Baptist discipline demanded a submersion of individuality and personal volition in the collective life of the community. An interpretation of spiritual gifts as a form of collective property carried this renunciation of self into the most important activities of the community. Baptists believed that "gifted brethren" received their powers from Christ and remained church property. The elders of the local Baptist association used this argument to discourage their ministers from preaching outside the baptized communities of the saints. The members of a gathered church could reclaim their freedom of association only if the community ceased to be "a true church of Christ," unsound in belief or persistent in some evil. Separation then became permissible "after her sin has been clearly held forth to her by the light of the word and all good means appointed and afforded of the Lord for her repentance and reformation have been used, according to the will of the Lord, with love and patience and meekness." Yet the means to judge a community's spiritual and scriptural purity remained murky, and Baptists who broke communion on pretense of higher authority could be "cast out to Satan." Baptists could not even depart from a community to attend another closer to their homes, as this kind of break violated the principle of church fellowship and "grieved the hearts of their brethren." In practice, an orderly separation could occur only after review and approval by the local community because acceptance in another group depended on the favorable testimonials.[236]

A system of admonition and excommunication existed to enforce this discipline. Particular Baptist communities resembled Independents in their insistence on discipline as a local prerogative. A community chose its minister and elders after a trial, election, and ordination by laying on hands, and this elite then shared responsibility for the "discovery of weakness" in the community. As souls lay in the balance of the disciplinary process, Baptists were generally cautious in pursuit of moral reclamation. The elders and concerned brethren usually admonished offenders in private. If admonition failed, excommunication branded the offender as "a heathen and a publican" in the open church. Baptist churches did not use excommunication, as did the traditional parish, to restore delinquents to moral and spiritual fellowship, but instead tended to cut their spiritual losses in response to frequent offenses. If repentance seemed possible, however, excommunication did not end the informal process of admonition. The excommunication of preachers was a different matter and created a more serious break. Baptists were forbidden to hear any minister excommunicated by the Baptist churches, although a local community could assign "some able brethren" to hear a prohibited sermon in order to refute the errors. To hear such a sermon voluntarily was to embrace the banned preacher and to "make void the church and null the act of the church by which he is excommunicated."[237]

The exclusivity practiced in the recruitment and in the constitution of Baptist communities served as a prelude to the open confrontation of gathered churches and the world, the unbaptized residue of humanity. The boundary between Baptists and the profane world existed for defensive purposes, not for concealment. Baptists represented their faith as a light or beacon to lead the saints from the corruption of the world into a protective citadel of godly community. The process of separation and the use of scripture and ritual to create boundaries symbolized the inner power of Christ and his elect. This godly community then confronted corruption in the relatively open relationship of the church and the profane world. Because the faithful had been commanded to "show forth" the death of the Lord, Baptist churches performed baptism and communion in the presence of the unregenerate. The excommunication of brethren was pronounced before the world "that they may see the church does not bear with sin and sinners and that it may mind them of the woeful condition of wicked men." Baptists excluded unbaptized neighbors from prayers only on special occasions.[238]

This separation from neighbors in the parish created a new social order, best described as the sanctified family. The traditional order of the parish, which was expressed in the arrangement of seats in the parish church, dissolved the family in a representation of the territorial parish, but families were undivided in Separatist assemblies as focal points of worship and symbols of spiritual unity. This movement of the family to the center of the sacred representation of society made a strict practice of the familiar Puritan injunction to make the family a church. Although John Geary of Tewkesbury, the most conspicuous local Puritan in the 1630s, never preached separation, sanctification of the family was an important theme in his published sermons.[239] The Baptists represented their community as Christ's family. This metaphor made Christ "the bridegroom" of the church, and the saints became his children. Members of the church addressed each other as brother and sister, and the only scriptural exceptions to this rule, which were allowed in the articles of faith, used the metaphor of parenthood and the category of "son" to describe kinship in the faith. The duties of brothers and sisters in a Baptist community resembled family responsibilities "in watching over each other and considering each other in respect of purity of doctrine, exercise of love, and good conversation."[240]

The centrality of family in sectarian communities explains the proliferation of rules for the formation of families and the conduct of households in the 1650s. An exclusive system of marital rules, created by the association of Baptist churches and sent to local communities in 1655, gave the gathered churches considerable influence over the process of family formation. These rules restricted marital choices to the small circle of "true believers in Christ," delineated by "a principle of grace." Although this insistence on the mere principle of grace preserved intercommunal marriages in simulacrum, the distribution of grace, in principle and practice, tended to be confined to the Baptist churches. The conventions that were sent to local Baptist churches in 1655 acknowledged a difference between unbelievers and persons of "pretended godliness" but considered a marriage to the latter "very inconvenient, uncomfortable, and dangerous." The faithful were enjoined to avoid this exposure "to continual temptation and clog from a bosom companion and yoke fellow."[241]

The family and household were the most important vehicles for the transmission of the faith in the Baptist community. Domestic relations were strictly controlled, and the various relations of the household were also examined for their impact on the collective life of Baptist churches. The Baptists promoted parental interest in children, and the association of churches instructed parents in 1656 to take personal responsibility for the education of their children, to raise them "in the nurture and admonition of the Lord." This familial education consisted of formal instruction in the Bible or "the things of the Lord" and of the personal exhortation "to walk closely with God." Despite insistence on the strict scriptural education of Baptist children, the association chided parents not to provoke children to the point of anger, lest youth be discouraged in the pursuit of godliness. Sensitivity to the intellectual peculiarities of children was encouraged, as long as indulgence did not become the toleration of evil in the home. Parents were advised "to chastise" children "even with severity" for "perverse" or "stubborn" persistence in sin. As the success or failure of household discipline, in general, and of a child's education, in particular, lay in the hands of God, the association admonished parents to pray.[242]

The relations of masters and servants posed unique problems in sectarian communities. Because servants were usually adolescents, or possibly young adults, and might bring their own religious identities into a household, this relationship was more difficult and potentially dangerous for the godly community than the relations of parents and children. The beliefs of masters and servants could not be assumed to coincide. If their servants were believers, the local association of churches directed masters in 1656 to acknowledge a spiritual equality and to perform the same duties to the servants as to other brethren. If the servants were unbelievers, the master had a moral and spiritual duty to rule for the good of the household. These servants were not to be suffered to pollute the godly home through a sinful life. The master was obligated to educate his unregenerate servants and to "hold forth the fruit of God to prepare them for the Lord." A master fulfilled in his household the same duty imposed on Baptists in the crusade against worldliness, to show the power of the elect in his own actions and "so walk as to show them a good example himself."[243]

Many saints experienced service as a matter of course, and this service sometimes placed the godly in unregenerate households. A system of rules protected the structure of authority in the household from the expression of spiritual equality or superiority in hierarchic relations. If masters were among the elect, the conventions of 1656 warned servants "not to take liberty to themselves" or neglect their duties. Yet this hierarchic relationship between spiritual equals remained potentially subversive, since masters and servants had the same duties of admonition and moral scrutiny imposed on all brethren. Despite unequal relations in the profane world, servants shared responsibility for the spiritual purity of the master's household, and "their relation as servants ought not to make them forget their relation in Christ's temple." This joint moral enterprise contravened traditional notions of household authority, and the Baptist association reminded servants to express views "in such a way and manner as is not disagreeable nor unsuitable to their relation." Yet the Baptist discipline generally *confirmed* customary forms of service and stressed loyalty among servants as a spiritual obligation. In 1656 the association ordered servants to obey reasonable commands "with reverence and singleness of heart" and to perform duties "as the servants of Christ doing the will of God." These rules honored the scriptural injunction to bear witness against sinful behavior but advised servants in disorderly house-holds to avoid "provoking and unsavory language" as well as unpleasant behavior. The Baptist discipline protected the household authority of unbelievers, and unregenerate masters received the honor due to "mas-ters and governors . . . that the name of God and his doctrine be not blasphemed." Yet the church acknowledged its duty to protect the saints from emissaries of Satan disguised in the forms of worldly authority. Servants were reminded to obey God before humanity and to disobey anything commanded against the rule of the Lord.[244]

This symbolic and structural dependence on family and household in sectarian communities affected the distribution of authority. The tradi-tional order in Tewkesbury Abbey had reproduced the formal relations of patriarchy. In the small, secluded, and often domestic assemblies of Sepa-ratists, the informal relations of family influenced the distribution of authority among men and women. Men controlled the Baptist church, and patriarchal symbols became structures of authority. The Baptist dis-cipline ordered women to avoid forms and contexts of speech that ex-pressed a denial of the "inferior of their sex and a usurpation of authority over the man." Women could not become elders or "stand up as rulers in the church" and were forbidden to teach, to "pass sentence" on forms of doctrine, or to speak in prayer "as the mouth of the church." But the construction of barriers to protect male authority obscures radical as-pects of this community. Baptist communities depended on the family for cohesion, discipline, and reproduction of the faith, and this interrela-tionship moved a flexible social institution into the heart of religious community. The practice of power in families often enhanced a widow's position and generally afforded women more influence than the rhetoric of formal patriarchy conceded. The liberation of feminine conscience in sectarian communities was measured less in admission to church ad-ministration than in opportunities to express faith and hope of salvation. After 1656 Baptist assemblies allowed women to make public professions of faith and desire of baptism, to participate in admonition, and to act as messengers between churches.[245] The power of separation clearly ap-pealed to more women than men, as the Baptist community in Tewkes-bury contained eighty-six women and forty-three men in 1663.[246]

The cultural importance of family in the creation of sectarian commu-nities raises questions about the social implications of the Revolution in the 1650s. Social historians tend to stress the continuity of basic structures in early modern society and to deny the relevance of such concepts as social revolution, save in the almost fantastic case of "an irreversible displacement of the social structure as a whole."[247] Keith Wrightson acknowledges the ambitious cultural revolution of the 1650s but stresses the failure of Puritan revolutionaries to create a godly nation. "The failure," he observes, "lay primarily in an inability to communicate meaningfully with the common people."[248] This view has received much support from investigations of the resistance to godly revolution and the resilience of loyalty to the Book of Common Prayer.[249] Yet the measure of revolution appears to be the successful implementation of a revolutionary program. Both interpretations read continuity as evidence of conservatism. Yet new forms of social order can arise only from familiar cultural idioms and conventions, and new movements carry the marks of the cultural order that creates them. A revolution occurs in the interrelationship of symbols and other forms of culture, such as social institutions. The symbolism of Independency and particular Baptism in the 1650s created a break in the cultural order, transformed the traditional interrelationship of family and parish, and thus constituted a social revolution.

The attempts to steer the corporation of Tewkesbury across nearly twenty years of war and political upheaval have left evidence of four critical moments, the reactions to political and military developments in the nation. The common council divided over the town's surrender to royalists in 1643, and Parliamentarian families sailed down the Severn to Gloucester. After years of painful service as a garrison for both sides, peace restored the unity of the corporation. The exiled families returned in 1646 and may have started to come back after Massey created a strong Parliamentarian garrison in 1644. The execution of the king ended three years of relative calm, as "Independents" and "royalists" petitioned parliament to excise the cancers from the corporation. These factions composed their dispute over the charter in 1649, but renewed complaints against the same men in 1656 and their removal from the common council by General Desborough reveal the persistence of suspicion. As divisions between the "well affected" and "malignants" came to dominate corporate politics, local officers tended to appeal factional disputes and crises to authorities in London.[250]

The experiences of war and revolution transformed religious communities in the northern vale. After 1643 successive garrisons undermined traditional structures of authority in the parish as well as in the corporation. A series of ordinances from parliament and Protector in the 1640s and 1650s rationalized and extended the discipline of the garrison community and made the parish an open church. As Presbyterian and Independent factions contested the ritual of this church, Baptists and Quakers resolved the problems of godly reformation in separation from the parish.[251] Although these conflicts over questions of authority and ceremony had divided the neighborhood since the late sixteenth century, the dissolution of the diocesan hierarchy and the bitter divisions created in the war added layers of hatred to the problems of the 1640s. Parish communities in the 1650s had been transformed beyond recognition.

The process of religious change affected other forms of culture, as the fragmentation of the parish expressed a shift from the territorial parish to the spiritualism of sectarian communities in the 1650s. This sectarian form of community embodied the most radical aspirations of the Revolution in the vale. Baptists were not the most radical group to emerge from the open church in the 1650s, but the symbolism and disciplinary code that differentiated Baptists from their neighbors placed the community alongside Quakerism on the radical spectrum.[252] These sectarian communities promoted a religious fellowship distinct from the parish that was expressed in the idiom of family relations, and after 1660 the recognition of this form of fellowship, the distinction between the Church of England and Dissent, made the Revolution a permanent feature of the cultural landscape. After the Restoration, the parish ceased to exist as a territorial community in its traditional form and became, instead, a community of sympathetic families represented in the traditional symbolism of the territorial church.

7

Astraea Redux:
Religious Conflict, Restoration,
and the Parish, 1660–1665

And what will they at best say of us and of the whole English name but
scoffingly, as of that foolish builder, mentioned by our Savior, who
began to build a tower and was not able to finish it?

> John Milton, *The Ready and Easy Way to Establish
> a Free Commonwealth* (1660)

At home the hateful names of parties cease
And factious souls are wearied into peace.

> John Dryden, *"Astraea Redux"* (1660)

Since the seventeenth century, the restoration of the Stuart monarchy in
1660 has played an important symbolic role in grand historical narratives. If such narratives were considered in their morphology, as are
familiar folk narratives, the Restoration would represent the magical
sleep, the supreme moment of collective forgetfulness. A rhetoric of
oblivion has been used repeatedly since 1660 to describe and interpret
the return of monarchy. As Dryden observed, "the hateful names of parties" vanished from the political landscape in 1660, and "factious souls
[were] wearied into peace."[1] Clarendon believed that the painful religious contortions of the 1650s had prepared the "natural inclinations
and integrity" of "hearts and affections" for the restoration of monarchy
and obedience to royal authority.[2] This attitude has been transformed in
modern historical narratives into a form of collective weariness. Charles
returned to a country in need of a rest, exhausted by the failures of
religious radicalism and constitutional innovation. The exhaustion of
the creative spirit in 1660 dominated the progressive narratives of David

Ogg and Godfrey Davies and the early revisionist account of John Kenyon.[3]

Critical assaults on progressive interpretations of the Civil War and Revolution have cast serious doubts on this interpretation of the Restoration as a social, political, and religious boundary, an interlude of forgetfulness between the emotional upheavals of the 1640s and the rational politics of the late seventeenth century. The loss of a historiographic convention has effectively reunified the seventeenth century around the evident persistence of familiar conflicts in the localities after 1660 and the deficiencies of power, policy, and authority in royal government itself.[4] Recent discussions of Charles II, the Cavalier Parliament, and various local communities have found in each context important continuities between the bitter divisions of the Civil War and the patterns of policy and conflict in the later seventeenth century.[5] Yet this emphasis on continuity and conflict makes the process of restoration itself more difficult to understand. If conflicts were unresolved, why was the restoration of the monarchy perceived as desirable? How did former enemies refashion identities to become allies and local leaders of the restoration process? These questions involve problems of local and national symbolism, identity, and power familiar not only to historians but also to anthropologists of modern Britain and other European nations. An interdisciplinary approach to the Restoration may thus offer a new perspective on the problem of political identity in 1660 and create a dialogue between historians and anthropologists interested in the symbolism and politics of belonging in local and national communities.[6]

As forms of community and governance dependent on the symbolism and authority of the government in London, corporations present problems of restoration appropriate to this interdisciplinary perspective. Historians have generally focused on a narrowly defined relationship between the corporations and the restored monarchy.[7] The local councils have been approached as the primary sources of power and identity in their communities, and the Restoration has been understood as a royalist invasion of corporate offices, an invasion less successful in some corporations than in others but independent of place in its motivations and designs. This approach has defined power and politics in secular terms. If religious issues have been raised, the issues have concerned the ability of specific groups to defy the penal laws and retain power in the corporation. The restoration of the parish itself and its distinctive forms of power and identity have received less attention, despite the significance of the parish in the ceremonial culture of corporations in the seventeenth century.[8] The corporate council in Tewkesbury and in many other places required members to participate in processions to parish churches on the Sabbath and maintained separate seats in local churches to symbolize the authority and dignity of the corporation in the ceremonial hierarchy of the parish. Before historians can ask the right questions about the process of restoration, this complex relationship between forms of religious community and civic community in corporations must be recovered. The nature of the relationship becomes clearer in the context of a particular corporation and parish and in the distinctive yet interrelated politics of belonging in both communities.

A description of Charles II's return and its immediate prelude survives in the form of rough notes scribbled in the account book of the Giles Geast charity in Tewkesbury. Like his neighbors in Tewkesbury, this anonymous local writer, perhaps Thomas Jeynes, a member of the common council, followed the public reports of factional conflict in the army in the late 1650s as a keenly interested but powerless spectator.[9] He marked the Lord Protector's death in the autumn of 1658 with a respectful contemplation of his victories in the field and further reflections on the transitory nature of worldly fame. His reaction to Cromwell's death differed from earlier commentaries on the mortality of kings. "This year upon the third day of September, 1658," the chronicle intoned, "died the Lord Protector whom upon the same day of the month in the years 1650 and 1651 had two eminent victories, the one at Dunbar, the other at Worcester, yet death conquered him who had been so eminent in arms. *Sic transit gloria mundi.*"[10] The metaphor of human vanity suggests a certain skepticism of prominent efforts, led by Andrew Marvell and others, to link Cromwell's death to the same forms of cosmological disturbance traditionally connected with royal deaths, a kingly representation already intimated in Marvell's commemoration of the first anniversary of the Protectorate in 1655.[11] Yet Cromwell's death clearly deprived the revolutionary polity of its most important political and religious symbol. The chronicle noted Richard Cromwell's succession as Lord Protector, but Richard never inspired in this local writer the same combination of fear, respect, and confidence.[12]

A chaos of factions seemed to follow the death of Oliver Cromwell.

The local account described the time between the dissolution of Richard's parliament in April 1659 and the army's restoration of the Rump in May as "an interregnum." The Protector's power "came to be clouded," and the members of the Long Parliament "began to have the sunshine of the army." On May 7, the surviving members of the Rump were invited to reassume the government "which God had prospered in their hands," and Richard Cromwell then faded from public view. But this literary love affair between the army and parliament soon dissolved in mutual suspicion. The local account of the schism focused on parliament's refusal to reform the command structure of the army in the wake of the petition from Lambert's soldiers in Derby. In October 1659 the army under Lambert once again barred the members from the House of Commons. Local anxiety was reflected in the chronicler's parenthetic remark: "now comes another interregnum."[13] These abrupt changes were a source of particular frustration to the writer, as the corporation was engaged in an expensive attempt to renew its charter.[14]

The same local scribe obtained sufficient news in 1660 to follow the movement of political struggle from a conflict between the army and the parliament to a conflict between factions in the army itself. The scribe's limited perception of the political process resolved this factional conflict into a struggle between the personalities of Lambert and Monk. Lambert had surfaced in local consciousness as the foremost representative of the military interest after his destruction of Booth's rebellion in the summer of 1659. In the local account, Lambert was represented, in the active prosecution of his command if not in formal rank, as the heart of the Committee of Safety formed to replace the Rump in October 1659. The chronicle focuses on the dramatic decisions and actions of individuals and demonstrates no awareness of the financial problems facing the Committee of Safety or of the political motives of the factions in the army. Lambert raced north to prevent Monk's advance on London from Scotland. Sir Arthur Hesilrige and the Portsmouth garrison then destroyed the Committee of Safety from behind, marching on London in the name of the Long Parliament. Lambert's soldiers deserted him in favor of Fairfax and the Rump, and Monk marched south to London, arriving in February 1660. These events of late 1659 and early 1660 were seen as expressions of the personal rivalries among army commanders.[15]

The remainder of the local narrative is a bare sketch of the relations between Monk and the restored Rump in February 1660. The writer juxtaposed Monk's early obedience to parliament, which was symbolized by his destruction of London's defenses, and his later commands to the Rump itself to restore the victims of previous purges, in order to portray Monk as a politician and manipulator. The grateful members of the restored House subsequently voted their own dissolution and sent the writs for a new parliament "which was then generally called a free parliament." This "free parliament" voted the return of the monarchy, and Charles II entered London on May 29, 1660, "in great triumph and joy to the people."[16]

This account of political vicissitudes in the late 1650s reproduces the superficiality of the "local version" of events. The chronicle described the return of monarchy as a chain of personalities and events seen from the outside and thus provides an unreflective image of the royal return as a process that was set in motion by forces and personalities beyond the local corporation and parish and that was concentrated in the factional politics of the army. This process was never described as a restoration, much less the Restoration. What did the return of the monarchy mean to this writer and his neighbors? The former supporters of the Protectorate retained administrative control in Tewkesbury. The Separatist communities remained to contest any reconstruction of diocesan and parochial institutions. These structures of communal life in the corporation and parish formed the context in which a process of restoration emerged from local debates, conflicts, and compromises over royal declarations and parliamentary legislation. The Restoration was therefore composed of many local events and assumed distinct forms according to the previous alignment of local factions.

The return of the king did not meet with universal enthusiasm in Tewkesbury. Three suicides were recorded in the borough council register in May 1661. Because of the severe religious prohibitions and property concerns involved, the council had never before recognized a death as an act of suicide. At least one of the suicides in 1661, Francis Godwin, had previously been prosecuted as a religious nonconformist.[17] A less extreme reaction surfaced in the attitudes of troopers in the Tewkesbury garrison. In the spring of 1660 soldiers were speaking openly against Monk's actions and seeking to arouse opposition in the local alehouses. In a speech at the White Hart in Tewkesbury, one soldier described Monk as "a rogue" and expressed his hope that "Lambert and his party should have a day for it." He dropped hints that Christopher Smith, the bailiff of Tewkesbury, would have "a troop" ready to serve Lambert on such a day. The second soldier had spoken at the Dog, saying that "Monk was a fellow of no principle and that no good was ever to be expected from him." Another had "reviled" and "dishonored" Monk at the White Hart, calling him "a monkey face." Monk immediately confronted the verbal attacks. He authorized Colonel Thomas Pury in Gloucester to call a court martial for the three soldiers and for other cases "tending to mutiny or sedition." But Pury was forbidden to impose any punishment extending to "life or member" without prior consultation with Monk.[18]

Despite this evidence of despair and criticism, many of the burgesses and freemen involved in the administration of the Protectorate favored reconciliation and accepted the pardon offered by Charles II in the Declaration of Breda.[19] William Neast of Twyning, the most prominent local supporter of the Protectorate, made a separate submission of his own.[20] The corporate council had been remodeled in 1656 by the forced exclusion of the Presbyterian faction, who were alleged reactionaries, but this rump council distanced itself from the remnant of Lambert's supporters in the local garrison by electing conservative representatives, Sir Henry Capel and Richard Dowdeswell, to the "free parliament" in April 1660.[21] These councilors had crossed ideological lines once before to elect a member capable of furthering local interests in London, but the election of 1660 constituted an abandonment of the Protectorate.[22] The motives behind the choice of conservative members became clear in the fortnight following Charles' return, as the council devised instructions for Richard Dowdeswell. Dowdeswell was ordered to prepare and present to the king an address from the corporation "declaring their joy in his return to this kingdom and humbly . . . laying hold of his Majesty's grace, offered by his declaration and letter."[23]

This effort to embrace the new regime through carefully chosen intermediaries succeeded in the first phase of the restoration process. The privy council intervened in November 1660 to reinstate the survivors of the group of eight councilors purged by Major General Desborough in 1656.[24] This action restored the common council of 1649. Among the councilors returned to their former places, Thomas Hale, Philip Hilly, Edward Jennings, John Man, John Slicer, Edward Wilson, and William Wilson had helped to steer the corporation through its vicissitudes as a royalist and parliamentary garrison in the 1640s; had supported Richard

Berrow and John Sclicer in the controversial corporate election of 1649; and had continued to serve in the highest corporate offices under the Commonwealth.[25] These councilors had been removed from office and had perceived their own participation in local government as compromised only after the declaration of a Protectorate. The first local restoration thus returned to the political and constitutional issues of 1649 and restored the council as it had existed under the Commonwealth and the early years of the Protectorate.

This settlement could not survive the new dispensation for corporations in the legislative program of the Cavalier Parliament. The second phase in the restoration process, a royalist reconstruction of the corporation, was marked by the political violence of a purge, several local lawsuits, and loud condemnations of corporate venality in the 1650s. This royalist restoration began to take shape in Tewkesbury in the summer of 1662, as institutions were established to implement the legislation passed by parliament the previous year. The Corporation Act established commissions to regulate the membership of corporate councils.[26] William Herbert, lord lieutenant of Gloucestershire, led the commission for Tewkesbury that included Sir Henry Capel and Richard Dowdeswell.[27] The bells of the abbey signaled the momentous arrival of Herbert and the other commissioners in August 1662.[28] After a brief investigation, the commission excluded William Neast and twelve of his supporters from the common council. The burgesses who were removed included John Bach, John Crafte, William Crafte, Thomas Jeynes, and Richard Yerrow.[29] A faction of royalists, headed by Thomas Nanfan and Conway Whithorne, replaced these supporters of the Protectorate.[30] Nanfan had served as a major in the armies of Charles I and Charles II, and three of his brothers had been killed in the king's service. His marriage to a daughter of William Hill, the former town clerk whose son was removed from the corporation in the purge of 1656, had consolidated his position in corporate politics. Conway Whithorne had supported the royalist cause in its various forms in the 1640s and 1650s. He circulated the petition in favor of episcopacy in 1642 and fought beside his father at the Battle of Worcester in 1651. Whithorne was related by marriage to the restored families of Man, Smithsend, and Jeynes.[31] John Man, Conway Whithorne, and Thomas Jeynes, son of the Thomas Jeynes who had carried Tewkesbury's surrender to the royalists in 1643, had been investigated as delinquents in the late 1640s.[32] But the purge stopped short of invasion. The royalist restoration removed only local supporters of the Protectorate, and councilors linked to the Commonwealth regime kept their places.

This purge of the common council inaugurated a general campaign to discredit the Protectorate. The removal of councilors was followed by a prolonged public investigation of their financial integrity. In January 1663 Richard Hill, the town clerk removed from office in the purge, was ordered to deliver "all the writings, books, and evidences belonging to the corporation" or face a lawsuit "in the name of the bailiffs and chamber."[33] The council appointed committees to question the suspected members, exclusively servants of the Protectorate, and several councilors were confronted by demands for their accounts. Richard Dowdeswell, member of parliament for the borough, may have played a role in the organization of this campaign and was certainly consulted for advice and approval before the initiation of the subsequent lawsuits.[34]

The new regime also established rules to liberate the restored council from the unsanctified practices of its counterpart under the Protectorate. These rules focused on the attendance of the full council and on the relationship between the council, the freemen of the corporation, and the inhabitants of the town. In the 1650s the common council had been reduced in size, and the most important decisions in the daily administration of the borough had passed to a smaller group of active burgesses. In 1662 the burgesses appointed by commission marked their restoration of the full council in rules of attendance that imposed stiff fines for lateness or absence from council meetings. These burgesses also sought to restore the boundaries of secrecy separating the council from the rest of the corporation and agreed to exclude from office any burgess found to have revealed "anything spoken or acted at any meeting of the common council."[35]

The royalist restoration of the borough in 1662 represented not only a change of personnel but also a reinterpretation of the public symbols of corporate identity and allegiance. The Corporation Act altered the ceremonies of installation in corporate office and inscribed an interpretation of the Civil War into the order of civic ritual. New ceremonial qualifications for corporate office were added to oaths already required by the corporations themselves. These new demands sought to bind local officers to king and church by the Oath of Allegiance and the Oath of Supremacy, bonds further strengthened by the reception of Anglican communion. But an additional oath and declaration required the acceptance of a royalist interpretation of events in the 1640s.[36] The oath enjoined nonresistance and denied the validity of any claim to take arms by the authority of the king against his person, in the manner of parliament. The declaration described the Solemn League and Covenant as an unlawful oath, despotically imposed against the liberties of the kingdom. As a result of this ceremonial innovation, the election of burgesses and the induction of corporate officers became a rudimentary history lesson and a public enactment of the royalist perspective on the Civil War.

This interpretation of the Civil War was associated with other symbols of corporate identity, the most important being the royal charter of the borough. The charter seems to have disappeared in the early days of the war. No evidence has been found to cast any light upon its mysterious departure. The "two skins of parchment" that remained from the original charter in 1672 suggest careless loss as readily as conspiracy or theft.[37] Yet the corporate council's interpretation of the event, current during the late 1660s and early 1670s, described the charter as "purloined and destroyed" in the 1640s by malcontents "inimical to all government."[38] The accuracy or inaccuracy of this interpretation is less interesting than the way in which it connects the radical cause in the Civil War to subversion of the charter, repudiation of the authority of law, and the annihilation of the corporation.

The local implementation of the Corporation Act thus demonstrates the high political price of the royalist restoration for the former supporters of the Protectorate regime. The local servants of the Protectorate had attempted to limit the adverse consequences of the royal return through preliminary contacts and cooperation, but the penalties imposed cannot have been wholly unanticipated. What were the motives for participation in a process that so quickly resulted in their own exclusion from the secular politics of the corporation? The process of restoration in the parish may provide an answer. If the former servants of the Protectorate experienced only defeat and exclusion in the royalist restoration of the corporation, the local pattern of religious settlement may have furnished a motive for their acceptance of the new regime.

To understand the appeal of Charles' return to heterogeneous groups is to perceive the general fear of religious extremism in the late 1650s. The process of religious separation created a social organism of intense spiritual power outside the institutional structure of the parish. Baptists in Tewkesbury had renounced local custom and hierarchy in the formal rules of their community yet professed obedience to the authority of the state. More radical groups like the Quakers and Fifth Monarchists departed from the Baptists in their exclusive reliance on the authority of personal revelation and mystic experience. This emphasis on personal experience over other forms of public authority, including scripture, made Quakerism appear antisocial and dangerous both to local supporters of the Book of Common Prayer and to Presbyterians and Independents.[39] The religious vision of prominent local Independents and supporters of the Protectorate, such as the armigerous Neast family of Twyning, called for the reorganization of the parish into a more exclusive religious community dominated by a spiritual elite. This spiritual elite included persons of different social status but preserved a hierarchy in the relationship between the elect and the remnant of the parish. Quakerism destroyed this hierarchy by emphasizing universal access to the authority of the light. To local Independents, the open church that harbored Quakerism thus began to symbolize the dissolution of social order.

The general fear of Quakers as antisocial spiritual levelers has dominated recent discussions of the religious motives for restoration.[40] The intensity of this common fear was occasionally expressed in acts of violence. In June 1660 Quakers were harassed and assaulted in the village of Tirley, southwest of Tewkesbury.[41] William Sparrow, a Quaker from Ross, had traveled to visit his friends and coreligionists in Tirley. Several villagers subsequently arrested Sparrow and assaulted one of his friends in an attack described by one participant as a civil action.[42] Richard Broadwell, another Quaker, went to the house of one of the villagers on the following day to request Sparrow's release but was lured into a room and accosted by Edward Perry, a servant of Richard Dowdeswell. Perry drew his sword and threatened to kill Broadwell unless he agreed to drink the king's health. In the confrontation that followed, Perry was physically restrained by his companions, as Broadwell fled from the house.

The distance between Quakers and other militant Protestants was expressed in a scuffle between George Fox and some Independents in Tewkesbury. In 1655 Fox held a night meeting in the town and then recounted its incidents in his journal. John Wells, the Independent minister of the parish, came to the meeting "with a great deal of rabble and rude people" and "boasted he would see whether he or [Fox] should have the victory." Fox then began to preach and "turned the people to the divine light, which Christ the heavenly and spiritual man had enlightened them withal; that with that light they might see their sins; and how that they were in death and darkness and without God in the world; and with the same light they might see Christ from whence it came, their savior and redeemer, who had shed his blood for them and died for them; who was their way to God, their truth and life." This approach to religious experience clearly repudiated election in favor of the mystical image of the "light of Christ" as a universal guide to salvation. In his exaltation of personal religious authority, Fox seemed to deny the principle of hierarchy and subordination in human society. The inevitable diffusion of religious authority in personal experience was repugnant to Independents, and Wells reportedly "began to rage against the light and denied it and so went away." His supporters remained behind and carried a "mischief . . . in their hearts" but were restrained, according to Fox, by the power of the Lord.[43]

A general fear of sectarian movements, and Quakerism in particular, formed the context of the first episcopal visitation held in Tewkesbury and its neighborhood. This visitation lasted from December 19, 1661, to September 9, 1662, as Convocation revised the Book of Common Prayer and created a conservative religious settlement.[44] The process of visitation and presentment reasserted the ceremonial authority and moral jurisdiction of the territorial church. Just as the local commissioners appointed by the Corporation Act created protective boundaries around the restored borough council, so the presentments made by churchwardens in the course of this visitation formed part of an effort to reconstruct the ceremonial boundaries of the parish church. Between October 1662 and March 1665, the consistory court focused almost exclusively on religious offenses and handled seventy presentments for seventy violations of the ceremonial code in the restored church. Cases of sexual indiscretion and lapses of discipline on the part of ecclesiastical officers accounted for twenty-five presentments and eighteen offenses.[45] Despite the narrowness of the formal settlement in the church, however, churchwardens did not prosecute Presbyterians and Independents in the Vale of Gloucester. The visitation was an unmistakable assault on Baptists and Quakers.[46]

The clerical leaders of moderate Nonconformist groups frequently failed to survive this reassertion of ecclesiastical boundaries. John Wells, the Independent minister of Tewkesbury, lost his benefice in 1662, and Robert Eaton, his more conservative replacement, acquired the benefice in the summer of the same year. Francis Harris, the other influential Independent minister in the neighborhood, suffered the same fate as Wells, losing the curacy of Deerhurst in 1662.[47] But the experience of the lay community was quite different, and only three Independents were prosecuted before 1665. These may have been leaders of an extremist faction in the group, since Thomas Atkinson, presented in 1663 as an Independent, was also described as a Fifth Monarchist.[48] Atkinson was the only person presented from the Neast connection, which was so closely associated with the interests of the Protectorate in the corporation.[49] Phillip Surman provides a stark contrast in his rapid recovery from exclusion. Surman, who was a member of Neast's family, suffered public humiliation when removed from the office of bailiff in 1662. He was nevertheless elected churchwarden in 1664.[50] Separatism was the principle of exclusion in the restored parish, and the Independents in Tewkesbury were reluctant to separate from a church that had borne their stamp in the 1650s.[51]

The visitation and the prosecutions that it produced formed a campaign against the most visible local Separatist movements, the Baptists and Quakers. The campaign was intended to mark the boundaries of the established church in prosecutions of the most conspicuous offenders. There was no systematic effort to prosecute the rank and file members of Separatist communities. Instead, the prosecutions focused on Separatists known to hold private religious meetings or conventicles in their homes. In 1663 Edwin Millington of Tewkesbury was presented for "keeping a conventicle of Anabaptists" in his house.[52] The Quakers who were presented, such as Samuel Mosse, Nathaniel Jeynes, Charles Tovy, and Joseph Underhill, were sufficiently prominent to hold the Stoke Orchard monthly meeting in their Tewkesbury homes.[53] This assault on conventicles was occasionally carried out in conjunction with the civil courts. In 1661 John Mansel and John Cooke of Deerhurst were indicted at the assizes in Gloucester for holding conventicles in their houses.[54]

The assault on the leadership and organizational base of Separatist movements was the primary objective of the visitation. But the assault on Separatism and the prosecutions of the early 1660s did occasionally touch the rank and file membership of local movements. The visitation court placed local religious life on trial and pronounced judgment on many less prominent Separatists presented for "offenses" ranging from nonattendance at church to more serious transgressions of the ritual cycle, such as keeping children unbaptized. The community of 135 Baptists that was centered on Tewkesbury had at least seventeen members presented in court, 13 percent of its total membership.[55] The number of prosecutions remained small and evenly distributed between movements. Of seventy presentments made between 1662 and 1665 for violations of the ceremonial code, thirty-five offenders can be positively identified as either Baptists or Quakers.[56]

The relatively small number of Separatists who were prosecuted supports an interpretation of the visitation as an attempt to establish boundaries rather than uniformity. The arrival of the bishop and the preparation of presentments was part of the larger process of marking the boundaries of the church and persuading neighbors outside the boundaries to cross over. Several local initiatives to restore the fabric of the abbey should be considered part of this attempt to reconstruct the traditional meanings of the parish church. In 1660 Independents still dominated the parish, but the churchwardens hired local workers to repaint and refurbish the royal arms in Tewkesbury Abbey.[57] The parish meeting then agreed to raise £112 for rebuilding the "great window" in the church.[58] Richard Cooke and Thomas Smith, churchwardens of Tewkesbury in 1657, were prosecuted in 1663 for their removal of the font from the church. The font stones were recovered from Richard Cooke's garden in 1664 and restored to their place in the abbey. Since the second churchwarden, Thomas Smith, was a Baptist, the recovery of the font publicly expressed the distinction in the restored parish between the sacred fabric of the parish church and Separatist sacrilege.[59] This restoration of the fabric and ceremonial architecture of the church was an important element in the creation of boundaries, an importance expressed in the presentation of an Independent and some Quakers for refusing to contribute to the levy.[60]

The creation of boundaries and the resulting confrontation with Separatism brought a small but significant group of Baptists back to the restored church.[61] Their return was a direct result of the boundary-making process in parochial restoration and of the relationship consequently formed between the Separatist religion of conscience and the restored religion of legal forms. The open church of the Protectorate had not only incorporated the Separatist groups but also had claimed as its spiritual mission the liberation of the many religious voices in the former regime. The only element of uniformity in this vision of the national church was the authority of conscience. The return of monarchy destroyed the political culture in which the pursuit of conscience had been defined as a civic virtue. Some of the most ardent Separatists of the 1650s found the subsequent devaluation of Separatism and its isolation beyond the boundaries of the restored church to be unacceptable. The lay preacher Edmund Jennings had "preached separation from the world" in the 1650s, but he made a break with the Baptist meeting and returned to the restored church in 1661.[62] Their exclusion from the national church also brought persecution and anxiety to many Separatists. If persecution remained below the level required to destroy movements, it nevertheless brought intense suffering to individuals. The experience of Thomas White, a Baptist of Tewkesbury, illustrates the power of this external pressure to conform. The local churchwardens presented White in 1662 and 1663 for his absence from the parish church. White then began to show some inconsistency in his attendance of the Separatist meeting. He was admonished for his disloyalty, apparently began to drink heavily, and was finally expelled from the Baptist community in 1663.[63]

The official and psychological pressure placed on the leadership and margins of Separatist movements in the restoration of the parish created and subsequently reinforced the distinction between the church and dissent. The importance of this boundary for local Presbyterians and Independents as well as for the shadowy community of Prayer Book Protestants helps to explain the diverse local support of the Restoration. The militant Protestant faction had splintered in the course of the 1650s, and a pervasive fear of spiritual levelers induced even Independents to favor the construction of formidable boundaries to protect the society of the elect from the destructive power of radical mysticism. Neast and his supporters on the Protectorate council chose to risk political exclusion in order to protect their vision of religious community. This cooperation between Presbyterians, Independents, and Cavaliers in the royalist restoration, an alliance superficially similar to the corporate and parochial politics of the early 1630s, saved the elect from the spiritually and socially subversive force of Quakerism. Yet this fragile alignment of diverse groups produced not the static relationships frequently implied by the concept of the Restoration but a form of belonging characterized as much by unresolved conflicts as by the shared desire to preserve social and religious hierarchy.

What is meant by restoration process? A process is defined by indeterminacy, the absence of closure or finality. This simple concept, applied to the return of monarchy in 1660, has already begun to shape a new historical perspective on the Restoration. Just as the progressive landmarks of the English Reformation have dissolved in contingency, the Restoration has ceased to stand as a monolithic event, defined once and for all in royal decrees and parliamentary statutes.[64] The local views and experiences of restoration in the corporation and parish of Tewkesbury make sense only in the context of the conflicts and alliances of the 1640s and 1650s. These experiences of restoration reveal a complex local politics of belonging in both corporation and parish, a politics of inclusion and exclusion. Nor did the restoration process resolve the related problems of authority, loyalty, and belonging or local identity. The experience of defeat was not the experience of destruction, and visions of the restored polity that were removed from power in the early 1660s survived to emerge in later conflicts and debates. The alliance of local Presbyterians and Independents produced in the first Restoration reappeared in slightly modified form in the local reaction to the Popish Plot in the late 1670s. The moment of restoration should not be assumed as the norm for relations between the factions in corporations.

The creation of boundaries between church and sect did not imply local consensus on the form of religious ritual to be practiced in the restored parish. Presbyterians, Independents, and Prayer Book Protestants agreed on the necessity of boundaries to protect formal hierarchy in the parish, but the precise relationship between prescribed forms of prayer and the authority of conscience in this restored hierarchy remained unclear. The parochial restoration thus failed to resolve old conflicts over authority and ritual in the church. Many of the Nonconformists who returned to the parish church in the early 1660s refused to accept the Restoration settlement as the last word on local religious practice. The first episcopal visitation distinguished Presbyterians, Independents, and Prayer Book Protestants as the restored parish and constructed boundaries to protect this form of belonging from sectarian neighbors. The restoration process thus represented neither a return to a homogeneous parish community nor a decisive break from the experience of the 1640s and 1650s in the corporation but represented rather, a redistribution of power among local factions expressed as an assault on sectaries and officers of the Protectorate. The fundamental questions of ritual and authority that had divided the neighborhood since the late sixteenth century had been rephrased but not resolved.

8

Bloody Stratagems and Busy Heads: Persecution, Avoidance, and the Structure of Religion, 1666–1689

In these distracted times, when each man dreads
The bloody stratagems of busy heads;
When we have fear'd three years we know not what,
Till witnesses begin to die o'th'rot,
What made our poet meddle with a plot?
> Thomas Otway, *Venice Preserved, or a Plot Discovered* (1682)

Let us now consider what a church is. A church seems to me to be a
free society of men, joining together of their own accord for the public
worship of God in such manner as they believe will be acceptable to
the Deity for the salvation of their souls. I say it is a free and voluntary
society.
> John Locke, *A Letter on Toleration* (1689)

In 1682 Thomas Otway used the metaphor of conspiracy in Venice to explore the catastrophic effects of division and faction in families and commonwealths. The nocturnal street scenes of *Venice Preserved,* performed and published in the aftermath of the Popish Plot and Exclusion Crisis, demonstrated the dark power of domestic conflict and senatorial faction to destroy intimate personal relationships—the friendship of Pierre and Jaffier, the marriage of Jaffier and Belvidera—as well as the institutions of the state and public order.[1] Otway's metaphoric representation of the crisis in 1682 assumed the close interrelationship of domestic order and public institutions. The familiar notion of the household as the foundation of political order makes the play more than a factional document, more than a royalist manifesto on the Popish Plot.

The broad themes of *Venice Preserved*, if not the details of its politics, mirrored deep concerns over both the constitution and the preservation of order in the corporation and parish of Tewkesbury. The interrelationship of the household, the parish, the civic community of the corporation, and the institutions of civil and ecclesiastical government in the kingdom remained sources of anxiety and conflict in Tewkesbury after the Restoration.

A recent discussion of political conflict in Restoration England has drawn attention to the importance of controversies inherited from the 1640s and 1650s in the development of conflict on constitutional and religious axes.[2] These axes of conflict in parliamentary and metropolitan politics were reproduced in distinctive local variations: in conflicts among the different forms of Anglicanism in the parish, in the politics of the distinction between the church and its sectarian neighbors, and in the impact of religious conflict on the civic community of the corporation in Tewkesbury. A similar process of variation affected local forms of antipopery, as Protestant diversity presented a more serious problem of public order than the small number of Catholics. John Miller's distinction between antipopery as an ideology and Catholics as a devotional community helps to explain why the local reaction to the Popish Plot and Exclusion Crisis in Tewkesbury focused on the dangerous conflicts among different kinds of Anglicans and Dissenters in the parish and never involved local Catholic families.[3] The most persuasive and relevant local lesson to be learned from the complex prejudice of antipopery concerned the general design to promote divisions among Protestants, as a prelude to conquest, and the need to enforce uniformity in the parish. A national crisis over a Catholic conspiracy became a local conflict among Protestants over the control of the parish church. Yet the most important form of local variation concerned the nature of the church itself. Anglican identity was disputed terrain in the Restoration parish, and the crisis of the late 1670s in Tewkesbury assumed the form of a bitter conflict between passionately held beliefs in a church based on law and a church based on conscience, both represented by advocates as the ideal of a national church loyal to the monarchy. The local evidence of a fight to control the parish and to shape its ceremonial discipline, a conflict over the nature of Anglican identity itself, raises important questions about the social depth of doctrinal coherence and "fundamental principles" in the Church of England.[4]

The boundaries created in the early 1660s shaped the structure of religious life in the vale in the fifteen years after the Restoration, as the practices of intermarriage and selective apprenticeship gradually brought familial relations into general agreement with religious boundaries. But the influence of formal boundaries was not expressed in the direct and oversimplified manner sometimes implied by the opposition of church and sect. Despite a structural transformation in the forms and practice of religion, prescriptive models—the abstract descriptions of religious order and practice contained in such sources as visitation articles—continued to represent forms of religious ritual in the parish as shared and uniform. The Anglican church was represented in such sources as an inclusive institution, despite the division of the parish into multiple fellowships based on family and household discipline. An ambivalent relationship existed between Anglicans and Dissenters. The prosecution of Dissenters would force an acknowledgment of separation and would place inclusive representations of the church at risk. Persecution in the courts was therefore nominal and focused on sensitive points of public order and property, such as the payment of tithes. If Dissenters kept the peace, their meetings were generally left undisturbed.

This pattern of relations should not be misconstrued as a form of toleration. The Anglican church encompassed several inclusive representations or models of the parish and its relationship to the national church. These abstract conceptions of the parish and church subsumed quite different positions on the relative authority of law and conscience in religion. Because the schisms of the 1650s had made inclusive representations of parish and church increasingly unreliable as descriptions of practice, Anglican models served as distinct approaches to the defense of an inclusive *fiction* from the consequences of separation. Toleration was neither stated nor implied. If the conception of the church based on law appeared more persuasive in a particular context than the conception of the church based on conscience, the relations between Anglicans and Dissenters could shift from avoidance to persecution.

Nor were Separatist groups bound to their neighbors by any alternative symbolism or formal code of values independent of religious difference. Dissenters assumed a marginal position as outsiders in their own parishes. The dubious position of Dissenters in local and national communities remained a source of emotional uncertainty and anxiety for their Anglican neighbors. In moments of crisis, local officers tended to enforce the legal boundaries of the Anglican church, and Separatist movements became a focus for fears of political conspiracy and social danger. The crises of the late 1670s produced a violent reaction rooted in the ambiguity of the social and religious space opened by the shadowy conception of Dissent.

The Popish Plot and Exclusion Crisis of 1678 and 1679 became a general crisis of political and religious authority that recalled the pattern of the early 1640s. In Tewkesbury, this crisis took the form of a conflict between local Protestant factions over the nature of authority in the church and corporation. Nonconformists inside and outside the parish church interpreted the plot as divine retribution for the moral irresponsibility of Charles II's regime. Francis Wells, the minister of Tewkesbury, preached a fiery sermon of moral indictment against Charles and his Court. Despite subsequent suspension from his ministry, Wells became the leader of a local revival of the movement for the further reformation of religious ceremonies in the parish. This movement was composed of veteran Nonconformists and former Parliamentarians who had returned to the established church in the 1660s. Wells and his supporters were opposed by an Anglican faction loyal to the Restoration settlement, a faction that included the chancellor of the diocese and most of the burgesses of the common council. In the early 1680s this faction of loyalist Anglicans deprived Wells of his benefice, and the prolonged controversy ended in a reactionary campaign of political and religious exclusion led by several former royalists.[5]

This campaign had a complex structure and history. The borough council produced by the Corporation Act had excluded numerous families from local government, and the subsequent attempt to reconstruct a more inclusive government in the late 1660s required a strategy to bring influential families back into corporate office and to protect royalist control of the borough. The council adopted a coercive system of controlled participation in the early 1670s to resolve this problem. Dissenters and Nonconformist Anglicans were threatened with fines and pressured to serve in the company of assistant burgesses and in the burdensome corporate offices of constable and surveyor of the highways. This policy achieved modest success in the 1670s but was condemned and abandoned in the aftermath of the Popish Plot and Exclusion Crisis. The leaders of the loyalist Anglican faction claimed that the reincorporated families had only used local office as a base from which to launch an-

other assault on royal authority and the church. Dissenters and Nonconformist Anglicans, forced into local office in the early 1670s, were driven
out in the early 1680s. This policy of exclusion from local office and a
simultaneous increase in the prosecution of religious offenses formed the
loyalist Anglican reaction to the crises of 1678 and 1679, a reaction
motivated by local loyalty to the legal boundaries of the church and
corporation created in the second Restoration of 1662.

These conflicts produced ample evidence of local anxiety over religious pluralism. The social and emotional implications of Separatism and
the psychological barriers to toleration may be clarified by reference to
the model of symbolic core and periphery in the cultural form of the
parish. Before the schisms of the 1640s and 1650s, participation in the
core rituals of parish religion placed the person in a fixed relationship to
the values and codes of behavior incorporated in the periphery. The
ambiguous notion of Dissent described groups that stood outside the
symbolism of parish rituals, in an uncertain relationship to the values
and behavioral expectations of the parish community. Dissenters seemed
dangerous because their discipline constituted an alternative to the parish, a core symbolism expressive of a religious community independent
of the parish church. The uncertainty of the moral identity created in
sectarian communities, seen from the perspective of neighbors in the
parish, had important social consequences. The ethical codes and behaviors prescribed in parish ritual included such diverse collective concerns
as the rules of sexual behavior and political loyalty. Separation from the
customary ritual cycle of the parish church made Dissent morally suspect
in the eyes of neighbors because it seemed to place Dissenters beyond the
boundaries of conventional moral and political behavior. To separate
from the symbolism of the parish community was to stand in uncertain
relationship to the behavioral codes and expectations that it sanctioned.

This politics of morality and religious difference helps to explain local
disputes over the legal boundaries of toleration in the 1680s. Prior to the
Revolution in 1688 and 1689, the local politics of religion produced
distinctive patterns of exclusion. Narrow regimes, marked by their exclusion of either loyalist Anglicans or Nonconformists, controlled local
government. The loyalist reaction in defense of the Restoration settlement in the early 1680s, for instance, culminated in the surrender of the
borough charter in 1684 and the acquisition of a more restrictive charter
early in the reign of James II. This new charter confined the parliamen-

tary franchise to the common council and established a more exclusive loyalist Anglican administration. The pattern of exclusion shifted, however, as James encountered opposition to the inclusion of Catholics in a policy of general toleration. The loyalist Anglicans were consequently removed from the council in 1687, and Dissenters were recruited as part of the royal campaign to construct local networks in favor of general toleration. This pattern shifted yet again in the autumn of 1688, as the attempt of the loyalist Anglican faction to restore the Jacobean charter of 1610 was frustrated only by the unexpected flight of James II.

The Revolution in 1688 and 1689 transformed this binary system of political exclusion because it produced a limited Protestant toleration and promoted a symbolism in which Dissenters and Anglicans participated in the same political community. This inclusion of Dissenters in the circle of order, enshrined in the Toleration Act, began to reshape political life in Tewkesbury between 1693 and 1698. Local sources describe this period as an "interregnum" in corporate government, and the institutions established by the charter were severely abbreviated. The common council appears to have survived in some form, minor offices continued to be filled, and the charities dependent on the incorporation of the borough operated continuously, but no bailiffs or senior officers were elected.

The factional politics of the 1690s revolved around the efforts of several influential local families to restore the Jacobean charter. In this fight for the control of the borough after the Revolution, Dissenters who were placed on the council in 1687 consolidated their political influence alongside the loyalist Anglican beneficiaries of James II's charter. Both groups were attacked by opponents as "regulators of the corporations" and enemies of the Revolution. Both groups had derived political advantage from the surrender of the charter and were represented as collaborators in the popish policies of James II. The local alliance of Anglicans and Dissenters had thus developed from the political vicissitudes of the 1680s, and this coalition finally secured the restoration of the Jacobean charter in 1698. The council that was nominated in the restored charter represented the first explicit incorporation of Anglicans and Dissenters as partners in the process of local government, a revolutionary change in the structure and politics of religious community.

After the violence and schism of the 1640s and 1650s, the structure of local religious life had become extremely complex. The divisions incorporated in the restored church after the visitation in 1662 ensured the persistence in the parish of diverse conceptions of how the church ought to be bounded and who ought to be considered its members. The sectarian communities had their own distinctive views of godly fellowship. The result of this diversity challenges narrow doctrinal conceptions of religious identity and makes it extremely difficult to describe a fixed relationship between church and sect. The religious culture of Tewkesbury and its neighboring parishes became the delicate product of a subtle process whereby the sacred and social relations were framed in the disputed idioms of ceremony and discipline. The existence of more than one frame, model, or ideal of religious community meant that the structure produced by this process could be influenced and even transformed by disturbances or conflict in the parish or in the broader communities, such as the diocese or kingdom, in which the parish participated. The structure of religion, the pattern of relations among diverse local groups and factions, became contingent and variable, not fixed by the terms of doctrine and law. Churchwardens were consistent neither in their prosecution of Dissenters and Nonconformists nor in the manner of prosecution. This variation in local attitudes to religious difference reflected the interactions of the multiple communities in which differences had symbolic significance and power. The national church and its diverse Separatist subcultures formed a spectrum of attitudes and relationships.

The dynamism in this diverse religious culture is difficult to recover and describe, but a discussion of three major problems may help to clarify the local situation and lay the foundation for interpretation. First, the existence of several distinctive ideals or prescriptive models of religious life in Restoration England can be demonstrated and the models described. These prescriptive models may be broadly classified as inclusive and Separatist in their views of membership. The inclusive model assumed different forms, identified here as the church of law and the church of conscience, that reflected different perceptions of the authority of law and conscience in church discipline and ceremonial practice. In the Vale of Gloucester, the Separatist models of religious life derived from Independent, Baptist, and Quaker notions of a boundary dividing the fellowship of the godly from the profane assemblies of the parish. Both inclusive and Separatist models were thus ideal conceptions of a single authoritative religious community.

Second, a considerable body of evidence survives, in the records of the ecclesiastical court and the local sects, to assess the relationship of prescriptive models to the local practice of religion and the building of religious communities. Practice need not conform to prescriptive models and may even contradict their basic premises. Patterns of kinship and neighborliness reveal some of the processes whereby religious difference was translated into social relations. In this behavioral context, prescriptive models of religious life appear as rather innocent fabrications remote from practice. The parish contained several socially articulated religious fellowships and had ceased even to approximate an inclusive religious community based on residence. Separatist notions of a distinct social and spiritual existence formed equally deceptive symbolic fictions. Dissenters lived in dangerous proximity to Anglican neighbors, and the exploration of the culture of Anabaptism in the previous chapter has already disclosed the symbiotic relationship between Separatist identity and the customary religious universe of the parish.

Third, and most difficult from the evidentiary perspective, are the implications of difference in prescription and practice for the process of interaction between the parish, the diocese, and the kingdom. The persuasive power of particular models of ceremony, discipline, and authority depended on conditions in the parochial, diocesan, and national communities in which the significance of religious difference was assessed and represented. The inhabitants of Tewkesbury and the other parishes of the northern vale defended their fictions, but the defense assumed different forms in response to variations in this contextual assessment of religious difference. One response to the presence of religious difference was a form of avoidance. Dissenters were frequently presented for conventional misdemeanors rather than for separation, and this practice corresponded closely to the rationale of the church of conscience. Churchwardens obscured religious difference in order to preserve the fiction of inclusion. In the late 1660s and early 1670s, the defense of this fiction involved accommodation of local conscience and avoidance of confrontation.[6] But a second response to religious difference was attack. In the national crises of the late 1670s, the same local officers adopted a strict position on the boundaries of lawful religious fellowship, the church of law, and used coercive means to enforce conformity and inclusion. Dissenters were prosecuted as Separatists for the first time since the episcopal visitation in 1662. The public position of the Anglican church on the issue of separation did not change decisively between 1666 and 1689, but variation in local perceptions of the significance of religious diversity resulted in a dynamic politics of religious forms or models.

The denizens of the vale embraced different and sometimes contradictory views of religious community in the 1660s, 1670s, and 1680s. This diversity was not created by the Restoration, but after the Restoration settlement of the parish in 1662, local faction and diversity were no longer framed by the common assumption of an inclusive church. Both the nature of distinctions in the restored parish and the reality of Separatism after the Restoration placed enormous pressure on traditional conceptions of the parish, and the relationship between prescriptive models and the practice of religion thus becomes a matter of considerable interest.

The Anglican church itself encompassed several distinct conceptions of its structure and membership. One such conception, the church of law, was articulated in many of the formal documents of the church. Gilbert Sheldon, Archbishop of Canterbury, provided a detailed description of this church of law in a letter to William Nicolson, Bishop of Gloucester.[7] After the passage of the second Conventicle Act in the spring of 1670, Sheldon wrote to Nicolson and the other bishops of his province to introduce his plan for "the peace and settlement of the church and the uniformity of God's service in the same."[8] The heart of the plan was Sheldon's injunction to the officers of the church to pursue "an exemplary conformity in their own persons and practice to his Majesty's laws and the rules of the church." Sheldon instructed the bishop of Gloucester to communicate the content of his letter to "parsons, vicars, and curates" of the diocese as well as to "chancellors, archdeacons, commissaries, officials, registers, and other ecclesiastical officers." The instructions maintained the practicality of an inclusive and uniform religious community, if only local officers could be made to "perform their duty to God, the king, and the church" in their "several capacities and stations" in the parishes of the diocese. An inclusive church would thus emerge from the local enforcement of law.

Sheldon's conception of parish and church made the local minister the embodiment of lawful religion. Strict reference to the Book of Common Prayer was to control the ceremonial conduct and discipline of the minister. This "due and reverent performance of so holy a worship" gave "honor to God" and enabled the minister "by his own example" to instruct the people of his parish in the proper doctrine. Divine service

consisted of the appointed prayers of the church, read "without addition
. . . or varying in substance or ceremony from the order and method set
down by the book." Ministers were also to represent their obedience and
practice of lawful religion by wearing "their priestly habit," the surplice
and hood, during the performance of the service.

The church of law expressed a fundamental lack of confidence in the
lay capacity to govern social and religious behavior in a responsible
manner. On the contrary, the laity needed to emulate a clerical model of
proper Christian conduct in order to achieve a virtuous life. The minister
provided such a model not only by performing the ceremonies of the
church in the lawful manner but also by observing a "strictness and
sobriety of life and conversation." An obedient and uniform orderliness
in religion and society would inevitably emerge from the minister's determined efforts to mold parish discipline in his own image by "checking
and punishing such as transgress and encouraging such as live orderly."
The minister provided "a pattern of good living" for his parishioners,
inculcating "virtue and religious deportment" by the force of his own
example.

The church of law demanded an assault on religious diversity. The
faithful servants of the Anglican church were missionaries in a wilder-
ness of Nonconformist and schismatic conceptions of religion. Officers
of the church had a duty to "persuade and win all nonconformists and
dissenters to obedience to his Majesty's laws and unity with the church."
If persuasion failed, Sheldon ordered his local officers to reduce refrac-
tory persons "by the censures of the church or such other good means
and ways as shall be most conducive thereunto." But neither persuasion
nor the strictures of the court exhausted the means to enforce uniformity.
The second Conventicle Act involved justices of the peace in the defense
of religious uniformity. The officers of the ecclesiastical hierarchy, from
the personnel of the court to the churchwardens in their respective parishes, were instructed to take particular notice of all "nonconformists
and holders and frequenters . . . of conventicles and unlawful assemblies
under pretense of religious worship." In particular, officers were enjoined to identify the preachers and teachers of conventicles and the
locations of the assemblies. Cities and towns of the diocese were to
receive close scrutiny, as Sheldon believed "the mischief" spread from
these urban sources into the smaller villages and hamlets.[9] The officers
were then directed to present the names of offenders to the justices and

to implore civil assistance in the suppression of unlawful assemblies. A systematic prosecution of religious difference could result, according to Sheldon, only in "a hearty affection to the worship of God, the honor of the king and his laws, and the peace of the church and kingdom."[10]

The church of law was characterized by an insistence on the authority of law and external agency in religion. This prescriptive model of the church maintained a connection between political loyalty, religious ceremony, and church discipline as foundations of order. The Restoration settlement had enshrined the necessary relationship of God, church, and king in the laws of the realm; moreover, the proper practice of religion was not so much a question of conscience as a question of conformity to this external standard, ideally represented in the ceremonial conduct and personal comportment of the Anglican minister. Conformity to the church of law surrounded personal faith in ceremonies that symbolized loyalty to king and church. The definitive symbols of this church were the Book of Common Prayer and the surplice.

The church of conscience is more difficult to reconstruct, as relatively few formal statements of the position have survived. The existence of alternative conceptions of the church was explicitly acknowledged by Sheldon himself. His letter to Nicolson called for obedience to the ritual order prescribed in the Book of Common Prayer, "wherein I hear and am afraid too many do offend."[11] As a protest against strict adherence to the prescribed forms of Anglicanism, the church of conscience held a more indulgent view of religious diversity. In 1669, Bishop Nicolson complained to the lord lieutenant and several justices that Dissenters assembled "in greater numbers and more daring than formerly." These assemblies persisted, according to Nicolson, in the "hope of . . . impunity . . . from their not being in the least suppressed."[12] Yet the church of conscience resembled the church of law in its inclusive representation of the parish. In the church of conscience, however, this inclusion was to be achieved by a relaxation of formal religious boundaries and an accommodation of the many local manifestations of lay piety.

This extension of boundaries was expressed in the ceremonies of the church. Ministers represented and sanctioned the authority of conscience by their spontaneous modification of the forms prescribed in the Book of Common Prayer and by their resistance to the surplice. Francis Wells, the curate of Tewkesbury, was admonished in the episcopal visitation of 1671 "to read prayers and wear the surplice."[13] Far from concealing their practice in the obscurity of remote parishes, supporters of the church of conscience used their position to confront the ecclesiastical hierarchy. In 1676 the ecclesiastical court ordered Wells to read prayers in front of the bishop and questioned his alteration of the form of the Absolution laid down in the Book of Common Prayer. Wells replied that he had not read in the prescribed manner because "it never was his custom so to do as to read the Absolution as the Book of Common Prayer directed."[14] By modifying his ceremonial practice in this way, Wells signified his sensitivity to similar qualms of conscience among his parishioners.

This concern to honor the authority of conscience is illustrated by a local incident in the early 1660s. In February 1661 a group of soldiers dragged some Quakers from their meeting place in Broad Campden and brought them before Thomas Overbury, a justice of the peace, to take the Oath of Allegiance. When the Quakers refused the oath, Overbury dutifully committed the group to prison. He nevertheless added his opinion that the Quakers were right not to swear if swearing was perceived as a question of conscience or was believed to be evil.[15] Overbury's decision to imprison the Quakers reflected the demands of the early Restoration and a commitment to the creation of boundaries for the new regime. By the late 1660s local officers like Overbury had ceased to prosecute separation that did not constitute an explicit challenge to public order.[16]

The boundaries of the church remained a focal point of conflict. As rules for the interaction of Anglicans and other local groups, however, the church of law and the church of conscience had important implications beyond the boundaries of Anglicanism. The issues addressed in conceptions of Anglican community were also confronted in Separatist visions of religious fellowship. An emphasis on conscience placed the Nonconformist Anglican model of community closer to moderate Dissent, in the form of Independency, on the spectrum of local belief. The fear and hatred of Dissenters in the church of law may have reflected an awareness of the Nonconformist element in the national church. Fears of a general Nonconformist conspiracy that included Dissenters were made credible by the persistence of controversies over authority and ceremonies in the church itself. In the early 1680s, for instance, local fears of Francis Wells and Nonconformist intentions in the parish community in Tewkesbury resulted in a general persecution of Dissenters. The factional conflicts in the parish communities of the national church always had the potential to incorporate the Dissenters, the outsiders in the parish.

The inclusive parish, in both its Anglican forms, was challenged by alternative conceptions of community based on separation from the church. After the Restoration, these minority views on the nature of religious community formed a subculture in a manner similar to the Baptist fellowship of the 1650s, although the process of restoration in the parish identified this subculture as dangerous and attempted to isolate its influence. This Separatist subculture comprised a spectrum of positions on the value and purpose of separation that included Independency, Anabaptism, and Quakerism, and in the form of Independency this spectrum of Dissent showed affinities to the restored parish. Despite their common Separatism, for instance, the Independents reviled the radical sects and represented their own groups as alternative visions of the church. The Independents had participated actively in the restoration of the monarchy, in part because of concern over the implications of radical sectarianism. But the distinctive quality of Dissent, common to all its forms, was the process of separation from the parish. The rationale and implications of this separation were most clearly expressed in the Separatism of the Quakers.

The Separatist model of religious fellowship sought to establish boundaries and to eliminate the influence of external values of any kind on the behavior of the initiates. In the prescriptive order of their monthly meeting in Stoke Orchard, the main assembly for the territory of Tewkesbury and its neighborhood, the Quakers represented the boundary that separated their group from the parish as a wall of blood constructed during long years of persecution. Ministers of the national church were described as "the priests of Baal" and "the fist of wickedness and bloody hands, who have had their hands in the blood of the brethren." Persecution in the service of the truth was thus a crucial element in Quaker identity. The climate of persecution and the boundaries that it produced were maintained and institutionalized in the life of the group. Quakers were instructed to collect formal descriptions of the "sufferings" of their coreligionists as symbols of "the murdering spirit of this world" from which the group had separated. These images of persecution and the wall of blood then became the symbolic "evidence" for the definitive Quaker metaphors of the parish as a modern Egypt and the Quakers as the chosen people in captivity. In the symbolism of captivity and flight, Quaker ritual was distinguished from the ceremonies of the national church as "the bread of life" from "the dishes and pleasures" of "the priest and his company."[17]

These boundaries identified Quakers as the sharers of a hidden truth and as the members of a distinct religious fellowship founded on the unity of the spirit in "one heart, one mind, and one soul." This model of community then required the exclusive influence of Quaker discipline over the internal life of the group. The codes of behavior prescribed for Quakers as the way to walk in the truth excluded the corrupt values and spurious authority of the world. Like other Nonconformist groups, the Quakers rejected conventional forms of conviviality, represented in the general order of the Stoke Orchard meeting as "pleasures, drunkenness, and gaming." This renunciation of the customary life of the parish removed Quakers from many of the situations in which neighborliness was represented and affirmed. The attempt to achieve an exclusive discipline is further illustrated by Quaker notions of the orderly marriage. If the fellowship decided a match was undesirable, conventional notions of honor and reputation were unconditionally subordinated to the group's order. The weekly and monthly meetings determined the legitimacy of marriages. Quakers who were married by ministers of the national church were to be presented and condemned in the quarterly meeting for submission to the spirit of Baal. The discipline of the meeting attempted to exclude conceptions of value and forms of authority beyond the boundaries of the group.[18]

These prescriptive models helped to define the structure of Restoration religion but should not be mistaken for descriptions of practice. In everyday life the residents of the northern vale were involved in complex social situations, and decisions did not necessarily conform to the rules enjoined in abstract representations of community. The behavior of individuals and groups often contradicted the assumptions and stereotypes implicit in the formal models of Anglicanism and Dissent. These stereotypes were instrumental in the creation of group boundaries and played a significant role in Anglican and Separatist models of religious fellowship, but local practice could be influenced by factors not considered in abstract assumptions and calculations. The practice of religion therefore tended to diverge from stereotypical representations of it.

A dependence on several unreliable assumptions and stereotypes undermined the inclusive conceptions of the parish. The church of law represented Nonconformity and Dissent as the deviance of a relatively small number of misdirected Anglicans who were seduced by cranks and malcontents. The church of conscience discarded this tendentious image of Nonconformity and Dissent as forms of deviance but retained an image of Dissent as the spiritual exile of Anglicans stricken in conscience and driven from the national church by its insistence on submission to the law in ceremonies and discipline. If Anglican ministers performed their pastoral duties, which were defined differently in the church of law and the church of conscience, most of the stray sheep, it was believed, would quietly return to the Anglican fold. Although these assumptions and stereotypes made an important contribution to arguments for an inclusive church, they were extremely unreliable as descriptions of Separatism.

The social organization of Nonconformity and Dissent in the parish of Ashchurch illustrates the distance between ideal and practice in local religious life.[19] Fragments of the local organization of Independents can be recovered from church court presentments, parish registers, and wills. In 1672 Richard Davison obtained a license to hold a meeting of Independents in his house in Ashchurch.[20] Davison lived in the hamlet of Natton, close to the center of the parish.[21] The other members of this fellowship were dispersed among the hamlets of Pamington, Fiddington, and Natton.[22] Despite its geographic diffusion, the group possessed a strong interfamilial organization, and the attraction of common religious belief was articulated in bonds of marriage and friendship. Davison's son married the daughter of Roger Long of Fiddington, and several members of the Long family belonged to the Independent meeting.[23] The Haines family of Natton and Pamington had developed significant links of friendship to Nonconformist families as early as the 1630s. John Purse of Pamington, presented as a Nonconformist in 1635, had been a close friend of Elizabeth Haines and served as one of the overseers of her will.[24] This Nonconformist connection was transferred to the next generation and expressed in the prosecution of Elizabeth's son, Richard Haines of Pamington, his wife Margaret, son Samuel, and daughter Margaret in the early 1670s.[25]

The evidence of wills indicates the importance of coreligionists in preparation for death and their frequent participation in the process as witnesses and overseers. Richard Olive, for instance, served as a witness for Roger Long of Fiddington. The Olive family was joined by marriage to the Haines family of Natton, cousins of the Haines family of Pamington.[26] Joseph Oakley witnessed the will of John Purse of Pamington. Oakley and Elinor Purse, the wife of John Purse, were prosecuted in the church court for not coming to church in the early 1670s.[27] Samuel Haines, the son of Richard Haines of Pamington, chose Phillip Surman of Tewkesbury and John Haines as his witnesses. Surman was the son-in-law of William Neast of Twyning, a pillar of the Independent regime under the Protectorate.[28] These families were connected at this critical moment in the life cycle by common forms of religious belief. Because the Independents were as opposed to the process of probate as to the other functions of the ecclesiastical court, the presence of coreligionists may have formed part of an informal process to establish or "prove" the legitimacy of a will.[29]

The boundaries of this fellowship were not limited by parish boundaries. Independents in the hamlets of Ashchurch were connected to similar clusters of families in Tewkesbury. Richard Davison's brother, William Davison of Tewkesbury, obtained a license in the early summer of 1672 to hold a meeting of Independents in his house.[30] Henry Lane of Tewkesbury, described as an Independent in the early 1660s, was related by marriage to Richard Haines of Pamington. Lane may have moved by the early 1670s or may have owned property in both Tewkesbury and Ashchurch, since he was prosecuted by the churchwardens of Ashchurch in the early 1670s for his absence from the parish church. Lane and Richard Haines had been prosecuted for Nonconformity in Ashchurch in the 1630s, and Haines had married Margaret Lane in the winter of 1633. His brother William Haines made his "landlord and very faithful friend" Henry Lane the overseer of his will in the early 1660s.[31] The fellowship of Independency clearly transcended the customary residential group of the parish, and the social organization of Independency showed a superficial resemblance to Baptist fellowship. The Independents were interconnected families identified not by the territorial boundaries of a parish but by the bonds of godly fellowship and shared views on the authority of scripture and conscience.

The evidence of Independency in Ashchurch indicates that the local organization of even the more moderate Dissenters contradicted the stereotype implicit in the inclusive models of the Anglican parish. Anglican views of Dissent consistently underestimated the qualitative, if not the statistical, significance of Separatism as a social phenomenon. Independency was neither the marginal religion of the mentally misaligned nor the enforced exile of tender consciences that were driven from the national church, but rather was a viable alternative to the form of religious fellowship symbolized by the parish. The persistence of local connections over time was particularly important in this context. Several of the important families in the group had been associated with Nonconformity since the early years of the seventeenth century. This connection was excluded from Anglican representations of Dissent, and formal recognition would have destroyed the most important fiction in the inclusive model of the parish, the fiction of social unity. The patterns of avoidance and persecution that characterized local reactions to religious difference from 1666 to 1689 resulted from Anglican efforts to protect this fiction.

The importance of stereotypes and fictions in the creation of boundaries was not unique to Anglicanism. Separatist models of fellowship were equally unreliable as descriptions of practice. If the inclusive parish required an unreliable representation of Dissent, Separatist fellowship depended on simplistic representations of a definitive break and withdrawal from customary codes of behavior and value. The most extreme assertion of this break came from the Quakers, and Quakers therefore provide the most interesting evidence of problems encountered in the process of separation from the parish. Traditional codes of behavior and courtship had a profound influence on the behavior of a Quaker named Anne Dobbins. In 1672 the Stoke Orchard monthly meeting warned Dobbins against marriage to "one of the world." Dobbins insisted that she had made the man a promise and that failure to honor her word would result in "a scandal to the truth." Although the meeting rejected her assessment of the situation, Dobbins refused to change her marriage plans. Despite her condemnation for this disorderly marriage, Dobbins does not appear to have been expelled from the group.[32] In 1680 Edward Edwards and Cornelius Grasstock of the monthly meeting agreed to caution the widow Salle against "disorderly walking" or "setting out her mind towards any man in order to marriage who does not make a profession of the truth."[33] The problem became important enough in 1677 for the monthly meeting to order one of its members to prepare a paper against "disorderly" marriages.[34]

The world of the traditional neighborhood and parish confronted Dissenters in the same way Dissent confronted the parish. Despite emotionally powerful symbols of their separation, Dissenters continued to dwell in the midst of parish communities and could not avoid some forms of neighborly interaction. The participation of Dissenters in the everyday life of their villages may seem too obvious for comment, but this participation involved Dissenters in a social life opposed to the symbols of separate fellowship. An emphasis on neighborliness, rather than spiritual difference, threatened to undermine the fiction of separation. The structure of religion after the Restoration reflected the efforts of Dissenters to protect both their fictions and the boundaries of their groups in the face of changing Anglican responses to their existence in the parish.

Structure usually refers to static relationships. The conventional idea of structure suspends interaction, defines relationships according to selected criteria, such as occupation or status, and produces a synchronic, static image of the order behind behavior. As an approach to religion, this idea of structure focuses on the set features of institutional order and doctrine. A fixed structure is produced by describing the organization of the parish, the diocese, and the sects as the institutional manifestations of doctrine. This approach cannot explain complex variations in the interaction of groups and factions. A different idea of structure might focus on doctrinal statements as prescriptive models and might consider the relationship between models and practice over time. This method results in a complex structure that is both generative and explanatory. The structure of religion described here encompassed the dynamic and often contradictory relationship of prescriptive order and practice in church and sect, generated diverse patterns of interaction, and explains alterations in the pattern. In the static form of structure, variation in the relations of local groups can result only from the impact of external forces. The dynamic idea of structure reveals, in the same evidence, the potential for internal transformation in religion.[35]

The structure of religion in Tewkesbury and the other parishes in the northern vale created diverse and seemingly inconsistent patterns of relationship between groups over time. The local response to religious difference in the 1670s is best described as a form of avoidance, in that the churchwardens refused to prosecute the forms of Separatism known to have had local organizations by the early 1670s. This pattern of avoidance seems to have involved more than a disinclination to prosecute neighbors. Many cases did come before the courts, but the offenders were prosecuted for customary offenses, such as absence from church or failure to receive communion, rather than for acts of separation. Prior to the rapid increase in prosecutions for Dissent in 1679, only one resident of northern Gloucestershire was prosecuted in the consistory court for participation in a conventicle. William Davison of Tewkesbury was presented in November 1677 for preaching in a conventicle held in King's Stanley, far beyond the boundaries of his own parish, and here the exception seems to prove the rule, because the decision to prosecute in Davison's case was complicated by his distance from home.[36] This refusal to enforce the penalties against Dissenters may have reflected a desire to avoid the social and cultural reality of separation.

After the Restoration, presentments in the church court differed from the pattern established in the first half of the seventeenth century.[37] Before the suspension of its activities in the summer of 1641, the consistory court had enforced standards of sexual comportment and civility. The court had helped to promote and protect both the ceremonial discipline of the parish and the standards of behavior exalted and sanctioned in the ceremonies of the church. The Restoration court, which concentrated on church discipline and ceremonial conformity, handled a much smaller number of sexual offenses than its predecessor. The court had lost its jurisdiction in matters now considered the concern of the justices of the peace. Between 1671 and 1697 the court processed only thirty-seven presentments for sexual offenses. These presentments represented a smaller number of offenses: ten cases of bastardy and fornication and twelve clandestine marriages. Sexual offenses thus represented only 6 percent of the 645 presentments made in the court, although the prosecution of bastardy revived in the late 1690s, and twelve cases were presented for Tewkesbury alone between 1699 and 1703.[38]

The court maintained its jurisdiction over cases of religious belief, ceremonial conformity, and church discipline, and the presentments for absence from church and failure to receive communion increased as the number of sexual offenses declined. Between 1671 and 1686 the court processed 470 cases of absence from church and failure to receive communion in the parishes of the northern vale, classes of offense that accounted for 76 percent of the court's business. A statistical assessment of the court's activity in Ashchurch, Deerhurst, Forthampton, Tewkesbury, Tredington, and Twyning becomes more difficult after the Restoration. The activities of local Nonconformists and Dissenters were not limited by parish boundaries, and several families from Tewkesbury and its vicinity were presented for misdemeanors committed in Boddington, Brockhampton, Gotherington, Oxenton, Stoke Orchard, and Woodmancote.[39]

The uneven distribution of cases over time and the descriptive ambiguity of the offenses handled by the court were no less important than the shifts in the composition of the court's business. Churchwardens did not confront Nonconformity and Dissent directly in the early 1670s. Despite Sheldon's forceful letter to the bishop of Gloucester in May 1670, no evidence survives of an "intensive campaign" against the sects in the northern vale. Of the 470 cases of absence from church and failure to receive communion presented in the church court between 1671 and 1686, only 63 were presented before 1678.[40] These cases often involved Dissenters, but participation in conventicles was not acknowledged in prosecutions before 1677. The small number of cases (fewer than two presentments per year for each of the six parishes) and the obscurity of the charge are difficult to reconcile to the accounts of persecution after the Restoration.[41] If the relationship between church and sect was a fixed antagonism from the Restoration to the Revolution, why were the local officers of the national church so reluctant to prosecute their adversaries? Why did the churchwardens of the 1670s refuse to prosecute neighbors for separation from the parish?

Although descriptions of offenses often remained the same, an important difference entered the records of prosecution in the late 1670s. Churchwardens identified conspicuous Dissenters in their presentments, and the number of cases presented increased dramatically. Of the 470 cases of absence from church and failure to receive communion presented from the six northern parishes of the vale between 1671 and 1686, 407 cases, 87 percent of the total presentments, appeared after 1678. John Cowell of Tewkesbury, a prominent Baptist, was presented in 1679 for absence from church and for the conventicle kept in his house. Cowell had been prosecuted in a less direct manner several years earlier as a performer of illicit marriages.[42] In the early 1680s the Quaker meeting places and the membership of local meetings were registered in the court, and the relationship of Quakers to the church began to approximate the stereotype of persecution that the group had long used to describe itself.[43] Dissenters were prosecuted as Separatists for the first time since the Restoration. As the position of the church on the issue of separation had remained the same, the explanation of this variation in perceptions of religious difference is not immediately apparent. The continuity in church policy on Dissent reduces the likelihood of external compulsion as an explanation for the variation in local attitudes. Why would the coercive power of the church have become so much more effective in the late 1670s? An explanation might be found in the structure of religion and in the local experience of events in the world beyond the parish. The variation in perceptions of religious difference may have resulted from reactions to the Popish Plot and the deadly danger it posed to the idea of an inclusive national church.

The patterns of avoidance and persecution are difficult to explain, but both make sense as reflections of a determined effort to protect the fiction of an inclusive church. An appreciation of lay conscience as a legitimate source of religious authority furnished the rationale for avoidance. In the church of conscience, Protestant unity was considered more important than the standard of ceremonial propriety established in law. The fears created by news of the Popish Plot, on the other hand, formed the national context in which local perceptions of religious difference and separation were transformed.[44] After the plot, the churchwardens and corporate officers of Tewkesbury came to perceive Nonconformity and Dissent as subversive impulses reminiscent of the pernicious radicalism of the early 1640s. Persecution became the means to preserve an inclusive church.

This transformation of attitudes left local traces. James Simpson, the town clerk of Tewkesbury, preserved the documents created by a dispute between the borough council and Francis Wells, the vicar of Tewkesbury. These sources reveal, in vitriolic detail, the controversy that developed among religious factions in Tewkesbury after Wells had delivered a provocative sermon in the early days of the plot's discovery. Simpson's papers make it possible to consider the local experience of the plot and the impact of local conflict, which was intensified if not created by the plot, on attitudes to the church of conscience and the church of law, the models of authority and community in the parish. The movement of the conflict from the parish and corporation in Tewkesbury to the consistory court in Gloucester, and from the consistory court to the Court of Arches in London, created important evidence of how shifts in the structure of religion affected the interrelationship of the parish, the diocese, and the provincial hierarchy of the national church.

The trouble began on Sunday, November 13, 1678. This day had been declared a fast day by parliament and "a day of humiliation to implore God's mercy in the further discovery of the plot against his Majesty's person . . ."[45] This decision to protect the king by calling a fast was no more than prudence. Charles was the semidivine head of a social and political hierarchy represented conventionally by the metaphor of a human body. He was joined to his subjects in such a way that the actions of the one could have acute spiritual and physical consequences for the other. A king could suffer for the misdeeds of his subjects, as a dissolute monarch could bring down divine wrath on his people. The fast day was a powerful means to prevent either misfortune. On these days, subjects withdrew from the profane world and purified themselves through the discipline of the fast. Collective sins were confessed in the fast day sermon and absolution humbly requested. The body of the realm was cleansed by this process of communal and individual sacrifice and confession.

Many of the social and religious assumptions necessary to successful public fasts had become untenable in the Vale of Gloucester by the late 1670s. An effective fast required a united community of penitents, for, in the hands of a faction, the fast might be used as a weapon to attack opponents. A general agreement on the sources of communal and national sin was a necessary consequence of this unity among believers. Confession might turn to indictment if factions used the occasion of the fast to advance rival interpretations of the evil in their midst. The fast of November 1678 was an attempt to unite local communities divided by decades of religious conflict; however, the occasion not only failed to evoke the desired unity but also produced a new intensity of acrimony.

Francis Wells, the vicar of Tewkesbury, presided over the fast in 1678. In the course of a long career, Wells had shown considerable hostility to the church of law. He received his M.A. from Gloucester Hall, Oxford, in 1629, and his enemies claimed in 1680 that "he was formerly a preacher to a regiment of the late rebels." Other sources indicate that his radicalism had millenarian overtones but stopped short of regicide, as Wells was said to have preached on the execution of John the Baptist on the Sunday after the death of Charles I.[46] The sermon Wells delivered on November 13, 1678, has not survived, so that his performance can be reconstructed only from the subsequent statements of churchwardens and magistrates.[47] The sermon was organized as a set of concentric confessions. It began with the national sins and the sins of the City, perceived as the bastion of finance, commerce, and avarice in London, and proceeded to the sins of town and country, before it narrowed down to "the particular sins of our town of Tewkesbury, for which this day we were to be humble."[48] But Wells was convinced that the sins of the body politic had a more fundamental source. The last box of vice and corruption that Wells opened for the assembled parish was reserved for King Charles himself. Wells later wrote to Sir Francis Russell, an important local landholder and one of the borough's members in the parliament, that "in confessing of the crying sins of the times," he had "confessed the sins of his Majesty." Wells perceived this confession as a duty and a means to procure divine pardon. The confession was made "not only in general, as thus we have sinned, we and our king, we and our princes, etc., but in particular, the sins of adultery and fornication and confessing these and naming of the king as deeply guilty of them and begging pardon for them for him . . ."[49] Russell had received only a modest account of the sermon. The churchwardens claimed that Wells had routinely enjoined the townspeople to be humble and then added abruptly that they should be humbler still "for the adultery, fornication, and whoredom of the king." According to the churchwardens, Wells invoked these royal sins as the reason that "the land did mourn."[50]

Responses to the sermon were in evidence before it was finished. Wells had started to discuss "the wonder of God's mercy" that Charles had been spared from such plots for so long "and not cut off in the midst of his sins," when Thomas Nanfan, the senior bailiff and highest legal officer in the borough, intervened. He told Wells that "it was not safe for the people to hear him farther on that subject" and asked him to desist. Wells refused, claiming that "he had said nothing but what he would justify," and continued to the end of his sermon.[51] By the end of the day, both Wells and his opponents on the common council had written to Sir Francis Russell for advice and support. Wells cautiously confessed to offending the magistrates but insisted that their behavior had "aggravated much the matter." Wells believed that the sermon had preserved the confessional spirit of the fast. His words had been spoken "out of real love and true loyalty to his Majesty, and out of zeal for God and discharge of a good conscience toward God and man." Wells had discovered, undoubtedly through his friends on the council, that his opponents had also drawn up a letter "somewhat untruly representing things to your honor." This knowledge had prompted Wells to write to request a letter that he was confident would stop any proceedings against him.[52] The letter from the council to Russell was also cautious. The councilors described the abrupt use of "very ill and reproachful words of his Maj-

esty" in the sermon. Wells had continued to preach despite the intervention of the senior bailiff, and the presence of "a very great congregation"
in the church underlined the threat to local law and order. The sermon,
in short, inclined "rather to sedition than otherwise, in this juncture of
time," and the burgesses closed their letter with a request for advice and
direction "to prevent calumny and danger therein."[53]

This early phase in the conflict contains information crucial to what
followed. Two points stand out. The first is the strong possibility that
Russell had supported the installation of Wells in the local benefice. The
advowson remained in the hands of the Crown, but it was customary for
the burgesses to put a candidate forward for confirmation by the bishop,
since the income of the benefice was largely at the corporation's disposal.[54] This circumstance usually meant consultation with one or more
of the prominent local gentlemen on the council, and after the Restoration no resident had a higher rank or better claim to be consulted in the
selection of the minister than had Sir Francis Russell. This relationship
between Wells and Russell affected the early development of the dispute
by making it impossible for Wells' opponents to attack him directly
without attacking Russell's local status and reputation. The risk of offending Russell created an incentive to negotiate a settlement with Wells
quickly and quietly.[55]

The second point concerns the hints contained in the letters of a
deeper source of schism in the parish. Wells represented "a good conscience toward God" as the heart of the fast. He had heeded the call of
conscience and confessed the sins of the king, but in this he had only
done his duty to God, to the community of the parish, and, ultimately, to
the king himself. Wells believed that the power of Christian community
resided in the authority of conscience. His exhortation to the king to
control the royal passions used the power of the body to shield the head,
as the parish community exerted its collective strength to enclose the
king in the moral armor of Christian values. The officers of the corporation presented a different account. They too perceived the fast as a day of
humiliation devoted to prayers for divine mercy and forgiveness, but
prayers for mercy were to be conducted in a decent and lawful manner.
Wells perceived his sermon as good conscience, but the invocation of
conscience to criticize the monarch sounded like "sedition" to the magistrates. Delivered to a large assembly in the early days of the plot, the
sermon was seen as a threat to law and the authority of government.

These representations of the church of conscience and the church of law would become more sharply defined over time.

Russell's response to these letters has not survived, but the actions of the next few weeks seem to reflect a general desire for a quiet solution. Wells preached a recantation sermon the next Sunday and declared that "if he knew of one drop of blood in his body that were factious and would not serve his Majesty, he would phlebotomize it, and if his hand should act anything to the damage of the king, he would rather cut it off."[56] He did not, however, confess to any unlawfulness in his conduct. This recantation was unsatisfactory to his opponents in the corporation, as it persisted in the elevation of unbridled conscience over the conscience that found God in the manner prescribed by law. The churchwardens of Tewkesbury, in conjunction with the burgesses who had written to Sir Francis Russell, prepared articles of complaint against Wells and presented the articles in the consistory court on December 3, 1678.[57]

The corporation of Tewkesbury had influence in the consistory court. Richard Parsons, chancellor of the diocese, presided over the court and numbered James Simpson, the town clerk of Tewkesbury, among his friends. Simpson would steer the corporation's case against Wells through both the consistory court and the Court of Arches.[58] This personal connection, as well as other factors, inclined diocesan institutions to look kindly on the corporate interest. Wells had confronted the diocesan authorities in the past. At a visitation in 1671, Parsons had admonished him to read prayers and to wear the surplice.[59] Wells was warned a second time in 1676, and the next year several Tewkesbury residents were prosecuted for involvement in clandestine marriages that Wells had conducted.[60] Wells had clearly failed to befriend Richard Parsons, and the apparent withdrawal of Sir Francis Russell's support deprived Wells of friends in the diocese and county who were powerful enough to help him oppose the articles presented by his opponents.

The faction opposed to Wells in the corporation wanted him suspended, but he was not bullied. Wells was in his seventies, and it was hoped his suspension would create a quiet time in which he could be persuaded to resign.[61] This calm was reflected in the vestry minutes that describe the joint efforts of Wells and the churchwardens to ensure delivery to London of sums collected for the rebuilding of St. Paul's Cathedral. As late as December 1, two days before his suspension, Wells was still able to work with a vestry composed primarily of his opponents.[62]

The petition for suspension was successful, but Wells used the procedural weapons available to him and made an open submission in the court. This submission to Parsons, who "cited a very fit piece of learning to convince him of his guilt and error," may have been a personal humiliation, but the act of submission had political uses, as it demanded reconciliation to the church and made prolonged suspension harder to justify. Wells rather cynically "requested Mr. Chancellor to be kind and merciful to him, to pity his age and infirmity, and to release his suspension with speed."[63] By the end of December, however, Wells seems to have realized that Simpson and Parsons could maintain his suspension indefinitely. Later evidence indicates that the corporation had started to pay outsiders to preach sermons, and Wells countered with a provocative signal to his parishioners that this practice subverted the bond between minister and parish. He sat through divine service and sermon with his hat on his head in the traditional Nonconformist sign of refusal to recognize the service as legitimate and make submission.[64]

The formal relationship between Wells and the common council emerges only at the late date of January 20, 1679, almost two months after his suspension. A full session of the council that included all six justices of the peace peremptorily resolved "that for want of a preaching minister, Mr. Wells be requested to resign."[65] Wells was summoned and confronted with the council's resolution. He tried once again to justify himself, claiming he had done nothing to deserve suspension, and refused to resign. In a terse note, it was ordered that a course should be taken "to force Wells by law to resign or else cause him to be deprived."[66] Despite these hard words, no drastic action was taken for another two-and-a-half months. The informal process of negotiation continued into early February, with increased chance of success, since Sir Francis Russell had returned from London after the dissolution of the parliament. At the council session of February 6, Russell being present, it was ordered that Wells be paid "so much of his salary of £10 *per annum* as was due him at Michaelmas last." Wells would also receive a bonus of £11 5s if he agreed to resign the cure of the parish upon request. After his resignation, the council would "give him a fair character, according to his desert," and help him collect "what benevolence he [could] get" from the town.[67] A compromise settlement had evidently started to form in the two weeks between the council sessions. Wells obviously wanted to avoid resignation in disgrace, and the orders of this February meeting furnish some slight evidence that he hoped to retain a curacy in the parish, perhaps agreeing to resign the vicarage in return for his arrears of salary. Sir Francis Russell added £10 on his own account to the sum offered by the council.[68] It remains uncertain whether Wells agreed to resign the whole of the benefice, but on February 7 he accepted the offer of compensation and agreed to resign the vicarage.[69] Local institutions resolved the conflict in a process of mediation, as had happened so many times in the past.

The compromise constructed by these ancient institutions lasted less than twenty-four hours. On February 8, Wells informed Sir Francis Russell that "upon more serious consideration" he could not resign his position, because "good hands" had assured him that the generality of the people did not desire his departure. Wells attacked the council and declared himself more obliged to serve his parishioners than "the desires of some few that perhaps may as soon be weary of another upon the least distaste." He also made an explicit statement of his position on the local role of the Anglican church. Wells claimed to know "the temper" of his parish "so well that if a stranger should be brought in, and them that they do not approve of, it will cause many more dissenting from the public, and so I may, by leaving them, be guilty of the hazard of their souls."[70] According to this view, the minister had a sacred duty to reflect on his performance of ceremony and to accommodate as many con-sciences as possible in the parish. An insensitive stranger might impose the orderliness of the church of law upon this local "temper" and force tender consciences out of the parish church to conventicles.

This letter had a decisive impact on the conflict between Wells and the council. The dispute had previously been defined primarily in terms of personal interest and reputation. Wells wanted his suspension lifted and to retain as much of his benefice as the corporation would allow. His opponents on the council insisted on his resignation but were prepared to negotiate compensation and possibly even the retention of a curacy. Defined in this way, the controversy lent itself to compromise, and local arbitration stood every chance of success as long as this interpersonal perspective on the conflict remained unchanged. Yet this perspective was not the only one possible. The "good hands" behind Wells in early Feb-ruary indicate that some of his parishioners interpreted the conflict in a different way. Supporters of the church of conscience perceived the sus-pension as part of an assault on the best reformed aspects of religion in the parish. This faction had returned to the restored church in the early 1660s but had refused to accept the Restoration settlement in the church as a permanent condition. In time, it was hoped, the ceremonies prescribed in the Book of Common Prayer might be modified in local practice. After exclusion from the common council in the second Restoration of 1662, several members of this faction returned to lesser positions in borough government and remained influential in business. They held a modest position in the parish church and waited.

The Popish Plot made this compromise untenable. The plot was the most acute spiritual crisis since the Restoration and was interpreted by many Protestants as divine retribution for past sins. Both factions in the church traced the crisis to their own conduct. Supporters of the church of law, particularly those who had served as justices of the peace, were aware that over two decades, they had all but made their peace with Nonconformity and Dissent. Many of their neighbors had been rumored to consort in the alleys behind Church Street, where conventicles were held, and virtually nothing had been done. Quakers had been prosecuted for tithe offenses, but most Dissenters had been left undisturbed. The Nonconformists in the parish had moved easily between conventicles and public service in Tewkesbury Abbey, but still justices and churchwardens had avoided confrontation. The plot was evidence that a mistake had been made. Anglicans on the council perceived their earlier avoidance of Nonconformity and Dissent as dangerous to both local administration and royal government. After the plot, strict adherence to orthodox Anglicanism became the only unequivocal sign of support for Charles II's regime.[71]

Wells and his supporters, who had long doubted the scriptural authority of many parts of the Book of Common Prayer, were forced by the ominous implications of the plot to undertake a similar examination of their past conduct. The result can be inferred only from their actions, but their provocative interpretation of the fast would seem to indicate that they too found themselves guilty of negligence. The Nonconformists in the parish had for almost twenty years compromised their consciences and had accepted, in the letter if not in the spirit, imposed forms of worship they believed were contrary to the word of God. It was possible that, in their acceptance of this church of law, imposed by royal decree, the king had been betrayed. Charles had behaved irresponsibly and would have to answer for the numerous sins of his person, but subjects who had made their peace with false ceremonies joined their king in the sin of idolatry.[72]

These distinct views on the nature of sin and the church, the church of conscience and the church of law, had made the fast day a local disaster and had remained a source of tension in the negotiations between Wells and the council after his suspension. The act of resignation forced the issue, and the speed of its reversal may indicate that, from the first, the resignation had been designed to test the minister's strength in the parish. The letter from Wells to Russell transformed this conflict from a dispute over interests to a fight between distinct visions of how the church should be ordered. The issue was no longer the income of the benefice but the ceremonies at the heart of the parish.

The ceremonial styles that divided supporters of Wells and Simpson in the 1670s had been a source of conflict in the parish since the 1590s, although the years had added layers of significance to the controversy over further reformation. The minister's attire and the proper form of the rites of passage had been sources of controversy as far back as local memory could reach. Yet attitudes toward reformation had been colored by the experiences of civil war, revolution, and the restoration of monarchy. These experiences had fostered a suspicion of religious diversity expressed in the church of law. The sermon Wells had preached in November 1678 and the fears evoked by the plot seemed to confirm this interpretation of religious difference as sedition and so enhanced the persuasive power of the church of law as a vision of the parish. It suddenly seemed both necessary and appropriate to prosecute Nonconformity and Dissent as a combined threat to the security of king and church. The significance of religious symbols, such as the surplice, extended beyond the ceremonies in the parish church to form part of a political commentary on the values and practices of Charles II's regime.

Wells and his supporters were identified by their hatred of the surplice and their denial of scriptural warrant to many parts of the Book of Common Prayer. Wells' rejection of the surplice was the most powerful symbolic expression of his devotion to the church of conscience and his subordination of the church of law to this principle. Richard Morgan, an iconoclastic glover, had shredded the surplice in 1641, and after a scandalous delay, the churchwardens of Tewkesbury had finally purchased a new surplice in the spring of 1678. According to Wells this new surplice quickly became too unclean to be worn.[73] On the first day that the reader wore the surplice, Wells reviled it in his sermon as "superstitious and an idol."[74] On the next Sunday the burgesses claimed Wells and his faction had conspired to fix "a scandalous and invective libel against the surplice" on a tree in the churchyard "to bring the decent ceremonies of the church into contempt."[75] This refusal of the surplice in the performance of communion and in funeral ceremonies appeared regularly in the lists of Wells's offenses compiled by James Simpson.[76]

As a ceremonial leader, Wells adopted a spontaneous approach to rituals of birth and death. This approach suited his own convictions and responded to the ceremonial needs of Nonconformists in the parish whose participation in the rites of the church could be secured only by concessions in the service.[77] Wells refused to wear the surplice in his conduct of a burial service in the summer of 1680. He was interrupted in this performance by the churchwardens and then entered the pulpit to preach, "but was by force prevented, whereby a great disturbance was occasioned."[78] In November 1681 Wells presided over another burial and led the procession into the churchyard, accompanied by the minister appointed to preach the funeral sermon. The deacon met the procession in the churchyard, wearing the surplice and holding the Book of Common Prayer. As the deacon began to read the sentences directed by the rubric, Wells asked "what that meant, and why the surplice, and what needed all that, and, when the sentences were all read over, the deacon beginning them again," Wells, "in a most contentious and unseemly manner, being all the while with his hat on his head, did all along rail at him for it, calling it a new business."[79]

Wells introduced modifications in most of the ceremonies of the parish. He made concessions to Nonconformists in his revision of the rules of baptism. Wells declared his opposition to the custom of charging the godparents to instruct the child in the Anglican catechism as preparation for the bishop's confirmation. In addition, Wells changed the ceremony of baptism to such an extent that he "left out the greatest part of the service [in his baptism for the child of Robert Wilkins], and so altered the residue that it was a great trouble to all who were present."[80] As the burgesses filed the only complaints, it is difficult to accept at face value their account of the general reaction to the omissions. Other Anglican ceremonies were simply abolished. Wells rejected the forms of ritual used to "church" women, the means whereby women who had undergone childbirth were restored to the church. In place of the prescribed ceremony, Wells used an extemporaneous prayer before his sermon to express thanks for the safe delivery of the women.[81]

The order of communion was a major source of contention. Simpson claimed that Wells did not consecrate more than half the wine delivered to communicants, a serious allegation of exclusive communion for the godly in the parish. When the consecrated bread or cup was delivered, Wells was said to omit the short prayer for that purpose appointed in the rubric.[82] This allegation was supported by William Jennings.[83] Jennings had been prepared to receive communion on Easter Sunday of 1677 and had seen the wine brought to the table. He was convinced the wine had not been consecrated before it was given to him and to other communicants. Wells also omitted the prayer stated in the rubric, and such practices had made Jennings reluctant to receive communion on subsequent holy days.[84]

A particular incident may help to convey the sentiments that such unilateral reforms evoked in the aftermath of the plot. In November 1680 William Jennings arranged his mother's funeral. Jennings was a burgess on the common council, as his father had been before him, and the burial of his mother was thus a civic occasion. Most of the members of the council, including its highest officers, would attend the ceremony, demonstrating by their presence a bond of friendship to Jennings, the honor of his family, and the solidarity and continuity of the corporation, even in the moment of death.

Jennings sent his servant on November 1 to inform Wells that another minister had been chosen to preach the funeral sermon. Funeral sermons were often preached by ministers other than the incumbent, but Wells interpreted this decision as yet another sign of the corporation's desire to silence him in his own parish and to deprive him of his fees. He made it clear that he would direct the funeral service and have the fees regardless who preached; and that night he sent his maid to the house of Edward Jennings, William's cousin, to deliver the threat "that if her master had not his fee he would keep all persons out of the pulpit."[85] This flurry of servants and messages continued the next day, when William Jennings replied that he who expected fees ought to perform some service. His mother's funeral was arranged for three o'clock in the afternoon of that day. If Wells was "ready to perform the Office of Burial as the Church of England appointed," he could have his fees. Wells answered "that he would do his duty."[86]

At the appointed hour, Wells arrived and was met in the churchyard by the sexton, who offered him the Book of Common Prayer and the surplice. Wells said "he would do other ways." As the magistrates and burgesses of the corporation looked on, Wells entered the church and went to the reading pew, where the book and the surplice were offered once more. The book was this time accepted, but the surplice was rejected. Wells remained seated in the pew for some time with his hat on his head, evidently in prayer. According to Jennings, Wells "was pleased" after a long silence to remove his hat and read the sentences, one psalm, and the lesson, in the course of which he seems to have made several alterations, described by Jennings as "mistakes."[87]

During the portion of the ceremony performed over the grave, Wells inserted an extemporaneous prayer for a sick child, contrary to the order of the Prayer Book, and the frayed tempers of a few mourners began to come apart. When Wells requested a candle to assist his reading, an argument erupted over the quality, position, and sufficiency of sunlight in the abbey. Wells was interrupted again as he tried to proceed with the ceremony by a minister offering to help him toward a more accurate reading of the text. The depositions end with the indignation of a conscience convinced of its possession of the moral high ground, as Wells sarcastically asked the visitor if he would presume to teach him.[88]

The rites of passage were not the only ceremonies Wells refused to perform in the prescribed manner. Robert Eaton, the master of Tewkesbury grammar school, testified that Wells made so many alterations in the routine performance of divine service "that if Wells had then read the service entire, without those alterations, he could not but have taken a particular notice thereof."[89] Some of the alterations had anti-Catholic overtones, and some inclined to a more austere interpretation of the human relationship to God. The Absolution became another spontaneous prayer and thus stressed the uncertainty of divine forgiveness. Because Wells disliked repetition, the Lord's Prayer was read only once in the service. Although the law required ministers to pray for "our gracious Queen Catherine," Wells referred to her as "our royal Queen Catherine," a variation taken by his critics as a slur upon the character of the Catholic queen and a denial of her state of grace. The phrase "bishops, priests, and deacons" contained in the Litany was replaced by "bishops, pastors, and curates" in an attempt to preserve the Church of England from the stain of Roman Catholic hierarchy. The removal of thanks for departed saints from the prayer for "Christ's church militant on earth" concluded the excision of popish elements from the Anglican service.[90]

These omissions and revisions amounted to a visual and verbal affirmation of the church of conscience in the parish, an affirmation magnified by the civic importance of Tewkesbury Abbey as a grand platform where the burgesses and corporate office holders displayed their status and authority. Before the plot, the accommodation of conscience had been a means to preserve the fiction of inclusion and the audience for the displays of power on the platform. After the plot, the conduct of Wells and his faction appeared to undermine the authority of the council in the civic and spiritual life of the community. Wells had continued his sermon despite the intervention of the bailiff and had denied the corporation's authority to intervene in the practice of religion. As far as the officers of the corporation were concerned, the further reformation of the late 1670s suddenly looked and sounded like the Independency of the late 1650s, and the burgesses later claimed that Wells had "endeavored to undermine and ruin our corporation."[91]

After his suspension, Wells made provocative appeals for public support, but the composition of his faction is difficult to define. Wells frequently invoked the principles of the church of conscience. In 1681 he declared that even Separatists should be allowed a voice in the choice of the minister.[92] According to his opponents, Wells usually entered the church as the service was being read, his hat on his head, and refused to stand up or make responses to any part of the service. He remained seated during the sermon, his head covered, in such a way that many residents of the parish, "whom he knew inclined to the like indecencies in that place," took "ill example" by him.[93] These accusations from biased sources are insufficient. The only concrete evidence of support for Wells is a set of nine depositions made in the consistory court and the Court of Arches, although four years of resistance to the common council obviously required more substantial support in the parish and corporation. The group that testified may not have been representative of local support for Wells, but the absence of additional sources makes this distortion the only alternative to ignorance.

Two staunch supporters had close connections to the Parliamentarian cause and the Protectorate in the 1640s and 1650s. Joseph Laight, a wealthy maltster and an assistant burgess in the 1670s, had fought for parliament in the Civil War and, after the Restoration, divided his time between the Anglican service in the abbey and the local conventicle of Independents.[94] Laight stood among the most prominent residents in the neighborhood of Barton Street, which was described in 1691 as pervaded by "a pestilential air of separation." His relationship to Wells probably dated from the 1650s, when the Independent John Wells, Francis' brother, had been the minister of Tewkesbury and had presided over a religious revolution.[95] William Hatton's links to the revolution were less direct. Hatton's father had signed the remonstrance sent by Gloucestershire Independents to Cromwell in June 1656 to demand a more aggressive defense of the "cause of Christ" against "Antichrist and his Kingdom" and to warn against the "spirit of vanity, slumber, and lukewarmness seizing so much upon the people of God themselves, even amidst the great salvations of the Lord."[96] Hatton, the elder, lost his place on the common council of Tewkesbury after the royalist Restoration in 1662.[97] William Hatton's career in the Restoration church was marked by a contempt for the hierarchy that may have reflected his father's views and certainly did not contradict them. As the rector of Cranham, Hatton became notorious for both ceremonial nonconformity and cheating at cards.[98] He was presented in the consistory court in 1677 for his performance of suspicious marriages.[99] Hatton's parishioners complained two years later that he refused to pay his proportion of a local rate. Seldom at a loss for words to express his feelings, Hatton told the constable of the hundred "that he did verily believe that he the said Hatton should be hanged for some of them, meaning the parishioners of Cranham." When the constable threatened to relay Hatton's words to the bishop or at least to make a report to the chancellor, Hatton replied, "A fart for my Lord Bishop and a turd for Mr. Chancellor."[100]

Support for Wells had a foundation in kinship and neighborhood. The interest of the Wells family had been established in Tewkesbury before the 1650s. Sarah Wells, sister of John and Francis, had married John Cox of Tewkesbury in the late 1630s, and the Laight family at that time had been intermarried with the Coxes for a decade.[101] Joseph Laight and Francis Wells were relatives by marriage. Sarah Cox and her daughter Mary, sister and niece to Francis Wells, also testified on his behalf in 1681.[102] This evidence of family connection should not be overemphasized, but the most vocal support for Wells consisted of three or four families that joined bonds of kinship to shared conviction. The subtle influence of neighborliness was also evident in the support for Wells.

Mathias Maide, like Joseph Laight an assistant burgess, had passed his childhood on Barton Street, not far from Laight's house.[103] Maide's father left a will that indicates the family's involvement in brewing on a large scale, and since Laight was a maltster only a few houses away, some contact between the households is not unlikely.[104] Joseph Laight and Mathias Maide had been the churchwardens who had served as witnesses when, upon induction to the vicarage of Tewkesbury in 1677, Wells had read the 39 Articles and had stated his controversial assent and consent to the Book of Common Prayer.[105] Both men testified for Wells in 1681.[106]

The complex role of neighborhood in religious conflict is illustrated by the situation of Francis Wells himself. Wells lived on Church Street, three houses away from William Hatton and George Olive, two of his strongest supporters.[107] But this stretch of Church Street also contained the houses of burgesses instrumental in the prosecution. Thomas Nanfan, the bailiff who had interrupted Wells and had attempted to stop his fast day sermon, lived next door to William Hatton.[108] Nanfan testified against Wells, describing Hatton as a vulgar man and George Olive as "a dangerous and mutinous fellow" who was Hatton's "great creature."[109] Nanfan, Robert Porter, Phillip Hilley, and William Jennings, all prominent burgesses and supporters of Simpson, lived only a few houses from Wells and his friends, who were clearly perceived as a blight on the neighborhood.[110] Because neighborhood comprised ideas, assumptions, and social relationships, opposed networks could exist side by side in the same street, and each faction could see itself as the proper embodiment of neighborliness. Neighborhood influenced this religious and civic conflict, not in the confrontation of spatially distinct groups in the town, but as diffuse networks that divided streets and stretched into lanes and alleys. Wells and Simpson both perceived their cause as the cause of Christian fellowship and neighborliness. This fight to control the abbey and its ceremony evoked, on both sides, networks of social relations that were defined in terms of neighborhood and believed by their advocates to speak for the interests of the entire parish community.

These networks were strikingly different in their social composition. Among those who testified for Wells were a maltster, a vintner, a clerical son of a mercer, a cooper, a domestic servant, and a poor almsman of the parish. The wealth and status of the craftsmen varied greatly, descending in the social hierarchy from the maltster Joseph Laight, worth roughly £500 in 1681, to the cooper George Olive, assessed for only one hearth in the hearth tax of 1671.[111] Joseph Face, the almsman, affirmed Wells's acceptance of the 39 Articles "as far as they agreed with scripture and no farther," and his deposition raises the question of support for Wells among the poor of the parish.[112] In a sermon preached after his suspension was lifted, Wells reviled the common council and accused the councilors of "dishonesty and injustice in their trust to him and the poor."[113] This may have been a rhetorical squib, but Wells may have known of the misallocation of charitable bequests to the parish. These resources were often used to finance the corporation's legal battles with adjacent parishes over the settlement of paupers.[114] Wells' conviction that he could carry a general vote against the council may also indicate an awareness of support extending beyond the middling sort to the quarter of the town's population too poor to pay the hearth tax in 1671.[115] Unfortunately, the evidence is too impressionistic to allow any definitive statement of the social distribution of this support.

Simpson's supporters present a quite different social profile. Of those residing in the town who testified for Simpson, five out of seven described themselves as gentlemen and served as burgesses on the common council.[116] All of Simpson's most vocal supporters were assessed for at least three hearths in the hearth tax of 1671, and the number of hearths ranged from three to six.[117] Differences in place of birth may have added emphasis to this difference in wealth and status. Seven out of nine of the witnesses for Wells had been born and raised in Tewkesbury, contrasting sharply with the witnesses for Simpson, seven out of nine of whom were born elsewhere and moved to the town as adults.[118] Thomas Nanfan came to Tewkesbury from Birtsmorton, Worcestershire, in the early 1650s, at the age of thirty. Charles Wynde arrived from New Fish Street, London, in the 1670s, at twenty-eight years of age. Robert Porter was twenty-six years old when he moved north to Tewkesbury from Gloucester in 1660.[119] Such evidence must be handled cautiously, as neither Wells nor his supporters ever expressed a view of their opponents as interlopers or outsiders. This difficult evidence nevertheless suggests that the controversy over the parish created factions composed of indigenous tradesmen and exogenous gentry.

Simpson and his faction were also marked by their support for the church of law and their revived loyalty to the Restoration settlement in the parish. They believed that the consistory court and the corporation should enforce the lawful order of worship prescribed in the Book of Common Prayer. This renewed loyalty to the Restoration settlement should be understood in relation to dreadful experiences in the Civil War, in a few cases the direct experience of combat and personal loss. Thomas Nanfan and Conway Whithorne had fervently supported the royalist cause in the 1640s and 1650s, and Nanfan had lost several members of his family in the war.[120] Whithorne and Nanfan had been placed on the council in Tewkesbury after the royalist Restoration in 1662 and had dominated the administration of justice in the borough for twenty-five years as senior justices of the peace.[121] Both had been restrained. Their position in the borough had not been used to persecute Dissenters in the 1660s and 1670s. The experience of royalist defeat, personal loss, and the religious radicalism of the 1650s had not created, in either Whithorne or Nanfan, advocates of a strict enforcement of law. But these experiences had created a view of the world inclined, in moments of crisis, to see the church of law and religious uniformity as the bulwarks that separated human society from anarchy. Nanfan saw the events of 1678 from a perspective born of his own experience, and the speed of his reaction to Wells' sermon reflected a fear and recognition, in those words and that crisis, of the ghost of crises past.

Several of the burgesses in 1678 had not been alive in the 1640s or had been small children, and their experience of the Civil War was indirect. The public representation of the war that was created in 1661 and 1662 may have exercised a formative influence on the attitudes of this group, as the civic ceremonies required by the Corporation Act had been performed consistently in the creation of burgesses since the royalist Restoration in 1662.[122] The oath of nonresistance and the declaration against the Solemn League and Covenant had become standard components of this civic initiation. A revulsion against the parliamentary cause in the Civil War had been joined to other symbols of the corporation, particularly its royal charter. The charter had disappeared in the early days of the war, and only "two skins of parchment" remained in 1672.[123] The councilors were persuaded that their charter had been "purloined and destroyed" in the 1640s by malcontents "inimical to all government."[124] This convenient and ultimately irrefutable interpretation of the war linked the parliamentary cause to subversion of the charter, the repudiation of law, and the annihilation of the corporation. The diffusion of such representations may have helped to create a council composed of second generation royalists who responded to the crisis of 1678 in much the same way as Whithorne and Nanfan.

The corporation and the parish were bitterly divided, and religious differences found expression in virtually every aspect of ceremonial and social life in the town. The structure of religion in the parish after the Restoration may help to explain the depth of animosity and the suddenness of the change. Christian ceremonies remained the ritual language used to express the phases of the life cycle, the concepts of civic responsibility, and, ultimately, the duty of loyalty to the monarchy. These multiple referents of religious belief and ceremony were joined in a ritual idiom used in the parish church, and each referent formed a layer of significance in the ceremony. The rites of the parish church created local communities and expressed a code of conduct founded on conceptions of duty, loyalty, and deference. In November 1678 a sermon created a sharp conflict between the multiple worlds of religion, expressed in different form in the church of conscience and the church of law. Perceptions of the plot as a conspiracy of Dissenters and Catholics to subvert the monarchy made the ceremonial directives of the church of law more attractive to many Anglicans, and the persecution of the ideas expressed in the sermon appeared the best means to protect the royal foundations of the church. On the other side of the issue, Nonconformists in the parish asserted the authority of conscience in 1678 to protect their church from the dangers of royal venality and popery. As the local enforcement of uniformity dates from the plot, the decisions of churchwardens seem to reflect this interplay of law and conscience. It is significant that the dispute in Tewkesbury began on a fast day, when the multiple worlds of religion were joined in a prayer that led to a bitter debate over the sins of the parish and the nation.

The profound structural conflict created by the sermon in Tewkesbury could not be resolved by local institutions, and the consistory court also failed to achieve a settlement acceptable to all parties. This court had participated in the symbolic creation of the parish for generations, and a variety of demands had drawn the corporation and the parish into the worlds of civil and ecclesiastical government since the sixteenth century; however, not since the restorations in 1660 and 1662 had authorities beyond the corporation intervened in a local conflict of such magnitude. The letter from Wells to Sir Francis Russell that announced the decision not to resign initiated a new phase in the conflict. The negotiations had ended in stalemate, and the failure of local institutions forced the disputants into a competition for the influence of institutions and persons of authority beyond the territorial boundaries of the community. The bishop of Gloucester in consistory court deprived Wells of the benefice in the summer of 1680. Wells rejected the decision of the court as corrupt and appealed his case to the Court of Arches, but the Arches confirmed the sentence of deprivation in 1681. After further difficulties in the execution of the sentence, Robert Frampton, newly elected Bishop of Gloucester, intervened at the request of Archbishop Sancroft to construct the compromise that seemed beyond local skill.

The techniques of this competition formed a powerful idiom in local culture. The movement of the conflict into courts of law demanded the translation of local interest into the language of law and procedure, but several lawyers in Tewkesbury had expertise in this form of translation, and the availability of this expertise blurred the distinction between the local style of mediation and the formal procedures of law. This process of translation imparted a dualism to statements in law not unlike the dualism inherent in the ceremonies of the parish. An assertion in law could express local values and aspirations in translated form, but could simultaneously articulate, through the construction of the homogeneous types of action characteristic of law, the bureaucratic priority of uniformity. Yet the ceremonies of the parish joined imperceptibly in the religious culture of the nation. The transition from local mediation to the courts required disputants to cross an institutional boundary. The power to cross this boundary was conferred by expertise in law or by the money to hire such expertise and by the financial reserves needed to press a lawsuit to conclusion, a substantial investment often spread over many years. The transition from mediation to the courts was thus political as well as cultural, and the conclusion of the dispute between Wells and the corporation was decided by the two related factors: expertise in the law and the extensive networks used by the corporation to influence events in the courts.

The friendship between James Simpson, town clerk of Tewkesbury, and Richard Parsons, chancellor of the diocese, influenced the conduct of the case in the diocese. This relationship had helped to secure the suspension of Wells and had also enhanced the corporation's ability to sustain the suspension while the case for deprivation was steered through the consistory court.[125] Parsons controlled the diocesan courts as both chancellor and surrogate for the archdeacon, an arrangement not unusual in Gloucester diocese, and may have used his position to help friends.[126] "As long as [Parsons] engrosses into his own hands all the business of my court as well as the bishop's court," wrote the archdeacon, Thomas Hyde, to Archbishop Sancroft in 1683, "nobody else can intermeddle nor have an opportunity of discovering his practices. Nobody else dare speak what they know, for fear of being persecuted by him."[127]

Parsons was as determined as Simpson to "swing the old hide of Wells" and was a constant source of advice and information.[128] In August 1680 after Wells had appealed his case to the Court of Arches, the corporation of Tewkesbury petitioned Archbishop Sancroft to hasten the notoriously dilatory procedure in the Arches.[129] Presentation was an important aspect of any petition, and Simpson therefore sent a first draft of the petition to Parsons for revision and approval. Parsons deleted some dubious claims against Wells, particularly the insinuations of his militancy in the Civil War, and also removed an account of the corporation's attempts to bribe Wells to resign, which Parsons felt "not so convenient to be mentioned."[130] Parsons also provided advice on procedure in the Court of Arches and often acted as intermediary between Simpson and the bishop of Gloucester.[131] Simpson received information about the bishop's schedule and travel plans that ensured quick responses to petitions and letters.[132] Parsons occasionally provided tips on how to petition the bishop to the best advantage and once approached the bishop directly on Simpson's behalf. After the bishop had passed sentence of deprivation but before the appeal had been processed by the Court of Arches, Parsons lobbied the bishop in support of Simpson's request that the appeal be ignored and a new minister inducted in Tewkesbury. The bishop agreed, on the condition that the induction be made quickly, but nothing further seems to have come of the scheme.[133]

Most networks have a circumscribed influence. Beyond certain boundaries, the control of events is opened to the influence of chance and competitive interests. Wells hoped to use the Court of Arches to reduce the influence of the powerful network that joined the officers of the corporation and diocese against him. The loss of corporate control that resulted from this appeal was made evident by the restoration of Wells to his benefice and the removal of his suspension, the necessary prelude to a definitive sentence from the Arches.[134] Wells boasted that, given the procedure in the Arches, he would be dead before the court finally made a decision.[135]

Simpson quickly recovered from this judicial defeat. Parsons and his friend Joseph Horner introduced Simpson to the procedure in the Arches. Horner, who was the notary public of the consistory court, had acted as Simpson's proctor in the deprivation case.[136] As Simpson soon discovered, commissions authorized to receive depositions from witnesses were used to collect evidence in the Arches. Separate local commissions sat for each of the parties in a lawsuit, but the commissioners were also required to cross-examine each group of witnesses on the basis of the questions submitted by the opposing party. Simpson carefully gathered information about the procedure, composition, and probable dates of the local commissions.[137] Although he could not interfere in the commission appointed for Wells, Simpson could and did use his influence to bolster the case presented by his own commission and witnesses. He consulted Parsons for a list of sympathetic commissioners who were likely to favor the corporation's cause.[138]

The commission convened in Tewkesbury Abbey in October 1681, and Simpson declined to present any new evidence. He attempted instead to undermine the credibility of the witnesses whom Wells presented in his defense.[139] Simpson's commissioners used a trick to persuade Joseph Face, the almsman, to sign a written statement that contradicted his earlier testimony.[140] These commissioners also tried to exclude Wells from the process and claimed that a procedural violation had negated his right to cross-examine Simpson's witnesses. It took a frantic note from Simpson's proctor in the Arches, informing him that the commission would be quashed, and much time and money lost, if Wells was not permitted to ask his questions, to restore a semblance of impartiality to the investigation.[141]

Simpson played an important role in this process as a mediator between the local council and the complex world of the courts. He enhanced the power of the corporation because he joined its interests to a wider network of influence and authority. Simpson was more than a link to this world: he possessed expertise that enabled him to operate as both translator and transmitter. Simpson translated vague local accusations against Wells into the language of petition and article, and this operation was a routine but necessary skill in his general performance of duties as town clerk. The combination of artistic and craft skills in this process of translation is conveyed by contemporary ideas of the expertise required to "frame" a petition or legal document.[142] Simpson's ability to translate the corporate interest into law was even more important. His case against

Wells was simple but brilliant. He prosecuted Wells in the consistory court on charges of improper induction to the vicarage.[143] This charge forced Wells to prove that, within two months of his induction, he had read the prescribed service from the Book of Common Prayer and had declared his acceptance of all the book contained, as the Act of Uniformity demanded. Wells faced a difficult task for reasons that bore little relationship to the justice of Simpson's charge.

The case turned on a few technical points. A copy of the 39 Articles was produced in court, subscribed by Wells in 1677 "with assent and consent" and endorsed by Joseph Laight and Mathias Maide, the churchwardens for that year. Yet neither Laight nor Maide could swear, when pressed, that Wells had actually read all the articles, for neither had the articles "without book, so as to know whether any alteration were made."[144] Laight believed that Wells had declared his "assent and consent" to the Book of Common Prayer but could not say precisely when Wells had been inducted to the benefice. He thus failed to prove that Wells had declared within the statutory limit of two months.[145] Wells never denied the other charges, and the bishop then pronounced the sentence of deprivation in August 1680.[146] Wells lost his benefice not because Simpson proved Wells' failure to declare assent and consent to the Book of Common Prayer but because Wells himself could not present sufficient evidence of his induction.

The distance between the local religious issues in Tewkesbury and the fine point of law used to remove Wells from the benefice is no less remarkable than the two years that passed before anyone perceived the illegality of the induction. Simpson's skill and influence in the courts enabled the council to mold the parish into the church of law. This power to speak the language of law was socially unequal, and after the appeal to the Court of Arches, the Nonconformist faction could not compete. William Jennings conveyed this inequality in an account of Simpson's examination of George Olive, the cooper. Simpson first asked Olive "whether he knew how much of the divine service the law required should be read." Olive replied that "he did not well know that." Simpson then asked whether Olive knew the 39 Articles, and again Olive had to admit his ignorance but added defensively that "Mr. Francis Wells did declare they were the nine and thirty articles which he read." Olive was also unaware that the law required Wells to declare his assent and consent to the Book of Common Prayer as well as the 39 Articles.[147] Joseph

Face, the almsman, did not know the number of articles and probably did not read well. Simpson's commissioners persuaded Face to sign a statement that Wells had declared his assent and consent to the 69 Articles.[148] The anxieties of Joseph Laight, George Olive, and Joseph Face mark the boundary between law and conscience. The law was bounded by a complicated procedure and a language that could transform an event into a phenomenon difficult even for witnesses to identify. Olive and Face did not know the law of induction, and Simpson's questions required support for Wells to be expressed in terms of this law. Conscience had no authority in law, and it was the corporation's mastery of the law that conveyed the power to control both the choice of the minister and the ceremonies of the parish.

James Simpson and Francis Wells used the court system to pursue a controversy that local institutions had failed to resolve. This strategy could not remove the bitterness of the conflict from the local arenas of corporation and parish; nonetheless, the persistence of serious religious conflict in the community and the use of the courts to control this conflict reflected the dependence of the corporation and parish of Tewkesbury on the officers and institutions of the national church after the Restoration. Local mediation had failed to resolve the conflict between Wells and the council in part because the locus of authority in the community was disputed. The corporation and the minister were forced to seek the assistance and authority of the courts in order to avoid the most destructive consequences of the conflict in the parish. Simpson and his faction soon learned that the authority of this law came at a price. Archbishop Sancroft confirmed the sentence of deprivation in December 1681 but also ordered a reluctant council to pay Wells the money previously offered for his resignation.[149] The protection of distinct visions of an inclusive parish had forced the minister and the council into dependence on a process of arbitration beyond local control. This dependence on the courts was an important part of the process whereby the rules and institutions of a national community were incorporated in local life.

The fear and controversy in Tewkesbury after 1678 made the differences between Anglicans and Dissenters appear more dangerous and ultimately led to persecution in the early 1680s. Because of the strictness of their separation and visibility of their difference, Quakers became particularly vulnerable in the new environment. A rich historical literature has examined the religious development of Quakerism from charismatic movement to sect or denomination, and recent scholarship has questioned the familiar account of quietism and decline in the Quakerism of the late seventeenth century.[150] Yet the importance of family and household in the reproduction of the sect has received less attention. The evidence of Independency in Ashchurch has revealed the importance of interfamilial connections in the social structure of the group. Quaker sources provide evidence of the *process* whereby religious differences became social differences expressed in the idiom of family relations. These sources reveal, in more detail than any other form of evidence, the shift from the residential parish to the family in the social structure of religious community. The minutes of the weekly and monthly meetings in Tewkesbury and Stoke Orchard provide ample evidence of the control over marriages and apprenticeships that helped to make religious differences into social differences and also reveal some of the recurrent problems of separation from the parish. Quakers assembled covertly in the villages near Tewkesbury and moved their meetings constantly to avoid detection, but the boundaries of the sect could be difficult to maintain in the everyday life of local villages. The Quakers, like other Dissenters, continued to confront the problems of a subculture in symbiotic relationship to the Anglican parish.

Quakers practiced a strict routine for the scrutiny of proposed marriages to ensure the preservation of spiritual integrity in the household and family. This routine generally delayed a marriage for several months and had two distinct phases. In the first phase, the match was proposed to the weekly or preparatory meeting, and fortunately the deliberations of this meeting can be recovered from the minutes of the women's weekly meeting in Tewkesbury recorded in the early 1680s.[151] Preparatory meetings had the narrowest territorial base of any Quaker group and seldom included members from more than two or three parishes. The members discussed the conduct and reputation of the couple and had "free liberty" to declare anything against the marriage.[152] These meetings did not have authority to approve a marriage but could eliminate matches if one partner or the other was known to have other commitments. The rejection of a match would have been an embarrassment to the partners and the meeting, and since all the matches in the minute book were accepted, the evidence suggests that only matches approved by the meeting were recorded in the book.[153] If the weekly meeting approved the couple, the proposed marriage was certified and passed to the monthly meeting for final permission to marry.

The presentation of a match to the monthly meeting initiated a second investigation. After a match had been presented to the meeting, at least two members were deputed to inquire into the circumstances of the courtship and the reputation of both partners. These deputies usually belonged to the same preparatory meeting as the person under examination and were forearmed with the names of informants. In 1673 Mary Walker and Elizabeth Woolams of Stoke Orchard were asked to assess the marital eligibility of their neighbor John Surman.[154] In first marriages, this inquiry often increased the premarital influence of parents as well as that of friends and neighbors. In 1680 the monthly meeting instructed Robert Milton and Anne Rickets to send a certificate signed by their parents as evidence of parental consent to their marriage.[155] After the monthly meeting had consulted her parents, Sarah Middleton of Tirley was ordered to secure £10 to the use of her mother before marriage, and several members of the Tirley meeting were appointed to see the condition honored.[156] This routine inquiry seems to have been rationalized relatively late in the development of the sect after the Restoration, probably in the 1670s. In 1673 seven members of the monthly meeting were deputed to attend marriages and to furnish certificates of the endorsement of a match and the freedom of the bride and groom from other commitments. These certificates were required if a Quaker from one of the four preparatory meetings, which were held in Cheltenham, Tewkesbury, Tirley, and Stoke Orchard under the jurisdiction of the monthly meeting in Stoke Orchard, desired to marry a Quaker from another area.[157] The investigative procedure became a fixture of Quaker social life and was used by the monthly meeting to evaluate forty-six proposed marriages from the end of 1671 to 1688.[158]

These methods did not always resolve doubts and conflicts over particular matches. An unspecified marriage was decried as inappropriate in the minutes for 1678. The match had apparently been forced on the meeting in a manner perceived as "contrary and out of the good order of friends," and the meeting renounced this procedure in the minutes as "a door opened for loose spirits" to assert their personal desires over the collective spiritual wisdom of the group. Doubtful cases could sometimes be decided by spiritual means. In 1683 the monthly meeting called for a special assembly "to wait upon the Lord to know his mind in the marriage depending between Joseph Colchester and Sarah Nellin."[159] The formation of a new Quaker family became, in this case, a literal act of God.

Selective apprenticeship was another means to reproduce Quaker beliefs in family and household. This process is difficult to recover because most families did not rely on the institutions of the sect to find acceptable households for their children. Yet the criteria used by the monthly and quarterly meetings to place poor children may furnish a general index of the priorities and interests of individual Quaker families. Both meetings made a financial contribution to ensure that poor families did not place their children beyond the boundaries of the sect. Between 1670 and 1681 the quarterly meeting contributed at least £25 to support apprenticeships for children of poor families in northern Gloucestershire, and the monthly meeting had collected smaller sums in 1674 and 1675, before the quarterly meeting began to assume financial responsibility.[160] This shift of responsibility increased the resources available for the children. The monthly meeting usually provided £3 or less with an apprentice, whereas the quarterly meeting generally offered £4 or £5 and sometimes included money for clothes.[161] These apprentices were almost invariably placed in Quaker families. The participation of the quarterly meeting in the selection process extended the search to the entire county and thus increased the number of acceptable households. A son of the widow Anne Clift, from a village close to Nailsworth in southern Gloucestershire, was sent by the quarterly meeting to Thomas Baker of Tewkesbury.[162] The monthly meeting in Stoke Orchard apprenticed Isaac Oakley's son to John Bissell of Dudley.[163] Children of the Phillips family, from the neighborhood around Westbury, were placed as far afield as Ross in Herefordshire.[164] These children were directed to Quaker families. In 1687 the monthly meeting agreed to "consider of a place" for Thomas Beale's son to be apprenticed.[165] The primary objective in placement was to circulate the children among Quaker families.

Most of the proposed marriages entered in the minutes were approved, but the few recorded instances of "disorderly" marriage raise important questions about the problems of separation and the familial structure of religious fellowship. Although control of marriage helped to preserve Quaker beliefs in the intimate circumstances of family life, such practices could also reproduce the ambiguous position of Quakers in local society. Quaker notions of religious fellowship and personal identity were based on the subordination of traditional ideas of honor and reputation to the authority of spiritual truth. Disorderly marriages were an unhappy indication of the difficulties that some couples experienced in withdrawal from a match once it had been publicly announced. In 1672 Thomas Baker and Sarah Beven were for unspecified reasons refused permission to marry. Baker and Beven rejected this decision and proceeded in their marriage. The monthly meeting sent deputies to admonish both Beven and Baker but finally declared the marriage disorderly. Baker ignored orders for his appearance before the meeting. Only after a year of admonition did he repent of his "disorderly" marriage and return to the meeting.[166] In the same year, problems surfaced in the courtship of John Surman and Joyce Bond. The couple apparently had a disagreement, and Surman spoke "rash words" against his fiancée in the presence of other Quakers. The meeting intervened to forestall further conflict by quashing the engagement, but Bond was deeply offended and reluctant to release Surman from his promise. The better part of a year passed in consultation with fellow Quakers before Bond agreed to relinquish her claim. Surman and Bond then resolved their differences in 1673 and were married.[167]

Beneath charges of disorderliness lay the difficult relationship between Quakerism and customary forms of behavior and identity. This problem was a constant source of concern and discussion in local meetings. Charles Tovy of Tewkesbury delivered a paper against disorderly marriages in the Stoke Orchard monthly meeting in 1677.[168] The quarterly meeting attempted to resolve the conflict of personal and collective interests in 1688 by advising couples to consult the "ancient friends" of their meeting before laying their plans before the monthly meeting. In this way, "advice may be given betimes, and the snares that attend many . . . may be prevented." The order was intended to protect the honor and public reputation of the parties to a match by ensuring that "when friends have proceeded so far as to lay [their proposed marriages] before the monthly meetings, there may be no occasion for an objection to hinder [their] accomplishment."[169]

Disorderly marriage represented only the most recurrent of the problems Quakers faced in their attempt to separate their fellowship from customary forms of behavior in local villages. The customary means to resolve conflict and represent status continued to exert a baleful influence. In 1693 the quarterly meeting issued a declaration that ordered friends to request the mediation of the monthly meeting before attacking each other in lawsuits. In the same year the quarterly meeting was also forced to issue an instruction to the monthly meetings against the "superfluous" display reported in local funerals.[170] The law and forms of material display belonged to communities of the profane world and must not be allowed to creep into the spiritual fellowship of the friends. Quaker beliefs had been established and preserved in family and household, but how were Quaker households and discipline to be consistently separated from the worldly behavior of their neighbors in the parish?

An answer to this difficult question may lie in the Quaker symbolism of suffering and persecution. Quakers began to construct an image of the distinctiveness and intensity of their suffering years before the persecution of the early 1680s. In 1676 officers of the parish avoided the issue of separation and made few presentments, but the Quaker quarterly meeting criticized friends for a failure to produce in sufficient quantities the descriptions of anti-Quaker "violence" known as sufferings.[171] The quarterly meeting appointed members of the monthly meeting in Stoke Orchard to prepare accounts of the suffering inflicted on the Quakers by local authorities. These documents, generally descriptions of tithe offenses, were then sent to an agent in Gloucester and forwarded to the annual meeting of Quakers in London. The annual meeting collected "sufferings" from Quaker meetings in every parish of England to produce an archive of collective pain.[172] Quakers frequently used "sufferings" to convey their problems and interests to sympathetic Anglicans in positions of authority. In 1677 the quarterly meeting ordered that the "sufferings" be collected and presented to the judge, the "moderate" justices, and the sheriff at the assizes in Gloucester.[173]

The most important characteristic of the "sufferings" was their depiction of local conflict as a fight for the fundamental principles of Quaker faith. After the Restoration, many Anglicans preferred to avoid the issues of dissent and separation from the parish. If Dissenters did not disturb the peace, officers of the parish left the conventicles undisturbed. Tithe disputes were interpreted and prosecuted as conventional disputes over property. The "sufferings" made no such concessions and interpreted each tithe dispute as a manifestation of the continuous effort of the profane powers to annihilate the truth.[174] Despite the absence of references to Quakerism in most lay prosecutions for tithe, the "sufferings" represented such conflicts as a reflection, not of the refusal to honor a form of payment, but of a deeper hatred of Quakerism itself. The quarterly meeting admonished an unspecified number of Quakers for failure to appreciate the significance of the tithe issue and for payments made to Richard Parsons, chancellor of the diocese, to prevent further prosecution.[175] A narrow conflict between the Quakers, the lay proprietors of tithes, and the Anglican church became a symbol of the barrier between the Quakers, the chosen people, and the Anglican parish, the Egyptian persecutors. A fictive world of continuous persecution maintained the difference and distance of the Quakers from the world of the parish. Quakers were differentiated from their neighbors by experience of the truth and willingness to suffer for it.

The Quakers provide the clearest evidence of the process whereby religious differences became social differences expressed in the form of family and household, but the influence of this process extended beyond Separatist groups. As the Anglican parish divided into factions and sects, the individual family became the focal point of its religious fellowship. The internal architecture of the parish church helps to illustrate this shift. In the first decade of the seventeenth century, the order of seats in the abbey had reflected the structure of the residential parish. The families of the parish had dissolved into a hierarchic representation of the residential community: husbands and wives did not share the same seats because the family was not the focus of worship. The household was the proper place for familial piety and discipline, and the ceremonies performed in Tewkesbury Abbey incorporated the family in the Christian neighborhood of the parish. In the late seventeenth century, the internal order of the parish community was reflected in the example of Thomas Hale, seated beside his wife in the "blue gallery." Hale's servant knelt just outside the entrance to the seat.[176] After decades of division and conflict in the parish, the family and household had coalesced in the parish church to form the social structure of public worship.

The controversies in the parish affected conceptions of belonging and participation in the civic order of the corporation in Tewkesbury. After the Restoration settlement, the connection between Nonconformity and treason enshrined in the Corporation Act ensured the exclusion of Dissenters from important offices.[177] James II intervened in the summer of 1687 to install Dissenters in prominent positions, but the factions and sects in the parish did not share local government after this reformation of the council. If Anglicans controlled the council, Dissenters were invariably excluded or placed in lesser offices, and the Dissenters returned the favor after their installation in 1687. The composition of the common council and recruitment to other local offices were closely related to the variations in local attitudes to religious difference. The enactment of religious toleration in 1689 transformed a dreary politics of exclusion in both parish and corporation, as Anglicans and Dissenters became lawful participants in the same civic community under the monarchy.

The refusal to acknowledge difference that marked the relationship of Anglicanism and Dissent in the late 1660s and early 1670s had its civic counterpart in a kind of forced inclusion. Dissenters were ordered to serve in such burdensome offices as constable and surveyor of the highways and were heavily fined for resistance. The common council treated resistance to the lesser offices and to the new oaths imposed by the Corporation Act as forms of conventional delinquency, and the religious difference between the delinquents and the Anglicans in control of the council appears only in other sources. The delinquents included the prominent Quakers Joshua Carte, Anthony Keare, and Joseph Underhill as well as the leader of the Independents, William Davison. In 1672 Henry Collett, an influential Independent, became a freeman and so liable to serve in local offices. He paid the corporation £6 for freedom from the office of constable.[178] As local avoidance of Dissent protected the fiction of an inclusive church, so the attempt to force Nonconformists and Dissenters into the less important corporate offices preserved the illusion of an inclusive civic community in the corporation.

The reconstruction of the company of assistant burgesses in 1673 was a product of this forced inclusion and provided a measure of its success. The Anglican council placed members of several influential families, excluded from government since the Restoration, in the subordinate position of assistants on the common council. Christopher and Thomas Atkinson and Thomas Skey, prominent names in the local history of Nonconformity and revolution, were among the newly coopted assistants. Christopher Atkinson had actively supported the Neast faction under the Protectorate. Thomas Atkinson was prosecuted in the consistory court as a Fifth Monarchist in the early 1660s. The Skey family had been linked to Nonconformity as early as the 1630s, and Thomas Skey was prosecuted in 1682 for his participation in conventicles.[179] The new company of assistants also included Joseph Laight and Mathias Maide, supporters of Francis Wells in the aftermath of the Popish Plot. This recruitment of assistants from the families of Nonconformists and Dissenters formed part of a conscious effort to enlist candidates for the lesser offices of local administration. In 1669 Christopher Atkinson and William Millington, a prominent Baptist, served as constables.[180] Thomas Jeynes and Phillip Surman, burgesses removed from the common council in 1662, were the surveyors of the highways in 1671.[181] Christopher Atkinson and the Quaker Anthony Keare became the surveyors in 1672, and in the same year, the Baptist leader John Cowell and the Quaker Thomas Baker served as overseers of the poor.[182]

This effort to include prominent Dissenters in local government may have reflected concern over spheres of influence beyond the direct control of the corporation. A small group of Dissenters, who refused to accept lesser positions on the common council, acquired control of the independent charity founded by Giles Geast in the 1550s. The board of this charity had previously furnished an administrative haven for councilors removed from the corporation in 1656.[183] The four feoffees of the charity held their places for life and selected replacements in the case of death. These replacements were usually chosen from the pool of "witnesses" instructed in how to keep the accounts and administer the charity. After the Restoration, the royalist faction on the council had retained a foothold among the feoffees of this substantial charity, but their influence slipped steadily and then disappeared in 1676. The Independents John Carver and Phillip Surman, removed from places on the common council in 1662, had the advantage in the vote over Phillip Hilley in 1676 and chose their friend, the Independent Thomas Jeynes, to replace the deceased Edward Jennings.[184] This control of the charity was a means to sustain the influence of the Independent faction among the poorest inhabitants of the borough. In the early seventeenth century, the rents collected from the properties of the charity had been distributed directly from house to house. An increase in the movement of poor "strangers" into the town in the 1630s had resulted in a more elaborate and less personal system of distribution, and the "violent" press of the crowd of poor residents in St. Mary's Lane and the Mill Bank in the late 1640s had led to a complex system of "tickets" devised to prevent some recipients from acquiring "two or three times" their share of money and coals.[185] But the officers of the charity still moved from house to house in the execution of their duties. The council's effort to force Dissenters into corporate offices in the 1670s should be understood in relation to the Independent faction's control over this autonomous charity that distributed relief funds directly to poor households. Tewkesbury had been under the control of the Independents in the 1650s, and Independents probably represented the largest group of Dissenters in town, although their numbers are difficult to calculate, in part because of their close relationship to the parish church. Over the course of twenty-one years between 1666 and 1687, a known Independent, usually either Phillip Surman or Henry Collett, served as receiver of the rents for the Giles Geast charity for nineteen years.[186]

After the controversy of the late 1670s, Dissenters were excluded from even the less influential civic offices. The persecution of Independents, Baptists, and Quakers in the consistory court corresponded to this exclusion of Dissenters from the civic community. A minimum of thirty-six Dissenters had served in the lesser local offices of churchwarden, constable, surveyor of the highways, and overseer of the poor between 1671 and 1680. In the next decade, only nineteen known Dissenters held these offices. The adherence to the church of law in the parish helps to explain the determination of Thomas Nanfan, Conway Whithorne, James Simpson, and other loyalist Anglicans in control of the council to drive Dissenters beyond the boundaries of the civic community represented by the circle of office holders.[187]

The clearest evidence of the motives behind the Anglican reaction is in the petition sent from the corporation to the Crown in 1682 to express abhorrence of the Earl of Shaftesbury's "association" and a second petition sent in 1683 to express a similar contempt for the Rye House Plot. The petition against Shaftesbury, prepared in June 1682, conveyed a "most unfeigned abhorrence and detestation of all manner of leagues and associations" organized by "any false Achitophel" against royal authority. A further assault on the defeated whigs represented Shaftesbury's daydreams of a Protestant association as a strategy to "[subvert] the best of governments in church and state" and to "miserably [involve] us in another unnatural civil war." The conclusion of the council's petition was an anthem to the circle of order: a "firm and hearty resolution" to defend the "sacred person" of the king and the royal prerogative against all invasions, and to protect "the succession of the Crown in its due and legal course of lineal descent and the true Protestant religion as now established by law, which never taught or practiced any kind of rebellion, against the hellish contrivances of all its popish and fanatic enemies."[188]

A second petition of support was prepared in the summer of 1683 in the wake of the Rye House Plot. The expressions used in this petition evoke the terms of the recently concluded battle to remove Francis Wells from the benefice in Tewkesbury. The local experience of religious conflict must have reinforced the common council's condemnation of the "desperate miscreants of fanatical and atheistical principles" responsible for the Rye House Plot. This description of the religious "enemies" of the monarchy was followed by a declaration of the "steady resolution" of the loyal citizens of Tewkesbury to defend "the imperial Crown" and the "government established by law both in church and state." The corporation entrusted the delivery of its petition to a group headed by Thomas Nanfan, the prominent opponent of Francis Wells and local symbol of Anglican loyalism, and James Simpson, the town clerk.[189]

This reaction culminated in the surrender of the borough charter in 1684. Although the loyalist Anglican faction on the council was the first and most obvious beneficiary of the new charter, the initial impetus for surrender came from outside the corporation. Henry Somerset, Duke of Beaufort, lord lieutenant of Gloucestershire, conveyed an order from Charles to the common council, in May 1684, to surrender their charter or expect a *quo warranto* procedure against it.[190] A *quo warranto* was an expensive and difficult lawsuit that required a corporation to show "by what right" their privileges were held and could lead to the annulment of a weak charter. The council was disturbed by this unsolicited intrusion in local affairs and expressed concern that unconditional surrender might endanger the £200 a year in "charitable uses" dependent on the incorporation of the borough. As Beaufort's deputies had inspected the corporate records in 1680 and declared themselves satisfied of the due observance of the Corporation Act, the councilors protested their ignorance of any "failure of duty" that could have justified the royal assault on their "ancient" privileges. In a concession made to avoid the cost of a *quo warranto* and to forestall the acquisition of a new charter, the council offered the Crown the right to approve bailiffs and other officers chosen in the corporation, volunteered to remove any members perceived as disaffected, and promised to elect the replacements recommended by the king.[191]

These efforts to avoid surrender were unsuccessful. In the summer of 1684, the councilors transferred the property of the corporation into the hands of trustees as a prelude to surrender.[192] A sparsely attended assembly of the council voted in early September to surrender the charter. Only thirteen of the twenty-four burgesses attended the session, and the vote was seven to six in favor of surrender. The loyalist Anglican faction was divided on the issue, as James Simpson voted in favor of the surrender and Thomas Nanfan opposed it.[193] The formal process of surrender and petition for a new charter was completed by the end of the following month.[194] But when Charles' sudden death on February 6, 1685, raised hopes of escape, the council seized the opportunity to prepare a loyal address of congratulations to James. Beaufort was approached to deliver the address and to ask James to reconsider the surrender of the charter "in regard of our want of money to defray the charges of a new one." This final effort to avoid the expense of a new charter failed, and the corporation was forced to surrender to the new king. The council reluctantly raised part of the money for the new charter from bequests to the poor. This money was carefully secured to the use of the poor at 5 percent interest from either the local tolls or lands of equal value "that no part of what belongs to the poor may be lost or diminished."[195]

The charter acquired in March 1686 had not been sought by the Anglican faction, but several of its provisions reinforced their position on the council and resolved disputes in their interest. Sir Francis Winnington, a skillful lawyer who had served as attorney-general to the Duke of York and solicitor-general to the Crown in the 1670s, and Richard Dowdeswell, Winnington's son-in-law, helped to acquire the charter. Winnington resided at Stanford Court in Worcestershire and had been extremely vocal in his denunciations of popery and in his support of royal power.[196] Dowdeswell was the grandson of the Richard Dowdeswell chosen for Tewkesbury in the Convention Parliament. He had connections to the Anglican faction on the council through James Simpson, his former clerk and lawyer. Dowdeswell and Sir Francis Russell attended the Duke of Beaufort in May 1685 to seek his assistance in hastening the charter.[197] This new charter made decisive changes in the form and personnel of the council. The traditional corporation of the bailiffs, burgesses, and commonalty was abandoned, and the corporation was newly constituted as the mayor, aldermen, and common council of the borough of Tewkesbury.[198]

The installation of its members in local office seemed to assure the control of this smaller corporation to the loyalist Anglican faction. Charles Hancock, Richard Dowdeswell's brother-in-law, served as the first mayor. John Man and William Saunders, veteran officers of the Anglican reaction, were ensconced in the new corporation as aldermen and justices of the peace. The Man family had been restored to the corporation in 1662 and supported the faction that included James Simpson, Thomas Nanfan, and Conway Whithorne. Saunders had entered the council in 1681 and was included alongside the bailiff William Jones, also nominated to the new council, in the group chosen in 1683 to present the corporation's abhorrence of the Rye House Plot to the king.[199] These officers promptly demanded recognition and obedience to the new hierarchy in the traditional form of civic ceremony. Among its early declarations, the new council "ordered that every member of this common council shall provide himself with a good black cloth gown faced with velvet, the mayor and aldermen their gowns only to be faced with fox fur, and that they attend Mr. Mayor severally with their gowns accordingly upon the Sunday next before Michaelmas day next to go with him to church."[200] James Simpson remained clerk of the council.[201] Thomas Nanfan, the ancient royalist, was dead by this time, and Conway Whithorne, almost seventy years old, seems to have retired from office.[202] A reduction in the size of the council from forty-eight to thirteen eliminated the company of assistants and thus removed most of the supporters of Francis Wells from the corporation.[203]

In addition to changes in the size and factional composition of the council, the new charter altered the parliamentary franchise in the borough. Tewkesbury had been troubled by franchise disputes since the elections of 1640 and had confronted the issue as recently as 1673. Yet the disputed notions of the franchise were not constant over time. In 1640, the controversy concerned whether the franchise extended only to freemen or included all the inhabitants except almsmen. In 1673 an election produced violence when it could not be decided whether the franchise included all the freemen or a smaller group of freemen, perhaps the holders of property that fronted one of the three main streets of the town. The new charter of 1686 restricted the franchise to the mayor, aldermen, and common councilors and ended many years of conflict.[204] This charter was a victory for the Anglican faction that had removed Francis Wells from the parish in 1681 but represented more to the corporation than factional politics. The council as a group had worked since the 1640s to incorporate the nearby hamlet of Walton Cardiff for purposes of taxation, and the new charter contained a statement of the hamlet's inclusion in the limits of the town.[205]

This final phase in the Anglican exclusion of Dissenters from the civic community was the first phase of serious opposition to Anglican control. James II's regime produced a distinctive pattern of civic politics, and the provisions of the new charter helped to create the pattern in Tewkesbury. James had retained the right to appoint and dismiss officers of the corporation and had manipulated local groups to create a platform for religious toleration. Support for this policy became a condition of participation in the civic community.[206] Yet the Anglican corporation, loyal to the Restoration settlement, returned Sir Francis Russell and Richard Dowdeswell to parliament in the election of 1685, representatives unlikely to favor a policy of toleration for Catholics.[207] James visited Tewkesbury on a progress in 1687 and subsequently used the provisions of the new charter to install more sympathetic officers.[208] By the middle of December 1687, Charles Hancock, John Man, William Saunders, and James Simpson, indeed all but two of the councilors appointed in the charter, had been dismissed "by his Majesty's mandamus."[209] Dissenters occupied the vacated places and sent James a declaration of thanks in February 1688 that promised to elect loyal members of parliament who were disposed to repeal the Test Act and the penal laws.[210]

The officers installed by the Crown differed from the Anglican faction on religious issues but not on points of administrative competence or social qualification for office. As far as local status was concerned, James had received accurate information and had appointed the same representatives of prominent families that the corporation had attempted to include in the civic community in the early 1670s. The Dissenters placed on the council in 1687 and 1688 had been excluded from high office in the borough since the Restoration but had accumulated years of administrative experience as governors of the Giles Geast charity. Henry Collett, Thomas Jeynes, and Phillip Surman had served as receivers of the rents since 1665.[211] Jeynes and Surman had been removed from corporate office in 1662 and returned to the council after years of exile.[212] James restored families that had been denied the honor of local office for many years. The Clarke, Millington, Skey, and Yerrow families had served the corporation in the 1640s and 1650s and had been removed at the Restoration.[213] On the other hand, several of the families "restored" to the council in 1662 had virtually no prior qualification for office save their position on political developments in the 1650s. The Smithsends and Steights, installed on the council in 1662, should not be differentiated from the Colletts and Surmans, installed in 1687, as the "natural" leaders in Tewkesbury. The Colletts and Surmans could be dangerous to the Anglican faction precisely because of their position as gentlemen in local society. More than one group in Tewkesbury possessed the social credentials, if not the religious qualifications, to serve in civic offices, and James exploited this situation.

Participation in the civic community of Tewkesbury under James II depended on support for toleration. Yet the exclusion of Anglicans loyal to the Restoration settlement in the church does not appear to have produced instability or disaffection from the monarchy. The excluded Anglicans accepted the new political conventions and placed pressure on the Crown to restore their faction to local office. James Simpson was undoubtedly dismayed to learn that "the stupendous and surprising news" of revolution in 1688 had frustrated his faction's nearly completed negotiations to restore the Jacobean charter of 1610.[214] The best illustration of Anglican response to the changes in the corporation in 1687 and 1688 is the sermon preached by John Matthews, the minister of Tewkesbury, to mourn the imprisonment of the seven bishops in June 1688.[215]

Matthews laid down a barrage of disclaimers to begin the sermon. He intended "not any reflections on royal councils" that were neither in his "power to fathom nor duty to examine." His sermon contained no "disloyal word" nor was it designed to "question the justice of a king's displeasure." Despite the disclaimers, the sermon used the conventional rhetorical strategies and texts available to Anglican preachers to encourage listeners in their "proper meditations" on the sufferings of the church under persecution. Matthews invoked the persecution of the early Christians to foster a mood of patient suffering, but how many of his hearers would have taken the imprisonment of Peter for acceptable or praiseworthy political conduct? The metaphor of persecution in the early church encouraged passive resistance but also placed public pressure on the monarchy to abandon its religious policies. Matthews sustained Anglican royalism but used the model of primitive Christianity as a criticism and as a description of the "duty" required to alleviate "the present perplexity" of the Anglican church.[216]

Matthews also kept a diary, and his entries in the late autumn of 1688 indicate no disposition to remove James or to dispute his claim to the throne. The diary rather contains endless prayers to keep the king from a "strong work of vengeance" and "rash, destructive councils." Matthews prayed for James to show "the patience, meekness, and clemency which were in his father." Several entries for October and November form a continuous lament "that the bond of unity, religion, and the sacrament should cause these breaches." Matthews was horrified by William's invasion and the possibility of war. He continued to pray for "peaceable councils" and for "the condescension of our king to avert this storm." One of his deepest fears, expressed after the landing, was that "many [would] be perverted from their duty and forget their oaths." As bloodshed seemed unavoidable, Matthews beseeched God not to make England "a seat of war and sacrifice of the sword."[217]

The Glorious Revolution arrived unsolicited in Tewkesbury like the crises of the Civil War, the Restoration, and the Popish Plot.[218] But the local experience of the Glorious Revolution, like the other national crises, resulted from the interrelationship of the structures in place in the local community and the new circumstances of their application. Although the evidence of the local experience of the Revolution in 1688 and 1689 is slight, a few fragments have survived. The form of government established by the charter of 1686 seems to have survived until 1693, and Thomas Jeynes served as mayor, an office created by this charter, until his death in 1692.[219] Perhaps the surrender of the charter in 1685 had been enrolled and thus remained unaffected by the proclamation that restored the corporate franchises in October 1688.[220] Thomas Jeynes' death in 1692 began a period described in local documents as an "interregnum of government" in the town.[221] Yet the institutional form of this interregnum is difficult to determine. Corporate charities, such as the Geast foundation, survived as did the administration of the parish. Offices were filled, but the process of selection remains mysterious. The vestry could continue to elect churchwardens and probably nominated surveyors of the highways and overseers of the poor, but constables and sergeants were customarily elected only by sessions of the common council.[222] The absence of borough government becomes even harder to understand in light of the parliamentary election held in 1695. Richard Dowdeswell and Sir Francis Winnington, sponsors of an effort to restore the Jacobean charter, were returned to parliament for Tewkesbury, but little evidence has survived to indicate election procedure, except the restriction of the franchise to freemen, which was a characteristic of local elections before the charter of 1686. A petition to parliament from the losing candidate, Richard Cocks of Dumbleton, baronet, claimed Winnington had "detained" the book of freemen used to determine voters in the election and had threatened Cocks' supporters with eviction from their homes.[223]

This hiatus was followed by the reconstruction of the corporation in the charter of 1698.[224] Local sources described the arrival of the new charter as the return of civilization after the night of anarchy. The celebration of renewal reflected the form of the new charter itself: a restoration of the generous Jacobean charter of 1610. One local officer, in notes recorded in the council book on the delivery of the new charter, referred to the grant of James II as "restrictive" and unpopular. He claimed that the charter had been "disliked" and abandoned in the early 1690s and that "no government or exercise of authority" had existed in the town under any of their former charters. The town was represented as "open" and vulnerable to all manner of factional conflicts before the timely intervention of William's regime to rebuild the civic community. The notes that precede the list of new officers describe William as a liberator, arrived in the borough to "restore" the "rights and liberties" surrendered to James II.[225]

This celebration of renewal may well have extended to the relations among the local religious groups, since the charter of 1698 represented the first incorporation of Anglicans and Dissenters in the same civic community.[226] The initial impetus for incorporation came from London in the form of a limited toleration for Protestants established in 1689, early in the affairs of the new regime.[227] But the *practice* of the inclusive pluralism prescribed in the Toleration Act resulted from the politics of the 1680s.[228] After the Revolution, loyalist Anglicans and Dissenters in Tewkesbury came under fire from local opponents as the "regulators of charters" and collaborators in the popish policies of James II.[229] Both groups had received considerable benefits from the discredited charter of 1686, and an alliance formed after the Revolution to protect their local influence. Anglican families, such as the Bulstrodes, made common cause with Dissenters, such as the Colletts and the Jeynses; and Sir Francis Winnington, who had been instrumental in the surrender of the charter in 1684, used his influence to connect this faction to Sir William Trumbull and the Earl of Sunderland in the 1690s.[230] A common implication in the dishonored charter of James II made radical supporters of toleration in the 1680s into allies of the Anglicans in the 1690s.

The local conflict reached its climax in the competition between Sir Francis Winnington and Sir Richard Cocks to acquire a new charter in 1695. Just as Winnington had connections to the Earl of Sunderland and to the Colletts and Bulstrodes in Tewkesbury, Cocks had friends at Court in Charles Berkeley, Lord Dursley, lord lieutenant of Gloucestershire, and John, Lord Somers, lord chancellor, as well as the local support of the Steight family in Tewkesbury.[231] After many frustrations, the alliance of Anglicans and Dissenters defeated the Cocks faction in the parliamentary election of 1695 and subsequently acquired the charter.[232] Cocks lost the election, but Lord Dursley then blocked the passage of the charter and forced a compromise over the appointment of officers, a compromise that excluded Sir Francis Winnington from the office of recorder.[233] Lord Dursley's maneuvers succeeded in part because the lords justices could not decide whether the charter's conditions—particularly the life terms of the recorder, town clerk, and chamberlain, and the exclusion of county justices from the corporation's jurisdiction—contradicted William's preferences stated in council.[234] Despite the loss of the lucrative recorder's office, Sir Francis Winnington and his son-in-law Richard Dowdeswell, the victorious parliamentary candidates in 1695, ultimately received credit for the acquisition of the charter, with some assistance in 1697 and 1698 from Sir Robert Tracy, a relative of Sir Richard Cocks appointed as the recorder in the new charter.[235]

Yet the nomination of Henry Collett, a leader of the Independents, to administer the oaths to the officers of the new corporation, and the appointment of Collett's son as the first town clerk, symbolized the inclusion of Dissenters in the restored civic community.[236] This inclusive pluralism could be justified in terms of both a statutory toleration, created by Crown and parliament, and a common social discipline. John Matthews, the Anglican minister, several times implied the shared principles of the sect and the parish in a common emphasis on the proper discipline of the family. Several of Matthews' marriage sermons articulated a rationale for toleration on the basis of this shared familial discipline, and his sermon for Thomas and Margery Kings in March 1698 argued that matters of doctrine were less important in the public life of religion than was the preservation of hierarchy and obedience in the family.[237] The civic community thus became a plural community in 1698. The formation of this community was neither deliberate nor inevitable; its rationale lay in the structure of religion and politics in Tewkesbury in the second half of the seventeenth century.

The cultural influence of religious difference in Tewkesbury after the Restoration assumed structural, social, and civic forms. The structural form involved the interrelationship of several ideals of religious community and the everyday practice of religion. The divergence of model or ideal and practice helps to account for the variations in the relationship of the Anglican church and its sectarian neighbors. Local reactions to religious difference, defined as avoidance and persecution, expressed a continuous effort to protect the notion of an inclusive church. The social form of difference resulted from the translation of religious belief into the idiom of family relations. This process resulted in a transition from a residential to a familial form of religious fellowship, from a discipline that was based on the residential parish to a discipline that built fellowship from networks of interrelated families. The civic form of difference was evident in the effect of religious boundaries on participation in local government and access to the power of office. These expressions of difference can be separated for the purposes of discussion and analysis but were interrelated aspects of the religious culture produced by the crises of the seventeenth century.

Beyond the crises lay the outlines of an inclusive pluralism in the civic community and parish of the 1690s. James II had helped to unite Anglicans and Dissenters, nationally by his promotion of Catholicism before the Revolution and locally by his introduction of a charter that laid the foundation for cooperation after the Revolution.[238] This transformation did not mean the end of religious conflict in the parish but did represent an important shift in the boundaries of religious and political community. The intervention of king and parliament in this process, to produce the legislative structure of toleration in 1689, marked a decisive moment in the history of interaction between local societies and the institutions of authority and government beyond their boundaries. The king and his officers in London intervened to manage the religious conflicts that local institutions seemed unable to resolve. The further construction of local and national interdependency lies in the eighteenth century, and its implications remain a subject of impassioned political debate.

Symbol and Boundary:
Religious Belief, Ceremony, and Social Order

The problem of the attitude towards the laws is the problem of the attitude towards the world.

Ernst Troeltsch, *The Social Teaching of the Christian Churches* (1911)

But a social system, which is simply a phase of a continuous evolution within human groups possessed of memory, cannot perish outright or at a single stroke.

Marc Bloch, *Feudal Society*, vol. 2 (1940)

The restoration of the Jacobean charter in 1698 marked the end of a phase in the cultural life of Tewkesbury and its rural neighborhood. Since the 1590s, parish communities in the Vale of Gloucester had participated in a process of debate and conflict that started in the inclusive order of the late Tudor and early Stuart parish, accelerated in the open parish of the Civil War, became more complex and ramified in the Anglican parish and the sects after the Restoration, and ultimately helped to create the limited toleration and Protestant civic community of the 1690s. This process has traditionally been viewed as a result of the Reformation in doctrine, as the rational application of doctrine to ethics and everyday life.[1] A more recent perspective, now a tradition itself, has interpreted the process as a reflection of nonrational elements in religious symbolism and the interrelationship of religious ceremonies and forms of community in early modern Europe.[2] This interpretation of the reformation process has not disregarded the doctrinal revolutions of the sixteenth and seventeenth centuries; rather, it has pursued the influence

323

and variations of doctrinal controversy into town and village in order to explore the impact of religious conflict on social and political boundaries, on the differentiation of elite and popular forms of religion, and on the process of social control implicit in the dominance of the former.

The records of particular places make this process less abstract and discover the personal and collective impact of the relationship between rational and nonrational elements in religion, as parishes combined the elements in their symbols and ceremonies. The symbols that were used in the rites of the parish church created Christian identity and in the process marked the boundaries of different forms of authority and community: the household, the parish, the corporation, the diocese, and the kingdom.[3] The controversies of the Reformation not only focused on the nature of Christian identity but also confronted the issues of Christian community and its boundaries: the forms of authority and community implicit in religious ceremonies. Symbols were to be used and understood in prescribed ways, and from the early 1600s, distinctions of conformity and nonconformity began to mark the boundaries of Christian fellowship. In Tewkesbury and the other parish communities of the northern vale, the boundaries deeply affected by these conflicts included the boundaries of place, social relationship, and civic community.

The conflicts of the Reformation process dissociated systems of religious belief and notions of place. As discussed in Chapter 1, ritual expressions of belief in the authority of custom had scratched the boundaries of the territorial and residential community of the parish into the landscape. The religious conflicts of the seventeenth century powerfully affected the shared landscapes defined by the custom of the parish. These customary landscapes had formed a primary communal element in the reciprocal relationship of locality and personal identity: residents of a parish were socialized into a particular manifestation of the customary system. The advocates of further reformation rejected this link between religious fellowship and territorial conceptions of place. Nonconformists refused to recognize the spatial boundaries of the parish as spiritual boundaries and so abandoned their parishes to hear sermons in other churches. This belief in the diffusion of spiritual authority, and the corrupt human origins of the parish, helps to explain the radical Nonconformist repudiation of the authority embodied in the system of parochial tithes. God did not exist in such customs, represented as the mere accretions of time elevated to divine status by corrupt priests and their idolatrous parishes, nor could the proper expressions of godliness be confined to the parish church. God could exist in a barn, behind a haystack, in a private house, in any place chosen for the assemblies of the saints.

This insistence on the boundaries of conscience as the authoritative boundaries of spiritual community removed the divine presence from particular places and from material objects and captured the holy spirit in the everyday lives and spontaneous assemblies of the saints. A barrier, represented as a "wall of blood" or less graphically as a separation of godly assemblies from assemblies of the world, began to divide Nonconformists from neighbors in the parish. Quakers frequently preferred imprisonment for the nonpayment of tithes to participation in the unholy community enshrined in parish custom.[4] The customary belief in the correlation of shared space and shared salvation did not survive conflicts over the spiritual authority of the parish. After the schisms of the 1640s and 1650s, many came to define spiritual fellowship not in terms of common residence and parochial neighborhood but in terms of sympathy of conscience and shared belief. These criteria of fellowship were not constrained by the boundaries of the parish. As sources of identity, religious community and locality had ceased to be synonymous.

Controversy over the authority of the parish influenced local patterns of social relationship. Parishes represented a distinctive form of neighborhood. As participants in a religious fellowship, residents of a parish were enjoined to honor common notions of charity and Christian fellowship. Participation in the core ceremonies of the parish, in particular the rites of passage and holy communion, symbolized the bond of charity and fellowship among residents of the parish. This notion of charity did not eliminate conflict, and disputes were endemic in the parish, but such conflicts tended to represent and affirm the values of parish community: the codes of behavior expressed in terms of custom and neighborhood. The processes of neighborly mediation, arbitration, and the resolution of conflict were essential to the reproduction of the customary system and did not affect attitudes to the ceremonial representation of custom and neighborhood in the parish church.

The religious conflicts of the seventeenth century created unprecedented divisions in parishes. These conflicts resisted local resolution and sometimes resulted in violence, because the sources of local authority, from the informal institutions of neighborhood and mediation to the formal institutions of the church courts, were included in the field of dispute. As local religious divisions became more explicit, the notions of social relationship and personal responsibility ceased to encompass the territorial boundaries of the parish. The contraction of religious fellow-ship into networks of interrelated households transformed the bounda-ries of charity and social responsibility. This analysis of Gloucestershire parishes as particular forms of religious fellowship, as distinctive con-figurations of symbolic boundaries, thus indicates a relationship between a transformation in the definition and experience of place and a transfor-mation of social relationships in the Reformation.

The interrelationship of religious symbols and public authority in early modern England meant that religious conflict by definition affected the boundaries of civic community in the corporation of Tewkesbury. As head of the Church of England, the authority of the monarch extended to religious matters, and royal leadership possessed a sacred quality. Eliza-beth I styled herself governor rather than head and acted more cau-tiously than her successors on the issue of religious uniformity, but from the Act of Supremacy in 1559 the monarchy possessed enormous power in its prerogative to articulate and enforce its religious views.[5] The Book of Common Prayer and the 39 Articles carried the royal sanction and symbolized the pastoral commitment of the Protestant monarchy. An attack on these symbols could easily be construed as an attack on the authority of the monarch to intervene in religious matters, and the Non-conformist insistence on the personal authority of conscience raised the question of political loyalties and intentions. The invocation of scripture and conscience did not lead inescapably to the subversion of monarchy, but the parish church displayed the royal arms, and the Book of Com-mon Prayer carried the impress of royal authority. The implications of radical departure from the prescribed ceremonies, such as the Saturday Sabbatarianism of the 1620s in Tewkesbury, seemed unmistakable to local officers.[6]

Sectarian departures from the parish church in the 1640s and 1650s were interpreted after the Restoration as separations from the civic com-munity protected by the authority of monarchy. This belief in the mutu-ally supportive relationship of parish church, monarchy, law, and social order had powerful consequences in 1662. The reaction to the early Quakers provides the best illustration of the belief that separation from the parish meant separation from civil society and ultimately had to end in the rule of blood and anarchy. This local sensitivity to the civil politics of religious symbolism endured in the later seventeenth century. In Tewkesbury, belief in the common boundaries of religious community and civic community emerged most forcefully in the Popish Plot, and the explosive interrelationship of religious symbolism, political authority, and personal allegiance began to lose its potency only in the aftermath of the Glorious Revolution. The limited toleration of 1689 represented the first tentative movement to dissociate personal loyalty to the monarchy from commitment to the Anglican parish.

The scenes of religious conflict in Forthampton and Tewkesbury that began this book were interrelated expressions of this process of reformation, a complex history that extended over more than a century and left traces in a variety of local evidence. The process was evident in the parochial disputes of Forthampton in 1606. Thomas Drake's invocation of conscience and scripture, and the departure of his supporters from their homes in Forthampton to receive communion from the more sympathetic hands of William Blackwell in the parish of Beckford, expressed the divisive power of Nonconformity.[7] Parish boundaries became barriers to the spiritual force of attraction among the godly. Drake's faction understood identity and responsibility not in terms of the parish but in terms of an exclusive network of interrelated families. Yet the broader implications of the religious symbolism used to create such factions remain obscure because the evidence produced in this dispute deliberately avoided discussion of sacramental issues and the 39 Articles. Richard Garner, the curate of Forthampton in 1606, believed that such a discussion might provoke violence in his parish.[8]

The variations of the Hickes narrative created in the 1630s reveal this broader context as well as the complex schemes of classification implicit in religious symbols. These narratives can be placed in relation to Henry Burton's Puritan cautionary tales as evidence of the relationship between local religious conflicts and the divisive national controversies over pollution and popish enemies in the Church of England in the 1630s. Peter Studley, the anti-Puritan author of the first Hickes narrative, and Burton, the author of a collection of Sabbatarian tales, consistently represented differences of religious belief and discipline as the tokens of religious enemies: the image-breaker and the Sabbath-breaker.[9] Studley used the mysterious incident of the desecrated cross in Tewkesbury to represent Thomas Hickes as a monstrous enemy of the sacred. Burton used similar literary techniques to represent opponents of the strict Sabbath as the enemies of God and the church. These stereotypic enemies that were created in the combative rhetoric of the Puritan and anti-Puritan literature of the 1630s and that were introduced in parish churches in the metropolitical visitation of 1635, helped to harden the religious factions of the 1610s into the more clearly defined interests that surfaced in the parliamentary elections of 1640 in Gloucestershire and Tewkesbury.[10]

The evidence created by the prosecution of Francis Wells and his faction in 1678 illustrates the continuity in the Reformation process across the Restoration, the persistence of divisions in the parish, and the significance of religious ceremonies in the civic community of Tewkesbury.[11] Wells created a storm in the corporation because his ceremonial style evoked memories of the Civil War and revived the exclusive fellowship of the godly parish in the 1650s. The controversy seems clearly linked to the earlier troubles of parish and nation. Yet the dispute that resulted in the removal of Wells from the benefice in Tewkesbury occurred in the early weeks of the Popish Plot, a crisis that divided the parish between conceptions of the church and conceptions of the enemy, and the crucial distinction between the church of conscience and the church of law could not have formed in the same fashion in the 1640s and 1650s. The cumulative experience of conflict and the influence of prior experience on subsequent behavior complicate the relationship between the problems in Forthampton in 1606 and in Tewkesbury in 1678. Despite this important caveat, the recurrent appeals to conscience and persistent assaults on the surplice and the Book of Common Prayer, as well as the impassioned apologies for the Book of Common Prayer and the 39 Articles, formed layers of continuity in a process of Reformation that transformed conceptions of authority, ceremony, and community in both parishes over time.

Appendixes

Notes

Manuscript Sources

Index

Tables

1. Total population, 1603–1710[a]

Parish	1603	1650	c. 1672	1710
Ashchurch	283 (376)	70:333	102:485	308
Deerhurst	202 (269)	130:618	86:409	620
Forthampton	94 (125)	60:285	68:323	160
Tewkesbury	1,600 (2,128)	1,000:4,750	471:2,237	2,500
Tredington	48 (64)	16:76	19:90	100
Twyning	280 (373)	60:285	78:371	600
Walton Cardiff	—	—	10:48	56

a. These figures furnish a sketch of local population in 1603, 1650, 1672, and 1710. The data for 1603 indicate communicants, people known by the minister to receive the sacrament. The age of communion is taken as fourteen years, a compromise between the twelve to thirteen years common in the late sixteenth century and the sixteen years ordered by canon law in 1604. A figure of 33 percent has been added on the right to allow for children under fourteen. The return for Forthampton is probably incorrect, since sixty-two men from the parish were listed for militia duty in 1608. Elrington has suggested that the 1603 return omits Swinley, a large hamlet in the parish, and is a return only for the village of Forthampton. See C. R. Elrington (ed.), *VCH Gloucester* (Oxford: Oxford University Press, 1968), vol. 8: 199. Of the other returns, the most questionable are Ashchurch and Deerhurst, large parishes where the distance to the church affected patterns of attendance.

The figures for 1650 came from the survey of church benefices in Gloucestershire. The survey recorded the number of families dwelling in a parish, indicated by the figure on the left. See C. R. Elrington, "The Survey of Church Livings in Gloucestershire, 1650," *TBGAS*, 83 (1964): 87–88. The estimate for Tewkesbury is extremely high, yielding a level of population not reached before the first quarter of the nineteenth century. A statement from the Committee for Plundered Ministers gave a figure of 2,500 communicants for the parish of Tewkesbury in 1649. See GRO: TBR A 1/1, p. 144.

The estimates for 1672 rest on hearth tax returns. The number of persons in the return, rated and exempt, is given on the left. The 1671–72 return is the best for Gloucestershire but

1. Total population, 1603–1710[a] (continued)

is not without its problems for investigation of the northern vale. None of the returns for Deerhurst include lists of exemptions, a significant drawback considering the number of poor people known to have resided in large hamlets such as Apperley. In the 1664 return for the much smaller hamlet of Deerhurst Walton, however, one-third of the inhabitants were exempt. On the strength of this return, one-third has been added to the 1672 returns for hamlets in the parish of Deerhurst, as a conservative estimate of the number of inhabitants too poor to pay the tax. The 1664 return for Forthampton also includes a list of exemptions and is therefore substituted in the table for the 1671–72 return. The figure for Ashchurch is a composite of the 1664 returns for the hamlets of Northway, Fiddington, and Pamington, which include exemptions, and the 1662 Michaelmas return for Aston on Carrant, which does not. See PRO: E 179/247/16 and E 179/116/554 for the 1664 return and the 1662 Michaelmas return.

The figures for 1710 are from Sir Robert Atkyns, *The Ancient and Present State of Gloucestershire,* 2nd ed. (London, 1768 [1712]), pp. 117, 202, 229, 381, 413, 415, 795. The most obvious errors are the estimates for Ashchurch, Forthampton, and Twyning. In the case of Forthampton, Atkyns appears to have underestimated the population of hamlets such as Swinley. The use of manorial records may have skewed the estimate for Ashchurch by omitting the landless, but the wild overestimate of the population in Twyning probably reflects a mistaken impression of the population dispersed in hamlets and isolated farms beyond the village of Twyning itself.

2. Distribution of population, 1608–1710 (percentage)[a]

Parish	1608	c.1672	1710
Ashchurch: Aston on Carrant	20	21	31
Fiddington and Natton	20	21	26
Northway and Newton	33	33	31
Pamington	28	26	26
Deerhurst: Apperley and Wightfield	70	73	50
Deerhurst	13	13	—
Deerhurst Walton	17	12	22
Forthampton: Down End	—	—	8
Forthampton	—	—	—
Swinley	—	—	23
Tewkesbury: Borough	94	96	—
Barton Street	(19)	(22)	
Church Street	(41)	(29)	
High Street	(40)	(48)	
Mythe and Mythe Hook	2	2	3
Southwick	4	2	—
Twyning: Green End	—	—	40
Hill End	—	—	—
Twyning	—	—	—
Shuthonger	—	—	—

a. The percentages for 1608 were calculated from the returns in John Smyth, *Men and Armour for Gloucestershire in 1608* (Gloucester: Alan Sutton, 1980). The figures for 1672 are based on the returns for individual hamlets in the hearth tax assessments used in Table 1. As the exempt were not listed by street, distribution in the town was calculated only for residents who paid the tax. The result thus represents the concentration of the affluent on the High Street. The percentages for 1710 are drawn from Atkyns and are reliable only for broad comparative purposes, as his unit of assessment was sometimes the house and sometimes the family. The absence of data on distribution in Forthampton and Twyning is disappointing, as both parishes contained large hamlets. See Elrington, *VCH Gloucester,* 8: 198; and Atkyns, *Gloucestershire,* p. 415.

3. Occupational structure, 1608[a]

Tewkesbury[b]
1. Agriculture, horticulture, fishing (24%): 10 yeomen, 5 husbandmen, 91 laborers, 2 gardeners, 3 fishermen, 6 servants
2. Provisions, retail (16%): 4 millers, 14 maltsters, 1 brewer, 10 bakers, 19 butchers, 1 cook, 1 fishmonger, 2 salters, 2 vintners, 3 innkeepers (2 chamberlains, 3 ostlers), 2 tapsters, 11 tipplers
3. Leather (13%): 18 glovers, 12 tanners, 1 currier, 1 tewgorer, 28 shoemakers, 1 cobbler, 2 saddlers
4. Cloth (10%): 3 drapers, 2 woolen drapers, 5 haberdashers, 12 mercers, 28 tailors
5. Shipping (6%): 23 mariners, 4 trowmen
6. Woodwork (6%): 7 carpenters, 7 joiners, 1 turner, 12 coopers
7. Textiles (5%): 1 clothworker, 8 weavers, 3 dyers, 1 wool dyer, 1 wool drier, 1 tucker, 5 shearmen, 5 feltmakers
8. metalwork (4%): 5 cutlers, 2 pewterers (one with 2 servants), 12 smiths
9. miscellaneous trades and retail (2%): 3 chandlers, 2 bottlemakers, 1 basketmaker, 1 roper, 1 turnmaker, 1 seveger
10. Building (1%): 2 masons, 2 slaters, 1 tiler, 2 glaziers
11. Transport (1%): 4 carmen, 3 carriers
12. Paper and books (1%): 1 stationer, 3 papermen, 1 parchmentmaker
13. Dealers (1%): 1 merchant, 1 peddler (with 1 servant), 2 chapmen, 1 horse courser
14. Professions (0.8%): 1 barber, 1 surgeon, 1 scrivener, 1 schoolmaster
15. Weapons and raw materials (0.5%): 1 fletcher, 1 bowyer, 1 saltpeterman
16. Other (4%): 16 gentlemen (one with one servant), 1 servant (master's occupation unspecified)
17. Unspecified (4%): 19

Ashchurch
1. Agriculture (57%): 12 yeomen, 20 husbandmen, 15 laborers, 15 servants
2. Crafts (13%): 2 tailors, 3 smiths, 1 collarmaker, 1 surgeon, 1 joiner, 1 wheeler, 1 weaver, 2 millers, 2 servants
3. Other (5%): 1 gentleman, 4 servants (master's occupation unspecified)
4. Unspecified (25%): 27

Deerhurst[c]
1. Agriculture (65%): 19 yeomen, 35 husbandmen, 12 laborers, 5 servants
2. Crafts (17%): 4 smiths, 5 tailors, 3 carpenters, 1 slater, 1 glover, 1 weaver, 1 musician, 3 badgers
3. Other (4%): 1 esquire, 1 gentleman, 2 servants to gentleman
4. Unspecified (15%): 16

3.   Occupational structure, 1608[a] (continued)

Forthampton
1. Agriculture (67%): 30 husbandmen, 11 laborers, 1 servant
2. Crafts (2%): 1 smith
3. Unspecified (32%): 20

Tredington
1. Agriculture (93%): 6 yeomen, 14 husbandmen, 8 servants
2. Crafts (7%): 2 smiths

Twyning
1. Agriculture (65%): 3 yeomen, 24 husbandmen, 6 laborers, 10 servants
2. Crafts (17%): 3 tailors, 1 smith, 1 weaver, 1 wool drier, 2 carpenters, 1 shoemaker, 2 servants
3. Other (11%): 5 gentlemen, 2 servants (master's occupation unspecified)
4. Unspecified (8%): 5

Walton Cardiff
1. Agriculture (68%): 3 yeomen, 3 husbandmen, 5 laborers, 2 servants
2. Crafts (11%): 2 weavers
3. Unspecified (21%): 4

a. Smyth, *Men and Armour,* pp. 86–87, 99, 114–127.
b. Including the hamlets of Southwick and the Mythe.
c. Six yeomen listed for the hamlets of Apperley and Wightfield were described as the "yeomen servants" of Thomas Cassey, esquire. Six husbandmen who were returned for the same hamlets of Apperley and Wightfield were described as Cassey's "husbandmen servants."

4. Occupations of testators, 1590–1690

Parish	1590–1615	1616–1640	1641–1665	1666–1690
Tewkesbury	2 gentlemen	1 gentleman	2 gentlemen	11 gentlemen
	11 yeomen	3 yeomen	2 yeomen	5 yeomen
	2 husbandmen	4 husbandmen	1 laborer	4 husbandmen
	1 shearman	1 laborer	2 weavers	1 shoemaker
	1 weaver	1 fisherman	2 tanners	1 glover
	1 tanner	1 weaver	4 bakers	1 butcher
	2 shoemakers	2 shoemakers	2 victuallers	1 brewer
	1 brewer	1 vintner	1 maltster	2 maltsters
	1 cook	1 cook	2 innkeepers	4 innkeepers
	2 bakers	2 innkeepers	2 mercers	3 bakers
	1 tailor	1 cutler	1 tailor	2 tailors
	2 smiths	1 smith	1 brazier	1 woolen draper
	1 cooper	1 cooper	1 ironmonger	2 mercers
	1 chandler	1 carpenter	1 cooper	2 cutlers
	1 saltpeterman	2 joiners	1 carpenter	1 brazier
	2 trowmen	1 linen draper	1 trowman	3 joiners
	1 chapman	1 chapman	1 chapman	1 owener
	1 clerk	1 clerk	2 masons	1 mariner
	1 slater	1 glazier	1 hallier	
	1 bottlemaker	1 bricklayer	1 clerk	
		1 clerk	1 minister	
Ashchurch	1 gentleman	1 gentleman	1 gentleman	12 yeomen
	3 yeomen	4 yeomen	4 yeomen	3 husbandmen
	4 husbandmen	1 husbandman	1 husbandman	1 tailor
			1 shoemaker	
Deerhurst	2 gentlemen	1 gentlemen	2 gentlemen	2 gentlemen
	9 yeomen	17 yeomen	7 yeomen	15 yeomen
	25 husbandmen	11 husbandmen	1 husbandman	2 husbandmen
	1 weaver	1 carpenter	1 carpenter	1 weaver
		2 blacksmiths	1 mason	
		1 baker	1 wheelwright	
Forthampton	6 yeomen	2 yeomen	1 yeoman	10 yeomen
	5 husbandmen	1 husbandman		
	1 blacksmith			
	1 clerk			
	1 pauper			

4. Occupations of testators, 1590–1690 (continued)

Parish	1590–1615	1616–1640	1641–1665	1666–1690
Tredington	1 gentleman 3 yeomen 4 husbandmen 1 laborer	3 yeomen 2 husbandmen		1 gentleman 2 yeomen
Twyning	7 yeomen 10 husbandmen 1 day laborer	1 esquire 2 gentlemen 12 yeomen 6 husbandmen	5 yeomen 1 tailor 1 weaver	1 gentleman 7 yeomen 1 weaver 1 broadweaver 1 blacksmith
Walton Cardiff	1 husbandman 1 weaver	2 yeomen 1 husbandman	1 husbandman	2 yeomen 2 husbandmen

5. Distribution of wealth by number of hearths, c. 1672[a]

Parish	1–2	3–5	6–9	10+	Exemptions
Ashchurch[b]	53	15	3	—	39
Deerhurst	52	10	3	1	24
Forthampton	24	13	—	1	30
Tewkesbury					
Southwick[c]	8	5	1	—	9
Mythe and Mythe Hook	5	1	1	1	—
Borough	136	101	22	4	186
Tredington	6	7	1	—	5
Twyning	37	16	7	1	17
Walton Cardiff[d]	7	3	—	—	2

a. This table is based on the hearth tax return for 1672 in PRO: E 179/247/14 or GRO: D 383. In the town, 72 percent of the population was exempt or paid for two hearths or less, 22 percent paid for between three and five hearths, and 6 percent paid for six hearths or more. In the rural hamlets of Southwick and the Mythe, the proportions were 71 percent, 19 percent, and 10 percent, respectively. The agricultural parishes surrounding Tewkesbury show a slightly different balance between the bottom and middle strata, with 79 percent of the population in the lower income category, 17 percent in the middle, and 5 percent in the highest.

b. The returns for Aston on Carrant do not include exemptions. The 1662 return has consequently been increased by 38 percent to match the 1664 exemptions for the other three hamlets in the parish.

c. Based on the 1664 return.

d. Based on the 1664 return.

6. Place of burial, 1590–1690

1590–1639
1. Ashchurch
   a. church: 2 gentlemen, 2 yeomen
   b. churchyard: 1 yeoman, 2 husbandmen
2. Deerhurst
   a. church: 1 gentleman, 1 yeoman, 2 husbandmen
   b. church or churchyard: 3 yeoman, 1 husbandman
   c. churchyard: 3 yeomen, 19 husbandmen, 1 weaver
3. Forthampton
   a. churchyard: 2 yeomen, 2 husbandmen, 1 blacksmith
4. Tewkesbury
   a. church: 2 gentlemen (1 former bailiff), 1 minister, 3 yeomen, 1 vintner
   b. church or churchyard: 5 yeomen, 2 husbandmen, 1 clerk, 2 cordwainers, 2 blacksmiths, 1 cook, 1 chandler
   c. churchyard: 2 yeomen, 1 husbandman, 1 trowman, 1 shearman, 2 weavers, 1 brewer, 1 shoemaker, 1 cordwainer, 1 blacksmith, 1 carpenter, 1 slater, 1 bottlemaker, 1 cooper, 1 laborer, 1 chapman
5. Tredington
   a. church: 1 gentleman, 1 yeoman
   b. church or churchyard: 1 yeoman, 3 husbandman
   c. churchyard: 2 yeomen, 2 husbandmen, 1 laborer
6. Twyning
   a. church: 2 yeomen
   b. churchyard: 7 yeomen, 13 husbandmen, 1 blacksmith

1640–1690
1. Ashchurch
   a. church: 2 yeomen
   b. church or churchyard: 1 yeoman, 1 husbandman
   c. churchyard: 2 husbandmen
2. Deerhurst
   a. church: 1 tailor
3. Tewkesbury
   a. church: 4 gentlemen, 1 mercer, 1 baker
   b. church or churchyard: 1 baker
   c. churchyard: 1 gentleman, 1 maltster, 1 baker, 1 brasier
4. Tredington
   a. church or churchyard: 1 yeoman
5. Twyning
   a. church or churchyard: 1 yeoman

7. Bequests to the parish, 1590–1690[a]

1590–1615
  81 (35%)
6 gentlemen, 1 widow of gentle family, 15 yeomen, 2 widows of yeomen, 24
  husbandmen, 1 widow of husbandman, 1 chapman
Total wills: 229

1616–1640
  23 (13%)
2 gentlemen, 1 spinster of gentle family, 8 yeomen, 1 spinster of yeoman family,
  3 husbandmen, 1 widow of husbandman, 1 minister
Total wills: 184

1641–1665
  3 (3%)
1 yeoman, 1 widow, 1 minister
Total wills: 110

1666–1690
  2 (1%)
1 yeoman, 1 widow
Total wills: 206

a. The figures under the chronological headings indicate, first, the number of wills that
included bequests to the parish that were proven during the specified period of time and,
second, the proportion that this number represented among the total number of wills from
the seven relevant parishes that were proven during the same period. When the testators
making these bequests to their parishes also stated their occupation or status, that
information is included in the second entry in the table.

8.   Bequests to the Poor, 1590–1690[a]

1590–1615
   70 (31%)
5 gentlemen, 1 widow of gentle family, 17 yeomen, 1 widow of yeoman, 15
   husbandmen, 1 widow of husbandman, 1 widow of brewer, 1 chapman, 1
   shoemaker
Total wills: 229

1616–1640
   37 (20%)
1 esquire, 1 gentleman, 1 widow of gentle family, 1 spinster of gentle family,
   13 yeomen, 1 widow of yeoman, 3 husbandmen, 1 widow of husbandman,
   1 daughter of husbandman,
1 blacksmith
Total wills: 184

1641–1665
   14 (13%)
2 gentlemen, 3 yeomen, 1 widow of yeoman, 1 mercer, 1 baker, 1 widow
Total wills: 110

1666–1690
   9 (4%)
3 gentlemen, 1 minister, 1 clerk
Total wills: 206

a. The figures under the chronological headings indicate, first, the number of wills that
included bequests to the poor that were proven during the specified period of time and,
second, the proportion that this number represented among the total number of wills from
the seven relevant parishes that were proven during the same period. When the testators
making these bequests to the poor also stated their occupation or status, that information is
included in the second entry in the table.

9. References to family, friends, and neighbors in preparation for death, 1590–1690[a]

1590–1615
  References to nuclear family: 397 (42%)
  References to kin relations: 333 (36%)
  References to friends and neighbors: 113 (12%)
  Total references: 937

1616–1640
  References to nuclear family: 324 (40%)
  References to kin relations: 326 (40%)
  References to friends and neighbors: 74 (9%)
  Total references: 813

1641–1665
  References to nuclear family: 191 (42%)
  References to kin relations: 185 (40%)
  References to friends and neighbors: 49 (11%)
  Total references: 458

1666–1690
  References to nuclear family: 298 (41%)
  References to kin relations: 338 (47%)
  References to friends and neighbors: 60 (10%)
  Total references: 722

a. The figures under the chronological headings express the references made in wills to the relations of the nuclear family, to kin relations, and to friends and neighbors as a proportion of the total number of references made in the wills proven during the specified period of time.

Accusations of Witchcraft in Tewkesbury[1]

The information of Susanna Vicaridge [ms damaged] of John Vicaridge, gentleman, taken upon oath [ms damaged] 20 February, 1666 (Lent Assizes, 1666).

Who deposes that one Isabell Sheene of Tewkesbury, widow, came several times to this examinate's house and offered her children cake, which being at first refused, was afterwards taken and eaten by them. And after this Isabell Sheene offered this informant a servant which she accepted of, and after not finding her for her turn, put her off again, which the said Isabell took ill and so expressed it, and shortly after Susanna this informant's daughter first fell ill, and after her son Thomas.

1. Susanna Vicaradge to the persons bewitched (£20)
    George Whittle of Tewkesbury, dyer (£20)
    John Parsons, gent, to the great strength of Margaret Vicaridge while the fit was on her (£20)
3. Robert Eaton, clerk, Margaret (£20)
2. £20 [apparently to Margaret's bewitchment]
    Samuel Kenricke, clerk, Margaret
    Edward Wilson of Tewkesbury, baker
    Thomas Boulter of Tewkesbury, mason
    Andrew Woolams of Tewkesbury
    Elizabeth Wight, widow
    Ann Cook of Tewkesbury, widow
    Edmund P[ierce?]

To Isabell Sheen [reputation as a witch]
   Thomas Hooper of Gloucester, brewer (£20)
   Katherine Newman, wife of Richard Newman of Stoke Orchard [ms
      damaged] of Tewkesbury (£20)
   Judith Torrent of Tewkesbury, singlewoman (£20)
   [Timothy Bishop, deleted]
   Edward Wilson of Tewkesbury, baker
   Mary Lawrence of Tewkesbury, widow (£20)
   Mary Kaner [Canner] of Tewkesbury, widow (£20)
   Joseph Bartholomew of Tewkesbury, shoemaker (£20)
   Martha Buggin of Tewkesbury, singlewoman (£20)
   Andrew Woolams of Tewkesbury, maltster
   Anne Cook of Tewkesbury, widow

To Anne Phillips for bewitching Robert Mallory
   [list of recognizances valued at] £20
   Robert Malory
   Samuel Kenrick, clerk
   Robert Eaton, clerk
   Elizabeth Wight, widow
   Edward Wilson of Tewkesbury, baker
   Thomas Boulter of Tewkesbury, mason
   Judith Palmer of Tewkesbury, singlewoman
   Thomas Roberts of Tewkesbury, yeoman
   Andrew Woolams of Tewkesbury, maltster
   Edmund Pierce
   Ann Hanly, wife of William Hanly

Examination of Isabell Sheene
   She says she is not guilty of bewitching the person of Margaret Vi-
      caridge as is charged upon her, or of using that devilish art to any
      other person or thing whatsoever.
   Isabell Sheene (mark)

Examination of Anne Phillips
   She says she is not guilty of bewitching the person of Robert Malory
      as is now charged against her.
   Anne Phillips (mark)

Notes

Abbreviations

Add	Additional
BL	British Library, London
Bodl	Bodleian Library, Oxford
CCC	Calendar of the Committee for Compounding, 1643–1660 (London, 1889)
CCAM	Calendar of the Committee for Advance of Money, 1642–1656 (London, 1888)
CSPD	Calendar of State Papers, Domestic Series, 1629–1696 (London, 1860–1964)
GCL	Gloucester City Library
GDR	Gloucester Diocesan Records
GRO	Gloucestershire Record Office, Gloucester
HMC	Historical Manuscripts Commission
KRO	Kent Record Office, Maidstone
LPL	Lambeth Palace Library, London
Ms	Manuscript
Mss Cranfield	Manuscripts of Lionel Cranfield, Earl of Middlesex
PM	Parish Microfilm
PRO	Public Record Office, London
RFTV	Records of Four Tewkesbury Vicars
TBGAS	Transactions of the Bristol and Gloucestershire Archaeological Society
TBR	Tewkesbury Borough Records
TT	Thomason Tracts
UCL	University College Library, London
VCH Gloucester	Victoria County History of Gloucester

Dates are given in Old Style, with the year beginning on January 1.

Introduction

1. This description of the confrontation and its background has been constructed from the accounts in GRO: GDR 100, Depositions: March 1606–

345

March 1609: Case of Office v. Drake and Edwards, Depositions of William Restell, Richard Garner, and John Cheston.

2. Among his horrors of nonconformity, Studley included the Evan family murders in Shropshire, attributed to a dispute among family members over the propriety of kneeling in communion. This story became the centerpiece in Studley's effort to define nonconformity as "unnatural" behavior. Peter Studley, *The Looking Glass of Schism,* 2nd ed. (London, 1635); and Peter Lake, "Puritanism, Arminianism, and a Shropshire Axe-Murder," *Midland History,* 15 (1990): 37–39. The several versions of the Hickes narrative were reprinted in James Bennett (ed.), *The Tewkesbury Yearly Register and Magazine,* 2 vols. (Tewkesbury: 1840, 1850), 2: 270–272.

3. Bennett, *Tewkesbury Yearly Register,* 2: 271.

4. Bennett, *Tewkesbury Yearly Register,* 2: 272.

5. S. R. Gardiner (ed.), "Reports of Cases in the Courts of Star Chamber and High Commission," *Camden Miscellany,* new series, 39 (1886): 244.

6. David Ogg, *England in the Reign of Charles II,* 2nd ed. (Oxford: Oxford University Press, 1956), pp. 1–34; Godfrey Davies, *The Restoration of Charles II, 1558–1660* (San Marino: Huntington Library, 1955), pp. 355–363; and J. P. Kenyon, *Stuart England,* 2nd ed. (Harmondsworth: Penguin, 1985), pp. 195–212.

7. Most of the documents from this case have been preserved in GRO: D 747/1, Papers of James Simpson, Town Clerk of Tewkesbury.

8. Patrick Collinson, *The Religion of Protestants: The Church in English Society, 1559–1625* (Oxford: Clarendon Press, 1982), p. 140.

9. The more recent contributions to this literature have been summarized by Peter Lake, "Defining Puritanism—Again?" in Francis J. Bremer (ed.), *Puritanism: Transatlantic Perspectives on a Seventeenth-Century Anglo-American Faith* (Boston: Massachusetts Historical Society, 1993), pp. 3–29.

10. Patrick Collinson, *The Elizabethan Puritan Movement* (London: Jonathan Cape, 1967), pp. 12–15, 26–27.

11. Collinson, *Religion of Protestants,* p. 189.

12. The nature of this moral crisis and the role of the churches in its resolution are discussed in Ernst Troeltsch, *The Social Teaching of the Christian Churches,* 2 vols. (London: George Allen & Unwin, 1931 [1911]), 1: 23–25, 2: 509, 849–850.

13. R. H. Tawney, *Religion and the Rise of Capitalism: A Historical Study* (Harmondsworth: Penguin, 1938 [1926]), p. 277. This book contained the first series of Holland Memorial Lectures, delivered by Tawney in 1922.

14. Max Weber, *The Protestant Ethic and the Spirit of Capitalism* (London:

George Allen & Unwin, 1930 [1904–1905]); and Max Weber, "The Protestant Sects and the Spirit of Capitalism," in H. H. Gerth and C. Wright Mills (eds.), *From Max Weber: Essays in Sociology* (New York: Oxford University Press, 1946 [1906]), pp. 302–322, 450–459; Troeltsch, *Social Teaching of the Christian Churches;* and Tawney, *Religion and the Rise of Capitalism.*

15. R. H. Tawney, "Forward," in Weber, *Protestant Ethic,* p. 1e.

16. Michael Walzer, *The Revolution of the Saints: A Study in the Origins of Radical Politics* (Cambridge, Mass.: Harvard University Press, 1965), p. 327.

17. The conception of ethos, for example, has become, in modified form, a commonplace in the social sciences. See Clifford Geertz, "Ethos, World View, and the Analysis of Sacred Symbols," in Clifford Geertz, *The Interpretation of Cultures: Selected Essays* (New York: Basic Books, 1973), pp. 126–141; and David E. Stannard, *The Puritan Way of Death: A Study in Religion, Culture, and Social Change* (New York: Oxford University Press, 1977).

18. Troeltsch, *Social Teaching of the Christian Churches,* 1: 447, 2: 991–993.

19. Tawney, *Religion and the Rise of Capitalism,* p. xiv.

20. The intellectual sources of this perspective, if not the connections to policy issues, are discussed in John Milbank, *Theology and Social Theory: Beyond Secular Reason* (Oxford: Blackwell, 1990), pp. 75–100.

21. William Haller, *The Rise of Puritanism* (New York: Columbia University Press, 1938), pp. ix, 127.

22. Haller, *Rise of Puritanism,* pp. 384–385, 421–432.

23. Haller, *Rise of Puritanism,* pp. 8, 83–127, 384.

24. M. M. Knappen, *Tudor Puritanism: A Chapter in the History of Idealism* (Chicago: University of Chicago Press, 1939), pp. xi–xii.

25. Knappen, *Tudor Puritanism,* pp. ix, xi–xii, 10–11, 348–349, 513–514.

26. Knappen, *Tudor Puritanism,* pp. 10–11. This point is another link between Knappen and Troeltsch. Troeltsch, *Social Teaching of the Christian Churches,* 2: 624.

27. Knappen, *Tudor Puritanism,* pp. 3–5.

28. Knappen, *Tudor Puritanism,* pp. 41–44, 339–340.

29. Haller, *Rise of Puritanism,* pp. ix, 405–406; Knappen, *Tudor Puritanism,* pp. 519–520.

30. Walzer, *Revolution of the Saints,* p. vii.

31. Michael Walzer, "Puritanism as a Revolutionary Ideology," *History and Theory,* 3 (1963): 59–60; and Walzer, *Revolution of the Saints,* p. 327.

32. Walzer, *Revolution of the Saints,* pp. 148–150, 177–183, 186–198, 327; Haller, *Rise of Puritanism,* pp. 138–167.

33. Walzer, *Revolution of the Saints,* pp. 264–267, 328.
34. Walzer, "Puritanism," 59–60; Walzer, *Revolution of the Saints,* pp. 327–328.
35. A. G. Dickens, *The English Reformation,* 2nd ed. (University Park: Pennsylvania State University Press, 1989), pp. 13–24, 56–60, 222–226, 391–396.
36. Collinson, *Elizabethan Puritan Movement,* pp. 14, 29–44.
37. Collinson, *Religion of Protestants,* p. 179.
38. Collinson, *Religion of Protestants,* p. 251.
39. Tawney, *Religion and the Rise of Capitalism,* pp. 123–125, 202, 230–231.
40. Tawney, *Religion and the Rise of Capitalism,* p. 233.
41. Christopher Hill, *The World Turned Upside Down: Radical Ideas During the English Revolution* (Harmondsworth: Penguin, 1972, 1975).
42. Christopher Hill, *Society and Puritanism in Prerevolutionary England* (Harmondsworth: Penguin, 1964), pp. 407–466.
43. Hill, *Society and Puritanism,* p. 417.
44. Hill, *Society and Puritanism,* p. 427.
45. Hill, *Society and Puritanism,* pp. 407–466; R. H. Tawney, *The Agrarian Problem in the Sixteenth Century* (London: Longman's, 1912); and Tawney, *Religion and the Rise of Capitalism,* pp. 209–210.
46. Keith Wrightson and David Levine, *Poverty and Piety in an English Village: Terling, 1525–1700,* 2nd ed. (Oxford: Clarendon Press: 1995 [1979]), pp. 103–109. Similar interpretations of the parish influenced by Hill's work may be found in David Underdown, *Revel, Riot, and Rebellion: Popular Politics and Culture in England* (Oxford: Clarendon Press, 1985), pp. 11–17, 24–40; and William Hunt, *The Puritan Moment: The Coming of Revolution in an English County* (Cambridge, Mass.: Harvard University Press, 1983), pp. 69–84, 327.
47. In the early seventeenth century, Puritanism and Protestantism appear to have been synonymous in Terling. This form of Protestant piety became nonconformity only in response to Laudian innovations in the 1630s. Wrightson and Levine, *Poverty and Piety,* pp. 159–160.
48. Wrightson and Levine, *Poverty and Piety,* pp. 29–31, 36–42, 166–167.
49. Martin Ingram, *Church Courts, Sex and Marriage in England, 1570–1640* (Cambridge: Cambridge University Press, 1987).
50. Other important contributions to the reconsideration of the institutional performance and social value of the ecclesiastical courts have been Ronald A. Marchant, *The Church Under the Law: Justice, Administration, and Discipline in the Diocese of York, 1560–1640* (Cambridge: Cambridge University Press, 1969); and Ralph Houlbrooke, *Church Courts and the*

People During the English Reformation, 1520–1570 (Oxford: Oxford University Press, 1979).

51. Ingram, *Church Courts, Sex and Marriage,* p. 123.

52. Ingram, *Church Courts, Sex and Marriage,* pp. 18–19.

53. Ingram, *Church Courts, Sex and Marriage,* pp. 72–83.

54. Margaret Spufford, *Contrasting Communities: English Villagers in the Sixteenth and Seventeenth Centuries* (Cambridge: Cambridge University Press, 1974), p. 239; and Margaret Spufford, "Puritanism and Social Control?" in Anthony Fletcher and John Stevenson (eds.), *Order and Disorder in Early Modern England* (Cambridge: Cambridge University Press, 1985), pp. 41–57.

55. Spufford, *Contrasting Communities,* pp. 239–300.

56. Spufford, *Contrasting Communities,* pp. 299–300. Ingram, *Church Courts, Sex and Marriage,* pp. 114–116, 118, also discusses the power of religion to create both vertical and horizontal social divisions.

57. Spufford, *Contrasting Communities,* p. 352.

58. Emile Durkheim and Marcel Mauss, *Primitive Classification* (Chicago: University of Chicago Press, 1961 [1903]), pp. 3–9.

59. Emile Durkheim, *The Elementary Forms of the Religious Life* (New York: Free Press, 1915 [1912]), p. 51; and Jean Delumeau, *Catholicism Between Luther and Voltaire: A New View of the Counter-Reformation* (London: Burns and Oates, 1971), pp. 129–130.

60. Mircea Eliade, *The Sacred and the Profane: The Nature of Religion* (New York: Harcourt, Brace, Jovanovich, 1957), pp. 10, 231.

61. Eliade, *Sacred and Profane,* pp. 8–18, 20–21.

62. Eliade, *Sacred and Profane,* pp. 162–201.

63. Peter Burke, *Popular Culture in Early Modern Europe* (London: Temple Smith, 1978), pp. xi–xii.

64. Keith Thomas, *Religion and the Decline of Magic: Studies in Popular Beliefs in Sixteenth and Seventeenth Century England* (London: Weidenfeld and Nicolson, 1971), pp. 3–21.

65. This literature has developed apace since the 1960s and has now reached the stately proportions of a tradition. The best introductions to the forms of popular culture, in addition to the works already discussed, are Natalie Davis, *Society and Culture in Early Modern France* (Stanford: Stanford University Press, 1975); and Barry Reay (ed.), *Popular Culture in Seventeenth-Century England* (London: Croom Helm, 1985).

66. Delumeau, *Catholicism Between Luther and Voltaire,* p. 129.

67. Delumeau, *Catholicism Between Luther and Voltaire,* p. 163. On the importance of ceremony in the creation of communities, see Natalie Davis, "The

Sacred and the Body Social in Lyon," *Past and Present,* 90 (1981): 40–70; Hunt, *Puritan Moment,* pp. 113–129; John Bossy, *Christianity in the West, 1400–1700* (Oxford: Oxford University Press, 1985); Underdown, *Revel, Riot, and Rebellion,* pp. 44–72; R. W. Scribner, "Cosmic Order and Daily Life: Sacred and Secular in Preindustrial Germany" and "Reformation, Carnival and the World Turned Upside Down," in R. W. Scribner, *Popular Culture and Popular Movements in Reformation Germany* (London: Hambledon Press, 1987), pp. 1–16, 71–101; Eamon Duffy, *The Stripping of the Altars: Traditional Religion in England, c. 1400–c. 1580* (New Haven: Yale University Press, 1992), pp. 131–154; and Christopher Haigh, *English Reformations: Religion, Politics, and Society Under the Tudors* (Oxford: Clarendon Press, 1993), pp. 25–39.

68. Edmund Leach, *Social Anthropology* (Glasgow: Fontana, 1982), p. 9.

69. Clifford Geertz, "Religion as a Cultural System," in Michael Banton (ed.), *Anthropological Approaches to the Study of Religion* (London: Tavistock, 1966), p. 5. Geertz's notion of symbolism in society is indebted to the work of Alfred Schutz, "Symbol, Reality, and Society," in Alfred Schutz, *Collected Papers I: The Problem of Social Reality* (The Hague: Martinus Nijhoff, 1962), pp. 287–356.

70. Geertz, "Religion as a Cultural System," 6.

71. Anthony P. Cohen (ed.), *Symbolising Boundaries: Identity and Diversity in British Cultures* (Manchester: Manchester University Press, 1986), pp. 1–19.

72. Cohen, *Symbolising Boundaries,* pp. 3–4; and Anthony P. Cohen, *Whalsay: Symbol, Segment, and Boundary in a Shetland Island Community* (Manchester: University of Manchester Press, 1987), pp. 1–21.

73. The best introductions to the definitions and conceptual problems of rites of passage are provided by Arnold Van Gennep, *The Rites of Passage* (London: Routledge and Kegan Paul, 1908); Victor Turner, *The Ritual Process: Structure and Anti-Structure* (Ithaca: Cornell University Press, 1969); and Max Gluckman (ed.), *Essays on the Ritual of Social Relations* (Manchester: Manchester University Press, 1962), pp. 1–52.

74. All quotations from Claude Lévi-Strauss, "History and Anthropology," in *Structural Anthropology* (New York: Basic Books, 1963), pp. 18, 21–22.

75. A similar view is expressed for a different purpose in Keith Wrightson, "Estates, Degrees, and Sorts: Changing Perceptions of Society in Tudor and Stuart England," in Penelope J. Corfield (ed.), *Language, History, and Class* (Oxford: Blackwell, 1991), pp. 30–52.

76. This approach to the distinction of sacred and profane reflects concerns over the relationship of "collective representations" and "practice" raised

in Edmund Leach, *Pul Eliya: A Village in Ceylon* (Cambridge: Cambridge University Press, 1961), pp. 296–306.

77. Scribner, "Cosmic Order and Daily Life," 2.

78. The case for the intimate interrelationship between religious, moral, and social conflict is most clearly and persuasively expressed in Wrightson and Levine, *Poverty and Piety,* pp. 110–141; and Underdown, *Revel, Riot, and Rebellion,* pp. 44–72.

79. On the general characteristics of godliness, see Keith Wrightson, *English Society, 1580–1680* (London: Routledge, 1982), pp. 199–221.

80. Scribner, "Cosmic Order and Daily Life," 2.

81. This discussion of the relationship between the sacred, ritual, and everyday life has been influenced by Eliade, *Sacred and Profane,* pp. 162–213.

82. This relationship of symbol to behavioral code recalls Simmel's distinction between "great forms" and other less comprehensive schemes for the organization and representation of social life. See Georg Simmel, *The Sociology of Religion* (New York: Philosophical Library, 1906), pp. 2–3.

83. This complex archive is described in Isabel M. Kirby, *Diocese of Gloucester: A Catalogue of the Records of the Bishop and Archdeacons,* 2 vols. (Gloucester: Gloucester City Corporation, 1968).

84. GRO: P 329 CW 2/1, Tewkesbury Churchwardens Accounts, 1563–1703.

85. GRO: TBR A 1/1–5, Borough Council Minutes; and D 2688, Giles Geast Charity Account Book.

86. GRO: D 4944 2/1, Tewkesbury Baptist Church Book; D 1340 B2/M1, Stoke Orchard Monthly Meeting, 1671–1783; and D 1340 C1/M3, Tewkesbury Women's Weekly Meeting.

1. Reverend Histories

1. Many studies of the physical geography of Gloucestershire exist, and I have nothing to add to them. The best introductions are H. P. R. Finberg, *The Gloucestershire Landscape* (London: Hodder and Stoughton, 1975); and William Marshall, *The Rural Economy of Gloucestershire,* 2 vols. (London, 1796). By far the best account of geography in the Tewkesbury area is C. R. Elrington (ed.), *VCH Gloucester* (Oxford: Oxford University Press, 1968), vol. 8.

2. Sir Robert Atkyns, *The Ancient and Present State of Gloucestershire,* 2nd ed. (London, 1768 [1712]), p. 380.

3. This drawing, dated 1804, was displayed in the Tewkesbury town hall in the 1960s and is reproduced in Elrington, *VCH Gloucester,* 8: 114.

4. These ferries became sources of diversion and relaxation in the nine-

teenth and early twentieth centuries. Some photographic evidence of their uses is reproduced in Charles Hilton (ed.), *Tewkesbury and the Vale of Gloucester in Old Photographs* (Gloucester: Alan Sutton, 1987), pp. 17, 73–75.

5. Several photographs of modern flood effects in Tewkesbury are included in Hilton, *Tewkesbury,* pp. 40, 72. See also Anthea Jones, *Tewkesbury* (Chichester: Phillimore, 1987), pp. 9, 13, 20.

6. Hilton, *Tewkesbury,* pp. 72, 102.

7. GRO: D 2688, Giles Geast Charity Book, f. 85v. Severn floods still force a few residents in the area south of Deerhurst to keep a boat. Vivid photographs of the Deerhurst floods are reproduced in Hilton, *Tewkesbury,* pp. 99, 101–102.

8. HMC, *13th Report, Appendix 2: Portland Mss* (London, 1893), p. 300.

9. GRO: P 329 IN 1/5, Burials, 7-4-1656.

10. Ordnance Survey, *Tewkesbury,* SO 83/93; Hilton, *Tewkesbury,* pp. 23–25; Elrington, *VCH Gloucester,* 8: 111–112.

11. Compare the rare photographs of structures in St. Mary's Lane to the photographs of buildings on the main streets reproduced in Hilton, *Tewkesbury,* pp. 35, 64 (St. Mary's Lane), 30–31, 47–48, 50–69, 71–72 (High Street, Church Street, and Barton Street). The lack of attention to the houses of the poor and the enthusiasm lavished on the main streets of the town provide fascinating evidence of attitudes to photographic preservation in the late nineteenth and early twentieth centuries.

12. Marshall, *Rural Economy,* p. 13.

13. John Bruges, esquire, won the cup. GRO: D 2688, Giles Geast Charity Account Book, f. 172r; and Elrington, *VCH Gloucester,* 8: 123.

14. Elrington, *VCH Gloucester,* 8: 112, 137–138.

15. See PRO, E 134, 13 Chas I/17 April/Easter 29, Deposition of George Harris.

16. GRO: GDR 89, Depositions, June 1601–March 1604: Case of Read v. Langston; and GRO: GDR 79, Depositions, April 1592–November 1597: Case of Read v. Langston, for the woad in Southwick.

17. Ordnance Survey, *Tewkesbury,* SO 83/93.

18. *True News Out of Herefordshire* (London, 1642). The battle reported in this pamphlet never happened.

19. The description in the next three paragraphs is based on Elrington, *VCH Gloucester,* 8: 34, 72, 196–198, 228, 236; and Atkyns, *Gloucestershire,* pp. 116–117, 201–202, 229, 413, 415.

20. Accusatory hands and heavy underlines mark the villagers from Walton Cardiff in the Tewkesbury parish registers of the seventeenth century. See

entries in GRO: P 329 IN 1/2–6; and Bennett, *Tewkesbury Yearly Register,* 2: 325.

21. Dan Beaver, "Conscience and Context: The Popish Plot and the Politics of Ritual, 1678–1682," *Historical Journal* 34 (1991): 301–304.

22. Elrington, *VCH Gloucester,* 8: 185.

23. Elrington, *VCH Gloucester,* 8: 172–175; a photograph of the Walton Spa pumproom before its demolition in 1961 is included in Hilton, *Tewkesbury,* p. 48.

24. John Smith reputedly killed the dragon, and the axe used to perform the heroic deed was a local attraction in 1714. Elrington, *VCH Gloucester,* 8: 36, 40. See the photographs of the raised paths and the construction of the "stanks" in Hilton, *Tewkesbury,* pp. 95, 106–107.

25. Elrington, *VCH Gloucester,* 8: 34.

26. Elrington, *VCH Gloucester,* 8: 44–45.

27. GRO: TBR B 2/41, Brief for Counsel as to Overlode Ferry, 1624.

28. Elrington, *VCH Gloucester,* 8: 197. The distance between households in the hamlets of Forthampton is evident in the photographs of Corner House Farm reproduced in Hilton, *Tewkesbury,* pp. 84, 90.

29. Elrington, *VCH Gloucester,* 8: 196.

30. GRO: D 2318 III/16, Deeds: Mythe and Mythe Hook, 1638.

31. GRO: P 329 IN 1/6, Burials, 21–10–1687. Orchards were also cultivated just south of Tewkesbury, around the hamlets of Deerhurst. See Elrington, *VCH Gloucester,* 8: 34.

32. GRO: D 2318 III/16, Deeds: Mythe and Mythe Hook; GDR 100, Depositions, March 1606–March 1609: Case of Margery Prickett v. Edward Rogers, Depositions of Richard Symons of Twyning and Thomas Orell of Tewkesbury; and Ordnance Survey, *Tewkesbury,* SO 83/93. The proximity of dwellings in the village of Twyning, as opposed to other parts of the parish, is also suggested by the photographs in Hilton, *Tewkesbury,* pp. 18–19.

33. GRO: GDR B4/3/34, Ashchurch (tithe), 1592/3, Giles Read v. William Holshippe; and GDR 79, Depositions, April 1592–November 1597: Case of Read v. Holsheep.

34. GRO: GDR 79, Depositions, April 1592–November 1597: Depositions of Walter Jeynes and John Carpenter.

35. GRO: GDR 79, Depositions, April 1592–November 1597: Depositions of George Morry and John Walker.

36. GRO: GDR 79, Depositions, April 1592–November 1597: Deposition of John Carpenter.

37. GRO: GDR 114, Depositions, 1611–1613: Case of Cartwright v. Shield

and Bick, Depositions of Thomas Greenwoe, Thomas Surman, and William Twinning; and GDR 121, Depositions, March 1613–February 1614: Case of Cartwright v. Shield and Bick, Depositions of Daniel Willis and John Diston.

38. Elrington, *VCH Gloucester,* 8: 115.

39. GRO: TBR B 2/41, Brief for Counsel as to Overlode Ferry, 1624.

40. Ibid.

41. Ibid. The ferries that moved between Tewkesbury and high points such as Mythe Hill during flood times were also organized on a customary basis, though no statement of the custom has survived. See GRO: GDR 100, Depositions, March 1606–March 1609: Case of Margery Prickett v. Edward Rogers; and D 2318 III/16, Deeds: Mythe and Mythe Hook: Lease to Wakeman in 1638 of "all that passage or ferry between the town of Tewkesbury and the Mythe Hill in time of floods, for carrying and recarrying all manner of persons and other things in boats, and the customs and duties for the same."

42. GRO: GDR 100, Depositions, March 1606—March 1609: Read v. Langston; and GDR B4/3/1173, Tewkesbury (tithe), 1594–1601, Giles Read v. Henry Langston; GDR 89, Depositions, June 1601–March 1604: Read v. Langston.

43. See Joan Thirsk, "Projects for Gentlemen, Jobs for the Poor: Mutual Aid in the Vale of Tewkesbury, 1600–1630," in Patrick McGrath and John Cannon (eds.), *Essays in Bristol and Gloucestershire History* (Bristol: Bristol and Gloucestershire Archaeological Society, 1976), pp. 147–169. This evidence from the 1590s lends support to Thirsk's argument that the cultivation of woad preceded tobacco in the region as a labor intensive project, although the woad was introduced by a relatively modest local farmer whose efforts predated the arrival in the vale of London merchants such as Baptist Hicks.

44. GRO: GDR 79, Depositions of John Jeynes, husbandman, Richard Tyrrett, yeoman, John Little, husbandman, and Robert Jenkins als. Jeynes, husbandman. Thirsk, "Projects for Gentlemen," 158, notes that woad was being tithed at Painswick, north of the clothmaking district around Stroud, by 1615.

45. GRO: GDR B4/3/35, Ashchurch, 1601 (tithe), John Roberts v. Roger Darston; and GDR 89, Depositions, June 1601–March 1604: Roberts v. Darston.

46. There was some uncertainty about Pamington's rights to pasture in the Homedowns. GRO: GDR 89, Deposition of John Jeynes.

47. In a rough breakdown, Northway received approximately forty acres, Newton twenty acres, Fiddington forty acres, Natton twenty acres, and

Pamington twenty acres. The remainder consisted of small enclosures like the one voted to John Darston "by the inhabitants of the hamlets, in regard of the pains he had taken for the same inhabitants about the same Homedowns." GRO: GDR B4/3/35, Roberts v. Darston; and GDR 89, Deposition of Edmund Roberts.

48. The quotation is from article 19 of the royal injunctions of 1559 reprinted in Gerald Bray (ed.), *Documents of the English Reformation* (Minneapolis: Fortress Press, 1994), p. 340. An excellent introduction to the ritual of perambulation, as to many other aspects of local custom, is John Brand (ed.), *Observations on the Popular Antiquities of Great Britain*, 3 vols. (London: George Bell and Sons, 1877), 1: 197–212.

49. Bray, *Documents*, p. 340.

50. Ibid.

51. See Underdown, *Revel, Riot, and Rebellion*, pp. 80–81, 90–91. On perambulations in northern Gloucestershire, see GRO: GDR 109, Depositions, April 1609–June 1611: Case of Taylor v. Harris (Deerhurst and the Leigh); P 329 [uncatalogued]: 3, 4 (Tredington); and PRO: E 134/29 Chas II/12 February/Easter 10, Depositions of James Cartwright, Thomas Cartwright, John Wadley, and Humphrey Jeynes (Tredington and Tewkesbury).

52. Brand, *Popular Antiquities*, 1: 204.

53. GRO: P 329 [uncatalogued]: 3; compare this certificate of participants in perambulation to the hearth tax return for 1672 in GRO: D 383.

54. GRO: GDR 109, Depositions, 1609–1611: Taylor v. Harris, Depositions of Thomas Bishop, William Hom, and Hugo Hampton; Taylor v. Bishop, Deposition of Richard Sharp, for the status of participants and descriptions of adolescent participation in the procession. The educational aspects of perambulation are a neglected subject.

55. On the issue of women and custom, see GRO: GDR 109, Depositions: Taylor v. Harris and Taylor v. Bishop, Depositions of Richard Sharp; GDR 159, Depositions, September 1625–May 1628: Hitches v. Smithsend, Depositions of Margery Balthropp, Joanna Flooke, Joanna Wyatt, and Margaret Phillips. See GRO: GDR 89, June 1601–March 1604: Read v. Langston, Deposition of John Little; and GDR 159, Hitches v. Smithsend, Depositions of Joanna Wyatt and Margaret Phillips, for examples of immigrants serving as authorities in disputes over custom.

56. GRO: GDR 109, Depositions: Taylor v. Harris, Depositions of Bishop, Hom, and Hampton.

57. GRO: GDR 109, Depositions: Deposition of Thomas Bishop.

58. GRO: GDR 89, Depositions: Case of Roberts v. Darston, Deposition of Edmund Roberts.

59. GRO: TBR B 2/41, Brief for Counsel as to Overlode Ferry, 1624.
60. Historians of colonial America, confronted by the radically different so-cial experiences in a slaveholding society, have been more sensitive than historians of early modern Britain to differential experiences of place and landscape. See Rhys Isaac, *The Transformation of Virginia, 1740–1790* (Chapel Hill: University of North Carolina Press, 1982), pp. 11–57; and Bernard Herman, *The Stolen House* (Charlottesville: University Press of Virginia, 1992), pp. 51–165. Isaac's work draws indirectly on the ideas developed in a number of essays by Alfred Schutz. See Alfred Schutz, "On Multiple Realities" and "Symbol, Reality, and Society" in *Collected Papers I: The Problem of Social Reality* (The Hague: Martinus Nijhoff Publishers, 1962), pp. 207–259, 287–356; and "The Stranger: An Essay in Social Psychology" in *Collected Papers II: Studies in Social Theory* (The Hague: Martinus Nijhoff Publishers, 1964), pp. 91–105. A strong argument for the intersection between landscape and emotional life is Yi-Fu Tuan, *Landscapes of Fear* (Minneapolis: University of Minnesota Press, 1979).
61. GRO: GDR 89, Depositions, 1601–1604: Trockmorton v. Wells, Deposi-tion of Thomas Alston, gentleman.
62. GRO: GDR 232, Depositions, 1678–1684: Case of Wriggan v. Jeynes, Deposition of Nicholas Smithsend.
63. GRO: GDR 109, Depositions, 1609–1611: Case of Taylor v. Bishop, Depo-sition of Hugo Hampton.
64. GRO: GDR 148, Depositions, May 1622–August 1625: Case of Hunt v. Miles, Deposition of Ralph Jeynes.
65. GRO: GDR 148, Depositions, May 1622–August 1625: Depositions of William Worley and Edward Knowles.
66. GRO: GDR 89, Depositions: Case of Throckmorton v. Wells, Deposition of Richard Harris.
67. GRO: GDR 232, Depositions: Case of Wriggan v. Jeynes, Deposition of John Jeynes, joiner.
68. See David Cressy, *Literacy and the Social Order: Reading and Writing in Tudor and Stuart England* (Cambridge: Cambridge University Press, 1980), pp. 118–141, for a discussion of the sociology of literacy.
69. A lease represented a legal relationship in written form but did not imply equality or solidarity between the parties involved. In 1623, William Jef-feries, a yeoman of Bredon, attributed his knowledge of tithing rights in the hamlet of the Mythe to a lease of tithes he had held seventeen years before. His subsequent knowledge of ownership was, however, based on having seen the servants of the alleged owner collecting payment. GRO: GDR 148, Depositions: Case of Savage v. Baugh, Deposition of William Jeffries.

70. GRO: GDR 148, Depositions: Depositions of William Jefferies and William Hayward. Hayward said the lords subsequently put their decision before the inhabitants for approval.

71. See Alfred Schutz, "Common Sense and Scientific Interpretation of Human Action" in *Collected Papers I: The Problem of Social Reality,* pp. 3–47; and Clifford Geertz, "Common Sense as a Cultural System," in *Local Knowledge: Further Essays in Interpretive Anthropology* (New York: Basic Books, 1983), pp. 73–93, for introductions to commonsense constructs in social life.

72. Brand, *Popular Antiquities,* 1: 197–198; and Wrightson, *English Society,* pp. 51–57, for a discussion of neighborliness.

73. GRO: GDR 127, Depositions, April 1616–November 1618: Case of Shaw v. Higgins.

74. GRO: GDR 127, Depositions, April 1616–November 1618: Deposition of John Harding.

75. GRO: GDR 127, Depositions, April 1616–November 1618: Depositions of John Harding, Thomas Harding, and Alice Mudge.

76. GRO: GDR 89, Depositions, June 1601–March 1604: Case of Roberts v. Darston, Depositions of Edmund Roberts and William Rayer.

77. GRO: GDR 89, Depositions, June 1601–March 1604: Case of Penryn v. Crees, Deposition of Thomas Neend. The enterprise covered four years, and although the rent was unspecified, the pasture was said to be worth about £12 a year. See GRO: W 1614/176 (Thomas Jordan) for the kinship between Neend and Jordan.

78. Some of the problems involved in reconstructing and interpreting the lives of the poor in early modern England are described in Paul Slack, *Poverty and Policy in Tudor and Stuart England* (New York: Longman, 1988), pp. 104–107.

79. The best source for parish poor relief in northern Gloucestershire is the Twyning vestry book that contains the accounts kept by overseers of the poor. The accounts are incomplete for the seventeenth century, starting in the 1660s and stretching into the eighteenth century. See GRO: P 343 VE 2/1, f. 23r.

80. This theme is explored in detail in A. L. Beier, *Masterless Men: The Vagrancy Problem in England, 1560–1640* (London: Methuen, 1985), pp. 8–12, 16–22, 38–40.

81. GRO: P 329 CW 2/1, p. 352.

82. GRO: P 343 VE 2/1, f. 19r.

83. As described and cited in Menna Prestwich, *Cranfield: Politics and Profits under the Early Stuarts* (Oxford: Clarendon Press, 1966), pp. 528–529.

84. GRO: GDR 81, Detection Book, October 1597. Stoolball was an early

form of cricket. See Underdown, *Revel, Riot, and Rebellion,* pp. 76–77, for further references to the game and its history.

85. The violence should not be underestimated. In 1593 Humfry Witcom of St. Nicholas in Gloucester, a servant of the widow Nevett, "died with a blow on the head at football." Both football and stoolball were popular sports in the vale. See GRO: P 154/15 IN 1/1, 10 March 1593.

86. GRO: GDR 122, Depositions, March 1614–April 1615: Bishop v. Cartwright, Deposition of Giles Bishop.

87. GRO: GDR 122, Depositions, March 1614–April 1615: Deposition of Humphrey Cosin.

88. GRO: GDR 121, Depositions, March 1613–February 1614: Case of Gremmett v. Chauntrell.

89. Chauntrell had already made over most of his estate to his younger brother in return for "meat, drink, and lodging during his natural life." GRO: GDR 121, Depositions, March 1613–February 1614: Deposition of William Darke.

90. GRO: GDR 121, Depositions: Case of Southerne v. Man, Deposition of Margery Carter.

91. GRO: GDR 127, Depositions, April 1616–November 1618: Case of Shaw v. Higgins, Deposition of Alice Mudge.

92. A detailed discussion of the transition from wife to widow may be found in Amy Louise Erickson, *Women and Property in Early Modern England* (London: Routledge, 1993), pp. 153–203.

93. GRO: GDR 114, Depositions, 1611–1613: Case of Eaton v. Greenway.

94. GRO: GDR 114, Depositions, 1611–1613: Depositions of Alice Willis and Margaret Wharton.

95. GRO: GDR 204, Depositions, January 1638–March 1640: Case of Beale v. Ward, Deposition of Thomas Smith.

96. GRO: GDR 168, Depositions, September 1628–March 1631: Case of Flucke and Weaver v. Beale and Beale, Depositions of Henry Wells, Anne Wells, and Jane Hart.

97. An account of the importance of widows and single people in local credit networks is provided by B. A. Holderness, "Credit in English Rural Society Before the Nineteenth Century, with Special Reference to the Period 1650–1720," *Agricultural History Review,* 24 (1976): 105; and "Credit in a Rural Community, 1660–1800: Some Neglected Aspects of Probate Inventories," *Midland History,* 3 (1975): 101–102. See Erickson, *Women and Property,* pp. 83–84, 203–204, for the social situation of single women.

98. GRO: GDR 221, Depositions, September 1670–February 1678: Case of Nind v. Nind, Deposition of Bridgett Yeend. This outburst appears to have been part of a passing dispute, as Jefferies als. Yeend eventually left the

whole of her estate to Joanne Yeend or Nind, the wife of a kinsman. GRO: W 1674/33, Elizabeth Jefferies als. Yeend.

99. The distinction between horizontal and vertical landscapes is discussed in Barbara Bender (ed.), *Landscape: Politics and Perspectives* (Oxford: Berg, 1993), p. 2.

100. See Thomas, *Religion and the Decline of Magic,* pp. 128–146.

101. James Howell, *Familiar Letters or Epistolae Ho-Elianae,* 3 vols. (London: Dent, 1903), 2: 72–73.

102. Ibid.

103. Peter Burke has made this distribution part of his argument for the separation of popular and elite cultures in early modern Europe. See Burke, *Popular Culture,* pp. 270–281. The incident described reflects important distinctions but not necessarily a separation between the worldview of formally educated gentility and the mental world of laborers.

104. Bodl: Rawlinson Ms B 323, ff. 287r-v.

2. Parts, Persons, and Participants in the Commonwealth

1. See Philip Abrams, *Historical Sociology* (Ithaca: Cornell University Press, 1982); and Charles Tilly, *As Sociology Meets History* (New York: Academic Press, 1981). An introduction to this debate is Alan Macfarlane, "History, Anthropology and the Study of Communities," *Social History,* 5 (1977): 634–635.

2. Pierre Bourdieu, *The Logic of Practice* (Stanford: Stanford University Press, 1990), pp. 1–21.

3. A fascinatingly complex statement of this problem is Leach, *Pul Eliya,* pp. 5–12, 296–306. See also Macfarlane, "History, Anthropology and the Study of Communities," 631–635; and Tim Ingold (ed.), *Key Debates in Anthropology* (London: Routledge, 1996), pp. 55–98.

4. The important variants of functionalism in British anthropology, in particular the influence of Durkheim on the form known as structural-functionalism, lie beyond the scope of this discussion. See A. R. Radcliffe-Brown, "On the Concept of Function in Social Science," in *Structure and Function in Primitive Society* (New York: Free Press, 1952), pp. 178–187.

5. Tilly, *Sociology Meets History,* pp. 101–103. A brilliant example of British functionalist ethnography is W. M. Williams, *The Sociology of an English Village: Gosforth* (London: Routledge and Kegan Paul, 1956).

6. The political aspects of symbolism and ritual are explored in Turner, *Ritual Process.* Social historians have adopted a similar approach to conflict in ritual. See Emmanuel Le Roy Ladurie, *Carnival in Romans* (New York: Braziller, 1979), pp. 93–152, 175–248; Natalie Zemon Davis,

"Charivari, Honor, and Community in Seventeenth-Century Lyon and Geneva," in John J. MacAloon (ed.), *Rite, Drama, Festival, Spectacle: Rehearsals Toward a Theory of Cultural Performance* (Philadelphia: Institute for the Study of Human Issues, 1984), pp. 42–57; and Robert Darnton, *The Great Cat Massacre and Other Episodes in French Cultural History* (New York: Basic Books, 1984), pp. 74–104.

7. Underdown, *Revel, Riot, and Rebellion,* p. 5. The parish of Wickham is described in similar terms in David Levine and Keith Wrightson, *The Making of an Industrial Society: Wickham, 1560–1765* (Oxford: Clarendon Press, 1991), p. 294.

8. David Underdown, *Fire From Heaven: Life in an English Town in the Seventeenth Century* (New Haven: Yale University Press, 1992), p. 85.

9. Macfarlane, "History, Anthropology and the Study of Communities," 636–638. The nongroup is discussed in detail in Jeremy Boissevain, "The Place of Non-Groups in the Social Sciences," *Man,* 3 (1968): 542–556.

10. The classic statement of this problem is Tawney, *Religion and the Rise of Capitalism,* pp. 188–189.

11. Underdown, *Revel, Riot, and Rebellion,* pp. 9–43; Underdown, *Fire From Heaven,* pp. 138–155; and George Orwell, *Coming Up for Air* (New York: Harcourt Brace Jovanovich, 1939).

12. Alan Macfarlane, *The Origins of English Individualism: The Family, Property and Social Transition* (Oxford: Blackwell, 1978), pp. 62–101; 130–164; Alan Macfarlane, *Marriage and Love in England: Modes of Reproduction, 1300–1840* (Oxford: Blackwell, 1986), pp. 119–147, 321–344; and Alan Macfarlane, "The Cradle of Capitalism: The Case of England," in *The Culture of Capitalism* (Oxford: Blackwell, 1987), pp. 170–190.

13. GRO: P 329 CW 2/1, p. 224.

14. The imaginary nature of communities is explored in Benedict Anderson, *Imagined Communities: Reflections on the Origin and Spread of Nationalism,* 2nd ed. (New York: Verso, 1991), pp. 5–7.

15. This discussion is indebted to Clifford Geertz's work on Balinese villages. See Clifford Geertz, "Form and Variation in Balinese Village Structure," *American Anthropologist,* 61 (1959): 991–992; and Clifford Geertz, "Tihingan: A Balinese Village," *Bijdragon Tot De Taal-Land-En Volkenkinde Von Nederlandech-India,* 120 (1964): 1–5.

16. See Tables 1 and 2 in Appendix 1 for the total population of the parishes and for the distribution of the population.

17. John Smyth, *Men and Armour for Gloucestershire in 1608* (Gloucester: Alan Sutton, 1980).

18. A. C. Percival (ed.), "A Survey of the Diocese of Gloucester," in *An Eccle-*

siastical Miscellany, Publications of the Records Section of the Bristol and Gloucestershire Archaeological Society (Gloucester: Bristol and Gloucestershire Archaeological Society, 1976), 11: 76–79.

19. E. A. Wrigley and R. S. Schofield, *The Population History of England, 1541–1871: A Reconstruction* (Cambridge: Cambridge University Press, 1981), pp. 565, 569; Anne Whiteman (ed.), *The Compton Census of 1676: A Critical Edition* (Oxford: Oxford University Press, 1986), pp. xxxiii–xxxiv; Marjorie McIntosh, *A Community Transformed: The Manor and Liberty of Havering, 1500–1620* (Cambridge: Cambridge University Press, 1991), p. 38; and A. C. Percival, "Gloucestershire Village Populations," *Local Population Studies,* 8 (1972): 43.

20. GRO: GDR 211, Depositions, October 1662–November 1669: Case of Coulding v. Hatton, Dobbins, and Holland, Deposition of Richard Thorne.

21. Wrigley and Schofield, *Population History,* Table A3.1.

22. The returns for large parishes such as Tewkesbury are the most likely to be estimates. See T. H. Hollingsworth, *Historical Demography* (Ithaca: Cornell University Press, 1969), pp. 82–84. A useful discussion of the surveys is C. R. Elrington, "The Survey of Church Livings in Gloucestershire, 1650," *TBGAS,* 83 (1964): 85–98.

23. A massive literature considers the hearth tax returns and their uses. Brief introductions and references are available in Alan Macfarlane, *A Guide to English Historical Records* (Cambridge: Cambridge University Press, 1983), p. 41; and W. B. Stephens, *Sources for English Local History,* 2nd ed. (Cambridge: Cambridge University Press, 1981), pp. 60–61.

24. The return is in PRO: E 179/247/14 or photostat in GRO: D 383. The mean household size is calculated in Peter Laslett, "Size and Structure of the Household in England Over Three Centuries," *Population Studies,* 23 (1969): 210–213.

25. See Tables 1 and 2 in Appendix 1.

26. I stress the tentative nature of the figures, which are based on the weak data for 1650 and 1672 except in the cases of Walton Cardiff (1672 and 1710), Tewkesbury (1603 and 1672), and Deerhurst (1603 and 1672). The survey of 1650 did not include information for Walton Cardiff and appears unreliable for Tewkesbury and Deerhurst.

27. Wrightson, *English Society,* p. 122.

28. The figures provided by Elrington, *VCH Gloucester,* 8: 35, 120, 175, 199, 229, 237, indicate a similar broad pattern of slow population growth in the sixteenth century.

29. Wrightson and Levine, *Poverty and Piety,* pp. 45–46; McIntosh, *Commu-*

nity Transformed, pp. 9–14; Spufford, *Contrasting Communities,* pp. 10–28; and Susan Dwyer Amussen, *An Ordered Society: Gender and Class in Early Modern England* (Oxford: Blackwell, 1988), pp. 15–16.

30. Wrightson, *English Society,* pp. 44–57.

31. Laslett, "Size and Structure of the Household," 211–213. A useful introduction to the vast literature on the family in early modern England is Ralph Houlbrooke, *The English Family, 1450–1700* (London: Longman, 1984), pp. 18–38.

32. Wrightson, *English Society,* pp. 44–45. David Cressy, "Kinship and Kin Interaction in Early Modern England," *Past and Present,* 113 (1986): 38–69, provides a useful corrective to the customary emphasis on the nuclear family. A sophisticated attempt to avoid the confusion of family and household is Rosemary O'Day, *The Family and Family Relationships, 1500–1900: England, France and the United States of America* (New York: St. Martin's Press, 1994), pp. 25–28.

33. Wrightson and Levine, *Poverty and Piety,* p. 92. Wrightson and Levine depend heavily on wills in questions of kin recognition. This approach places a great deal of emphasis on evidence created by one social situation, albeit a situation of crucial significance in the life cycle. The range of kin mentioned in wills could be "narrow and shallow" without diminishing the importance of kinship ties in other contexts.

34. Rosemary O'Day has observed that ideas of patriarchy and partnership were not mutually exclusive. See O'Day, *Family and Family Relationships,* pp. 52–58.

35. GRO: W 1613/206.

36. GRO: GDR 221, Depositions: September, 1670–February, 1678: Case of Office v. Flucke.

37. GRO: W 1626/127, John Fisher, fisherman.

38. O'Day has recently used the distinction between "prescriptive" and "descriptive" families to clarify and emphasize the practical importance of kinship. See O'Day, *Family and Family Relationships,* pp. 73–80, 87–94.

39. The sociology of wills is examined in detail in Chapter 3. See Table 9 in Appendix 1 for a social profile of the references made in wills.

40. The term *cousin* was also used occasionally in reference to relations currently defined as grandchildren, such as the son of a son. Several of the categories of relatives described as cousins may be found in GRO: W 1604/109, 1605/40, 1614/201, 1662/211.

41. GRO: W 1605/45, 1651/80, 1662/239, 1671/164, 1683/130, 1687/168.

42. GRO: W 1622/33, 1679/20, 1681/21.

43. Of the testamentary references made to nonresident kin in the northern

vale from 1590 to 1690, 5 percent to 7 percent were made to grandchildren. Such relatives by marriage as mothers-in-law, fathers-in-law, sons-in-law, and daughters-in-law accounted for another 5 percent to 7 percent of the references. Sons-in-law formed the dominant subgroup in this category at 64 percent to 70 percent of the references. A second group of relatives by marriage composed of brothers-in-law and sisters-in-law accounted for an average of just over 5 percent of testamentary references. Parental kin relations such as uncles and aunts amounted to less than 1 percent of the references.

44. See Keith Wrightson, "Kinship in an English Village: Terling, 1500–1700," in Richard M. Smith (ed.), *Land, Kinship and Lifecycle* (Cambridge: Cambridge University Press, 1984), pp. 329–332; Wrightson and Levine, *Poverty and Piety,* pp. 82–91; and McIntosh, *Community Transformed,* pp. 86–87.

45. The will involved the household of Buckle himself, his sons-in-law Thomas Smith of Forthampton and William Beale of Tirley, and his nephew Walter Buckle of Uckington. Additional visits came from the household of Giles Ward, described only as the brother-in-law of Thomas Smith of Forthampton, Buckle's son-in-law. GRO: GDR 204, Depositions: January 1638–March 1640: Case of Beale v. Ward, Depositions of Thomas Smith and Walter Buckle.

46. GRO: GDR 204, Depositions: January 1638–March 1640: Case of Beale v. Ward, Depositions of Thomas Smith and Walter Buckle. Beale married a daughter of Thomas Buckle's wife Isabel by a previous marriage. The deposition of Walter Buckle suggests that Beale and his wife resided in the village of Tirley, southwest of Tewkesbury across the Severn.

47. Ibid.

48. This theme is explored on a general scale in O'Day, *Family and Family Relationships,* pp. 129–135.

49. This incident may not have been the first problem that Henry had with his mother. One witness described Christian Hatton as "without good discretion," and another observed "that old people often take occasion before it be offered to be angry." GRO: GDR 65, Depositions: February 1586–March 1592: Case of Hatton v. Hatton, Depositions of Edward Hatton and Helen Edwards als. Hatton.

50. The social significance of godparentage in parish communities is considered at length in Chapter 3.

51. Examples of the many different forms of commitment required of friends may be found in GRO: W 1594/114, 1611/156, 1615/4, 1638/151, 1645/89.

52. GRO: W 1592/151. The placing of Alice's portion in the hands of trustees outside the family was a condition imposed on Clarke's wife as executor of the will.
53. GRO: W 1593/132.
54. GRO: W 1638/151.
55. GRO: W 1681/211.
56. GRO: W 1612/53. The estate was instead administered by Francis Guy, the widow of the deceased.
57. GRO: W 1626/254.
58. In one hundred years of testamentary records, I have found only six instances of friends' refusing to perform the duties required in wills. These cases survive as GRO: W 1612/53, 1626/254, 1639/227, 1671/168, 1680/110, 1686/104, 1687/37. The will proved in 1671 does not document a refusal to serve but does include an alternative provision in case a friend refused to serve as a guardian.
59. This discussion of neighborhood has been influenced by the post-humously published investigations of Philip Abrams that are presented in Martin Bulmer, *Neighbors: The Work of Philip Abrams* (Cambridge: Cambridge University Press, 1986), pp. 3–14, 17–26, 27–43, 83–99. Abrams conceived neighborhood as a pattern of exchange formed by the interaction of personal interest, material constraint, and conventional notions of reciprocity. He was critical of earlier definitions of neighborhood based on notions of selflessness or altruism.
60. See Ronald Frankenberg, *Village on the Border: A Social Study of Religion, Politics and Football in a North Wales Community* (London: Cohen and West, 1957); H. J. Gans, *The Urban Villagers: Group and Class in the Life of Italian-Americans* (New York: Free Press, 1962, 1982); and Michael Young and Peter Willmott, *Family and Kinship in East London* (London: Routledge and Kegan Paul, 1957).
61. The villages in the neighborhood of Tewkesbury contributed £12 2s 10d in bushels of malt and wheat to help finance the festival. GRO: P 329 CW 2/1, pp. 130–131.
62. Keith Wrightson has made the most insightful recent arguments on the nature of early modern neighborhoods. But Wrightson does not consider the importance of distance between neighbors and generally interprets neighborhood as an organic form of solidarity, a social response to the "shallow" kinship system of early modern England. See Wrightson, "Kinship in an English Village," 329–332.
63. Abrams traced the modern perception of past neighborhoods as more intimate than their modern counterparts to the replacement of neighborhood reciprocity by the welfare provisions of the state. Yet the historical

existence of higher levels of mutual aid does not mean distance was any less important in the differentiation of neighbors from friends and kin. See Bulmer, *Neighbors*, pp. 91–95.

64. David Rollison uses a list of participants in a communal event as evidence to support an objective definition of neighborhood in southern Gloucestershire. Unfortunately, he does not explore the possibility of more than one such definition, and neighborhood becomes a simple form of plebeian solidarity. David Rollison, "Property, Ideology and Popular Culture in a Gloucestershire Village, 1660–1740," in Paul Slack (ed.), *Rebellion, Popular Protest and the Social Order in Early Modern England* (Cambridge: Cambridge University Press, 1984), p. 313.

65. GRO: GDR 127, Depositions: April 1616–November 1618: Case of Best v. Bennett, Deposition of Gilbert Turbervile. The emphasis is mine.

66. GRO: W 1602/60.

67. GRO: W 1590/30.

68. GRO: GDR 168, Depositions: September 1628–March 1631: Case of Fluck and Weaver v. Beale and Beale, Depositions of Henry and Alice Wells.

69. This comment is not intended to reduce the complex phenomenon of witchcraft to problems of neighborhood. An excellent recent discussion of witchcraft as an inversion of "good neighborhood" is Annabel Gregory, "Witchcraft, Politics and 'Good Neighborhood' in Early Seventeenth-Century Rye," *Past and Present*, 133 (1991): 31–35, 55–58. Gregory's argument is a sophisticated modification of the standard accounts in Thomas, *Religion and the Decline of Magic,* pp. 546–560; and Alan Macfarlane, *Witchcraft in Tudor and Stuart England: A Regional and Comparative Study* (London: Routledge and Kegan Paul, 1970), pp. 168–177.

70. GCL: Smyth of Nibley Papers, vol. 16, f. 57.

71. Ibid. The servant is not named in the record, but Anne Phillips and Isabel Sheene were apparently examined at the same time. Phillips was examined for *maleficium* against Robert Malory. Seven of the ten witnesses against her came from Tewkesbury and had also appeared against Sheene. Phillips denied any involvement in *maleficium*.

72. Eaton supported the account of *maleficium* but not the declaration against Isabel Sheene. Appendix 2 contains John Smyth's list of witnesses and recognizances against Sheene and Phillips.

73. Smyth does not record the decision of the grand jury, and the "information" may not have proceeded to indictment. The evidence in Smyth's papers is weak and suffers from the lack of a confession. GCL: Smyth of Nibley Papers, vol. 16, f. 57. On the desirability, if not necessity, of the confession in the sixteenth century, see Macfarlane, *Witchcraft*, pp. 19–20.

74. The best introductions to the prescriptive aspects of neighborhood are F. G. Bailey (ed.), *Gifts and Poison: The Politics of Reputation* (Oxford: Blackwell, 1971); and J. G. Peristiany (ed.), *Honor and Shame: The Values of Mediterranean Society* (London: Weidenfeld and Nicolson, 1966). An elegant statement of the relationship between the values of neighborhood and the philosophical and moral systems implied by the term *worldview* is Robert Redfield, *The Little Community: Viewpoints for the Study of a Human Whole* (Chicago: University of Chicago Press, 1955), pp. 81–95.

75. GRO: GDR 148, Depositions: May 1622–August 1625: Case of Cartwright v. Collett, Depositions of Jane Benson, Elizabeth Jeynes, Prudence Fluck.

76. Susan Amussen maintains that sexual behavior was more important in feminine than in masculine reputation. There is an excellent general discussion of the politics of reputation in Amussen, *Ordered Society*, pp. 98–104.

77. Several historical studies have approached defamation and slander as forms of collective moral scrutiny and social control. This approach links defamation to knowledge of sexual impropriety and, in the tradition of sociological functionalism, tends not to address the manipulative aspects of social institutions such as gossip. An example of this approach is J. A. Sharpe, *Defamation and Sexual Slander in Early Modern England: The Church Courts at York* (York: Borthwick Institute, 1980), pp. 19–20.

78. This account of the election and its aftermath is derived from GRO: GDR 168, Depositions: September 1628–March 1631: Case of Vaughan v. Canner, Depositions of John Kiffin, Margaret Lloyd, Thomas Jeynes, Thomas Rayer, Quinborough Johnsons, and Catherine Simmons.

79. The use of subsidy lists to resolve questions of status is problematic. The lists were made by local assessors and were then approved by commissioners for the county. These assessments often reflected political relations rather than status, as local assessors sought to increase or diminish the assessments of rivals, clients, and friends. The upward movement of the Vaughan family reflected in the subsidy lists nevertheless seems to have been acknowledged by Thomas Vaughan as well as his neighbors. Vaughan himself served as one of the assessors in 1626. He assessed himself the lesser rate for goods rather than lands but maintained the increase in the value of his assessment from 1624. The potential for manipulation and favoritism in the assessment of subsidies is discussed in A. Hassell Smith, *County and Court: Government and Politics in Norfolk, 1558–1603* (Oxford: Clarendon Press, 1974), p. 115.

80. GRO: TBR A 1/1, ff. 8–9, 11–12, 14, 20, 24, 31, 33.

81. Christopher Canner was Elizabeth Canner's husband. GRO: W 1649/5.

82. Vaughan also ranked fourth in the assessment of the fifteenth in 1624. His

name was recorded in a separate list, among the four most highly assessed persons in the borough. GRO: TBR A 1/1, f. 12.

83. Vaughan also loaned the corporation £200 in 1626, and Canner was among the burgesses present to secure the loan. GRO: TBR A 1/1, p. 371.

84. GRO: D 2688, Giles Geast Charity Account Book, ff. 69v, 71v.

85. This conflict may indicate a motive, in addition to deference, for the frequent selection of outsiders in borough elections. As a result of the local competition for status, burgesses may have preferred to select an outside candidate rather than risk the promotion of local families to more powerful positions.

86. A general discussion of mobility and its local impact is Wrightson, *English Society,* pp. 40–44, 130–148.

87. A discussion of stereotypic aspects of the scold is David Underdown, "The Taming of the Scold: The Enforcement of Patriarchal Authority in Early Modern England," in Anthony Fletcher and John Stevenson (eds.), *Order and Disorder in Early Modern England* (Cambridge: Cambridge University Press, 1985), pp. 119–121.

88. I do not deny the importance of gossip as a punishment for known "offenses" and thus as a form of social control. In most cases, however, historians lack the evidence needed to differentiate the manipulation of stereotypes from the use of gossip to defend the moral boundaries of a community.

89. Vaughan recruited several of his Welsh neighbors to attest the legitimacy of his birth. GRO: GDR 168, Depositions: September 1628–March 1631: Case of Vaughan v. Canner, Depositions of John Kiffin and Margaret Lloyd.

90. An attempt to discredit witnesses was common practice in seventeenth-century lawsuits. See the examples from Norfolk in Amussen, *Ordered Society,* pp. 98–104.

91. GRO: GDR B4/1/2484. These documents are incorrectly catalogued as part of an adultery case prosecuted in 1615. A comparison of the lists of interrogatories and the depositions from 1628 indicates that the documents came from the same defamation case.

92. A synthesis of recent work on lineage is provided in Felicity Heal and Clive Holmes, *The Gentry in England and Wales, 1500–1700* (Stanford: Stanford University Press, 1994), pp. 20–47.

93. Wrightson, *English Society,* pp. 36–37, 42–43, 110. See McIntosh, *Community Transformed,* pp. 53–65, for detailed evidence of service and apprenticeship in an Essex community.

94. William Harrison, *The Description of England* (New York: Dover, 1968), p. 100. The characteristics of unilineal and cognatic descent groups are

compared in Robin Fox, *Kinship and Marriage: An Anthropological Perspective* (Harmondsworth: Penguin, 1967), pp. 41–53.

95. Many examples of genealogies may be found in records of the local visitations made by heralds. The heralds were royal officers appointed to preserve the hierarchy of ranks among lineages and to prevent common abuses, such as false pedigrees. See Sir John Maclean and W. C. Heane (eds.), *The Visitation of the County of Gloucester, 1623* (London, 1885); and T. Fitz-Roy Fenwick and Walter C. Metcalfe (eds.), *The Visitation of the County of Gloucester, 1682–1683* (Exeter, 1884).

96. Harrison, *Description of England,* pp. 95–97, 100–103, 113–115.

97. The best general descriptions of the status hierarchy are Sir Thomas Smith, *De Republica Anglorum* (Cambridge: Cambridge University Press, 1982), pp. 64–77; and Harrison, *Description of England,* pp. 94–123.

98. An excellent introduction is Anthony Fletcher, "Honor, Reputation and Local Officeholding in Elizabethan and Stuart England," in Fletcher and Stevenson, *Order and Disorder,* pp. 92–94.

99. Harrison, *Description of England,* pp. 100–102, 113–114.

100. Smith, *De Republica Anglorum,* pp. 66–70. Thirsk has also commented on the predominance of parish gentry in the Vale of Tewkesbury. See Thirsk, "Projects for Gentlemen," 151.

101. James Bennett's lavish praise of the Tracys in 1830 is testimony to the longevity of the family's local status and influence. See James Bennett, *The History of Tewkesbury* (Tewkesbury, 1830), pp. 437–438; and W. R. Williams, *The Parliamentary History of the County of Gloucester* (Hereford, 1898), pp. 233–234.

102. GRO: D 760/36; Williams, *Parliamentary History of Gloucestershire,* p. 234.

103. Williams, *Parliamentary History of Gloucestershire,* pp. 233–237, 242.

104. Sir Robert Tracy played a role in the restoration of the Tewkesbury borough charter in 1698. GRO: D 2688, Giles Geast Charity Account Book, f. 146v. The Russells had little influence in the neighborhood of Tewkesbury before the Restoration. Sir Francis Russell represented Tewkesbury in parliament from 1673–1681, 1685–1687, and 1689–1690. Sir William Russell, father of Francis and commander of the royalist garrison of Worcester in the Civil War, was the first baronet. See Williams, *Parliamentary History of Gloucestershire,* p. 243.

105. Harrison, *Description of England,* pp. 101–102.

106. GRO: D 760/36.

107. GRO: D 760/36. Tracy's reference to Mr. Baptist Hickes may have been a calculated insult. Hickes was knighted in 1603 and should have been

styled *Sir* Baptist Hickes. Williams, *Parliamentary History of Gloucestershire*, p. 234.

108. Smith, *De Republica Anglorum*, p. 67.
109. GRO: W 1641/10.
110. Harrison, *Description of England*, pp. 96–97.
111. Elrington, *VCH Gloucester,* 8: 36–41, 202, 230–231.
112. Smith, *De Republica Anglorum*, pp. 66, 70–71.
113. Harrison, *Description of England*, p. 113.
114. The relationship of honor, the status of arms, and political violence is explored in Mervyn James, "English Politics and the Concept of Honor" (1978), reprinted in Mervyn James, *Society, Politics and Culture: Studies in Early Modern England* (Cambridge: Cambridge University Press, 1986), pp. 308–314, 333–335.
115. Smith, *De Republica Anglorum*, p. 77.
116. Smith, *De Republica Anglorum*, p. 72; and Harrison, *Description of England*, p. 114.
117. Smith, *De Republica Anglorum*, p. 72; and Harrison, *Description of England*, p. 114.
118. Smith, *De Republica Anglorum*, p. 70.
119. See GRO: TBR A 1/1, pp. 223–292 (freemen), 299–318 (apprentices), 366, 370, 372; TBR A 1/2, p. 14; Bennett, *History of Tewkesbury*, pp. 199–200; and Christopher Elrington, "Records of the Cordwainers' Society of Tewkesbury, 1562–1941," *TBGAS*, 83 (1966): 164–174.
120. Elrington, "Records of the Cordwainers' Society," 166, 169. The role of companies in civic ceremonies and politics has been discussed in its late medieval context by Charles Phythian-Adams, "Ceremony and the Citizen: The Communal Year at Coventry, 1450–1550," in Peter Clark and Paul Slack (eds.), *Crisis and Order in English Towns, 1500–1700: Essays in Urban History* (Toronto: University of Toronto Press, 1972), pp. 57–85.
121. See Table 3 in Appendix 1 for the occupational structure of the vale in 1608. The description of social structure in this section relies heavily on Smyth's militia survey of 1608, testamentary records, and the 1672 hearth tax return.
122. GRO: W 1601/12 and 1609/185.
123. HMC, *13th Report, Appendix 2*, p. 300.
124. Bennett, *History of Tewkesbury*, p. 380.
125. Harrison, *Description of England*, pp. 393, 395.
126. Smyth, *Men and Armour,* pp. 118–119; and Elrington, *VCH Gloucester,* 8: 173.
127. Elrington, *VCH Gloucester,* 8: 34–35.

128. The numbers and activities of the Gloucestershire badgers are described in David Rollison, *The Local Origins of Modern Society: Gloucestershire, 1500–1800* (London: Routledge, 1992), pp. 52–55.

129. GRO: I 1646/33 and 1677/82.

130. See Table 4 in Appendix 1 for the occupations of testators. Of 732 wills made in the parishes of the northern vale from 1590 to 1690, 395 (54 percent) contain information about occupations.

131. See the depositions in PRO: SP 19/116, ff. 237v, 246r-v, 255r-v, 256r, 263r.

132. See PRO: E 112/407/341 for some of the characteristics and problems of the Welsh trade.

133. Probate inventories from Gloucestershire survive in smaller numbers than wills, and the vale has been enlarged to create a collection of inventories for analysis. The inventories from the nearby parishes of Alderton, Ashleworth, Bishop's Cleeve, Boddington, Charlton Kings, Clifford Chambers, Corse, Elmstone Hardwicke, Hasfield, Kemerton, Leigh, Oxenton, Stoke Orchard, Tirley, Uckington, and Woolstone have been added to inventories from the seven parishes of the northern vale. Charlton Kings, which was a large agricultural parish southwest of Cheltenham, is included because of its similarity in social structure and proximity to a market town.

134. This is not to deny the pressure on small farmers in the sixteenth and seventeenth centuries, but probate records are not sufficient evidence of changes in the distribution of land. See Spufford, *Contrasting Communities,* pp. 46–57.

135. GRO: TBR A 1/1, f. 28.

136. This relationship is explored in John Walter and Keith Wrightson, "Dearth and the Social Order in Early Modern England," in Slack, *Rebellion, Popular Protest and the Social Order,* pp. 108–128.

137. GRO: TBR A 1/1, p. 17. Alye's legacy of £7 12s to the poor of Tewkesbury was distributed in doles of two pence. At twelve pence per shilling and twenty shillings per pound, this yields 912 recipients of charity.

138. *CSPD, Charles I* (London, 1860), v. 4 (1629–1631): 445.

139. See Table 5 in Appendix 1 for the distribution of wealth based on the number of hearths.

140. GRO: I 1678/86. Prichett's total estate was valued at £33.

141. GRO: I 1691/198.

142. GRO: I 1715/190. Etheridge's total estate was valued at £20.

143. GRO: I 1707/3. Wintell's total estate was valued at £11.

144. GRO: I 1684/227.

145. GRO: I 1688/158.

146. GRO: I 1689/114. Deagle's total estate was valued at £143.

147. PRO: PROB 4/2441. Cooke's total estate was valued at £456.

148. GRO: I 1702/187.

149. GRO: I 1711/173.

150. Smyth, *Men and Armour,* pp. 86–87.

151. GRO: W 1631/191 and 1642/25. See the will of Gilbert Turberville, yeoman, in GRO: W 1627/56, for the acquisition of leasehold property.

152. This land was owned by William, Lord Craven, an absentee royalist landlord in the 1650s, but "residing beyond sea, in the Netherlands or Holland," in the 1630s when Turberville leased the land. See GCL: Smyth of Nibley Papers, vol. 12, f. 20. Lord Craven's career is described in Lawrence Stone, *The Crisis of the Aristocracy, 1558–1641* (Oxford: Clarendon Press, 1965, 1979), pp. 120, 266.

153. GCL: Smyth of Nibley Papers, vol. 12, f. 20.

154. See Geertz, "Religion as a Cultural System," 12–24, for a general discussion of religious symbols and for the power to produce general models of existence as a definitive characteristic of religious symbolism.

155. See the discussion of feuds and litigation in Anthony Fletcher, *A County Community in Peace and War: Sussex, 1600–1660* (London: Longman, 1975), pp. 54–57; and Heal and Holmes, *Gentry,* pp. 175–177.

156. My account of the Vicaries murder is based on PRO: STAC 8/18/17. This set of documents is used to good effect in William Bradford Willcox, *Gloucestershire: A Study in Local Government, 1590–1640* (New Haven: Yale University Press, 1940), pp. 221–222.

157. In 1608 this principle was confirmed in an election dispute, and the charter of 1698 included a formal description of the practice. See GRO: TBR A 1/2, p. 5; D 2688, Giles Geast Charity Book, f. 53v; and charter of 1698 printed in Bennett, *History of Tewkesbury,* pp. 392–393.

158. GRO: TBR A1/2, Borough Ordinances, 1639, nos. 2, 15.

159. GRO: TBR A1/2, Borough Ordinances, 1639, no. 10.

160. GRO: TBR A1/2, Borough Ordinances, 1639, no. 11.

161. GRO: TBR A1/2, Borough Ordinances, 1639, no. 6.

162. GRO: TBR A1/2, Borough Ordinances, 1639, no. 16.

163. GRO: TBR A1/2, Borough Ordinances, 1639, nos. 23, 25.

164. The arrangement of seats is reconstructed from pew rentals in the churchwardens' accounts for the years 1590 to 1640. GRO: P 329 CW 2/1, pp. 107, 110, 240–242, 557.

165. GRO: TBR A 1/2, Borough Ordinances, 1608, no. 1.

166. GRO: TBR A 1/2, Borough Ordinances, 1639, no. 3.

167. A borough ordinance required churchwardens to present accounts in the

council chamber before "the yielding up of their account and choosing of new churchwardens in the parish church openly after Easter." GRO: TBR A 1/2, Borough Ordinances, 1608, no. 10.

168. See the descriptions of the parish in S. L. Ware, *The Elizabethan Parish in Its Ecclesiastical and Financial Aspects* (Baltimore: Johns Hopkins University Press, 1908); Tawney, *Religion and the Rise of Capitalism*, pp. 158–159; and Troeltsch, *Social Teaching of the Christian Churches*, 1: 221.

169. GRO: P 329 IN 1/3, f. 23.

170. GRO: P 329 CW 2/1, pp. 107, 209. The sexton was paid £1 6s 8d for this duty.

171. GRO: P 329 CW 2/1, p. 254. The Tewkesbury churchwardens' accounts cover the years 1563 to 1700 in an unbroken sequence and provide a unique source for the history of Gloucestershire. The other parishes in the vale do not offer accounts of equal detail for the years before 1660; therefore, this discussion of the parish relies heavily on the evidence for the town.

172. A record of this transaction is preserved in GRO: TBR A 1/1, pp. 127–129.

173. An inventory of the church goods drawn up in 1585 included "players' apparel" frequently loaned to nearby villages for festivals. GRO: P 329 CW 2/1, pp. 87, 55–88.

174. The churchwardens were £21 short of the sum required and had to levy a parish rate to make up the difference. GRO: P 329 CW 2/1, pp. 130–131.

175. GRO: P 329 CW 2/1, p. 200.

176. GRO: P 329 CW 2/1, p. 249.

177. GRO: P 329 CW 2/1, pp. 202, 221, 253.

178. GRO: P 329 CW 2/1, pp. 201, 205, 221, 227, 232, 238, 242, 253. The accounts for 1609–1610 provide a monthly breakdown of expenses.

179. GRO: P 329 CW 2/1, pp. 177, 252.

180. GRO: P 329 CW 2/1, p. 224.

181. GRO: P 329 CW 2/1, p. 251 *et passim*. The churchwardens' accounts may be opened at any point for evidence of this mobility in the abbey.

182. GRO: P 329 CW 2/1, p. 107.

183. GRO: P 329 CW 2/1, p. 199.

184. GRO: P 329 CW 2/1, pp. 359, 411. The brief for Falkenham raised only £1 4s but may have been affected by a levy of £112 for church repairs at the time of the collection. The brief for Knaresborough returned a meager 7s 9d. Underdown describes a pattern of substantial response to such requests in the wealthier community of Dorchester in *Fire From Heaven*, pp. 125–128.

185. GRO: P 329 CW 2/1, p. 255. William Hill, the town clerk of Tewkesbury, attempted to follow the events in Germany in the 1620s. In 1620, Hill

recorded the coronation of Frederick of the Palatinate and Elizabeth "our king's daughter and his wife" as rulers in Bohemia "by which means there are great wars in Germany, the success whereof rests on God's providence." In 1622, 69 contributors from Tewkesbury raised £15 10s for a royal collection "toward the regaining the Palatinate." GRO: D 2688, f. 65v; TBR A 1/1, p. 10.

186. UCL: RFTV, vol. 9: Sermons on Public Events and Occasions, 1691–1708.

187. Ibid.

188. Ibid.

189. The procedure and personnel of the consistory court is described in detail in F. S. Hockaday, "The Consistory Court of the Diocese of Gloucester," *TBGAS*, 46 (1924): 195–287; and Ralph Houlbrooke, *Church Courts and the People During the English Reformation, 1520–1570* (Oxford: Oxford University Press, 1979), pp. 21–54.

190. Isabel M. Kirby, *Diocese of Gloucester,* 2 vols. (Gloucester: Gloucester City Corporation, 1967–1968), 1: xvi–xix, 1–18, describes the boundaries and visitation records of the diocese.

191. The issues of power and the political uses of the church courts in the vale are discussed in Beaver, "Conscience and Context," 293.

192. GRO: GDR 100, Depositions, March 1606–March 1609: Case of Dorothy Little v. Thomas Moore, Depositions of John Little, Peter Parsons, and Ralph Nutting. A problem in the use of this evidence is the performative aspect of the deposition itself. A witness might have an interest in the misrepresentation of another's words, but a performance conforms to rules and conventions even in the extreme case of a lie. As my concern is the nature of performance, not the truth or falsehood of any particular statement, the depositions become more reliable evidence.

193. This account of Moore's words and motives is drawn from the testimony of Peter Parsons, a friend and supporter of the Littles. GRO: GDR 100, Depositions, March 1606–March 1609: Deposition of Peter Parsons.

194. Moore's allegations were made in a complex social situation. There was a high risk of miscommunication and a failed performance. Little's journeyman was distracted by work and misunderstood the direction of the assault. He believed that Moore had reserved the "cow's grass in heaven" for Little's former journeyman, a man named Jacksons, and thus missed the point of the entire episode. GRO: GDR 100, Depositions, March 1606—March 1609: Deposition of Ralph Nutting.

195. Apparitors were officers of the court who carried citations to parish churches and made sure the orders of the court were implemented. They were empowered to investigate cases in their deaneries and often received reports of misdeeds from the neighbors. See F. D. Price, "Elizabethan Ap-

paritors in the Diocese of Gloucester," *Church Quarterly Review,* 134 (1942): 37–55.

196. GRO: GDR 79, Depositions: April 1592–November 1597: Case of William Downbell v. Barbara Downbell, Deposition of Thomas Richards.

197. For local influence in the Elizabethan consistory court, see F. D. Price, "An Elizabethan Church Official: Thomas Powell, Chancellor of Gloucester Diocese," *Church Quarterly Review,* 128 (1939): 100, 108; and Price, "Elizabethan Apparitors," 47–51.

3. Under the Hand of God

1. Some of the important classes of documents produced by parish rituals and politics are discussed in W. E. Tate, *The Parish Chest: A Study of the Records of Parochial Administration in England,* 3rd ed. (Chichester: Phillimore, 1983 [1969]), pp. 43–125; and Macfarlane, *Guide to English Historical Records,* pp. 114–121.

2. This approach to ritual is best described as the "thick description" advocated in Clifford Geertz, "Thick Description: Toward an Interpretive Theory of Culture," and "Deep Play: Notes on the Balinese Cockfight," in Clifford Geertz, *The Interpretation of Cultures* (New York: Basic Books, 1973), pp. 3–30, 412–453. See also Turner, *Ritual Process,* pp. 1–43, 94–130.

3. This discussion is based on an analysis of 732 wills proved in the consistory court of Gloucester diocese between 1590 and 1690. The funeral sermons were written in the late seventeenth century and form part of the manuscript collection of the sermons and diaries of John Matthews, the vicar of Tewkesbury from 1689 until his resignation in 1728, in the library of University College, London. The epitaphs were collected on the ground and culled from Bennett, *Tewkesbury Yearly Register,* and Thomas Dingley, *History From Marble,* 2 vols. (London: Camden Society, 1867, 1868).

4. The European context of the English movement for a scriptural Christianity is discussed in Dickens, *English Reformation,* pp. 13–24.

5. Spencer identified the social response to death as one of the "rudimentary forms" of "the religious idea and religious sentiment" underlying the practice of ancestor worship. See Herbert Spencer, *The Principles of Sociology,* 3 vols. (London: Williams and Norgate, 1897), 3: 95–97.

6. Van Gennep, *Rites of Passage,* pp. 146–165.

7. A national overview of the issues of ritual discussed in this chapter has been provided in David Cressy, *Birth, Marriage and Death: Ritual, Religion, and the Life-Cycle in Tudor and Stuart England* (Oxford: Oxford University

Press, 1997). Yet the best local histories often make virtually no reference to burial practices or preparation for death. See Spufford, *Contrasting Communities;* and Wrightson and Levine, *Poverty and Piety.* The interests of the Cambridge Group for the History of Population and Social Structure have influenced the demographic bias in historical studies of death. See John Walter and Roger Schofield (eds.), *Famine, Disease, and the Social Order in Early Modern Society* (Cambridge: Cambridge University Press, 1989).

8. Keith Wrightson and David Levine, "Death in Whickham," in Walter and Schofield, *Famine, Disease, and the Social Order,* pp. 129–165. The discussion is part of the richly detailed study of Wickham in Levine and Wrightson, *Making of an Industrial Society,* pp. 281–294. See also McIntosh, *Community Transformed,* pp. 83–85.

9. See GRO: W 1619/129, 1621/146, 1641/65, 1673/174, for allusions to death as the final stage of the Christian pilgrimage.

10. Of 732 wills from the vale, 179 (24 percent) were prepared for women. An obvious bias is the absence of married women excluded by their husbands' legal ownership of the family property. See GRO: W 1676/92 for a rare example of a married woman's will.

11. By the 1670s and 1680s, the letters of administration and the accounts demanded in the probate court cost around £2. As the estate of a poor householder ranged between £5 and £10, the incentive to evade the court is obvious. See GRO: W 1684/274, 1685/334, 1685/480. An example of a will brought into the court only after an intrafamilial dispute over its legitimacy is in GRO: GDR 168, Depositions: September 1628—March 1631: Case of Elizabeth Waters, Deposition of Henry Wells.

12. See, for instance, the three cases for Tewkesbury in GRO: GDR 75: Court Book, 1594–1596.

13. See GRO: W 1639/252 for one of many examples of a will made by a sick person lying in bed.

14. GRO: GDR 79, Depositions: April 1592–November 1597.

15. See GRO: W 1593/109, 1604/85, and 1622/71 for references to "dangerous days" as a reason to make a will.

16. GRO: W 1664/136

17. GRO: W 1664/66.

18. Goodman survived this premonition of his death by three years. GRO: W 1637/132.

19. GRO: W 1594/73.

20. GRO: W 1663/228. Weber interpreted this notion of stewardship as a subordination to possessions rather than to divine will. See Weber, *Protestant Ethic,* pp. 162, 170.

21. GRO: W 1612/44.
22. GRO: W 1606/32.
23. GRO: W 1644/96.
24. GRO: W 1629/110.
25. GRO: W 1660 and 1661/156.
26. GRO: GDR 89, Depositions: June 1601–March 1604: Case of Smith v. Braine, Deposition of Giles Flucke.
27. GRO: W 1616/234, 1621/6, 1621/146, 1625/5, 1625/36, 1628/179, 1641/65, 1664/136.
28. This aspect of wills became the focus of intense debate in the 1970s, as historians began to use wills as sources for the study of popular religious beliefs. See Margaret Spufford, "The Scribes of Villagers' Wills in the Sixteenth and Seventeenth Centuries and Their Influence," *Local Population Studies,* 7 (1971): 28–43; Matlock Population Studies Group, "Wills and Their Scribes," *Local Population Studies,* 8 (1972): 55–57; R. C. Richardson, "Wills and Will-Makers in the Sixteenth and Seventeenth Centuries: Some Lancashire Evidence," *Local Population Studies,* 9 (1972): 33–42; Bernard Capp, "Will Formularies," *Local Population Studies,* 14 (1975): 49–50; Eric Poole, "Will Formularies," *Local Population Studies,* 17 (1976): 42–43; Margaret Spufford, "Will Formularies," *Local Population Studies,* 19 (1977): 35–36; M. L. Zell, "The Use of Religious Preambles as a Measure of Religious Belief in the Sixteenth Century," *Bulletin of the Institute of Historical Research,* 50 (1977): 246–249; J. D. Alsop, "Religious Preambles in Early Modern English Wills as Formulae," *Journal of Ecclesiastical History,* 40 (1989): 19–27; and McIntosh, *Community Transformed,* pp. 188–193. This debate has not diminished the importance of preambles as evidence of the *general beliefs* of testators, in particular the important belief in the appropriateness of the preamble itself, although the work of Capp and Alsop on the printed formulae in circulation from the middle of the sixteenth century should make historians wary of assuming that the *words* in a preamble were the exact words of testators.
29. These wills were admitted in the consistory court and passed probate without comment. See GRO: W 1621/77.
30. GRO: W 1593/109, 1603/20, 1605/157, 1618/45, 1627/182, 1629/151, 1631/43, 1649/31, 1686/372.
31. It therefore seems to me difficult to argue that the preambles referring to salvation by election do not reflect some form of belief in predestination.
32. GRO: W 1598/2, 1616/220, 1634/139, 1638/184, 1662/239.
33. This bequest was made in a wide variety of forms. See GRO: W 1594/114,

1599/11, 1602/35, 1616/234, 1624/102, and 1631/47 for just a few examples.

34. The vast majority of scribes in the vale were laymen. Of twenty scribes identified for wills made between 1590 and 1665, only seven were of clerical status. A further group of twenty laymen have been only uncertainly identified as scribes by the comparison of their signatures to the body of the will.

35. GRO: W 1599/11, 1604/59.

36. The last will bearing Edwards' distinctive formula is GRO: W 1613/136.

37. See GRO: W 1608/114 for an example of this formula.

38. GRO: W 1662/19.

39. GRO: W 1612/44.

40. John Turberville, a clerical witness to Hampshire's will, may have recommended this form. GRO: W 1612/134.

41. GRO: Dispersed Wills I: 1687/353.

42. GRO: W 1660 and 1661/156

43. GRO: W 1625/25. The notion of stewardship is expressed in countless wills. See GRO: W 1619/129, 1621/146, 1625/136, 1634/33, 1638/133, 1639/52, 1641/65, and 1669/192 for a few of the many examples.

44. GRO: W 1625/136.

45. GRO: W 1643/40.

46. GRO: W 1617/119.

47. GRO: W 1683/130.

48. The opposite was also true. An estate troubled by intrafamilial disputes did not bode well for the fate of the soul in the afterlife.

49. The payment of debts commonly preceded the entrance of relatives into full enjoyment of the property. Friends could be empowered as overseers to seize the property if debts went too long unpaid. GRO: W 1639/227, 1648/33.

50. See GRO: W 1632/24 for a reference to the enumeration of debts as a confession. Several wills describe the publication of debts as a primary motive in the making of a will. See GRO: W 1593/111, 1600/112, 1602/118.

51. GRO: W 1594/25.

52. The debt was the significant sum of £5. GRO: W 1612/155, 1636/146.

53. GRO: W 1640/62.

54. GRO: W 1637/15. Alice was particularly close to her brother's family. Before her death, Richard Pitt had given his sister a lease of a room or set of rooms in his house in Tewkesbury. This was probably a provision for her old age. Alice lived in her own house at the time of her death.

55. Ibid. Alice also made a less magnificent but substantial bequest to the family of a more distant kinsman.

56. GRO: W 1668/143.

57. The same creative power is evident in the wills of elderly parents, which could use bequests to grandchildren to cultivate relations between the households of married daughters and sons. See GRO: W 1675/185, 1689/15.

58. The calculations of the Cambridge Group have produced a rough expectation of life at birth in the seventeenth century of 38 years for the period between 1566 and 1621 and 32 years for the quarter century centered on 1675. As the mean age of first marriage was roughly 23.5 for women and 26.5 for men, many parents probably died before their children were placed as servants or apprentices. These children were recognized as dependents, who were in need of a substantial commitment in care and resources, and were therefore considered before other relations in the will. This circumstance does not mean that other relations were perceived as insignificant or that the English kinship system was shallow. The kin group excluded from the will was not defined as dependent. See Wrigley and Schofield, *Population History,* pp. 234–236; and Peter Laslett, *The World We Have Lost: Further Explored* (London: Methuen, 1983), p. 83.

59. GRO: W 1647/71.

60. GRO: W 1645/34.

61. GRO: W 1663/228.

62. GRO: W 1601/32. Ricketts also provided marriage portions for several of his daughters by his first marriage, apparently unmarried and in their minorities at the time of his death.

63. These witnesses were exclusively women and not invariably relatives of the deceased. See the certificates of burial in woolen from the 1680s and 1690s recorded in GRO: P 329 IN 1/6, Baptisms, Marriages, and Burials, 1683–1778.

64. GRO: W 1627/70. Crowds of over one hundred persons were not uncommon at funerals in the seventeenth century, and many of these attendants were almost certainly poor neighbors drawn by the customary distribution of alms. See Clare Gittings, *Death, Burial, and the Individual in Early Modern England* (London: Croom Helm, 1984), pp. 151–152.

65. GRO: W 1634/117.

66. GRO: W 1644/26. This bequest may have been a return for efforts expended in the performance of George's will and may thus have been separate from the funeral party.

67. GRO: W 1629/151.

68. GRO: W 1605/157.

69. GRO: W 1673/104. It is impossible to determine the percentage of this bequest spent on the funeral party, but other arrangements made for the burial indicate it was a more lavish affair than the burial of the husbandman to which it has been contrasted.

70. This duality expressed many of the characteristics of liminality explored in Victor Turner, *The Forest of Symbols* (Ithaca: Cornell University Press, 1967), pp. 93–111. See also Turner, *Ritual Process*, pp. 94–165. The evidence of social structure in this liminal moment complicates Turner's idea of the liminal space as a source of power, described as *communitas*, beyond the conventional structures of society.

71. The distribution of charity might occur at a number of different points in the mortuary process. If the sum allocated was large, poor householders assembled in the church after the burial to receive alms. See GRO: TBR A 1/1, p. 17. Otherwise the distribution was probably made from house to house in the manner of other local charities. See GRO: D 2688, Giles Geast Charity Account Book, f. 83v. The distribution of alms did not always occur on the day of burial. Some wills postponed the event as much as a year after death. Because the distribution of charity was generally overseen by the deceased's friends, however, the death commemorated was doubtless made apparent to the recipients of alms on the day of the disbursement. See GRO: W 1614/114, 1619/54, 1624/109; and TBR A 1/1, p. 17.

72. GRO: W 1681/80.

73. GRO: W 1635/16.

74. GRO: W 1663/147.

75. GRO: W 1631/47.

76. GRO: W 1648/53.

77. The wills from the vale make only one reference to mourning clothes. John Roberts of Fiddington, a gentleman, left £20 to his son for mourning clothes and similar sums to other relatives. See GRO: W 1632/46. Because the gentry families of the northern vale were a "parish gentry," and relatively poor by the standards of aristocratic families such as the Berkeleys to the south, elaborate processions in full mourning may have been rare.

78. GRO: W 1641/1.

79. GRO: W 1614/114.

80. GRO: W 1673/104. Because she was unmarried and her brother lived in London, neighborliness may have been particularly important to Mary Roach.

81. GRO: W 1687/353.

82. GRO: W 1613/108.

83. See GRO: W 1640/27, 1645/55, 1673/105, and 1687/353 for the ministers

named to preach funeral sermons. The earliest reference to a funeral sermon in a local will occurred in 1598. GRO: W 1598/3.

84. UCL: RFTV, vol. 13, Sermons for Funerals of Named Persons, 1691–1712: Sermon for Joseph Laight. Matthews based his sermon on 1 Corinthians 15: 43 and the Anglican office of burial.

85. Matthews took his metaphors from 1 Corinthians, St. John, and Acts.

86. Brand, *Popular Antiquities,* 2: 203.

87. Brand, *Popular Antiquities,* 2: 204, 208–209.

88. The largest bell in Tewkesbury Abbey was named "the messenger of death" in a special inscription. See Dingley, *History From Marble,* 2: 349.

89. See GRO: W 1590/9, 1605/157, 1608/114, 1612/44, 1612/107, 1618/87, 1629/151, 1668/98 for references to ringers and bell-ringing in the arrangement of funerals.

90. GRO: W 1629/151.

91. The hierarchy of bells is evident in Dingley, *History From Marble,* 2: 349.

92. See Table 6 in Appendix 1 for a classification based on wills that mention both occupation and place of burial.

93. GRO: W 1666/139.

94. GRO: W 1641/10.

95. GRO: W 1599/62, 1660 and 1661/26. Of the Bingleys honored in the church, one was a husbandman and the other a tailor. The family may have held property that carried a customary right to burial in the church.

96. GRO: W 1681/91.

97. GRO: W 1644/122.

98. GRO: W 1611/23, 1617/118. The Izode family was represented in Smyth, *Men and Armour,* p. 87.

99. This evidence from the northern vale provides a contrast to the record of burials in Whickham. The requests for specific burial sites declined in Whickham after the first decade of the seventeenth century, but the six requests for emotionally significant burial sites in the vale parishes occurred after 1640. I am skeptical of generalization from wills on this point, because failure to specify their burial arrangements in wills does not necessarily mean people no longer cared where they were buried. See Wrightson and Levine, "Death in Whickham," 164.

100. GRO: W 1678/65.

101. GRO: W 1687/353.

102. GRO: W 1671/130.

103. The recipient of an epitaph or a monument sometimes oversaw the project before death. See Beaver H. Blacker (ed.), *Gloucestershire Notes and Queries* (London, 1881), 1: 356, 462.

104. The description of grave markers as "speaking stones" is taken from an epitaph of the 1620s published in Blacker, *Gloucestershire Notes and Queries*, 1: 161.

105. Boylston's husband probably prepared this epitaph, but the marker's description of her status mentions her father as well. See Bennett, *Tewkesbury Yearly Register*, 2: 350.

106. Bennett, *Tewkesbury Yearly Register*, 2: 367–368.

107. Bennett, *Tewkesbury Yearly Register*, 2: 352.

108. Dingley, *History From Marble*, 2: 339.

109. Dingley, *History From Marble*, 2: 338.

110. Blacker, *Gloucestershire Notes and Queries*, 1: 84. This image of the earth as mother may express a notion of the person as composed of flesh, defined as a feminine element, and spirit, defined as a masculine element. This distinction would be hard to prove but might provide insight into commonplace images of death as a return to original parents, God and earth, and help to clarify notions of passage to the grave as a passage home.

111. Blacker, *Gloucestershire Notes and Queries*, 1: 162.

112. Blacker, *Gloucestershire Notes and Queries*, 1: 53.

113. Van Gennep, *Rites of Passage*, p. 11.

114. See Table 7 in Appendix 1 for the number and proportion of wills that contained bequests to the parish.

115. See Table 8 in Appendix 1 for the number and proportion of wills that made charitable donations to the poor.

116. GRO: W 1598/62, 1601/89.

117. GRO: W 1594/181, 1598/151.

118. GRO: W 1614/114.

119. GRO: W 1601/170.

120. In the case of border settlements, however, bequests might include the poor families of nearby hamlets beyond the boundaries of the parish. See GRO: W 1593/109.

121. GRO: W 1602/98. I understand this slightly ambiguous phrase to mean households accepted by the parish officers for poor relief.

122. Anne Ferrers of Ashchurch made a special bequest "to each of my godchildren whom I have christened." See GRO: W 1590/39, 1602/93, 1605/118, 1612/85 and 114, 1612/205, 1613/136, 1614/176, 1619/136, 1632/18, 1634/33, 1635/125, 1636/97, 1644/26, 1681/91, 1685/235 for instances of godchildren receiving the same Christian name as their godparents. Anne Ferrers' bequest is in GRO: W 1605/1.

123. Brothers and sisters frequently stood as godparents to the children of

siblings. See GRO: W 1590/39, 1611/153, 1613/136, 1620/39, 1621/48, 1622/70, 1632/18, 1636/97, 1641/1, 1641/137 for the variety of relations subsumed in godparentage.

124. GRO: W 1627/70, 1636/97.
125. Of 413 wills proved between 1590 and 1640, 65 referred to godchildren.
126. GRO: TBR A 1/2, pp. 13, 38.
127. This information is from the accounts kept between 1649 and 1666, but the cost of a grave remained stable in the seventeenth century. See GRO: P 329 CW 2/1, pp. 329–388; and W 1671/164 for Thomas Tusten's bequest of £5 to construct a monument in the church.
128. GRO: W 1614/228. This is the only reference to funeral expenses before 1641.
129. GRO: W 1641/49.
130. GRO: W 1648/9. Funerals may have become more expensive after the Restoration. The base cost in the higher ranks of the status hierarchy was probably £5. In 1664, Mary Roach of Walton Cardiff insisted that "at least" £5 be spared from her estate for her funeral. In 1668 John Hancock, a yeoman of Twyning, left £5 5s for his funeral, and Thomas Tusten of Tewkesbury reserved £5 for his funeral in 1671. See GRO: W 1668/98, 1671/164, 1673/104.
131. See Tables 7 and 8 in Appendix 1 for bequests to the parish and to the poor before 1640. These figures are difficult to interpret, in part because of the scale of the local crisis in the 1590s. The substantial involvement of small farmers or husbandmen in the work of poor relief testifies to the scale of the calamity, in the course of which more than 560 people died in Tewkesbury in the years 1592 and 1593 alone. I believe the reduction in bequests before 1640 reflects the return of the demographic and economic regime to the familiar cyclical patterns of the vale after the great seizure of the 1590s. There is also a strong likelihood that the combination of plague and poor harvests reduced the number of small farmers in the early 1600s.
132. Permanent charities that made annual disbursements to poor householders were endowed in 1601, 1614, 1617, 1625, 1629, 1631, 1632, and 1636. See GRO: W 1601/170, 1614/114, 1632/46, 1636/146; TBR A 1/1, pp. 44–51, 175; TBR A 1/2, p. 3; and Bennett, *History of Tewkesbury,* pp. 228–237.
133. GRO: W 1598/3. See GRO: W 1592/123, 1593/44, 1601/89, 1612/197, 1623/12 for further gifts of grain and bread.
134. GRO: W 1612/197.
135. GRO: D 2688, Giles Geast Charity Account Book, f. 83v.
136. GRO: D 2688, Giles Geast Charity Account Book, f. 94v.

137. See Dickens, *English Reformation,* pp. 339–361; and Patrick Collinson, "A Comment Concerning the Name of Puritan," *Journal of Ecclesiastical History,* 31 (1980): 483–488. The general characteristics of the Elizabethan Settlement are discussed in G. R. Elton, *The Tudor Constitution: Documents and Commentary* (Cambridge: Cambridge University Press, 1960, 1982), pp. 395–399.

138. On the traces of this attitude in the reform campaign of the sixteenth century, see Knappen, *Tudor Puritanism,* p. 15; and Collinson, *Elizabethan Puritan Movement,* pp. 370–371.

139. UCL: RFTV, vol. 13, Sermons for Funerals of Named Persons, 1691–1712: Sermon for Joseph Laight. This sermon is used a second time to illustrate how funeral sermons can be viewed as formal elements of the ritual process and as political statements, employing the conventional images of death for particular purposes. The local context of the sermon helps to clarify its political aspects.

140. An early rejection of corporeal resurrection is described in Felicity Heal, "The Family of Love and the Diocese of Ely," in Derek Baker (ed.), *Schism, Heresy, and Protest* (Cambridge: Cambridge University Press, 1972), p. 218. Anglicans and Dissenters supported their views from 1 Corinthians, 15: 35–54.

141. Stannard, *Puritan Way of Death,* p. 101; Weber, *Protestant Ethic,* p. 105; Collinson, *Elizabethan Puritan Movement,* p. 370.

142. See the similar statements of Puritan clerics in the diocese of Chester, related in R. C. Richardson, *Puritanism in Northwest England: A Regional Study of the Diocese of Chester* (Manchester: Manchester University Press, 1972), p. 30.

143. GRO: W 1639/227.

144. GRO: W 1641/137.

145. GRO: W 1643/40.

146. GRO: W 1666/139.

147. GRO: W 1664/69.

148. See Tables 7, 8, and 9 in Appendix 1 for bequests to the parish, bequests to the poor, and references to family, friends, and neighbors in preparation for death, 1590–1690.

149. GRO: W 1635/23. Geary was suspended from his ministry in 1634 for nonconformity. GRO: GDR 186, Detection Causes: March–November 1634.

150. GRO: W 1645/55.

151. Of 316 wills proved from 1641 to 1690, only 13 made provision for godchildren. The institution of godparentage obviously did not cease to exist, but the relations of godparents and godchildren, an important ex-

pression of parish community, were not invoked in the process of preparation for death.

152. Baptists in Tewkesbury probably had a separate place of burial as early as the 1650s. The Quakers used a local barn for burials in 1670. See Elrington, *VCH Gloucester,* 8: 163.

153. A similar analysis of death as a moment of articulation between the family and external groups is Daryll Forde, "Death and Succession: An Analysis of Yako Mortuary Ritual," in Max Gluckman (ed.), *Essays on the Ritual of Social Relations* (Manchester: Manchester University Press, 1962), pp. 89–123.

4. Circumcisions of the Heart

1. The importance of Pauline Christianity in sixteenth-century religious conflict is discussed in Troeltsch, *Social Teaching of the Christian Churches,* 1: 404, 2: 467–477; Haller, *Rise of Puritanism,* p. 8; and Dickens, *English Reformation,* pp. 82–91.

2. Bossy, *Christianity in the West,* pp. 91–114.

3. Patrick Collinson, "England," and Bob Scribner, "A Comparative Overview," in Bob Scribner, Roy Porter, and Mikulas Teich (eds.), *The Reformation in National Context* (Cambridge: Cambridge University Press, 1994), pp. 90, 221–222.

4. John E. Booty (ed.), *The Book of Common Prayer, 1559* (Washington: Folger, 1976), p. 18.

5. "An Admonition to the Parliament" (1572), in W. H. Frere and C. E. Douglas (eds.), *Puritan Manifestos* (London, 1907, 1959), p. 14.

6. M. M. Knappen (ed.), *Two Elizabethan Puritan Diaries: Richard Rogers and Samuel Ward* (1933), pp. 106–107.

7. Rosemary O'Day, *The Debate on the English Reformation* (London: Methuen, 1986), p. 11.

8. Troeltsch, *Social Teaching of the Christian Churches,* 1: 404, 2: 464; Knappen, *Tudor Puritanism,* pp. 10–11; and Haller, *Rise of Puritanism,* pp. 297–302.

9. Edmund Grindal, "Letter 89: To the Queen, 20 December, 1576," in W. Nicholson (ed.), *The Remains of Archbishop Grindal* (London, 1843), pp. 376–390.

10. "Peter Wentworth's Speech, 8 February" (1576) in T. E. Hartley (ed.), *Proceedings in the Parliaments of Elizabeth I* (Leicester, 1981), 1: 430.

11. Collinson, *Religion of Protestants,* pp. 141–188.

12. Collinson, *Religion of Protestants,* pp. 153–164; and William Haller, *Foxe's*

Book of Martyrs and the Elect Nation (London: Jonathan Cape, 1963), pp. 82–109.

13. *Book of Common Prayer,* pp. 22–33.

14. *Book of Common Prayer,* pp. 14–21.

15. *Book of Common Prayer,* pp. 5–13.

16. As introductions to a growing literature, see Collinson, *Religion of Protestants,* pp. 191–220; John Morrill, "The Religious Context of the English Civil War" (1984), reprinted in John Morrill, *The Nature of the English Revolution* (New York: Longman, 1993), pp. 45–68; and Donald A. Spaeth, "Common Prayer? Popular Observance of the Anglican Liturgy in Restoration Wiltshire," in S. J. Wright (ed.), *Parish, Church, and People: Local Studies in Lay Religion* (London: Hutchinson, 1988), pp. 125–151.

17. *Book of Common Prayer,* p. 309.

18. This view has been developed in many distinguished contributions to the study of religion in the sixteenth and seventeenth centuries. See Tawney, *Religion and the Rise of Capitalism,* pp. 123–125, 128–129; Hill, *Society and Puritanism,* pp. 141–211; Hunt, *Puritan Moment,* pp. 130–155; Wrightson and Levine, *Poverty and Piety,* pp. 110–141; Wrightson, *English Society,* pp. 206–221; and Underdown, *Revel, Riot, and Rebellion,* pp. 44–72.

19. This important distinction between religion and social control is made to good effect in McIntosh, *Community Transformed,* pp. 240–258.

20. Willcox, *Gloucestershire,* p. 142.

21. GRO: TBR A 1/2, Borough Ordinances, 1608, no. 6.

22. Willcox, *Gloucestershire,* p. 142.

23. "Sabbatarianism in Manchester, 1616" in R. C. Richardson and T. B. James (eds.), *The Urban Experience: English, Scottish, and Welsh Towns, 1450–1700* (Manchester: Manchester University Press, 1983), pp. 142–143; and Collinson, *Religion of Protestants,* pp. 170–171, 199–200.

24. See F. D. Price, "An Elizabethan Church Official: Thomas Powell, Chancellor of Gloucester Diocese," *Church Quarterly Review,* 128 (1939): 94–112; "Elizabethan Apparitors in the Diocese of Gloucester," *Church Quarterly Review,* 134 (1942): 37–55; "The Abuses of Excommunication and the Decline of Ecclesiastical Discipline under Queen Elizabeth," *English Historical Review,* 57 (1942): 106–115; and "Bishop Bullingham and Chancellor Blackleech: A Diocese Divided," TBGAS, 91 (1972): 175–198. Price's argument is reiterated in Houlbrooke, *Church Courts and the People,* p. 53.

25. *More Strange News: Of Wonderful Accidents Happening by the Late*

Overflowing of Waters in Somersetshire, Gloucestershire, Norfolk, and Other Places of England (London, 1606), A4.

26. *More Strange News,* A8.

27. *More Strange News,* B3–4.

28. *More Strange News,* B3. David Underdown provides a rich illustration of this notion of providence in his account of local reactions to the fire in Dorchester in 1613. See Underdown, *Fire From Heaven,* pp. 1–5, 90–129.

29. Troeltsch, *Social Teaching of the Christian Churches,* 1: 241–245, 395–397, 2: 528–539; Walzer, *Revolution of the Saints,* p. 35; and Thomas, *Religion and the Decline of Magic,* pp. 78–96.

30. Anthony Fletcher, "Factionalism in Town and Countryside: The Significance of Puritanism and Arminianism," in Derek Baker (ed.), *The Church in Town and Countryside* (Oxford: Blackwell, 1979), pp. 292–293.

31. Nicholas Tyacke, *Anti-Calvinists: The Rise of English Arminianism, c. 1590–1640* (Oxford: Clarendon Press, 1987), pp. 9–15.

32. Tewkesbury and its environs were hit by plague six times between 1592 and 1624. The most severe outbreak occurred in April 1593 and lasted through May 1594. In the course of the year, 150 houses were infected, 560 people died, and many inhabitants fled the town. GRO: TBR A 1/1, pp. 322, 328, 329, 341, 342; D 2688, f. 69v.

33. This relationship between wealth, power, and social discipline has been found in many other local communities. See Wrightson and Levine, *Poverty and Piety,* pp. 127–128.

34. Another problem is the absence of any pattern of presentments to distinguish "Puritan" churchwardens from other local office holders. The conflation of religious belief and social discipline is pronounced in Wrightson and Levine, *Poverty and Piety,* pp. 133–137, 140–141, 156–158.

35. Articles survive for the episcopal visitations of 1607 and 1622, and for the first metropolitical visitation of Archbishop Abbot in 1612. See GRO: GDR 102, Episcopal Visitation of Diocese and Cathedral, 1607; GDR 115, Visitations, 1612–1619; and GDR 146, Episcopal Visitation, 1622.

36. See Kenneth Fincham, *Prelate as Pastor: The Episcopate of James I* (Oxford: Oxford University Press, 1990), pp. 112–176, on the politics of episcopal visitation and justice.

37. See Price, "An Elizabethan Church Official," 94–112; "Elizabethan Apparitors in the Diocese of Gloucester," 37–55; "The Abuses of Excommunication," 106–115; and "Bishop Bullingham and Chancellor Blackleech," 175–198.

38. Price, "Bishop Bullingham and Chancellor Blackleech," 189. See presentments for the seven relevant parishes in GRO: GDR 66, Detection Causes: April–August 1591 and December 1591–September 1592. This volume

records thirty-three presentments in all, but only twenty-three cases had reached the stage of personal appearance.

39. GRO: GDR 66, Detection Causes: April–August 1591 and December 1591–September 1592, ff. 43v and 57r [Richard Burford of Deerhurst], f. 86v [Thomas Powten of Tredington], and f. 69v [John Smith of Deerhurst].

40. Fincham, *Prelate as Pastor,* p. 147; Willcox, *Gloucestershire,* p. 239; Kirby, *Diocese of Gloucester,* 1: 125.

41. Willcox, *Gloucestershire,* p. 239.

42. GRO: GDR 100, Depositions: March 1606–March 1609: Case of Office v. Drake and Edwards, Deposition of Richard Garner; GDR 96, Episcopal Visitation: 1605, Winchcombe Deanery; and GDR 97, Detection Causes: September 1605, f. 118r. Archdeacons continued to conduct visitations, and a primary responsibility in the 1680s seems to have been the collection of transcripts of the local parish registers. See GRO: P 329 IN 1/6, Baptisms, Marriages, and Burials, 1683–1778, 3–6–1680.

43. Fincham, *Prelate as Pastor,* pp. 114–115.

44. GRO: P 329 CW 2/1, pp. 101, 107; GDR 66, Detection Causes: April–August 1591; December 1591–September, 1592, f. 48v.

45. The role of the "common fame" of an offense in its presentment is recorded in GRO: GDR 66, Detection Causes: April–August, 1591; December, 1591–September 1592, f. 46v [James Southen of Tewkesbury]; GDR 67, Office Causes: June 1591-June 1592 [William Flook of Apperley]; and GDR 75, Detections: 1594–1596, f. 46v [John Hale of Tewkesbury].

46. GRO: GDR 116, Detection Causes: October 1612–March 1613 [William Worley of Ashchurch].

47. GRO: TBR A 1/1, pp. 341–342.

48. A similar institutional inertia has been uncovered in the visitation records of Chichester diocese in the 1620s. See Fletcher, *County Community,* p. 85.

49. The fluctuations in such presentments in other parts of the country could conceivably reflect deeper social changes. Amussen argues that the early seventeenth-century presentments in Norfolk expressed the tensions of "capitalist development" in the area. See Amussen, *Ordered Society,* pp. 95–133, 164–165.

50. GRO: GDR 66, Detection Causes: April–August 1591; December 1591–September 1592.

51. GRO: GDR 66, Detection Causes: April–August 1591; December 1591–September 1592, f. 82v.

52. See R. H. Tawney and Eileen Power (eds.), *Tudor Economic Documents,* 3 vols. (London: Longman, 1924), 2: 328–334 and 346–362, for the stat-

utes of 1572, 1576, and 1597 that established the system of parish poor relief in England.

53. GRO: GDR 66, Detection Causes: April–August 1591; December 1591–September 1592, ff. 2v and 5v [Humfrey Huss and Alice Webb of Tewkesbury]; 40v [Richard Shelton and Anne Watts of Deerhurst]; 46v [James Southen and Joanna Wood of Tewkesbury]; 122r and 124r [Thomas Bishop and Jocosa Gnat of Tewkesbury].

54. On the many problems of enforcement and the relatively low levels of church attendance and participation in communion in Elizabethan parish communities, see Thomas, *Religion and the Decline of Magic,* pp. 159–166; Wrightson and Levine, *Poverty and Piety,* pp. 156–157; and Collinson, *Religion of Protestants,* pp. 210–212.

55. The official position on church attendance is considered in Dickens, *English Reformation,* p. 278.

56. GRO: GDR 66, Detections: April–August 1591; December 1591–September 1592, f. 48v.

57. GRO: GDR 66, Detections: April–August 1591; December 1591–September 1592, f. 46r-v.

58. Leslie Bradley, "An Enquiry into Seasonality in Baptisms, Marriages, and Burials, Part I: Introduction, Methodology, and Marriages," *Local Population Studies,* 4 (1971): 21–40, reprinted in Michael Drake (ed.), *Population Studies from Parish Registers* (Matlock: Local Population Studies, 1982), pp. 1–13 (p. 9); and Thomas, *Religion and the Decline of Magic,* p. 620.

59. Bradley, "An Enquiry into Seasonality in Baptisms, Marriages, and Burials," 8–10. Bradley found the second period of prohibition, comprising roughly two weeks in May, to be infrequently observed in the twelve parishes he studied.

60. The bishop's judgment has not survived, but Audrey was still curate of Tewkesbury in 1593. See GRO: GDR 66, Detections: April–August 1591; December, 1591–September 1592, f. 9r; GDR 73, Episcopal Visitation of the Diocese and Cathedral, 1594, p. 29; and W 1593/36, Henry Tovy of Tewkesbury.

61. Haigh, *English Reformations,* pp. 274–275; Spufford, *Contrasting Communities,* pp. 171–172; Wrightson and Levine, *Poverty and Piety,* p. 12.

62. The court ruled Symes could continue without a license, as long as he did not describe himself as a surgeon. GRO: GDR 66, Detections: April–August 1591; December 1591–September 1592, f. 129.

63. GRO: GDR 100, Depositions: March 1606–March 1609: Case of Office v. Drake and Edwards, Depositions of William Restell, Richard Garner, and John Cheston.

64. GRO: GDR 67, Office Causes: June 1591–June 1592 [Surman].

65. Cooke was a servant of the Cassey family of Deerhurst, known in the diocesan courts for their devout Catholicism. The publicity given to Cooke's penance for a common sexual offense was probably calculated to embarrass the family. See GRO: GDR 67, Office Causes: June 1591–June 1592 [Cooke]; and GDR 75, Detections: 1594–1596 [Parker].

66. See GRO: GDR 66, Detections: April–August 1591; December 1591–September 1592, ff. 82v, 83r; GDR 67, Office Causes: June 1591–June 1592, Case of John Surman of Forthampton; and GDR 75, Detections: 1594–1596, ff. 55r, 58r, for the variety of penitential forms.

67. GRO: GDR 75, Detections: 1594–1596, ff. 58r, 89r.

68. The Christian social doctrine of love, described in its earliest phase as a veritable "religious communism of love," has been explored in Troeltsch, *Social Teaching of the Christian Churches,* 1: 62.

69. GRO: P 329 CW 2/1, pp. 119, 140; D2688, Giles Geast Charity Account Book, ff. 53v, 54v, 55v, 58v, 60v, 61v, 63v, 66v, 67v, 71v, 73v, 74v.

70. See Ingram, *Church Courts, Sex, and Marriage,* pp. 52–53, 340–363, for a more detailed account of excommunication and its effectiveness.

71. Ingram, *Church Courts, Sex, and Marriage,* p. 53.

72. Ingram, *Church Courts, Sex, and Marriage,* p. 53. The process of issuing a *significavit* and acquiring the writ was prolonged, expensive, and infrequently used. See Price, "Abuses of Excommunication," 112–115.

73. Presentments survive for the years 1591–1592, 1594–1597, 1599–1600, 1602–1603, 1605, 1610, 1612–1613, and 1616–1617. These years correspond roughly to the schedule of episcopal visitations, and the chances of a large group of presentments not having survived are therefore slight. The churchwardens of Ashchurch, Deerhurst, Forthampton, Tewkesbury, Tredington, and Twyning presented 576 people for 480 offenses during this period. In the years 1594–1597 and 1599–1600, 290 people were presented for 242 offenses. Figures are drawn from GRO: GDR 66, Detection Causes: April–August 1591; December 1591–September 1592; GDR 75, Detections: 1594–1596; GDR 76, Detection Causes: 1594–1597; GDR 81, Detection Causes: October 1597; GDR 87, Detection Causes: September 1599–December 1600; GDR 91, Detection Causes: July 1602–March 1603; GDR 97, Detection Causes: September 1605; GDR 111, Detection Causes: October–December 1610; GDR 116, Detection Causes: October 1612–March 1613; and GDR 125, Detection Causes: June 1616–March 1617.

74. McIntosh has identified a similar response to crisis in the impact of immigration and a sharp decline in real wages on presentments for sexual misdemeanors in Havering. McIntosh, *Community Transformed,* pp. 254–255.

75. GRO: GDR 91, Detection Causes: July 1602–March 1603.

76. GRO: GDR 66, Detection Causes: April–August 1591; December 1591–September 1592; GDR 75, Detections: 1594–1596; GDR 76, Detection Causes: 1594–1597; and GDR 81, Detection Causes: October 1597.

77. The prices per bushel of various kinds of produce were listed in 1597 as follows: wheat (12s 6d), barley (8s), beans (8s), malt (8s), fitches (5s), oats (3s). Even the imported rye was sold at 5s and 6s per bushel. These prices can be compared with those that preceded the fear of dearth in 1607: wheat (3s), barley (2s 4d), malt (2s 4d), pulse (18d). GRO: TBR A 1/1, ff. 21r-v, 28r.

78. The average age of marriage in the late sixteenth and early seventeenth centuries was 23.5 for brides and 26.5 for grooms. This age could have been lower or higher, depending on a family's social status and wealth. See Laslett, *World We Have Lost,* pp. 82–84.

79. GRO: GDR 76, Detection Causes: 1594–1597; D 2688, Giles Geast Charity Account Book, an incomplete list of the disbursements for 1636 inside the cover.

80. Flucke moved his family south from Deerhurst to the larger settlement of Apperley shortly after the birth of his grandson and was therefore suspected of attempting to evade detection. GRO: GDR 76, Detection Causes: 1594–1597, f. 269r. This case is unique in its prosecution of the female offender and the male offender's father. Giles Flucke was twenty-four years old at the time of the presentment and thus no longer a minor. GRO: P 112 IN 1/1, 18-11-1570: Giles Flucke, son of William Flucke.

81. GRO: GDR 66, Detection Causes: April–August 1591; December 1591–September 1592; GDR 75, Court Book: 1594–96; GDR 76, Detection Causes: 1594–97; GDR 81, Detection Causes: October 1597; and GDR 87, Detection Causes: September 1599–December 1600.

82. The form of penance itself was relatively mild, as the Jefferies were ordered to appear with the white rod during divine service but were permitted to stand in their usual attire. See GRO: GDR 76, Detection Causes: 1594–1597, f. 82v.

83. GRO: GDR 75, Detections: 1594–1596, f. 90v.

84. GRO: GDR 76, Detection Causes: 1594–1597, f. 63v.

85. GRO: GDR 76, Detection Causes: 1594–1597, f. 269v.

86. GRO: GDR 76, Detection Causes: 1594–1597, ff. 271v [Twyning], 270r [Ashchurch and Tredington], 269r [Deerhurst], 268r [Forthampton].

87. The enforcement of licenses and the prosecution of curates who performed clandestine marriages to increase their fees are recorded in GRO: GDR 75, Court Book: 1594–1596, f. 51r-v; GDR 81, Detection Causes: October 1597 [Curtis]; GDR 87, Detection Causes: September 1599–De-

cember 1600, pp. 165, 183, 195; GDR 97, Detection Causes: September 1605 [Rickardes]; and GDR 125, Detection Causes: June 1616–March 1617 [Graver].

88. The evidence of more systematic episcopal regulation of schools in the late 1590s and early 1600s is in GRO: GDR 76, Detection Causes: 1594–1597, f. 267r [Thomas Rogers of Tewkesbury]; GDR 81, Detection Causes: October 1597 [Thomas Rogers and John Terrett of Tewkesbury]; GDR 87, Detection Causes: September 1599–December 1600, p. 153; and GDR 97, Detection Causes: 1605 [Thomas Restall of Forthampton].

89. GRO: GDR 75, Detections: 1594–1596, f. 89r.

90. See John Colet, "Sermon to the Convocation at St. Paul's," in Elizabeth M. Nugent (ed.), *The Thought and Culture of the English Renaissance* (The Hague: Martinus Nijhoff, 1969), p. 363.

91. The general importance of anticlericalism in the process of reformation is discussed in Dickens, *English Reformation,* pp. 320–321.

92. The clerical leadership in northern Gloucestershire participated in a more general process of educational and ethical reform among the late Elizabethan clergy. See Dickens, *English Reformation,* p. 363; Collinson, *Religion of Protestants,* pp. 92–114; Richardson, *Puritanism in Northwest England,* pp. 47–53. A similar local chronology of reformation in Dorchester is described in Underdown, *Fire From Heaven,* pp. 19–24.

93. Audrey served the cure in Tewkesbury until 1594. Curtis arrived in 1597 and was followed by Fox in 1602. Wright was curate of Ashchurch from 1592–1594 and was succeeded by Ashby, who served until 1599. Blackwell was frequently invited by Fox to preach in Tewkesbury and became the curate in 1608. See GRO: GDR 73, Episcopal Visitation: 1594, pp. 29, 33; GDR 80, Episcopal Visitations, 1597–1602, pp. 38–39, 113, 231; GDR 91, Detection Causes: July 1602–March 1603 [Case of Blackwell under presentments for Tewkesbury]; and GDR 107, Episcopal Visitation, 1609.

94. GRO: GDR B4/1/995.

95. I Kings, 12: 31, 13: 33.

96. GRO: GDR 89, Depositions: June 1601–March 1604: Case of Barnard v. Winsmore, Depositions of Robert Mayle and John Brewer.

97. Winsmore was accused of many other profanations of his office, and therefore I have reproduced only the most public and documented examples of his behavior. GRO: GDR 89, Depositions of Robert Mayle and Edward Nuttinge.

98. GRO: GDR 80, Episcopal Visitations, 1597–1602, p. 232.

99. GRO: GDR 96, Episcopal Visitation, 1605.

100. GRO: GDR 66, Detection Causes: April–August 1591; December 1591–September 1592.

101. GRO: GDR 75, Detections: 1594–1596, f. 58r; GDR 76, Detection Causes: 1594–1597, ff. 64r, 66v, 266r, 271r; GDR 81, Detection Causes: October 1597; and GDR 87, Detection Causes: September 1599–December 1600, ff. 155r, 162r-v, 164v-165r, 181v, 183v-184r, 185r, 186r-187r.

102. GRO: GDR 81, Detection Causes: October 1597.

103. GRO: GDR 81, Detection Causes: October 1597.

104. GRO: GDR 87, Detection Causes: September 1599–December 1600, f. 164v.

105. GRO: GDR 91, Detection Causes: July 1602–March 1603, p. 137.

106. See also GRO: GDR 91, Detection Causes: July 1602–March 1603, p. 217, for the lack of charity among neighbors as grounds for withdrawal from communion. Presentments for nonreception of communion reached an annual peak of 28 in 1605. See GRO: GDR 97, Detection Causes: September 1605.

107. These figures were culled from GRO: GDR 66, Detection Causes: April–August 1591; December 1591–September, 1592; GDR 75, Court Book: 1594–1596; GDR 76, Detection Causes: 1594–1597; GDR 81, Detection Causes: October 1597; and GDR 87, Detection Causes: September 1599–December, 1600.

108. On a related issue, see the discussion of Puritan attitudes to "idle words" as a form of sensuality in Weber, *Protestant Ethic,* pp. 157, 261.

109. GRO: GDR 76, Detection Causes: 1594–1597, f. 107v.

110. GRO: GDR 81, Detection Causes: October 1597; and GDR 87, Detection Causes: September 1599–December 1600, ff. 154r-v, 185v.

111. GRO: GDR 81, Detection Causes: October 1597; and GDR 87, Detection Causes: September 1599–December 1600, f. 184r.

112. GRO: GDR 87, Detection Causes: September 1599–December 1600, f. 154v.

113. On the surface, this local conflict resembled the famous controversies between Prayer Book Puritans and Genevan Puritans that had divided English Protestants since the 1550s. See Dickens, *English Reformation,* p. 347.

114. GRO: GDR 76, Detection Causes: 1594–1597, f. 270r; and GDR 91, Detection Causes: July 1602–March 1603, Case of Humphrey Fox of Tewkesbury.

115. GRO: GDR 66, Detection Causes: April–August 1591; December 1591–September 1592, f. 46r. The use of common bread in communion, contrary to the royal injunctions of 1559, is discussed in Collinson, *Elizabethan Puritan Movement,* p. 367.

116. See Dickens, *English Reformation,* pp. 277, 359–360; Collinson, *Elizabethan Puritan Movement,* pp. 92–97; and Richardson, *Puritanism in North-*

west England, pp. 23–26, 75–76, for perceptions of the surplice as a symbol of catholic sacrifice and reactions to its use.

117. GRO: GDR 91, Detections: July 1602–March 1603.

118. GRO: GDR 100, Depositions: March 1606–March 1609: Case of Office v. Drake and Edwards, Depositions of William Restell, Richard Garner, and John Cheston. The importance of psalms for many Nonconformists is discussed in Collinson, *Elizabethan Puritan Movement,* pp. 359–360.

119. This episode is recounted in GRO: TBR A 1/2, p. 23. The doctrinal issues and politics of Saturday Sabbatarianism are discussed in David S. Katz, *Sabbath and Sectarianism in Seventeenth-Century England* (Leiden: Brill, 1988), pp. 1–20.

120. GRO: GDR 100, Depositions: March 1606–March 1609: Case of Office v. Drake and Edwards, Depositions of William Restell and Richard Garner.

121. GRO: GDR 91, Detections: July 1602–March 1603; GDR 100, Depositions: March 1606–March 1609: Case of Office v. Drake and Edwards, Depositions of William Restell, Richard Garner, and John Cheston. Collinson, *Religion of Protestants,* p. 246.

122. GRO: GDR 97, Detection Causes: September 1605, f. 135r; and GDR 100, Depositions: March 1606–March 1609: Case of Office v. Drake and Edwards, Depositions of William Restell and John Cheston.

123. GRO: GDR 100, Depositions: March 1606–March 1609: Case of Office v. Drake and Edwards, Deposition of William Restell.

124. Puritanism as a combination of Troeltsch's ecclesiastical and sectarian elements has been a persistent theme in the work of Patrick Collinson. See Collinson, *Elizabethan Puritan Movement,* p. 14; and Collinson, *Religion of Protestants,* pp. 268–273.

125. GRO: GDR 76, Detection Causes: 1594–1597, f. 31r.

126. GRO: P 329 CW 2/1, p. 133; D 2688, ff. 54v, 58v.

127. The curacies of Fox and Drake have left traces in GRO: GDR 80, Episcopal Visitations: 1597–1602, p. 231; GDR 96, Episcopal Visitation: 1605, Winchcombe Deanery; GDR 97, Detection Causes: September 1605, f. 118r; GDR 102, Episcopal Visitation: 1607, Winchcombe Deanery; and GDR 100, Depositions: Case of Office v. Drake and Edwards, Depositions of William Restell and Richard Garner.

128. GDR 102, Episcopal Visitation: 1607, Winchcombe Deanery.

129. See the references in Wrightson, *English Society,* pp. 183–221; Wrightson and Levine, *Poverty and Piety,* pp. 110–172; Underdown, *Revel, Riot, and Rebellion,* pp. 9–72; Amussen, *Ordered Society,* pp. 175–176; and Rollison, *Local Origins of Modern Society,* pp. 37–39.

130. See GRO: GDR 76, Detection Causes: 1594–1597, f. 266r; GDR 91, Detection Causes: July 1602–March 1603; GDR 100, Depositions: March 1606–

March 1609: Case of Office v. Drake and Edwards, Depositions of William Restell, Richard Garner, and John Cheston; TBR A 1/2, p. 23; and Smyth, *Men and Armour,* pp. 115–116, 121–127.

131. The usefulness of an approach to Puritanism as "a distinctive style of piety and divinity" is discussed in Lake, "Defining Puritanism," 6–7, and can be extended to include distinctive nonconformist styles.

132. Collinson perceives local variation as relatively unimportant and emphasizes the uniformity of Puritan mentality and discipline. See Collinson, *Religion of Protestants,* p. 247.

133. GRO: GDR 91, Detections: July 1602–March 1603.

134. Collinson, *Religion of Protestants,* p. 212.

135. The evidence from the northern Vale of Gloucester stands in contrast to the power and cohesion of Nonconformity in market towns in the dioceses of Chester, Canterbury, and Peterborough. See Richardson, *Puritanism in Northwest England,* pp. 13–15; Peter Clark, *English Provincial Society from the Reformation to the Revolution: Religion, Politics, and Society in Kent* (Cranbury: Associated University Presses, 1977), pp. 168–169; and W. J. Shiels, *The Puritans in the Diocese of Peterborough, 1558–1610* (Northampton: Northampton Record Society, 1979), pp. 23–35.

136. This point is based on a comparison of the names culled from the sources listed in the previous footnote and the churchwardens identified in GRO: P 329 CW 2/1.

137. George Shaw's occupation and the standing of his family are revealed in the will of John Shaw, his brother. GRO: W 1606/41, John Shaw; TBR A 1/2, p. 23.

138. GRO: GDR 97, Detection Causes: September 1605, f. 135r; and GDR 100, Depositions: March 1606–March 1609: Case of Office v. Drake and Edwards, Depositions of William Restell and John Cheston.

139. GDR 102, Episcopal Visitation, 1607: Information of Henry Hatton of Forthampton.

140. GRO: GDR 91, Detections: July 1602–March 1603.

141. GRO: TBR A 1/2, p. 23.

142. GRO: GDR 89, Depositions: June 1601–March 1604: Case of Barnard v. Winsmore, Deposition of Robert Mayle.

143. Drake lived in the same house during the time of his suspension from the cure of Forthampton. GRO: GDR 100, Depositions: March 1606–March 1609: Case of Office v. Drake and Edwards, Depositions of William Restell, Richard Garner, and John Cheston.

144. GRO: W 1602/35 and 1624/102, John and Margery Alcocke; and GDR 100, Depositions: March 1606–March 1609: Case of Office v. Drake and Edwards, Deposition of John Cheston. The Alcockes never held parochial office.

145. The distribution of Nonconformity across social classes in Forthampton recalls Margaret Spufford's description of Orwell in Cambridgeshire and provides a contrast to scattered rural nonconformity in the Wiltshire parishes of Keevil and Wylye. See Spufford, *Contrasting Communities,* pp. 300–306; and Ingram, *Church Courts, Sex, and Marriage,* pp. 114–123.

146. This pattern of rural cohesion and urban diffusion in Nonconformity differs markedly from the standard patterns as described in Collinson, *Religion of Protestants,* pp. 170, 276.

147. GRO: GDR 100, Depositions: March 1606–March 1609: Case of Office v. Drake and Edwards, Depositions of William Restell, Richard Garner, and John Cheston.

148. Ibid.

149. GRO: GDR 100, Depositions: March 1606–March 1609: Case of Office v. Drake and Edwards, Depositions of Richard Garner and John Cheston.

150. GRO: GDR 100, Depositions: March 1606–March 1609: Case of Office v. Drake and Edwards, Deposition of John Cheston.

151. GRO: GDR 100, Depositions: March 1606–March 1609: Case of Office v. Drake and Edwards, Deposition of William Restell.

152. Ibid.

153. Collinson's account of ministers discussing their "country congregations" at Hampton Court includes a hint of this mentality. See Collinson, *Religion of Protestants,* p. 200.

154. Dickens identifies the potential clerical leadership of this faction in his discussion of local curates who survived the Elizabethan Settlement but remained committed to traditional forms of ritual. Dickens, *English Reformation,* pp. 30–31.

155. GRO: P 329 CW 2/1, p. 87; F. L. Cross and E. A. Livingstone (eds.), *The Oxford Dictionary of the Christian Church,* 2nd ed. (Oxford: Oxford University Press, 1974, 1983), pp. 45, 153.

156. The powers attributed to bells are described in Thomas, *Religion and the Decline of Magic,* pp. 31, 32, 49, 255, 493.

157. GRO: GDR 73, Episcopal Visitation: 1594, p. 29 [Walter Rogers]; and GDR 80, Episcopal Visitations: 1597–1602, p. 39 [Richard Curtis].

158. GRO: GDR 75, Detections: 1594–1596, f. 149r.

159. Turner was notorious for leaving church at the start of the sermon. GRO: GDR 65, Depositions: February 1586–March 1592: Case of John Audrey v. Henry Turner, Depositions of Robert Dale, Richard Mitchell, William Little, and Roger Keare; and GDR 67, Office Causes: June 1591–June 1592: Case of Office v. Henry Turner.

160. Brand, *Popular Antiquities,* 2: 84.

161. GRO: GDR 159, Depositions: September 1625–May 1628: Case of Hitches v. Smithsend, Deposition of Joanna Wyatt.

162. Ibid.

163. GRO: GDR B4/3/1178, Tewkesbury, 1627 (tithe), William Hitches v. Nicholas Smithsend.

164. Ibid.

165. Ibid.

166. A useful general overview of the kinds of problems confronted by Catholics in the vale is John Bossy, "The Character of Elizabethan Catholicism," *Past and Present,* 21 (1962): 39–59. See also John Bossy, *The English Catholic Community, 1570–1850* (New York: Oxford University Press, 1976), pp. 75–194, for an ethnography of the English Catholic community in the seventeenth century and for the small number of Catholic families in Gloucestershire.

167. GRO: GDR 87, Detection Causes: September 1599–December 1600, pp. 164, 185; GDR 97, Detection Causes: September 1605, f. 150r; and GDR 125, Detection Causes: June 1616–March 1617, pp. 32–33. The Catholicism of the Casseys is discussed in "Old Catholic Families," *TBGAS,* 74 (1955): 128–152.

168. GRO: GDR 97, Detection Causes: September 1605, f. 150r.

169. GRO: W 1624/40, John Eagles of Deerhurst.

170. GRO: GDR 97, Detection Causes: September 1605, f. 150r.

171. See the references in Wrightson, *English Society,* pp. 183–221; and Underdown, *Revel, Riot, and Rebellion,* pp. 9–72. A broad spectrum of variation in the local intensity and experience of this reformation of manners is recognized in Levine and Wrightson, *Making of an Industrial Society,* pp. 295–308.

172. Attempts to disentangle the issues of religion and social control include Spufford, *Contrasting Communities,* pp. 239–271, 298–318; Ingram, *Church Courts, Sex, and Marriage,* pp. 70–124; and McIntosh, *Community Transformed,* pp. 240–258.

5. A Circle of Order

1. Conrad Russell, *The Causes of the English Civil War* (Oxford: Oxford University Press, 1990), pp. 58–60.

2. Nicholas Tyacke, "Puritanism, Arminianism, and Counterrevolution," in Conrad Russell (ed.), *The Origins of the English Civil War* (London: Macmillan, 1973), pp. 129–137; and *Anti-Calvinists,* pp. 125–130, 166–167, 180.

3. Tyacke, *Anti-Calvinists,* pp. 166–167.

4. Kevin Sharpe, "The Personal Rule of Charles I," in Howard Tomlinson (ed.), *Before the English Civil War: Essays on Early Stuart Politics and Government* (London: Macmillan, 1983), pp. 62–63, 75; Kevin Sharpe,

The Personal Rule of Charles I (New Haven: Yale University Press, 1992), pp. 360–363.

5. Peter White, *Predestination, Policy, and Polemic: Conflict and Consensus in the English Church from the Reformation to the Civil War* (Cambridge: Cambridge University Press, 1992), pp. 1–12, 238–255, 272–312.

6. Julian Davies, *The Caroline Captivity of the Church: Charles I and the Remoulding of Anglicanism* (Oxford: Clarendon Press, 1992), pp. 3, 11–14, 24–33.

7. Andrew Foster, "Church Policies of the 1630s," in Richard Cust and Ann Hughes (eds.), *Conflict in Early Stuart England: Studies in Religion and Politics* (London: Longman, 1989), p. 207.

8. Tyacke, *Anti-Calvinists*, p. 195.

9. Thomas G. Barnes, *Somerset, 1625–1640: A County's Government during the "Personal Rule"* (Cambridge, Mass.: Harvard University Press, 1961), pp. 172–280; Paul Slack, "Religious Protest and Urban Authority: The Case of Henry Sherfield, Iconoclast, 1633," in Derek Baker (ed.), *Schism, Heresy, and Religious Protest* (Cambridge: Cambridge University Press, 1972), p. 295; and Fletcher, "Factionalism in Town and Countryside," 291.

10. Kirby, *Diocese of Gloucester*, pp. 10–11.

11. GRO: D 2688, Giles Geast Charity Account Book, f. 69v.

12. Bradford is recorded as bailiff in GRO: D 2688, f. 74v.

13. GRO: D 2688, f. 72v. Bradford had evidently seen one of several chronograms, which were used to express violent fantasies of Buckingham's death, in circulation in the late 1620s. See examples in BL: Harley Ms 4931, f. 9r; Add Ms 29492, f. 55v; Add Ms 15227, f. 41v; Sloane Ms 826 f. 181v; and Bodl: Tanner Ms 465, f. 100.

14. Collinson, *Religion of Protestants*, pp. 89–90; and GRO: GDR 115, Visitations, 1612–1619: Episcopal Visitations, 1616, 1619.

15. "Godfrey Goodman," in *Dictionary of National Biography* (Oxford, 1922), p. 131; GRO: GDR 157, Episcopal Visitation, 1625; GDR 166, Episcopal Visitation, 1628; and GDR 186, Detection Causes: March–November 1634.

16. GRO: GDR 189, Visitation by Archbishop Laud's Commissioners, 1635.

17. GRO: GDR 97, Detection Causes: September 1605; GDR 111, Detection Causes: October–December 1610; GDR 116, Detection Causes: October 1612–March 1613; and GDR 125, Detection Causes: June 1616–March, 1617.

18. A book of presentments made in 1619 was too badly damaged to be consulted in the spring of 1988. GRO: GDR 134, Detection Causes: Winchcombe Deanery, 1619.

19. Presentments for the years 1631–1634 are in GRO: GDR 174, Detection

Causes, Winchcombe Deanery: 1631, 1634, 1635, 1636, 1637; GDR 176, Detection Causes: May 1631–February 1632; GDR 181, Detection Causes: March–September 1633; and GDR 186, Detection Causes: March–November 1634.

20. Wrightson and Levine have observed a similar pattern of decline in Terling. See Wrightson and Levine, *Poverty and Piety,* p. 119.

21. Presentments for 1635 and 1637 are in GRO: GDR 174, Detection Causes: 1631, 1634, 1635, 1636, 1637; GDR 191, Detection Causes: October 1635–March 1637; GDR 195, Detection Causes: January–March 1637; and GDR 202, Detection Causes: February 1638–April 1641.

22. GRO: GDR 176, Detection Causes: May 1631–February 1632; and GDR 174, Detection Causes: 1631, 1634, 1635, 1636, 1637.

23. GDR 174, Detection Causes: 1631, 1634, 1635, 1636, 1637.

24. GRO: GDR 176, Detection Causes: May 1631–February 1632, p. 16; and GDR 174, Detection Causes: 1631, 1634, 1635, 1636, 1637.

25. GRO: GDR 174, Detection Causes: 1631, 1634, 1635, 1636, 1637.

26. GRO: GDR 191, Detection Causes: October 1635–March 1637; GDR 195, Detection Causes: January–March 1637.

27. GRO: GDR 174, Detection Causes: 1631, 1634, 1635, 1636, 1637.

28. Ibid.

29. Ibid.

30. The court ordered the churchwardens of Twyning and Forthampton to make similar certifications in September 1634 but never recorded a return from either parish. Deerhurst was inexplicably omitted from the examination of certificates. GRO: GDR 174, Detection Causes: 1631, 1634, 1635, 1636, 1637.

31. "The Declaration of Sports" (1633), in S. R. Gardiner (ed.), *Constitutional Documents of the Puritan Revolution* (Oxford, 1889), pp. 34–35. See also J. P. Kenyon (ed.), *The Stuart Constitution,* 2nd ed. (Cambridge: Cambridge University Press, 1986), pp. 116, 136.

32. Underdown, *Revel, Riot, and Rebellion,* pp. 66–68.

33. GRO: GDR 181, Detection Causes: March–September 1633.

34. GRO: GDR 176, Detection Causes: May 1631–February 1632, p. 16. Downbell's father was probably Stephen Donneble, a tippler, listed as an elderly inhabitant of Church Street in the militia survey of 1608. See GRO: W 1611/153, 1649/31; Smyth, *Men and Armour,* p. 124.

35. In 1649 the town clerk estimated the number of freeman at "above 300" or roughly 70 percent of the eligible males in a town of 2,000 inhabitants. This proportion was probably affected by the "very great number of poor having crept into the town since the beginning of the wars," but the fines required by the corporation would have prevented the poorest members

of the community from becoming freemen at any time. See GRO: TBR A1/1, pp. 153, 159. The status of male offenders presented between 1631 and 1633 may be recovered from GRO: TBR A 1/2, pp. 67, 76, 90, 94, 116, 128, 149, 168.

36. See GRO: GDR 73, Episcopal Visitation: 1594, p. 29; GDR 102, Episcopal Visitation: 1607; GDR 115, Visitations: 1612–1619, vol. 1, ff. 111r, 217r, for the Hamptons in parochial office. See GRO: W 1612/107 for the Smithsends.

37. Smyth, *Men and Armour,* pp. 127–128. Stocke still owed the money at the time of Lawrence Hampton's death in 1613. GRO: W 1613/157.

38. GRO: W 1640/148.

39. GRO: GDR 191, Detection Causes: October 1635–March 1637.

40. GRO: GDR 174, Detection Causes: 1631, 1634, 1635, 1636, 1637.

41. Barry Reay, "Popular Religion," in Reay, *Popular Culture,* pp. 92–93.

42. GRO: GDR 174, Detection Causes: 1634 [2], 1635 [4]; GDR 191, Detection Causes: October 1635–March 1637 [1]; and GDR 202, Detection Causes: February 1638–April 1641 [8].

43. Ware, *Elizabethan Parish,* p. 11.

44. GRO: GDR 75, Detection Causes: 1594–1596 [Forthampton]; GDR 97, Detection Causes: September 1605 [Forthampton]; GDR 116, Detection Causes: October 1612–March 1613 [Forthampton]; and GDR 125, Detection Causes: June 1616–March 1617 [Deerhurst].

45. The presentments for 1631–1640 are in GRO: GDR 174, Detection Causes, Winchcombe Deanery: 1631, 1634, 1635, 1636, 1637; GDR 176, Detection Causes: May 1631–February 1632; GDR 181, Detection Causes: March–September 1633; and GDR 202, Detection Causes: February 1638–April 1641.

46. Tyacke, *Anti-Calvinists,* pp. 181–182, 188–192, 199–209.

47. Peter Lake, "Antipopery: The Structure of a Prejudice," in Cust and Hughes, *Conflict in Early Stuart England,* pp. 91–92; and "Puritanism, Arminianism, and a Shropshire Axe-Murder," 37–39.

48. Fletcher, "Factionalism in Town and Countryside," 294, 300; Lake, "Antipopery," 72.

49. Peter Studley, *The Looking Glass of Schism,* 2nd ed. (London, 1635); and Henry Burton, *A Divine Tragedy Lately Acted* (1636, 1641). James Bennett reproduced the version of the Hickes narrative contained in the first edition of Studley's book in *Tewkesbury Yearly Register,* 2: 270–272. Bennett's copy of the book is important, as it contained "manuscript observations . . . evidently written about the time of its publication and probably by one who had some personal knowledge of the party." Bennett also reprinted a certificate sent by the bailiffs of Tewkesbury to Studley's oppo-

nent, Richard More, a Shropshire magistrate. More attempted to demonstrate that Studley's general account of the relationship between religious nonconformity, mental illness, and monstrous acts depended on lies, misinformation, and insensitivity to local context.

50. "Henry Burton," in *Dictionary of National Biography*, pp. 457–459; Tyacke, *Anti-Calvinists*, pp. 157–158, 227–228; Lake, "Antipopery," 95; and Haller, *Rise of Puritanism*, pp. 250–252.

51. "Henry Burton," 457; Tyacke, *Anti-Calvinists*, pp. 157–158, 227–228.

52. Burton, *Divine Tragedy*, p. 1.

53. Lake, "Antipopery," 73.

54. Burton, *Divine Tragedy*, pp. 3, 9–11, 15, 17.

55. Burton, *Divine Tragedy*, p. 12.

56. Burton, *Divine Tragedy*, p. 17.

57. Burton, *Divine Tragedy*, pp. 4, 10.

58. Burton used this trope from Psalm 107.43 in *Divine Tragedy*, p. 2.

59. Burton, *Divine Tragedy*, pp. 8–9.

60. Burton, *Divine Tragedy*, p. 7.

61. Burton, *Divine Tragedy*, pp. 11–12, 23–24, 35–37.

62. Burton, *Divine Tragedy*, p. 28.

63. Burton, *Divine Tragedy*, pp. 3–4.

64. Burton, *Divine Tragedy*, p. 29.

65. Burton, *Divine Tragedy*, p. 35–36.

66. Burton, *Divine Tragedy*, p. 35.

67. Burton, *Divine Tragedy*, p. 14.

68. Burton, *Divine Tragedy*, pp. 8–9.

69. Burton, *Divine Tragedy*, pp. 4, 11.

70. Burton, *Divine Tragedy*, pp. 28–29.

71. Burton, *Divine Tragedy*, pp. 37–38.

72. Burton, *Divine Tragedy*, pp. 26, 29.

73. Burton, *Divine Tragedy*, p. 28.

74. Lake, "Puritanism, Arminianism, and a Shropshire Axe-Murder," 37–39, 50–60.

75. Studley, *Looking Glass of Schism*, A5–6.

76. Studley, *Looking Glass of Schism*, pp. 2–4.

77. Studley, *Looking Glass of Schism*, pp. 192–193.

78. Studley, *Looking Glass of Schism*, p. 190.

79. Studley, *Looking Glass of Schism*, pp. 147–151; Bennett, *Tewkesbury Yearly Register*, 2: 270–271.

80. *More Strange News*, A4–5, B3–4.

81. GRO: GDR 66, Detection Causes: April–August 1591; and December 1591–September 1592, f. 46r.

82. Bennett, *Tewkesbury Yearly Register*, 2: 271.

83. Studley conceded this point in the second edition of his book. Studley, *Looking Glass of Schism,* p. 38.

84. Bennett, *Tewkesbury Yearly Register,* 2: 272.

85. See Studley's response to More included in the second edition of *Looking Glass of Schism,* pp. 31–56; Lake, "Puritanism, Arminianism, and a Shropshire Axe-Murder," 37, 56–60.

86. An important point also addressed in Lake, "Puritanism, Arminianism, and a Shropshire Axe-Murder," 49–50.

87. S. R. Gardiner (ed.), "Reports of Cases in the Courts of Star Chamber and High Commission," *Camden Miscellany,* new series, 39 (1886): 244.

88. Ibid.

89. GRO: GDR 174, Detection Causes: 1631, 1634, 1635, 1636, 1637.

90. I have also included the companions of Humphrey Fox presented in 1635 for absence from divine service and failure to receive communion. GRO: GDR 174, Detection Causes: 1631, 1634, 1635, 1636, 1637.

91. Fox described the circumstances of his suspension in *CSPD, Charles I* (London, 1873), v. 14 (1639): 199. See GRO: GDR 91, Detection Causes: July 1602–March 1603, for his relationship to Blackwell. *CSPD, Charles I* (London, 1877), v. 15 (1639–1640): 582, implied the link between Fox and Geary.

92. GRO: GDR 174, Detection Causes: 1631, 1634, 1635, 1636, 1637; GDR 176, Detection Causes: May 1631–February 1632; and GDR 186, Detection Causes: March–November 1634.

93. GRO: GDR 115, vol. 2, Visitations, 1612–1619: Episcopal Visitation, 1616, p. 333.

94. Elrington, *VCH Gloucester,* 8: 201.

95. Collinson, *Religion of Protestants,* p. 90; GRO: GDR 115, vol. 2, Visitations, 1612–1619: Episcopal Visitation, 1616; Episcopal Visitation, 1619, p. 479; GDR 146, Episcopal Visitation, 1622.

96. *CSPD, Charles I,* v. 14 (1639): 199; GRO: GDR 157, Episcopal Visitation, 1625; GDR 166, Episcopal Visitation, 1628.

97. GRO: GDR 186, Detection Causes: March–November 1634.

98. "Godfrey Goodman," in *Dictionary of National Biography,* pp. 131–132.

99. GRO: GDR 186, Detection Causes: March–November 1634.

100. Ibid.

101. *CSPD, Charles I* (London, 1866), v. 9 (1635–1636): 87, 94, 101, 131, 481; and A. G. Matthews (ed.), *Calamy Revised* (Oxford: Clarendon Press, 1934), p. 301.

102. Elrington, *VCH Gloucester,* 8: 45, 155, 185, 207, 234.

103. GCL: Survey of Abbey Lands in Tewkesbury, 1632, p. 7; and *CSPD, Charles I,* v. 15 (1639–1640): 582. Mary Cooper was Baptist Hickes' daughter.

104. GRO: GDR 100, Depositions: March 1606–March 1609, Depositions of

Richard Garner and John Cheston. *CSPD, Charles I,* v. 15 (1639–1640): 582.

105. GRO: GDR 186, Detection Causes: March–November 1634.

106. GRO: GDR 202, Detection Causes, Winchcombe Deanery: February 1638–April 1641.

107. GRO: GDR 195, Detection Causes: January–March 1637; and PRO: E 134, 29 Charles II/12 February/Easter 10, Deposition of Humphrey Jeynes.

108. GRO: GDR 174, Detection Causes: 1631, 1634, 1635, 1636, 1637.

109. Ibid.

110. GRO: GDR 181, Detection Causes: March–September 1633; GDR 174, Detection Causes: 1631, 1634, 1635, 1636, 1637.

111. GRO: GDR 174, Detection Causes: 1631, 1634, 1635, 1636, 1637.

112. I have traced the names in GRO: GDR 174, Detection Causes: 1631, 1634, 1635, 1636, 1637 through the wills listed as 1605/35 (Salisbury), 1614/176 (Jorden), 1618/50 (Slicer), 1623/70 (Ockell), in order to reconstruct the status and interconnections of several nonconformist families in Ashchurch.

113. GRO: GDR 174, Detection Causes: 1631, 1634, 1635, 1636, 1637.

114. GRO: GDR 174, Detection Causes: 1631, 1634, 1635, 1636, 1637.

115. GRO: D 2688, List of Disbursements, 1635.

116. GRO: GDR 174, Detection Causes: 1631, 1634, 1635, 1636, 1637.

117. Ibid.

118. Tyacke, *Anti-Calvinists,* pp. 181–223. In this discussion, Laud is assumed to be responsible for the views expressed and the actions taken during the visitation conducted in his name. I concede that the orders may have come from Charles. I also concede that the commissioners' actions may not reflect the personal views of either Charles or Laud. Still, the visitation was conducted in the archbishop of Canterbury's name, and subtle distinctions of this kind did not affect reactions to the visitation in the vale. Sharpe, *Personal Rule,* pp. 333–345.

119. Sharpe views Laud's religion as a balance between devotional action and the word. Laud's visitation commissioners, however, paid little attention to sermons and focused exclusively on the position of the communion table, the physical condition of churches, and church property. Sharpe, *Personal Rule,* p. 328.

120. GRO: GDR 174, Detection Causes: 1631, 1634, 1635, 1636, 1637; and GDR 189, Visitation by Archbishop Laud's Commissioners, 1635. Sharpe maintains that this rhetoric of pollution addressed a serious problem, but I have found no further references to dogs in over a century of ecclesiastical records. Sharpe, *Personal Rule,* pp. 340–341.

121. GRO: GDR 174, Detection Causes: 1631, 1634, 1635, 1636, 1637.

122. See GRO: P 329 CW 2/1, pp. 189, 203, 219, 233, 239 for the agricultural uses of the churchyard in Tewkesbury.
123. Davies, *Caroline Captivity of the Church,* p. 223. Davies cites GRO: P 329 CW 2/1, p. 248, the accounts of the churchwardens of Tewkesbury for 1627. I have not checked references to other accounts in the diocese.
124. The expenses of the churchwardens of Tewkesbury and the local rates levied in the 1630s are contained in GRO: P 329 CW 2/1, pp. 267, 270, 274, 277, 280, 281, 283, 284, 287, 291.
125. GRO: P 329 CW 2/1, p. 286.
126. GRO: GDR 191, Detection Causes: October 1635–March 1637; and GDR 195, Detection Causes: January–March 1637.
127. GRO: P 329 CW 2/1, pp. 278–279, 281, 283, 285, 289.
128. This distrust may have been compounded in 1635 by the conviction of six apparitors, including the apparitor of Winchcombe deanery, for the misappropriation of funds collected on briefs for victims of a fire in Shropshire. GRO: GDR 191, Detection Causes: October 1635–March 1637.
129. Presentments for the late 1630s are in GRO: GDR 174, Detection Causes: 1631, 1634, 1635, 1636, 1637; and GDR 202, Detection Causes: February 1638–April 1641. See *CSPD, Charles I* (London, 1869), v. 12 (1637–1638): 156 for the dearth of 1637–1638.
130. GRO: P 329 CW 2/1, pp. 288, 292; GDR 174, Detection Causes: 1631, 1634, 1635, 1636, 1637. Tewkesbury did not have a formal vestry before 1660. The rather shadowy parish assembly consisted of the bailiffs and justices of the corporation "and diverse others of the parish." See GRO: P 329 CW 2/1, pp. 283, 285, 288, 292.
131. Lake, "Puritanism, Arminianism, and a Shropshire Axe–Murder," 57–59.
132. GRO: GDR 174, Detection Causes: 1631, 1634, 1635, 1636, 1637.
133. GRO: GDR 195, Detection Causes: January–March 1637.
134. Ibid.
135. *CSPD, Charles I,* v. 14 (1639): 159, 198–199, 266–267.
136. John Allibond, rector of Broadwell, to Peter Heylyn, 24-3-1640, in *CSPD, Charles I,* v. 15 (1639–1640): 582.
137. Ibid.
138. GRO: D 2688, Giles Geast Charity Account Book, f. 79v.
139. Ibid.
140. GRO: TBR A 1/1, f. 82.
141. James Howell, *Familiar Letters,* 2: 72–73.
142. A Puritan perspective on omens and marvels, developed in the literary remains of William Whiteway and Denis Bond of Dorchester, is discussed in Underdown, *Fire From Heaven,* pp. 53–54.

143. Sir Robert Tracy also attempted unsuccessfully to revive his family's parliamentary interest in Tewkesbury in the months before this election. KRO: Sackville Mss: Mss Cranfield: William Hill to Middlesex, 15-12-1639.

144. KRO: Sackville Mss: Mss Cranfield: Roger Plevy and Thomas Hale, Bailiffs of Tewkesbury, to Middlesex, 12-10-1640.

145. The corporation chose traditional candidates in this election. Alford had married Lady Mary Cooper, daughter of Baptist Hickes, Viscount Campden, in 1632, and had thus acquired property and political capital in Tewkesbury. Hill mentioned Alford's candidacy in December 1639. Anthony Ashley Cooper benefited from the Hickes interest and from marriage into Lord Thomas Coventry's family. See Mary Frear Keeler, *The Long Parliament, 1640–1641* (Philadelphia: American Philosophical Society, 1954), pp. 47–48, 82–83, 146; GCL: Survey of Abbey Lands in Tewkesbury, 1632; and KRO: Sackville Mss: Mss Cranfield: William Hill to Middlesex, 15-12-39.

146. GRO: D 2688, Giles Geast Charity Account Book, f. 85v.

147. Ibid.

148. John Craven of London was Lord Thomas Coventry's brother-in-law, and the Craven family owned several properties in Tewkesbury and Ashchurch. See *Journals of the House of Commons*, v. 2 (April 1640–March 1643): 23; Keeler, *Long Parliament*, pp. 47–48, 146; GRO: D 184 M 1, Survey of the Manor of Pamington, 1652; D 184 M 17, Survey of the Manor of Mythe Hooke, 1652.

149. Thomas Hale, a bailiff of the borough, received the blame for this third return, although the journal states "that he that returned the third indenture, it appears not, he committed a misdemeanor," and the Commons quickly rescinded its order of November 9 to prosecute Hale for delinquency. A sergeant at arms nevertheless escorted Hale to London and kept him in custody until December 3, 1640. Keeler, *Long Parliament*, p. 48; *Journals of the House of Commons*, 2: 23, 44.

150. The Commons did not enforce an order to exclude the members until the committee of elections had decided the case. Alford assumed his place for Arundel in Sussex. Stephens did not enter parliament until after the second Tewkesbury election. *Journals of the House of Commons*, 2: 23, 239; *Journals of the House of Commons*, v. 3 (March 1643–December 1644): 352; and Keeler, *Long Parliament*, pp. 48, 82, 141, 146, 350.

151. *Journals of the House of Commons*, 2: 313; and *Journals of the House of Commons*, 3: 378–379. The description of the returns is deceptive, because the bailiffs were election officers and perforce were present for both returns. Cooke and Alford were the common council's choice. Cooke and

Stephens were the choice of freeholders in the town. The bailiffs returned both decisions.

152. *Journals of the House of Commons*, 2: 22; and *Journals of the House of Commons*, 3: 352.

153. See the discussion of multiple returns in Mark Kishlansky, *Parliamentary Selection: Social and Political Choice in Early Modern England* (Cambridge: Cambridge University Press, 1986), pp. 117–120. Kishlansky's discussion stresses the pivotal importance of the Short Parliament elections in many constituencies.

154. The links between Sir Robert Cooke, Edward Stephens, and the Nonconformist interest are described in a letter from John Allibond, rector of Broadwell, to Peter Heylyn, 24-3-1640, in *CSPD, Charles I*, v. 15 (1639–1640): 580–583.

155. Edward Hyde, Earl of Clarendon, *The History of the Rebellion and Civil Wars in England*, ed. W. D. Macray, 6 vols. (Oxford: Clarendon Press, 1888), 1: 331, 330–333; and John Geary, *Judah's Joy at the Oath* (London, 1641), A2r-v.

156. Geary learned of the "parliamentary vow" from his friend Nathaniel Stephens, a sympathetic member of parliament for Gloucestershire, and dedicated the sermon to him. Geary, *Judah's Joy*, A2r-v.

157. Geary, *Judah's Joy*, Dr.

158. Geary, *Judah's Joy*, D3r-v; John Geary, *Vindiciae Voti* (London, 1641), ff. E2r-E3r. The second tract argued against Henry Burton's view of the Protestation as a justification for separation from the Church of England. Geary's sermon and reply to Burton were published together in 1641.

159. Geary, *Judah's Joy*, A2r-v.

160. GRO: TBR A 1/2, Borough Ordinances, 1639, no. 8.

161. This is almost certainly the county petition described in HMC, *5th Report, Part I* (London, 1876), p. 345. I have found no evidence in the northern vale of the earlier county petition for relief from "grievous impositions and taxes and . . . extreme and unlimited power of ecclesiastical government" printed as *Humble Petition of the Inhabitants of the County of Gloucester* (London, 1642), A2r.

162. Journal of Sir Simonds D'Ewes, 19-2-1642, in Willson H. Coates, Anne Steele Young, and Vernon F. Snow (eds.), *The Private Journals of the Long Parliament: 3 January to 5 March 1642* (New Haven: Yale University Press, 1982), p. 418.

163. GRO: GDR 174, Detection Causes: 1631, 1634, 1635, 1636, 1637.

164. GRO: D 2688, f. 85v; Allibond to Heylyn, 24-3-1640, in *CSPD, Charles I*, v. 15 (1639–1640): 580–583.

165. Allibond to Heylyn in *CSPD, Charles I*, v. 15 (1639–1640): 580–583;

Journals of the House of Commons, 2: 589; and Journal of Sir Simonds D'Ewes, 27-5-1642, in Vernon F. Snow and Anne Steele Young (eds.), *The Private Journals of the Long Parliament: 7 March to 1 June 1642* (New Haven: Yale University Press, 1987), pp. 377–378.

166. Foster, "Church Policies of the 1630s," 198–210.

167. As an assistant burgess in 1620, Plevy had recanted his heterodox views of the Sabbath. Plevy was a burgess in May 1639 when a council ordinance excluded *professed* Catholics and Nonconformists from the office. GRO: TBR A 1/2, Borough Ordinances, 1639, preamble; and D 2688, f. 84v.

6. To Unchurch a Church

1. In the most important local account of the war, John Corbet, a Puritan minister in Gloucester, argued it was just as important to deny the enemy quiet possession of the Vale of Gloucester as to control it. See John Corbet, *An Historical Relation of the Military Government of Gloucester* (London, 1645), pp. 5–10, 32–34, for evidence of the strategic importance of the northern vale.

2. 17 Car. I, c. 11, "An Act for repeal of a branch of a statute primo Elizabeth concerning commissioners for causes ecclesiastical," in Kenyon, *Stuart Constitution,* pp. 206–207; and Ingram, *Church Courts, Sex, and Marriage,* pp. 367–369.

3. The archdeacon held a visitation in the spring of 1642, but no presentments appear to have been made. GRO: GDR 207, Archdeacon of Gloucester's Visitation, 1642.

4. Kenyon, *Stuart Constitution,* pp. 175–183.

5. Wrightson, *English Society,* pp. 17–118.

6. Andrew Marvell, "An Horatian Ode upon Cromwell's Return from Ireland" and "The First Anniversary of the Government Under His Highness the Lord Protector," in *Complete Poetry* (London: Dent, 1984), pp. 56, 93–94.

7. Marvell, "The First Anniversary of the Government Under His Highness the Lord Protector," in *Complete Poetry,* pp. 95, 101.

8. Marvell, "A Poem upon the Death of His Late Highness the Lord Protector," in *Complete Poetry,* p. 105.

9. Marvell, "The First Anniversary of the Government Under His Highness the Lord Protector," in *Complete Poetry,* pp. 96, 99–100; John Morrill, "Cromwell and His Contemporaries," in John Morrill (ed.), *Oliver Cromwell and the English Revolution* (London: Longman, 1990), pp. 262, 271.

10. J. C. Davis, "Cromwell's Religion," in Morrill, *Oliver Cromwell,* p. 182.

11. Claire Cross, "The Church in England, 1646–1660," in G. E. Aylmer

(ed.), *The Interregnum: The Quest for Settlement, 1646–1660* (London: Macmillan, 1972), pp. 104–110.

12. Davis, "Cromwell's Religion," and Anthony Fletcher, "Oliver Cromwell and the Godly Nation," in Morrill, *Oliver Cromwell,* pp. 198–208, 219–225.

13. Davis, "Cromwell's Religion," 202.

14. Fletcher, "Oliver Cromwell and the Godly Nation," 231.

15. Davis, "Cromwell's Religion," 191–192; Blair Worden, "Toleration and the Cromwellian Protectorate," in W. J. Shiels (ed.), *Persecution and Toleration* (Oxford: Oxford University Press, 1984), pp. 201, 205–210, 213–215, 225–228.

16. Roy Sherwood, *The Court of Oliver Cromwell* (London: Croom Helm, 1977), pp. 158–167.

17. Sherwood, *Court of Oliver Cromwell,* pp. 165–166; and Ogg, *England in the Reign of Charles II,* pp. 1–2.

18. Ronald Hutton, *The Restoration: A Political and Religious History of England and Wales, 1658–1667* (Oxford: Clarendon Press, 1985), pp. 4, 21–123. Hutton's fine discussion of factional politics in the late 1650s is marred by his argument that local life in the 1650s "carried on much as before the wars and revolution." This statement disregards the connections between political and religious order that Hutton emphasizes in other contexts.

19. John Morrill, *The Revolt of the Provinces: Conservatives and Radicals in the English Civil War, 1630–1650* (London: Longman, 1976, 1980), p. 46; and Corbet, *Historical Relation,* pp. 23–24.

20. *True News Out of Herefordshire* (London, 1642). The battle is supposed to have occurred on November 16, 1642.

21. *True News Out of Herefordshire,* pp. 3–6. The royalists allegedly lost 2,500 slain and 1,200 prisoners in this battle.

22. GRO: TBR A 1/1, ff. 99v–100r.

23. PRO: SP 19/116, ff. 227–231.

24. Corbet, *Historical Relation,* p. 12.

25. Clarendon, *History of the Rebellion,* 2: 336–337.

26. PRO: SP 19/116, f. 228v.

27. PRO: SP 19/116, f. 228r-v.

28. PRO: SP 19/116, f. 228v.

29. GRO: TBR A 1/1, ff. 98r-v.

30. Clarendon, *History of the Rebellion,* 2: 440.

31. Clarendon, *History of the Rebellion,* 2: 441.

32. Clarendon, *History of the Rebellion,* 2: 445.

33. Clarendon, *History of the Rebellion,* 2: 440–448, 501.

34. Corbet, *Historical Relation*, pp. 21–22.

35. PRO: SP 19/116, f. 229r.

36. GRO: D 2688, f. 87v. Clarendon reports of the assault on Cirencester "not so few as two hundred killed upon the place and above one thousand taken prisoners." See Clarendon, *History of the Rebellion*, 2: 447; and Corbet, *Historical Relation*, p. 21.

37. PRO: SP 19/116, ff. 229r, 245r; Corbet, *Historical Relation*, pp. 23–24.

38. Corbet, *Historical Relation*, p. 23.

39. PRO: SP 19/116, f. 229r.

40. Corbet, *Historical Relation*, pp. 23, 58.

41. PRO: SP 19/116, f. 229v; Corbet, *Historical Relation*, pp. 23–24.

42. PRO: SP 19/116, ff. 229r-v.

43. GRO: D 2688, f. 89v; Corbet, *Historical Relation*, p. 30.

44. Corbet, *Historical Relation*, p. 24.

45. GRO: TBR A 1/1, p. 152; and TBR A 1/2, p. 44.

46. PRO: SP 19/116, f. 229v.

47. *CCC* (London, 1889), pp. 85–86.

48. PRO: SP 19/116, ff. 228r, 229v, 236.

49. PRO: SP 19/116, f. 229v; and GRO: D 2688, f. 87v.

50. PRO: SP 19/116, ff. 229v-230r.

51. GRO: TBR A 1/1, pp. 119–120; and Elrington, *VCH Gloucester*, 8: 148.

52. PRO: SP 19/116, f. 245r; and GRO: D 2688, f. 89v.

53. GRO: TBR A 1/1, pp. 119–120.

54. GRO: TBR A 1/2, pp. 42–43.

55. GRO: D 2688, f. 87v.

56. GRO: TBR A 1/2, Borough Ordinances, c. 1608, no. 10. See the examples of this presentation of accounts in GRO: P 329 CW 2/1, pp. 298, 307, 311, 314.

57. GRO: P 329 CW 2/1, p. 317.

58. GRO: P 343 VE 2/1, ff. 8–9.

59. GRO: P 343 VE 2/1, ff. 7v, 8v; Elrington, "Survey of Church Livings," 87–88.

60. See the accounts of John Weaver of Boddington printed in Bennett, *Tewkesbury Yearly Register*, 2: 466.

61. GRO: P 343 VE 2/1, ff. 8v, 12v. An order to make churchwardens collect the money for maimed soldiers and the old clothes, including "any linen surplices left in the parishes," for poor soldiers is recorded in *Journals of the House of Commons*, 4: 345.

62. Charles Carlton, *Going to the Wars: The Experience of the British Civil Wars, 1638–1651* (London: Routledge, 1992), pp. 150–154.

63. Ann Hughes, *Politics, Society, and Civil War in Warwickshire, 1620–1660* (Cambridge: Cambridge University Press, 1987), pp. 169–170.

64. PRO: SP 19/116, ff. 227v, 236r-v; and GRO: D 2688, f. 87v.

65. PRO: SP 19/116, ff. 227v, 230r, 236r.

66. GRO: D 2688, f. 89v; and Corbet, *Historical Relation*, p. 64.

67. Corbet, *Historical Relation*, p. 65.

68. GRO: TBR A 1/1, pp. 119–120, 122; and Corbet, *Historical Relation*, pp. 63–64.

69. GRO: TBR A 1/1, p. 122.

70. See the series of ordinances in 1644 and 1645 "for the raising and maintaining of horse and foot for the garrison of Gloucester and for the counties of Gloucester, Hereford, Monmouth, Glamorgan, Brecknocke, and Radnor" in TT E 47 (12), E 274 (1), E 286 (7).

71. GRO: TBR A 1/1, p. 142.

72. GRO: TBR A 1/1, pp. 130, 132–133, 136–138, 142–143.

73. GRO: TBR A 1/1, pp. 133–134, 136–137.

74. GRO: D 2688, f. 89v.

75. Carlton, *Going to the Wars*, pp. 152–153.

76. Bennett, *Tewkesbury Yearly Register*, 2: 466.

77. GRO: TBR A 1/1, p. 116. The bailiffs also recorded a loan of "about £100" to the soldiers "duly repaid within a month or six weeks after."

78. GRO: TBR A 1/1, p. 116.

79. PRO: SP 19/116, f. 224v.

80. PRO: SP 19/116, ff. 223v-224r.

81. Corbet, *Historical Relation*, pp. 32–33, 93–95.

82. GRO: D 2688, f. 89v.

83. GRO: TBR A 1/1, p. 125.

84. GRO: TBR A 1/1, pp. 127–129.

85. GRO: TBR A 1/1, pp. 140–141. Only twenty-five names were included in this list, and the caption indicates that the schedule was part of a scheme to muster a larger labor force composed of residents from the three main streets.

86. PRO: SP 19/116, f. 293r.

87. Sir William Waller's maneuvers in the vicinity of Tewkesbury in March and early April 1643 are reported in *Mercurius Aulicus* (13), March 26–April 2, 1643, p. 162; *Mercurius Aulicus* (14), April 2–9, 1643, p. 169; *Mercurius Aulicus* (15), April 9–16, 1643, pp. 186–187; *Perfect Diurnal of the Passages in Parliament* (44), April 10–17, 1643, f. 4v; *The Victorious and Fortunate Proceedings of Sir William Waller* (London, 1643), TT E 97 (2); and Corbet, *Historical Relation*, pp. 30–33.

88. Corbet, *Historical Relation*, pp. 33–34.

89. PRO: SP 19/116, ff. 225v-226r.

90. Corbet, *Historical Relation*, pp. 33–34; and *Mercurius Aulicus* (15), April 9–16, 1643, pp. 188–189.

91. Corbet, *Historical Relation*, pp. 33–34; *Mercurius Aulicus* (15), April 9–16, 1643, pp. 188–189; and *Mercurius Aulicus* (16), April 16–23, 1643, p. 201. Cooke was a member of parliament for the town.

92. GRO: D 2688, f. 89v.

93. Henry Foster, *A True and Exact Relation* (London, 1643), ff. Br-v. The Earl of Essex's presence in Tewkesbury and activities in the northern vale in September 1643 are reported in GRO: D 2688, f. 88v; *A True Relation of the Late Expedition* (London, 1643), ff. B2r-v; and *Perfect Diurnal* (9), September 11–18, 1643, ff. 3v-4v.

94. Corbet, *Historical Relation*, p. 67.

95. PRO: SP 19/116, f. 291r.

96. Canner added that "he never killed any man in his life, either when he was a soldier or otherwise, in heat of blood or cold blood." PRO: SP 19/116, f. 287r.

97. Corbet, *Historical Relation*, pp. 101–104.

98. Corbet, *Historical Relation*, p. 59.

99. Corbet, *Historical Relation*, pp. 58–59; and *Perfect Diurnal* (14), October 16–23, 1643, p. 107.

100. Corbet, *Historical Relation*, p. 59.

101. GRO: D 2688, f. 89v; Corbet, *Historical Relation*, p. 64.

102. Corbet, *Historical Relation*, pp. 93–95; *A Diary or Exact Journal of Proceedings in Both Houses of Parliament* (4), June 6–13, 1644, pp. 30–31; *Perfect Occurrences of Parliament* (25), June 7–14, 1644, f. 1r.

103. This phrase is borrowed from Tuan, *Landscapes of Fear*, pp. 3–10.

104. PRO: SP 19/116, ff. 237v, 246r-v, 255–256, 263.

105. Bennett, *Tewkesbury Yearly Register*, 2: 466.

106. [Bruno Ryves], *Mercurius Rusticus: The Country's Complaint* (1647), pp. 159–166.

107. *Perfect Diurnal* (30), February 12–19, 1644, pp. 233–234; and Corbet, *Historical Relation*, p. 105.

108. Bennett, *Tewkesbury Yearly Register*, 2: 466–467; and Corbet, *Historical Relation*, p. 124.

109. There are many allusions to Irish and Welsh soldiers, both in stereotype and local experience, in GRO: D 2688, ff. 86v, 89v; Corbet, *Historical Relation*, pp. 58–59, 64–65; *Perfect Diurnal* (17), November 6–13, 1643, p. 135; *Perfect Diurnal* (18), November 13–20, 1643, p. 139; and *True News Out of Herefordshire*, pp. 3–6.

110. GRO: TBR A 1/1, p. 117.

111. KRO: Sackville Mss: Mss Cranfield, William Underhill to Middlesex, 8-5-1643.

112. KRO: Sackville Mss: Mss Cranfield, William Underhill to Middlesex, 26-9-1643. Essex demanded the twentieth part of estates in Tewkesbury for Gloucester garrison and evidently extended this rate to the countryside around the town. See Foster, *True and Exact Relation*, f. Br.

113. KRO: Sackville Mss: Mss Cranfield, William Underhill to Middlesex, 8-7-1634, 26-9-1643.

114. PRO: SP 19/116, f. 225r.

115. GRO: D 2688, f. 93v.

116. B. D. Henning (ed.), *The House of Commons: 1660–1690* (London: Secker and Warburg, 1983), 3: 480–482; and David Underdown, *Pride's Purge: Politics in the Puritan Revolution* (Oxford: Oxford University Press, 1971), pp. 29, 138, 144, 147, 159, 194–195, 197.

117. John Stephens was elected in 1645 to replace Sir Robert Cooke. Cooke died in 1643, but the royalist garrison in Tewkesbury in 1644 and months of uncertain Parliamentarian control of the town in 1645 presumably delayed the new election. See *Journals of the House of Commons*, 4: 259; PRO: SP 16/116, ff. 228r, 231r; Keeler, *Long Parliament*, p. 141; Henning, *House of Commons*, 3: 481; and Underdown, *Pride's Purge*, pp. 105, 138, 291.

118. Underdown, *Pride's Purge*, pp. 264–265. An entry in the Tewkesbury council register repeats a parliamentary act of September 10, 1649, "concerning oaths to mayors and other officers," and adds the engagement to new oaths for the bailiffs, justices of the peace, and freemen. GRO: TBR A 1/1, pp. 150–151, 153.

119. *Journals of the House of Commons*, v. 4 (December 1644–December 1646): 629; GRO: TBR A 1/1, p. 116.

120. There was a sharp fight for the Severn bridge at Upton. The local skirmishes prior to the Battle of Worcester are reported in *Several Proceedings in Parliament* (100), August 21–28, 1651, pp. 1543–1544; *Perfect Diurnal* (90), August 25–September 1, 1651, pp. 1250–1252; *The Modern Intelligencer* (5), August 26–September 3, 1651, p. 32; and *Several Proceedings in Parliament* (100), August 28–September 4, 1651, pp. 1556–1559.

121. HMC, *12th Report, Appendix, Part IX: Beaufort, Donoughmore Mss* (London, 1891), p. 518. A detachment of royalist soldiers visited the town before Cromwell's arrival and may have demanded supplies. *Perfect Passages from the Parliaments* (55), August 22–29, 1651, p. 362.

122. GRO: P 329 CW 2/1, pp. 332, 335.

123. GRO: TBR A 1/1, p. 142.

124. Christopher Hill, *The Century of Revolution, 1603–1714,* 2nd ed. (New York: Norton, 1980), pp. 97–98; and Kenyon, *Stuart Constitution,* pp. 322–324. See GRO: D 2688, ff. 98v, 105v, 106v, for local awareness of the army's political influence.

125. GRO: TBR A 1/1, p. 148.

126. GRO: TBR A 1/1, p. 117.

127. GRO: TBR A 1/1, p. 116.

128. GRO: TBR A 1/1, p. 117.

129. GRO: TBR A 1/1, p. 147.

130. GRO: TBR A 1/1, pp. 144, 145, 147, 162.

131. GRO: TBR A 1/1, p. 145.

132. GRO: TBR A 1/1, p. 162.

133. Hill, *World Turned Upside Down;* J. F. McGregor and B. Reay (eds.), *Radical Religion in the English Revolution* (Oxford: Oxford University Press, 1984); and G. E. Aylmer, "Collective Mentalities in Mid Seventeenth-Century England: III. Varieties of Radicalism," *Transactions of the Royal Historical Society,* 5th Series, 58 (1988): 1–25, provide fine introductions to a vast literature.

134. Edward Stephens, member of parliament for Tewkesbury, served on this committee. See *Ordinance of the Lords and Commons for the Garrison of Gloucester* (London, 1644), TT E 47 (12), pp. 3–4.

135. *CCC,* pp. 85–86, 1949.

136. The evidence against Dowdeswell came from such "witnesses" as Joseph Lewis of Tewkesbury, a button maker, a man whom Dowdeswell, as an attorney, had prosecuted in the Tewkesbury court of record. According to further testimony in the inquiry, Lewis vowed revenge against Dowdeswell. These kinds of personal animosities make it difficult to evaluate the evidence of delinquency. PRO: SP 19/116, ff. 216r, 227r-231r, 295r. Dowdeswell did not appear in the county list of 1648.

137. *CCC,* p. 87; GRO: D 2688, ff. 35v, 41v, 48v, 49v, 58v, 68v, 73v, 80v, 85v; and TBR A 1/2, pp. 43–44.

138. *CCC,* p. 86; PRO: SP 19/116, ff. 268r, 269r; and GRO: D 2688, f. 88v, for Theophilus Alye as bailiff in 1643.

139. *CCC,* p. 86; and Journal of Sir Simonds D'Ewes, 19-2-1642, in Coates, Young, and Snow, *Private Journals,* p. 418.

140. The county committee described Rowles as an attorney, an unusual occupation in the rural hamlet of Pamington. Rowles may have worked in the Tewkesbury court of record. *CCC,* p. 85; *CCAM* (London, 1888), p. 859; GRO: W 1614/114; and W 1632/46. Roberts did not appear in the county list of 1648.

141. *CCC*, pp. 1822–1823; GRO: TBR A 1/1, p. 159. Gwynnett did not appear in the county list of 1648.

142. *CCC*, p. 85; *CCAM*, p. 1271. In 1650, the corporation purchased Cowles's fee farm in the parish, deducted from his sequestered property and valued at £44 11s 5d ob per year, to create a permanent fund "for the benefit of the almsmen and other poor of this town." The purchase is recorded in GRO: D 2688, f. 95v.

143. As a result of his marriage to Lady Mary Cooper in 1632, Alford controlled the Hickes properties in Tewkesbury described in GCL: Survey of Abbey Lands in Tewkesbury, 1632; and *CCC*, p. 85.

144. PRO: SP 19/116, ff. 216r, 237v, 271r.

145. *CCC*, p. 87.

146. GRO: TBR A 1/1, p. 145; and *CCC*, p. 87.

147. *CCC*, p. 87; and GRO: TBR A 1/1, pp. 72–73.

148. *CCC*, p. 87; and *CCAM*, p. 859.

149. Corbet, *Historical Relation*, p. 24.

150. GRO: TBR A 1/2, pp. 43–44; TBR A 1/1, p. 144; Bennett, *Tewkesbury Yearly Register*, 2: 325–326; and Beaver, "Conscience and Context," 300–304.

151. GRO: TBR A 1/2, p. 44.

152. GRO: TBR A 1/2, p. 44; and TBR A 1/1, p. 144.

153. GRO: TBR A 1/1, p. 152.

154. GRO: TBR A 1/1, p. 152; and GRO: GDR 174, Detection Causes: 1631, 1634, 1635, 1636, 1637.

155. GRO: TBR A 1/1, p. 152; and D 1340 B2/M1, pp. 15, 21.

156. GRO: TBR A 1/1, p. 152; and D 4944 2/1, pp. 21–22.

157. GRO: TBR A 1/1, p. 152; and Bodl: Rawlinson Ms A 39, f. 528. Few names are more common in the northern vale than Jeynes. A family of this name owned a substantial landed estate in Southwick, known as Jeynes Farm, and the royalist Thomas Jeynes, a gentleman, probably came from this family. Another branch of Jeyneses practiced trades in Tewkesbury, and the Independent Thomas Jeynes may have been the son of a wealthy joiner of the same name, a friend of the joiner Francis Godwin, prosecuted in 1635 for sitting at divine service. GRO: TBR A 1/1, pp. 70, 77; W 1598/163; W 1633/91; and GDR 174, Detection Causes, 1631, 1634, 1635, 1636, 1637.

158. GRO: TBR A 1/2, p. 44, for a list of burgesses in 1647. The faction's petition to parliament in 1649 came from "Christopher Atkinson, other well affected of the common council, assistants, and other inhabitants." PRO: SP 24/5, f. 115r.

159. Matthews, *Calamy Revised,* pp. 134, 555.
160. GRO: TBR A 1/1, p. 152; TBR A 14/2; and D 2688, f. 85v.
161. Williams, *Parliamentary History of Gloucester,* pp. 54–57.
162. GRO: TBR A 1/1, p. 152; and W 1670/209.
163. GRO: W 1684/155.
164. Bulstrode married Edward Hatch's daughter. The Hatch family ranked among the wealthiest families in the town in the subsidy lists of the 1620s. Much of the estate lay east of the town in Walton Cardiff. Edward Hatch and a group of eight justices, bailiffs, and common councilors of Tewkesbury petitioned John Thurloe to accept a parliamentary seat from the town in 1658. GRO: D 2688, f. 94v; TBR A 1/1, pp. 11, 14, 20, 24, 68; and Thomas Birch (ed.), *Collection of the State Papers of John Thurloe,* 7 vols. (London, 1742), 7: 572.
165. GRO: D 2688, f. 94v.
166. William Wright allegedly sued Bach over quarters assigned by the bailiffs. See GRO: D 2688, f. 95v, for Bach as the junior bailiff in 1650; and PRO: SP 24/7, ff. 50r, 107v, 120v, 125.
167. PRO: PROB 4/5294; GRO: W 1684/155; and I 1684/352. William Jeffries of Twyning possessed an estate in livestock and provisions valued at £212 9s 4d in 1663. GRO: I 1663/20.
168. GRO: GDR 174, Detection Causes: 1631, 1634, 1635, 1636, 1637.
169. The conflict may have started as early as February 1648, when William Hill, town clerk, Edward Jennings, bailiff, and Richard Dowdeswell were presented as delinquents to the Committee for Advance of Money. *CCAM,* pp. 857, 859.
170. This was William Hill's opinion, expressed in GRO: D 2688, f. 94v.
171. GRO: D 2688, f. 94v; *CCAM,* p. 1170. Edward Wilson and William Wilson had been questioned for delinquency and discharged in 1645. *CCAM,* p. 43.
172. GRO: TBR A 1/1, p. 152.
173. The accused councilors, in turn, presented Christopher Atkinson, John Bach, and William Crofte as delinquents to the Committee for Advance of Money. The committee laconically recorded "no proceedings" in the entire convoluted affair. *CCAM,* p. 1170.
174. GRO: TBR A 1/1, p. 153.
175. GRO: TBR A 1/1, pp. 152–153.
176. The 18 councilors were John Man, William Hill, William Wilson, Thomas Hale, Edward Jennings, William Whitledge, Thomas Hale, the elder, Richard Mince, John Millington, John Slicer (for Richard Berrow), John Carver, Thomas Clarke, Phillip Hilly, Christopher Smith, Edward Wilson,

Edward Phelps, Richard Berrow (for John Slicer), and Thomas Skey (for Richard Berrow). GRO: TBR A 1/1, p. 150; and TBR A 1/2, p. 43.

177. *CCAM,* p. 1170; and GRO: TBR A 1/1, p. 153.

178. GRO: TBR A 1/1, pp. 152–153.

179. GRO: TBR A 1/1, pp. 154–155.

180. Clement Barksdale, *A True Account of a Dispute at Winchcomb Parish Church* (London, 1653); and GRO: TBR A 1/1, p. 147.

181. GRO: TBR A 1/1, pp. 158–159. The corporation failed to obtain a new charter under the Protectorate. GRO: D 2688, f. 103v; *Mercurius Politicus* (437), October 7–14, 1658, p. 912; and *CSPD, Commonwealth* (London, 1885), v. 12 (1658–1659): 99, 152, 274.

182. Clarendon, *History of the Rebellion,* 5: 374–379; GRO: TBR A 1/1, p. 150; TBR A 1/2, pp. 43, 46; TBR A 1/3, p. 6; and *State Papers of John Thurloe,* 4: 396. Nathaniel Hill assumed the office of town clerk in place of his father in October 1650.

183. GRO: TBR A 14/2.

184. Matthews, *Calamy Revised,* p. 275; and Baxter, *Autobiography of Richard Baxter,* p. 84.

185. GRO: TBR A 1/1, pp. 144, 162; PRO: SP 25/77, p. 499; SP 25/78, pp. 429, 803, 858–859; and Elrington, *VCH Gloucester,* 8: 155.

186. Cooper eventually sat for Wiltshire rather than Tewkesbury in this parliament. Francis St. John, eldest son of Oliver St. John, was elected in Cooper's place but never sat for the town before parliament's dissolution. GRO: D 2688, f. 99v; and Williams, *Parliamentary History of Gloucester,* p. 238.

187. *CSPD, Commonwealth,* v. 12 (1658–1659): 117. Thomas Holtham had been presented alongside Humphrey Fox in 1635 for refusal to hear divine service and failure to receive communion in the parish church. See GRO: GDR 174, Detection Causes, 1631, 1634, 1635, 1636, 1637. Thomas Jeynes supported Wells in a scandal over contraband books reported in *Mercurius Politicus* (288), December 13–20, 1655, p. 5823.

188. This incident was described in *Mercurius Politicus* (288), December 13–20, 1655, pp. 5821–5823; and *The Publick Intelligencer* (12), December 17–24, 1655, pp. 189–190.

189. *Mercurius Politicus* (288), pp. 5821–5822.

190. *Mercurius Politicus* (288), p. 5822.

191. Richard Neast was William Neast's brother. *Mercurius Politicus* (288), p. 5823; Fenwick and Metcalfe, *Visitation of the County of Gloucester,* p. 125.

192. *Mercurius Politicus* (288), p. 5822; *Publick Intelligencer* (12), p. 189.

193. *Mercurius Politicus* (288), p. 5823.
194. *Publick Intelligencer* (12), p. 189.
195. Ibid.
196. GRO: TBR A 1/2, p. 43; D 2688, f. 95v.
197. GRO: P 329 CW 2/1, p. 303.
198. GRO: D 2688, f. 95v.
199. Clement Barksdale, *The Winchcomb Papers Revived* (London, 1675), p. 6.
200. GRO: D 2688, f. 95v.
201. Matthews, *Calamy Revised*, p. 249; Bodl: Rawlinson Ms A 39, f. 528; GRO: GDR 210, Detection Causes: October 1662–November 1663; P 329 CW 2/1, pp. 353, 354, 359, 379; D 4944 2/1, Tewkesbury Baptist Church Book, p. 10.
202. GRO: TBR A 1/2, p. 46.
203. Poverty in Tewkesbury increased in the 1640s, and the economy of the northern vale recovered only slowly from the war. In 1648 a disastrous harvest produced high wheat prices of 10s the bushel. The price of rye climbed to 8s and malt to 6s the bushel, despite imports of "outlandish corn" from Bristol. Many poor families moved into Tewkesbury from its rural neighborhood in the late 1640s. An excellent harvest in 1654 finally brought relief, when the price of wheat dropped to 16d or 17d the bushel, and bushels of barley sold for 13d and 22d. In October Robert Jennings, a justice of the peace for the borough, dramatically carried "a handful of good wheat" into a session of the borough court to announce the new low prices. GRO: D 2688, ff. 88v, 89v, 93v, 99v; TBR A 1/1, p. 159; and *Several Proceedings in Parliament*, October 19–26, 1654, p. 4196.
204. GRO: TBR A 1/2, p. 48.
205. GRO: P 329 CW 2/1, pp. 310, 318; and Ronald Hutton, *The Rise and Fall of Merry England: The Ritual Year* (Oxford: Oxford University Press, 1994), p. 208.
206. GRO: P 329 CW 2/1, p. 367.
207. GRO: P 329 CW 2/1, p. 324.
208. GRO: P 329 CW 2/1, pp. 324, 327, 330, 331, 333, 337, 339, 343, 346, 352.
209. GRO: P 329 IN 1/3, *passim*; and Christopher Durston, *The Family in the English Revolution* (Oxford: Blackwell, 1989), pp. 66–86.
210. This argument for a relationship between civil intervention in the marriage process and the rise of secular political sovereignty is made in Walzer, *Revolution of the Saints*, p. 188.
211. Barksdale, *Winchcomb Papers Revived*, p. 6.
212. Clement Barksdale printed the substance of this debate in *A True Account of a Dispute at Winchcomb Parish Church* (London, 1653) and reprinted

the account in *The Winchcomb Papers Reviewed* (London, 1657) and *The Winchcomb Papers Revived* (London, 1675).

213. Barksdale, *Winchcomb Papers Revived*, p. 4; and Barksdale, *Winchcomb Papers Reviewed*, pp. 1–15.

214. GRO: TBR A 1/1, p. 160; Matthews, *Calamy Revised*, pp. 256, 490–491, 519; and A. G. Matthews (ed.), *Walker Revised* (Oxford: Clarendon Press, 1948), pp. 173, 191–192, 285.

215. Barksdale, *Winchcomb Papers Revived*, pp. 6–7.

216. Barksdale, *Winchcomb Papers Revived*, p. 50.

217. Barksdale, *Winchcomb Papers Revived*, pp. 43–44.

218. Barksdale, *Winchcomb Papers Revived*, p. 49.

219. GRO: P 329 CW 2/1, p. 339.

220. Cultural change is a classic problem of anthropological inquiry. Despite different field areas and methods, the following studies provide an introduction to the analysis of culture over time. Clifford Geertz, *The Social History of an Indonesian Town* (Westport: Greenwood Press, 1965), pp. 119–152; F. G. Bailey (ed.), *Debate and Compromise: The Politics of Innovation* (Totowa, New Jersey: Rowman and Littlefield, 1973), pp. 6–8; Sidney W. Mintz, *Caribbean Transformations* (Baltimore: Johns Hopkins University Press, 1974), pp. 246–247; and Marshall Sahlins, *Historical Metaphors and Mythical Realities: Structure in the Early History of the Sandwich Islands Kingdom* (Ann Arbor: University of Michigan Press, 1981), pp. 3–8.

221. GRO: D 1340 B2/M1, Stoke Orchard Monthly Meeting, pp. 15, 21; and D 4944 2/1, Tewkesbury Baptist Church Book, pp. 21–22. On the significance of the tithe controversy in the differentiation of Baptists from the Church of England, see GRO: D 4944 2/1, Tewkesbury Baptist Church Book, pp. 6, 8.

222. GRO: TBR A 1/1, pp. 144–145, 147, 161–162.

223. The Baptists in the Tewkesbury neighborhood participated in the Warwick Baptist association discussed in Hughes, *Politics, Society, and Civil War,* pp. 317–318. See GRO: D 4944 2/1, Tewkesbury Baptist Church Book, p. 1.

224. GRO: D 4944 2/1, Tewkesbury Baptist Church Book, p. 6.

225. Dick Hebdige, *Subculture: The Meaning of Style* (London: Methuen, 1979), pp. 1–19.

226. On the Baptist movement in a broader Christian context, see Weber, *Protestant Ethic*, pp. 144, 153, 254, 264; Weber, "Protestant Sects," 313–314, 317, 452–453; and Troeltsch, *Social Teaching of the Christian Churches*, 1: 328–349, 2: 691–699, 706–709. On the issues of the 1640s and 1650s, see J. F. McGregor, "The Baptists: Fount of All Heresy," in J. F.

McGregor and B. Reay (eds.), *Radical Religion in the English Revolution* (Oxford: Oxford University Press, 1984), pp. 23–63.

227. GRO: D 4944 2/1, Tewkesbury Baptist Church Book, pp. 4–5, 8, 32.

228. GRO: D 4944 2/1, pp. 5–6, 8, 12–13.

229. GRO: D 4944 2/1, p. 23.

230. GRO: D 4944 2/1, pp. 4, 9–10.

231. The complex relationship between Baptists and the ecstatic and millenarian movements of the 1640s and 1650s is discussed in Troeltsch, *Social Teaching of the Christian Churches*, 2: 706–714; and McGregor, "Baptists," 23–63.

232. GRO: D 4944 2/1, pp. 15, 17. The scriptural reference in the Baptist church book is from 1 Corinthians, 14.3.

233. Bernard S. Capp, *The Fifth Monarchy Men: A Study in Seventeenth-Century English Millenarianism* (Totowa, New Jersey: Rowman and Littlefield, 1972), pp. 172–194; and GRO: D 4944 2/1, p. 29.

234. GRO: D 4944 2/1, p. 30.

235. GRO: D 4944 2/1, pp. 3–4, 7, 17.

236. GRO: D 4944 2/1, pp. 28–29, 32–34, 36.

237. GRO: D 4944 2/1, pp. 11, 15, 35, 37.

238. GRO: D 4944 2/1, pp. 15–17.

239. John Geary, *The Character of an Old English Puritan or Nonconformist* (London, 1646), p. 5.

240. GRO: D 4944 2/1, pp. 4–5, 13, 30; and Fletcher, *County Community*, p. 64.

241. GRO: D 4944 2/1, pp. 5, 7.

242. GRO: D 4944 2/1, p. 14.

243. Ibid.

244. GRO: D 4944 2/1, pp. 20–21.

245. GRO: D 4944 2/1, p. 18.

246. See the coded membership list in GRO: D 4944 2/1, pp. 38–39.

247. Wrightson, *English Society*, pp. 214–220; and Laslett, *World We Have Lost*, p. 183.

248. Wrightson, *English Society*, p. 215.

249. Morrill, "The Nature of the English Revolution," in Morrill, *Nature of the English Revolution*, pp. 18, 25–26; and Hughes, *Politics, Society, and Civil War*, pp. 322–323. Ann Hughes warns that the changes of the 1640s and 1650s may have *created* Anglicanism in Warwickshire.

250. A general process of administrative centralization in the 1650s is discussed in Underdown, *Pride's Purge*, pp. 297, 301, 307. Ann Hughes discusses a similar process of political polarization in Hughes, *Politics, Society, and Civil War*, pp. 289–290.

251. The factional conflict in the corporation of Tewkesbury provides a con-

trast to the general indifference of many new local regimes to "religious novelties" described in Underdown, *Pride's Purge,* pp. 318, 321, 331.

252. Underdown, *Pride's Purge,* p. 330.

7. *Astraea Redux*

1. John Dryden, "*Astraea Redux*: A Poem on the Happy Restoration and Return of His Sacred Majesty Charles the Second" (1660), ll. 311–312, in Keith Walker (ed.), *John Dryden* (Oxford: Oxford University Press, 1987), p. 17.

2. Edward Hyde, Earl of Clarendon, *The Life of Edward Earl of Clarendon and Continuation of His History of the Grand Rebellion,* 3 vols. (Oxford: Clarendon Press, 1827), 1: 320–321, 327–328.

3. Ogg, *England in the Reign of Charles II,* pp. 1–34; Davies, *Restoration of Charles II,* pp. 355–363; and Kenyon, *Stuart England,* pp. 195–212.

4. Hutton, *Restoration,* pp. 1–119; John Miller, "The Later Stuart Monarchy," in J. R. Jones (ed.), *The Restored Monarchy, 1660–1688* (London: Macmillan, 1979), pp. 30–47.

5. Ronald Hutton, *Charles II* (Oxford: Clarendon Press, 1989), pp. 1–165; Paul Seaward, *The Cavalier Parliament and the Reconstruction of the Old Regime* (Cambridge: Cambridge University Press, 1989), pp. 1–8; and Paul Seaward, "Gilbert Sheldon, the London Vestries, and the Defense of the Church," Gary S. De Krey, "London Radicals and Revolutionary Politics, 1675–1683," and Jonathan Barry, "The Politics of Religion in Restoration Bristol," in Tim Harris, Paul Seaward, and Mark Goldie (eds.), *The Politics of Religion in Restoration England* (Oxford: Blackwell, 1990), pp. 49–73, 133–189.

6. Some recent examples of this anthropology include Cohen, *Belonging* and *Symbolising Boundaries;* and John Borneman, *Belonging in the Two Berlins* (Cambridge: Cambridge University Press, 1992).

7. The literature on corporations in the late seventeenth century is extensive. The best overview is Paul Halliday, *Dismembering the Body Politic: Partisan Politics in England's Towns, 1650–1730* (Cambridge: Cambridge University Press, 1998). See J. H. Sacret, "The Restoration Government and Municipal Corporations," *English Historical Review,* 45 (1930): 232–259; John Miller, "The Crown and the Borough Charters in the Reign of Charles II," *English Historical Review,* 50 (1985): 53–78; Judith J. Hurwich, "'A Fanatick Town': The Political Influence of Dissenters in Coventry, 1660–1720," *Midland History,* 4 (1977): 15–47; and four articles by Michael Mullett: "The Politics of Liverpool, 1660–1688," *Transactions of the Historical Society of Lancashire and Cheshire,* 124 (1972): 31–56; "'To

Dwell Together in Unity': The Search for Agreement in Preston Politics, 1660–1690," *Transactions of the Historical Society of Lancashire and Cheshire,* 125 (1974): 61–81; "'Deprived of Our Former Place': The Internal Politics of Bedford, 1660–1688," *Bedford Historical Record Society,* 59 (1980): 1–42; and "Conflict, Politics and Elections in Lancaster, 1660–1688," *Northern History,* 19 (1983): 61–86.

8. The excellent work on the restoration of the church has focused primarily on the reconstruction of administrative functions and has not identified the restoration of the parish as a problem distinct from the revival of the institutional structure of the church. See I. M. Green, *The Reestablishment of the Church of England* (Oxford: Oxford University Press, 1978), pp. 1–36, 117–142, 179–201.

9. GRO: D 2688, ff. 104v, 105v, 106v, 107v. This tentative attribution of authorship is based on a comparison of signatures in the register. Jeynes became a feoffee of the charity in 1677.

10. GRO: D 2688, f. 104v.

11. Andrew Marvell, "A Poem upon the Death of His late Highness the Lord Protector," ll. 112–134, and "The First Anniversary of the Government under His Highness the Lord Protector," ll. 201–204, 387, in *Complete Poetry,* pp. 99, 104, 108.

12. GRO: D 2688, f. 104v. Ronald Hutton has begun to rehabilitate Richard Cromwell's reputation, but the few local references to Richard present him as a pale reflection of his father. Hutton, *Restoration,* p. 41.

13. GRO: D 2688, f. 105v.

14. GRO: D 2688, f. 103v; *Mercurius Politicus* (437), October 7–14, 1658, p. 912. These efforts almost succeeded in October 1658 but failed in February 1659. *CSPD, Commonwealth,* v. 12 (1658–1659): 99, 152, 274.

15. GRO: D 2688, ff. 105v, 106v.

16. GRO: D 2688, f. 106v.

17. Godwin had been prosecuted as a Nonconformist in the 1630s. GRO: TBR A 1/3, p. 9; GDR 174, Detection Causes: 1631, 1634, 1635, 1636, 1637.

18. *HMC, 5th Report, Part I,* p. 361.

19. GRO: TBR A 1/3, p. 132. This list contains the names of remarkably few Baptists and Quakers. John Surman of the Quakers was the only identified Separatist to claim pardon, and his Separatism is known only from sources in the early 1670s. Compare the names in the list of pardon seekers to the names in GRO: D 4944 2/1, Tewkesbury Baptist Church Book, pp. 38–39, and D 1340 B2/M1, Stoke Orchard Monthly Meeting, 1671–1783, pp. 3, 6, 9, 17.

20. GRO: TBR A 1/3, p. 134.

21. Before the restoration of the excluded councilors in late November 1660

and the purge of the radicals in 1662, the council elected conservative members in Capel and Dowdeswell. GRO: D 2688, f. 106v.

22. In January 1659 the corporation chose Robert Long to sit for the borough. Although Long was a royal familiar, he had legal expertise invaluable to a corporation seeking the renewal of its charter. Williams, *Parliamentary History of Gloucestershire*, pp. 241–242.

23. GRO: TBR A 1/3, p. 2.

24. GRO: TBR A 1/3, p. 6.

25. GRO: TBR A 1/1, pp. 132, 150; TBR A 1/2, pp. 43–44; TBR A 1/3, p. 6; and D 2688, ff. 93v, 94v, 95v, 96v, 97v, 98v, 99v, 100v. In addition to the order from the council, Edward and William Wilson, Thomas Hale, John Man, Philip Hilly, and Edward Jennings had acquired writs of mandamus from the Court of King's Bench to regain their positions on the common council. Thomas Wilson also received a mandamus to regain the office of burgess, but lists of burgesses from the 1660s in GRO: TBR A 1/3 suggest he was not restored. The records of mandamus are in PRO: KB 21/14, Crown Side Rule Books: Easter, 1660–Hilary, 1662, f. 17v.

26. On the Corporation Act, see Sacret, "Restoration Government and Municipal Corporations," 246–252; Ogg, *England in the Reign of Charles II*, pp. 198, 517–519; and Miller, "The Crown and the Borough Charters," 59–66.

27. GRO: TBR A 1/3, p. 20.

28. GRO: P 329 CW 2/1, p. 372.

29. GRO: TBR A 1/3, pp. 19–20. The other burgesses excluded were Phillip Surman, John Carver, Thomas Clarke, William Hatton, Robert Buggin, Bartholomew Reade, and Henry Symonds. Richard Hill was also removed from the office of town clerk.

30. Ibid. The commission appointed to the common council Conway Whithorne, Thomas Nanfan, Thomas Jeyne, John Man, the younger, George Jeyne, Nicholas Steight, Richard Smithsend, Thomas Kings, and Thomas Smithsend. Edward Wilson replaced Phillip Surman in the office of bailiff. Edward Jennings became a justice of the peace in place of John Carver. George Jeyne replaced Richard Hill in the office of town clerk.

31. These marriage alliances are recorded alongside the royalist background of Nanfan and Whithorne in Fenwick and Metcalfe, *Visitation of the County of Gloucester, 1682–1683*, pp. 124–125, 200. See Coates, Young, and Snow, *Private Journals of the Long Parliament*, p. 418, for Whithorne's circulation of a petition in support of episcopacy.

32. *CCC*, pp. 85–87, 1949.

33. GRO: TBR A 1/3, p. 32.

34. Dowdeswell had remained in the neighborhood throughout the 1650s

and may have received inside information on borough politics. The Protectorate councilors questioned were John Bache, Thomas Clarke, John Carver, and Thomas Jeynes. GRO: TBR A 1/3, pp. 17–18, 29.

35. GRO: TBR A 1/3, pp. 17–18.

36. Ogg, *England in the Reign of Charles II*, pp. 198, 517–519; Sacret, "Restoration Government and Municipal Corporations," 246–252; Miller, "The Crown and the Borough Charters," 59–66. On the enforcement of the Corporation Act in Tewkesbury, see GRO: TBR A 1/3, pp. 21, 33, 63; TBR A 1/4, Council Minutes for 6-4-1680 and 15-7-1680.

37. GRO: TBR A 1/3, f. 101.

38. GRO: D 2688, f. 118v; Bennett, *History of Tewkesbury*, p. 208.

39. The number of Prayer Book Protestants in northern Gloucestershire is impossible to estimate, and loyalty to the Book of Common Prayer was never stated as a motive for local action or protest. The churchwardens of Tewkesbury had to purchase a new Book of Common Prayer in 1661. GRO: P 329 CW 2/1, p. 367.

40. Barry Reay, "The Quakers, 1659, and the Restoration of the Monarchy," *History*, 63 (1978): 193–213, and "The Authorities and Early Restoration Quakerism," *Journal of Ecclesiastical History*, 34 (1983): 69–84. Reay's interpretation of militant Quakerism and the restored monarchy is incorporated in Hutton, *Restoration*, pp. 10–11.

41. GRO: D 1340 A1/A1, Quaker Sufferings: Tirley.

42. GRO: D 1340 A1/A1, Quaker Sufferings: Tirley.

43. This incident was recorded in Norman Penney (ed.), *The Journal of George Fox*, 2 vols. (Cambridge: Cambridge University Press), 1: 197.

44. GRO: GDR 209, Episcopal Visitation: 1661–1662.

45. Because Baptists and Quakers were often prosecuted for such offenses as absence from church, the distinction between cases produced by the different conceptions of church discipline in the parish and cases resulting from avowed Nonconformity is difficult to sustain for presentments made after the Restoration. GRO: GDR 210, Detection Causes: October 1662–November 1663; and GDR 212, Detection Causes: July 1663–March 1665.

46. This evidence complicates the interpretation of the Restoration settlement in the church as the general assault of the gentry on Puritanism. The practical boundaries of the settlement may have depended on the character of the first visitation. See Green, *Reestablishment of the Church of England*, pp. 179–180.

47. Matthews, *Calamy Revised*, pp. 249, 519; GRO: GDR, Register Copies, vol. 1667–1683, pp. 16–17; and GDR 209, Episcopal Visitation: 1661–1662. The description of Eaton as conservative is based on his acceptance of ordination by the bishop of Dublin after the outbreak of the Civil War.

48. GRO: GDR 210, Detection Causes: October 1662–November 1663.

49. Christopher Atkinson was Neast's son-in-law. GRO: W 1670/209.

50. GRO: P 329 CW 2/1, p. 377. Surman was Neast's son-in-law. GRO: W 1670/209.

51. The first reliable evidence of an Independent conventicle in the neighborhood of Tewkesbury dates from the Licensing Act of 1672. Henry Collett, Thomas Skey, and William Davison were described in 1672 as congregational ministers and were licensed to hold meetings in their own houses. *CSPD, Charles II* (London, 1899), v. 13 (1672): 99, 196.

52. GRO: GDR 210, Detection Causes: October 1662–November 1663.

53. GRO: GDR 210, Detection Causes: October 1662–November 1663; and D 1340 B2/M1, pp. 19, 24, 41, 47. The Stoke Orchard monthly meeting included the weekly meetings of Cheltenham, Stoke Orchard, Tewkesbury, and Tirley.

54. PRO: ASSI 5/1/7, f. 1r. Mansel was probably a Baptist. GRO: GDR 210, Detection Causes: October 1662–November 1663.

55. The Quakers did not keep a membership list, so that their numbers are impossible to estimate. GRO: GDR 210, Detection Causes: October 1662–November 1663; GDR 212, Detections: July 1663–March 1665; and D 4944 2/1, Tewkesbury Baptist Church Book, pp. 38–39.

56. I have identified seventeen Baptists and eighteen Quakers. This is a conservative estimate, as I have rejected cases in which a family name alone is associated with one group or the other. The names of Haines and Slicer, for instance, are found in the records of the Quaker meeting in Tewkesbury, but Richard Haines, Mary Haines, and Samuel Slicer, presented in 1665 for absence from church, have not been identified individually and therefore have not been counted as Quakers. GRO: D 1340 C1/M3, Declaration of 1700. The problems of positive identification are summed up in the case of the widow Tovy of Tewkesbury, presented in 1663 for allowing her husband to be buried contrary to the order of the Church of England. Tovy is a name associated with both the Baptist and the Quaker movements in Tewkesbury, and thus the woman in question is virtually impossible to identify with any certainty. GRO: D 4944 2/1, pp. 31–32; D 1340 B2/M1, *passim.*

57. GRO: P 329 CW 2/1, p. 362.

58. GRO: P 329 CW 2/1, p. 359.

59. GRO: P 329 CW 2/1, pp. 359, 379.

60. See the presentation of John Bache, Edward Hawkins, and Samuel Mosse in GRO: GDR 210, Detection Causes: October 1662–November 1663.

61. The cases of five Baptists who returned to the established church are contained in GRO: D 4944 2/1, pp. 129–130. The language of "return" among Nonconformists implied more than mere attendance at church.

Thomas and Maria Baker of Deerhurst certified their church attendance in 1662 but did not abandon their Quakerism. The continuity of the Quaker meeting and membership across the Restoration is impossible to establish, as records do not survive for the Quakers of northern Gloucestershire in the early 1660s. GRO: GDR 210, Detection Causes: October 1662–November 1663; and D 1340 B2/M1, pp. 1, 26.

62. GRO: D 4944 2/1, pp. 129–130.
63. GRO: D 4944 2/1, p. 129.
64. Haigh, *English Reformations,* pp. 288–295.

8. Bloody Stratagems and Busy Heads

1. Aline Mackenzie Taylor, *Next to Shakespeare* (Durham: Duke University Press, 1950), pp. 45–59.
2. Tim Harris, *Politics Under the Later Stuarts: Party Conflict in a Divided Society* (London: Longman, 1993), pp. 8–13.
3. John Miller, *Popery and Politics in England, 1660–1688* (Cambridge: Cambridge University Press, 1973), pp. 67–90.
4. John Spurr, *The Restoration Church of England, 1646–1689* (New Haven: Yale University Press, 1991), pp. 105–165, 379; and John Spurr, "'Virtue, Religion and Government': The Anglican Uses of Providence," in Harris, Seaward, and Goldie, *Politics of Religion,* p. 30.
5. The terms *whig* and *tory* were never used in local accounts of faction. I have chosen to refer to a loyalist Anglican faction and a Nonconformist faction because groups in Tewkesbury consistently appeared on the same side of the issues in the Popish Plot and Exclusion Crisis, and attitudes to the Restoration settlement in the church were the most clearly articulated principle of action. See the discussion of parties in Harris, *Politics Under the Later Stuarts,* pp. 80–82.
6. The coexistence of this strategy and strategies of coercion or persecution complicate the interpretation of Restoration England as a persecuting society. This interpretation emphasizes a particular ideal of the church and disregards both other ideals and the evidence of local practice. Mark Goldie, "The Theory of Religious Intolerance in Restoration England," in O. P. Grell, J. I. Israel, and Nicholas Tyacke (eds.), *From Persecution to Toleration* (Oxford: Clarendon Press, 1991), pp. 331–332.
7. GRO: GDR 220, Visitation Book: 1670–1677, ff. 2–3.
8. The second Conventicle Act imposed a fine of £20 on any persons holding a conventicle in their house and mobilized civil authority in defense of religious uniformity, as substantial fines were imposed on negligent justices of the peace, and constables were permitted to force entry in

search of conventicles. See the general account in Ogg, *England in the Reign of Charles II*, p. 207.

9. GRO: GDR 220, Visitation Book: 1670–1677, ff. 2–3.

10. In 1681, the main features of the church of law were incorporated in the visitation articles of Robert Frampton, the newly elected Bishop of Gloucester. GRO: GDR 240, Episcopal Visitation, 1681: Articles of Visitation, pp. 3–4.

11. GRO: GDR 220, Visitation Book: 1670–1677, ff. 2–3.

12. BL: Add Ms 33,589, f. 75

13. GRO: GDR 223, Episcopal Visitations: 1671–1673.

14. GRO: GDR 227, Detection Causes: April 1676–January 1677.

15. GRO: D 1340 A1/A1, Quaker Sufferings.

16. Michael R. Watts, *The Dissenters: From the Reformation to the French Revolution* (Oxford: Clarendon Press, 1978), pp. 244–249.

17. GRO: D 1340 B2/M1, Stoke Orchard Monthly Meeting, 1671–1783, pp. 2–3, 7–8.

18. GRO: D 1340 B2/M1, pp. 1, 3–4.

19. The behavior of those described as Nonconformists indicates a relatively close relationship to the church. The religious practice of Nonconformists included both private meetings in conventicles and public worship in the parish church. If presented for absence from church, Nonconformists had less difficulty than strict Dissenters in obtaining a certificate of attendance, although participation in communion might remain a problem. See the church court's absolution of several members of the Haines family in GRO: GDR 224, Detection Causes: September 1671–July 1673.

20. *CSPD, Charles II*, v. 13 (1672): 400, 402.

21. GRO: W 1683/103.

22. The distribution of Nonconformists and Dissenters among the hamlets of Ashchurch is indicated by the presentments in GRO: GDR 243, Episcopal Visitation, 1682. This pattern of dispersion in both central and marginal hamlets does not conform to Alan Everitt's interpretation of rural Nonconformity as evidence of Anglican failure to serve the religious needs of large rural parishes. Ashchurch was a large parish, roughly 4,300 acres, but Pamington and Natton were both less than a mile from the parish church. See Alan Everitt, "Nonconformity in Country Parishes," *Agricultural History Review*, 18 (1970): 189–191; and Spufford, *Contrasting Communities*, pp. 298–300.

23. GRO: W 1683/103, 1684/249. Richard Davison, son of Richard Davison of Natton, yeoman, married Hannah Long, the daughter of Roger Long of Fiddington, yeoman. Henry Long and Samuel Long, the sons of Roger Long, were presented and excommunicated in the late summer of 1686

"for refusing conformity with the church and for not receiving the sacrament." GRO: GDR 259, Detection Causes: 1686–1708.

24. GRO: GDR 174, Detection Causes: 1631, 1634, 1635, 1636, 1637; W 1631/43.

25. GRO: GDR 224, Detection Causes: September 1671–July 1673; PM 19/1. The several branches of the Haines family in Ashchurch are often difficult to distinguish. The Independent group in the family consisted of Richard Haines (ch. 16-10-1609), his wife Margaret (m. 17-2-1633), his daughter Margaret (ch. 31-10-1647), and his son Samuel (ch. 29-10-1649).

26. GRO: W 1626/178, 1684/249; PM 19/1 (16-1-1614, marriage of Mary Haines and Robert Olive). Anne Olive, the wife of Richard Olive, was prosecuted alongside Davison and Haines in the early 1670s. Richard Olive was the son of Mary Haines and Robert Olive.

27. GRO: W 1682/105; GDR 224, Detection Causes: September 1671–July 1673.

28. GRO: W 1670/209. John Haines was presented alongside several other members of the Independent meeting in the early 1670s. GRO: GDR 224, Detection Causes: September 1671–July 1673.

29. In the parish of Ashchurch, three of the four testamentary cases presented in 1685 concerned families of Dissenters. The Oakley, Rowles, and Keare families were each prosecuted for retaining unproven wills. See GRO: GDR 252, Detection Causes: 1684–1688.

30. GRO: W 1683/103; and *CSPD, Charles II*, v. 13 (1672): 196, 216.

31. GRO: GDR 210, Detection Causes: October 1662–November 1663; GDR 224, Detection Causes: September 1671–July 1673; GDR 174, Detection Causes: 1631, 1634, 1635, 1636, 1637; PM 19/1; W 1663/228.

32. The name Anne Dobbins does not reappear in the records after the condemnation of her disorderly marriage, but no formal mention of expulsion is made. GRO: D 1340 B2/M1, Stoke Orchard Monthly Meeting, 1671–1783, pp. 6, 8, 9.

33. GRO: D 1340 B2/M1, p. 79.

34. GRO: D 1340 B2/M1, p. 54.

35. This discussion of structure has been influenced by Anthony Giddens, *Central Problems in Social Theory: Action, Structure, and Contradiction in Social Analysis* (Berkeley: University of California Press, 1979), pp. 9–95; and Derek Gregory, *Regional Transformation and Industrial Revolution: A Geography of the Yorkshire Woolen Industry* (London: Macmillan, 1982), pp. 1–25.

36. GRO: GDR 231, Visitation Book, 1677–1678. The disinclination of churchwardens to prosecute conventicles in the church court does not appear to have coincided with any increase in the number of such cases handled by the quarter sessions, but the sessions archive is poor for

Gloucestershire in the seventeenth century. GRO: Q/SIb 1, Quarter Sessions Indictments, 1660–1668.

37. The presentments for the years 1671 to 1708 are contained in GRO: GDR 224, Detection Causes: September 1671–July 1673; GDR 227, Detection Causes: April 1676–January 1677; GDR 230, Detection Causes: 1677–1680; GDR 231, Visitation Book, 1677–1678; GDR 233, Detection Causes: July 1678–September 1679; GDR 235, Detection Causes: September 1679–April 1680; GDR 239, Detection Causes: 1680–1681; GDR 241, Detection Causes: June 1681–July 1682; GDR 243, Episcopal Visitation, 1682; GDR 244, Detection Causes: September–December 1682; GDR 245, Detection Causes: October 1682–February 1683; GDR 247, Detection Causes: October 1683–March 1684; GDR 252, Detection Causes: 1684–1688; GDR 259, Detection Causes: 1686–1708.

38. GDR 259, Detection Causes: 1686–1708.

39. GRO: GDR 224, Detection Causes: September 1671–July 1673; GDR 227, Detection Causes: April 1676–January 1677; GDR 230, Detection Causes: 1677–1680; GDR 231, Visitation Book, 1677–1678; GDR 233, Detection Causes: July 1678–September 1679; GDR 235, Detection Causes: September 1679–April 1680; GDR 239, Detection Causes: 1680–1681; GDR 241, Detection Causes: June 1681–July 1682; GDR 243, Episcopal Visitation, 1682; GDR 244, Detection Causes: September–December 1682; GDR 245, Detection Causes: October 1682–February 1683; GDR 247, Detection Causes: October 1683–March 1684; GDR 252, Detection Causes: 1684–1688; GDR 259, Detection Causes: 1686–1708.

40. The absence of full quarter sessions records demands caution on this point. On the persecution of the early 1670s, see Ogg, *England in the Reign of Charles II,* p. 207; and Watts, *Dissenters,* pp. 244–249.

41. Watts, *Dissenters,* pp. 221–262.

42. Cowell was an elder of the Baptist church in the early 1660s. GRO: D 4944 2/1, Tewkesbury Baptist Church Book, pp. 38–39. His appearances in the church court are recorded in GRO: GDR 230, Detection Causes: 1677–1680; GDR 233, Detection Causes: July 1678–September 1679.

43. GRO: GDR 241, Detection Causes: June 1681–July 1682.

44. On the national context of the Popish Plot, see Miller, *Popery and Politics,* pp. 154–162; and John Kenyon, *The Popish Plot* (Harmondsworth: Penguin, 1972), pp. 1–36.

45. Bodl: Tanner Ms 147, f. 148.

46. Joseph Foster (ed.), *Alumni Oxonienses* (Oxford, 1892), p. 1595; Matthews, *Calamy Revised,* p. 519; and GRO: GDR 223, Episcopal Visitations: 1671–1673; GDR 227, Detection Causes: April 1676–January 1677; D 747/1, Petition of Corporation to Bishop Elect of Gloucester.

47. GRO: GDR B4/1/2500; GDR 232, Depositions: February 1678–January

1684: Depositions of Thomas Nanfan, William Jennings, Mathias Maide, Phillip Hilly, and Nicholas Staight; Bodl: Tanner Ms 147, ff. 128, 130; and GRO: D 747/1.

48. GRO: GDR B4/1/2500.

49. Bodl: Tanner Ms 147, f. 130.

50. GRO: GDR B4/1/2500.

51. Bodl: Tanner Ms 147, f. 128.

52. Bodl: Tanner Ms 147, f. 130.

53. Bodl: Tanner Ms 147, f. 128.

54. GRO: D 747/1, Simpson to Bishop of Gloucester, March 1682.

55. Russell has been identified as a whig activist and was in London when Wells acquired letters patent under the great seal for presentation to the vicarage. Russell's subsequent failure to stand behind Wells was an early indication of the distance between prominent whig landholders and populist religious radicals. See Henning, *House of Commons*, 3: 361–362; and Peter Earle, *Monmouth's Rebels: The Road to Sedgemoor, 1685* (New York: St. Martin's, 1977), pp. 191–194.

56. GRO: GDR B4/1/2500.

57. Ibid.

58. GRO: GDR B4/1/2500.

59. GRO: GDR 223, Episcopal Visitations: 1671–1673. Parsons had acted as surrogate for John Nicholson, the chancellor.

60. GRO: GDR 227, Detection Causes: April 1676–January 1677; GDR 230, Detection Causes: 1677–1680.

61. Matthews, *Calamy Revised*, p. 519; and GRO: TBR A 1/4, 20-1-1679.

62. GRO: P 329 CW 2/1, p. 435.

63. GRO: GDR B4/1/2500.

64. GRO: TBR A 1/4, 4-11-1679; D 747/1. This practice was not invariably subversive in the national context, but in the local milieu Wells had adopted a style of Nonconformist protest evident since the early 1600s. See Spurr, *Restoration Church*, pp. 204–205.

65. GRO: TBR A 1/4, 20-1-1679.

66. Ibid.

67. GRO: TBR A 1/4, 6-2-1679.

68. Bodl: Tanner Ms 147, f. 136; and GRO: D 747/1.

69. GRO: D 747/1.

70. GRO: D 747/1, Francis Wells to Sir Francis Russell.

71. LPL: Arches Case 9783, Bbb. 502/3.

72. LPL: Arches Case 9783, Bbb. 502/2; and GRO: D 747/1, Simpson to Thomas Haslewood, esquire, with articles against Wells.

73. GRO: P 329 IN 1/4, f. 35; GDR 232, Depositions: February 1678–January

1684: Deposition of Mathias Maide, 1679; and LPL: Arches Case 9783, Bbb. 488/6.

74. GRO: D 747/1.

75. GRO: D 747/1; and LPL: Arches Case 9780, D 2229 and 2230, fiche no. 12066, f. 59.

76. GRO: D 747/1.

77. My assumption is that Wells knew precisely what he was doing when he altered the form of the service. His opponents consistently presented him as a senile old man no longer in control of his actions, but his surviving letters indicate he was at least as sane as any of the other parties to the dispute. See Bodl: Tanner Ms 147, ff. 130, 134; and GRO: D 747/1, Francis Wells to Sir Francis Russell.

78. Bodl: Tanner Ms 147, f. 132a.

79. Ibid.

80. Ibid.

81. GRO: D 747/1; and LPL: Arches Case 9780, D2229 and 2230, fiche no. 12066, f. 61r-v.

82. GRO: D 747/1; and LPL: Arches Case 9780, D2229 and 2230, fiche no. 12066, f. 60r-v.

83. LPL: Arches Case 9783, Bbb. 502/4, Deposition of William Jennings. Of all Simpson's supporters, Jennings was most inclined to favor Wells, perhaps because Jennings was related by marriage to William Hatton, one of Wells's most steadfast adherents.

84. GRO: GDR 232, Depositions: February 1678–January 1684: Deposition of William Jennings.

85. GRO: D 747/1.

86. Ibid.

87. Ibid.

88. Ibid.

89. LPL: Arches Case 9783, Bbb. 502/3.

90. Ibid.

91. GRO: D 747/1.

92. Bodl: Tanner Ms 147, ff. 134, 136.

93. Bodl: Tanner Ms 147, f. 132a.

94. LPL: Arches Case 9783, Bbb. 502/3. See PRO: PROB 11/421/149 for Laight's occupation and wealth. His links to Nonconformists down to his death in 1691 are described in UCL: RFTV, vol. 13, Funeral Sermon for Joseph Laight.

95. UCL: RFTV, vol. 13, Funeral Sermon for Joseph Laight; Bodl: Rawlinson Ms A 39, f. 528.

96. Bodl: Rawlinson Ms A 39, f. 528.

97. GRO: TBR A 1/3.
98. LPL: Arches Case 9783, Bbb. 502/3, Deposition of Edward Baker.
99. GRO: GDR 230, Detection Causes: 1677–1680.
100. LPL: Arches Case 9783, Bbb. 502/3, Deposition of Edward Baker.
101. GRO: W 1628/39; P 329 IN 1/4, 21-2-1640; P 329 IN 1/2, f. 105.
102. LPL: Arches Case 9783, Bbb. 488/6.
103. GRO: W 1665/99. The position of houses is indicated by hearth tax returns in PRO: E 179 247/14 or in the photostat of the return in GRO: D 383. See GRO: TBR A 1/4, list inside front cover, for Maide as an assistant burgess.
104. GRO: W 1665/99; and PRO: E 179 247/14 or GRO: D 383.
105. LPL: Arches Case 9780, D 2229 and 2230, fiche no. 12064, f. 30v.
106. LPL: Arches Case 9783, Bbb. 488/6.
107. PRO: E 179 247/14 or GRO: D 383.
108. Ibid.
109. LPL: Arches Case 9783, Bbb. 502/3, Deposition of Thomas Nanfan.
110. PRO: E 179 247/14 or GRO: D 383.
111. LPL: Arches Case 9783, Bbb. 488/6; and PRO: E 179 247/14 or GRO: D 383.
112. LPL: Arches Case 9783, Bbb. 502/2, Deposition of Joseph Face.
113. Bodl: Tanner Ms 147, f. 132a.
114. GRO: TBR A 1/4, 20-1-1678. It could be argued that this fight to restrict the number of paupers allowed to settle in the town increased the council's power to assist the remnant in its care, thus indirectly satisfying the demands of charity. The bequest, however, was clearly intended for direct disbursement among the poor.
115. Bodl: Tanner Ms 147, f. 136; and PRO: E 179 247/14 or GRO: D 383.
116. LPL: Arches Case 9783, Bbb. 502/3.
117. PRO: E 179 247/14 or GRO: D 383.
118. LPL: Arches Case 9783, Bbb. 502/3 and Bbb. 488/6.
119. Ibid.
120. Fenwick and Metcalfe, *Visitation of the County of Gloucester, 1682–1683,* p. 125.
121. GRO: TBR A 1/3, f. 19; and TBR A 1/4, *passim.*
122. GRO: TBR A 1/3, pp. 21, 33, 63; and TBR A 1/4, Council Minutes for 6-4-1680, 15-7-1680.
123. GRO: TBR A 1/3, f. 101.
124. GRO: D 2688, Giles Geast Charity Account Book, f. 118v; Bennett, *History of Tewkesbury,* p. 208.
125. GRO: D 747/1.
126. Bodl: Tanner Ms 147, f. 190; and Eward, *No Fine But A Glass Of Wine,* p. 208.

127. Bodl: Tanner Ms 147, f. 190.

128. GRO: D 747/1, Parsons to Horner, 9-10-1680.

129. GRO: D 747/1, Petition to the Archbishop, October–November 1680.

130. GRO: D 747/1, Petition to the Archbishop as revised by Parsons, 13-10-1680; and Parsons to Simpson, 13-10-1680.

131. GRO: D 747/1, Parsons to Horner, 9-10-1680.

132. GRO: D 747/1, Parsons to Simpson, undated [September 1680].

133. Ibid.

134. GRO: D 747/1, Inhibition to Simpson from the Arches, 23-8-1680.

135. GRO: D 747/1, Petition of Burgesses to Archbishop, October–November 1680.

136. GRO: D 747/1, Parsons to Horner, 9-10-1680; and Horner to Simpson, 25-4-1681.

137. GRO: D 747/1, Nixon to Simpson, 21-4-1681 to 11-10-1681; and Horner to Simpson, 25-4-1681.

138. GRO: D 747/1, Parsons to Simpson, undated [October 1681].

139. GRO: D 747/1, Simpson's Allegation against Wells in the Arches; and Nixon to Simpson, 29-9-1681.

140. This statement has survived as LPL: Arches Case 9783, Bbb. 502/2.

141. GRO: D 747/1, Nixon to Simpson, 11-10-1681.

142. GRO: D 747/1, Petition to the Archbishop, October–November 1680; and Petition to Bishop Elect of Gloucester, undated [1681].

143. GRO: D 747/1, Articles against Wells in Consistory Court, 28-3-1679.

144. LPL: Arches Case 9780, D 2229 and 2230, fiche no. 12064, f. 30v; and GRO: GDR 228, ff. 116v-117.

145. GRO: GDR 228, ff. 116v-117.

146. GRO: D 747/1, Copy of Bishop's Definitive Sentence, 2-8-1680.

147. LPL: Arches Case 9783, Bbb. 502/3, Deposition of William Jennings.

148. LPL: Arches Case 9783, Bbb. 502/2.

149. Bodl: Tanner Ms 147, f. 189.

150. The different views of Quakerism after the Restoration are discussed in Barry Reay, *The Quakers and the English Revolution* (London: Temple Smith, 1985), pp. 103–122; and David Scott, *Quakerism in York, 1650–1720* (York: Borthwick Institute, 1991), pp. 1–3, 9–21, 31–32.

151. GRO: D 1340 C1/M3, Women's Weekly Meeting. It should be noted that the formal influence of the weekly meeting was brought to bear only after the completion of the courtship.

152. GRO: D 1340 C1/M3, Women's Weekly Meeting, p. 8.

153. The record of approved marriages may be incomplete, as seven marriages were entered in the minutes of the women's meeting in Tewkesbury between 1681 and 1694, but none were recorded between 1683 and 1691. GRO: D 1340 C1/M3, Women's Weekly Meeting.

154. GRO: D 1340 B2/M1, Stoke Orchard Monthly Meeting, 1671–1783, p. 20.
155. GRO: D 1340 B2/M1, pp. 78–79.
156. GRO: D 1340 B2/M1, pp. 65, 71, 77.
157. GRO: D 1340 B2/M1, p. 17.
158. GRO: D 1340 B2/M1, Stoke Orchard Monthly Meeting, 1671–1783.
159. GRO: D 1340 B2/M1, p. 102.
160. GRO: D 1340 A1/M1, Quarterly Meeting, 1671–1733.
161. GRO: D 1340 B2/M1, pp. 30, 34, 44–45, 47, 78, 84, 89, 92.
162. Robert Silvester, generally connected to Nailsworth in minutes of the quarterly meeting, was instructed to send Clift to Tewkesbury. GRO: D 1340 A1/M1, Quarterly Meeting, 1671–1733: 27-12-1693.
163. GRO: D 1340 B2/M1, p. 34.
164. GRO: D 1340 A1/M1, Quarterly Meeting, 1671–1733: 31-3-1692, 26-3-1696, 30-9-1697.
165. GRO: D 1340 B2/M1, p. 120.
166. GRO: D 1340 B2/M1, pp. 1, 6, 8–9, 26. Baker's statement of repentance refers to Beven as his "former" wife, making it unclear whether the marriage was dissolved by death, mutual consent, or the unilateral decision of one of the partners.
167. GRO: D 1340 B2/M1, pp. 6–7, 9, 12, 14, 16, 20–22.
168. GRO: D 1340 B2/M1, p. 54.
169. GRO: D 1340 A1/M1, Quarterly Meeting, 1671–1733: 31-3-1688.
170. GRO: D 1340 A1/M1, Quarterly Meeting, 1671–1733: 27-9-1693, 27-12-1693.
171. GRO: D 1340 A1/M1, Quarterly Meeting, 1671–1733: 27-12-1676.
172. The production of "sufferings" is described in GRO: D 1340 B2/M1, p. 112; D 1340 A1/M1, Quarterly Meeting, 1671–1733: 27-12-1676, 26-12-1677, 28-12-1681, 29-6-1682, 27-12-1682, 23-12-1685, 31-6-1686, 26-6-1690, 30-6-1692, 26-9-1695, 29-9-1698, 28-9-1699.
173. GRO: D 1340 A1/M1, Quarterly Meeting, 1671–1733: 26-12-1677.
174. GRO: D 1340 A1/A2, Quaker Sufferings, pp. 24, 69, 207.
175. GRO: D 1340 A1/M1, Quarterly Meeting, 1671–1733: 26-9-1695.
176. GRO: P 329 CW 2/1, Tewkesbury Churchwardens' Accounts, 1563–1703, 5-9-1683. This illustration is from a redistribution of seats in 1683 that offers ample evidence of the coherence of families and servants in the parish assembly.
177. A different pattern has been found in a detailed investigation of Coventry. Dissenters in Coventry quickly recovered prominence in the corporation after the Restoration, perhaps because much of the Dissent in the town was Presbyterian and more inclined to occasional conformity and comprehension. See Hurwich, "'A Fanatick Town,'" 17–23.

178. GRO: TBR A 1/3, pp. 88–89, 94, 97–98, 104, 106, 115, 119–120. In 1672 Collett obtained a license to minister to Independents in his house. Collett had supported the Crown in the Civil War and received a pardon in 1686 for his refusal to take the Oaths of Allegiance and Supremacy. *CSPD, Charles II,* v. 13 (1672): 44, 99, 140; and *CSPD, James II* (London, 1964), v. 2 (1686–1687): 119.

179. GRO: W 1670/209; GDR 210, Detection Causes: October 1662–November 1663; GDR 174, Detection Causes: 1631, 1634, 1635, 1636, 1637; GDR 244, Detection Causes: September–December 1682. The organization of the Neast faction has already been discussed.

180. Millington was an elder of the Baptist church in the 1690s. GRO: D 2688, Giles Geast Charity Account Book, f. 115v; D 4944 2/1, Tewkesbury Baptist Church Book, p. 28.

181. GRO: TBR A 1/3, p. 19; D 2688, f. 117v.

182. GRO: D 4944 2/1, pp. 38–39; D 1340 B2/ M1, Stoke Orchard Monthly Meeting, 1671–1783, p. 48; D 2688, f. 118v.

183. GRO: D 2688, ff. 106v, 107v; TBR A 1/3, p. 6.

184. GRO: TBR A 1/3, p. 19; D 2688, ff. 122v, 123v.

185. GRO: D 2688, ff. 83v, 94v.

186. GRO: D 2688, ff. 112r-134r.

187. I have attempted to identify only the officers listed in GRO: D 2688, Giles Geast Charity Account Book. This source does not consistently list all the local officers for a given year. Another problem has been the identification of Nonconformists and Dissenters in the records. If a person was not presented in the courts or was not significant enough, in the case of the Quakers, to appear in the minutes of the local meetings, it is not possible to identify their religious inclinations.

188. GRO: TBR A 1/4, 13-6-1682.

189. The council minutes suggest the Duke of Beaufort may have been an intermediary in the presentation of both petitions. GRO: TBR A 1/4, 13-6-1682, 16-7-1683.

190. GRO: TBR A 1/4, 30-5-1684.

191. GRO: TBR A 1/4, 6-6-1684.

192. GRO: TBR A 1/4, 10-7-1684; 19-8-1684.

193. GRO: TBR A 1/4, 2-9-1684. Samuel Hawling, William Jennings, John Man, Robert Porter, William Saunders, James Simpson, and Samuel Smith voted for the surrender of the charter. Thomas Bartholomew, John Dobbins, Richard Dowdeswell, Henry Hatton, Theophilus Holland, and Thomas Nanfan voted against it.

194. I have found no outline of concessions to be sought in a new charter. The petition in the council minutes refers only to "such limitations and re-

strictions as shall be most conducive to your Majesty's service." GRO: TBR A 1/4, 23-10-1684.

195. GRO: TBR A 1/4, 13-3-1685; 17-3-1685; 24-3-1685; 11-5-1685; 22-9-1685.

196. "Sir Francis Winnington," in *Dictionary of National Biography*, p. 668; Henning, *House of Commons*, 3: 746–747. Winnington lost his office because of his support for the exclusion of James from the succession.

197. GRO: TBR A 1/3, p. 128; TBR A 1/4, 11-5-1685; Williams, *Parliamentary History of Gloucestershire*, p. 244.

198. *CSPD, James II*, v. 2 (1686–1687): 41; Bennett, *History of Tewkesbury*, pp. 379, 383; and GRO: TBR A 1/5, pp. 247, 258.

199. *CSPD, James II*, v. 2 (1686–1687): 41; GRO: TBR A 1/3, pp. 6, 19–20; TBR A 1/4, 25-10-1677, 27-10-1681, 16-7-1683.

200. GRO: TBR A 1/5, p. 255.

201. *CSPD, James II*, v. 2 (1686–1687): 42; GRO: TBR A 1/5, p. 258.

202. GRO: W 1685/332; Bennett, *Tewkesbury Yearly Register*, 2: 375.

203. *CSPD, James II*, v. 2 (1686–1687): 41; GRO: TBR A 1/5, p. 258. The new corporation consisted of the Duke of Beaufort as high steward and Charles Hancock as mayor. Beaufort and Hancock joined John Man, John Peyton, and William Saunders as aldermen and justices of the peace. The common councilors were Thomas Bartholomew, Samuel Hawling, William Jennings, William Jones, George Moore, James Simpson, William Wilson, and Charles Wynde.

204. *CSPD, James II*, v. 2 (1686–1687): 42; Bennett, *History of Tewkesbury*, p. 385; and GRO: D 2688, Giles Geast Charity Account Book, f. 85v; TBR A 1/3, p. 110.

205. *CSPD, James II*, v. 2 (1686–1687): 41; Beaver, "Conscience and Context," 300–304; Bennett, *Tewkesbury Yearly Register*, 2: 325–326; and Bennett, *History of Tewkesbury*, p. 384.

206. The broader implications of this policy and James II's appeal to Dissenters are discussed in Miller, *Popery and Politics*, pp. 214–228.

207. Williams, *Parliamentary History of Gloucestershire*, p. 243.

208. GRO: TBR A 1/5, p. 203; D 2688, Giles Geast Charity Account Book, f. 134v.

209. GRO: TBR A 1/5, p. 203. This new corporation consisted of Thomas Hitchman as mayor; Henry Collett, Thomas Jeynes, and Phillip Surman as aldermen; and Joseph Clarke, Henry Dobbins, William Jones, John Lane, William Millington, George Moore, William Pay, Thomas Skey, and Jonathan Yerrow as common councilors.

210. Henning, *House of Commons*, 1: 244; and Miller, *Popery and Politics*, pp. 214–215.

211. GRO: D 2688, Giles Geast Charity Account Book, f. 111v.
212. GRO: TBR A 1/3, p. 19.
213. GRO: TBR A 1/1, pp. 148, 150, 155; TBR A 1/3, p. 19.
214. Bennett, *Tewkesbury Yearly Register,* 1: 38.
215. UCL: RFTV, vol. 9, Sermons on Public Events and Occasions, 1691–1708.
216. UCL: RFTV, vol. 9, Sermons on Public Events and Occasions, 1691–1708.
217. UCL: RFTV, vol. 15, Pious Maxims, Meditations, and Occasional Observations. On the general context of fear and violence in 1688, see Miller, *Popery and Politics,* pp. 259–261.
218. This attitude has been described for the political nation in W. A. Speck, *Reluctant Revolutionaries: Englishmen and the Revolution of 1688* (Oxford: Oxford University Press, 1988), pp. 213–215.
219. GRO: D 2688, Giles Geast Charity Account Book, ff. 137r, 138r, 139r, 140r.
220. This is Christopher Elrington's view, expressed in *VCH Gloucester,* 8: 149.
221. GRO: D 2688, Giles Geast Charity Account Book, f. 141r. In May 1693 Sir Francis Winnington and Richard Dowdeswell, described as "burgesses of Tewkesbury," petitioned the Crown to "revive and confirm" the privileges held by the corporation before the "interruptions" and "irregular proceedings" of the new charter. *CSPD, William and Mary* (London, 1903), v. 4 (1693): 156–157.
222. I have found no evidence to indicate that the vestry conducted such elections. The names of these officers are recorded in GRO: D 2688, Giles Geast Charity Account Book, ff. 137r, 138r, 139r, 140r, 141r, 142r, 143r, 143v-144v, 145v, 146v, 147v.
223. *Journals of the House of Commons,* v. 11 (November 1693–November 1697), p. 343; and Williams, *Parliamentary History of Gloucestershire,* p. 244.
224. The charter's arrival in Tewkesbury and the election of officers are described in GRO: TBR A 1/5, f. 1r-v. The charter is printed in Bennett, *History of Tewkesbury,* pp. 387–415.
225. GRO: TBR A 1/5, f. 1r-v.
226. Ibid. The council nominated in the charter of 1698 consisted of Henry Dobbins and Joseph Jones as bailiffs; Theophilus Holland, Robert Porter, Nicholas Steight, and Charles Wynde as justices of the peace; and Thomas Bartholomew, Henry Collett, the younger, Richard Dowdeswell, Abraham Farren, Thomas Hale, John Jeynes, William Jones, Daniel Kemble, Francis Leight, William Steight, Robert Tracy, Thomas Warkman, William Wilson, and Nicholas Wrenford as principal burgesses. Algernon Capel, Earl of Essex, became high steward.
227. The limitations of the Toleration Act are emphasized in Spurr, *Restoration*

Church, pp. 376–377; and in Speck, *Reluctant Revolutionaries,* p. 185. Despite its qualifications, the statute was the foundation of a more inclusive civic community in Tewkesbury, reflected in the different religious views of the officers chosen in 1698. A broader chronological perspective on the significance of the Toleration Act is developed in Nicholas Tyacke, "The 'Rise of Puritanism' and the Legalizing of Dissent, 1571–1719," in Grell, Israel, and Tyacke, *From Persecution to Toleration,* p. 41.

228. The importance of practical concerns in the creation of the Toleration Act and in the general intellectual issues of toleration is discussed in John Dunn, "The Claim to Freedom of Conscience: Freedom of Speech, Freedom of Thought, Freedom of Worship?" in Grell, Israel, and Tyacke, *From Persecution to Toleration,* p. 172; and Weber, *Protestant Ethic,* p. 242.

229. Bodl: English History Ms b209, Writings of Sir Richard Cocks, c. 1682–1701, f. 38.

230. Bodl: English History Ms b209, Writings of Sir Richard Cocks, c. 1682–1701, f. 38; and HMC, *Report on the Mss of the Marquess of Downshire, vol. 1: Papers of Sir William Trumbull* (London, 1924), pp. 477, 550.

231. Bodl: English History Ms b209, Writings of Sir Richard Cocks, c. 1682–1701, f. 38; D. W. Hayton (ed.), *The Parliamentary Diary of Sir Richard Cocks, 1698–1702* (Oxford: Clarendon Press, 1996), pp. xxxvi–xxxvii; 321–322. In a letter dated September 1695, Cocks thanked "Mr. Steight" for his promise of support in the anticipated parliamentary election. Nicholas Steight had not attended the session of the common council that voted to surrender the charter in 1684, and the family was prominent in local office in the 1690s. William Steight served as churchwarden in 1693 and 1694 and as bailiff in 1699. Both Nicholas and William Steight became burgesses under the new charter in 1698. GRO: TBR A 1/4, 2-9-1684, TBR A 1/5, ff. 2r, 4r; D 2688, Giles Geast Charity Account Book, ff. 141r, 142r, 147v.

232. The charter reached the great seal in 1696 but stalled after the death of Henry, Lord Capel of Tewkesbury, in May 1696. Capel had been nominated as the high steward in the new charter. HMC, *Report on Mss Downshire, vol. 1: Papers of Sir William Trumbull,* pp. 676–677. The warrant for this charter, prepared in 1695, is printed in *CSPD, William and Mary* (London, 1906), v. 5 (1694–1695): 462–463.

233. Bodl: English History Ms b209, Writings of Sir Richard Cocks, c. 1682–1701, f. 38; HMC, *Report on Mss Downshire, vol. 1: Papers of Sir William Trumbull,* pp. 473, 477–478; *CSPD, William and Mary,* v. 5 (1694–1695): 486; Sir Francis Winnington had been named as recorder in the warrant for the charter printed in *CSPD, William and Mary,* v. 5 (1694–1695): 462–463.

234. *CSPD, William and Mary* (London, 1913), v. 7 (1696): 268.

235. GRO: D 2688, Giles Geast Charity Account Book, f. 146v; TBR A 1/5, f. 2r; and HMC, *Report on Mss Downshire, vol. 1: Papers of Sir William Trumbull*, p. 748. Sir Robert Tracy's mother was Dorothy, daughter of Sir Thomas Cocks of Castleditch, Herefordshire, brother of Sir Richard Cocks. "Sir Robert Tracy," in *Dictionary of National Biography*, p. 1069; and *Burke's Peerage and Baronetage*, 105th ed. (London: Burke's Peerage, 1975), p. 246. On the activities and offices of Sir Richard Cocks, see Williams, *Parliamentary History of Gloucestershire*, pp. 62, 244–245; and Bennett, *Tewkesbury Yearly Register*, 2: 431–432.

236. GRO: TBR A 1/5, f. 1r-v. Prior to the parliamentary election in 1695, Sir Francis Winnington had written to Sir William Trumbull on behalf of John Collett, a clerk in the stamped paper office. Winnington recommended Collett "to be warehousekeeper or distributor of stamped paper," perhaps as a preelection favor to the Collett family. See HMC, *Report on Mss Downshire, vol. 1: Papers of Sir William Trumbull*, p. 550.

237. UCL: RFTV, vol. 12, Marriage Sermons, c. 1693–1699, f. 7r-v. In this context, it would be helpful to know more about the joint participation of Anglicans and dissenters in local societies for the reformation of manners in the eighteenth century.

238. Miller, *Popery and Politics*, p. 226.

Conclusion

1. Weber, *Protestant Ethic*, pp. 95–128; Troeltsch, *Social Teaching of the Christian Churches*, 2: 576–625, 691–694; Haller, *Rise of Puritanism*, pp. 10, 178–179, 259–261; and David Little, *Religion, Order, and Law: A Study in Prerevolutionary England* (New York: Harper & Row, 1969), pp. 33–131.

2. Delumeau, *Catholicism Between Luther and Voltaire*, pp. 175–202; Burke, *Popular Culture*, pp. 207–243; Reay, "Popular Religion," in Reay, *Popular Culture*, pp. 91–128; and Scribner, *Popular Culture*, pp. 1–47.

3. Spurr, *Restoration Church*, pp. 166–167.

4. Barry Reay, "Quaker Opposition to Tithes, 1652–1660," *Past and Present*, 86 (1980): 99, 105–110, 112.

5. Collinson, *Religion of Protestants*, pp. 1–21; and Wallace T. MacCaffrey, *The Shaping of the Elizabethan Regime: Elizabethan Politics, 1558–1572* (Princeton: Princeton University Press, 1968), pp. 402–403.

6. Katz, *Sabbath and Sectarianism*, pp. 1–20.

7. GRO: GDR 100, Depositions: March 1606–March 1609: Case of Office v. Drake and Edwards, Deposition of John Cheston.

8. GRO: GDR 100, Depositions: March 1606–March 1609: Deposition of Richard Garner.

9. Peter Studley, *The Looking Glass of Schism*, 2nd ed. (London, 1635); Henry Burton, *A Divine Tragedy Lately Acted* (London, 1636, 1641); and Bennett, *Tewkesbury Yearly Register*, 2: 270–272.

10. Lake, "Antipopery," 72–73.

11. GRO: D 747/1, Papers of James Simpson, Town Clerk of Tewkesbury.

Appendix 2

1. GCL: Smyth of Nibley Papers, vol. 16, f. 57.

Manuscript Sources

Bodleian Library

English History Manuscripts: Ms b209, Writings of Sir Richard Cocks, c. 1682–1701.

Rawlinson Manuscripts: Ms A 39, Petition of Gloucestershire Independents to the Lord Protector, 1656; Ms B 323, Visitation Book of Richard Parsons.

Tanner Manuscripts: Tanner Ms 147.

British Library

Additional Manuscripts: Add Ms 33, 589.

Gloucester City Library

Smyths of Nibley: Smyth Papers, vols. 12, 16.

Manorial Surveys: Survey of the Manor of Tewkesbury, 1632.

Gloucestershire Record Office

Giles Geast Charity: D 2688, Giles Geast Charity Account Book.

Gloucester Diocese

Consistory Court: GDR 65, Depositions: February 1586–March 1592; GDR 66, Detection Causes: April–August 1591 and December 1591–September 1592; GDR 67, Office Causes: June 1591–June 1592; GDR 75, Detections: 1594–1596; GDR 76, Detection Causes: 1594–1597; GDR 79, Depositions: April 1592–November 1597; GDR 81, Detection Book, October 1597; GDR 87, Detection Causes: September 1599–December 1600; GDR 89, Depositions: June 1601–March 1604; GDR 91, Detection Causes: July 1602–March 1603; GDR 97, Detection Causes: September 1605; GDR 100, Depositions: March 1606–March 1609; GDR 109, Depositions, April 1609–June 1611; GDR 111, Detection Causes: October–December 1610; GDR 114, Depositions, 1611–

1613; GDR 116, Detection Causes: October 1612–March 1613; GDR 121, Depositions, March 1613–February 1614; GDR 122, Depositions, March 1614–April 1615; GDR 125, Detection Causes: June 1616–March 1617; GDR 127, Depositions, April 1616–November 1618; GDR 148, Depositions, May 1622–August 1625; GDR 159, Depositions, September 1625–May 1628; GDR 168, Depositions: September 1628–March 1631; GDR 174, Detection Causes, Winchcombe Deanery: 1631, 1634, 1635, 1636, 1637; GDR 176, Detection Causes: May 1631–February 1632; GDR 181, Detection Causes: March–September 1633; GDR 186, Detection Causes: March–November 1634; GDR 191, Detection Causes: October 1635–March 1637; GDR 195, Detection Causes: January–March 1637; GDR 202, Detection Causes: February 1638–April 1641; GDR 204, Depositions, January 1638–March 1640; GDR 210, Detection Causes: October 1662–November 1663; GDR 211, Depositions, October 1662–November 1669; GDR 212, Detection Causes: July 1663–March 1665; GDR 221, Depositions, September 1670–February 1678; GDR 224, Detection Causes: September 1671–July 1673; GDR 227, Detection Causes: April 1676–January 1677; GDR 230, Detection Causes: 1677–1680; GDR 232, Depositions, February 1678–January 1684; GDR 233, Detection Causes: July 1678–September 1679; GDR 235, Detection Causes: September 1679–April 1680; GDR 239, Detection Causes: 1680–1681; GDR 241, Detection Causes: June 1681–July 1682; GDR 244, Detection Causes: September–December 1682; GDR 245, Detection Causes: October 1682–February 1683; GDR 247, Detection Causes: October 1683–March 1684; GDR 252, Detection Causes: 1684–1688; GDR 259, Detection Causes: 1686–1708.

Consistory Court Papers

GDR B4/3/34, B4/3/35, Ashchurch; GDR B4/1/995, Forthampton; GDR B4/3/1173, B4/3/1178, B4/1/2484, B4/1/2500, Tewkesbury.

Probate

Wills (W), 1590–1690; Inventories (I), 1550–1715.

Visitation

GDR 73, Episcopal Visitation of the Diocese and Cathedral, 1594; GDR 80, Episcopal Visitations, 1597–1602; GDR 96, Episcopal Visitation, 1605; GDR 102, Episcopal Visitation of Diocese and Cathedral, 1607; GDR 107, Episcopal Visitation, 1609; GDR 115, Visitations, 1612–1619; GDR 146, Episcopal

Visitation, 1622; GDR 157, Episcopal Visitation, 1625; GDR 166, Episcopal Visitation, 1628; GDR 189, Visitation by Archbishop Laud's Commissioners, 1635; GDR 207, Archdeacon of Gloucester's Visitation, 1642; GDR 209, Episcopal Visitation: 1661–1662; GDR 220, Visitation Book: 1670–1677; GDR 223, Episcopal Visitations: 1671–1673; GDR 231, Visitation Book, 1677–1678; GDR 240, Episcopal Visitation, 1681; GDR 243, Episcopal Visitation, 1682.

Parishes

Deerhurst: P 112 IN 1/1, Parish Register; Tewkesbury: P 329 CW 2/1, Churchwardens Accounts, 1563–1703; P 329 IN 1/2, P 329 IN 1/3, P 329 IN 1/4, P 329 IN 1/5, P 329 IN 1/6, Parish Registers; Twyning: P 343 VE 2/1, Twyning Vestry Book.

Baptists

D 4944 2/1, Tewkesbury Baptist Church Book.

Quakers

D 1340 A1/A1, Sufferings; D 1340 A1/M1, Quarterly Meeting, 1671–1733; D 1340 B2/M1, Stoke Orchard Monthly Meeting, 1671–1783; D 1340 C1/M3, Tewkesbury Women's Weekly Meeting.

Quarter Sessions

Q/SIb 1, Quarter Sessions Indictments, 1660–1668.

Tewkesbury Corporation

TBR A 1/1, Council Register; TBR A 1/2, Council Register; TBR A 1/3, Council Register; TBR A 1/4, Council Register; TBR A 1/5, Council Register; TBR B2/41, Brief for Council as to Overlode Ferry, 1624; D 747/1, Papers of James Simpson, Town Clerk of Tewkesbury.

Kent Record Office

Sackville Manuscripts

Manuscripts of Lionel Cranfield, Earl of Middlesex.

Lambeth Palace Library

Court of Arches

Arches Case 9780, D 2229, D 2230; Arches Case 9783, Bbb. 488/6, Bbb. 502/2, Bbb. 502/3, Bbb. 502/4.

Public Record Office

Assize

ASSI 5/1/7.

Exchequer

E 112/407/341 (Bill); E 134/13 Chas I/ 17 April/ Easter 29 (Bill and Depositions); E 134/29 Chas II/12 February/Easter 10 (Bill and Depositions); E 179/247/14, E 179/247/16, E 179/247/554, Hearth Tax Returns.

Star Chamber

STAC 8/18/17.

State Papers

SP 19/116; SP 25/77; SP 25/78.

Probate

PROB 4; PROB 11.

University College Library

Records of Four Tewkesbury Vicars, c. 1680–1770: vol. 9, Sermons on Public Events and Occasions, 1691–1708; vol. 12, Marriage Sermons, c. 1693–1699; vol. 13, Sermons for Funerals of Named Persons, 1691–1712; vol. 15, Pious Maxims, Meditations, and Occasional Observations.